STEP BY STEP INTO EPF

A Guide to Employees' Provident Fund

STEP BY STEP INTO EPF

A Guide to Employees' Provident Fund

Ram Niwas Bairwa

Notion Press

Old No. 38, New No. 6

McNichols Road, Chetpet

Chennai - 600 031

First Published by Notion Press 2016

Copyright © Ram Niwas Bairwa 2016

All Rights Reserved.

ISBN 978-93-5206-506-6

This book has been published in good faith that the work of the author is original. All efforts have been taken to make the material error-free. However, the author and the publisher disclaim the responsibility.

No part of this book may be used, reproduced in any manner whatsoever without written permission from the author, except in the case of brief quotations embodied in critical articles and reviews.

Contents

Preface	*xxiii*
Application of The EPF & MP ACT, 1952	**1**
Chapter 1: The Act	**3**
I. A Retrospect	3
II. Aims and Object	5
III. Act is Subject to Consumer Protection Act	7
IV. Effect of SIC Act, 1985	8
V. Interpretation	9
VI. Power of Central Govt. to give directions	10
VII. Power of Central Govt. to make rules	11
VIII. Jurisdiction of Courts	12
Chapter 2: Applicability of the Act	**15**
I. The Extent	16
II. Act Applies by its own force	16
III. Establishment, means	17
IV. Exclusions	18
V. State Act: Prevalence over Central Act	23
VI. Infancy Protections	27
VII. Coverage of Factory Establishment	28
VIII. Coverage of Non-factory establishments	29
IX. Effect of Section 2A	29
X. Engaged 20 or more employees	30
XI. Contractor Establishment – whether covered independently	39
XII. Specified Industry	42
XIII. Voluntary Application of the Act	43
XIV. Establishment once covered cannot go out of the Act	44
XV. Special Notification for Coverage under Sec. 3	45
XVI. Power to add to Schedule- I	45
XVII. Industries in Schedule – I and notified classes of stablishments	46
XVIII. No retrospective application	48
XIX. Application of Schemes	48
Chapter 3: Interpretation and Definitions	**51**
I. Interpretation	51
II. Definitions	53

A.	Definitions under the Act	53
B.	In the Employees' Provident Funds Scheme, 1952	58
C.	In the Employees' Pension Scheme, 1995 Paragraph 2. – Definitions	61
D.	Definitions under the Employees' Deposit-Linked Insurance Scheme, 1976	62
III.	Speaking Order	63

Administration and Management   65

Chapter 4: Statutory Body   67
    I. Appropriate Government   68
    II. Central Government   68
    III. Governing Body   68

Chapter 5: Administrative set-up   75
    I. Appointment of Officers and Staff   77
    II. Service Conditions   77
    III. Powers related to Scheme   77
    IV. Responsibility related to administration of Schemes   78
    V. Defective or delayed service to subscribers   78
    VI. Financial Management   78

Chapter 6: Statutory and quasi-judicial Authorities   79
    I. Statutory Authorities in Administration   79
    II. Inspectors   81
    III. Powers of Inspector   85
    A. Quasi-judicial authorities   86
    B. Judicial authorities   86

Chapter 7: Employer   87
    I. Importance of Employer   87
    II. Who is employer?   88
    III. Powers and duties of an employer   89
    IV. Allotment of Account numbers   93
    V. Duties of contractor   94

Products & Services   95

Chapter 8: The Schemes   97
    I. Framing of Employees' Provident Funds Scheme, 1952   98
    II. Application of the Scheme   99
    III. Recognition under the Income Tax Act   100
    IV. Framing of Employees' Family Pension Scheme, 1971   101
    V. Framing of Employees' Pension Scheme, 1995   102
    VI. Framing of the Employees' Deposit-linked Insurance Scheme, 1976   103

Chapter 9: Contributions — 105
    I. Contributions — 107
    II. Pay or wages for contributions — 108
    III. Other elements of pay or wages — 112
    IV. Contributions, liability for payment of — 115
    V. Liability of a contractor's employees' contribution and recovery from contractor — 116
    VI. Waiver of demand for contributions — 118
    VII. Contribution, on higher pay or at the higher rate — 119
    VIII. Contribution to the Pension Fund — 120
    IX. Contribution on higher pay or wages under EPF, 1995 — 120
    X. Non–deduction of contribution- by omission or by clerical mistake — 121
    XI. Non–payment of Contributions and other due — 121
    XII. Non payment of contribution deducted from employees pay — 121
    XIII. Contribution to the Insurance Fund — 122
    XIV. Administration Charges — 122
    XV. Rate of contribution in the past — 122

Chapter 10: Membership — 123
    I. Eligibility for Membership — 126
    II. Resolution of dispute regarding membership of an employee — 126
    III. Excluded employee — 127
    IV. Member withdrawn his P.F. amount in full — 128
    V. Pay exceeding Rs. 15,000 P.M., the statutory limit — 128
    VI. Membership continues even after pay exceeding Rs. 15,000/- — 129
    VII. The apprentices or the trainees or the learners — 129
    VIII. Membership to an "excluded employee" — 130
    IX. Declaration on getting employment — 130
    X. Nomination and declaration — 131
    XI. Membership Employees' Pension Scheme, 1995 — 133
    XII. Membership Employees' Deposit-Linked Insurance Scheme, 1976 — 134
    XIII. Retention of membership — 134

Chapter 11: Benefits — 135
    I. The Provident Fund — 135
    II. Transfer of PF Account — 135
    III. Rate interest applicable year-wise — 136
    IV. Advance payments from P.F. Account (as withdrwal) — 137
    V. Final payment to the member him-self — 138
    VI. Final payment on death of a member — 139
    VII. Modes of payments — 140
    VIII. Pensions — 142
    IX. Eligibility — 142

X.	Pensionable salary	143
XI.	Amount of Pension	143
XII.	Widow Pension	146
XIII.	Scheme Certificate	146
XIV.	Withdrawal benefit	147
XV.	Commutation and Return of Capital	147
XVI.	Payment of monthly pensions	147
XVII.	Insurance Benefit	148

Chapter 12: Safe-Guards — 149

I.	Protection against attachment	149
II.	Employer not to reduce wages	150

Exemptions from the Schemes — 153

Chapter 13: Exemptions — 155

I.	Exclusion and exemption, difference between	162
II.	Pre-requisite for the exemption	164
III.	Exemption to an establishment	164
IV.	Exemption to a person or a class of employees	165
V.	Relaxation pending exemption and the terms and conditions	166
VI.	Scope of Section 17	172
VII.	Formation P.F. Trust and Application for exemption	172
VIII.	Functions of the Board of Trustees	174
IX.	Cancellation of Exemption	174
X.	Exemption from Employees' Pension Scheme, 1995	180
XI.	Exemption from Employees' Deposit Linked Insurance Scheme, 1976	182
XII.	Investment pattern w.e.f. 01.04.2015	184

Default Management — 185

Chapter 14: Determination of dues — 187

I.	Authorities under, and Scope of section 7A	190
II.	Role of a Provident Fund Inspector	192
III.	Speaking Order	193
IV.	Onus	196
V.	Time limit for disposal of an inquiry	199
VI.	Dispute regarding applicability	200
VII.	Determination of dues	200
VIII.	Ex-parte order determining the dues	201
IX.	Setting aside the ex-parte order	202
X.	Determination of Escaped dues	202
XI.	Review of the orders	202

Chapter 15: Levy of damages And Interest — 207
  I. 1988 amendments = effects with regard to the powers of authority and previous defaults, proceedings initiated thereafter — 209
  II. One answer to many — 209
  III. Levy of damages: a quasi-judicial process — 211
  IV. Default leading to damages — 212
  V. Limitation of levy of damages — 212
  VI. Damages- whether for loss — 213
  VII. Contribution not deducted or wages not paid — 213
  VIII. Damages for pre-discovery period — 214
  IX. Establishment registered with B.I.F.R. - levy of damages — 216
  X. Waiver of, or reduction in damages — 217
  XI. Interest on belated remittances — 217

Chapter 16: E.P.F. Appellate Tribunal — 219
  I. Matters which can be appealed against — 222
  II. Application for appeal — 223
  III. Finality of the order of the Tribunal — 223
  IV. Procedure of Appeal and Tribunal — 224

Chapter 17: Recovery of the dues — 237
  I. Amounts Due for which Recovery is enforced — 241
  II. Priority of payment of contributions over other debts. — 242
  III. Liability in case of transfer of establishment — 243
  IV. Modes of Recovery and Authorities to enforce Recovery — 244
  V. Recovery by an authority other than Recovery Officer — 244
  VI. Recovery by a Recovery Officer — 247
  VII. Attachment and sale of the property of — 247
  VIII. Arrest of employer and his detention in prison — 249
  IX. Appointment of Receiver for management of property of the establishment or the employer — 249
  X. Transfer of certificate of other Recovery Officer — 249
  XI. Corrections in and/or stay on the Recovery Certificate — 250
  XII. The Recovery Rules — 250

Chapter 18: Penalties — 285
  I. Offences under the Act and penalties — 288
  II. Persons liable to be charged for offence — 290
  III. Authority to file complaint in the Court — 295
  IV. Cognizable Offence, Scope of — 296
  V. Power of court to make order — 296

Chapter 19: Supplements

I.	Schedule I to the EPF & M.P. Act Act, 1952	297
II.	List of other establishments Notified under section 1(3) (b) of the Act:	302
III.	Schedule II to the EPF & M.P Act, 1952	309
IV.	Schedule III to the EPF & M.P. Act, 1952	310
V.	Schedule IV to the EPF & M.P. Act, 1952	311
VI.	EPF A.T. (Procedure) Rules, 1997	224
VII.	EPF A.T. (Condition of Service) Rules, 1997	234
VIII.	Schedule II to the Income Tax Act, 1961	251
IX.	Schedule III to the Income Tax Act, 1961	269
X.	Income Tax (Certificate Proceedings) Rules, 1962	269
XI.	The Employees' Provident Fund Scheme, 1952	312
XII.	The Employees' Pension Scheme, 1995	397
XIII.	The Employees' Deposit-Linked Insurance Scheme, 1976	424
XIV.	Form No. 9 (Application for Review u/s. 7-B	295

Provision Finder

Sec.	Particulars	Chapter	Pages
1	Short title, extent and application	2	12
2	Definitions	3	48
2A	Establishment to include all departments and branches	2	26
3	Power to apply Act to an establishment which has a common provident fund with another establishment	2	41
4	Power to add to schedule I	2	41
5	Employees' Provident Funds Scheme	8	87
5A	Central Board	4	60
5AA	Executive committee	4	62
5B	State Board	4	62
5C	Board of Trustees to be body corporate	4	63
5D	Appointment of officers	5	67
5DD	Acts and proceedings of the Central Board or its Executive Committee or the State Board not to be invalidated on certain ground	4	63
5E	Delegation	4	63
6	Contributions and other matters which may be provided for in the Scheme	9	95
6A	Employees' Pension Scheme	8	90
6B	[XXX]-	-	
6C	Employees' Deposit-Linked Insurance Scheme	8	92
6D	Laying of Schemes before Parliament	8	94
7	Modification of scheme	8	94
7A	Determination of moneys due from employers	14	171
7B	Review of orders passed under Section 7A	14	173
7C	Determination of escaped amount	14	174
7D	Employees' Provident Funds Appellate Tribunal	16	201
7E	Term of Office	16	202
7F	Resignation	16	202
7G	Salary and allowances and other terms and conditions of service of Presiding Officer	16	202
7H	Staff of the Tribunal	16	202
7I	Appeals to Tribunal	16	203
7J	Procedure of Tribunal	16	203

7K	Right of appellant to take assistance of legal practitioner and of Government, etc. to appoint presenting officers	16	203
7L	Orders of Tribunal	16	203
7M	Filling of vacancies	16	204
7N	Finality of orders constituting a Tribunal	16	204
7O	Deposit of amount due, on filing appeal	16	204
7P	Transfer of certain applications to Tribunal	16	204
7Q	Interest payable by the employer	15	199
8	Mode of recovery of moneys due from employers17	219	
8A	Recovery of moneys by employers and contractors7	80	
8B	Issue of certificate to the Recovery Officer	17	220
8C	Recovery Officer to whom certificate is to be forwarded	17	220
8D	Validity of certificate and amendment thereof	17	221
8E	Stay of proceedings under certificate and amendment or withdrawal thereof	17	221
8F	Other modes of recovery	17	226
8G	Application of certain provisions of Income Tax Act	17	233
9	Fund to be recognised under Act 11 of 1922	8	87
10	Protection against attachment	12	136
11	Priority of payment of contributions over other debts	17	222
12	Employer not to reduce wages, etc.	12	137
13	Inspectors	6	71
14	Penalties	18	267
14A	Offences by companies	18	268
14AA	Enhanced punishment on certain cases after previous conviction	18	269
14AB	Certain offences to be cognizable	18	269
14AC	Cognizance and trial of offences	18	269
14B	Power to recover damages	15	189
14C	Power of court to make orders	18	270
15	Special Provisions relating to existing provident funds	2	140
16	Act not to apply to certain establishments	2	15
16A	Authorising certain employers to maintain provident fund accounts	19 19	141
17	Power to exempt	13	141
17A	Transfer of Accounts	11	123
17AA	Act to have effect notwithstanding anything contained in Act 31 of 1956	8	93
17B	Liability in case of transfer of establishment	17	223
18	Protection of action taken in good faith	6	73
18A	Presiding Officer and other officers to be public servants	6	73
19	Delegation of powers	4	63

19A	[XXX]	-	-
20	Power of Central Government to give directions	1	9
21	Power to make rules	1	10
22	Power to remove difficulties	1	10
	Schedule -I	19	280
	List of classes of industries Notified	19	285
	Schedule -II	19	292
	Schedule -III	19	294
	Schedule -IV	19	296
	EPF Appellate Tribunal (Procedure) Rules, 1997	16	206
	EPF Appellate Tribunal (Condition of Service) Rules, 199	16	215
	Schedule II to Income Tax Act, 1961	16	233
	Schedule III to Income Tax Act, 1961	16	251
	Income Tax (Certificate Proceedings) Rules, 1962	16	252
	The Employees' Provident Fund Scheme, 1952	19	297
	The Employees' Pension Scheme, 1995	19	414
	The Employees' Deposit-Linked Insurance Scheme, 1976	19	424

The Employees' Provident Funds Scheme, 1952

Sec.	Particulars	Pages
	Chapter-I	
	PRELIMINARY	
1	Short title and application	312
2	Definitions	325
	Chapter-II	
	BOARD OF TRUSTEES, EXECUTIVE COMMITTEE AND REGIONAL COMMITTEES	
3	Election of certain members of the Executive Committee	329
4	Regional Committee	329
5	Terms of Office	330
6	Resignation	331
7	Cessation and restoration of trusteeship	331
8	Disqualifications for trusteeship or membershipof Regional Committee	331
9	Removal from Trusteeship or membership of a Regional Committee	332
10	Absence from India	332
11	Meetings	333
12	Notice of meeting and list of business	333
13	Chairman to preside at meetings	333
14	Quorum	333
14A	Nomination of a substitute during the absence of a trustee/member of the Central Board/Regional Committee	334
15	Disposal of business	334
16	Minutes of meetings	335
17	Acts of a Regional Committee not invalid by reason merely of any vacancy in, or defect in the Constitution, etc.	335
18	Fees and allowances	335
	Chapter-III	
	APPOINTMENT AND POWERS OF COMMISSIONER AND OTHER STAFF OF BOARD OF TRUSTEES	
19	Central Provident Fund Commissioner and Financial Adviser and Chief Accounts Officer	338
20	[x x x]	338
21	Opening of regional and other offices	338

22	Secretary of the Central Board or Regional Committee	338
22A	Appointment of Officers and employees of the Central Board	
23	Information of appointments of the Central Board	
24	Administrative and Financial Powers of the Commissioner	338
24A	Delegation of powers by the Central Board	339
25	Powers of the Central Government until the Central Board is constituted	339

Chapter-IV
MEMBERSHIP OF THE FUND

26	Classes of employees entitled and required to join the Fund	340
26A	Retention of membership	341
26B	Resolution of doubts	341
27	Exemption of an employee	341
27A	Exemption of a class of employees	342
27AA	Terms and conditions of exemption	342
28	Transfer of accumulations from existing Provident Funds	346

Chapter-V
CONTRIBUTIONS

29	Contribution	348
30	Payment of contributions	348
31	Employer's share not to be deducted from the members	349
32	Recovery of a member's share of contribution	349
32A	Recovery of damages for default in payment of any contribution	349
32B	Terms and conditions for reduction or waiver of damages	350

Chapter-VI
DECLARATION, CONTRIBUTION CARDS AND RETURNS

33	Declaration by persons already employed at the time of the institution of the Fund	351
34	Declaration by persons taking up employment after the Fund has been established	351
35	Preparation of Contribution Cards	351
36	Duties of Employers	351
36A	Employer to furnish particulars of ownership	352
36B	Duties of Contractors	353
37	Allotment of Account Numbers	353
38	Mode of payment of contributions	353
39	Fixation of administrative charges	354
40	Contributions to be entered in the contribution card	354
40A	Supply of passbooks to the members	354
41	Currency of contribution cards	354
42	Renewal of contribution cards	355
43	Submission of contribution cards to the Commissioner	355
44	Custody of contribution cards	355

45	Inspection of cards by members	355
46	Production of cards and records for inspection by the Commissioner or Inspector	355
47	Supply of cards and Forms to employers	356
48	Current Account	356

Chapter-VII
ADMINISTRATION OF THE FUND, ACCOUNTS AND AUDIT

49	Administration Accounts	357
50.	Provident Fund Account	357
51	Interest Suspense Account	357
52	Investment of moneys belonging to Employee's Provident Fund	357
53	Disposal of the Fund	357
54	Expenses of Administration	357
55	Form and manner of maintenance of Accounts	358
56	Audit	358
57	Inter-State transfer of members	358
58	Budget	358
59	Members' Accounts	359
60	Interest	359

Chapter-VIII
NOMINATIONS, PAYMENTS AND WITHDRAWALS FROM THE FUND

61	Nomination	361
62	Financing of Members' Life Insurance Policies	361
63	Conversion of policy into a paid-up one and payment of late fee etc.	362
64	Assignment of Policies to the Fund	362
65	Bonus on policy to be adjusted against payments made from the Fund	363
66	Reassignment of policies	363
67	Recovery of amounts paid towards Insurance Policies	363
68	[x x x]	363
68A	[x x x]	363
68B	Withdrawal from the Fund for the purchase of a dwelling house/flat or for the construction of a dwelling house including the acquisition of a suitable site for the purpose	363
68BB	Withdrawal from the Fund for repayment of loans in special cases	368
68BC	Withdrawal/financing from the Fund for the purchase of a dwelling house/flat or the construction of a dwelling house including the acquisition of a suitable site by the Member	368
68C	[x x x]	
68D	[x x x]	
68E	Computation of period of membership	370
68F	[XXX]	370

68G	[XXX]	370
68GG	[XXX]	370
68H	Grant of advances in special cases	371
68I	[XXX]	371
68J	Advance from the Fund for illness in certain cases	372
68K	Advance from the Fund for marriages or post-matriculation education of children	373
68L	Grant of advances in abnormal conditions	373
68M	Grant of advance to members affected by cut in the supply of electricity	374
68N	Grant of advance to members who are physically handicapped	374
68NN	Withdrawal within one year before the retirement	362
68NNN	Option for withdrawal at the age of 55 years for investment in Varishtha Pension Bima Yojana	375
68NNNN	Option for withdrawal on cessation of employment	375
68O	Payment of withdrawal or advance	375
69	Circumstances in which accumulations in the Fund are payable to a member	375
70	Accumulations of a deceased member to whom payable	377
70A	Payment of provident fund accumulations in the case of a person charged with the offence of murder	378
71	[XXX]	378
72	Payment of Provident Fund	378
73	Annual statement of member's account	381

Chapter-IX
MISCELLANEOUS

73A	[x x x]	382
74	Annual report on the work and activities of the Board and its audited accounts	382
75	Issue of copies of Member's Accounts, Annual Reports etc.	382
76	Punishment for failure to pay contribution, etc.	382
77	Conduct of business of the Central Board	383
78	Power to issue directions	383
79	Special provisions relating to factories and other establishments in respect of which applications for exemption are received	370
79A	Filing application for review	383
79B	Time limit for communicating the views of the Central Board to the appropriate Government on a proposal for grant of exemption to an establishment	383
79C	Composition of the Board of Trustees of the exempted establishments and he terms and conditions of service of the trustees	384

Chapter-X
[Special Provisions]*
*(Heading to this Chapter has snot been given, for convenience this heading has been gioven)

80	Special provisions in the case of Newspaper Establishments and Newspaper Employees	386
81	Special provisions in the case of cine-workers	388
82	Special provisions in respect of certain employees	390
83	Special provisions in respect of international workers	391

The Employees' Pension Scheme, 1995

1.	Short title, commencement and application	397
2	Definitions	397
3	Employees' Pension Fund	398
4	Payment of contribution	399
5	Recovery of damages for default in payment of any contribution	399
6.	Membership of the Employees' Pension Scheme	399
6A	Retention of Membership	400
7	Option for joining the Scheme	400
8	Resolution of doubts	400
9	Determination of eligible service	400
10	Determination of pensionable service	401
11	Determination of pensionable salary	401
12	Monthly Member's Pension	402
12A	Option for Commutation (Omitted)	404
13	Options for return of capital (Omitted)	404
14	Benefits on leaving service before being eligible for monthly member's pension	404
15	Benefits on permanent and total disablement during the service	404
16	Benefits to the family on the death of a member	405
16A	Guarantee of Pensionary Benefits	407
17	Payments on Exercise of Option	407
17A	Payment of pension	407
18	Particulars to be supplied by the employees already employed at the time of commencement of the Employees' Pension Scheme	408
19	Preparation of contribution cards	408
20	Duties of employers	408
21	Employer to furnish particulars of ownership	408
22	Duties of contractors	409
23	Allotment of account numbers	409
24	Declaration by persons taking up employment after the fund has been established	409
25	Employees' Pension Fund Account	409
26	Investment of the Employees' Pension Fund	409

27	Disposal of the Fund	410
28	[x x x]	410
29	Forms of account	410
30	Audit	410
31	Rounding up of the benefits	410
32	Valuation of the Employees' Pension Fund and review of the rates of contributions and quantum of the pension and other benefits	410
33	Disbursement of pension and other benefits	410
34	Registers, records, etc.	411
35	Power to issue directions	411
36	Regional Committee	411
37	Annual Report	411
38	Application of the provisions of Employees' Provident Funds Scheme, 1952	411
39	Exemption from the operation of the Pension Scheme	411
39A	Submission of Return	412
39B	Transfer Value	412
40	Information to the Central Government	412
41	Interpretation	412
42	Punishment for failure to submit return, etc.	412
43	Payment of pension in the case of a person charged with the offence of murder	401
43A	Special provisions in respect of International Workers	413
44	Repeal and Savings	414
	Table-A	415
	Table-B	416
	Table-C	418
	Table-D	422
	Table-E	423

The Employees' Deposit-Linked Insurance Scheme, 1976

1	Short title, commencement and application	424
2	Definitions	424
3	Administration of the Scheme	424
4	Regional Committee	424
5	Delegation of power by the Central Board	424
6	Administrative and financial powers of the Commissioner	425
7	Contribution	425
8	Mode of payment of contribution	425
8A	Recovery of damages for default in payment of any contribution	425
8B	Terms and conditions for reduction or waiver of damages	426
9	Employer's contribution not to be deducted from the wages of the employees	426
10	Duties of employers	426
11	Inspection of records and registers by the Commissioner or Inspector	427
12	Supply of forms to employers	427
13	Administration Account	427
14	Deposit-linked Insurance Fund Account	427
15	Investment of moneys belonging to the Insurance Fund	427
16	Interest	427
17	Disposal of the Insurance Fund	427
18	Expenses of Administration	428
19	Forms and manner of maintenance of accounts	428
20	Audit	428
21	Budget	428
22	Scales of assurance benefit and the minimum average balance to be maintained by an employee	429
23	Assurance benefit to whom payable	430
24	Assurance amount - How to be paid	431
25	Registers, Records, etc.	431
26	Annual Report on the working of this Scheme	431
27	[XXX]	431
28	Special provisions in respect of which applications are received for exemption from the provisions of this Scheme	431
29.	Punishment for failure to submit returns etc.	432

Preface

Now-a-days, when the documentation and working is going paperless, it is becoming hard to keep memory active for the documents and relevant references in mind to be critical and analytical towards professional assignments. So happens in the Government controlled organization, especially, in an organization claims to be dedicated towards the social security of the working-class. Can it be possible to implement the Act and the Schemes in its true spirit? Any individual may have a critical observations, but that may be a blasphemy, but the Judiciary has right to comment all about it. Only two quotes are enough to back why this book is necessary for the officers and the staff of the EPF Organisation and also for the employers and other professionals.

The Calcutta High Court, in the case of **R.P.F.C., W.B. vs. the Gauripore Co. Ltd [1992 Lab.I.C. 1515- (Cal.)]** has been very much critical in observing that-*"on behalf of the Regional P.F. Commissioner, it has been stated that about a sum of Rs. 113 crores is due on account of arrears of PF dues in respect of different establishments in this state alone. This is possible because of laches and gross negligence on the part of the Regional P.F. Commissioners in the performance of their duties, if not something more. In view of the same, the establishment concerned has been able to obtain an interim order or another, in one writ petition after another, sometimes in respect of the very same period, obtaining order of injunction against prosecution pending or impending against the directors and other officers, thereafter making default after paying one or more installments granted by court."* Neither the employers nor the authorities have been spared. But, who is punished, ultimately, It is the subscriber/ member only who suffers.

In an another case, Bombay High Court critically observed that *"if, it needed 17 years to issue a notice which only required turning of pages of a register with a view to seeing the date of payment, it is difficult to lunderstand what sort of administration of this social welfare legislation is being done by the authorities concerned in the state of Maharashtra. This case isa glaring example of the way the social welfare legislations are being dealt with and administered."* **[K.T. Rolling (P) Ltd.]**

I think, this book will be able helpful to address such matters.

In last, I am very much thankful to my readers, admirers, well wishers whose belief in me has been encouraging me to be with them, through all my books, including this one. I happy that I could be able to bring this book again to you in a new format and edition.

138, Mahatma Gandhi Nagar,	RAM NIWAS BAIRWA,
DCM, Ajmer Road, Jaipur-302021.	Phone: 0141-2353751,
30th October, 2015	Mob.: 09414986422
	e-mail: brniwas@gmail.com

Step by Step Into

Into

Application of the Employees' Provident Funds and Miscellaneous Provisions Act, 1952

Chapter 1

The Act

> ***Brief badinage-***
>
> *It is tough to be confined between the lines of a statute, specially, when it is intended to fulfill social security obligations, and taking liberty to go beyond, is also not permitted, because the law is blind. Is it really true that the law is blind? It depends on the person, who is interpreting the law, for whose care it is being interpreted and what is to be achieved by such go, is a matter of debate which can be left for the seminars, forums, media or so on, but when a law is discussed, really it is tough to remain between the lines of a statute. So, it is easy to say something by quoting the authority of judicial pronouncements, whether you agree with that or not. Of course, one may mention his disagreements with the particular judgement, whether that established a good law or not.*

I. A Retrospect

The Concept of Contributory Provident Fund was first introduced by **Tata Iron & Steel Company Ltd., (TISCO) in 1920.** Thereafter, the Government of India took various steps to introduce various/different Labour Laws which was a result of Nation-wide strike by Industrial Labourers in different industrial centers. The Government took steps to introduce Provident Fund by enacting Provident Fund Act, 1925 which was not compulsory for the labourers or the employees.

In 1937 Cawnpore *(Kanpur)* Labour Inquiry Commission was set up and proposed to introduce Contributory Provident Fund for Industrial employees but, it was not taken up in the proirity. In 1942, 3rd Labour Minister's Conference also discussed the Introduction of Contributory Provident Fund and accordingly, in 1944 the draft Provident Fund Rules were finalized and circulated amongst different State (the then provincial) Governments for approval, but it could not be materialized as no turn-up. The Labour Investigation Committee, 1946 summed up the position of provident funds in private industries as follows-

"The whole problem of provision against old age or death of breadwinners legitimately falls within the scope of social security and it is a matter for consideration whether either the initiation or management of schemes of provident funds, gratuities and pensions should be left to employers themselves. Of course, so long as there are no schemes of social security introduced in a particular industry or area, the existing private schemes of provident funds, etc. shall be allowed to continue under the management of employers. The existing schemes in this connection do not appear to be very liberal, and specially in regard to the employers' contribution to provident funds of workers, the restrictions on withdrawal of employer's contribution seems to be somewhat unsatisfactory.

If provisions against old age or death of breadwinner is intended to stabilize the industrial worker in employment, the employer's contribution, which is really in consideration for permanent service by the worker, should, as far as possible, be made available to him on early retirement, etc. The absence of social security measures like provident funds, gratuities and pensions in most concerns has largely contributed to the migratory character of Indian labour, and is one of the most important causes of large labour turnover in factories. Though, some of the large employers have instituted tolerably good schemes, the number of such employers is very small. During the last few years, however, some progress has been achieved in this direction. Generally speaking, provident funds are most common, gratuities are given only in some cases and pensions are rather rare. Only some of the provident funds are registered, whilst most are not. In cases of unregistered funds, the amount standing to the worker's credit is attachable, but not so in the case of registered funds. We are of opinion that all provident funds, wherever they exist, shall be compulsorily registered and treated as trust."

In 1947, the Board of Reconciliation for Coal Mines recommended for institution of Contributory Provident Fund for the Coal Mines Employees. The Industrial Committee on Coal Mines in 1948 expressed the need of introduction of Provident Fund for the Coal Mines employees. Accordingly, the 'Coal Mines Provident Fund Ordinance' was promulgated which became the 'Coal Mines Provident Fund and Miscellaneous Provisions Act, 1948' as it exists today.

In April, 1948 the Indian Labour Conference further underline the need of introduction for Contributory Provident Fund for industrial workers in 1950 the Standing Committee of Labour also recommended for the same and finally the Labour Minister's Conference in 1951 approved the introduction of Provident Fund Accordingly. 'Employees' Provident Fund Ordinance' in 1951 was promulgated on 16.11.1951 which was converted into **'Employees' Provident Fund Act, 1952'** w.e.f. 14.4.1952.

After enactment of Provident Fund Act, a Scheme for institution of Contributory Provident Fund was introduced w.e.f. 1.11.1952.

On demand of Pension Scheme by different Labour Organisations in sixties, an amendment was brought into, by an ordinance, to introduce Family Pension Scheme and the name of the Act was changed as 'Employees' Provident Fund & Family Pension Act, 1952.' The Employees' Family Pension Scheme,1971 was introduced w.e.f. 1.3.1971.

After 5 years, a compulsory Insurance Scheme was introduced in 1976 for which once again an ordinance was promulgated to amend the Provident Fund Act and the Act was renamed as **Employees' Provident Fund & Miscellaneous Provisions Act, 1952** and Employees' Deposit Linked Scheme,1976 was introduced w.e.f. 1.8.1976.

The 20 years' currency of Family Pension Scheme necessitate to meet the demand of institution of a Pension Scheme for the Industrial Workers covered under the Provident Funds Act and steps were taken by the Government to introduce Old-age Pension Scheme. For this purpose, again an ordinance to amend the Act was promulgated to facilitate introduction of Employees' Pension Scheme on 16.10.1995. Accordingly the 'Employees' Pension Scheme, 1995' was introduced w.e.f. 16.11.1995 replacing the old Employees' Family Pension Scheme, 1971.

Legislative history and List of Amending Acts:

+ORDINANCE – 16.11.1951
+ BILL PASSED – 25.03.1952
+BECAME THE ACT – 14.04.1952
+EPF SCHEME, 1952 – 01.11.1952
+EFP SCHEME, 1971 – 01.03.1971
+EDLI SCHEME, 1971 – 01.08.1976
+EPS, 1995 – 16.11.1995

1. The Employees' Provident Funds (Amendment) Act, 1953 (37 of 1953),
2. The Employees' Provident Funds (Amendment) Act, 1956 (94 of 1956),
3. The Repealing and Amending Act, 1957 (36 of 1957),
4. The Employees' Provident Funds (Amendment) Act, 1958 (22 of 1958),
5. The Employees' Provident Funds (Amendment) Act, 1960 (46 of 1960),
6. The Employees' Provident Funds (Amendment) Act 1963 (28 of 1963),
7. The Employees' Provident Funds (Amendment) Act, 1965 (22 of 1965),
8. The Labour Provident Fund Laws (Amendment) Act, 1971 (16 of 1971),
9. The Employees' Provident Funds and Family Pension Fund (Amendment) Act, 1973 (Act 40 of 1973),
10. The Labour Provident Fund Laws (Amendment) Act, 1976 (Act 99 of 1976),
11. The Delegated Legislation Provisions (Amendment) Act, 1985 (Act 4 of 1986),
12. The Employees' Provident Funds and Miscellaneous Provisions (Amendment) Act, 1996 (25 of 1996),
13. The Employees' Provident Funds and Miscellaneous Provisions (Amendment) Act, 1998 (10 of 1998),
14. The Repealing and Amending Act, 2001 (30 of 2001).

II. Aims and Object:

As mentioned above, the object of the need of an old age security measure was underlined in the Labour Investigating Committee of 1946. However, an enactment carries its Aims & Objects in the form of "Statement of Objects & Reasons," so this Act also has. Even then, It becomes necessary for the judiciary to persistedly, reiterate the aims and objects at different points of time to remind the every stake holder under the Act not to forget the obligations they have to hold high.

So, the Supreme Court has done by underlining the object of the Act in the case of **_Balveer Kaur & Others V/s Steel Authority of India & Others_** and also in the case of **_T.K. Meenaxi & Another V/s Steel Authority of India & Others – [2000 (6) SCC 493: AIR 2000 SC 1596:]_** that the Employees'

Provident Fund & Miscellaneous Provisions Act, 1952 is a beneficial piece of legislation and can amply described as Social Security Legislation. The object of the Act is to ensure brighter future of the employee as concerned on his retirement and for the benefit of the dependents in the case of his earlier death.

Further, the object of the Act is that all the employees of an establishment or factory engaged in any industry specified in schedule-1 or class of establishments to which the provisions of the Act are applicable, should make a provision of Provident Fund *[Delhi Clothe & General Mills Company Ltd. V/s RPFC UP – 1961 (2) LLJ-444]*. The same view has also been expressed by the Supreme Court in the case of *Mohd. Ali & Ors V/s UOI & Another – [1963 (A) LLJ 536; AIR 1964 SC 980]*, the underlined idea behind the provisions of the Act is to bring all kinds of employees within its fold as and when the Central Government might think fit after reviewing the circumstances of each class of the establishment. The statement of Objects and Reasons of this Act was published in the Gazette on 23.02.1952 part II, S.2, p.67, which reads as under-

"The question of making some provision for the future of the industrial worker after he retires or for his dependents in case of his early death, has been under consideration for some years. The ideal way would have been provisions through old age and survivors' pensions as has been done in the industrially advanced countries. But, in the prevailing conditions in India, the institution of a pension scheme can not be visualized in the near future. Another alternative may be for provision of gratuities after prescribed period of service. The main defect of a gratuity scheme, however, is that the amount paid to a worker or his dependents would be small, as the worker would not him-self be making any contribution to the fund. Taking in account the various difficulties, financial and administrative, the most appropriate course appears to be the institution compulsory of contributory provident funds in which both the worker and the employer would contribute. Apart from other advantage, there is the obvious one of the cultivating among the workers a spirit of saving something regularly. The institution of a provident fund of this type would also encourage the stabilization of a steady labour force in industrial centers."

"The subject of legislation for compulsory institution of contributory provident funds in industrial undertakings was discussed several times at tripartite meetings in which representatives of the Central and State Governments and of employers and workers took part. A large measure of agreement was reached that there should be such legislation. Further, a non-official Bill on this subject was introduced in the Central Legislature in 1948 and was withdrawn only on an assurance given that Government itself would soon consider the introduction of a comprehensive Bill. The view that the proposed legislation should be undertaken was lastly endorsed by the Conference of Provincial Labour Ministers held in January, 1951. It may be added that a statutory Contributory Provident Fund already exists for workers in coal mines, covering about 3,00,000 persons. This has been in operation for about five years and is working very satisfactorily."

"The Bill provides for institution, in the first instance, of contributory provident funds in the six major organized industries named in Schedule I; except undertakings owned by the Central or a State Government or by a local authority. There is also a provision empowering the Central Government, by notification, to add other industries to the Schedule or to apply the Act to industrial undertakings employing less than fifty persons."

"To avoid any hardship to new establishments, a provision has been made for exempting them for a period of three years and similar exemptions are given to other establishments which are less than three years old till they have been in operation for a period of three years in all. The rate of contribution will be 6¼ percent of the total emoluments of worker, the worker and the employer each contributing these amounts. Further, the scheme could empower payment of a higher subscription by the worker at their option."

"Where provident funds exist in private industry, contributions are usually a percentage of the basic wages. Unlike government departments, wages in private industry have not, however, been rationalized and there are very great variations in the level of basic wages in private industry, even in different units in the same industry. If, contributions are reckoned on the basis of basic wage only, there will, therefore, be wide changes in the degree of benefit received. This will be unfair to the workers and may also penalize those employers who have brought the level of basic wages more in accord with current requirements. Government appreciates that dearness allowance is a variable factor depending on the cost of living. Nevertheless, for the reasons explained, Government is satisfied that contributions to the provident fund should be on the basis of basic pay plus dearness allowance. This should not be construed as, in any way, implying that dearness allowances on the existing rates are to be recognized as a permanent measure."

"Most of the details relating to the Fund will be settled in accordance with a scheme which, in the interest of uniformity, will be framed by the Central Government. The administration will, to a large extent, be decentralized in regard to undertakings falling within the sphere of State Governments."

"Where provident funds offering equal or more advantageous terms are operating efficiently, provision has been made for them to continue subject to certain safeguards in the interest of the workers."

"This Bill when enacted will repeal and re-enact an Ordinance promulgated on the same lines on the 15th November, 1951."

III. Act is Subject to Consumer Protection Act:

The Provident Fund Act is considered to be a Social Security Act for over six decades, the expectations of the beneficiaries are becoming higher to get better services in the era of Globalization. The Consumer Protection Act, 1986 was passed in India to safeguard the interest of costumers and the service seekers. It has been the view of the authorities that the being a Government Department and Government Organisation, the actions or services being given under the Act cannot be censured at any level by other authorities. This euphoria was broken by the Supreme Court in the case of Shiv Kumar Joshi who filed a complaint before District Consumer Forum in Haryana and after getting favourable verdict P.F. authorities brought the order of the District Forum to the State Forum and on failure there, to the National Forum and Supreme Court. The Supreme Court held that **collection of administrative charges is Service Charge. It can not, legally claim that the facilities provided by the 'Scheme' were not "service" or the benefits under the scheme being provided were free of charge. A perusal of the scheme clearly and unambiguously indicate that that is a "service" within the meaning of Sec. 2(1) (o) and the member is a "consumer" within the meaning of Sec. 2(1) (d) of the Consumer Protection Act, 1986 (68 of 1986). Therefore, it is applicable to the E.P.F. Scheme, 1952** *[RPFC Vs. Shiv Kumar Joshi – 2000 Lab. I.C. 232 (SC)].*

In respect of Employees' Pension Scheme, 1995, some of the High Courts have held that no charge is taken from either the employer of from the employee for the services being given under the Scheme, hence it does not fall under the lenses of the Consumer Protection Act. And other do not consider so because the administration charges paid under the EPF Scheme is also considered and proportionately pooled for the administrative expenses of the Pension Scheme.

IV. Effect of Sick Industrial Companies (Special Provisions) Act, 1985:

For the revival and rehabilitaion of sick companies, a special Act has been enacted namely **Sick Industrial Companies (Special Provisions) Act, 1986** which provides certain relief to the sick industrial companies declared sick u/s 4 of the Act. Under Section 22, there are special immunes provided for such companies with regard to taxation and other liabilities. But the immune provided u/s 22 is not available as far the Provident Fund dues which are not penal damages. Accordingly while drafting/approving a revival scheme by the Board of Industrial and Financial Reconstruction, a special mention is provided in the scheme with regard to payment of contribution to pay in installments and with regard to payment of damages, it is recommended for waiver by the appropriate authority.

However, different views have been taken by the different courts. In the case of *SLM Manek Lal Industries Vs. R.P.F.C. [1997 (2) LLJ-283 (Guj.)]*, the Gujarat High Court has observed that Proceeding under the Act for recovery of P.F. dues by way of execution distress etc. could not be taken against a company which is declared sick industry by B.I.F.R. in view of Section 22 of Sick Industrial Companies (Special Provisions) Act, 1985. The proceeding remains suspended.

On the contrary, in the case of *Universal Paper Mills Ltd. and others Vs. R.P.F.C. and others – [20001 (2) LLJ 1193; 2001 (91) FLR 591; 2002 LLR 41; 2001 (99) FJR 199]* another court has taken a view that the company has no right to take shelter under section 22 of the Sick Industrial Companies (Special Provisions) Act, 1985 in respect of statutory liabilities and the employees are entitled to have their statutory benefits under EPF & MP Act and thereby any default on the part of the employer under the said Act cannot attract the said section 22 or can get away taking an advantage of the Section. [***Also see Digpal Singh Vs. U.O.I. 2002 LIC 3547; 2003 (I) LLJ 876)].***

The Orissa High Court has also taken similar view that the provisions of Section 22(1) of the Sick Industrial Companies (Special Provisions) Act, 1985 would not apply to statutory dues of an employee covered under the P.F. Scheme *[Industrial Development Corp. of Orissa Ltd. and another Vs. R.P.F.C.II and another- 2002 (I) LLJ 774; 2002 (92) FLR 945]*.

V. Interpretation:

Thus the object of the Social Security Act has clearly been defined by Apex court and Accordingly it need be interpreted while implementing the provisions of the Act.

The Act was enacted in conformity with the **Directive Principles of the State** as laid down in constitution and being the matter of Labour Welfare it has been put in the **concurrent list** of the **seventh schedule to the constitution of India**. Accordingly the Act came into being and further it is being amended to provide more benefits to the larger population employed in different industries and also to families connected to them. As it is to fulfill the social obligations it has been termed as Beneficial Legislation and requires to be interpreted to advance the constitutional directives it bears. No labour legislation, no special legislation, no economic legislation can be considered by the court without applying the principle of social justice in interpreting the provisions of these law *[Prakash Cotton Mills (P) Ltd. vs. State of Bombay 1957(2)LLJ.490]*. It is the duty of the courts to interpret the Act in such a manner as to give effect to the intention of the legislature and not to put a very narrow construction which may defeat the object of the Act *[Kumpur Textile Finishing Mills Vs. R.P.F.C., AIR 1955 Punjab 130]*.

In Construing the provisions of the Act if, two views are reasonably possible the courts should prefer the view which helps the achievement of the object, though, for such purpose, the stretching the word to an unreasonable degree is not proper *[RPFC V/s Shibu Metal Works – [1965 (1)LLJ 473]*. Further in the case of *Nazeena Traders (P) Ltd Vs. RPFC –[AIR-1965 AP 200; 1966 (1) LLJ 334]*, the Andhra Pradesh High Court have held the Employees' Provident Fund Act *fit* to as a beneficial legislation enacted as a measure of Social Justice and should be constituted liberally as to confer benefits on the employees to the maximum extent.

The employees' Provident Fund Act is a social legislation and the canons of construing a social legislation are very different from the canons of construing a taxation law. The court must not countenance any subterfuge which would defeat the provisions of a social legislation and the court must even, if necessary, strain the language of the Act in order to achieve the purpose which the legislature had in placing this legislation on the statute book. Therefore, not only the court must disapprove all subterfuges to defeat a social legislation, but must actively try to prevent such subterfuges succeeding in their object" *[J.G. Vakharia Vs. R.P.F.C. [(1957) 1 LLJ 448]*. Any construction which would facilitate evasion of the provisions of the Act would as far as possible be avoided *[Sayaji Mills Ltd. Vs. R.P.F.C.-AIR1985 S.C. 323; 1985 SCC (L&S) 310]*. Interpretation of the Act is to be in consonance with the upliftment and betterment of the working conditions of the employees as such *[Bhaskara Ceramic Industries vs. R.P.F.C. A.P.- [1991 Lab. I.C. 1138 (A.P.)]*

Further, the is not an exercise in linguistic discipline. It is emerging as an important therapy in the disorder of social metabolism…. There is accordingly a growing recognition by courts that a statute should be constructed, rather than interpreted, with due regard to its avowed object and to its character. The avowed object of the Act is to provide adequate security to the worker in old age and infirmity. It is a welfare legislation and it should be construed so as to give necessary effect to that object. [*Ramesh Metal Works Vs. State, (1962) 1 LLJ 169: AIR 1962 All 227*]

In the case of *Jayakar Rao N. Shetty Vs. R.P.F.C. [(1993) 2 LLJ 78: 1993 Lab IC 561:]* their Lordships underlined that "It cannot be doubted that the provisions of residential accommodation is one of the objects which is dealt with by the Scheme. All that the petitioners are asking is withdrawal of amounts lying to the credit of their respective funds. If the right which is specifically sought to be bestowed to the petitioners by Paragraph 68-B is denied by putting artificial and restricted interpretation… The very object of the Act and the Scheme will be defeated."

The Supreme Court in the case of *Srikanta Datta Narsimha Raja Vs. Enforcement Officer, [(1993) 3 SCC 217:1993 Lab IC 1359]* have observed that "Meticulous lexicographic analysis of words and phrases and sentences interpretative functioning of the court is to reflect the contemporary needs and the prevailing values consistent with the constitutional and legislative declaration of the policy envisaged in the statute under consideration."

In the dictionary meaning of the word "Interpretation" as per The Concise English Dictionary is:

"To explain the meaning of, to translate from one language into another, to expound, to make intelligible, to find out the meaning of, to construe or understand (in a particular way), to represent the meaning of or one's idea of artistically. (1984 edition – reprint 1985.)"

The interpretation of any provision of the Act depends on the motive it has and strictly it can not be interpreted grammatically. The responsibility to interpret the provisions of the fact does not depend only on the judicial authorities but by and large it is the duty of the authorities who exercise their powers conferred on them to decide a particular issue coming up for his decision.

Usually the order of the court and/or the Supreme Court is taken as law on the matter, but the Article 141 of the Constitution expressly provide that the order of the Court shall be from law only, when it is expressly mentioned or declared by the Supreme Court (or by the High Courts), otherwise all the decisions or orders of the Supreme Court or other High Courts are confined to the given case only as per Article 141 of the Constitution. Besides, the interpretations given by the Court the administrative authority are also bound to interpret the provisions while giving any decision in the given matter. By and large the interpretation given by the authority are more useful and giving sufficient material for the courts to decide the matter before them basing on the findings of the Administrative Authority. That is why the administrative authorities, while acting as a quasi-judicial authority are required to follow the principle of natural justice and pass a speaking order. The passing of the Speaking Order by an administrative authority is a judicial compulsion on them so that his biasness or pre-concepts may not work.

VI. Power of Central Govt. to give directions:

Section [1][20. Power of Central Government to give directions:

The Central Government may, from time to time, give such directions to the Central Board as it may think fit for the efficient administration of this Act and when any such directions is given, the Central Board shall comply with such direction.]

---
1. Sub. For Sec. 19A by Sec. 22 of Act 33 of 1988 (w.e.f. 1.7.1997)

Legislative reference–

By sec. 22 of the Act 33 of 1988, the sec. 19 A has been replaced and it has been given effect from 1st July, 1997. Originally, sec. 19 and sec.19A was added vide Act 37 of 1953. Sec. 19A was entitled "Power to remove difficulties" and was a remedy in case any difficulty was to arise in giving effect to the provisions of the Act and particularly, in cases where the applicability was disputed. This was a remedy which has now been replaced by sections 7D to 7P with the setting-up of the E.P.F. Appellate Tribunal.

Para 78: Power to issue directions. – (1) The Central Government may, from time to time, issue such directions to State Governments, the Central Board or any other authority, under this Act or Scheme as it may consider necessary for the proper implementation of this Scheme or for the purpose of removing any difficulty which may arise in the administration thereof including difficulties in the matter of payment of accumulations in the Fund to members after they cease to be such members.

^{1}[* * *]

(3)The authority to whom any directions are issued under this paragraph shall comply with such directions.

---
1. Sub-paragraph (2) Omitted by G.S.R. 1845, dated the 28.11.1963.

Beyond the statutory provisions and interpretation of them by the administrative authorities and the judiciary, by various courts, there is a specific provision in the Act itself to the effect that if any difficulty is faced in implementing the provisions of the Act, the Central Government has been authorized to give direction to remove that difficulty, and such direction is binding on the Board as well as all other parties related to that.

Similar provisions have been made in the EPF Scheme, 1952 under paragraph 78, which also has similar force of a statutory provision.

VII. Power of Central Govt. to make rules:

Section ^{1}[21. Power to make rules –

(1) The Central Government may, by notification in the Official Gazette, make rules to carry out the provisions of this Act.

(2) Without prejudice to the generality of the foregoing power, such rules may provide for all or any of the following matters, namely:-

      (a) the salary and allowances and other terms and conditions of service of the Presiding Officer and the employees of a Tribunal;

      (b) the form and the manner in which, and the time within which, an appeal shall be filed before a Tribunal and the fees payable for filing such appeal;

(c) the manner of certifying the copy of the certificate, to be forwarded to the Recovery Officer under sub-section (2) or section 8C; and

(d) any other matter which has to be, or may be, prescribed by rules under this Act.

(3) Every rule made under this Act shall be laid, as soon as may be after it is made, before each House of Parliament, while it is in session, for a total period of thirty days which may be comprised in one session or in two or more successive sessions, and if, before the expiry of the session immediately following the session or the successive sessions aforesaid, both Houses agree in making any modification in the rule or both Houses agree that the rule should not be made, the rule shall thereafter have effect only in such modified form or be of no effect, as the case may be; so, however, that any such modification or annulment shall be without prejudice to the validity of anything previously done under that rule.]

---
1. Inserted by Act 33 of 1988, Sec. 25 (w.e.f. 1.8.1988).

Section [1][22. **Power to remove difficulties** – (1) If any difficulty arises in giving effect to the provisions of this Act, as amended by the Employees' Provident Funds and Miscellaneous Provisions (Amendment) Act, 1988, the Central Government may, by order published in the Official Gazette, make such provisions, not inconsistent with the provisions of this Act, as appear to it to be necessary or expedient for the removal of the difficulty:

Provided that no such order shall be made after the expiry of a period of three years from the date on which the said Amendment Act receives the assent of the President.

(2) Every order made under this section shall, as soon as may be after it is made, be laid before each House of Parliament.]

---
1. Inserted by Act 33 of 1988, Sec. 25 (w.e.f. 1.8.1988).

VIII. Jurisdiction of the Courts:

The Punjab & Haryana High Court, in he case of *R.P.F.C. vs. Dr. O. P. Mittal and another-[2011 LLR. 1254 (P. & H. HC)]* has clarified that when a specific remedy is provided in a particular statute, it has to be availed and no other recourse under any other Act will be permissible. When the jurisdiction of the **Civil Court** is barred by the provisions of EPF & MP Act, filing of civil suit will not be maintainable.

A part cannot be allowed to overcome or avoid such statutory injunction by seeking a prayer in a civil court in such a manner so as to make it appear that apparently, the order passed under Section 7A of the Act is not challenged, though in effect and in substance the relief, if granted, would result in nullifying the order passed under Section 7A of the Act – *[U.O. I. and other vs. Narayan Bannappa Pakkanvar- 1989 Lab. I.C. 854 (Karn.)].*

No relief which has an effect of nullifying the order under Section 7A of the Act can be granted by a civil court. The plaintiff, by cleverly wording the prayer in the plaint, cannot be allowed to defeat or overcome the bar contained in sub-section (4) of Section 7A. All the trapping of a judicial proceeding are granted into the process of determination to be made under Section 7A of the Act by declaring it deemed to be judicial proceedings within the meaning of Section 193 and 228 and for the purpose of Section 196 of Indian Penal Code and vesting powers in authority under Section 7A as vested in a court under the Civil Procedure Code. Even after, if the employer feels aggrieved by the order, it is open to him to challenge the same under Article 226 or 227 or both of the Constitution. (Now he remedy rests with the EPF Appellate Tribunal w.e.f. 1st July, 1997).

Chapter 2
Applicability of the Act

> ### *Brief badinage -*
>
> *Unlike other enactments, the Employee' Provident Funds and Miscellaneous Provisions Act, 1952 **is not enforced** in the first instance, **but it applies to** an establishment. Rather, it has been the intention to make the industries participative in the implementation of the social security schemes in India. Dint of that the Act was not made applicable to all the industries or establishments, and also granted relief of five years and then three years as infancy period to allow for financially sustainability. Similar thing happened with the additions to Schedule I, which finally leave no room to escape any department from the coverage. There is no scope for the authorities to intervene in application of the Act, except by the Inspector appointed under section 13 of this Act who has been authorized to indulge with the employers to ensure that the employer is performing well as required by the Act. Except Inspectors, all other authorities are meant to administer the Scheme, not to share the enforcement. But, the employers cannot be expected to be saints. They try to add to their profits not by noble deeds only, but by cut in their employees' benefits. When, it is done intentionally, the authorities begin to play their role of enforcing this Act, for which, they have subsequently been authorized or empowered to take action under section 7A, 14B etc. From this point, the application and the enforcement has created so many laws, written and unwritten, between and beyond the lines of the law. What is written in the statute book is open.*

Section-1. Short title, extent and application. [1][(1) This Act may be called the Employees' Provident Fund and Miscellaneous Provisions Act, 1952.]

(2) It extends to the whole of India except the State of Jammu and Kashmir.

[2][(3) Subject to the provisions contained in section 16, it applies-

(a) to every establishment which is a factory engaged in any industry specified in Schedule I and in which [3][twenty] or more persons are employer, and

(b) to any other establishment employing [3][twenty] or more persons or class of such establishments which the Central Government may, by notification in the Official Gazette, specify in this behalf:

Provided that the Central Government may, after giving not less than two months' notice of its intention so to do, by notification in the Official Gazette, apply the provisions of this Act to any establishment employing such number of persons less than [3][twenty] as may be specified in the notification.]

⁴[(4) Not with standing anything contained in sub-section (3) of this section or sub-section (1) of section 16, where it appears to the Central Provident Fund Commissioner, whether on an application made to him in this behalf or otherwise, that the employer and the majority of employees in relation to any establishment have agreed that the provisions of this Act should be made applicable to the establishment, he may, by notification in the Official Gazette, apply the provisions of this Act, to that establishment on and from the date of such agreement or from any subsequent date specified in such agreement.]

⁵[(5) An establishment to which this Act applies shall continue to be governed by this Act notwithstanding that the number of persons employed therein at any time falls below twenty.]

⁶[* * *]

1.	Substituted by Sec. 17 of Act 99 of 1976.
2.	Substituted by Sec. 2 of Act 94 of 1956.
3.	Substituted by Sec. 2 of Act 46 of 1960 for the figures 'fifty' (w.e.f. 31.12.1960).
4.	Substituted by Sec. 2 of Act 33 of 1988 (w.e.f. 1.8.1988).
5.	Substituted by Sec. 2 of Act 46 of 1960 for the figures 'fifty' (w.e.f. 31.12.1960).
6.	Proviso deleted by Sec. 13 of Act 16 of 1971 (w.e.f. 23.4.1971).

Legislative reference –

Sub Section (3) was amended by substituting by the Act 94 of 1956 splitting into clause (a) & (b). The number of employees required for application was substituted by "Twenty" in 1960.

Sub Section (4) was substituted by Act 33 of 1988 delegating the powers of notification to the Central Provident Fund Commissioner instead of the Central Government and providing applicability with a retrospective date but after the agreement between employer and the employees.

Proviso to Sub Section (5) was deleted in 1971 by Act 16 of 1971. By virtue of the proviso any covered establishment employing less than 15 for a continuous period of 12 months could go out of the coverage of the Act.

*****

I. The Extent:

The Act extends to whole of India except State of Jammu & Kashmir due to constitutional embargo. There is a separate law for Jammu and Kashmir, namely - The Jammu and Kashmir Employees' Provident Funds And Misc. Provisions Act, 1961 with Employees' Provident Funds Scheme, 1961 and Employees' Deposit linked Insurance Scheme, 2000. No pension scheme is available under that Act.

II. Act Applies by its Own Force:

The application ofl the Act does not require any attention or initiation of the authorities but it applies by its own force. There are inbuilt provisions provisions which provide a mechanism to apply the Act to an establishment. As soon as the conditions laid down in this Section are satisfied, the employer of the establishment is required to implement the Act to his establishment. The employer of the establishment is required to examine the tests and decide the date from which the Act is to be applied. The tests are- whether the business activities of the establishment fall under any industry as mentioned in the Schedule-I or the activity of the establishment is covered by any activity classified by any of the Notification issued under proviso to Section 11 (3) (b).

Despite the inbuilt directives, if an employer fails to implement the Act, then the authorities have to take initiative to verify whether the provisions of the Act are applicable to the establishment or not! For the purpose of such investigations, Inspector appointed under section 13 of the Act and armoured with the powers of search and seizure as provided in the Code of criminal Procedure, 1973 (previously it was of 1898) as they apply to any search and/or seizure made under the authority of a warrant issued under Section 94 of the said Code (of 1898). In this way, the powers of an Inspector appointed under the Act can be invoked by him before the Act is made applicable to an establishment.

Though, the Act applies by its own force and the authorities are simply to ensure compliance by the employer and ensuring compliance by self by the authorities by completing the accounts of the PF members. However, only the Inspector is empowered to enforce the Act by virtue of the provisions of section 13 (2) which, inter-alia provides for invoking powers mention in section 94 of the Criminal Procedure Code.

To determine the applicability of the Act to an establishment, there is no geographical barrier. Therefore, the authorities i.e. Inspectors appointed under section 13 have powers to enter into investigations anywhere in the country where an establishment is found to exist, to ascertain whether the provisions of the Act are applicable or not to that establishment.

Application of the Act and the Schemes are on different footings, this is to be kept in mind.

Application of the Act is subject to the provisions of Section 16 which lay down certain conditions that exist in respect of an establishment which put embargo on the application of the Act to such an establishment.

III. Establishment, means:

The establishment has not been defined in the Act, although it has been used in the statute everywhere. It covers different types of establishments to be covered under the Act. Industries and classes of establishments, which are governed and defined to be an incorporated persons under different Acts are considered to be establishments for the purpose of this Act. Establlishment as defined in the Shop and Establishments Act is considered proper while defining an establishment in this Act. The Madras High Court has made it clear that the word 'establishment' has not been defined in the EPF Act, 1952, though that word has been used in several provisions ofl the Act, and also in other terms used in definition section. An 'establishment,' therefore must be given its ordinary meaning and it means an organization which employ persons between whom and the establishment the relationship of employee and employer comes to ixist- *[Sri Varadaswami Transport (P) Ltd. vs. RPFC, Madras – AIR 1965 Mad. 466: 1966 (I) LLJ. 699].*

The term 'establishment' is used in its broad sense, meaning any organization of business or industry and not ain narrow sense meaning a fixed and sizeable place of business or residence together with all things which are essential part of it. The Identity ofnon-factory establishment depends on particular ownership or management of it and not any place at which itk is situated at a particular point of time. A Circus is, thus an establishment within the sub-section because wherever it goes, its proprietorship and management remains the same-*[K. Gopalan vs. U.O.I. – 1973 lab.I.C. 287]*.

Further, to construed the word 'establishment,' **if** 'internal aids' are not available, 'external aids' can be taken to under-stand its meaning. Those may be in the nature of 'popular understanding' of the said word in the industrial field, available in dictionary and historical background of the Act.

The dictionary meaning of the word 'establishment' in the Collins Dictionary is as under-

"**Establish-** v.t. set up; settle; prove- **establishment-** n. establishing; church system established by law; permanent organized body, full number of egiment, etc.; household; business; public institution."

Thus, it is clear that the word establishment is not limited to a narrow meaning; but, has a broad meaning. For the purpose of this Act, the establishment includes a factory and other institutions or set-ups, business which have been notified by the Central Government in exercise of the powers conferred on it by Section 1 (3).

However, beyond the nature of business or activities, establishments may be of different categories according to their set-up, incorporation or ownership. Section 16, for the purpose of exclusions from the Act, defines the establishments in 5 categories-

(1) The establishments registered under Co-operative Societies Act prevailing in the respective States.

(2) The establishment belonging to the Central Government or a State Government.

(3) The establishment under the control of the Central Government or of a State Government.

(4) The establishments set-up under a Central of a Provincial or a State Government, and

(5) Other establishments, not falling under any of the above categories.

IV. Exclusions:

In a recent case, a PIL was moved to the Kerala High Court for exclusion/exemption, which was disposed off by deciding that whether a particular class of establishment can be included or excluded under the EPF & MP Act, 1952 or the Scheme framed there under; is clearly a legislative function which cannot be considered by the Court in a Public Interest Litigation. The underlying idea behind the provision of the Act is to bring all kinds of employees within the fold of the Act as and when the Central Government might think fit, after reviewing the circumstances of the each class of establishments- *[George Issac, Managing Partner, Malabar Coast Products, Kottayam vs. Assistant Regional Provident Fund Commissioner and Others. 2015 LLR. 844 (Ker. HC)]*.

Section 1(3) opens with words- "Subject to the provisions contained in section 16, it applies" means, application of the Act is subject certain exclusions which have been mention in section 16.

Section **16. Act not to apply to certain establishments–**

[1]**[(1) This Act shall not apply–**

(a) **to any establishment registered under the Co-operative Societies Act, 1912 (2 of 1912), or under any other law for the time being in force in any State relating to Co-operative societies employing less than fifty persons and working without the aid of power; or**

²[(b) to any other establishment belonging to or under the control of the Central Government or a State Government and whose employees are entitled to the benefit of contributory provident fund or old age pension in accordance with any Scheme or rule framed by the Central Government or the State Government governing such benefits; or

(c) to any other establishment set up under any Central, Provincial or State Act and whose employees are entitled to the benefits of contributory provident fund or old age pension in accordance with any scheme or rule framed under that Act governing such benefits;
³[* * *]

⁴[* * *]

⁵[(2) If the Central Government is of opinion that having regard to the financial position of any class of 6[establishments] or other circumstances of the case, it is necessary or expedient so to do, it may, by notification in the Official Gazette, and subject to such conditions, as may be specified in the notification, exempt ⁷[whether prospectively or retrospectively,] that class of ⁶[establishments] from the operation of this Act for such period as may be specified in the notification.

1.	Substituted by Act 46 of 1960, S.5.
2.	Substituted by Act 33 of 1988, S.21 (w.e.f. 1.8.1988)
3.	The word "or" omitted by Act 10 of 1998, S.5 (i) (w.e.f. 22.9.1997)
4.	Clause (d) and Explanation thereto omitted by Act 10 of 1998, S.5 (ii) (w.e.f. 22.9.1997)
5.	Inserted by Act 37 of 1953, S.15
6.	Substituted by Act 94 of 1956, S.3
7.	Inserted by Act 33 of 1988, S.21 (w.e.f. 1.8.1988)

Legislative reference–

The section was first amended in 1960 and thereafter in 1988 by incorporating clauses (b), (c) & clause (d) providing for certain exclusions for certain categories of establishments. The clause (d) which provided for infancy protections for newly set up establishments was done away vide amending Act 10 of 1998 w.e.f. 22.9.1997.

The sub-section 2 was inserted in 1953 to provide for exclusion by Central Government by issue of notification in respect of certain class of establishments of which economic and other conditions required so.

*****

There are two types of exclusion mentioned in the section 16,

-one is, the exclusion from the application before its application; and

-the other is, exclusion after the application of the Act to an establishment.

Section 16 opens with the words- **"This Act shall not apply"**

Sub-section (1) of Section 16 deals with the exclusion of former category and sub-section (2) of that section, deals with the latter category of establishments, therefore, the go in the both the categories is different. The conditions laid-down in sub-section (1) are considered before coverage of an establishment is finalized and code number is issued; whereas the cases falling under sub-section (2) are, partly considered before coverage of an establishment and partly after an establishment is covered and the conditions laid down in the sub-section (2) created thereafter. Such creation of conditions may be by virtue of a notification issued by the Central Government or by a High Court or the Supreme Court orders in a particular matter.

There happen such cases where any of the conditions laid-down in sub-section (1) created after the Act applied and need to be excluded thereafter. In such circumstances, the case for exclusion, and therefore, de-coverage is required to be done by the appropriate authority to whom the powers to decide any dispute regarding application of the Act has been given, by passing a speaking order to that effect under Section 7A. Suo-moto exclusion by the administrative authorities or by the employer can be term as violation and a default by itself on account of the either end. In some cases, the intervention of the judiciary allowing exclusion after application of the Act, also require the same go of passing a speaking order by the appropriate authority under Section 7A.

The immunes provided by sub-section (1) are-

(1). establishments registered under Cooperative Societies Act, not working with the aid of power and employing less than 50 persons;

(2). establishments belonging to or under the control of the Central or a State Government and employees of which are in receipt of benefits of contributory provident fund or old-age pension as per scheme or rules framed the Central of the State Government;

(3). establishments established under a Central or a State Act and employees of which are entitled to benefits of contributory provident fund or old-age pension as per rules framed under the said Act.

1. Establishments under Co-operative Societies Act-

In respect of establishments registered under Cooperative Societies Act, the condition for application of the Act is that it should employ 50 or more persons as against the 20 persons as provided in section 1(3), if it is not run or working with the aid of power. If a Cooperative Society, it may be engaged in any industry or falling under any class of establishment notified for the purpose of Section 1(3) (b) and working with the aid of power, it is treated at par with other establishments as mentioned in section 1(3) clause (a) or (b). In such cases the provisions of clause (b) & (c) under section 16 (1) do not apply, although, one may claim that cooperative societies are always established under the central or a state Act, hence, these should be entitled to the immune available under clause (b) or (c) of section 16 (1) as the case may be. But, before going for such a claim, it has to be seen whether there is any provision of institution of a provident fund under the said Cooperative Societies Act? If, such a provision is absent in that Act, than no cooperative society is entitle to any immune provided by the section 16 except that of clause (a) of section 16 (1).

The Gujarat High Court has interpreted the use of power by an establishment under Cooperative Societies Act. Their Lordship have observed that petitioner, a Cooperative Bank, claims that it was not using electric power and hence with less than 50 employees, it was not liable to be covered by the Act. Rejecting the contention, that the petitioner was not using electric power, it was observed that the Bank works with the aid of power not only for the purpose of lighting and cooling to the employees and customers work place but also for its computers and other gadgets used in the Bank in providing effective service to the customers. If on this ground alone the petitioner wanted the authorities to hold that the provisions of the Act are not applicable, the same has no substance and hence rejected- *[Mansa Nagrik Sahakari Bank Ltd. Vs. R.P.F. Commissioner- 2003 III CLR 177 (Guj. H.C,)]*. In some cases, dispute of employment strength has been a matter of concern where the cooperative establishment does not use power. In such cases, the workers used to be members of that cooperative society, hence claims exclusion. Here, certain parameters to be observed. If the member-workers get payment for the production-work done for the society, in any nature are to be treated as workers and not the share-holders exclusively, whether, they get share in profit monthly or annually, in addition to the value of the work performed or production done by them.*[refer the case of..*

2. **Establishments belong to Central or State Governments-**

There is no doubt about the establishments belonging to the Central Government or a State Government. Such establishments are directly controlled by the concerned government through its ministries. However, the qualifying clause for exclusion is that the employees of such establishments are required to be entitled to the benefit of contributory Provident Fund or Old Age Pension **in accordance with any scheme or rule framed by the concerned Central or the State Government governing such benefits**. If there is no such scheme or rule to govern the CPF or the Old Age Pension benefits, the exclusion is not available to such establishments even that belong to the Central or State Government.

3. **Establishments under the control of the Central or State Governments-**

The word "**control**" has become a crucial and critical and controversial too, as far the application of the Act is concerned. For the different interpretations of the word "**control**" have come up. In a democratic country, where state and society is governed by different laws and the power of enacting a law is given to the parliament or a state legislature by the Constitution.

The State or Central Government (administration) – the executive body-has general and superior control over all the spheres of the society, specifically, the activities being carried out for advancement of society, as the Constitution has made it compulsory being a welfare State. As such every sphere, every section, every activity is governed by a particular law or a set of laws in that particular section or sphere. By virtue of it the Central or the State Government has control over that within such law and sphere. That is a wider scope of "under the control of the Central or a State Govt."

By this, no one can mean that a particular establishment or a class of establishment is "under the control of that Government." In fact "sphere" as used in the different laws can not mean of having "control on a class of establishment" as envisaged in Section 16(1) (b) and also in Sec. 2(a) of the EPF & MP Act and also relatively in Sec. 2(b) or the Industrial Employment (Standing Orders) Act, 1946, which defines the "Appropriate Government" and used the phrase "under the control of the Central Government."

The word "Control" has been discussed at length by the Patna High Court in the case of "***Sindri Workers Union Vs. Commissioner of Labour***" – *[AIR 1959 Pat. 36; 1959 (2) LLJ- 53]* and by the Supreme Court in the case of "***Heary Engg. Mazdoor Union Vs. State of Bihar***" – *[AIR 1970 SC 82; 1969 (2) LLJ-549; 1969 (i) SCC 765]* decided under Sec. 2(a) (i) of I.D. Act, 1947. The observation of the Patna High Court was, "It is not disputed on behalf of the respondents that the President holds the majority share in the industrial establishment, not in his personal capacity but in his capacity as the head of the Central Government……. The powers of the President are circumscribed by the articles of association, but … the President holds the majority of directors of the company and also the authority to remove any director from his office in his absolute direction."

"It is also clear from the article of association that the management of the company is subject to full control of the president not only in the matters of policy, but also in other matter….. It is, therefore, manifest that under the articles of association, the President has got complete control over the working of the industrial establishment, and therefore, the appropriate Government under Sec. 2(b) of the Act XX of 1946 is the Central Government and not the State Government. As a matter of law, Government enterprises may take various forms in a welfare State. It may take, for example, the form of the departmental administration or a departmental project, it may also take legal form of a joint stock Company in which the Government holds the majority of shares or the totality of shares and so there is complete Government control under the articles of association and under the provisions of the Company law."

4. Public Sector Undertakings

There is also a third type of Government enterprises, popularly known as the Public Sector undertakings, which are established by a separate state or Central government. However, the question of the legal form of the Government enterprises has no real bearing under Sec. 2(b) of Act XX of 1946. The test for finding out whether an industrial establishment is controlled by the Central Government under Sec. 2(b) is a realistic test, whether the Central Government has control over an industrial establishment under the articles of association, in the case of a private Company or by the provisions of special statute in the case of a public sector undertaking. The appropriate Government under Sec. 2(b) of Act XX of 1946 is the Central Government and not the State Govt."

An industrial establishment set up under a Central or State Act known as Public Sector undertakings. Such establishment is set up by an Act, but the legislation does not provide any privilege to the employees of such industries, but allows to implement other labour legislations. Therefore, all the public sector undertakings are required to implement the P.F. Act. Then the judgements in educational institutes' case requires a review at the academic level as well as at the judicial level.

5. Establishment Set-up by an Act

There are certain establishments, which are set-up by a Central or a State Act and specific provision as to contributory Provident Fund or Old Age Pension is made for the benefit of the employees of such establishment. A scheme or rules are required to framed under the said provision. If, it is a fact that employees are getting benefit of Contributory Provident Fund or Old Age Pension as per the Scheme or Rules so framed, the establishment is not suppose to implement the provisions of the P.F. Act. However, if, instead of framing a scheme or rules, it is notifies that the provisions of the P.F. Act should apply than the P.F. Act will apply, no exclusion is available in such a case as in the Working Journalists (Condition of Service) and Misc. Provisions Act, 1955 and Cine workers and Cinema Theatre Workers (Regulation of Employment Act, 1981, the paragraphs 80 and 81 respectively have been inserted to give effect to, but no such provisions have been made with regard to the Building and Construction Workers' Condition Service) Act.

Applicability of the Act

6. Exclusion by Central Government under sub-section (2)

The Central Goernment, after it considerations, may notify such industry or class of establishment to which the Act would not apply despite the fact that that industry or the class of establishment stands notified under Section 4 or under proviso to sub-section 1 (3) (b) of the Act. There was a notification under this sub-section lastly issued vide notification No. S.O. 1431 dated 14th May, 2010 in respect of establishments registered under Societies Registration Act, 1860 or any of the similar Act of a State in force. It's currency expired on 31.03.2015. Thereafter, the Cenctral Government has not considered it to extend, and thus denotified vide G.O.I. Letter No. S-35013/1/2015 –SS.II dated 20.08.2015 circulated vide C.P.F.C. letter No. Coord/1(1) 2010/Notification u/s 16(2)/24366 dated 07.09.2015.

As on date there is notification under sub-section (2) exists w.e.f. 01.04.2015.

V. State Act: Prevalence over Central Act:

Why the question that, whether a State legislation will prevail over a Central Legislation or a Central legislation will prevail over a State Act arises? Definitely, Article 254 (2) is quoted in support of the reply to the question. Here, again the scope of the subject matter, 'Prevalence of an Act enacted later by a State Government' becomes relevant.

If a legislation contain directions about the subject matter, like Contributory Provident Fund, the later enactment must contain that subject mater with a wider scope and a greater force equal to or more than that what is available in the earlier enactment. Secondly, the proviso to the Article 254 (2) must be regarded and taken into account where by, it is provided that the parliament may amend, enhance, vary or repeal the law. The relevant provision of Article 254 (2) reads as under.

"(2) where a law made by legislature of a State, with respect to one of the matters enumerated in the concurrent list contains any provision repugnant to the provisions or an existing law with respect to that matter, than the law so made by the legislature of such State shall, if it has been reserved for consideration of the President and has received his assent, prevail in that State:

Provided that nothing in the clause shall prevent parliament from enacting at any time any law with respect to the same matter including a law adding to, amending, varying or repealing the law so made by the legislature of the State."

The proviso has expressly given the powers to the parliament to enact any law with respect to the same matter, including adding to, amending, varying or repealing the law so made by the legislature of a State. There appears no law that has been enacted by the parliament in that manner.

The High Court of Bombay, in the case of *Security Guards Board of Greater Bombay and Thane District and others V/s R.P.F.C. – [1991 Lab IC 1855 – Bombay]* has held, for the first time, that the Security Guards Board for Greater Bombay and Thane districts established under the Maharashtra Private Security Guards (Regulation of Employment and Welfare) Act, 1981, is not covered by the Central Act i.e. E.P.F. & M.P. Act, 952; as the P.F. Act would fall in entry 24 of the Concurrent List, in the constitutional arrangement. The P.F. Act and the Act of 1981 are vitally different. The supervising authority and many other features indicate a radical difference between the two enactments. The Act of 1981 together with the scheme framed there under will have primacy over the P.F. Act of 1952.

The reason behind that judgment was provision for exclusion of an establishment which falls within the scope of section 16 (1) (b) or (c). And what is the scope of that section, will be discussed in this chapter, Step 3 (Applicability). However, such interpretation belies the version given by the Supreme Court, depriving the workers from the Pension Schemes available under the EPF & MP Act, 1952.

However, the High Court of Kerala has taken a different view that the P.F. Act applied to establishment where 20 or more persons are employed, but, the Kerala Motor Transport Workers' Welfare Fund Act, 1985 applies only to such establishments to which the Central Act does not apply. Both the central and the state Acts can, therefore, simultaneously, apply in their respective areas of operation. Therefore, there is no repugnancy as envisaged by Article 254(i) of the Constitution of India. That apart, the State Act had received the assent of the President and the same would prevail over the Central Act even if the same in deemed to have occupied the field *[Unni Mammu Haji Vs. State of Kerala – 1989 (2) LLJ 493 (Ker.)]*.

Further, a case under that came up before the Hounorable High Court of Kerala in which it was held that Motor Transport undertakings covered under EPF Act are out of purview of Kerala Motor Transport Workers Welfare Fund Act. Though the petitioner's establishment was covered under the provisions of the Employees' Provident Funds and Miscellaneous Provisions Act, 1952, the authorities appointed under the provisions of Kerala Motor Transport Workers' Welfare Fund Act, 1985 directed the petitioner to comply with and pay contributions under the provisions of K.M.T.W. Welfare Fund Act, 1985. Writ petition filed by the petitioner challenging said order, was rejected by the Learned Single Judge. Hence this writ appeal.

The Court held that in view of the proviso to Section 4 of the Act, once the establishment viz. Motor Transport Undertaking is covered by the provisions of Provident Fund Act, 1952, either under Sub-section (3), or Sub section (4), these Motor Transport Undertakings are kept out of Section 4 of the Kerala Motor Transport Workers' Welfare Fund Act, 1985. The learned Single Judge has proceeded on the wrong assumption that it was never the intention of the State legislature by enacting the proviso to Section 4 (1) of the Welfare Fund Act, to permit employers and majority of the employees to voluntarily go under the net of Provident Fund Act and thereby depriving the employees of more beneficial provisions available under Welfare Fund Act. This wrong assumption has led the learned Single Judge to reject the writ petition. These are two legislations, one framed by the Central

Government and the other by the state Government with the avowed object of assisting the employees working in the establishment. The conclusion reached by the observations made by the Division Bench of this Court in *Unni Mamu Haji's case (supra)*. This Court cannot accept the reasoning and the conclusions reached by the Single Judge. Hence the impugned judgement is set aside and also the demand notice issued by the respondent under the provisions of erala Motor transport Workers' Welfare Fund Act, 1985. Appeal allowed- *[Hymavathi vs. Special By. Tehsildar. – 2008 (119) FLR 279 (Kerala HC)]*.

After enacting a law by a state legislature, the parliament has enacted a law for adding new provisions for making new schemes, from time to time, for the benefit of the PF members and their families. Recent enactment is the Act 25 of 1996, the Employees' Provident Fund & Miscellaneous Provisions (Amendment) Act, 1996 which has provided for framing of a Pension Scheme, known as "the Employees' Pension Scheme, 1995." Whether the amending Act of 1996 can be treated an Act passed by the Parliament subsequent to an Act passed by a State legislation enacted prior to the Act 25 of 1996? Thus, the EPF & MP Act, 1952 with amendment by Act 25 of 1996 is not to prevail over such a State legislation? A fair answer can be affirmative only.

Besides, these judicial pronouncements, it may be a matter of discussions in the judicial circle and in the academic circles that if a comprehensive amendments facilitating for a fresh Scheme is brought in subsequent to the enactment of the State Act which also quote the accent of the President, will it prevail over the State Act? In 1995 to introduce Pension Scheme an amendment was brought into the Act which is a comprehensive social security scheme but by virtue of the interpretation given by the High Court of Bombay the benefit of the Pension Scheme is not available to employees of such establishments who are availing benefit of Section-16(1) (c) of the Act. This is a situation where the purpose of the Social Security Legislation is defeated by rude and inflexible interpretation of the enactments.

This situation has also taken to interpret adversely in the case of *Laxmi Bai K Vs RPFC A.P. – [2006 (I) LLJ.27]* when it ruled that "Hard cases make bad law" [Black's Dictionary 6th Edition] is a phrase used to indicate judicial decisions which, to meet a case of hardship to a party, are not entirely consonant with the true principles of law. The Andhra Pradesh High Court held that even when the petitioner's plight deserves sympathy, no relief can however be granted contrary to law. This is the way to remain confined between the lines of a statute despite the fact that the Objet of the particular enactment has a wider scope.

But, in the case of *Balbari Vidya Mandir and others vs. State and others*, the single Judge of Rajasthan High Court has taken a different view while interpreting the word "control" occurred in section 16 (1) (b). The view taken by the single Judge has been confirmed by a Division Bench *[Union of India vs. Shree Digamber Jain Secondary School and others – 2003 I CLR 233 (Raj. DB)]* and by the Supreme Court also *[Regional P.F. Commissioner vs. Sanatan Dharma Girls Secondary School and others-AIR 2007 SC 276: 2007 I LLJ 458: 2007 (1) SCC 268: 2007 (112) FLR 314:]*. The case was filed by some 25 schools situated in various parts of Rajasthan which were getting grant-in-aid from the

Government of Rajasthan. The Act was extended to the six categories of institution, popularly and broadly known as 'Educational Institutes' vide Notification No. S.O. 986 dated 19.2.1982 (published in the gazette on 6.3.1982). After upholding validity of the notification by Supreme Court by order dated 8.1.1988, schools receiving grant-in-aid from the state government were feeling uncomfortable in implementing the Act, The Central Government also issued direction under paragraph 78 of the EPF Scheme, 1952 circulated vide Central P.F. Commissioner's circular No. 19(3)94/E-1/18675 dated 03.7.2000. In the mean-time, the state legislature of Rajasthan passed an Act, namely- The Rajasthan Non-Government Educational Institutions Act, 1989 with a provision of making P.F. rules for the benefit of the employees of such institutions, empowering the state government for the same. The state government, accordingly notified the rules known as The Rajasthan Non-Government Educational Institutions (Recognition, Grant-in-aid and Service Conditions) Rules, 1993 (w.e.f. 1.1.1993) in which provisions for P.F. mainly for the institution which were in receipt of grant-in-aid. A provision empowering the state government to grant exemption to any or a class of institutions from the operation the P.F. instituted under the said rules. In 1997, the state government issued a notification exempting all aided educational institutes from the operation of the above P.F. provision under the state rules. Aggrieved by the State Government's notification, some schools filed writ petitions in the High Court and the single Judge decided the writ and ordered that-

(1) the State Government has right to recognize an educational institute and also the right to de-recognise that, therefore, the institutions are under the control of the State Government for the purpose of section 16 (1) (b) of the Act of 1952;

(2) there is a provision for contributory provident in the rules made by the state government under the said State Act of 1989 known as 'the Rajasthan Non-Government Educational Institutions (Recognition, Grant-in-Aid and condition service) Rules, 1993 for the benefits of such employees;

(3) the State Act of 1989 was passed after the Central Act of 1952, and both the Acts are on a subject falling under the Concurrent List under the Constitution as such both the Acts have been given ascent by the President of India under Article 254(2), hence the later Act of 1989 will prevail over the Central Act of 1952;

(4) with a view to the above, the institutions of the petitioners were not covered by the Act of 1952;

(5) the powers of the State Government under the State Rules to exempt any or a class of institutions from the operation from all or any of the provision of the said Rules is unconstitutional, therefore the order of the state government issued in 1997 exempting all educational institutes receiving grant-in-aid from the government of Rajasthan, was illegal.

After confirmation of this judgment by the Division Bench, all the educational institutions in Rajasthan were allowed to go out of the EPF Act, 1952 by the regional administration of the EPFO, said to be with the concurrence of the HO. Many of the schools other then the aided ones also did not extended the PF benefits neither under the Central Act nor under the state Rules.

The interpretation does not seem to be a good at any level. It seems to be a mixture of 2 clauses (b) & (c) of section 16 (1) as "control" has been taken from clause (b) and shelter of Article 254 (2) has been taken from clause (c).

On the other hand, this interpretation may lead to another constitutional complication for the State Government under **Article 12 of the Constitution**. All the Educational Institutions in Rajasthan may claim to be employees of the State and the benefits accordingly.

Article 12 of the Constitution reads as under:

"In this part, unless the context otherwise requires, the 'State' includes the Government and Parliament of India and the government and the legislature of each of the state and all local or other authorities within the territory of India or under the Control of the Government of India."

In both the situations, as stated above, the employees of the educational establishments under the control of the state government of Rajasthan are required to enjoy the CPF or Old Age Pensionary benefits, but, unfortunately, they are not getting any thing like PF and pension.

Any establishment, which is not required to implement the provisions of the Act, that shall enjoy benefit of exclusion.

This unfortunate situation has drawn back the state of affairs of a social security enactment despite views expressed by the Apex Court in the early days of the Republic till to day [refer **RPFC V/s Shibu Metal Works – 1965 (1)LLJ 473; Nazeena Traders (P) Ltd V/s RPFC – AIR-1965 AP 200; 1966 (1) LLJ 334; J.G. Vakharia V. R.P.F.C. (1957) 1 LLJ 448; Sayaji Mills Ltd. Vs. R.P.F.C.-AIR1985 S.C. 323; 1985 SCC (L&S) 310; Bhaskara Ceramic Industries vs. R.P.F.C. A.P.- 1991 Lab. I.C. 1138 (A.P.); Srikanta Datta Narsimha Raja V. Enforcement Officer, (1993) 3 SCC 217:1993 Lab IC 1359** etc.].

VI. Infancy Protections:

Clause (d) of Section 16 (1) was deleted w.e.f. 22.9.1997 wherein it was provided that an establishment, other than those specified in clauses (a) to (c) were not required to implement the Act for 3 year from the date of its set up. This 3 years period was suppose to be a breathing time for a new establishment which can sustain itself financially and then ready to bear the burden under the Act.

This condition has been of great importance for an establishment and if it has been a unit of an establishment already in existence and running its business, it is clubbed together with the existing establishment by the authorities and the infancy protection of 3 years was usually denied. On this ground litigations have come up in the past before different courts.

Promised Estoppels

With effect from 22.9.1997 the infancy protection as provided in clause (d) of Sub-section (1) of Section 16, was deleted and every establishment which was existed on that date were required to implement the provisions of the Act. Most of the establishment which were existed on that date & setup prior to that date claimed for infancy protection for three years. But, the department did not allow and enforced demand of contribution from 22.9.1997. Such establishments took the matter before the courts. The courts Bombay High Court and the Rajasthan High Court took the stand that when an establishment was existing prior to the date of which the amendment was brought in into the Act were entitled to the benefits of infancy period of three year from the date of set-up. Thus the demand from 22.9.1997 was not legal. In such cases the Supreme Court also confirmed this contention and rule that any amendment in the Act cannot take away the benefit which it was entitled to as on the date of appointment. It was the promised right given by the law to the establishment set up before 22.9.1997, but did not complete a period of three years' infancy. Such establishment is entitled to avail the breathing time of three years and required to report compliance after completion of three years that may occur after a date of the amendment. [*See the case of Sangam Spinners vs. R.P.F.C.-I - 2008(I)CLR424 (SC); 2008-I-LLJ.661(SC)*].

Since the infancy protection has been done away, court cases on this matter have become irrelevant now, hence not given here. However, the Supreme Court judgment in the above case is, rather relevant in other matters where a question of promised estoppels may attract.

VII. Coverage of a Factory Establishment:

Initially the Act was made applicable to Factory establishments only that too which were engaged in the industries specified in Schedule-I. Therefore, the application of the Act to an establishment, which is factory has its own category which is defined and included in Schedule-I. Ancillary activities to the factory carrying out manufacturing activities including the Head Office or/and the Registered Office were covered with the factory. At present, practice has reversed and factories, the manufacturing units are treated as part of the Head Office or the Registered Office, as if the Head Office activities are the main and the manufacturing activities are ancillary to the Head Office (?).

When a question arises whether a particular establishment is a factory and whether it is engaged in any industry specified in schedule-I or not. The word "Factory" has been defined in Section 2(g). The expression "engaged" in section 1(3)(a) indicates what is the production on commercial basis or is a primary concern where sole intention is to impart training to the students of an educational institute and the products manufactured by the students are not sold nor does the institute derive any monetary benefits out of such production, it cannot be said that institute is engaged in the production of such goods-*[Victoria Jubilee Technical Institution vs. R.P.F.C.- 1980(I) LLJ.254]*. On the other hand, in the case of **Andhra University vs R.P.F.C. and other-*[AIR 1986 SC 463; 1986 Lab.I.C. 103]***, while disapproving the judgement of Calcutta High Court in the case of **Vishwa Bharati vs. RPFC,** the Supreme Court held that the publication department of the University is an establishment engaged in production or publication of books and materials for students which is sold on cost, hence the publication department is an establishment under the Act.

[**Note**- This case was for the period prior to extension of the Act to the Universities and Educational Institutions.]

The Supreme Court has taken a different view but, with a difference, in the case of **Cemendia Co. Ltd. Vs. Bachu Bhai N. Rawal- *[AIR 1987 SC 1956; 1987 Lab.IC.1648; 1988 (I) LLJ.138]*** wherein it has been observed that a workshop run by the company, which is engaged in "building and construction" for maintenance of its machinery and equipment and not undertaking any work of outsiders is not an establishment engaged in "Engineers and Engineering Contractors, not being exclusively engaged in building and construction," hence not covered under section 1(3)(a) of the Act.

To decide whether a particular factory is engaged in a particular activity is decided by its manufacturing process. The manufacturing process is the process right from procurement of raw material to dispatch of finished goods. As such, this may involve various activities being performed in different departments, which were, in beginning years were not included in the scheduled activities, hence section 2A was inserted to cover all the employees under the Act.

VIII. Coverage of Non-factory establishments:

The provision to extend the Act to non factory establishments was brought in into the statute book by the Act 94 of 1956 by substituting sub-section (3) with classification through clauses (a) and (b) and the first notification was in respect of the *Tea Plantations (other than the tea plantations in the State of Assam), Coffee Plantations, Rubber Plantations, Cardamom Plantations, Pepper Plantations and then to the Mines of Iron-ore etc.* in the beginning of 1957. A contributory provident funds scheme was already working for the tea plantation workers in the state of Assam, hence, with a view to extend the PF benefits to plantation workers in other part of the country.

There has not been a suggested schedule for such 'other establishments,' and power to notify by the Central Government not provided in any other section but, in the proviso to clause (b) itself the Central Government has been authorized to issue notifications for the purpose of the clause.

Further, an arrangement for the future has also been made that if, at any point of time, it is considered necessary that the provisions of this Act be extended to any establishment employing less than 20 employees, the Central Government may do it by giving a notice for not less than two months of its intention so to do, then it may do so. But, as far as the question of factory establishments is concerned, clause (a) is required to be amended by an amending Act.

IX. Effect of Section 2A:

Section [1][2A. **Establishment to include all departments and branches. – For the removal of doubts, it is hereby declared that where an establishment consists of different departments or has branches, whether situate in the same place or in different places, all such departments or branches shall be treated as parts of the same establishment.**]

> 1. Substituted by Act 46 of 1960, s.5.

Legislative reference:

This section was first inserted in 1960 with a view to remove doubts regarding coverage of employees employed in branches or different departments of an establishment. At that time the industries inserted in the Schedule I were 10 only and most of the industries used to have various departments within the same factory premises and branches for the purpose of marketing of the products and procuring raw material for the factory was situated in different parts of the country. Employees employed wherein were not extended the Provident Fund benefits thought the branches of the departments were forming part of the establishment. Therefore, the factory establishments or other establishments owned by a company could not be treated to be a composite unit or part of the establishment. Every such establishment which is having different entity or existence had to be treated as an independent establishment for the purpose of this Act.

This provision was inserted in 1960, that is after adding non-factory establishments in section 1(3) in 1956. Obviously, unlike the factory establishments, other establishment have different characteristics business scope.

Section 2A is merely a declaratory and explanatory and it is not intended to amend or alter the law previously existing- *[Uma Shankar Srivastava vs. State of U.P.- S.C. N. Vol. No. VI P.19 dated 16.10.1964].*

We find that the High Court is wholly un-justified in the reaching of the above conclusion that both M/s. Naraini Udyog, Kota and M/s. Modern Steels, Kota, being two independent companies can not be clubbed together. It is time as found by the High Court that they are registered as two independent units and represented separately by the members of a Hindu un-divided joint family. Nevertheless, the Commissioner recorded as a fact the functional unity and integrity between the two concerns. In the ultimate analysis the employer gets the maximum out turn of his production by ensuring health to its employers which is the fundamental right of the latter'-*[R.P.F.C., Jaipur vs. M/s Naraini Udyog and others- 1996 (2) LLJ.1063 (SC)].*

Again, the Supreme Court has underlined the same principle in the case of *R.P.F.C. vs. Dharamsi Morarji Chemicals Co. Ltd. - [1998 (II) CLR 151 (SC)]* by observing that the respondent company established a factory in Roha in 1977 which originally running a factory at Ambernath since 1921. It was held that besides common ownership, there is no evidence of inter connection between the two. There is also no evidence of common, supervisory, financial or managerial control. The products manufactured are different and work force is different. Hence infancy allowed.

The tests and criteria to determine different establishments or units as a whole are discussed by the A.P. High Court in the case of *Andhra Cement Co. Ltd, Vijaywada vs. R.P.F.C. and others- [1988 (2) LLJ.453 (AP)].* However, it is relevant to mention that principle of inter-dependency of to different establishments was, first outlined by the Supreme Court in the case of Associated Cement Companies Ltd. Vs. their workmen - *[AIR. 1960 S.C. 56]* which was a case under Industrial Disputes Act. On the basis of that case, Allahabad High Court in the case of Delhi Cloth and General Mills Co. Ltd. Vs. RPF Commissioner, UP- *[AIR 1961 All.309; 1961 (2) LLJ 444; 20 FJR 410]* declared that it Dourala Sugar Mill was part of the DCM hence was not entitled to the infancy.

Since, the infancy protection has been done-away w.e.f. 22.9.1997, cases of clubbing cases have limited to the employment strength only.

X. Engaged, 20 or more employees:

The purpose of putting limitation of twenty employees as cut off point is to see that unnecessary burden should not be put on the employer, if he is a small employer not capable of bearing the burden. The same was the purpose for providing infancy period. But, the Act also provides that where new branches and units are opened. Then those units also should be considered as part of the same establishment. It was held that where the employer grows in such a manner that he opens one after another branch in different names, including one or the other members of the family as a partner in order to deprive the workmen of the fruits of growth, and keeps the number of employees less than 20

Applicability of the Act

in each firm, the law cannot be a mute spectator- *[Regional P.F. Commissioner vs. M/s Nath Traders and others- 2007 (1) Lab.I.C. 826: 2007 LLR. 378 (Delhi HC)].*

The expression 'Engaged' in Section 1 (3) (a) indicates the commercial production as primary concern. Where sole intention is to impart training to the students of an educational institute and the products manufactured by the students are not sold, nor does the institute derive any monetary benefits out of such production, it can not be said that the institution is engaged in the production of such goods - *[Victoria Jubilee Technical Institution vs. R.P.F.C.- 1980 (1) LLJ. 254].*

The burden to prove strength of employees, contrary to the assertion of E.P.F. Authority, lies upon the employer since the required records of employees, as employed, are always in possession of the employer- *[J.K. college of Nursing & Paramedicals vs. Union of India & Others- 2011 LLR. 1013 (Delhi HC)]. Coverage* of an establishment under the Act is justified when the management fails to produce the attendance or payment of wages records to prove employment of less than 20 persons- *[Ajmeri Gold Fingers vs. Asstt. P.F. Commissioner and another-2013 LLR. 1127 (Bom. HC)].*

An establishment having 20 or more employees on its roll is covered under the E.P.F. & M.P. Act, 1952. Proceedings under Section 7A of the Act are justified when an establishment is having 20 or more employees on its roll but not making compliance of the Act by depositing the contributions as per scheme under the Act. Once the employer's authorized representative or a responsible official has verified the number of employees to be more than 20, denial by the employer later on that number of employees were not 20 or more than 20 or less than 20, is not sustainable – *[M/s. Sachdeva Maternity & General Hospital vs. Presiding Officer, E.P.F Appellate Tribunal & another- 2015 LLR. 837 (P 7 H H.C.)].*

Another major condition to apply the Act to an establishment is the '**number of persons employed.**' For application of the Act, number of employees have been put 20 or more to be employed in an establishment. How the numbers are counted, has been an area of inviting disputes. In the times, when every establishment is going for out-sourcing employees or work in certain areas and of certain nature, it is general concept of the employer to disown the statutory liability of P.F. in respect of the persons not directly employed by the employer. A confusion has been prevailing over the employment of number of employees, after few judgements by the Supreme Court, especially in the case of *Food Corporation of India vs. Provident Fund Commissioner – [(1990) 1 SCC. 68: 1990 (60) FLR. 15: 1990 1 CLR. 720: 1990 SCC (L & S) 1]* whereby it was insisted upon that while assessing the dues under the PF Act, the beneficiaries have to be identified so that amount so assessed and recovered could be credited to the beneficiaries accounts. In the cases of coverage, insisting for a list of beneficiaries is not warranted as the Act applies as soon as the employment strength reaches 20 despite the fact that some of them may not be entitled for membership. This misunderstanding prevailed before the EPF AT in a case which was taken before the Punjab & Haryana High Court where it was held that once the employer's authorized representative or a responsible official has verified the number of employees to be more than 20, denial by the employer later on that number of employees were not 20 or more than 20 or less than 20, is not sustainable- *[Sachdeva Maternity & General Hospital vs. Presiding Officer, Employees' Provident Fund Appellate Tribunal and Another- 2015 LLR. 837 (P & H HC)].* Prior to this judgement, many other judgements were given by various High courts at various point of time.

To resolve this, one has to depend on the definition given in the Act. The 'employee' has been defined in section 2(g), which reads as under:-

[2][**(f)** *"employee"* **means any person who is employed for wages in any kind or work, manual or otherwise, in or in connection with the work of** [1][**an establishment**] **and who gets his wages directly or indirectly from the employer,** [2][**and includes any person,-**

(i) **employed by or through a contractor in or in connection with the work of the establishment;**

(ii) **engaged as an apprentice, not being an apprentice engaged under the Apprentices Act, 1961 (52 of 1961) or under the standing orders of the establishment**].

---

1. Substituted by sec. 3 of Act 94 of 1956 for the words "a factory."
2. Substituted by sec. 3 of Act 33 of 1988 (w.e.f. 1.8.1988).

Legislative reference-

The definition was widened by substituting the ending words by clauses (i) and (ii) by the Act 33 of 1988.

By going through the definition, there are certain facts which come out of the definition which help and lead to a concrete and unambiguous conclusion. These are- a person,

(1) *employed **for wages**, who gets directly or indirectly from the employer,*

(2) employed **in any kind of work**, manually or otherwise, in or in connection with the work of an establishment,

(3) employed **by a contractor**,

(4) employed **through a contractor**, in connection with the work of the establishment,

(5) engaged as **an apprentice**–

– **not being** under the Apprentices Act, 1961, and

– **not being** under the standing orders of the establishment.

(1) Employed for wages:-

What does employed mean? As per section 1 (3) (a), the Act would apply to a factory when it appears that twenty of more persons were, **ordinarily employed** therein. "Are employed" has to be read as "are ordinarily employed"-*[Inspector, EPF vs. Alwin Concrete Blocks and Tiles Mfg. Co.-AIR 1974 SC 337; (1974) 3-SCC. 717; 1974 Lab.I.C. 770; 1974 (I) LLH. 276]*. For the purpose of the E.P.F. Act, the "number of persons employed" is to be determined by taking into account the general requirement of the establishment for its regular work, which should have a commercial nexus with its financial capacity and stability. If a factory is compelled to employ additional hands for an accidental purpose or for a very short period, than they cannot be considered. Similarly, if an establishment regularly requires certain number of persons for its business for whole of the year or for a long time then they will be considered for coverage, employment of 20 persons on a single day are excessive-*[R.P.F.C. vs. T.S. Hariharan – AIR 1971-SC 1519; 1971 (I) LLJ. 416]*.....The employment must be contained as employment in the regular course of business of the establishment. Such employment, obviously, would not include employment of a few persons for a short period on account of some passing necessity or some temporary emergency beyond the control of the company. This must necessarily require determination of the question in each case of its own peculiar facts-*[Chetram vs. R.P.F.C. Orissa 1972 (I) LLJ. 60 9 SC)].*

For the purpose of this Act, a person is treated as an employee when he is working in or for the establishment for wages. If a person works for the establishment without intention to get wages, he is not an employee. This clearly means that there must be a person called employer and another person, who with intention to get wages, working under the superintendence of the former which in its finality bears the relationship of **master and servant**, of course, the later may be getting his wages directly or indirectly from the employer.

The principle of *relationship of master and servant* was led-down by the Supreme Court in a case under Shops and establishments Act *[Silver Jublee tailoring vs. Chief Inspector of Shops and Establishments and another-1974 (I)-SCR 747],* in which it has been held that the question is not whether, in practice, the work was done subject to a direction and control exercised by an actual supervision or whether an actual supervision was possible, but, whether **ultimate** authority over the man in the performance of his work resided in the employer so that he was subject of the latter's orders and directions. This relationship of employer and employee does not cease when an employer stops his business, but, it ceases only when it is terminated in accordance with the law-*[Imambhai Gulam Husein Shaikh vs. R.P.F.C.- 23 CLR 581].*

(2) **Employed in any kind of work, manually or otherwise, in or in connection with the work of an establishment:-**

The second condition, which is put in the definition clause, is that the person may performing *any kind of work,* which *may be manually of otherwise,* but *must be in or in connection with work of the establishment.* Here, three conditions have been put leaving no corner for any dispute. This covers all type of employees whether he is employed on regular or permanent, or temporary or casual basis or he may be engaged to work on piece-rate basis. Further, he may be employed through a contractor or by a contractor, he is an employee.

'Any kind of work' can be determined by the manufacturing process or the total stock of the business activities, which definitely should be for the purpose of the business of manufacturing activities of the establishment. This vary fact has been underlined by the Supreme Court in seventies in the case of *Silver Jublee tailoring vs. Chief Inspector of Shops and Establishments and another-[1974 (I)-SCR 747],* wherein it has been ruled that the workers are not obliged to work for the whole day in the shop, is not very much material. There is of course, no reason why a person, who is only employed **part-time**, should not be a servant and it is doubtful whether regular **part time service** can be considered, even prima-facie, to suggest may thing other than a contract of service. According to the definition in section 2(14) of the Shops and Establishments Act, even if he is principally employed in connection with the business of the shop, he will be a 'person employed.' Therefore, even if he accepts some work from other tailoring establishments or does not work whole time in a particular establishment, that would not in any way, derogate from his being employed in the shop where he is principally employed.

A **person can be a servant of more than one employer**. A servant need not be under the exclusive control of one master-*[Patwardhan Tailors Poona vs. Their Workmen- 1960 (I) LLJ. 722]*. Any person employed for wages for any kind of work in or in connection with the work of the establishment regardless of the place where he worked in connection with the employer's establishment, would be an employee within the meaning of the Act. Under the statutory definition, even if a person is not wholly employed, if he is principally employed in connection with the business of the shop, he would be a person employed within the meaning of the statutory language-*[Satish Plastic vs. R.P.F.C.- (1982) 44 FLR 207]*.

Women members of Charitable Trust/Society – paid on piece rate basis- The women, who came to the establishment of the petitioner to manufacture eatables out of raw materials supplied to them by the trust are nothing, but, workers and the authorities under the Act were more than justified in covering the establishment under the Act. The fact that they were employed to become members of the trust before they were allowed to work cannot change their legal status as employees. On the basis of the admitted facts and circumstances of the case, there is hardly any doubt that the relationship between the so called associate members and the trust is that of employer and employee and the authorities have properly and correctly covered the establishment under the provisions of the Act- *[Shree Kutchi Oshwal Mahila Mandal vs. U.O.I. and others, - 1992 Lab.I.C. 1449 (Bomb.)]*.

Similar view has been taken by the Madhya Pradesh High Court in the case of *Shree Mahila Griha Udyog Lijjat Papad vs. U.O.I. and another-[1994 Lab.I.C. 1308 (M.P.); (1994) 2 LLJ. 610]* which was confirmed by the Supreme Court *[Shree Mahila Griha Udyog Lijjat Papad vs. U.O.I. and another- 1999 (4) LLN. 64 (SC)]* ordering that the Act be applied from 1.4.1999 that is prospectively to the Jabalpur Branch of the appellant. The M.P. High Court earlier held that the petitioner society was formed for the upliftment of down-trodden ladies to provide them with work and infuse self sufficiency. The society takes ladies who actually work with them as members the ladies are paid remuneration for the work done by them on the basis of its quantity. Ultimate control of Jabalpur branch vests either in the Managing Committee or in the Branch Committee or the Sanchalika. The women members have no power to control it. They cannot claim ownership of the branch except wages for work done. Therefore, they cannot be termed as 'employer' in view of the status aforesaid in relation to the establishment. Even if the position of the member is considered in general law, they could not be termed as 'employers.' They do not contemplate an employer without financial control or management and supervision of the establishment. It must be held that since employees get their wages from Sanchalika or Branch Committee who would be 'employer' in relation to the establishment in question and the member working for wages in the establishment and manufacturing Papad, Badies etc. are 'employees' of the establishment within the meaning of Section 2(f) of the Act and are entitled to the benefits thereof. The EPF Act does not make any distinction between directly engaged or engaged through contractor and a casual employee and regular employee. For coverage of P.F., even piece rated workers would also be counted- *[Jaggi & Co. vs. E.P.F. Appellate Tribunal and another- FLR (116)2008 P. 326 (Delhi HC); 2008 LLR.126 (Delhi HC)]*.

Weaver of a Weavers Coop. Society, who are **members of the society**, do the work in connection with the work of the petitioner establishment, they are also paid wages on the basis of their work. The Woven Cloths are sold by the petitioner society.

Applicability of the Act

The yarn is supplied by the petitioner to the weavers. Thus, it is clear that the weavers are engaged for the work in connection with the work of the petitioner. There is, thus, relationship of employer and employee between the society and their weavers/workers-*[Madathnpath Weavers" Co-oriduction & Sales Society Ltd. Vs. R.P.F.C.- 1997 Lab.I.C. 2957 (Mad.); 1998 (I) LLJ. 824 (Mad.)].*

In *Gandhi Vanita Ashram vs. Provident Fund Commissioner, [(1996) 73 FLR 1612 (P&H)],* it has been held that the crucial test for applying the provisions of the Act to an institution imparting vocational training is the existence of relationship of master and servant between the institution concerned and the trainees. A Governmental institution running on no profit no loss basis and getting merely non-recurring grant from the government started training centers to train destitute women and widows in vocational courses so that they could have self-employment or seek employment in other organizations. Such trainees were paid a nominal amount for the work done by them. The institution had no control over the trainees. In such circumstances it was held that such payment was not salary, nor were the trainees employees of the institution. The mere fact that the textile clothes prepared by the trainees were being supplied to various departments of the government did not make such an institution, a commercial organization. Hence, the Act was held to be inapplicable to such an institution.

An un-reported judgement in the case of *Moideen Beary Bajpe, SK vs. R.P.F.C. Karnataka- [UP No. 3075 / 1974]* of Karnataka High Court go further while observing relying on the case of *R.P.F.C. vs. T.S. Hariharan- [AIR 1971 SC 1519]* that **Changulies means day-labourers.** These labourers are employed for seasonal operation in the estate. The operations like picking, manufacturing and weeding are stated to be the work in the coffee estate. The said works are not un-connected with agricultural operations in the estate nor could they be said to have been necessitated by any act of emergency. These are regular work in every coffee estate which are to be attended to every year. Therefore, changulies workers employed for that purpose cannot be excluded for determining the strength of the establishment.

A **Sweeper** working for more than one establishment, situated in the street and paid regularly by the establishment, he is an employee for the purpose of the E.P.F. and M.P. Act- *[Merta Oil Mills Co. vs. R.P.F.C. – (1992) 65 FLR. 537 (Raj.)].* Similar view has again been expressed by the same court in the case of *Railway Employees' Cooperative Banking Cociety vs U.O.I.- [1980 Lab.I.C. 1212 (Raj.)]* that where a cooperative Banking Society engaged a **sweeper,** who worked twice or thrice a week, a **night watchman,** who kept a watch on other shops in the locality also and a **gardener,** who came for work ten days in a month, they must be held to be 'employees.'

(3) **Contractors' employees-**

What is the scope of 'contractor?' The meaning of this term has come in the PF vocabulary from Bombay High Court through the case of *Tata Engineering and Locomotive Co. Ltd. Vs. U.O.I.- [1991 Lab.I.C. 49; 2 CLR 595; 62 FLR 191 (Bom.); (1990) 2 LLN. 1194].* The contractor contemplated by section 8A is one who is a mere front or headman of the principal employee. It does not cover a registered cooperative society which was engaged in business of various types and in addition to that whose employees attended to the work of conservancy at an employer's factory, nor does it cover a supplier of certain goods to such employer. Hence, the employer could not, under section 7A be asked to supply particulars of workers employed by such cooperative society or of workers employed by **such supplier.**

Employment through or by contractors has been an area, which has provided many ways and means for avoidance of labour laws. Rather the way of employment of persons in any type of work has been a gift to the Indian economy very much suitable to the bureaucratic system of administration. However, it has become fate of the Indian society and economy; therefore, the laws framed draw attention to look towards them, and so the EPF Act has taken care of them, of course, as late as in 1988 by substituting certain provisions by amending Act 33 of 1988.

Employment by or through a contractor and their entitlement for the PF membership has been discussed at length by the Andhra Pradesh High Court in the case of *G.V.V. Swamy vs. R.P.F.C and others- [1987 Lab.I.C. 719 (AP)].* Merely, because the periods of various contracts of the petitioners were for limited period or months that does not make the employee casual labour. The employee continued to work with the contractor in the various contracts and were not appointed as casual labour. On the facts of the present case, there can be no dispute that the employees of the contractor, though, not directly employed by the principal employer, were, however employed by the contractor in connection with the work of the principal employer. Hence the provisions of the P.F. Act became applicable to them.

Today, a common thinking is working on this point that is, treating all the contractors as establishments for the purpose of this Act. This view has rendered the persons being employed by or through contractors are hardly getting their social security membership for a longer period which may render a better social security benefit to them of to their families in the times, it is actually required and meant for.

For the purpose of this Act, while considering the contractors' labour, the principal employer cannot be out of scene, he always remains there on scene and he is made responsible legally and the definition also speaks so. Thus, the employment of contractor labour can be of *three* natures, namely,

(i) **Employed by a contractor-**
(ii) **Employed through a contractor, in connection with the work of the establishment,**
(iii) **Self-employed on contract basis.**

(i) **Employed by a contractor–**

Employed by a contractor means the contractor has been awarded with a particular job to be completed within the specified time and for the money agreed for. In this category, the principal employer is concerned for the work as per the specifications and standards and not for the working hours, the wages being paid to the workers and other working conditions, if the work is being performed out of the premises of the principal employer. This type of contractor is an establishment having certain infrastructure to complete the given job with the standers of skills, which may be called 'giving expert service.'

(ii) **Employed through a contractor-**

In this category, person employed by the establishment is not recruited by it under the normal recruitment procedure and/or the Standing Orders, but, called through a known agent. Such persons are paid on daily basis or piece rate basis till his services are required by the establishment, and thus, his term of contract of employment comes to an end. For such employments, authorities have taken care by making certain provisions and putting certain conditions with a view to take care under that particular enactment. This type of employment can never be an employment under the classification 'expert services' and the principal employer is fully responsible for the person employed as such.

(iii) Self-employed on contract basis-

This type of employment has also emerged especially in government under-takings by way of engaging a person on piece rate contract and such person is paid only when he raises bill for that. This may be argued that he is a contractor and not covered under the definition of the 'employee' with the logic that who will bear the employer's share and the cost of administrative charges? It is true that he is a contractor, but under which category! Whether, he is engaged by or through a contractor? And, whether, he is working in or in connection of the work of the establishment? If the answer to the former is 'no' then he has to be treated to have been engaged by the establishment it-self, may be the terms of employment and the payment of emoluments differ than those prevailing in the employment environment. The answer to the later is definitely 'affirmative' then there remains nothing to keep that poor fellow out of the reach of this Act.

Another point, which makes it different from the above two categories, is the provisions in Section 8A. This section has intended towards smooth compliance under the Act in respect of the contractors' employees by the contractors by giving certain powers to the employer to get amounts recovered from the contractor payable by the contractor under the Act. Under this Act, the responsibility for reporting compliance has been laid on the employer only, which is also supportive to the definition of 'employee.' This position regarding **Counter Holders in Apana or Super Bazar** has been clarified by the Gujrat High Court by observing that the R.P.F.C. held that the employees engaged by counter holders in the premises of petitioner co-operative society running Apna Bazar are employees of the petitioner cooperative society. It was challenged by the petition. Various conditions imposed upon counter holders clearly go to show that counter holders are working as agents or contractors. Thus, there is no illegality in the order of the *R.P.F.C. [Ahmedabad Cooperative Departmental Stores Ltd. Vs. U.O.I.- 1997 (II) CLR 123 (Guj)].* **Where no contractor has been appointed** and wages were paid through the union leaders who the members of union and employees' of the company the employees are not of a contractor appointed but of the company *[G.M. ONGC Contractual Workers Union- CLR (II) 2008 P. 988 (SC)].*

(iv) In or in connection with the work of the establishment-

This term has rendered to maximum litigation. Major question on this account which is raised is whether the particular employment is in connection with the work of the establishment or not. Again, this question can be dealt with by referring the 'manufacturing or manufacturing process' or the 'total activities or the business of the establishment.' Without considering either of the aspects, any conclusion on the issue may lead to a whimsical one and the litigation in the court of law.

Hitherto, numerous landmark judgements have come out of the Apex Court and various High Courts. It is very difficult to mention all those here, but, such judgements, which have the force of law, are referred here.

The Andhra Pradesh High Court has discussed these points at length in the case of *G.V.V. Swamy Vs. R.P.F.C and others- [1987 Lab.I.C. 719 (AinP)].* By a notification of the Central

Government No. GSR 1069 dated 23.9.1980 (w.e.f. 31.10.1980), the Act was made applicable to 'building and construction contractors.' Consequent to that, such contractors became liable. Prior to that, the principal employers were responsible for the PF compliance in respect of contractors except those which were covered under 'engineers and engineering contractors, not being exclusively engaged in building and construction industry.' Certain such contractors were already employed by Hindustan Ship Yard, Vishakhapattanam, which before the said date was liable as principal employer in respect of the persons employed by the contractors. The question of the liability, if any, of the contractor vis-à-vis the Hindustan Ship Yard in respect of the amounts payable by the Ship Yard for the pre 31.10.1980 period in respect of persons employed by the contractors arose. The court examined the various provisions of the E.P.F. Scheme, 1952 and amendments thereof and particularly in view of paragraph 30, 32, and 36-B of the Scheme held that for the period prior to 31.10.1980 the contractors were liable to pay to the Hindustan Ship Yard their own contribution as the employers' share together with other charges and the contribution payable by their employees mentioned in the Act and the Scheme. It was further held that the Hindustan Ship Yard was entitled to deduct these amounts from the amounts payable to the contractors. Prior to 31.10.1980 the contractors were not directly liable to the authorities under the Act, but their principal employer.

Among other cases, the Supreme Court judgement on **Home-Workers** in Beedi Industry, is the land mark. In the case of *P.M. Patel and Sons and other vs. U.O.I. [AIR 1987 SC 447; 1986 Lab.I.C. 1410; 1986 (I) LLJ.88 (SC)],* the Apex Court has held that to be an employee, it is necessary that the relationship of master and servant should exist with the employer. In the context of the condition and circumstances in which the home workers of a single manufacturer go about their work including the receiving of raw material, rolling the beedies at home and delivering them to the manufacturer, subject to the right of rejection. There is sufficient evidence of the requisite degree of control and supervision for establishing the relationship of master and servant between the manufacturer and the home-worker. It must be remembered that rolling of beedies is not of a sophisticated nature requiring control and supervision at the time of work. It is performed by thousands of illiterate workers, young and old, men and women with equal facility and it does not require a high order of skill. In the circumstances, the right of rejection can constitute in itself and effective degree of supervision and control. The same view has been expressed by Madras High Court in the case of *S.P. Abdul Rahim and Sons vs. R.P.F.C. and another-[1996 (I) LLJ. 1134 (Mad.)].*

In the case in the case of *S.K. Nasiruddin Beedi Marchant (P) Ltd. Vs. R.P.F.C. and other- [1991 (I) LLJ.19]* that a producer or manufacturer can not be made liable to contribute towards the Provident Fund of a workman, who is not employed by the producer. The content of the word 'employee' has, however, under gone radical change. It is, obvious, that if, wages are paid to a person for production in connection with the industry, the worker would become employee of the manufacturer. The wages may be paid to him directly by the employer him-self or indirectly from the employer through a contractor. The definition takes in its sweep not only the persons engaged in the premises of the employer. Naturally, they are spread out at different places and do not work in the establishment of the employer. Yet, they are in the category of workers, who get their wages from the employer. When, beedi worker gets his wages directly from the employer, there is no difficulty in appreciating that he is an employee of the manufacturer. Even, if he gets his wages through a contractor, retained by or in connect with the employer. Home-worker, therefore, employed either by an employer or by a contractor must be held to be an employee of the employer.

(5) **Engaged as an apprentice-**

The definition of 'employee' excludes apprentices of two kind namely–

– **not being under the Apprentices Act, 1961, and**

– **not being under the standing orders of the establishment.**

There is no dispute regarding the apprentices engaged under the Apprentices Act, 1961, which are governed by the conditions mentioned in that Act, hence excluded from the 'employee.' In the paragraph 2(f) (iv) of the E.P.F. Scheme, 1952, the 'apprentice' has been defined through the Explanation, which was substituted prior to the Apprentices Act, 1961 was enacted. It says '**An apprentice means a person who, according to the certified standing orders applicable to the factory or establishment, is an apprentice, or who is declared to be an apprentice by the authority specified in this behalf by the appropriate Government.**'

Now, the situation stands changed after 1961. The apprentices are those, who are engaged under the Apprentices Act. 1961, but still the relevance of the standing orders prevail. It is with regard to the persons engaged by giving them the category of 'Trainees,' 'Learners' or so.

Under the Industrial Employment (Standing Orders) Act, 1946, every industry is require to prepare standing orders get it approved by the appropriate authority and notify. In fact these orders use to be the rules of discipline in that industry. If, there is a provision in the standing orders for engaging learners of trainees, there must be a scheme of training describing therein the period of training, the areas of training, the stipend and periodical increase in it, periodical skill test and procedure for valuing the performance etc. Any person under-goes training as per that scheme, than he is treated as a learner or a trainee otherwise an employee.

XI. Contractor Establishment - whether covered Independently:

After the new-economic order under Globalisation, out-sourcing has become a common phenomenon to engage employees through contractors thereby responsibility under this Act is also being shifted on the shoulders of the contractors' them-selves instead of the principal employer. It is true that no provision of this Act permits for recognize a contractor as an independent establishment and covered separately under the Act, even than it is going on, and change of contractor every year or after a short spell, another contractor appears on scene asking for a separate coverage with same work force which has been working with the ousted contractor. This is all being done under the industry schedule head specified as 'Expert services,' though, the contractor does not happen to be an establishment rendering expert services. 'Expert services' have been explained in the notification No. GSR 805 dated 17.05.1971 as "Establishments rendering expert services, such as supply of personnel, advice on domestic or departmental enquiries, special services in rectifying pilferage, thefts and pay rolls irregularities, to factories and establishments." Most of the contractor establishment do not qualify the criterion prescribed in that notification.

As appears in the definition of 'employee' "**... employed by or through a contractor**" clears the fog. Where persons are employed by a **contractor can be (not exclusively) an establishment**

rendering expert services depending on the tests to determine whether a particular contractor establishment is engaged in rendering expert services or not. If the contractor establishment does not qualify the tests, then, it is simply 'taking persons employed through a contractor' and the principal employer cannot absolve of his obligation under this Act. However, the back ground of identifying and defining a contractor-establishment in the Act may clarity through a light on this point.

For the first time, vide notification No. GSR 346 dated 07-03-1962, activities by which some establishments can be termed as a contractor establishment was listed. Such activities, which are popularly known as 'trading and commercial establishments' carrying-out the business, namely- **importers, advertisers, commission agents and brokers and commodity and stock exchanges.** Un-dobdtedly, such establishments may also work as contractors, but after that notification, such establishments may be treated as 'trading & commercial establishments under the Act.

Similarly, the establishments notified vide notification No. GSR 1398 dated 17-09-1964, which are the establishments **of Attorneys, Chartered or registered accountants, Cost and Works Accountants, Medical practitioners and medical specialists, Architects and expressly, the Engineers and engineering contractors, but not exclusively engaged in building and construction industry** are contractor establishments, but notified separately to term as an establishment.

Further, the establishments of **Railway Booking Agencies run by contractors or other private establishments on commission basis** (notification No. GSR 505 dated 17-03-1972); establishments engaged in **building and construction industry** (Notification No. GSR 1069 dated 23.09.1980); Establishments engaged in **stevedoring, loading and unloading of ships** (notification No. GSR 611(E) dated 23.11.1981); the establishments engaged in **Railways for construction, maintenance, operation and commercial services of Railways** (Notification No. GSR 401 dated 10.11.2005); and establishments engaged in **marketing, servicing and usage of a computer including manufacturing** (notification No. SO 4356 dated 16.11.2007) are also of the nature of a contractor establishments, but have further been classified as establishments just to avoid any litigation. These establishments can also be grouped under a common head of '**expert services**,' but, ultimately, it will be wrong go, because, the entry of 'expert services' as notified vide notification No. GSR 805 dated 17-05-1971 expressly includes a clarification viz. '**such as supplying of personnel, advice on domestic or departmental enquiries, special services in rectifying pilferage, theft and pay roll irregularities, to factories and establishments**' does **not include the supply of labour to a factory or to an establishment**, because, by including the labour in personnel may lead to wrong resulting in change of meaning, the definition of the 'employee' and the soul of the Act defeated. Unfortunately, this version is being practiced. This erring go has also has a history.

In the middle of ninety sixties, the Government of India established a force known as the Central Industrial Security Force (C.I.S.F.) for providing security to sensitive Government of India undertakings as it was not possible for such undertakings to recruit security experts. After some time, the bigger private establishments under the same threat also asked for the assistance of the CISF, but the Government did not accept the request, however, it allowed to get such personnel from some agencies having such expertise and personnel, therefore, the entry of the such establishments was notified vide notification No. GSR 505 dated 17-05-1971 just to recognize them as independent establishments.

Again a problem arose in the PSUs which were enjoying exemption either under section 17 (1) of the Act or relaxation under paragraph 79 of the EPF Scheme, 1952 that the PSUs were extending PF benefits to the employees on the roll through their PF trusts, but, the employees employed by or through contractors were not being enrolled as PF members and the PF authorities took initiation for assessing the dues in respect of contractor employees, and the PSUs were not in a position to dilute those dues, hence, again the matter was discussed at higher level and it was decided the PSUs to go for exemption under paragraph 27A of the Scheme for a class of employees instead of under section 17 which is meant for the whole of the establishment, and the compliance in respect of the contractors' employees, the establishments may continue to report as un-exempted establishment. After some time, the PSUs insisted for a separate code number for the contractors, which, by the higher intervention, was made operative, and when the PF Inspectors were refrained from frequent visits to the establishments, they could not do anything except supporting the applications for separate code numbers by contractors just to add up the number of coverage in their account and facilitating the contractors to play for evasions and to increase number of non-complying establishments.

A high gray area in relation to contractors is the franchisee. Whether a franchisee is a contractor of the principal establishment? The answer came from Madras High Court in the case of ***R.P.F.C, Tirunellveli vs. Prabha Beverages Pvt. Ltd. And another-[2009 LLR. 972 (Madras)]*** in an appeal against the order of EPF Appellate Tribunal. It was observed that a franchisee establishment functioning under the contract for distribution of bottled soft drinks will be distinct one and neither an establishment nor contractor, hence it will not be treated as part of the manufacturing company to be covered under the EPF Act as an extension of the establishment.

A franchisee being a distinct establishment, employing more than 20 employees, will be entitled to infancy benefit (before September, 1997).

Coverage of a franchisee establishment under the EPF Act by the Authorities is to be cancelled and also recovery of Rs. 3,40,240.80 P. towards contribution is liable to be refunded with interest @ 9% per annum because it was not an extension of the manufacturing company i.e. Parle (Export) Pvt. Ltd.

Similarly, where canteen was in the premises of the school for which the school had no control or supervision over it, it is not justified to extend the PF benefits to the workers of the canteen. Moreover, the approach of malafied and bias by the Enforcement Officer cannot be brushed aside. In his earlier inspection, he has not insisted to cover the employees in the canteen but, only when his daughter studying in the school failed he has tried to club the canteen with school. The High Court remanded the matter to the Commissioner to pass a fresh order in accordance with law- ***[Kerala Sareeram Model School through its Trust-in-charge, A.P.R. Nair vs. U.O.I. and others-2006 LLR. 383 (Jharkhand H.C.)]***.

In case, all employees/workers employed by the contractor were paid salary by contractor and contractor had also been allotted a separate code number. Here it is contractor who had employed the workers and deputed at premises of establishment. It is the employer who has to made the contribution at first instance. Hence, the contractor has to pay the contribution. And the PSEB i.e. the establishment could not be held liable for making the contribution on account of employees employed by the contractor.

So long so the code number is not allotted to the contractor, it is the liability of the establishment to pay provident fund on account of the employees employed by the contractor and thus in essence, it is the liability of the PS establishment to pay and not that of the contractor to pay contribution.

On going through the plain language of Section 2 (e) and (f) it envisages that the employer means in relation to an establishment the person who is the 'authority' which has the ultimate control over the affairs of the establishment would be the employer or not. The definition of employee has to be read in conjunction with the definition of employer and as per the definition of employer (supra) the employee would mean a person who is employed for wages in any kind of work, manual or otherwise in or in connection with the work to an establishment, and getting his wages 'directly' or 'indirectly' from the employer.

It is the contractor which has relationship of employer and employee and the PSEB i.e. the establishment has no control over the service conditions of the employees employed by the contractor, therefore could not be held liable for making the contribution employed by the contractor. *[M/s. Calcutta Construction Company vs. Regional P.F. Commissioner and others. – 2015 (146) FLR 579 (P & H H.C.)]*.

XII. Specified Industry:

An establishment which is a factory engaged in an 'industry' specified in schedule I and employing 20 of more persons, will attract the provisions of the Act even if being run by a larger organization carrying on other activities not covered by the Act- *[Andhra University vs. R.P.F.C (1985) 4 SCC 509; (1986) 1 LLJ. 155; 1986 SCC (L&S) 134]*.

The case of *Nazeena Traders (P) Ltd. Vs. R.P.F.C. [AIR 1965 AP 200; (1966) I LLJ. 334]* has been the case whereby the concept of clubbing two industries was ruled by the AP High Court. It says that the scope of section 1(3) (A) of the EPF Act, 1952 is not limited to factories exclusively engaged in the industries enumerated in Schedule I to the Act and the fact that a factory carries on one industry which is included in Schedule I while the other industry carried on by the same factory does not come within its purview does not absolve the employer form the obligations impugned by the Act if the total strength of the employees in the industries exceeds the required number. The concept of a Composite establishment has been taken up by the Supreme Court in the case *of Associated Industries (P) Ltd. Vs. R.P.F.C. Kerala- [AIR 1964 SC 314; 1963 (2) LLJ.652 (SC)]* that where the Industrial activities are independent and the factory is running separate industry within the same premises and as part of the same establishment and under the same license as in the petitioner's case, it can not be accepted that, in such cases, enquiry would be relevant as to which of the industries is dominant and primary and which is not. There the High Court was plainly right in rejecting the appellant's case that its factory did not attract the provisions of section 1(3)(a) of the Act. The case of *R.P.F.C. vs. Shrikrishna Metal Mfg. Co.- [AIR 1962 SC 1536]* is also on the same lines.

One of the points that an organization run on no profit basis whether is an establishment or not! The answer is given in the case of *Christian Association for Radio and Audio Visual Service (CURAVS), Jabalpur vs. R.P.F.C. [1979 Lab.I.C. 283]* that the petitioner society was not a spiritual or religious organization, but was run on no profit no loss basis. The activity of the petitions was to render specialized service to Christian Churches and institutions in the field of radio, television and audio visual aids by selling books and pictures and renting out films. It was being aided by Churches and Charitable Organisations. There was a systematic activity in pursuance of the object of petition.

There was an organized co-operation between petitioner and its employees for production and distribution of goods and services calculated to satisfy human needs and wants. Simply, because petitioner was being aided by Churches and other organisations, it did not cease to be a trading and commercial establishment. It is covered by Notification dated 7.3.1962 issued under the EPF Act.

XIII. Voluntary Application of the Act:

An establishment, which covered by the provisions of section 16 and by virtue of that, it is not coverable under section 1(3) of the Act, can get the Act applied voluntarily under sub-section (4). The sub-section has been re-drafted by the Act 33 of 1988 with a view to dispose of the cases of voluntary coverage swiftly. Now, the main conditions are-

* the Central Provident Fund Commissioner is authorize to issue notification;
* it can be done whether an application has been made to him or other-wise;
* the employer and the majority of employees should agree for such application;
* such application can be from the date of such agreement or from a date subsequent to it or form a date specified in such agreement.

Obviously, voluntary coverage under the Act depends and reaches its finality when a notification is issued, otherwise it leaves many legal complications. Prior to the amendment of 1988, the provision was–

> **"(4) Notwithstanding anything contained in sub-section (3) of this section or sub-section (1) of section 16, where it appears to the Central Government, whether on an application made to it in this behalf or otherwise, that the employer and the majority of employees in relation to any establishment have agreed that the provisions of this Act should be made applicable to the establishment, it may by notification in the Official Gazette, apply the provisions of this Act to that establishment."**

The difference is clear as to the process for voluntary application of the Act.

Whether voluntarily covered establishment can go out of the Act? There is no provision in the Act for any establishment to go out of the Act except sub-section (5). However, in the case of ***Sampath Kumaran & Co. vs. R.P.F.C. -[1974 Lab.I.C. 602; (1973 44 FJR 191]***, it has been held that it is elementary that if persons can do an act for their benefit, but, contemporaneously burdened with obligation, they would be in order, at any time thereafter, to seek for a relief of such obligation created by their own voluntary act of commission, by once again expressing in unequivocal terms, their desire not to be burdened any more with such liabilities or obligations. This is reflected in section 21 of the General Clauses Act. But, under which provision of the Act? The provisions of section 1(3), whether such establishment, if covered under or not, to be examined before any action to be taken in honour of the above judgement.

XIV. Establishment once covered Cannot go out of the Act:

There is no provision in the Act as to end the application of the Act to an establishment. Sub-section (5) of section 1 provides that an establishment once covered under the Act will continue to be covered under the Act until the establishment ceases to exist.

However, it is open for the Central Government, by invoking the provisions of section 16(2), it may issue a notification excluding any establishment or a class of, then, such establishment will remain out of the purview of the Act for the period specified in the notification.

In many cases, various High Courts and the Supreme Court subsequently, declared an establishment or a class of establishments falling under section 16 (1) (b) or (c) led to avail holiday from the application of the Act. At this stage of age and time, the E.P.F. & M.P. Act, 1952 does not provide for the Provident Funds only, but have brought incomparable Pension Scheme and the Insurance Scheme within its wings leaving behind all the common known social security schemes, compatible to the Provident Funds.

However, an establishment involves in running a factory with administrative and branch offices, whether at one place or at different places and the employment strength of all these, if they constitute an integral, whole must be aggregated to find out whether the mischief of the Act is attracted or not. Once such establishment is covered, the falling of number of employees below twenty would not take it out of the purview of the Act- *[Leo Mercantile Corporation, Madras vs. The Secretary, Ministry of Labour, G.O.I.- 1987Lab.I.C. 557 (Mad.)].*

The Kerala High Court has also taken similar view in the case of **Kottathala Handloom Industrial Co-op. Society vs. Enforcement Officer,- [2008 III C.L.R. 464 (Kerala H.C.)]** that the petitioner is a cooperative society which had at one point of time 50 employees in its employment and was therefore covered by the provisions of E.P.F. & M.P. Act. But later on the strength of the employees fell below 50 (and even below 20). Thereafter, the petitioner did not send its returns and payment of contribution to the Commissioner as required by the Act, hence a prosecution was launched against the petitioner for non-compliance of statutory obligations. The petitioner therefore, filed a petition under section 482 of the Criminal Procedure Code and invoked its inherent powers to quash the prosecution.

The petitioner contended that the employees strength had fallen below 50 long before the relevant dates with reference to which the allegations of non-compliance are made. The Enforcement Officer respondent on the other hand contended that it is irrelevant whether the employment strength had fallen below 50 or below 20 as the establishment if it is once covered under the Act, shall continue to be covered under the Act, whatever be the fall in the employment strength.

The only question before the High Court was whether such an establishment which is already covered under the provisions of the Act shall cease to be covered when the employment strength falls below 20/50. The High Court pointed out the legislative history behind section 1(5) unmistakably conveys that under no circumstances the establishment can claim that it ceases to be covered on the ground of fall of employment strength below 50 or 20. Establishment which is once covered whether under section 1(5) or under section 16(1) shall continue to be covered and the fall in employment strength cannot be advanced as a ground to justify the claim of cessation of coverage takes place automatically. Hence the petition was dismissed.

XV. Special Notification for Coverage under Sec. 3:

Section [1][3. **Power to apply Act to an establishment which has a common provident fund with another establishment–**

Where immediately before this Act becomes applicable to an establishment there is in existence a provident fund which is common to the employees employed in that establishment and employees in any other establishment, the Central Government any, by notification in the Official Gazette, direct that the provisions of this Act shall also apply to such other establishment.]

> 1. Substituted by Act 94 of 1956, s.5.

This provision is occasional and related to such establishment which is a member of a common provident fund prior to application of this Act, by virtue of the coverage of an establishment participating in the common provident fund, the other establishment to which this Act does not apply, the Central Government has been empowered to extend the provisions of this Act to such other establishment by way of issuing a notification in the Official Gazette. This is, perhaps, with a view to make operative smoothly the provisions of section 15 without disturbing the existing provident fund management by the Trust.

XVI. Power to add to Schedule I-

Section 4. **Power to add to schedule I – (1) The Central Government, may by**

notification in the Official Gazette, add to schedule I any other industry in respect of the employees whereof it is of opinion that a Provident Fund Scheme should be framed under this Act and thereupon the industry so added shall be deemed to be an industry specified in Schedule I for the purpose of this Act.

(2) All notifications under sub-section (1) shall be laid before Parliament, as soon as may be, after they are issued.

> *Schedule I and the list of other establishment notified under clause (b) of sub-section (1) of section 1 are given at the end of this chapter.*

Section 4 authorises the Central Government to add any other industry in the Schedule I, without bringing any amending Act because, the Schedule I is the part of the Act and any provision or part of it can be amended only by way of an amending Act. By making provision of section 4, that necessity has been removed for this limited cause. Therefore, the Schedule I has been enlarged by way of notifications over a period of 60 years.

XVII. Industries in Schedule I and notified classes of Establishments:

Whether an establishment falls under an industry specified in the Schedule or a class of establishments notified under clause (b) of sub-section (3) of section 1 has been discussed hereinabove, however, there are specific cases which have been discussed by various High Courts and Supreme Court. The same are relevant to refer here.

(i) Application to Minority Institutions- The fact that the constitution provides, in Article 30 (1) that all minorities, whether based on religion or language, shall have the right to establish and administer educational institutions of their choice, does not mean that the state cannot make laws of any nature with respect to those institutions, like the E.P.F. & M.P. Act, 1952, which has been enacted for the benefits of the workers in an establishment. Even if a Provident Find is being maintained in the establishment under the Provident Funds Act, 1925, the provisions of E.P.F. & M.P. Act, 1952, can be made applicable to such institutions under section 1(3)(b)- *[Christian Medical Collage and Brown Memorial Hospital, Ludhiana vs. R.P.F.C. Chandigarh- 1982 Lab.I.C. 952; 1988 (2) LLJ. 379 (SC)].*

(ii) Chit Funds, Not covered by the Act - The financial establishment other then banks, as notified vide G.S.R. No. 1458 under section 1(3)(b) of the Act must be engaged in the activities of borrowing, ending and advancing of money and dealing with either monetary transactions with a view to earn interest. If we read the word "and" as conjunctive, than only such of those financial establishments engaged in monetary transactions with a view to earn interest would be covered by the Act. The meaning of the word "interest" is obviously, a return for the money advanced. The commission earned by a foreman, who renders some service to the subscribers by collecting moneys, conducting auctions or distributing prize amounts to the subscribers after taking a security from him to assure subscribers obligation to pay the balance installments, as per scheme of chit fund business. The commission earned by him for the services rendered by him has been equated in the impugned order of the Govt. applying the Act to the petitioner establishment engaged in the business of chit of kuris, to interest. In chits, there is no element of interest earned by foreman. He earns commission not exceeding 5 percent. Hence, the petitioner establishment is not covered by the Act.- *[Sundaram Finance Corporation & another vs. R.P.F.C. Madras & Others- 1989 (I) MLJ. 356].*

(iii) Clinic without in patient – whether an establishment of "Medical Practitioners" or a "Hospital or Dispensary"- In order to make it an establishment of a medical practitioner and specialists (under notification of 1964), it is not the ownership, control or management that counts. It is the business transacted there that is material, otherwise the beneficent provisions could easily, be defeated by keeping ownership, management and control in somebody else. A clinic or a dispensary or a pharmacy or by whatever name it is called, is an establishment of medical practitioner and specialists.

The notification of 1973 was published only for the purpose of bringing – in such other institutions which could successfully escape from the previous one using the word "Hospital," because, hospitals are likely to be taken out of purview of establishment of medical practitioners and specialists. The primary object of the notification is to give benefit to employees and not to exclude an establishment on the ground that in- patients are not admitted- *[K.B. Jacob vs. R.P.F.C. – 1987 Lab.I.C. 1139 (Ker.)]*

Further more, the same High Court ruled that the facility for hospitalization is not a condition precedent to make an institution a hospital, even though, in most of the hospitals that facility may also be there. If a hospital coming under notification of 1973, it need not be included in that of 1964 and vice-versa. Either way, it is an establishment covering under the Act and Scheme-*[E.P.F. Inspector, Trichure vs. the Poly Clinic (P) Ltd. -1989 Lab.I.C. 969; 1989 (2) llj. 562 (Ker.)]*.

(iv) **Manufacturing of artificial limbs** – requires both the engineering skill and scientific skill and is, therefore, covered under the head "electrical, mechanical and general engineering products" and not as an hospital despite it is manufactured and fixed in disabled person- *[Navedac Prosthetic Centre vs. R.P.F.C.- (1996) 2 LLN. 738 (P&H)]*.

(v) **Solicitor's Firm**- an establishment- The analogy of the Industrial Disputes Act in the matter of "Employees' Provident Funds Acts" can not and should not be imported. Further, that an establishment coming under section 1(3) (b) should be read as **ejusdem generies** with clause (a)- *[M.G.Poddar vs. R.P.F.C.- 1971 (1) LLJ. 381 (Cal)]*.

(vi) **Advocate Firm** ;- Coverage of a firm of advocates under the Act by the Provident Funds Authorities under the head "Attorneys" is not sustainable because of the fact that the word 'Attorney' has been deleted from the Advocates Act, 1961- *[The ACME Company Ltd. Vs. U.O.I. – 2005(I) LLJ.250; 2004 LLR 1054]*.

(vii) **Mess run by I.I.T. not covered:-** The test to be applied in, does the establishment sought to be covered under the Act has the avowed purpose of running messes? If it is so then the establishment would be covered by Notification No. 299 dated 24.03.1973which applies the Act to the messes other than military messes. In this case, the hostel statutorily required to run by the institution, can not be construed as merely a place of sojourn or a lodging. The mess attached to the hostel was incidental or as subsidiary to a greater object of imparting education by an institution. Therefore, the mess is not an independent establishment to which the provisions of the Act could be applied-*[Indian Institute of Technology, Madras vs. R.P.F.C. Madras- 1979-54 FJR 429]*.

(viii) **Circus** – It is in the very nature of the circus business that its working can not be continuous in the sense of working day in and day out. It has to give rest to artists. It has to avoid rains as it works in tents and not in buildings. It also has to spend time in traveling. These hindrances are inevitable. But the intention of a person who carries on the circus business is to work continuously excepting those intervals which can not be avoided in the nature of things. A circus is, therefore, a continuous business and not a casual business. It would be casual only if people come together for a particular performance only without the intention of carrying on a business over a period of time by repeating the performance at suitable time and places. It can not therefore, be said that circus as a business is not an establishment within the meaning of section 1(3)(b) of the Act *[K. Gopalan vs. Union of India- 1973 Lab.I.C. 287.]*.

(ix) **Saw Mills includes saw mills used for cutting stone and metal-** The Rajasthan High Court interpreted the 'Saw Mills' that meaning of the expression "Saw Mills," occurring in the notification GSR 1232 dated 7.9.1962, is not restricted to saw-mills cutting wood. In absence of any qualifying words to justify such a restricted meaning, the said expression has to be given a sufficiently wide meaning so as to cover even saw mills engaged in cutting stone or metal- *[Raghunandan Prasad & Co. vs. Union of India- 1989 Lab.I.C. 1701; (1989) 1 LLN 788; (1989) 42; (1989) 1 CLR 641 (Raj. DB)]*.

(x) "Textile" includes 'Khadi' – In *Sahara Zila Khadi Gramodyog Sangh Vs. Union of India-[(1996) 2 CLR 678; (1996) 3 LLN 246 (Pat.DB)]*, the Patna High Court held that the Act was enacted for the benefit of the employees in factories and in similar establishments. Therefore, being a beneficial legislation, the Act had to be construed liberally with a view to see that the object of the Act was achieved by providing maximum benefit to the employees engaged in industry and similar establishments. Accordingly the High Court interpreted the word 'textile' occurring in Schedule I widely so as to cover Khadi.

(xi) "Trading and Commercial Establishments"- It includes even an establishment run on no loss no profit basis as well as an establishment run with financial aid form others- *[Christian Association for Radio and Audio Visual Service vs. R.P.F.C. – 1979 Lab.I.C. 283 (MP.DB)]*.

In another case, the appellant was engaged in the business of **equipment leasing and merchant banking.** The Karnataka High Court held that the said activities fell within the scope of the notification dated 7.3.1962. The High Court further held that the said activities were intimately concerned with the goods constituting a commercial establishment if not a trading establishment- *Can Bank Financial Services Ltd. Vs. R.P.F.C. – (1998) 1 LLJ.92; (1997) 3 LLN 575; (1997) 2 CLR 734 (Kant.DB)]*.

And, where the dominant activity of an establishment was only purchasing of yarn and getting the same manufactured into bed-sheets and towels by handloom weavers, mere incidental sale of such finished goods would not make such an establishment a trading and commercial establishment- [Chennimalai Weavers' Coop. P. & S. Society vs. Govt. of India- 1981 Lab.I.C. 203 (Mad)].

XVIII. No retrospective application:

Having once accepted the stand of the employer in respect of the applicability of the Act, the Commissioner cannot try to review the situation after a period of fifteen years for applying thee Act retrospectively when no new facts had come on record nor was it contended that the number of persons employed had exceeded twenty in the meantime- *[Ratanlal vs. R.P.F.C. – 1977 Lab.I.C. 1765 (Del)]*.

However, if after an enquiry, an order is made under section 7A directing the employer to make payment for pre-discovery period, it cannot be said that the Act has been applied retrospectively. An order under section 7A does not apply the Act or the Scheme retrospectively but only seeks to enforce it from the date it should have been implemented by the employer- *[Shapoorji Nusserwanji & Co. vs. Trustees of E.P.F.- (1970) 37 FJR 569 (Bom)]*.

Further, If after issue of a notification extending the Scheme framed under the Act, the commissioner does not take steps to collect the dues from an employer and demands the contribution after about two years for the whole period, it cannot be said that retrospective effect has been given to the provisions of the Act- *[Bajarang Lal Padia vs. Stat of Orissa- 1975 Lab.I.C. 830]*.

XIX. Application of the Schemes:

There are 3 Schemes framed under this Act, and provision application each scheme has been mentioned in the schemes.

(i) The Employees' Provident Funds Scheme, 1952:-

An independent provision as to application of the Employees' Provident Funds Scheme, 1952 has been made in the Scheme itself in paragraph 1. Sub-paragraph 3 provides its application to the establishment to which the Act applies, subject to the provisions of Section 16 and 17. Clause (a) of the sub- para excludes the application of the Scheme to the Tea factories in the State of Assam and in clause (b), the dated of application of the Scheme to different classes of establishments from different points of time, that is with effect from or after a subsequent date of issue of notification under Section 4 or under clause (b) of sub-section (3) of Section 1. It is not necessary that the scheme applies automatically on the issue of notification under above sections, but a separate notification under para 1 (3) (b) is necessary for application of the Scheme. If such notification is issued on a subsequent date and the date of application in the notification is not notified, than the Scheme is to apply from the date of the publication of the notification in the official Gazette.

Some cases where application of the EPF Scheme, 1952 is postponed for some time under certain conditions. Those conditions have been laid-down in Section 15.

In the Section 15, special provisions have been made in respect of the establishments where a Provident Fund scheme already exists. Such condition may occure in respect of an industry or a class of establishments notified under section 4 of section 1 (3) (b). Such cases are rare now as almost every type of industry has been notified. However, where exemption was granted to an establishment under section 17 (1) or under paragraph 27 A and require cancellation or revocation on failure under conditions laid-down under paragraph 27AA of the EPF Scheme, 1952, especially condition 29, the establishment is given a time to get the exemption re-notified or till a notification by the appropriate government is issued withdrawing such exemption, the establishment is required to continue to maintain PF accounts under its PF Rules or Scheme.

(ii) The Employees' Pension Scheme, 1995:-

The Employees' Pension Scheme was introduced on 16.11.1995 replacing the Employees' Family Pension Scheme, 1971. Application of the EPS, 1995 is automatic with the application of the EPF Scheme, 1952. No separate notification ir required.

(iii) The Employees' Deposit-Linked Insurance Scheme, 1976:-

Application of this Scheme is also automatic with the application of the EPF Scheme, 1952. No separate notification is required.

Chapter 3

Interpretation and Definitions

> **Brief badinage–**
>
> *Given definitions in a legislation are the guide understand and interpret its provisions. Definitions usually denotes the specific meaning assigned to the certain words within the context and fulfilling the object the legislation carries. Further, it depends upon the authorities to interpret the provisions in a way that it leads to achieve the goal for which the legislation was brought on the statute book.*

I. Interpretation-

The object of the Social Security Act has clearly been defined by Apex court and Act and it need be interpreted accordingly while implementing the provisions of the Act.

The Act was enacted in conformity with the **Directive Principles of the State** as laid down in constitution and being the matter of Labour Welfare, it has been put in the **concurrent list** of the **seventh schedule to the constitution of India**. Accordingly, the Act was came into being and further was amended several times to provide more benefits to the larger population employed in different industries and also to families connected to them as it is to fulfill the social obligations it has been termed as Beneficial Legislation. Therefore, it requires to be interpreted to advance the constitutional directives it aimed to. Provisions of a labour legislation, or a special legislation, or an economic legislation cannot properly be interpreted by the courts without applying the principle of social justice *[Prakash Cotton Mills (P) Ltd. vs. State of Bombay 1957(2) LLJ.490]*. It is the duty of the courts to interpret the Act in such a manner as to give effect to the intention of the legislature and not to put a very narrow construction which may defeat the object of the Act *[Kumpur Textile Finishing Mills vs. R.P.F.C., AIR 1955 Punjab 130]*.

In Construing the provisions of the Act, if two views are reasonably possible, the courts should prefer the view which helps the achievement of the object, though, for such purpose, the stretching the word to an unreasonable degree is not proper *[RPFC V/s Shibu Metal Works – 1965 (1)LLJ 473]*. Further in the case of **Nazeena Traders (P) Ltd V/s RPFC – [AIR-1965 AP 200; 1966 (1) LLJ 334]**, the Andhra Pradesh High Court have held the Employees' Provident Fund Act *fit* to as a beneficial legislation enacted as a measure of Social Justice and should be constituted liberally as to confer benefits on the employees to the maximum extent.

The employees' Provident Fund Act is a social legislation and the canons of construing a social legislation are very different from the canons of construing a taxation law. The court must not countenance any subterfuge which would defeat the provisions of a social legislation and the court must even, if necessary, strain the language of the Act in order to achieve the purpose which the legislature had in placing this legislation on the statute book. Therefore, not only the court must disapprove all subterfuges to defeat a social legislation but must actively try to prevent such subterfuges succeeding in their object" [*J.G. Vakharia V. R.P.F.C. (1957) 1 LLJ 448*]. Any construction which would facilitate evasion of the provisions of the Act would as far as possible be avoided [*Sayaji Mills Ltd. Vs. R.P.F.C.-AIR1985 S.C. 323; 1985 SCC (L&S) 310*]. Interpretation of the Act is to be in consonance with the upliftment and betterment of the working conditions of the employees as such [*Bhaskara Ceramic Industries vs. R.P.F.C. A.P.- 1991 Lab. I.C. 1138 (A.P.)*].

Further, the is not an exercise in linguistic discipline. It is emerging as an important therapy in the disorder of social metabolism..... There is accordingly a growing recognition by courts that a statute should be constructed, rather than interpreted, with due regard to its avowed object and to its character. The avowed object of the Act is to provide adequate security to the worker in old age and infirmity. It is a welfare legislation and it should be construed so as to give necessary effect to that object [*Ramesh Metal Works V. State, (1962) 1 LLJ 169: AIR 1962 All 227*].

In the case of *Jayakar Rao N. Shetty V. R.P.F.C. [(1993) 2 LLJ 78: 1993 Lab IC 561]* their lordship underlined that "It cannot be doubted that the provisions of residential accommodation is one of the objects which is dealt with by the Scheme. All the petitioners are asking is withdrawal of amounts lying to the credit of their respective funds. If the right which is specifically sought to be bestowed to the petitioners by Paragraph 68-B is denied by putting artificial and restricted interpretation... The very object of the Act and the Scheme will be defeated."

The Supreme Court, in the case of *Srikanta Datta Narsimha Raja V. Enforcement Officer, [(1993)3 SCC 217: 1993 Lab. I.C. 1359]* have observed that "Meticulous lexicographic analysis of words and phrases and sentences interpretative functioning of the court is to reflect the contemporary needs and the prevailing values consistent with the constitutional and legislative declaration of the policy envisaged in the statute under consideration."

In the dictionary meaning of the word "Interpretation" as per The Concise English Dictionary is:

"To explain the meaning of, to translate from one language into another, to expound, to make intelligible, to find out the meaning of, to construe or understand (in a particular way), to represent the meaning of or one's idea of artistically. (1984 edition – reprint 1985.).

The interpretation of any provision of the Act depends on the motive it has and strictly it cannot be interpreted grammatically. The responsibility to interpret the provisions of the fact does not depend only on the judicial but by and large, it is the duty of the authorities who exercise their powers conferred on them to decide a particular issue coming up for his decision.

Usually the order of the court and/or the Supreme Court is taken as law on the matter, but the **article 141 of the constitution expressly provide that the order of the court shall be termed as law, only when it is expressly mentioned by the Supreme Court, otherwise all the decisions** or orders of the Supreme Court or other High Courts are confined to the given case only as per Article 141 of the Constitution. Besides, the interpretations given by the Court, the administrative authorities are also bound to interpret the provisions while giving any decision in the given matter. By and large the interpretation given by the authority are more useful and giving sufficient material for the courts to decide the matter before them basing on the findings of the Administrative Authority. That is why the administrative authorities, while acting as a quasi-judicial authority, are required to follow the principle of natural justice and pass a speaking order. The passing of the Speaking Order by an administrative authority is a judicial compulsion on them so that his biasness or pre-concepts may not work. Even these works the order may find certain material information for a proper and judicious decision in the matter by the Appellate Authorities.

II. Definitions-

A dictionary of certain words and phrases used in the EPF & MP Act, 1952 has been given in Section 2. Certain other words and phrases have been put in the paragraphs 2 with the heading "Definitions" in the respective Schemes framed under the Act.

A. Definitions under the Act:-

Section 2. Definitions

In this Act, unless the context otherwise requires, -

1[(a) *"appropriate Government"* **means –**

    (i) **in relation to an establishment belonging to, or under the control of, the Central Government or in relation to, an establishment connected with a railway company, a major port, a mine or an oil-field or a controlled industry 2 [or in relation to an establishment having departments or branches in more than one State], the Central Government; and**

    (ii) **in relation to any other establishment, the State Government;]**

> 1. Substituted for clause-(a). by sec. 2 of Act 22 of 1958.
> 2. Substituted by Sec.2 of Act 22 of 1965.

In this Act, the insertion of the definition of 'appropriate government is relevant to section 13 and section 17 of the Act and also for the purpose of paragraph 27A of the EPF Scheme, 1952 whereunder it appoints Inspectors and notifies the exemption granted to an establishment in respect of which it is the appropriate government, respectively.

1[(aa)] *"authorised officer"* **means the Central Provident Fund Commissioner, Additional Central Provident Fund Commissioner, Deputy Provident Fund Commissioner, Regional Provident Fund Commissioner or such other officer as may be authorized by the Central Government, by notification in the Official Gazette;]**

1. Inserted by sec. 3 of Act 33 of 1988 (w.e.f. 1.8.1988)

(b) *"basic wages"* **means all emoluments which are earned by an employee while on duty or 1[on leave or on holidays with wages in either case] in accordance with the terms of the contract of employment and which are paid or payable in cash to him, but does not include -**

- (i) **the cash value of any food concession;**
- (ii) **any dearness allowance (that is to say, all cash payments by whatever name called paid to an employee on account of a rise in the cost of living), house-rent allowance, overtime allowance, bonus, commission or nay other similar allowance payable to the employee in respect of his employment or of work done in such employment;**
- (iii) **any presents made by the employer;**

1. Substituted by sec. 3 of Act 33 of 1988 (w.e.f. 1.8.1988)

Explanation given under section 6 which further includes certain elements of pay for the purpose of payment of contribution under the Schemes is reproduced here for instant reference.

Explanation I. – **For the purposes of this section dearness allowance shall be deemed to include also the cash value of any food concession allowed to the employee.**

Explanation II. – **For the purposes of this section, "retaining allowance" means allowance payable for the time being to an employee of any factory or other establishment during any period in which the establishment is not working, for retaining his services.**

The basic wages for the purpose of the Act has been an area where disputes have come up because the quantum of wages creates volume of liability on the employer. That is why the employers pay remunerations in different names and heads to his employees with the intension to minimize the liability under the Act which he is under the obligation to pay. With a view to protect the interests and impose certain barriers on the employer, Section 12 has been put in the statute so that no employer can reduce the wages etc. However, under various agreements and awards on wages, different heads of payment have been created just to minimize the liability of the employer, not only under the Act but under other labour laws like Bonus Act, Payment of Gratuity Act etc. Despite the protective provisions, the tactics of the employers to avoid liability is an omni-presence. The judiciary has actively and wisely interpreted the essence of the wages. In the definition itself includes the cash value of food concession, Dearness Allowance which includes all cash payments by whatever name it is called, paid to an employee on account of a rise in the cost of living, House Rent Allowance, Bonus, Over Time

Allowance, Commissions and other similar allowances and the presence made by the employer have been excluded. On the other hand the Dearness Allowance and Food Concessions have been included for the purpose of payment of contribution under the Act.

Detailed discussion on this issue is available under Section 6 in Chapter No. 4.

(c) *"contribution"* **means a contribution payable in respect of a member under a scheme 1 [or the contribution payable in respect of an employee to whom the Insurance Scheme applies];**

1. Inserted by Act 18 of 1976 (w.e.f. 1.8.1976)

(d) *"controlled industry"* **means any industry the control of which by the Union has been declared by a Central Act to be expedient in the public interest;**

1[(e) *"employer"* **means –**

- **(i)** in relation to an establishment which is a factory, the owner or occupier of the factory, including the agent of such owner or occupier, the legal representative of a deceased owner or occupier and, where a person has been named as a manager of the factory under clause (f) of sub-section (1) of section 7 of the Factories Act, 1948 (63 of 1948), the person so named; and
- **(ii)** in relation to any other establishment, the person who, or the authority which, has the ultimate control over the affairs of the establishment, and where the said affairs are entrusted to a manager, managing director or managing agent, such manager, managing director or managing agent;]

1. Substituted by sec. 4 of Act 94 of 1956.

Despite this definition, a clarificatory provision has also been made under Section 14A where, for the purpose of penalties, the employer has widely been defined. It reads as under:-

Explanation:- For the purpose of this section-

- (a) "company" means any body corporate and includes a firm and other association of individuals; and
- (b) "director" in relation to a firm means a partner in the firm.

    This has given a wider scope not to be strict with the dictionary meaning of a given word.

(f) *"employee"* **means any person who is employed for wages in any kind or work, manual or otherwise, in or in connection with the work of 1 [an establishment] and who gets his wages directly or indirectly from the employer, 2 [and includes any person, -**

(i) employed by or through a contractor in or in connection with the work of the establishment;

(ii) engaged as an apprentice, not being an apprentice engaged under the Apprentices Act, 1961 (52 of 1961) or under the standing orders of the establishment];

---
1. Substituted by sec.3 of Act 94 of 1956 for the words "a factory."
2. Substituted by sec. 3 of Act 33 of 1988 (w.e.f. 1.8.1988)

The definition of the employee is very much clear and invites no dispute. However, for the purpose of counting number of employees at the time of coverage it is disputed that a person is an employee or not. This has also been discussed in various judgments by various courts and Government of India has also been given power to issue directions under paragraph 78 of the E.P.F. Scheme, 1952. The detailed discussion on this point is available in Chapter-2.

1[(**ff**) "*exempted employee*" means an employee to whom a Scheme 2[or the Insurance Scheme, as the case may be,] would, but for the exemption granted under 3[***] section 17, have applied;

(**fff**) "*exempted 4[establishment]*" means 4[an establishment] in respect of which an exemption has been granted under section 17 from the operation of all or any of the provisions of any Scheme 2[or the Insurance Scheme, as the case may be,] whether such exemption has been granted to the 4[establishment] as such or to any person or class of persons employed there in;

---
1. Inserted by sec. 3 of Act 37 of 1953.
2. Inserted by sec. 18 of Act 99 of 1976.
3. Omitted by sec.2 a of Act 28 of 1963.
4. Substituted by sec.3 of Act 94 of 1956.

(**g**) "*factory*" means any premises, including the precincts thereof, in any part of which a manufacturing process is being carried on or is ordinarily so carried on, whether with the aid of power or without the aid of power:

1[(**gg**) ***

(**ggg**) ***]

---
1. Omitted by sec. 3 of Act 25 of 1996 (w.e.f. 16.11.1995)

(**h**) "*Fund*" means the Provident Fund established under a Scheme;

(**i**) "*industry*" means any industry specified in Schedule I, and includes any other industry added to the Schedule by notification under section 4;

Interpretation and Definitions

¹[(ia) *"Insurance Fund"* means the Deposit-linked Insurance Scheme framed under sub-section (2) of section 6C:]

(ib) *"Insurance Scheme"* means the Employees' Deposit Linked Insurance Scheme framed under sub-section (1) of section 6C;]

²[(ic)* *"manufacture" or "manufacturing process"* means any process for making, altering, repairing, ornamenting, finishing, packing, oiling, washing, cleaning, breaking up, demolishing or otherwise treating or adapting any article or substance with a view to its use, sale, transport, delivery or disposal;]

---
1. Inserted by sec. 18 of Act 99 of 1976 (w.e.f. 1.8.1976)
2. Substituted by sec.2 of Act 28 of 1963 and re-numbered by Act 99 of 1976.

(j) *"member"* means a member of the Fund ;

(k) *"occupier of a factory"* means the person, who has ultimate control over the affairs of the factory, and, where the said affairs are entrusted to a managing agent, such agent shall be deemed to be the occupier of the factory ;

¹[(kA) *"Pension Fund"* means the Employees' Pension Fund established under Sub-section (2) of section 6A;

(kB) *"Pension Scheme"* means the Employees' Pension Scheme framed under sub-section (1) of section 6A;]

---
1. Inserted by sec. 3 of Act 25 of 1996 (w.e.f. 16.11.1995)
---

¹[(ka) "Prescribed" means prescribed by rules made under this Act;

(kb) "Recovery Officer" means any officer of the Central Government, State Government or the Board of Trustees constituted under section 5A, who may be authorized by the Central Government, by notification in the Official Gazette, to exercise the powers of a Recovery Officer under this Act;]

---
1. Inserted by sec. 3 of Act 33 of 1988 (w.e.f. 1.8.1988).
---

¹[(l) "Scheme" means the Employees' Provident Funds Scheme framed under Section 5;]

²[(ll) "superannuation," in relation to an employee, who is the member of the Pension Scheme, means the attainment, by the said employee, of the age of fifty-eight years.]

³[(m) "Tribunal" means the Employees' Provident Funds Appellate Tribunal constituted under section 7D.]

---
1. Substituted by sec. 14 of Act 16 of 1971.
2. Inserted by sec.3 of Act 25 of 1996 (w.e.f. 16.11.1995).
3. Inserted by sec. 3 of Act 33 of 1988 (w.e.f. 1.8.1988)

B. Definitions under the EPF Scheme, 1952:-

Paragraph 2.- Definitions – In this Scheme, unless the context otherwise requires, -

(a) "Act" means the 'The Employees' Provident Funds [1][and Family Pension Fund] Act, 1952 (19 of 1952);

(b) [2][xxx]

---
1. Substituted by GSR 320 dated 16.02.1972 (w.e.f. 13.2.1971).
2. Deleted by GSR 1845 dated 28.11.1963.

(c) "children" means legitimate children and includes adopted children if the Commissioner is satisfies that under the personal law of the member adoption of a child is legally recognized;

[3][(d) "Commissioner" means a Commissioner of Employees' Provident Fund appointed under section 5D of the Act and includes a Deputy Provident Fund Commissioner and a Regional Provident Fund Commissioner;]

---
3. Substituted by GSR 1845 dated 28.11.1963.

(e) "continuous service" means uninterrupted service and includes service which is interrupted by sickness, accident, authorized leave, strike which is not illegal, or cessation of work not due to the employee's fault;

(f) "excluded employee" means-

[4][(i) an employee who, having been a member of the Fund, withdrew the full amount of his accumulations in the Fund under clause (a) or (c) of paragraph 69;]

[5][(ii) an employee whose pay at the time he is otherwise entitled to become a member of the Fund, exceeds [6][six thousand five hundred rupees] per month;

Explanation- "Pay" includes basic wages with dearness allowance, [7][retaining allowance (if any)] and cash value of food concessions admissible thereon;]

[8][(iii) xxx]

[9][(iv) an apprentice;

Explanation – An apprentice means a person who, according to the certified standing orders applicable to the factory or establishment, is an apprentice, or who is declared to be an apprentice by the authority specified in this behalf by the appropriate Government;]

---
4. Substituted by GSR 1122 dated 19.9.1960
5. Added by GSR 1337 dated 16.4.1957
6. Substituted by GSR 326(E) dated 04.5.2001 (w.e.f. 01.6.2001)
7. Added by GSR 201 dated 08.02.1961
8. Omitted by GSR 1467 dated 02.12.1960
9. Substituted by GSR 331 dated 15.01.1958

Interpretation and Definitions

Note:- The definition of 'excluded employee' stands modified/ amended in relation to –

1. The Newspaper establishments vide paragraph 80;

    (2) For paragraph 2(f), the following shall be substituted, namely-

    (i) an employee who, having been a member of the Fund, has withdrawn the full amount of his accumulations in the Fund under clause (a) or (c) of sub-paragraph (1) of paragraph 69;

    (ii) an apprentice.

    Explanation.- 'Apprentice' means a person who, according to the standing order applicable to the newspaper establishment concerned, is an apprentice or who is declared to be an apprentice by the authority specified in this behalf by the appropriate Government.

2. the Cine-workers, including cinema theatres, under para 81;

    (f) "Excluded employee" means-

    (i) a cine-worker, who having been a member of the Fund had withdrawn the full amount of accumulations in the Fund under clause (a) or (c) of sub-paragraph (1) of paragraph 69;

    (ii) a "cine-worker," whose wages at the time hs is otherwise entitled to become a member of the Fund exceeds on thousand and six hundred rupees per month and where such remuneration is by way of a lump-sum exceeding fifteen thousand rupees.

    Explanation.- "wages" means "wages" as defined in clause (k) of section 2 of the Cine Workers and Cinema Theatre Workers (Regulation of Employment) Act, 1981 (50 of 1981).

3. the disabled employees employed by the establishment, under para 82,

    (f) "Excluded employee" means-

    (i) a person with disability, who having been a member of the Fund has withdrawn the full amount of his accumulation under clause (a) or clause (c) of sub-paragraph (1) of paragraph 69;

    (ii) a person with disability, whose pay at the time he is otherwise entitled to become a member of the Fund, exceeds twenty-five thousand rupees per month;

    (iii) an apprentice.

4. in respect of International Workers, under paragraph 83-

    (f) "Excluded employee" means an International Worker, who is contributing to a social security programme of his/her country of origion, either as a citizen or resident, with whom India has entered into a social security agreement on reciprocity basis and enjoying the status of detached worker for the period and terms, as specified in such an agreement.

    [10][(ff) "International worker" means-

    (a) an Indian employee having worked or going to work in a foreign country with which India has entered into a social security agreement and being eligible to

> *avail the benefits under a social security programme of that country, by virtue of the eligibility gained or going to gain, under the said agreement;*
>
> *(b) an employee other than an Indian employee, holding other than an Indian passport, working for an establishment in India to which the Act applies;]*

10. Added by GSR 706 (E) dated 01.10.2008 (w.e.f. 01.10.2008).

(g) "family means –

[11][(i) in the case of a male member, his wife, his children, whether married or unmarried, his dependant parents and his deceased son's widow and children:]

Provided that if a member proves that his wife has ceased, under the personal law governing him or the customary law of the community to which the spouses belong, to be entitled to maintenance she shall no longer be deemed to be a part of the member's family for the purpose of this Scheme, unless the member subsequently intimates by express notice in writing to the Commissioner that she shall continue to be so regarded, and

[11][(ii) in the case of a female member, her husband, her children, whether married or unmarried, her dependant parents, her husband's dependent parents and her deceased son's wife and children:]

Provided that if a member by notice in writing to the Commissioner expresses her desire to exclude her husband from the family, the husband and his dependant parents shall no longer be deemed to be a part of the member's family for the purpose of this Scheme, unless the member subsequently cancels in writing any such notice.

Explanation- In either of the above two cases, if the child of a member [of, as the case may be, the child of a deceased son of the member] has been adopted by another person and if, uner personal law of the adopter, adoption is legally recognized, such a child shall be considered as excluded from the family of the member;

11. Substituted by GSR 351 dated 03.03.1966.

(h) "financial year" means the year commencing on the first day of April;

(i) "Government Security" shall have the meaning assigned to it in the Public Debt "Act, 1944
(18 of 1944);

(j) "Inspector" means a person appointed as such under section 13 of the Act;

(k) "quarter" means a period of three months commencing on the first day of January, the first day of April, the first day of July and the first day of October of each year;

[12][(kk) "seasonal factory" means a factory which is exclusively engaged in the manufacturing of [13][tea, sugar, rubber, turpentine, rosin, indigo, lac, fruit and vegetable preservation industry, rice milling industry, dal milling industry, cashewnut industry, stemming or redrying of tobacco leaf industry, tiles industry, hosiery industry, oil milling industry,

licensed salt industry, jute bailing or pressing industry, fire works and percussion cap industry, ice or ice-cream industry or cotton ginning and pressing industry];

[14][(kkk) "seasonal establishment" means a plantation of tea, coffee, rubber, cardamom or pepper,

[15][a coffee curing establishment, a fire clay mine or a gypsum mine;]]

(l) "trustee" means a member if a Board of Trustees; and

(m) All other words and expressions shall have the meaning respectively assigned to them in the Act.

---

12. Added by GSR 1660 dated 21.7.1956.
13. Added by different notifications from 1956 to 1972.
14. Added by SRO 1363 dated 26.4.1957.
15. Substituted by GSR 12 dated 22.12.1969.

C. Definitions under the EPF Scheme, 1995:-

Paragraph 2 – Definitions- In this Scheme, unless the context otherwise requires-

(i) "Act" Means the Employees' Provident Funds and Miscellaneous Provisions Act, 1952 (19 of 1952);

(ii) "Actual service" means the aggregate of periods of service rendered from the 16th November, 1995 or from the date of joining any establishment, whichever is later, to the date of exit from the employment of the establishment covered under the Act;

(iii) "Commissioner" means a Commissioner for Employees' Provident Funds appointed under Section 5D of the Act;

(iv) "Contributory service" means the period of actual service rendered by a member for which contribution to the fund have been [1][received or are receivable];

(v) "Eligible member" means an employee who is eligible to join the Employees' Pension Scheme;

(vi) "Existing member" Means an existing employee who is a member of the Employees' Family Pension Scheme, 1971;

(vii) "Family" means:

   (1) wife in the case of male member of the Employees Pension/fund;

   (2) husband in the case of a female member of the Employees' Pension Fund; and

(3) sons and [2][xxx] daughters of a member of the Employees' pension Fund;

Explanation:- The expression 'sons' and 'daughters' shall include children [1][legally adopted by the member].

(viii) "Pension" means the pension payable under the Employees' pension Scheme and also includes the family pension admissible and payable under the Employees' Family Pension Scheme, 1971 immediately preceding the commencement of the Employees' Pension Scheme, 1995 with effect from 16th November, 1995;

(ix) "member" means an employee who becomes a member of Employees' Pension Fund in accordance with the provisions of this Scheme;

[3][Explanation:- An employee shall cease to be the member of Pension Fund from the date of attaining 58 years of age or from the date of vesting admissible benefits under the Scheme, whichever is earlier.]

(x) "Non contributory service" is the period of 'actual service' rendered by a member for which no contribution to the Employees' Pension Fund has been [1][received or are receivable];

(xi) "Orphan" means a person, none of whose parents is alive [2][xxx];

(xii) "Past service" means the period of service rendered by an existing member from the date of joining Employees' Family Pension Fund till 15th November, 1995;

(xiii) "Pay" means basic wages, with dearness allowance, retaining allowance and cash value of food concession admissible, if any;

(xiv) "Pension Fund" means the Employees' Pension Fund set up under sub-section (2) of section 6A of the Act;

(xv) "Pensionable service" means the service rendered by the member for which contributions have been [1][received or are receivable];

[1][(xvi) "Permanent total disablement" means such disablement of permanent nature as incapacitates an employee for all work which he/she was capable of performing at the time of disablement, regardless whether such disablement is sustained in the course of employment or otherwise];

(xvii) "Table" means Table appended to this Scheme;

(xviii) The words and expression defined in the Act but not defined in this Scheme shall have the same meaning as assigned to them in the Act.

1.	Substituted by GSR 134 dated 28.02.1996 (w.e.f. 16.03.1996)	
2.	Deleted by GSR 134 dated 28.02.1996 (w.e.f. 16.03.1996)	
3.	Added by GSR 66 dated 22.02.1999 (w.e.f. 06.03.1999)	

D. Definitions under the EDLI Scheme, 1976:-

Paragraph 2 – Definitions- In this Scheme, unless the context otherwise requires-

(a) "Act" Means the Employees' Provident Funds and Miscellaneous Provisions Act, 1952 (19 of 1952);

(b) "assurance benefit" means a payment linked to the average balance in the Provident Fund Account of an employee, payable to a person belonging to his family or otherwise entitled to it in the event of death of the employee while being a member of the Fund;

(c) all other words and expressions used herein but not defined shall have the meaning respectively assigned to them in the Act or the Employees' Provident Funds Scheme, 1952.

III. Speaking Order:

Among administrative circles, when they discuss about a Speaking Order, it is defined in different ways by different persons. Some may insist for a better linguistic form, some may insist for a model format for it, some may prefer to give exhaustive details, some may express their egos and concepts through the it. Many authorities use to draft it in a way as if it is for a competitive examination, in which the facts and retrospect of the case is found absent. In a good Speaking Order, besides all the grammatical, linguistic excellence, detail of facts and their relevance with the chronology of events and legislative references are seen and those facts are discussed in a way they are expected as explained in the Evidence Act. In the Evidence Act it is expected from a judicial or quasi-judicial authority that a material facts or evidence or witnesses are discussed to establish whether those are relevant to the case under consideration and those lead to a judicious conclusion. If it is not found in an order it cannot be a good Speaking Order.

The need of passing a Speaking Order is required u/s 7A, 14B, 7Q, of the Act and Para 26B of the Scheme by the authorities upon whom the powers have been conferred to give a decision under those provisions. If it is not found judicious and self contained order, the Higher Judicial Authority may take a different view and may pass comments on the authorities for that accordingly. Patna High Court has underlined this state of affairs in the case *of Inter-state Transport Agency, Sitamarhi Vs. R.P.F.C. Patna-[1993 Lab I.C. 940 (Pat.)]* that Section 7A comes into play only when someone, who should have himself come forward, does not do so. Then the sums payable is determined under section 7A and if he commits default in making the contribution, he is subjected to imposition of penal damages under Section 14-B of the Act. Under both the provisions, there must be an enquiry for determining the amount due by providing "reasonable opportunity." As a matter of fact, the authorities under this Section are vested with the powers conferred under the Civil Procedure Code and particularly, they have to conduct the enquiry in a fair and reasonable manner. It cannot be said that no proper and effective hearing has been provided under section 7A of the Act, as is expected from a judicial or quasi-judicial authority. Section 7A ensures just fair enquiry.

Any abuse to power and act of mala-fide is not justifiable before the High Court and Supreme Court.

Further, to protect the interest of the employees, the authority is vested with the powers to summon any record for evidence, to examine any witness in person or on oath, admit any affidavit or issue commission for examination of a witness, as he deems proper and reasonable. Further, the employer is bound to be given a reasonable opportunity for representing his case. Thus, the provision of this Section prescribes a wholesome procedure for conducting enquiry for the purpose of determining the amount due from the employer under any provision of the Act and Schemes.

Some times, it may happen that on a particular point, different opinions of different courts lead to so many administrative inconveniences. To remedy such situation, certain mandatory provisions have been made which are taken as an authority on that particular point. Such provision is available in section 20 and also in the corresponding provision in paragraph 78 of the Employees' Provident Funds Scheme, 1952.

Step by Step Into EPF

Administration and Management

Chapter 4

Statutory Body

Brief badinage–

Administration under legislation specially, when it is aimed to provide certain financial benefits to a large number of population under a social security scheme, becomes a sensitive area requiring humanitarian considerations with devotion. It becomes more relevant when a large number of the beneficiaries are illiterate and un-aware of their rights and bound to bow for the reasons of feudal social back-ground they lived-in thousands of years and inherited. In such a social back-ground, the concept of administration of the EPF & MP Act becomes more relevant. The administration the Act is two partite, one is the employer of the employee and the other is the Central Board of Trustees, which by-and-large known as the Government, and the third one is the beneficiary for whom the legislation has been enacted and schemes have been framed. That is the very reason that the Act has not been made enforceable, but expected from both the ends i.e. the employer and the authorities to comply with it. Therefore, when an employer fails to report compliance, he becomes a defaulter and the enforceable part of the legislation is invoked. On the other hand, the Central Board of Trustees is legally, under obligation to complete the compliance required to be reported on its part, that is keeping accounts of the monies received by it in the members' respective accounts and intimate about to the concerned members and part-with the benefits in time. But, as one can see, both the ends are defaulters, and when two defaulters come together, what happens is the 'corruption.' When beneficiaries seek for their dues, the employers' and the CBT's staff is comfortable to take something from the beneficiaries, and when the employer defaults, the authorities invoking enforceable provisions, it is easy to manage the things. In both situations, the member, the employee, the beneficiary is under the edge of hammer. Hence, it is the call of the time that the compliance on the part of the CBT to be ensured first by revisiting the system of administration and re-engineering the operational part professionally, not making castle in the air in a bureaucratic fashion but make it a regular feature to educate its own staff as well as the employers and the employees with a view to make awareness among them.

Of-course, the finances are like blood-cells of an organization, its quality and quantity spell the total health and working of that organization. Any decay in it speaks a lot about, and, it is not possible here to discuss all about, however, it is a subject which may engage a separate book. Therefore, without going into deep discussion on this issue, it is simple and relevant here to mention that the globalization of the business, the EPF organization also came under threat and scan. This has started with the coming up of private Insurance companies and

> *simultaneously release of the OASIS report targeting the huge corpus with the EPFO which is being invested in secured security areas, whereas the market wanted it to be available to the them. Hence, the EPF organization went for re-engineering, re-inventing itself, but with foeticide of initial part one. Thanks to the philosophy of the Indian masses, even the so-called pro-market champions have not gone for that. The most popularized New Pension Scheme could hardly get few thousand members (3500) enrolled in its first year after the 'Pension Regulatory Authority' came into being. The Indian masses have shown their faith in the EPF & MP Act, 1952 and the Schemes framed their under. The administrators, the EPF organization and the employers have to uphold that faith shown in them by the Indian working people by a sound, solid and visible financial management.*

Unlike other enactments, the EPF & MP Act, 1952 is not managed by the Government itself, but a tripartite body has been created to keep away the workers money merge with the revenue exchequer of the government for heavenly mis-use by its bureaucratic set up with an overall control over it to ensure security of the money and thereby, the faith of the workers. Accordingly, the authorities play their rolls at different levels and stages.

I. Appropriate Government-

Appropriate Government has been defined in section 2 (a) – See the text at page No...
    It is relevant to issue notification for appointment of Inspectors under section 13 and for grant of exemption under section 17 (1) and under paragraph 27A.

II. Central Government-

In this Act, the Central Government has been authorized to keep overall control and to issue notification for framing the schemes, to frame Rules, for various other purposes including, to issue direction under section 20.

III. Governing Body -

A. Central Board of Trustees-

Section [1][5A. Central Board.– (1) The Central Government may, by notification in the Official Gazette, constitute, with effect from such date as may be specified therein, a Board of Trustees for the territories to which this Act extends (hereinafter in this Act referred to as the Central Board) consisting of the following [2][persons as members], namely:-

    (a)   [3][a Chairman and a Vice-Chairman] to be appointed by the Central Government;

[4][(aa)   the Central Provident Fund Commissioner, Ex- officio;]

(b) not more than five persons appointed by the Central Government from amongst its officials;

(c) not more than fifteen persons representing Governments of such States as the Central Government may specify in this behalf, appointed by the Central Government;

(d) [5][ten persons] representing employers of the establishments to which the Scheme applies, appointed by the Central Government after consultation with such organizations of employers as may be recognized by the Central Government in this behalf; and

(e) [5][ten persons] representing employees in the establishments to which the Scheme applies, appointed by the Central Government after consultation with such organizations of employees as may be recognized by the Central Government in this behalf.

(2) The terms and conditions subject to which a member of the Central Board may be appointed and the time, place and procedure of the meetings of the Central Board shall be such as may be provided for in the scheme.

(3) The Central Board shall [6][subject to the provisions of section [6][[7][and section 6C] administer the Fund vested in it in such manner as may be specified in the Scheme.

(4) The Central Board shall person such other functions as it may be required to person by or under nay provisions of the Scheme [8][, the [9][Pension] Scheme and the Insurance Scheme].

[10][(5) The Central Board shall maintain proper accounts of its income and expenditure in such form and in such manner as the Central Government may, after consultation with the Comptroller and Auditor-General of India, specify in the Scheme.

(6) The accounts of the Central Board shall be audited annually by the Comptroller and Auditor – General of India and any expenditure incurred by him in connection with such audit shall be payable by the Central Board to the Comptroller and Auditor-General of India.

(7) The Comptroller and Auditor-General of India and any person appointed by him in connection with the audit of the accounts of the Central Board shall have the same rights and privileges and authority in connection with such audit as the Comptroller and Auditor-General has, in connection with the audit of Government accounts and, in particular, shall have the right to demand the production of books, accounts, connected vouchers, documents and papers and inspect any of the offices of the Central Board.

(8) The accounts of the Central Board as certified by the Comptroller and Auditor-General of India or any other person appointed by him in this behalf together with the audit report thereon shall be forwarded to the Central Board which shall forward the same to the Central Government along with its comments on the report of the Comptroller and Audit-General.

(9) It shall be the duty of the Central Board to submit also to the Central Government an annual report of its work and activities and the Central Government shall cause a copy of the annual report, the audited accounts together with the report of the Comptroller and Audit-General

of India and the comments of the Central Board thereon to be laid before each House of Parliament.]

1. Inserted by Act 28 of 1963, Sec. 4.
2. Substituted by Act 33 of 1988, Sec. 4, for the words "persons" (w.e.f. 1.8.1988).
3. Substituted by Act 33 of 1988, Sec. 4, for the words "a Chairman" w.e.f. 1.8.1988)
4. Inserted by Act 33 of 1988, Sec. 4 (w.e.f. 1.8.1988)
5. Substituted by Act 33 of 1988, Sec. 4, for the words "six persons" (w.e.f. 1.8.1988)
6. Inserted by Act 16 of 1971, Sec. 15,
7. Inserted by Act 99 of 1976, Sec. 19 (deemed to have come into force from 1.8.1976)
8. Substituted by Act 99 of 1976, Sec. 19, for the words "and the Family pension Scheme" (deemed to have come into force from 1.8.1976)
9. Substituted by Act 25 of 1996, Sec. 4, for the words "Family Pension" (w.e.f. 16.11.1995).
10. Sub-Sec. (5) to (9) inserted by Act 33 of 1988, Sec. 4 (w.e.f. 1.8.1988)

Legislative reference:

Section 5A was added by Act 28 of 1963. Prior to that there was no provision in the Act to constitute a Board of Trustees Sec. Paragraph 3 of the Employees' Provident Funds Scheme, 1952 provided for constitution of a Board which stands replaced w.e.f. 1st July, 1989 by the provision of election procedure of Executive Members.

By the Act 33 of 1988, the section was amended and sub-sections (5) to (9) were inserted, making the Board responsible for maintenance of accounts, auditing by the Comptroller and Auditor General of India and preparing the annual report and laying the accounts and the report of C.A.G before the Parliament.

B. Executive Committee-

Section ¹[5AA. **Executive Committee.–** (1) The Central Government may, by notification in the Official Gazette, constitute, with effect from such date as may be specified therein, an Executive Committee to assist the Central Board in the performance of its functions.

(2) The Executive Committee shall consist of the following persons as members, namely:-

(a) a Chairman appointed by the Central Government from amongst the members of the Central Board;

(b) two persons appointed by the Central Government from amongst the persons referred to in clause (b) of sub-section (1) of section 5A;

(c) three persons appointed by the Central Government from amongst the persons referred to in clause (c) of sub-section (1) of section 5A;

(d) three persons representing the employers elected by the Central Board from amongst the persons referred to in clause (d) of sub-section (1) of section 5A;

(e) three persons representing the employees elected by the Central Board from amongst the persons referred to in clause (e) of sub-section (1) of section 5A'

(f) the Central Provident Fund Commissioner, ex-officio.

(3) The terms and conditions subject to which a member of the Central Board may be appointed or elected to the Executive Committee and the time, place and procedure of the meetings of the Executive Committee shall be such as may be provided for in the Scheme.]

> 1. Inserted by Act 33 of 1988, Sec. 5.

C. State Board -

Section [1][5B. State Board. – (1) The Central Government may, after consultation with the Government of any State, by notification in the Official Gazette, constitute for that State a Board of Trustees (hereinafter in this Act referred to as the State Board) in such manner as may be provided for in the Scheme.

(2) A State Board shall exercise such powers and perform such duties as the Central Government may assign to it from time to time.

(3) The terms and conditions subject to which a member of a State Board may be appointed and the time, place and procedure of the meetings of a State Board shall be such as may be provided for in the Scheme.]

> 1. Inserted by Act 28 of 1963, Sec. 4.

This section has not so far been acted upon, as if it has not been notified to implement. However, Regional Committees are being constituted for each state by a notification issued by Chairman, CBT as provided for under paragraph 4 of the EPF Scheme, 1952.

D. Related and referred provisions:-

Section [1][5C. Board of Trustees to be body corporate. – Every Board of Trustees constituted under section 5A or section 5B shall be a body corporate under the name specified in the notification constituting it, having perpetual succession and a common seal and shall by the said name sue and be sued.]

> 1. Inserted by Act 28 of 1963, Sec. 4

Section [1][5DD. Acts and proceedings of the Central Board or its Executive Committee or the State Board not to be invalidated on certain grounds. – No act done or proceeding taken by the Central Board or the Executive Committee constituted under section 5AA or the State Board shall be questioned on the ground merely of the existence of any vacancy in, or any defect in the constitution of, the Central Board or the Executive Committee or the State Board, as the case may be.]

> 1. Inserted by Act 33 of 1988, Sec. 7 (w.e.f. 1.8.1988).

Section [1][5E. Delegation.– [2][The Central Board may delegate to the Executive Committee or to the Chairman of the Board or to any of its officers and a State Board may delegate to its Chairman or to any of its officers], subject to such conditions and limitations, if any, as it may specify, such of its powers and functions under this Act as it may deem necessary for the efficient administration of the Scheme [3][, the [4][Pension] Scheme and the Insurance Scheme]].

> 1. Inserted by Act 28 of 1963, Sec. 4
> 2. Substituted by Act 33 of 1988, Sec.8 (w.e.f. 1.8.1988)

3.	Substituted by Act 99 of 1976, Sec. 20, for the words "and the Family Pension Scheme" (deemed to have come into force from 1.8.1976).
4.	Substituted by Act 25 of 1996, Sec.4, for the words "Family Pension" (w.e.f. 16.11.1995).

Section [1][19. **Delegation of powers** - The appropriate Government may direct that any power or authority or jurisdiction exercisable by it under this Act, [2][the Scheme, [3][the [4][Pension] Scheme or the Insurance Scheme]] shall, in relation to such matters and subject to such conditions, if any, as may be specified in the direction, be exercisable also–

(a) where the appropriate Government is the Central Government, by such officer or authority subordinate to the Central Government or by the State Government or by such officer or authority subordinate to the State Government, as may be specified in the notification; and

(b) where the appropriate Government is a State Government, by such officer or authority subordinate to the State Government as may be specified in the notification.]

1.	Substituted by Act 37 of 1953, Sec.17 in place of the original section.
2.	Substituted by Act 16 of 1971, Sec. 29,
3.	Substituted by Act 99 of 1976, Sec.37 (deemed to have come into force from 1.8.1976)
4.	Substituted by Act 25 of 1996, Sec.4, for the words "Family Pension" (w.e.f. 16.11.1995).

(I) - Central Board of Trustees:

This Board has been referred as the C.B.T. Vide amending Act 33 of 1988, its composition was enlarged and made it of 43 members. Earlier, the Central Provident Fund Commissioner (CPFC) was to be the Secretary of the CBT without any membership virtues, was not authorized to vote in the meetings of the CBT. From 1988, the CPFC has also been made a member of the CBT on the equal footings of the other member and also to work as a secretary.

The combination of the CBT is as under-

Chairman	01
Vice Chairman	01
Central Government representative	05
State Governments' representative	15
Employers' Organisations' representative	10
Employees' Organisations' representative	10
Central P.F. Commissioner – ex-officio	01

By the Act 33 of 1988, a subordinate body of the CBT was also made by inserting section 5AA, called the Executive Committee, and the members to it are nominated out from the CBT itself. The CPFC has to work in this Committee as Secretary also.

Since, no State Board has been constituted in any State, provision for constitution of a Regional Committee for each state, where the Regional Office of the CBT is situated. The power to constitute the Regional Committee has been given to the Chairman, CBT under paragraph 4 of the EPF Scheme,

1952. The numbers of the members in the Regional Committee may vary from Region/State to State. The respective Regional Commissioner in-charge is the secretary of the Regional Committee, vide paragraph 22 of the Scheme, however, he has not been put as member in the Regional Committee.

The procedure of appointment of members, meetings and business transaction etc. have been prescribed in the Scheme of 1952. Related references of paragraphs are:-

Paragraph 3 – **Election of certain members of the Executive Committee–**

Paragraph 4 – **Regional Committee -**

Paragraph 5 – **Term of office-**

Paragraph 7 – **Cessation and restoration of trusteeship-**

Paragraph 8 – **Dis-qualification for trusteeship or membership of a Regional Committee-**

Paragraph 9 – **Removal from trusteeship or membership of a Regional Committee –**

Paragraph 10 – **Absence from India –**

Paragraph 11 – **Meetings –**

Paragraph 12 – **Notice of meeting and list of business –**

Paragraph 13 – **Chairman to preside at meetings –**

Paragraph 14 – **Quorum –**

Paragraph 14A – **Nomination of a substitute during the absence of a trustee/member of the Central Board/Regional Committee –**

Paragraph 15 – **Disposal of business –**

Paragraph 16 – **Minutes of meetings –**

Paragraph 17 – **Acts of a Regional Committee not invalid by reason merely of any vacancy in, or defect in the Constitution, etc.-**

Paragraph 18 – **Fees and allowances –**

Paragraph 77 – **Conduct of business of the Central Board-**

(II). Body corporate:

Under section 5C, the Board of Trustees, (CBT) and all State Boards have been given the status of a Corporate Body. To be a Body Corporate has an independent status before the law and is responsible for any action for which it can be sued. For its identity, it has perpetual succession and is also authorized to have a common seal. However, in most of the cases, CBT is not made a party but, Regional P.F. Commissioners are made party before a High Court or Supreme Court.

(III). Statutory powers:

Un-doubtedly, all the powers are vested in the CBT from the provisions of the Act and the Schemes, but, it performs certain statutory duties relating to-

- **Advise on Exemption Application** - CBT is required to give view and opinion to the appropriate Government in the cases where application for exemption under section 17 has been made to the appropriate Government, the time limit prescribed under paragraph 79 B for such opinion which is fixed as three months;

- **Rate of Interest** – Every year, CBT is required to give its recommendation to the Central Government for declaration of rate of interest under paragraph 60 of the EPF Scheme;

- **Waiver of damages** – Damages levied under section 14 B read with paragraph 32-B of EPF Scheme, 1952 and paragraph 8-B of EDLI Scheme, 1976 can be waived by the CBT on the terms and conditions as laid down under those paragraphs. But, the CBT has not been authorized to waive damages levied under paragraph 5 as no provision corresponding to proviso to section 14B regarding waiver of damages has been made in the Employees' Pension Scheme, 1995.

(IV). Administrative and financial powers:

All the administrative and financial powers are vested in the CBT, as it is evident, every time for such sanction, the meeting of the CBT cannot be convened, therefore, vide paragraph 24A, the CBT can delegate its powers to its Chairman exercise of which is subject to laying before the CBT for its approval.

Opening of offices is the main administrative power of the CBT. Besides, all the officers and staff is sanctioned by it and appointed under section 5D of the Act.

Some of the powers have been entrusted to the Executive Committee to ease the burden of the CBT, and some it discusses before the matter is put before the CBT for its final decision.

The CBT and the Executive Committee have setup their sub-committee for different purposes. There are three sub- committees of the CBT, namely-

1. Sub-Committee for Finance and Investment,
2. Sub-Committee for Exempted Establishments, and
3. Sub-Committee for Information Services.

Similarly, there two sub-committees set-up under the Executive Committee, namely-

1. Sub-Committee for Pension Implementation, and
2. Sub-Committee for Building and Construction.

Chapter 5

Administrative Set-up

The administrative setup under the Act, other than the CBT and executive committee is as under:

(i) Head Office: headed by the Central P.F. Commissioner, assisted by 2 Additional Central P.F. commissioners, Additional Central O.F. Commissioners (Grade I & II), then Regional P.F. Commissioner (I & II), Assistant P.F. Commissioners in hierarchy supported by staff.

(ii) Zonal Offices: headed by Additional Central P.F. Commissioners (Grade I) assisted by Regional P.F. Commissioner (II)/Assistant P.F. Commissioner, and other staff.

(iii) Regional Offices: headed by Regional P.F. Commissioner (I) and assisted by Regional P.F. Commissioners (II), Assistant P.F. Commissioners, Accounts Officers, Enforcement Officers (as Inspectors) and other staff and Sub-Regional Offices.

(iv) Sub-Regional Offices: Headed by Regional P.F. Commissioner (II) assisted by Assisted Commissioners, Accounts Officers, Enforcement Officers and other staff.

Appointment and other service conditions are laid down in section 5D.

Section [1]**[5D. Appointment of officers** – (1) The Central Government shall appoint a Central Provident Fund Commissioner who shall be the chief executive officer of the Central Board and shall be subject to the general control and superintendence of that Board.

(2) The Central Government may also appoint [2][a Financial Adviser and Chief Accounts Officer] to assist the Central Provident Fund Commissioner in the discharge of his duties.

(3) The Central Board may appoint [3][subject to the maximum scale of pay, as may be specified in the Scheme, as many Additional Central Provident Fund Commissioner, Deputy Provident Fund Commissioner, Regional Provident Fund Commissioner, Assistant Provident Fund Commissioners and] such other officers and employees as it may consider necessary for the efficient administration of the Scheme [4][the [5][Pension] Scheme and the Insurance Scheme].

(4) No appointment to [6][the post of the Central Provident Fund Commissioner or an Additional Central Provident Fund Commissioner or a Financial Adviser and Chief Accounts Officer or any other post under the Central Board carrying a scale of pay equivalent to the scale of pay of any Group 'A' or Group 'B' post under the Central Government] shall be made except after consultation with the Union Public Service Commission:

Provided that no such consultation shall be necessary in regard to any such appointment –

(a) for a period not exceeding one year ; or

(b) if the person to be appointed is at the time of his appointment –

(i) a member of the Indian Administrative Service, or

(ii) in the service of the Central Government or a State Government or the Central Board in a [7][Group 'A' or Group 'B' post].

(5) A State Board may, with the approval of the State Government concerned, appoint such staff as it may consider necessary.

(6) The method of recruitment, salary and allowances, discipline and other conditions of service of the Central Provident Fund Commissioner, [8][and the Financial Adviser and Chief Accounts officer] shall be such as may be specified by the central Government and such salary and allowances shall be paid out of the fund.

[9][(7) (a) The method of recruitment, salary and allowances, discipline and other conditions of service of the Additional Central Provident Fund Commissioner, Deputy Provident Fund Commissioner, Regional Provident Fund Commissioner, Assistant Provident Fund Commissioner and other officers and employees of the Central Board shall be such as may be specified by the Central Board in accordance with the rules and orders applicable to the officers and employees of the Central Government drawing corresponding scales of pay:

Provided that where the Central Board is of the opinion that it is necessary to make a departure from the said rules or orders in respect of any of the matters aforesaid, it shall obtain the prior approval of the Central Government.

(b) In determining the corresponding scales of pay of officers and employees under clause (a), the Central Board shall have regard to the educational qualifications, method of recruitment, duties and responsibilities of such officers and employees under the Central Government and in case of any doubt, the Central Board shall refer the matter to the Central Government whose decision thereon shall be final.]

(8) The method of recruitment, salary and allowances, discipline and other conditions of service of officers and employees of a State Board shall be such as may be specified by that Board, with the approval of the State Government concerned.]

---

1. Inserted by Act 28 of 1963, Sec. 4
2. Substituted by Act 33 of 1988, Sec. 6, for the words "as many Deputy Provident Fund Commissioners, Regional Provident Fund Commissioners and other officers whose maximum monthly salary is not less than five hundred rupees as it may consider necessary" (w.e.f. 1.8.1988)
3. Inserted by Act 33 of 1988, Sec. 6 (w.e.f. 1.8.1988).
4. Substituted by Act 99 of 1976, Sec. 20, for the words "and the Family Pension Scheme" (deemed to have come into force from 1.8.1976).
5. Substituted by Act 25 of 1996, Sec. 4, for the words "Family Pension" (w.e.f. 16.11.1995).
6. Substituted by Act 33 of 1988, Sec. 6 (w.e.f. 1.8.1988)
7. Substituted by Act 33 of 1988, Sec. 6 (w.e.f. 1.8.1988), for the words and figures "Class I or Class II post."
8. Substituted by Act 33 of 1988, Sec. 6 (w.e.f. 1.8.1988), for the words "Deputy Provident Fund Commissioner and Regional Provident Fund Commissioner."
9. Substituted. By Act 33 of 1988, Sec. 6 (w.e.f. 1.8.1988).

I. Appointment of Officers and Staff:

This section was amended extensively by the Act 33 of 1988. Previously, the Central Government was the appointing authority in respect of all group 'A' officers. From August, 1988, the power of appointment of all officers have been given to the CBT, which, in turn, has delegated the powers under paragraph 24A of the Scheme to its Chairman. To regulate the appointments, the CBT has also notified Recruitment Rules in respect of all cadres separately and amended from time to time as the time required. However, all these are subject to approval of the Central Government. There is also a rider in sub-section 9 that all the recruitments with respect of qualification, pay and other condition of service shall be as applicable to the respective cadre under the Central Government and any deviation from that is required the approval of the Central Government.

II. Service Conditions:

The Rules governing the service conditions and other service matters are mentioned in the 'Employees; Provident Funds (Officers and other Employees and Condition of Service) Regulations, 2008.' Prior to the present set of regulations, 'The Employees' Provident Funds (Staff and Condition of Service) Regulations, 1962' were in force. The rules of 2008 are appended here at the end as Annexure. The Central Provident Fund Commissioner and Financial Advisor and Chief Accounts Officer are appointed by the Central Government only.

III. Powers related to Scheme:

The administration of the Schemes is the responsibility of officers appointed under this section, therefore, different officers have been delegated with different powers as mentioned in paragraph 24 of the Scheme and in respective paragraphs of the Scheme. Those are-

Para 26 (6) -	Enrolment of an excluded Employee & permission to Contribute on higher salary	Asstt. PF Commissioner and above,
Para 26 B -	Resolution of membership dispute	Regl. PF Commissioner,
Para 27 -	Individual exemption from PF Scheme	Regl. PF Commissioner,
Para 79 -	Grant of Relaxation pending exemption	Regl. PF Commissioner,
Para 32(1) - III proviso	Permitting deduction of employees' share for past period	Inspector,
Para 68-H - (1A)	permitting advance from employer's share	Asstt. PF Commissioner,
Para 72 -	Accepting guardianship/ Lunatic certificates for payment of benefits	Commissioner/Chairman, CBT,

For all other purposes, the Commissioner or any officer authorized by him.

The Commissioner has been defined in paragraph 2 (d) which reads as under–

Paragraph **2 (d) "Commissioner" means a Commissioner of Employees' Provident Fund appointed under section 5D of the Act and includes a Deputy Provident Fund Commissioner and a Regional Provident Fund Commissioner.'**

Administrative and Financial Powers of the Commissioner are enumerated in paragraph 24.

IV. Responsibility related to administration of Schemes:

As mentioned in the 'Brief badinage' above, the employer is responsible to report compliance to the CBT in respect of and employee as mentioned in Chapter V and VI of the Scheme, but, the CBT is also responsible to complete the compliance by maintaining record of the employee as required to be completed under paragraph 50, 51, 53, 55, 57, 59, 60 and in the Chapter VIII of the Scheme. Most important, out of those are the matters related to maintaining proper record of monies received by it on behalf of the employees deposited by the employers and income from investments, keeping individual accounts of employees/members and crediting interest properly every year and intimating there-about to the member concerned. And, the ultimate part of compliance on the part of the CBT is to keep the members' will properly, given and obtained in form No. 2 as provided for in paragraph 60 and give service to the members them-selves or the family members in the event of death of a member or paying advance/withdrawals for various purposes as mentioned in Chapter VIII.

V. Defective or delayed service to subscribers:

When a service is found to be defective on the part of the CBT, the Consumer Protection Act, 1985 comes to rescue the service seeking subscriber and the delayed service is condemned by the EPF and other Schemes themselves, that the Commissioner, responsible for such delay has to pay interest on the amount paid beyond 30 days. Such provision has been made in paragraph 72 of the EPF Scheme and similar provisions are available in the Employee' Pension Scheme and in the EDLI Scheme also.

VI. Financial Management:

Another important responsibility of the CBT/department is to manage finances received by it with a view to get and give a better return to the subscribers and timely completion of the records and budget, which can exhibit the financial health and managerial skills of the department. Sufficient provisions have been made in the Scheme for that purpose and also for creating a better and technologically compatible infrastructure.

Chapter 6

Statutory and Quasi-Judicial Authorities

Like any other enactment dealing with public specially in terms of money, it is obvious that default may take place. As a remedy to it, quantum in default is to be determined, thereafter, recovery of the same is to be enforced. Since all such actions are of judicial nature, the authority to exercise such statutory power are defined and vested with the powers of either quasi-judicial in nature or judicial one.

I. Statutory Authorities in Administration-

In the administrative setup as mentioned herein above, there is only one authority is the statutory authority under this Act, who has been armed with vast powers, that is the Inspector. In addition to it, 'Authorised Officer' and the 'Recovery Officer' are also statutory authorities.

Section – 13. Inspectors. (1) The appropriate Government may, by notification in the Official Gazette, appoint such persons as it thinks fit to be Inspectors for the purposes of this Act, [1][the Scheme, [2][the [3][Pension] Scheme or the Insurance Scheme]] and may define their jurisdiction.

(2) Any Inspector appointed under sub-section 1 may, for the purpose of inquiring into the correctness of any information furnished in connection with this Act or with any [2][Scheme or the Insurance Scheme] or for the purpose of ascertaining whether any of the provisions of this Act or of any [2][Scheme or the Insurance Scheme] have been complied with [4][in respect of] [5][an establishment] to which any [2][Scheme or the Insurance Scheme] applies or for the purpose of ascertaining whether the provisions of this Act or any [2][Scheme or the Insurance Scheme] are applicable to any [5][establishment] to which the [2][Scheme or the Insurance Scheme] has not been applied or for the purpose of determining whether the conditions subject to which exemption was granted under section 17 are being complied with by the employer in relation to an exempted [5][establishment].-

(a) require an employer [6][or any contractor from whom any amount is recoverable under section 8A] [7][to furnish such information as he may consider necessary] [8][****];]

(b) at any reasonable time [9][and with such assistance, if any, as he may think fit, enter and search] any [5][establishment] or any premises connected therewith and require any one found in charge thereof to produce before him for examination any accounts, books, registers and other documents relating to the employment of persons or the payment of wages in the [5][establishment];

(c) examine, with respect to any matter relevant to any of the purposes aforesaid, the employer [6][or any contractor from whom any amount is recoverable under section 8A], his agent or servant or any other person found in charge of the [5][establishment] or any premises connected therewith or whom the Inspector has reasonable cause to believe to be or to have been, an employee in the [5][establishment];

[9][(d) make copies of, or take extracts from, any book, register or other document maintained in relation to the establishment and, where he has reason to believe that any offence under this Act has been committed by an employer, seize with such assistance as he may think fit, such book, register or other document or portions thereof as he may consider relevant in respect of that offence];

(e) exercise such other powers as the [2][Scheme or the Insurance Scheme] may provide.

[10][(2A) Any Inspector appointed under sub-section 1 may, for the purpose of inquiring into the correctness of any information furnished in connection with the [3][Pension] Scheme or for the purpose of ascertaining whether any of the provisions of this Act or of the [3][Pension] Scheme have been complied with in respect of an establishment to which the [3][Pension] Scheme applies, exercise all or any of the powers conferred on him under clause a, b, clause c, or clause d sub-section 2.]

[11][[12][(2B)] The provisions of the Code of Criminal Procedure, 1898 (5 of 1898) shall, so far as may be, apply to any search or seizure under sub-section 2 [13][or under sub-section 2A, as the case may be,] as they apply to any search or seizure made under the authority of a warrant issued under section 98 of the said Code.]

[14][(3) xxx]

1. Substituted by Section 24 of by Act 16 of 1971.
2. Substituted by Section 29 of by Act 99 of 1976.
3. Substituted by Section 4 of by Act 25 of 1996.
4. Inserted by Section 11 of by Act 37 of 1953.
5. Substituted by Section 3 of by Act 94 of 1956 in place of 'Factory.'
6. Added by Section 9 of by Act 28 of 1963.
7. Added by Section 9 of by Act 28 of 1963.
8. Few words Deleted by Section 11 of by Act 37 of 1953.
9. Substituted by Section 9 of by Act 28 of 1963.
10. Added by Section 24 of by Act 16 of 1971.
11. Added by Section 9 of by Act 28 of 1963.
12. Renumbered by Section 24 of by Act 16 of 1971.
13. Inserted by Section 24 of by Act 16 of 1971.
14. Sub-section(3) deleted by Section 17 of Act 33 of 1988.
* Now it is Criminal Procedure Code, 1973 (2 of 1974) and the referred Section 98 is Section 94 thereof.

Section 2.

[1][(aa)] *"authorised officer"* means the Central Provident Fund Commissioner, Additional Central Provident Fund Commissioner, Deputy Provident Fund Commissioner, Regional Provident Fund Commissioner or such other officer as may be authorized by the Central Government, by notification in the Official Gazette;]

²[(kb) "Recovery Officer" means any officer of the Central Government, State Government or the Board of Trustees constituted under section 5A, who may be authorized by the Central Government, by notification in the Official Gazette, to exercise the powers of a Recovery Officer under this Act;]

---

1. Section 18 and 18A Substituted by Section 24 of Act 33 of 1988.
2. Added by Section 3 of Act 33 of 1988. w.e.f. 1.8.1988.

Section ¹[18. **Protection of action taken in good faith**— No suit, prosecution or other legal proceeding shall lie against the Central Government, a State Government, the Presiding Officer of a Tribunal, any authority referred to in section 7A, an Inspector or any other person for anything which is in good faith done or intended to be done in pursuance of this Act, the Scheme, the ²[Pension] Scheme or the Insurance Scheme.]

Section ¹[18A. **Presiding Officer and other officers to be public servants**-The Presiding Officer of a Tribunal, its officers and other employees, the authorities referred to in section 7A and every Inspector shall be deemed to be public servants within the meaning of section 21 of the Indian Penal Code (45 of 1860).]

---

1. Added by Section 24 of Act 33 of 1988. w.e.f. 1.8.1988.
2. Substituted by Section 4 of Act 25 of 1996. w.e.f. 16.11.1995.

II. Inspectors:

Inspectors under the Act happens to be a watch dog, who is supposed to ensure implementations of that particular Act within the frame-work provided there for. There are many enactments under which the highest authority is designated by the word "Inspector." Unfortunately, the time has made the intelligence-wing a tool in the hands of superior authorities which has dignified "Inspector" adversely. However, the statutory support to it has attracted higher authorities to enjoy the powers of an Inspector" by themselves, that is why, over a period of time, under the EPF Act too, administrative authorities are also included in the term "Inspector" who are authorized to exercise the powers as mentioned under section 13, specially, in sub-section (2) of that section. Inspectors appointed by the Appropriate Government by notification in the official gazette. Following administrative officer have been notified to Inspectors-

1. All Enforcement Officers within their defined territorial jurisdiction;
2. All Assistant Provident Fund Commissioners;
3. All Regional Provident Fund Commissioners;
4. All Additional Central Provident Fund Commissioners, and
5. The Central Provident Fund Commissioner for whole of India.

Notification to appointment of inspectors u/s. 13(1)–

[1][S-O. 1913.-In exercise of the powers conferred by sub-section (1) of Section 13 of the **Employees' Provident Funds and Miscellaneous Provisions Act, 1952** (19 of 1952) and in supersession of the notification of the Government of India in the Ministry of Labour and Employment number S.O. 2935, dated the 13th October, 2008, except as respects things done or omitted to be done before such supersession, the Central Government hereby appoints the officers holding the posts specified in column (2) of the table below in the office specified in column (3) of the said table to be Inspectors for the area specified in column (4) thereof, for the purposes of the said Act and the Schemes framed there under in relation to any establishment belonging to, or under the control of the Central Government or in relation to an establishment connected with a railway company, a major-port, a mine or an oil-field or a controlled industry or in relation to an establishment having department or branches in more than one State, namely:-

Table

S. No. (1)	Officers (2)	Office (3)	Area (4)
1.	(i) Central Provident Fund Commissioner (ii) Additional Central Provident Fund Commissioner (Compliance) (iii) Regional Provident Fund Commissioners (iv) Enforcement Officers	Employees Provident Fund Organisation Head Office, New Delhi	Whole of India except the State of Jammu and Kashmir
2.	(i) Additional Central Provident Fund Commissioner (ii) Assistant Provident Fund Commissioners (iii) Enforcement Officers	Zonal Office of Employees' Provident Fund Organisation, Hyderabed.	The States of Andhra Pradesh Orissa and the Yanam area of the Union Territory of Puducherry.
3.	(i) Additional Central Provident Fund Commissioner (ii) Assistant Provident Fund Commissioners (iii) Enforcement Officers	Zonal Office of Employees' Provident Fund Organisation, Delhi.	The National Capital Territory of Delhi and the State Uttarakhand.
4.	(i) Additional Central Provident Fund Commissioner (ii) Assistant Provident Fund Commissioners (iii) Enforcement Officers	Zonal Office of Employees' Provident Fund Organisation, Mumbai.	The States of Maharashtra Chhattisgarh.
5.	(i) Additional Central Provident Fund Commissioner (ii) Assistant Provident Fund Commissioners (iii) Enforcement Officers	Zonal Office of Employees' Provident Fund Organisation, Ahmadabad.	The States of Gujarat, Madhya Pradesh, and Union Territories of Daman and Diu and Dadra and Nagar Haveli.
6.	(i) Additional Central Provident Fund Commissioner (ii) Assistant Provident Fund Commissioners (iii) Enforcement Officers	Zonal Office of Employees' Provident Fund Organisation, Faridabad.	The States of Haryana and Rajasthan

Statutory and Quasi-Judicial Authorities

7. (i) Additional Central Provident Fund Commissioner (ii) Assistant Provident Fund Commissioners (iii) Enforcement Officers	Zonal Office of Employees' Provident Fund Organisation, Bangalore	The States of Karnataka and Goa
8. (i) Additional Central Provident Fund Commissioner (ii) Assistant Provident Fund Commissioners (iii) Enforcement Officers	Zonal Office of Employees' Provident Fund Organisation, Chandigarh	The States of Punjab, Himachal Pradesh and the Union Territories of Chandigarh
9. (i) Additional Central Provident Fund Commissioner (ii) Assistant Provident Fund Commissioners (iii) Enforcement Officers	Zonal Office of Employees' Provident Fund Organisation, Chennai	The States of Tamil Nadu, Kerala, and Union Territories of Lakshadweep. Puducherry except Yanam area
10. (i) Additional Central Provident Fund Commissioner (ii) Assistant Provident Fund Commissioners (iii) Enforcement Officers	Zonal Office of Employees' Provident Fund Organisation, Kanpur	The States of Uttar Pradesh and Bihar.
11. (i) Additional Central Provident Fund Commissioner (ii) Assistant Provident Fund Commissioners (iii) Enforcement Officers	Zonal Office of Employees' Provident Fund Organisation, Kolkata	The States of West Bengal. Jharkhand, Assam, Arunachal Pradesh, Nagaland, Manipur, Meghalaya, Mizoram, Tripura, Sikkim and Union Territory of Andaman and Nicobar Islands.
12. (i) Regional Provident Fund Commissioners (ii) Assistant Provident Fund Commissioners (iii) Enforcement Officers	Regional or Sub-Regional Offices of the Employees' Provident Fund Organisation in the State of the National Capital Territory of Delhi.	The National Capital Territory of Delhi.
13. (i) Regional Provident Fund Commissioners (ii) Assistant Provident Fund Commissioners (iii) Enforcement Officers	Regional or Sub-Regional Offices of the Employees' Provident Fund Organisation in the State of Andhra Pradesh and the Yanam area of the Union Territory of Puduchery.	The State of Andhra Pradesh, and the Yanam area of the Union Territory of Puducherry.
14. (i) Regional Provident Fund Commissioners (ii) Assistant Provident Fund Commissioners (iii) Enforcement Officers	Regional or Sub-Regional Offices of the Employees' Provident Fund Organisation in the State of Assam, Arunachal Pradesh, Nagaland, Manipur, Meghalaya, Mizoram and Tripura.	The States of Assam, Arunachal Pradesh, Nagaland, Manipur Meghalaya, Mizoram and Tripura.
15. (i) Regional Provident Fund Commissioners (ii) Assistant Provident Fund Commissioners (iii) Enforcement Officers	Regional or Sub-Regional Offices of the Employees' Provident Fund Organisation in the State of Bihar.	The State of Bihar.
16. (i) Regional Provident Fund Commissioners	Regional or Sub-Regional Offices of the Employees'	The State of Chattisgarh

(ii) Assistant Provident Fund Commissioners (iii) Enforcement Officers	Provident Fund Organisation in the State of Chattisgarh.	
17. (i) Regional Provident Fund Commissioners (ii) Assistant Provident Fund Commissioners (iii) Enforcement Officers	Regional or Sub-Regional Offices of the Employees' Provident Fund Organisation in the State of Goa.	The State of Goa.
18. (i) Regional Provident Fund Commissioners (ii) Assistant Provident Fund Commissioners (iii) Enforcement Officers	Regional or Sub-Regional Offices of the Employees' Provident Fund Organisation in the State of Gujarat and Union Territories of Daman and Diu and Dadraand Nagarllaveli.	The State of Gujarat and Union Territories of Daman and Diu and Dadra and Nagar Haveli.
19. (i) Regional Provident Fund Commissioners (ii) Assistant Provident Fund Commissioners (iii) Enforcement Officers	Regional or Sub-Regional Offices of the Employees' Provident Fund Organisation in the State of Haryana.	The State of Harayana.
20. (i) Regional Provident Fund Commissioners (ii) Assistant Provident Fund Commissioners (iii) Enforcement Officers	Regional or Sub-Regional Offices of the Employees' Provident Fund Organisation in the State of Himachal Pradesh.	The State of Himachal Pradesh.
21. (i) Regional Provident Fund Commissioners (ii) Assistant Provident Fund Commissioners (iii) Enforcement Officers	Regional or Sub-Regional Offices of the Employees' Provident Fund Organisation in the State of Jharkhand.	The Slate of Jharkhand.
22. (i) Regional Provident Fund Commissioners (ii) Assistant Provident Fund Commissioners (iii) Enforcement Officers	Regional or Sub-Regional Offices of the Employees' Provident Fund Organisation in the State of Karnataka.	The State of Karnataka.
23. (i) Regional Provident Fund Commissioners (ii) Assistant Provident Fund Commissioners (iii) Enforcement Officers	Regional or Sub-Regional Offices of the Employees' Provident Fund Organisation in the State of Kerala, the Union Territory of Lakshdweep and in the Mahe area of the Union Territory of Puducherry.	The State of Kerala and Union Territory of Lakshadweep and the Mahe area of Union territory of Puducherry.
24. (i) Regional Provident Fund Commissioners (ii) Assistant Provident Fund Commissioners (iii) Enforcement Officers	Regional or Sub-Regional Offices of the Employees' Provident Fund Organisation in the Stale of Madhya Pradesh.	The State of Madhya Pradesh.
25. (i) Regional Provident Fund Commissioners (ii) Assistant Provident Fund Commissioners (iii) Enforcement Officers	Regional or Sub-Regional Offices of the Employees' Provident Fund Organisation in the State of Maharashtra.	The State of Maharashtra.
26. (i) Regional Provident Fund Commissioners	Regional or Sub-Regional Offices of the Employees'	The Slate of Orissa.

(ii) Assistant Provident Fund Commissioners (iii) Enforcement Officers	Provident Fund Organisation in the State of Orissa.	
27. (i) Regional Provident Fund Commissioners (ii) Assistant Provident Fund Commissioners (iii) Enforcement Officers	Regional or Sub-Regional Offices of the Employees' Provident Fund Organisation in the State of Punjab and Union Territory of Chandigarh.	The State of Punjab and Union Territory of Chandigarh.
28. (i) Regional Provident Fund Commissioners (ii) Assistant Provident Fund Commissioners (iii) Enforcement Officers	Regional or Sub-Regional Offices of the Employees' Provident Fund Organisation in the State of Rajasthan.	The State of Rajasthan.
29. (i) Regional Provident Fund Commissioners (ii) Assistant Provident Fund Commissioners (iii) Enforcement Officers	Regional or Sub-Regional Offices of the Employees' Provident Fund Organisation in the State of Tamil Nadu and the Union Territory of Pudueherry except the Mahe and Yanam areas.	The State of Tamilnadu and Union Territory of Pudueherry except the Mahe and Yanam areas.
30. (i) Regional Provident Fund Commissioners (ii) Assistant Provident Fund Commissioners (iii) Enforcement Officers	Regional or Sub-Regional Offices of the Employees' Provident Fund Organisation in the State of Uttarakhand.	The States of Uttarakhand.
31. (i) Regional Provident Fund Commissioners (ii) Assistant Provident Fund Commissioners (iii) Enforcement Officers	Regional or Sub-Regional Offices of the Employees' Provident Fund Organisation in the State of Uttar Pradesh.	The States of Uttar Pradesh.
32. (i) Regional Provident Fund Commissioners (ii) Assistant Provident Fund Commissioners (iii) Enforcement Officers	Regional or Sub-Regional Offices of the Employees' Provident Fund Organisation in the States of Sikkim, West Bengal and Union Territory of Andaman and Nicobar Islands.	The States of Sikkim, West Bengal and Union Territory of Andaman and Nicobar Island.

* *Notifications S.O. 2935 dated 13.10.2008. Published in Gazette of India dated 18.10.2008.*

III. Powers of Inspector:

Powers of Inspector have specifically been mentioned in the section it-self. However, *in J & J Dechane vs. R.P.F. Inspector – [(1960) 1 LLJ 765 (AP)]* relying on **State of Madras vs. V.G. Row, AIR 1952 SC 196 and Virendra vs. State of Punjab, AIR 1957 SC 896],** it was held that the powers conferred on the Inspector under section 13(2) for the purpose of ascertaining whether the provisions of the Act were applicable to any particular establishment or, in other words, to implement the provisions of the Act, could not be considered to be arbitrary or unreasonable.

No suit against an Inspector is maintainable as a Provident Fund Inspector is appointed by the Appropriate Government and his services are controlled by the Government. He performs public duties. Hence, notwithstanding that he is paid from the Central Provident Fund and not by the

Government, he is a public officer within the definition contained in Section 2 (17) (h) of the CPC. Therefore, a suit filed without a notice under Section 80 of the CPC, for restraining him from enforcing the provisions of the Act cannot sustain.-*[Union of India vs. Narayan Bannppa Pakkanavar, -1989 Lab. I.C. 854 (Kant).]*

In many court cases, the **Gazette notification** has been insisted to be produced, but the High Court of Rajasthan held that the complainant failed to produce the Gazette but in the complaint and in his statement proved his appointment as Provident Fund Inspector under Section 13 of the Act. In such circumstances, taking judicial notice under section 57 of the Evidence Act of his appointment, the burden to contradict the said statement lay on the other party- *[Provident Fund Inspector vs. Jhoomarlal Swarooplal Tiwari- (1994)69 FLR (Sum) 22.].*

A. Quasi-judicial Authorities-

Quasi-judicial authorities are those mentioned in section 7A to resolve the disputes as defined under sub-section (1), those are-

All Assistant Provident Fund Commissioners,

All Regional Provident Fund Commissioners,

All Additional Central Provident Fund Commissioners, and

The Central Provident Fund Commissioner.

Functions and other matters have been discussed in **Step-6, Default Management, Determination of Dues.**

B. Judicial Authorities-

Judicial authorities have exclusive powers to decide any dispute with-in their sphere and jurisdiction. The Recovery Officer, who is protected by the Judicial Officers (Protection) Act, 1850 and the Presiding Officer of the Employees' Provident Fund Appellate Tribunal are the judicial authorities in the legal terms.

The powers jurisdiction and functions of Recovery Office have been discussed in Step 6 (Default Management) Step 16 (Recovery of the Dues) and the powers, jurisdiction, function & procedure of the EFF Appellate Tribunal have been discussed in Step 18.

Chapter 7

Employer

Under the Act, the employer is the main roll-player, without which no one can imagine the implementation of the social security schemes. 'Employer' has been defined in section 2 (e)-

Section 2. [1][(e) *"employer"* means –

(i) **in relation to an establishment which is a factory, the owner or occupier of the factory, including the agent of such owner or occupier, the legal representative of a deceased owner or occupier and, there a person has been named as a manager of the factory under clause (f) of sub-section (1) of section 7 of the Factories Act, 1948 (63 of 1948), the person so named; and**

(ii) **in relation to any other establishment, the person who, or the authority which, has the ultimate control over the affairs of the establishment, and where the said affairs are entrusted to a manager, managing director or managing agent, such manager, managing director or managing agent;]**

---
1. Substituted by Sec. 4 of Act 94 of 1956.

In addition to this definition, a clarificatory provision has also been made under section 14A where, for the purpose of penalties, the employer has widely been defined. It reads as under:-

Explanation:-For the purpose of this section-

(a) **"company" means any body corporate and includes a firm and other association of individuals; and**

(b) **"director" in relation to a firm means a partner in the firm.**

I. Importance of Employer:

For the administration the EPF & MP Act, 1952 and the Schemes framed there-under, the first initiation is taken by the employer only. As it is an inherent essence of the Act that it applies by its own force, it is only the employer, who has to take initiation to implement the Act as soon as the conditions as laid-down in Section 1 are fulfilled and intimate the concerned administrative authority of the CBT to complete the administrative formalities of issue of a Code number and guide for reporting of compliance, etc.

Secondly, all the information and documentation in respect of an employee is completed and submitted to the authorities by the employer only, No record is created by the authorities except processing the information etc. supplied by the employer.

II. Who is employer?:

Who is an employer responsible for the implementation of the Act, has been defined in Section 2 (e) of the Act. The definition of employer is in two parts-one, in relation to an establishment which is a factory; and the other is, in relation to other establishments. This two way definition has been provided by the amendment Act 94 of 1956 by which the Act facilitated its application to the other establishments other than the factories, accordingly, the term 'employer' was defined on deferent footings. Therefore, it goes–

Owner or occupier or its agent and the Factory Manager as required to be appointed and designated so under Section 7 (1)(f) of the Factories Act, 1948. Occupier by designation so is also required to be appointed or declared under the Factories Act. However, the owner of a factory can be a person, or incorporated person either a company registered under the Companies Act or a Partnership Firm registered under the Partnership Act. And,

In relation to other establishments, the employer is the person, who has ultimate control over the affairs of the establishment. Where the owner is a body incorporated either under Companies Act, or under Partnership Act or under Registration of Societies Act or under Cooperative Societies Act or so, to whom the affairs of the establishment have been assigned, is the owner for the purpose of this Act, whether he/she is a manager, or managing director or the managing agent. A director of a company included in the declaration under columns 8 and 11 of Form 5-A as one of the persons in charge of, and responsible to, the company for the conduct of the business of the establishment, has been held to be liable, under section 14-A for non-compliance with the provisions of the Act and Schemes in not depositing the contribution. Supreme Court has explained this position in the case of *Shrikanta Datta Narasimharaja Wodiyar vs. Enforcement Officer, Mysore- [(1993) 3 SCC 217;1993 SCC (L&S) 751; (1993) 2 LLN 69]* that clause (i) and (ii) of Section 2 (e) are wide in their sweep. In clause (i) there are included not only the owner or occupier but even the agent or manager. When it comes to establishments other than factory it is not confined to owner or occupier but to all those who have control over, or are responsible for affairs of, the company. It includes even a director.

The Owner - In the PF Act, owner has not been defined, however, it is used in section 85 (2) of the Factories Act, 1948 and the Honourable Bombay High Court, had occasion to delineate the 'owner' in the case of *Jamnabai PurshottamAsar vs. State of Maharashtra [(1964) 2 LLJ 7; AIR 1964 Bom. 267]* –

"The owner who was within the contemplation of the legislature, was a person who bore some relationship with the workers who were working on the premises. A person who is merely the owner of a place on which the premises of the factory aare situate, as for example, the Port Trust in the present case, or a person who is merely the owner of the premises in which the machinery is installed or who again is merely the owner of the machinery with the help of which the manufacturing process is carried on, cannot be deemed to be an owner such as is contemplated by sub-section (2) of section 85. The proviso to sub-section (1) also emphasizes that the 'owner' contemplated by section 85 must be a person who in some manner is concerned with the manufacturing process carried on in the place in respect of which the power is conferred on the State Government to issue a notification. If the 'owner' as contemplated by clause (ii) of the non-obstante clause and the proviso to sub-section (1) of Section 85 must mean a person who is either connected with the manufacturing process or is concerned directly or indirectly with the persons engaged in the manufacturing process, the word 'owner' which occurs in sub-section (2) of Section 85 must bear a similar meaning."

Managing Agent- Section 2 (25) of the Companies Act defines the Managing Agent as under- "Managing Agent means any individual, firm or body corporate entitled, subject to the provision of this Act, to the management of the whole, or substantially the whole, of the affairs of a company by virtue of an agreement with company, or by virtue of its memorandum or article of association, and includes any individual, firm or body corporate occupying the position of a managing agent, by whatever name called.

Receiver- Where the receiver appointed under the orders of the court had full control over the affairs of the establishment and the existing staff subject to the court's supervision in certain matters, it was held that it could not be said that the partnership firm was the employer. In fact, the receiver would be the employer under section 2(e) *[Provident Fund Inspector vs. Venkatachalam Chettiar- (1970) 1 LLJ 455]*.

Liquidator- A liquidator having the ultimate control for all practical purposes over the affairs of a factory including the power to carry on the factory or to sell it as a going concern is "employer" under the Act. But if the liquidator is asked to wind up a factory and close it down, the liquidator will not be liable under the Act because it will not longer be a factory engaged in the specified industry- *[Mahalaxmi Cotton Mills Ltd (in Liquidation), in re, AIR 1960 Cal. 199]*.

Partnership firm- In case of a firm, all the partners are treated as employer and the mere fact that the partnership firm has been dissolved would not absolve them from liability to pay provident fund dues *[Mukhtiar Sing Sodhi vs. RPFC, -1972 ALL LJ 265]*. However, the definition of the expression "employer" makes it clear that ordinarily all the partners of a firm are not liable to be punished in criminal cases, but only the person who has ultimate control over the affairs of the establishment, or the manager, managing director, or managing agent who has ultimate control over the affairs of the establishment is liable to be prosecuted under section 14 (1A) and 14 (1B)- *Anantharamaih Woolen Factory vs. State- 1981 Lab IC 538; (1981) 1 LLN 170 (Kant)]*.

III. Powers and duties of an employer:

In fact, every action of the CBT in administration of the Act and the Schemes is based on the compliance made by the employer, therefore, his duties are vital and powers in certain matter have also been given to the employer. Special power has been given to an employer with respect to a contractor, who is engaging workers for the work of, and deploying workers for an employer, as far reporting of compliance in respect such employees is concerned,

Under section 8A, the employer is authorized to recover the dues paid by him under paragraph 30 of the EPF Scheme in respect of employees employed by a contractor. It goes as under-

Section [1]**[8A. Recovery of moneys by employers and contractors.–** (1) [2][The amount of contribution (that is to say, the employer's contributions as well as the employee's contribution in pursuance of any Scheme and the employer's contribution in pursuance of the Insurance Scheme)] and any charges [3][***] for meeting the cost of administering the Fund paid or payable by an employer in respect of an employee employed by or through a contractor may be recovered by such employer from the contractor, either by deduction from any amount payable to the contractor under any contract or as a debt payable by the contractor.**

(2) A contractor from whom the amounts mentioned in sub-section (1) may be recovered in respect of any employee employed by or through him, may recover from such employee the employee's contribution [4][under any Scheme] by deduction from the basic wages, dearness allowance and retaining allowance (if any) payable to such employee.

(3) Notwithstanding any contract to the contrary, no contractor shall be entitled to deduct the employer's contribution or the charges referred to in sub-section (1) from the basic wages, dearness allowance, and retaining allowance (if any) payable to an employee employed by or through him or otherwise to recover such contribution of charges from such employee.

Explanation given under section 6 which further includes certain elements of pay for the purpose of payment of contribution under the Schemes.

1.	Ins. by Act 28 of 1963, sec. 8 (w.e.f. 30-11-1963).
2.	Subs. by Act 99 of 1976, sec. 25, for certain words (w.e.f. 1-8-1976).
3.	The words "on the basis of such contribution" omitted by Act 33 of 1988, sec. 13 (w.e.f. 1-8-1988).
4.	Ins. by Act 99 of 1976, sec. 25 (w.e.f. 1-8-1976).

Besides, obtaining declaration from the employees in form No. 11 and 2 and passing these over to the authorities and submission of monthly returns with payments and annual returns as prescribed by the Commissioner on completion of a financial year for recording the moneys in the individual accounts of the members. The foremost duty of the employer is to render assistance to the CBT in making correct payment to the right claimant, which is the soul of the Act and the Schemes and the completion of the Compliance under the Act. The following paragraphs of the EPF Scheme describe the duties of an employer–

Paragraph 33. **Declaration by persons already employed at the time of institution of the Fund.–**

Paragraph 34. **Declaration by persons taking up employment after the, Fund has been established.–**

Paragraph 35. **Preparation of contribution cards.–**

Paragraph 36. **Duties of Employers.–**

On the part of an employer, it is must that all relevant information in formats prescribed are submitted to the authorities to ensure proper service to his employees– Subscribers to P.F. There are many forms prescribed, but few important from on which the fool proof compliance by the employers & authorities is based are discussed with here under, despite the fact that the EPFO has introduced networking services by seeking compliance on-line and giving service with add of the networking system.–

FORM No. 11

(1) **Utility:-** To ascertain the entitlement of an employee for PF membership.

(2) This form is to be filled in for each and every employee taking up employment in the establishment at the time of coverage.

(3) This form is also to be filled in for each and every new employee joining the establishment after the date of coverage.

Employer

(4) After obtaining the information in this from, the employer shall decide about the entitlement of an employee to become PF member as per the flowchart given here under:-

(5) If any employee is entitled to become member of PF as per above flowchart and he is also getting pension under EPS'95, then the full employers' contribution is to be deposited in A/c No. 1, i.e., Provident fund and in no case any contribution is to be made towards pension fund, i.e., A/c No. 10.

(6) This form is not to be filed with the PF department but is to be retained by the employers themselves for verification by PF authorities in future, when required.

FORM No. 09

(Para 36(1) of EPF Scheme, 1952 & Para 20 of EPS, 1995)

In the networking environment, the information required to be submitted in form 9 is uploaded as "employee master" which creates a permanent record on the system. The columns are almost the same as detailed below, simultaneously, description of form 9 is also given.

1. It should be filled up only on one side.
2. It should be laminated on other side.
3. Entries should be made after leaving one row blank. This blank row is for officer use.
4. A copy of Form 9 should be retained by the employer and should be updated with reference to Form No. 5 and 10.
5. In column No. 2, the Account number should be started from one onwards in sequential manner.
6. No employee should be given more than one Account Number and also one Account Number should not be allotted to more than one employee.
7. If any employee, who is given PF Account Number and after sometime leaves the establishment and then rejoins the establishment, in this case if his earlier PF Account Number is not closed, then the same account number will continue, otherwise, new account number may be allotted.
8. No abbreviation is to be used with respect to name of employee and father's name. For ex. AMIT KUMAR VERMA should not be written as A.K. VERMA.
9. Date of Birth (DOB) is an important information and due care should be taken to fill up the correct date of birth. Pension benefits is related to DOB, and once filled this will not be allowed to change under normal circumstances.
10. Every page should be signed by the employer /authorized officer with his official send of designation.
11. The information and authorization sheet giving information of the establishment, attached to Form No. 9 should be signed by the employer only and not by his authorized officer.

    The employer may authorize any office of his off to attest, sign and submit various forms and returns to the EPF department on his behalf. The officer so authorized should be reliable and responsible officer of the employer.
12. Any change in the authorized officer should be intimated through specimen signature card duly attested by the employer only.
13. The designation of the authorized officer should be mentioned.
14. This form is to be submitted to EPF office within 15 days of receipt of coverage letter.

FORM No. 05

(Para 36(2)(a) of EPF Scheme, 1952)

Form No. 5 and 10 has become irrelevant in the networking environment. It is supplemented by addition a new employee master and also adding in the monthly contribution information uploaded.

1. It should be submitted to EPF Office within 15 days of close of each month.

2. No abbreviation is to be used with respect to name of employee and father's name. For ex. **AMIT KUMAR VERMA** should not be written as **A.K. VERMA.**

3. Date of Birth (DOB) is important information and as such due care should be taken to fill up the correct date of birth.

Pension benefits is related to DOB, and once filled this will not be allowed to change under normal circumstances.

4. Any employee qualifying to become member of the fund during the preceding month on joining or on rejoining the establishment, the detail of such employee should be furnished as in Form No. 5.

In case an employee rejoins, his/her earlier PF Account No. if not already closed, should be continued. If earlier P.F. account number is closed than a new account number be allotted.

5. Form No. 2 should also be enclosed for all such new members.

6. If there is no such employee joining the establishment during the preceding month, a "NIL" return should be filed with EPF Office.

FORM No. 10

(Para 36(2)(b) of The EPF Scheme, 1952 & Para 20(2) of The EPS, 1995)

1. The details of members leaving the service during the month should be given in this form.

2. It should be submitted to EPF Office within 15 days of close of each month.

3. No abbreviation is to be used with respect to name of employee and father's name. For ex. **AMIT KUMAR VERMA** should not be written as **A.K. VERMA.**

4. In column Number 6 the reason for leaving service should be clearly mentioned.

If the reason of leaving service is discharge/dismissal/termination or on other similar ground, then in the remarks column the details of any court case pending should also be mentioned.

5. If there is no such employee leaving the establishment during the preceding month, a "NIL" return should be filed with EPF Office.

FORM 5-A

(Para 36-A of The EPF Scheme, 1952 & Para 21 of The EPS, 1995)

Paragraph [1][**36A. Employer to furnish particulars of ownership.–** Every employer in relation to a factory or other establishment to which the Act applies on the date of coming into force of the Employees' Provident Funds (Tenth Amendment) Scheme, 1961, or is applied after that date shall furnish [2][in duplicate] to the Regional Commissioner in Form No. 5A annexed hereto. [3][particulars of all the branches and departments, owners], occupiers, directors, partners, manager or any other person or persons who have the ultimate control over the affairs of such factory or establishment and also send intimation of any change in such particulars, within fifteen days of such change, to the Regional Commissioner by registered post and in such other manner as may be specified by the Regional Commissioner]:

[4][Provided that in the case of any employer of a factory or other establishment to which the Act and the Employees' Family Pension Scheme, 1971, shall apply the aforesaid Form may be deemed to satisfy the requirements of the Employees' Family Pension Scheme, 1971, for the purpose specified above.]

1.	Added by G.S.R. 1457, dated 21st February, 1961.
2.	Ins. by G.S.R. 1714, dated 1st September, 1966.
3.	Subs. by G.S.R. 1836, dated 7th December, 1965.
4.	Ins. by G.S.R. 320, dated 16th February, 1972.

1. This form is related to particulars of ownership of the establishment.

2. This form is to be submitted in duplicate within fifteen days of receipt of Code Number. Any change subsequently requires to be intimated to the EPF Office through a fresh Form Number 5A in duplicate within 15 days of such change.

3. In column Number 11 of Form 5A, the details of such persons should be mentioned who is/are having the ultimate control over the affairs of establishment, for example, CEO, MD, Managing Partner, General Manager etc.

4. This form should not be signed by the authorized officer of the establishment but by the employer himself only. Detail discussion Chapter 3, Step-11 (Contribution be referrred)

IV. Allotment of Account numbers:

Paragraph 37. **Allotment of account numbers.**–On receipt of the information referred in sub-paragraphs 33, 34 and 36, the Commissioner shall promptly allot an Account Number to each employee qualifying to become a member and shall communicate the Account Number to the member through the employer.

In certain matter, there happens to be a system defined which proves to be a turning point & key for the smooth management; any deviation from that leads to a mess in future. In the case of administration of the Act and the Schemes, obligation casted upon the authorities by paragraph 37 has the same gravity. By taking liberty of not following the mandate of para 37 by the authorities has automatically given liberty for not maintaining the records of the schemes properly, which has ultimately resulted is creating the scene of the day when the authorities are facing and struggling for worthy survival in the competitive market threat.

It is evident that if the authorities would have continued to allot account numbers to the P.F. member on receipt of Form 9 or 5 the authorities would have been under obligation to check the correctness of the information being supplied by the employer through deferrent forms/returns, there after the basic record of members in form No. 9 would have been competed before proceeding for prepation of individual accounts of members and no room for wrong or multiple accounts would have happened and there by, the service to subscribers would have been at an appreciable height and would be ready to face any threat of competition. But, unfortunately, the run of the track led to some what where nobody wanted to go, perhaps, except wee heinous.

Related provision of EPS, 1995–

Paragraph **23. Allotment of account** [1]**[numbers].**— (1) For purposes of this Scheme, where the member has already been allotted or is allotted hereafter an account number under the Employees' Provident Funds Scheme, 1952, he shall retain the same account number.

(2) In the case of employees of the establishments exempted from Employees' Provident Funds Scheme, 1952 under section 17 of the Act, who are members of the Employees' Family Pension Fund the account number already allotted shall be retained by them.

(3) In the case of employees of the establishment exempted from the Employees' Provident Funds Scheme, 1952 under section 17 of the Act, who are not members of the Employees' Family Pension Fund but opt to become members of Employees' Pension Fund and in case of new employees of such establishments, fresh account numbers shall be allotted by the Commissioner.

---
1. Subs. by G.S.R. 134, dated 28th February, 1996 (w.e.f. 16-3-1996).

Despite these provisions, while submitting form No. 9 or 5, the employers use to allot account numbers to members in a serial number. Some time, one person was allotted more than one account number or one account number was allotted to more than one person. Such happened due to not exercise of checks by the employer or a senior responsible person. Now, the EPFO has taken initiative to allot a 'unique account number' (UAN) which will remain with the member till his life. There will be no effect on change of the employer. Whenever a new person joins a new establishment, the employer has to obtain his UAN through Form No. 11 and list it out in his monthly contribution roll.

V. Duties of Contractor:

1. Under EPF Scheme, 1952–

Paragraph [1]**[36B. Duties of Contractors** — Every contractor shall, within seven days of the close of every month, submit to the principal employer a statement showing the recoveries of contributions in respect of employees employed by or through him and shall also furnish to him such information as the prinicpal employer is required to furnish under the provisions of the Scheme to the Commissioner.]

---
1. Subs. by G.S.R. 1845, dated 28th November, 1963.
---

2. Under Employees' Pension Scheme, 1995–

Paragraph **22. Duties of contractors.**–Every contractor shall, within seven days of the close of every month, submit to the principal employer a statement showing the particulars in respect of employees employed by or through him in respect of whom contributions to the Employees' Pension Fund are payable and shall also furnish to him such information as the principal employer is required to furnish under the provisions of this Scheme to the Commisioner.

Step by Step Into EPF

> *Product*
> *and*
> *Services*

Chapter 8

The Schemes

> *Brief badinage–*
>
> *The heading which has been chosen for this chapter, the 'Products and Services' rather, does not suit to statutory schemes which have been framed under a parliamentary enactment. When every benefit and availability of those are defined by law, there is no choice to alter or modify the products and give any exclusion from those to any person entitle to it, leads to an offence. However, with a view to present the schemes in an attractive form, an excuse is taken for the suggested heading.*

Employees' Provident Funds Scheme, 1952:

Section 5. Employees' Provident Funds Scheme.– [1][(1)] The Central Government may, by notification in the Official Gazette, frame a scheme to be called the Employees' Provident Fund Scheme for the establishment of provident funds under this Act for employees or for any class of employees and specify the [2][establishments] or class of [2][establishments] to which the said Scheme shall apply [3][and there shall be established, as soon as may be after the framing of the Scheme, a Fund in accordance with the provisions of this Act and the Scheme].

[4][(1A) The Fund shall vest in, and be administered by, the Central Board constituted under section 5A.

(1B) Subject to the provisions of this Act, a Scheme framed under sub-section (1) may provide for all or any of the matters specified in Schedule II.]

[3][(2) A Scheme framed under sub-section (1) may provide that any of its provisions shall take effect either prospectively or retrospectively on such date as may be specified in this behalf in the Scheme.]

---
1. Renumbered as sub-section (1) of Sec. 5 by Act 37 of 1953, Sec. 4.
2. Substituted by Act 94 of 1956, Sec.3, for "factories."
3. Inserted by Act 37 of 1953, Sec. 4.
4. Inserted by Act 28 of 1963, Sec. 3.

Section 9. Fund to be recognised under Act 11 of 1922.– For the purpose of the Indian Income-tax Act, 1922 (11 of 1922), the Fund shall be deemed to be a recognised provident fund within the meaning of Chapter IX-A of that Act:

Provided that nothing contained in the said Chapter shall operate to render ineffective any provision of the Scheme under which the Fund is established, which is repugnant to any of the provisions of that Chapter or of the rules made there under-

I. Framing of Employees' Provident Funds Scheme, 1952:

As has already been mentioned in Chapter 1, after a long debate and discussions, the government of India could decide to make a statutory provident fund for the benefits of industrial workers on the lines which was working for the workers in Coal Mines and Tea Plantations in Assam. To get enabled for the same, the Central Government, through the Governor-General of India, an Ordinance was promulgated on 15th November, 1951 and after becoming it an Act in March, 1952, the Employees' Provident Funds Scheme, 1952 was made applicable from 1st November, 1952, initially on Six big Industries by the Central Government in exercise of conferred on it by Section 5 of the Act making provision therein on the matters mentioned in the Schedule II attached to that Act, which reads as under-

Schedule II

[1][See Section 5 (1B)]

MATTERS FOR WHICH PROVISION MAY BE

MADE IN A SCHEME-

1. The employees or class of employees who shall join the Fund, and the conditions under which employees may be exempted from joining the Fund or from making any contribution.

2. The time and manner in which contribution shall be made in the Fund by the employers and by, or behalf of employees, [2][(whether employed by him directly or by or through a contractor)], the contribution which an employee may, if he so desires, make under [3][xxx] section 6, and the manner in which such contribution may be recovered.

[2][2A. The manner in which employees' contribution may be recovered by contractors from employees employed by or through such contractors.]

3. The payment by the employer of such sums of money as may be necessary to meet the cost of administering the Fund and the rate at which and the manner in which the payment shall be made.

[1][4. The constitution of any committee for assisting any Board of Trustees.]

[1][5. The opening of regional and other offices of any Board of Trustees.]

6. The manner in which accounts shall be kept, the investment of moneys belonging to the Fund in accordance with any directions issued or conditions specified by the Central Government, the preparation of the budget, the audit of accounts and the submission of reports to the Central Government.

7. The conditions under which withdrawal from the Fund may be permitted and any deduction or forfeiture may be made and the maximum amount of such deduction or forfeiture.

8. The fixation by the Central Government in consultation with Board of Trustees concerned of the rate of interest payable to members.

9. The form in which an employee shall furnish particulars about himself and his family whenever required.

10. The nomination of a person to receive the amount standing to the credit of a member after his death and the cancellation or variation of such nomination.

11. The registers and records to be maintained with respect to employees and the returns to be furnished by employers ²[or contractors].

12. The form or design of any identity card, token or disc for the purpose of identifying any employee, and for the issue, custody and replacement thereof.

13. The fee to be levied for any of the purposes specified in this Schedule.

14. The contraventions or defaults which shall be punishable under sub-section (2) of section 14.

15. The further powers, if any, which may be exercised by an Inspector.

16. The manner in which accumulation in any existing provident fund shall be transferred to the Fund under section 15, and the mode of valuation of any assets which may be transferred by the employers in this behalf.

17. The conditions under which a member may be permitted to pay premium on life insurance from the Fund.

18. Any other matter ²[which is to be provided for in the Scheme or] which may be necessary or proper for the purpose of implementing the Scheme.

1.	Substituted by Act 28 of 1963, Sec. 13. (w.e.f. 30.11.1963)
2.	Inserted by Act 28 of 1963, Sec. 13. (w.e.f. 30.11.1963)
3.	Omitted by Act 28 of 1963, Sec. 13. (w.e.f. 30.11.1963)

II. Application of the Scheme:

An independent provision as to application of the Employees' Provident Funds Scheme, 1952 has been made in the Scheme itself in paragraph 1. Sub-paragraph 3 provides its application to the establishment to which the Act applies, subject to the provisions of section 16 and 17. Clause (a) of the sub-paragraph (3) excludes the application of the Scheme to the Tea factories in the State of Assam and in clause (b), the application of the Scheme to different industries and classes of establishments from different dates, that is with effect from or from a subsequent date of issue of notification under section 4 or under clause (b) of sub-section (3) of section 1. It is not necessary that the scheme applies automatically on the issue of notification under above sections, but a separate notification under paragraph 1 (3) (b) is necessary for application of the Scheme. If such notification is issued on a subsequent date and the date of application in the notification is not notified, than the Scheme is to apply from the date of the publication of the notification in the official Gazette. There are so many such examples. In the case of Educational establishments, the Notification under Section 1(3) (b) was published on 6th March, 1982 and the notification of application the Scheme was published on 6th July, 1982, thus the liability of the employers of such establishments started from 1st August, 1982 only, and not from 1st April, 1982.

III. Recognition under the Income Tax Act:

The Provident Fund is in the nature of savings for the old-age security, it required an immunity to be given from the Income-Tax, therefore, a specific provision has been made in the Act itself that the Fund established under the Act shall be a recognized Fund and the savings and the interest earned thereon will not attract the Income Tax liability. Although, the reference of the Income Tax Act, 1922 has been mentioned in the section 9, and the Income Tax Act, 1961 has replaced that Act, a due reference is required to be mentioned in this Act.

On the similar footing, all exempted provident funds are also required to take a recognition certificate from the Income Tax Authorities for the purpose of the immune aforesaid. In Finance Bill, 2006, it has been made mandatory that every private provident fund is to be got notified under section 17 of the EPF and MP Act, 1952 failing which no immune will be available to such funds. Therefore, every private provident fund is required to get the establishment covered under the PF Act first and then get exemption notified under section 17 of the Act of 1952.

Employees' Pension Scheme, 1995

In 1971, by an ordinance, the Act was amended to frame a pension scheme called 'the Employees' Family Pension Scheme, 1971' which was made applicable w.e.f. 1st March, 1971. Under that scheme, family pension was available to a family member of a deceased member of that scheme with a lump sum amount as a Life Assurance Benefit, if the death occurred while in service only, otherwise a lump sum amount was being paid.

In 1995, that scheme was replaced by a comprehensive pension scheme which is applicable from 16.11.1995. The enabling provisions to frame the pension scheme has been made under section 6-A with the supporting provisions in Third Schedule, which are reproduced here-under-

Section [1][**6A. Employees' Pension Scheme.**– (1) **The Central Government may, by notification in the Official Gazette, frame a scheme to be called the Employees' Pension Scheme for the purpose of providing for** –

(a) superannuation pension, retiring pension or permanent total disablement pension to the employees of any establishment or class of establishments to which this Act applies; and

(b) widow or widower's pension, children pension or orphan pension payable to the beneficiaries of such employees.

(2) Notwithstanding anything contained in section 6, there shall be established, as soon as may be after framing of the Pension Scheme, a Pension Fund into which there shall be paid, from time to time, in respect of every employee who is a member of the Pension Scheme,-

(a) such sums from the employer's contribution under section 6, not exceeding eight and one-third per cent. Of the basic wages, dearness allowance and retaining allowance, if any, of the concerned employees, as may be specified in the Pension Scheme;

(b) such sums as are payable by the employers of exempted establishments under sub-section (6) of section 17;

(c) the net assets of the Employees' Family Pension as on the date o the establishment of the Pension Fund;

(d) such sums as the Central Government may, after due appropriation by Parliament by law in the behalf, specify.

(3) One the establishment of the Pension Fund, the Family Pension Scheme (hereinafter referred to as the ceased scheme) shall cease to operate and all assets of the ceased scheme shall vest in and shall stand transferred to, and all liabilities under the ceased scheme shall be enforceable against, the Pension Fund and the beneficiaries under the ceased scheme shall be entitled to draw the benefits, not less than the benefits, they were entitled to under the ceased scheme, from the Pension Fund.

(4) The Pension Fund shall vest in and be administered by the Central Board in such manner as may be specified in the Pension Scheme.

(5) Subject to the provisions of this Act, the Pension Scheme may provide for all or any of the matters specified in Schedule III.]

(6) The Pension Scheme may provide that all or any of its provisions shall take effect either prospectively or retrospectively on such date as may be specified in that behalf in that scheme.

(7) A Pension Scheme, framed under sub-section (1) shall be laid, as soon as may be after it is made, before each House of Parliament, while it is in session, for a total period of thirty days which may be comprised in one session or in two or more successive sessions, and if, before the expiry of the session immediately following the session or the successive sessions aforesaid, both Houses agree in making any modification in the scheme or both Houses agree that the scheme should not be made, the scheme shall thereafter have effect only in such modified form or be of no effect, as the case may be; so, however, that any such modification or annulment shall be without prejudice to the validity of anything previously done under that scheme.].

1. Substituted by Act 25 of 1996, Sec. 5 (w.e.f. 16.11.1995).

IV. Framing of Employees' Family Pension Scheme, 1971:

From the very beginning it was under consideration to introduce a scheme of Social Security benefits for the industrial workers, the pension has been a centre point together with the consideration of provident fund, the Government could not introduce it for the reasons that the supportive infrastructure did not exist. In the late sixties, it could get attention of the Government. But, again, the Government was not in a position to satisfy all the demands of various sectors of labours, therefore, an Ordinance was promulgated in March, 1971 which enabled the Central Government to make a family pension Scheme to provide pensions to the family members who dies **while in Service**. The scheme was notified by the Central Government and made applicable w.e.f. 1st March, 1971, in exercise of powers conferred on it by newly inserted Section 6A of the Act making provision therein on the matters mentioned in the Schedule III added to the Act, making it optional to join it, for the persons who were already enjoying P.F. membership as on 28th February, 1971.

The application of this Scheme was simultaneous with the application of the **Employees' Provident Funds Scheme, 1952.**

The application of the **Employees' Family Pension Scheme, 1971** was simultaneous with the application of the E.P.F. Scheme, 1952, but, in respect of a newly covered establishment, which was covered retrospectively, there was an administrative arrangement that the **Employees' Family Pension Scheme, 1971** would apply from the date of issue of the letter of coverage through which the Code number used to be issued. This interpretation was criticized by the High Court of Gujrat in the case of **Gitaben Arvindkumar Sheth vs. Union of India [(1995) 2 LLN 226].** The writ was filed on denial of family pension to the widow of the member who became P.F. member from 1st April, 1990, by the coverage order dated 31st May, 1990, hence, the family pension membership was reckoned from 1st May, 1990. The member expired on 26th July, 1990 and due to not having a reckonable service of 3 months to make the widow entitled for family pension. The High Court observed that there was no provision in Employees' Family Pension Scheme, 1971 to deny family pension membership from the date from which he was entitle to the provident fund membership. P.F. membership of the deceased member commenced form 1st April, 1990, as such the Family Pension membership also commences from 1st April, 1990, thus having completed the reckonable service of 3 months as required under the Employees' Family Pension Scheme, 1971, the widow was entitled to the family pension under the Employees' Family Pension Scheme, 1971.

The order of the High Court was not appealed by the department and it got its finality.

By that time, the Central Government decided to introduce the Employees' Pension Scheme replacing the Family Pension Scheme, 1971.

V. Framing of Employees' Pension Scheme, 1995:

The twenty years existence of the Employees' Family Pension Scheme raised the expectation of the workers to demand for an old age pension scheme. By that time, many major changes were made in the P.F. scheme including that of enhancement of rate of contribution and wage ceiling for contribution, hence, the Government decided to replace the Family Pension Scheme by a comprehensive pension scheme, and its introduction 1st April, 1993 was announced in the Parliament in Budget Session in 1993, but it could not get the mandate for the reason mainly, due to the demand of the old age pension as an additional benefit without any curtailment of existing structure of contribution that was being credited to the members P.F. accounts. Ultimately, after two and half year of the announced date of 1st April, 1993, again an Ordinance was promulgated on 16th October, 1995 to enable the Central Government for making a new pension scheme, and the Scheme was notified on 16th November, 1995 by the Central Government, in exercise of powers conferred on it by Section 6A (substituted) of the Act making provision therein on the matters mentioned in the substituted Schedule III attached to that Act, which is known as the **Employees' Pension Scheme, 1995.**

Un-like the Family Pension Scheme, this scheme was made compulsory for all the existing members of the old Family Pension Scheme, with a rider provision for the members of family pension scheme who ceased their membership between 1st April, 1993 and 16th November, 1995 and who could be entitled to the benefits under the new scheme, to join it and get benefit available under the new scheme.

Employees' Deposit-linked Insurance Scheme, 1976-

Section [1][6C. Employees' Deposit-linked Insurance Scheme.– (1) The Central Government may, by notification in the Official Gazette, frame a scheme to be called the Employees' Deposit-linked Insurance Scheme for the purpose of providing life insurance benefits to the employees of any establishment or class of establishments to which this Act applies.

(2) There shall be established, as soon as may be after the framing of Insurance Scheme, a Deposit-linked Insurance Fund into which shall be paid by the employer from time to time in respect of every such employee in relation to whom he is the employer, such amount, not being more than one per cent. Of the aggregate of the basic wages, dearness allowance and retaining allowance (if any) for the time being payable in relation to such employee as the Central Government may, by notification in the Official Gazette, specify.

Explanation.– For the purposes of this sub-section, the expressions "dearness allowance" and "retaining allowance" have the same meanings as in section 6.

(3) [2][* * *]

(4) (a) The employer shall pay into the Insurance Fund such further sums of money, not exceeding one-forth of the contribution which he is required to make under sub-section (2), of the Central Government my, from time to time, determine to meet all the expenses in connection with the administration of the Insurance Scheme other than the expenses towards the cost of any benefits provided by or under that Scheme.

(b) [3][* * *]

(5) The Insurance Fund shall vest in the Central Board and be administered by it in such manner as may be specified in the Insurance Scheme.

(6) The Insurance Scheme may provide for all or any of the matters specified in Schedule IV.

(7) The Insurance Scheme may provide that any of its provisions shall take effect either prospectively or retrospectively on such date as may be specified in this behalf in that Scheme.

1.	Inserted by Act 99 of 1976, Sec. 21 (deemed to have come into force from 1.8.1976).
2.	Sub-sec. (3) omitted by Act 25 of 1996, Sec. 6 (w.e.f. 16.11.1995).
3.	Clause (b() of sub-section (4) omitted by Act 25 of 1996, Sec. 6 (w.e.f. 16.11.1995).

Section [1][17AA. Act to have effect notwithstanding anything contained in Act 31 of 1956 - The provisions of this Act shall have effect notwithstanding anything inconsistent therewith contained in the Life Insurance Corporation Act, 1956 (31 of 1956).]

1.	Inserted by Act 99 of 1976 Sec. 35 (w.e.f. 1.8.1976)

VI. Framing of the Employees' Deposit-linked Insurance Scheme, 1976:

Like pension to the workers as a Social Security measures, introduction of an insurance scheme was also under consideration for years together. Therefore, in 1976, it was decide to introduce an insurance scheme for the provident fund members under the E.P.F. Act 1952. To implement this scheme, once again an Ordinance was promulgated on 1st August. 1976 and The **Employees' Deposit-linked Insurance Scheme,1976** was notified providing for payment of a lump-sum amount to the recipient of the provident fund of a deceased member who dies while in service, calculated on the basis of the deposits in the provident fund account. This Scheme applies as soon as the Employees' Provident Funds Scheme applies to an establishment.

By the Act 99 of 1976, which repealed the Ordinance, renamed the Act as the **Employees' Provident Funds and Miscellaneous Provisions Act, 1952.**

The Central Government in exercise of conferred on it by Section 6C (inserted by the Act 99 of 1976) of the Act making provision in the Insurance on the matters mentioned in the Schedule IV attached to that Act.

Section [1][**6D. Laying of Schemes before Parliament.** – Every scheme framed under section 5, section 6A and section 6C shall be laid, as soon as may be after it is framed, before each House of Parliament, while it is in session, for a total period of thirty days which may be comprised in one session or in two or more successive sessions, and if, before the expiry of the session immediately following the session or the successive sessions aforesaid, both Houses agree in making any modification in the scheme, or both Houses agree that the scheme should not be framed, the scheme shall thereafter have effect only in such

modified form or be of no effect, as the case may be ; so however, that any such modification or annulment shall be without prejudice to the validity of anything previously done under that scheme.]

---
1. Inserted by Act 4 of 1996, Sec. 2 and Sch.

Section 7. Modification of Scheme.– (1) The Central Government may, by notification in the Official Gazette add to, [1][amend or vary either prospectively or retrospectively, the Scheme, the [2][Pension] Scheme or the Insurance Scheme, as the case may be.]

[3][(2) Every notification issued under sub-section (1) shall be laid, as soon as may be after it is issued, before each House of Parliament while it is in session, for a total period of thirty days, which may be comprised in one session or in two or more successive sessions, and if, before the expiry of the session immediately following the session or the successive sessions aforesaid, both Houses agree in making any modification in the notification, or both Houses agree that the notification should not be issued, the notification shall thereafter have effect only in such modified form or be of no effect, as the case may be ; so, however, that any such modification or annulment shall be without prejudice to the validity of anything previously done under that notification.]

---
1. Substituted by Act 99 of 1976, Sec. 22, for the words "amend or vary the Scheme or the family Pension Scheme, as the case may be" (deemed to have come into force from 1.8.1976).
2. Substituted by Act 25 of 1996, Sec. 4, for the words "Family Pension" (w.e.f. 16.11.1995)
3. Inserted by Act 4 of 1986, Sec. 2 and Sch.

# Chapter 9

Contributions

Section ¹[6.] Contributions and matters which may be provided for in Scheme.- The contribution which shall be paid by the employer to the Fund shall be ²[ten per cent.] of the basic wages, ³[dearness allowance and retaining allowance (if any)] for the time being payable to each of the employees ⁴[(whether employed by him directly or by or through a contractor)], and the employee's contribution shall be equal to the contribution payable by the employer in respect of him and may ⁵[if any employee so desires, be an amount exceeding ²[ten per cent.] of his basic wages, dearness allowance and retaining allowance (if any), subject to the condition that the employer shall not be under an obligation to pay any contribution over and above his contribution payable under this section]:

⁵[Provided that in its application to any establishment or class of establishments which the Central Government, after making such inquiry as it deems fit, may, by notification in the Official Gazette specify, this section shall be subject to the modification that for the words "²[ten per cent.]," at both the places where they occur, the words ⁶["12 per cent."] shall be substituted:]

Provided further that where the amount of any contribution payable under this Act involves a fraction of a rupee, the Scheme may provide for rounding off of such fraction to the nearest rupee, half of a rupee, or quarter of a rupee.

⁷[Explanation I.] – For the purposes of this ⁸[section] dearness allowance shall be deemed to include also the cash value of any food concession allowed to the employee.

⁹[Explanation II. – For the purposes of this ⁸[section], "retaining allowance" means allowance payable for the time being to an employee of any factory or other establishment during any period in which the establishment is not working, for retaining his services]

¹⁰[(2) * * *]

¹⁰[(3) * * *]

---

1. Sub-sec. (1) of Sec. 6 numbered as s. 6 by Act 28 of 1963, s.5
2. Substituted by Act 10 of 1998, s. 2, for "eight and one-third per cent." (w.e.f. 22.9.1997)
3. Substituted by Act 46 of 1960, s.4.
4. Inserted by Act 28 of 1963, s.5.
5. Substituted by Act 33 of 1988, s.9 (w.e.f. 1.8.1988).
6. Substituted by Act 10 of 1998, s.2, for "ten per cent." (w.e.f. 22.9.1997).
7. Re-numbered as Explanation, by Act 46 of 1960, s. 4.
8. Substituted by Act 28 of 1963, s.5.
9. Inserted by Act 46 of 1960, s.4.
10. Sub-sec. (2) and (3) omitted by Act 28 of 1963, s.6

Legislative reference:

The content of this section is not only the Contribution, but other material provisions which were proposed to be provided in the Scheme have also been included. For such provisions sub-section (1A) and (1B) inserted in 1956, but, in 1963, those provisions were inserted in section 5 as sub-section 1B and deleted from section 6. Thereafter, section 6 exclusively deals with the matters related to contributions only.

Referred and related provisions-

Section 2 (c)- *"contribution"* means a contribution payable in respect of a member under a scheme 1[or the contribution payable in respect of an employee to whom the Insurance Scheme applies];

1.	Inserted by Act 18 of 1976 (w.e.f. 01.8.1976).

Section 2 (b)-*"basic wages"* means all emoluments which are earned by an employee while on duty or ¹[on leave or on holidays with wages in either case] in accordance with the terms of the contract of employment and which are paid or payable in cash to him, but does not include -

- (i) the cash value of any food concession;
- (ii) any dearness allowance (that is to say, all cash payments by whatever name called paid to an employee on account of a rise in the cost of living), house-rent allowance, overtime allowance, bonus, commission or nay other similar allowance payable to the employee in respect of his employment or of work done in such employment;
- (iii) any presents made by the employer;

1.	Substituted by Sec. 3 of Act 33 of 1988 (w.e.f. 1.8.1988).

Explanation given under section 6 which further includes certain elements of pay for the purpose of payment of contribution under the Schemes.

Paragraph 29. Contribution.- (1) The contributions payable by the employer under the Scheme shall be at the rate of ten per cent. of the basic wages, dearness allowance (including the cash value of any food concession) and retaining allowance (if any) payable to each employee to whom the Scheme applies:

Provided that the above rate of contribution shall be twelve per cert. in respect of any establishment or class of establishments which the Central Government may specify in the Official Gazette from time to time under the first proviso to sub-section (1) of section 6 of the Act.

(2) The contribution payable by the employee under the Scheme shall be equal to the contribution payable by the employer in respect of such employee:

Provided that in respect of any employee to whom the Scheme applies, the contribution payable by him may, if he so desires, be an amount exceeding ten per cent, or twelve per cent., as the case may be, of his basic wages, dearness allowance and retaining allowance (if any) subject to the condition that the employer shall not be under an obligation to pay any contribution over and above his contribution payable under the Act.

(3) The contributions shall be calculated on the basis of basic wages, dearness allowance (including the cash value of any food concession) and retaining allowance (if any) actually drawn during the whole month whether paid on daily, weekly, fortnightly or monthly basis.

(4) Each contribution shall be calculated to the nearest rupee, 50 paise or more to be counted as the next higher rupee and fraction of a rupee less than 50 paise to be ignored.

I. Contributions:

The structure of the Provident Fund is contributory, hence the Fund is credited with the contributions made by the employer and equal amount of contribution is given by the member him-self. Therefore, the definition has been constructed in a way in which contributions under all the Schemes framed under the Act have been included.

In section 6, the rate of contribution has been defined. Initially, the rate of contribution was fixed as six and a quarter percent of the pay. By the amending Act 33 of 1988, it was fixed as 8 and one third percent w.e.f. 1st August, 1988 and w.e.f. 22nd September, 1997, the rate of contribution has been fixed as ten percent of wages.

In this section it-self, a rider has been provided through the proviso which authorizes the Central Government, **to enhance the rate of contribution** in respect of certain class of industries or establishments by a notification in the Official Gazette,. Accordingly, prior to 1st August, 1988, the enhanced rate of contribution was 8 percent. After the amendment by Act 33 of1988, such notification could be issued only on 17th May, 1989, specifying the classes of establishments and industries to which the enhanced rate of contribution was made applicable. W.e.f. 22nd September, 1997, the rate of contribution has further been revised by the Act 10 of 1998 making it ten percent and in the proviso, twelve percent from a retrospective date, a notification under proviso issued Vide SO 320 (E) dated 9th April,1997 is remained valid after the Act 10 of 1997. The notification enhancing the rate of contribution is reproduced here-under—

SO 320 (E), dated April 9, 1997 – In exercise of the powers conferred by the first proviso to section 6 of the Employees' Provident Funds and Miscellaneous Provisions Act, 1952 (19 of 1952) and in super session of the notifications specified in Schedule I to this notification except a respects things done or omitted to be done before such super session, the Central Government after making necessary inquiry into the matter hereby specifies with effect from the first day of May, 1997 every establishment and class of establishments other than those specified in Schedule II, to which the said proviso shall apply. The words "eight and one-third percent" at both the places where they occur, the words "ten percent" shall be substituted.

Schedule I

(i) SO No. 360 dated the 17th May, 1989

(ii) SO No. 1837 dated the 29th June, 1990

(iii) SO No. 627 (E) dated the 31st August, 1994

(iv) SO No. 126 (E) dated the 1st March, 1995

Schedule II

Establishments to which the first proviso to Section 6 shall not apply:

(i) Any establishment in which less than twenty persons are employed;

(ii) Any sick industrial company as defined in clause (o) of sub-section (1) of Section 3 of the Sick Industrial Companies (Special Provisions) Act, 1985 (1 of 1986) and which has been declared as such by the Board for Industrial and Financial Reconstruction established under Section 4 of the Act, for the period commencing on and from the date of registration of the reference in the Board and ending either on the date by which the net worth of the said company becomes positive in terms of the orders passed under sub-section (2) of Section 17 of that Act or on the last date of implementation of the scheme sanctioned under Section 18 of that Act;

(iii) Any establishment which has at the end of any financial year accumulated losses equal to or exceeding its entire net worth that is, the sum total of paid-up capital and free reserves and has also suffered cash losses in such financial year and the financial year immediately preceding such financial year.

Explanation -For the purpose of clause (iii) "cash loss" means loss as computed without providing for depreciation;

(iv) Any establishment in the,-

    (A) Jute industry;

    (B) Beedi industry;

    (C) Brick industry;

    (D) Coir industry other than the spinning sector; and

    (E) Guar gum factories.

Note: Section 6 as amended by Act 10 of 1998 w.e.f. 22.9.1997 prescribes the rate of contribution at 10%. This, in effect, supersedes the notification S.O. 320(E) dated 9.4.1997. Hence, the rate of 10% would apply from 22.9.1997 to all the establishments till a new notification is issued by the Central Government under the first proviso to Section 6 enhancing this rate of contribution to 12% in respect of the establishments as may be specified in that notification.

The subject matter and the context in which a particular word is used are of great importance. A restricted meanings of certain words in definitions in Section 2 should not be applied to the words 'contribution,' 'scheme' and 'fund' occurring in Section 6. These words should rather, be interpreted so as to apply even to a private provident fund scheme in force in an establishment exempted under section 17. Therefore, if there is a default in contribution by an exempted establishment, the same amounts to contravention of Section 6 and is punishable under section 14 (1A)- *[N.K. Jain vs. C.K. Shah- (1991) 2 SCC 495; 1991 SCC (L&S) 656; 1991 Lab.I.C. 1013].*

II. Pay or wages for contributions:

What shall be the contribution is determined with reference to the basic-wages or the pay. Basic wages has been defined in Section 2(b), but for the purpose of calculation of contribution, some elements of pay which have been kept out of the definition of basic wages, have also been included. Step by step, the ingredients and nomenclature mentioned in the definition should be taken to under-stand the basic wages.

Basic-wages is all emoluments,

\+ earned while on duty, or

\+ on leave or on holidays, and

\+ paid by directly or indirectly by the employer;

It does not include

\# cash value of food concession,

\# dearness allowance (all cash payments by whatever name called, paid on account of a rise in the cost of leaving),

\# house-rent allowance,

\# overtime allowance,

\# bonus,

\# commission, and

\# similar allowance payable to an employee for his employment or for work done in such employment; and

\# any present made by the employer.

But, for the purpose of payment of contributions, by putting explanations under Section 6, dearness allowance, cash value of food concession and the retaining allowance paid in seasonal establishments have also been included. Similar inclusion has been made in paragraph 29 in which the word 'basic-wages' has been enriched with these supplementary elements of emoluments for the purpose of contributions. Therefore, the area of dispute remains the commissions, other similar allowances to meet the rise in the cost of living, and the presents made by the employer.

Earned while on duty means pay for the defined duty timings mutually agreed, but not in contravention to the law in force regulating the employment like the Factories Act or the Industrial Disputes Act or similar other laws. For example, 8 hours defined duty period is the normal duty period, any emoluments earned for work within that period is basic wages and for work beyond that duty period, that becomes overtime allowance for which a different rate of pay/ wages is applicable.

Authorised leave with wages and weekly and other authorized holidays are also treated as duty, hence the earning for those periods is also basic wages which is subject to contribution. If an employee works on holiday he is paid with additional pay for that day which will not be termed as pay, but is an extra income falls under over-time or extra pay for holiday.

Bombay High Court, in the case of *Hindustan Lever Employees' Union vs. Regional P.F. Commissioner, Maharashtra and Goa- [1995 Lab.IC 775 (777); (1995) 1 LLN 767; (1995) 2 LLJ 279; (1995) 71 FLR 46]* stretched the meaning of the word 'leave with wages' to an extent not acceptable by any end, but the authorities took it as extra scope to get additional contribution on payment of encashment of accumulated leave on retirement of leaving the job of the employer until the Supreme Court did not intervened in the matter.

There are few important judgements which explain the earnings while on duty, which seems to be a complex of piece-rate or quantitative production during normal duty hours and payment for such quantity of production which is more than the normal production within the normal duty hours is termed as incentive, or production bonus or good work reward or so.

In the case of **Amal Kumar Ghatak vs. R.P.F. Commissioner-[(1980) 2 LLJ 308 (Cal)]**, the Calcutta High Court has held that extra leaf price paid in the tea garden to pluckers who pluck more tea than the normal fixed was the 'basic wages.' It also held that the case of Bridge and Roof Co. was distinguishable and had no application to this case. The extra leaf price was not payment for something which was done beyond the regular working hours and therefore, **it could not be overtime.** Overtime means work done not on time but thereafter. Extra leaf price, therefore, could not be "overtime allowance" which is excluded from the definition of "basic wages" be Section 2 (b) (ii). Further, it has also been mentioned that from the dictionary meaning, it is certain that overtime is some-thing which is done not on time, but thereafter. If extra work is done on time, the same, in view of the above, would not come within the definition of overtime and as such, the payment received by the workmen for extra work within the normal duty hours, would not be overtime and should be subject to provident fund contribution being part of basic wages.

Prior to this case, there have been occasion before the Supreme Court to decide two petitions of similar nature, one, known as *Bridge and Roof Co vs. Union of India –[(1962) 2 LLJ 490; AIR 1963 SC 1474; (1963) 3 SCR 978]* and the other was *Jay Engineering Works Ltd. Vs. Union of India-[(1963) 2 LLJ 72; AIR 1963 SC 1480]*.

In the Bridge & Roof case, in addition to basic wages and dearness allowance payable to workers, the company had two production bonus schemes, one for hourly-rated workers and the other for the rest. The main feature of the two schemes was that production bonus began to be paid on certain rates specified in the two schemes when the output reached a particular specified minimum per year and that no production bonus was to be paid when the output was less than the prescribed minimum for the year. The question before the court was whether production bonus was to be treated as 'basic wages' under the Act so as to be taken into account in calculating the amount of contribution under Section 6 of the Act. Their lordship reviewed the definition of the term 'basic wages' as given in the Act, examined the contentions raised on behalf of the parties and observed that the fact that the exceptions contain even presents made by the employer shows that though the definition mentions all emoluments which are earned in accordance with the terms of the contract of employment, care has been taken to exclude presents which would ordinarily not earned in accordance with the terms of the contract of employment. Similarly, though the definition includes 'all emoluments' which are paid or payable in cash, the exception excludes the cash value of any food concession, which in any case was not payable in cash. The exceptions, therefore, do not seem to follow any logical pattern which would be in consonance with the main definition.... Dearness allowance, which an exception in the definition of 'basic wages' is included for the purpose of contribution by Section 6 and the real exceptions, therefore, in clause (ii) are the other exceptions besides dearness allowance which has been included through Section 6.

"This brings us to the consideration of the question of bonus, which is also an exception in clause (ii)."

"We are, therefore, of the opinion that there is no reason why when the word 'bonus' is used in clause (ii) without any qualifying word, it should not be interpreted to included all kind of bonus which were known to industrial adjudication before 1952 and which must, therefore, be deemed to be within the knowledge of the legislature....... We are, therefore, of the opinion that production bonus of this type is excluded from the definition of 'basic wages' in section 2(b)." The Supreme Court reaffirmed its earlier judgement in the case of *Titagarh Paper Mills Co. Ltd. Vs. Workmen- [AIR 1959 SC 1095; 1959 Supp (2) SCR 1002; (1959) 2 LLJ 9].*

In the *Jay Engineering Works Ltd. Case*, the question of production bonus was involved. The petitioner company and its workmen entered into an agreement in August, 1958 for establishment of a production bonus scheme although some kind of production bonus on a more or less straight piece rate system was in force from as far back as 1947. As per the scheme of 1958, a certain proportion of the production was taken to correspond to the minimum basic wages and dearness allowance fixed by the awards, and this was termed as 'quota.' The production above the quota was paid for at piece rate. But, there was a 'norm' also fixed which was much higher than the 'quota' and every workman was normally expected to produce the 'norm,' as the minimum production. If the workman did not produce the 'norm,' he would be guilty of misconduct. Thus this scheme had two bases or standards in the shape of a 'quota' and a 'norm,' the quota being much lower than the norm, while a typical production above that base or standard is production bonus. The question before their lordship was whether in this peculiar scheme, production bonus could be said to start immediately after the first base (the quota) or it could only start after the second base (the norm). Their lordship took note of the fact that in a typical production bonus scheme, the worker is not bound to produce more than the base or standard even though he may do so in order that his earning may go up and held "the real base of the production bonus scheme in force in the petitioner company is the norm and not the quota and therefore, payment up to the norm whether made in one form or the other, is basic wage for the purpose of the Act.

When production bonus is not linked with productivity, it will be deemed as 'basic wages' for provident fund contributions – *[Daily Pratap vs. R.P.F.C and others – 1999 LLR 1 (SC); 1999 (1) CLR 2; 1998 (80) FLR 894].*

[There is no dispute that **wages or pay for the leave period or holidays** is not a part of the basic wages, but an unforeseen situation arose when the Bombay High Court, in the case of *Hindustan Lever Employees' Union vs. Regional P.F. Commissioner, Maharashtra and Goa- [1995 Lab.IC 775 (777); (1995) 1 LLN 767; (1995) 2 LLJ 279; (1995) 71 FLR 46]* ordered that the payment of leave encashment is subject to provident fund. Hindustan Lever Limited has its private provident fund trust and contribution on leave encashment paid on un-availed leave was being paid by the employer also. After a period, that payment was withdrawn by the company. The employees filed a writ claiming restoration of the payment of contribution on the leave encashment by invoking Section 12 of the Act. The High Court held that since the leave is earned during the duty and payment on account of un-availed leave was, of course was payment for duty and once the benefit on that payment has been given by the employer, now that cannot be withdrawn by the employer under Section 12 of the Act. That judgement was taken seriously and such demand was started to rise in other cases also. But, after some time, such demand was withdrawn by the authorities].

Splitting up of wages in conveyance, lunch and medical allowances was examined by the commissioner and an order of demand of contribution was made. It was challenge by a writ that the PF Commissioner had no power to examine the splitted wages for the purpose of contribution. The Karnataka High Court agreed that the decision of the Commissioner and approval by the Single Judge that the splitting up of he pay of the employees under several heads was only a subeterfuge to avoid payment of contribution to the provident fund by the employer, thus the Commissioner was right in examining the splitting up of pay- *[M/s. Group 4 Securities guarding Ltd, Bangalore vs. R.P.F.C. and others – 2004 Lab.I.C. 2075; 2004 (2) LLJ. 1142; 2004 LLR. 540; 2004 (102) FLR 374].*

The Supreme Court also upheld this decision of the Devision Bench of Karnataka H.C.

Many other High Courts also confirmed this order saying that Conveyance, Lunch and Medical allowances are included in the definition of 'basic wages'- *[Gujrat Cypromet Ltd. Vs. A.P.F.C. – 2004 (3) CLR 485; 2004 (103) FLR. 908; also see Surya Roshni Ltd. Vs. EPF- 2011- LLR 568 (M.P.) and the Management of Raynold Pens India Pvt. Ltd. & Other vs. R.P.F.C. (II), Chennai – 2011-LLR 876 (Mad)].*

*The question of **minimum wages*** is also a matter of concern for many employers. Most of the employer split up the minimum wages into different heads like house rest allowance, conveyance allowance, special allowance or so with a view to reduce his liability under the Act. Some employers took it as eroding the minimum wages guaranteed under the law, but Madhya Pradesh High Court did not agree with this contention while deciding the case of **Khemchand Motilal Tobacco Products Ltd. Vs. Union of India- [(1995) 1 LLN 1002; (1995) 2 CLR 360 (MP-DB)]**. It has been held therein that the amount of contribution made by the employee/employer ultimately reaches the hands of the employee or his legal representative. Hence, the contention that the employees' contribution erodes the minimum wages guaranteed under the law, is without substance.

III. Other elements of pay or wages:

Besides the formal wages as discussed above, certain elements of remuneration paid to any employee whether form part of wages or not, have been raised before various courts from time to time, and rulings thereon have importance with regard to wages.

Notice pay as a payment made by way of consideration for terminating the contract of employment of a permanent employee without notice, that payment is not part of the emoluments earned by him, while on duty or on leave, and cannot, therefore, be included with in the definition of basic wages- *[India United Mills vs. R.P.F.C. Bombay-AIR 1960 Bom. 203; 1959 (2) LLJ 733].*

Similarly, **Ad-hoc payment** is considered. Whenever, there is a package deal, the question of earning or not earning the payment, agreed to be paid does not arise. Therefore, though, the adhoc payment is part and parcel of emoluments, it would not be basic wages as it does not have the characteristic of being earned while on duty. The Ad-hoc payment in question is more in the nature of a present made by the Employer, though it may not be a present in the conventional sense of the term.

The payment of Rs. 450, a lump-sum ad-hoc payment, partakes the character of other allowances agreed to be paid by the employer as the employees agreed to make this payment not towards the arrears of wages, but, instead of the arrears of revised wages and revised house rent allowance.-

[Associated Cement Company Ltd. And other vs. R.M. Gandhi, R.P.F.C. and others -1992 Lab.IC 2110 (Guj)].

Arrears paid due to wages increase: When an award gives revised pay scales, the employees become entitle to revised emoluments and where the said revision is with retrospective effect, the arrears paid to the employees, as a consequence, are the emoluments earned by them while on duty. If the original emoluments earned by the employees are "basic wages," there is no justification to hold the substituted emoluments, as a result of the award are not "basic wages"- *[Prantiya Vidyut Mandal Mazdoor Federation and others vs. Rajasthan State Electricity Board and others- 1992 Lab.IC 1790; 1993 (1) LLJ. 222 (SC)].*

Special Allowance paid by the employer to the employees as a result of an agreement entered into between the parties was not agreed to be treated by employees and employer as part of basic wages or dearness allowance which could be subject to provident fund contribution. As a matter of fact, even the Regional P.F. Commissioner, merely stated that as per section 6 of the Act special allowance should be deemed to be dearness allowance without giving any reason. Needless to say that an officer like the appellant has no power to deem something to be something else which it is not, it being the prerogative only of the legislature-[*R.P.F.C. , EPF vs. Southern Alloy Foundries (P) Ltd.- 1981 Lab.IC 472 (Mad-DB)].* "Special allowance" payable under "settlement" between employer and employees is to be included in "basic wages"- *[Mangalore Ganesh Beedi Works vs. A.P.F.C. -2002 Lab.IC 1578 (Karn)].* In another case, the authority held that the special allowance mean 'wages' with in Sec. 2(b) of the EPF & MP Act and contribution demanded. It is held that since the workmen were required to work, the money paid therefore under whatever name partakes the character of basic wages only. The mutual agreement between the parties has no force and any agreement contrary to provisions of the statute too. The petitioner has not made out any case which would require any interference, Petition dismissed. –*[Gordon Woodroffe Ltd vs. Regional Commissioner, EPF- 2002 Lab.IC 653 (Mad)].*

Special allowance paid to employees not under any contract of employment, settlement or award but purely out of the management's own will and pleasure does not form part of wages. Hence, the employer is not liable to pay provident fund contribution on such allowance- *[R. Ramanathan Chettiar Jewellers vs. Regional Commissioner, EPF- (1998) 2LLJ 945; 1998 4 LLN 783; (1999) 1 FLR 559 (Mad)].*

When contractor agency was paid as 'karigar' charges after deducting TDS for specialized work of embroidery and printing, such amount will not attract PF contribution. When the status of person as employee is to be determined, it should be seen whether such person has an obligation to report for duty next day. Payment made to karigars for knitting and printing through the contractor, who are specialized in particular work of embroidery, will not attract provident fund contribution hence order of the P.F. Authority covering such karigars as employees has been rightly se aside by EPF Appellate Tribunal. For determining as to whether a person is an employee, it is to be seen whether there is some continuity in his employment i.e. to see whether he has and obligation to report for duty every day – *[The Regional P.F. Commissioner, Mumbai vs. M/s syndicate Overseas Pvt. Ltd. - 2001 LLR 953 (Bom. H.C.)].*

Agreement with employer not to pay contribution: The employers' agreement with the employees not to deduct contribution does not discharge the employer of his obligation in law to make payment. The term of the settlement which provides that there shall be no deduction only mean that the company has agreed to take on the liability also. It is the duty of the employer to contribute towards Provident Fund- *[Shree Changdeo Sugar Mills and other vs. U.O.I. and another- 2001 (2) SCC 519; 2001 SCC (L&S) 457; AIR 2001 S.C. 557; 2001 (88) FLR 939].*

Back wages awarded by Court: The petitioner terminated service of the workman on 7.6.1982. In ensuing litigation an award was passed on 27.9.1991directing the petitioner to reinstate workman and pay him 75% back wages. Workman was reinstated in service and he was paid back wages in the sum Rs. 61,079.10 p. Petitioner did not deduct amount of Provident Fund from said amount of back wages nor did it make statutory contribution.

Pursuant to the complaint made by workman in respect of contribution of P.F. amount by the employer on back wages paid to him, an inquiry was made under Section 7A of the Act and thereafter, under paragraph 26-B of the Scheme and impugned order dated 21.4.1999 was passed holding that back wages awarded to workman constituted basic wages and petitioner was liable to make its contribution to the provident fund.

Feeling aggrieved by aforesaid order, petitioner has filed this petition on the ground that back wages and therefore no liable for P.F. contribution.

The workman was reinstated with continuity of service. The continuity of service does not carry the meaning the period spent on duty. The purpose to allow continuity in service would be that such period would not be treated as break in service for the purpose of service benefits. In absence of specific order that such period should be treated as period on duty, such period cannot be held to be the period spent on duty. Besides the fact that Labour Court has awarded only a part of back wages, would also tend to show that the period of absence from duty.

When the court awarded back wages for the period employee was kept away from duty, what the Court does is to award damages. Thus the amount of damages or the compensation awarded would not constitute 'basic wages' as envisaged by the Act, the petitioner was under no statutory obligation to make statutory contribution of P.F. under the Act. As such, impugned order of P.F. Commissioner is quashed.- *[Swasik Textile Engineers (P) Ltd. Vs. Virijibhai Mavjibhai Rathod- 2008 CLR 953 (Guj)].*

When the workman, pending the writ petition, in which the award for his reinstatement in service is under challenge, settles the dispute with the management and takes monetary compensation, he cannot be treated to be in service of the said management for relevant period, for the purpose of EPF contribution.

EPF Appellate Tribunal held that – (i) Authority cannot contribute for the period for which respondent No. 3 workman neither worked nor agreed to be treated as on duty; (ii) no reliance can be placed on the interim order passed by this court; (iii) the amounts paid to respondent No. 3 – workman makes no reference to wages and hence no contribution can be claimed from the petitioner; (iv) order passed by the Tribunal confirming the order passed by 2nd respondent is not sustainable and hence set aside- *[Universal Brakes (P) Ltd., Coimbatore vs. Pesiding Officer, EPF Appellae Tribunal and others – 2011 III CLR 662 (Mad. H.C.)].*

Commission being paid by the employer under various conditions to different categories of employees in addition to salary, for example, shop pool commission, individual transaction commission, hire-purchased commission, service and repair commission, aggregate commission, etc. The commission and salary varied with the category of shop where a person was posted and the employer's case was that it was inherent in a wage structure which is evolved for sales promotion or is efficiency oriented, that the basic wages are far below than what are paid in concerns which have no commission or incentive oriented scheme. The Commissioner came to the conclusion that some of the categories were extremely low-paid and that the whole or part (depending on the category of employees) of the commission must be added to the basic wages or salary for the purpose of computation of the contribution postulated by the Act. It was held by the Delhi High Court that the Commissioner seemed to have completely forgotten that salaries or wages were fixed on the basis of letters of appointment or contract of service and the Commissioner's approach appeared to have been to fix fair wages rather than determine the question before him that commission was being paid as subterfuge for basic wages. Therefore, the commission, in any case, stood excluded from the definition of wage, whether one look the statutory definition or the definition in the petitioners' rules. The High Court also observed that 'the plea of subterfuge would have been tenable if it could be demonstrated that the commission payable to the employees was so fixed that a minimum of a specified sum would be payable to each employee irrespective of the work done by him. That is not so.' *[Usha Sales Ltd. Vs. R.P.F. Commissioner- 1980 Lab.IC 546; (1980) 1 LLN 452 (Del-DB)].*

In *Padiyur Sarvodaya Sangh vs. Union Of India* [(1999) 2 LLN 224 (Mad)], besides the monthly paid staff of the petitioner-Sangh, there were artisans who worked as home-workers. They either purchase their raw material from, and sold their finished products to, the petitioner-Sangh or were provided with raw materials by the petitioner Sangh itself which subsequently collected their finished products by paying the difference of value of finished products and raw materials. In such circumstances, it was held that the **difference in the value of the finished products and raw materials was nothing but wages.**

Payment made to transporters towards reimbursement of cost of feeding and maintaining animals is not 'basic' wages under Section 2(b) - *[Mohd. & Sons vs. J.M. Pandya- 1979 Lab.IC (NOC) 115 (Raj)].*

IV. Contributions, liability for payment of:

As soon as the Act becomes applicable to an establishment, the employer in relation to that establishment is under obligation to pay contributions as above to the statutory Fund in accordance with the provision of paragraph 30. It does not require any notice from the authority to pay the contributions. However, a system has been developed that until a notice issuing a Code No. is received by the employer, the payment is delayed for that period, which results in invoking of Section 14 B and section 7Q. This has simultaneously, raises demand for Waiver of the contributions.

Apart from the initial compliance, the employer is required to pay the contributions and other charges every month up to the fifteenth day. Paragraph 30 (1) clearly requires the employer that '**in the first instance,**' he has to pay both the contributions payable by him-self as the employer's share and the employees' contribution and, also in respect of the employees employed by or through a contractor, irrespective whether the pay or wages have been disbursed or not, along with other charges as levied by the Scheme. A such, it is the prime responsibility of the principal employer to pay the dues, any delay is a default on the part of the employer.

Once again a question was raised before Delhi High Court through LPA 727/2014 by the *Builders' Association of India and others vs U.O.I. and others,* decided on 16.10.2015 that contribution if paid by the builders in respect of workers engaged for a short term job, they will never claim that contribution. Their Lordship answer this question that on this argument the employers can not be allowed to avoid payment and defeat the very purpose of the Act. Employers' are bound to pay contribution as per section 6 of the Act and it is the employees who claim it directly from the Commissioner. How it is paid is the responsibility of the commissioner. *[The case has not reported till the script was finalized].*

As regards the recovery of the contributions and other charges paid by the principal employer, care has been taken by the Supreme Court while disposing of the appeal filed by **Orissa Cement Ltd. vs. Union of India- *[AIR 1962 SC 1402; (1962 1 LLJ 493].*** Where the government issued two notifications making amendments in the Scheme, the effect of which was to extend the benefits of the Scheme to contract labour without giving the employer the correlative right to recover the amount of members' share of the contribution from the wages of contract labour, it was held that the amended Scheme operated unfairly and harshly on persons employing contract labour. It resulted in discrimination between those who employed contract labour and those who employed direct labour, and therefore, could not be said to be reasonable. Accordingly, the two notifications were struck down as unconstitutional and void.

As a result of this judgement, Section 8A was added on the statute book.

V. Liability of a contractor's employees' contribution and recovery from contractor:

The opening line of paragraph 30 makes the principal employer responsible for payment of contribution and other charges payable by him and on behalf of his employees including those employed through by his contractor in the first instance. Thereafter, the liability paid by the employer on behalf of the contractor, is recoverable by the employer from the next bill raised by the contractor under the mandate given by **Section 8A**, therefore, there is not escape and excuse for both, the employer and the contractor.

Thus, an employer is liable to pay contributions even with regard to to employees employed through a contractor – *[Himachal Pradesh Nagar Vikas Pradhikaran vs. R.P.F.Commissioner- (1998) 2 LLJ 267 (HP-DB)].*

Contribution not deducted from the employees employed through a contractor, no relief is available to the employer. This question was answered by Patna High Court (DB) in the case of ***Central P.F. Commissioner vs. S.K. Nasiruddin Beedi Merchant Ltd. –[(1999) 1 LLJ 360 (Pat. DB) reversing the single judge order – SK Nasiruddin vs. C.P.F. Commissioner - (1997) 75 FLR 471].*** The respondent could not deduct the employees' contribution for the period from October, 1985 to 3.5.1993 from the wages of Home-Workers because of pendency of litigation on the question of the applicability of the Act in respect of such Home-Workers and claimed relief from payment of employees' contribution. The said litigation was ultimately decided against the respondent and on

3.5.1993 the Supreme Court granted six months' time to the respondent to furnish the names of all the Home-Workers to the PF Commissioner after collecting the same, if necessary, from the contractors. The respondent complied with the Supreme Court Order. The High Court held that the mere fact that the respondent was seeking its remedy before a court of law is by itself no ground for holding that in the event the respondent failing before the court of law, the liability should be extinguished. If, Such were the law, any liability imposed by law would be defeated by challenging any order passed for the enforcement of that liability. Moreover, in law the respondent was obliged to made deductions from the wages of the employees and to deposit their contribution in accordance with the scheme. Having failed to do so, it can not be permitted to argue that its liability was extinguished or that the same should be waived because of its own failure to act in accordance with law.

The liability to pay Provident/fund is the liability of the principal employer even is respect of an employee under a contractor. It is open to the principal employer to recover the same from the contractor under Section 8A of the Act. The fact that the petitioner (the employees under contractors) are covered by the scheme is not relevant to decide their status – *[Petroleum Workers Union Hindustan Petroleum Corp. Ltd. Chennai and other vs. HPCL Mumbai and others – 2004 (2) LLN 451]*. Further, if the authority finds that though the contractors are covered by the scheme and contribution has not been made by the contractors, then only the liability can be fastened upon the principal employer for compliance of the statutory provisions - *[Proto Pumps and Motors Pvt. Ltd. Vs. Asstt. P.F. Commissioner, EPFO, Surat and others – 2004 Lab.IC 2993; 2004 LLR 1145]*.

In case **contractor disputing applicability of the Act**- the petitioner contractor of Rajasthan Housing Board contended that since, in the construction work different kinds of labour are required for different jobs, it had no regular employee and that engaged labour as per its requirement and that, therefore, its workmen were not employees with in Section 2(f). Therefore, no amount of contribution was due from the petitioner in respect of its workmen and that therefore, the respondent Board could not deduct any amount of contribution from the petitioner's running bills. In such circumstances, it has been held by the Rajasthan High Court that until the dispute, as to the applicability of the Act and liability to pay contribution was adjudicated under Section 7-A of the Act, the principal employer could not by issuing a unilateral order direct the petitioner to deposit the contribution nor could it deduct such amounts from the running bills of the contractor- *[Parvati Construction Co. vs. Rajasthan Housing Board- (1998) 2 LLJ 970 (Raj)]*.

Compensation/wages awarded by court do not attract provident fund contribution, when minimum wages not paid, intention of law is to give compensation to workman and not to penalize the employer. Respondent employee has been paid less than the minimum wages as provided under the said Act. Respondent obtained the order from the Authority under the Act to pay amount due with compensation at ten times the same. Impugned order is challenged by this petition. While modifying the order for compensation, the court observed that what is to be kept in mind while awarding such compensation is the intention behind the provision, which is to compensate the workman, and not to penalize the employer. In the impugned award the reasoning adopted by the authority, while granting the maximum quantum of compensation awarded to the respondent shows that the Authority appears to be more inclined to punish the employer i.e. the petitioner herein, rather than compensating the workman. There is no gainsaying the fact that the authority under Minimum Wages Act exercises quasi-judicial powers. It appears in the case at hand, that only factor that appears to have weighed with the authority is that the employer was a public sector under-taking. Such an interpretation is wholly un-called for. It would amount to creating a special category of employers in whose cases, no flexibility whatsoever compensation must always be granted. Following the law laid down by Supreme Court in *Perena Sahayog*, the court modified the order for payment of compensation to the amount equal to the wages awarded. Writ petition disposed off accordingly- *[Kerala Automobiles Ltd. Vs. Naveetha P (Mrs) – 2008 (III) LLJ 530 (Del)].*

Similarly, the V.R.S. optees are not entitled for the settlement benefits arrived after VRS, since the settlement covered only on roll employees- *[Vijay Kumar and others vs. Whirlpool of India and others- 2008 LLR 227 (SC)].*

VI. Waiver of Demand for Contributions:

If no demand for contribution is made by the authorities under the Act for few years, it cannot be said that the demand has been waived *[N.K. Jain vs. C.K. Shah- (1991) 2 SCC 495; 1991 SCC (L&S) 656; 1991 Lab.I.C. 1013]. In* fact the authorities have no power of waiver under the Act or the Scheme- *[K.R. Subbier Tape Factory vs. RPF Commissioner- (1970) 2 LLJ 109].* The Government cannot grant exemption or option to the employees in respect of their past contributions. This is clearly against the statutory mandate of Section 6 and paragraph 29 of the Scheme– *[Alliminium Corpn. Of India Ltd. Vs. RPF Commissioner- SIR 1958 Cal 570; (1959) 1 LLJ 249].*

However, in cases of belated or retrospective application of the Act and Scheme, relief has been given by the Supreme Court itself to the Cinema theatres, to which the Act was made applicable by virtue of Section 24 and 25 of the Cine Workers and Cinema Theatre Workers (Regulation of Employment) Act, 1981and the notification No. GSR 347 was issued on 30.4.1986 applying the Act w.e.f. 01.10.1984. The Supreme Court held that – 'The payment of employees' contribution by the employer with the corresponding right to deduct the same from the wages of the employees could only for the current period during which the employer has also to pay his contribution. In the instant case, for the period from October 1, 1984 upto the date of impugned notification the employer has paid full wages to the employees since during that period, there was no scheme applicable to his establishment. By retrospectively applying the scheme, the employer cannot be saddled with the liability to pay the employees' contribution for the retrospective period, since he has no right to deduct the same from the future wages payable to the employees. The employer could not have made the deduction prior to the impugned notification dated April 30, 1986 since the Scheme was not then applicable.

It was not possible for the employer to make deduction from subsequent wages of the workmen with the consent in writing of the Inspector as required under the third proviso to para 32(1) of the Scheme, since the third proviso could be taken advantage of by the employer only where no deduction has been made from the wages of the employees due to accidental mistake or clerical error when the scheme is operative which is not the case here.' *[District Exhibitors Association vs. Union of India – (1991)3 SCC 119; 1991 SCC (L&S) 822; (1991) 2 LLJ 115].*

In another case in which the Supreme Court has clarified whether employer's share could be waived in such a retrospective application. Reverting the High Court decision, wherein the employer was allowed to pay employer's share of contribution from the date of the judgement e.i. 24.11.1994 while the notification was issued by the Central Government on 30.4.1986, the Supreme Court held that the relief granted in respect of payment of employees' share of contribution but the relief granted to the theatre owners and licensees was improper. Hence, it was directed that such owners/licensees to deposit their share of contribution towards provident fund from the date they filed the writ petitions in the High Court- *[Union of India vs. Murugan Talkies – (1996) 1 SCC 504; 1996 SCC (L&S) 326].*

VII. Contribution, on Higher Pay or at the Higher Rate:

Under paragraph 29, there is a provision that a member can contribute to the Provident Fund at a higher rate of contribution than the prescribed in Section 6, but the employer will not be under obligation to pay matching contribution as the contribution is first defined which payable by the employer and the employee is to pay equal contribution. The employer may contribute at the statutory rate only.

In paragraph 29, how the contribution has been defined, is relevant to see. Sub-paragraph (1) opens with words – '**The contribution payable by the employer……**' mean in the first instance, the contribution is calculated as the liability of the employer, not of the employee. In sub-paragraph (2), it requires that '**the contribution payable by the employee under the Scheme shall be equal to the contribution payable by the employer in respect of each employee**':

'**Provided that in respect of any employee to whom the Scheme applies, the contribution payable by him may, if he so desires, be an amount exceeding ten per cent, or twelve per cent., as the case may be, of his basic wages, dearness allowance and retaining allowance (if any) subject to the condition that the employer shall not be under an obligation to pay any contribution over and above his contribution payable under the Act.**'

Now, refer the relevant wordings in paragraph 26 (6), '**Notwithstanding anything contained in this paragraph, an officer not below the rank of an Assistant Provident Fund Commissioner may, on the joint request in writing of any employee of a factory or other establishment to which this Scheme applies and his employer, enroll such employee as a member or allow his to contribute more than rupees** [2]**[fifteen thousand] of his pay per month if he is already a member of the Fund and thereupon such employee shall be entitled to the benefits and shall be subject to the conditions of the Fund provided that the employer gives an undertaking in writing that he shall pay the administrative charges payable and shall comply with all statutory provisions in respect of such employee.**'

Interpretation of these provisions together reveals that the employer obliged to pay contribution on the pay prescribed by the Scheme or as agreed to pay under paragraph 26 (6) that is higher than the prescribed pay, with the administration and other charges payable, and equal amount of contribution is payable by the employee.

Proviso to sub-paragraph (2) of paragraph 29 permits an employee to contribute at a higher rate of contribution than the prescribed in the Scheme, that is 10 % or 12%, and obviously, the employer is not under obligation to pay the contribution at the additional higher rate of contribution. Both the additional contributions, on higher salary and at the higher rate cannot be mixed together. Both have their own spares and scopes. But, unfortunately, the Supreme Court, in the case of *Marathwada Gramin Bank Karmachari Sanghathan and another vs. Management of Marathwada Gramin Bank and others; Marathwas Regional Rural Bank Employees' Union vs. Management of Marathwada Gramin Bank and others – [2011 (9) SCC 620: 2011 (4) LLJ. 305: 2011 (4) LLN. 472: 2011 (4) Lab.I.C. 4449: 2011 (131) FLR. 754: 2011 LLR. 1130]* has not laid down a good law. This was a peculiar case put the department on test and it failed. The case was filed by the employees of the bank under Section 12 of the EPF Act against the refusal by the management to continue to contribute on the higher salary it was being paid by it for over 2 decades. The plea was taken that proviso to paragraph 29 (2) allows to flee from the additional liability. The Supreme Court also took decision on this proviso in isolation. It may be noted that the EPF department was not a party in this case at any level, but it affected the open go practiced over years. When it came to be clarified internally, the arsenal did not work with the fused bullets and opted out to file any review petition or appeal.

VIII. Contribution to the Pension Fund:

There is no separate contribution for pension fund, but it segregated from the employer's share of P.F. Contribution @ 8.33% of the pay. The remaining part of employer's PF contribution remains in the P.F. account of the member credited.

The exempted funds also go accordingly and pay pension contribution out from the employer's share of O.F. Contribution. Section 17 and Section 6 and paragraph 29 contains such provisions.

W.e.f. 01.09.2014, a provision has been added in paragraph 6 of the EPS, 1995 which debars the persons in receipt of pay more than 15,000 p.m. at the time of joining the Provident Fund and also restricting contribution payment on a pay more than 15,000 p.m. This has been done by amending paragraph 11.

IX. Contribution on Higher Pay or Wages undr EPS, 1995:

In sub-paragraph (6) of paragraph 26, an Assistant Commissioner may permit member to contribute P.F. contribution on a higher wages than the statutory limit, but the employer will not be under obligation to pay matching contribution on such higher pay, however, the employer is to under-take that he will be liable to pay administrative charges on such higher pay on which contribution is charges.

But, in the **Pension Scheme**, the position is different. There is a provision in the pension scheme to contribute on a higher pay than the statutory limit in the proviso under paragraph 11, but it is possible when the employer also pays P.F. Contribution on a higher pay, because there is no separate contribution under pension scheme, but segregated from the employer's share in to the Provident Fund. If, the employer is not paying contribution on higher pay, then in no way, pension contribution be on higher pay. However, w.e.f. 01.9.2014 the said proviso under paragraph 11 of the EPS, 1995 has been amended and facility to contribute on a higher salary has been taken away. By amending paragraph 6, employees in receipt of pay more than 15,000 p.m. at the time of joining the Fund, and who was not a EPS member earlier, will not be entitled to become a member of EPS, 1995 despite he may become member of PF by obtaining a sanction/permission under paragraph 26 (6).

X. Non-deduction of Contribution- by Omission or by Clerical Mistake:

Paragraph 32 provides that if contribution payable by an employee has not been deducted from the pay for which the contribution is due, that escaped deduction can not be deducted from the pay for the period it does not relate. In such case, the employer has to bear the employee's contribution also. But, there may be cases where deduction of employee's contribution could not be deducted from his pay by a clerical mistake or omission, such omitted contribution may be deducted from the pay which does not relate to the contribution period, with the written permission of the Provident Fund Inspector only, otherwise, the deduction will be illegal and the employer may be asked to bear that contribution.

XI. Non-payment of Contributions and other Dues:

It was contended on behalf of the employer in the case of *Calicut Modern Spinning & Weaving Mills Ltd. Vs. R.P.F.C. [1982 Lab.IC 1422; (1982) 1 LLJ 440 (Ker)];* that the mode of payment was provided in Para 38 of the Scheme and Paragraph 30 only provided as to who should make the contributions, that the obligation on the employer to pay contribution arose only when wages in respect of the relevant period were paid and that Section 14-B would not be attracted in cases where the employer was disabled from paying wages to the employees in time for reasons beyond his control, e.g. a lock out, strike, etc. These contentions were not accepted by the Kerala High Court. It was held that paragraph 38 of the Scheme obliged the employer to make the payment within 15 days of the close of every month and paragraph 30 cast an obligation on the employer to pay the contributions payable by himself and on behalf of the member employed by him in the first instance. The word 'in the first instance' did not mean only for the first time. They meant payment of contribution voluntarily by the employer for every month irrespective of the fact whether wages have been paid or not.

In paragraph 30 and 38 of the Scheme, it is provided that the contributions and other dues payable under the Act and Schemes shall be paid within 15 days of the close of the month, i.e. the 15th of every month is the due date for payment of the dues. Thereafter, it becomes a case of non-payment and termed as default. In such default two-way penal actions have been provided in the Act-

First, levy of penal damages as provided under Section 14-B read with paragraph 32 A of EPF Scheme, paragraph 5 of Pension Scheme and paragraph 8A of the Insurance Scheme; and a simple interest @ 12 p.a. in all cases for the period of default.

Second, filing a criminal case in the appropriate court of law under Section 14 or 14AA as the case may be for which imprisonment and fine or both can be awarded.

XII. Non-Payment of Contribution Deducted from Employees Pay:

There may cases where provident fund contribution has been deducted from the pay of an employee or employees and not deposited within the prescribed time limit with the authorities, it attracts an additional offence under Section 405 of Indian Penal Code, by virtue of the explanation under that Section which punishable under Section 406–409 of I.P.C. By virtue of the explanation under Section

405, the deducted amount of provident fund contribution is deemed to be entrusted to the employer for the purpose of paying to the authorities thereby it becomes misappropriation of the entrusted money.

XIII. Contribution to the Insurance Fund:

There is no contribution to the Insurance Scheme by the employees. It is funded by the employers only with a nominal contribution @ 0.5% and administration charges @ 0.01% only of the pay which is limited to Rs. 6,500/- p.m. W.e.f. 01.09.2014, the pay limit has been raised to Rs.15,000 p.m.

XIV. Administration Charges:

Administration charges for the administration of the Fund is also payable by the employer fixed by the Central Government with the consent of the C.B.T. under paragraph 39 of the Scheme. At present, the rate of administration charges, as fixed **w.e.f. 01.8.1998 is 1.1 %** of the pay on which P.F. contribution is paid. Prior to that, it was 0.65 % w.e.f. 01.10.1986. W.e.f. 01.01.2015, the rate of administration charges has been reduced to 0.85% with minimum charges payable Rs. 500 p.m. Under EDLI Scheme too the minimum administration charges has been fixed as Rs. 200 p.m.

Incentive Scheme for employers:

Government of India, vide Notification No. S.O. 443 (E) dated 10 February, 2016 has announced an incentive scheme for employer. The Scheme is in 2 categories and qualifying conditions for both are:-

Performance fields	Achievement for 10 %	Achievement for 5 %
Providing details in Form No 11 (New)	80 % of new members or above	60 % of new members or above
Seeding of AADHAAR	80 % of above or above	70 % of above or above
Seeding of Bank details	100 % of above (i)	80 % of above (i)
Seeding of Pan details	Wherever applicable	Wherever applicable
UAN activation	100 % of above (i)	60 % of above (i)

The incentive is applicable w.e.f. 01.01.2016 fork one year for the time being and payable quarterly; but performance will be calculated on monthly basis.

The procedure for claiming the incentive will be as would be circulated by the Central P. F. Commissioner.

XV. Rate of Contribution in the Past:

The rate of contribution as it is applicable today has been made applicable w.e.f. 22.9.1997, which is 10 % and 12 %. Prior to it, 8.333% was applicable w.e.f. 1.8.1988 and 10 % as enhanced rate was made effective from 17.5.1989 i.e. from 1.6.1989. Before that it was 6.25 % and 8 %.

Similarly, the pay limit, as is today is prevailing from 1.6.2001 which is Rs. 6500/-. Prior to it Rs. 5000/- was effective from 1.11,1990 and before that it was 3500/- per month for the purpose of contribution. Now, w.e.f. 01.09.2014 the pay limit has been raised to Rs. 15,000 p.m. for all the three Schemes.

Chapter 10

Membership

> **Brief badinage–**
>
> *The ultimate aim of the enactment and framing of different Schemes under that is to provide security when a worker gets old and rendered jobless, and also to his family some relief in the event of death of a earning workman of the family. Hence, it achieves its object only when all the workmen of an industry to which it applies, are enrolled as members of the Schemes. If for any reason, any worker is kept out of the membership of the Schemes, the very purpose of the enactment if defeated. That situation becomes more painful when a social security scheme is much talked about as bandwagon. The law then becomes a showpiece of printed papers in the library of the laws, and also when the authorities whom the work of interpretation of the provisions of the law is assigned, if they too go with the above mentioned type of version and translation.*

To go ahead, certain provisions are to be understood first-

Section 2 (f) *"employee"* means any person who is employed for wages in any kind or work, manual or otherwise, in or in connection with the work of [1][an establishment] and who gets his wages directly or indirectly from the employer, [2][and includes any person,-

(i) employed by or through a contractor in or in connection with the work of the establishment;

(ii) engaged as an apprentice, not being an apprentice engaged under the Apprentices Act, 1961

(52 of 1961) or under the standing orders of the establishment];

---
1. Substituted by Sec. 3 of Act 94 of 1956 for the words "a factory."
2. Substituted by Sec. 3 of Act 33 of 1988 (w.e.f. 1.8.1988).

Provisions of the Employees' Provident Fund Scheme, 1952-

Paragraph 2 (f) – "excluded employee" means-

[1][(i) an employee who, having been a member of the Fund, withdrew the full amount of his accumulations in the Fund under [2][clause (a) or (c) of] sub-paragraph (1) of paragraph 69;]

[3][(ii) an employee whose pay at the time he is otherwise entitled to become a member of the Fund, exceeds [4][fifteen thousand] rupees per month;

Explanation- "pay" includes basic wages wit dearness allowance, [5][retaining allowance (if any)] and cash value of food concessions admissible thereon;]

6[(iii) xxx].

7[(iv) an apprentice;

Explanation- An apprentice means a person who, according to the certified standing orders applicable to the factory or establishment, is an apprentice, or who is declared to be an apprentice by the authority specified in this behalf by the appropriate Government.]

1.	Substituted by S.R.O. 331 dated 15.01.1958 (w.e.f. 25.01.1958).
2.	Inserted by G.S.R. 1122 dated 19.09.1960 (w.e.f. 24.09.1960).
3.	Substituted by S.R.O. 1337 dated 16.04.1957 (w.e.f. 31.05.1957).
4.	Substituted by G.S.R. 326(E) dated 04.05.2014 (w.e.f. 01.09.2014).
5.	Added by G.S.R. 201 dated 08.02.1961 (w.e.f. 31.12.1960).
6.	Omitted by G.S.R. 1467 dated 02.12.1960 (w.e.f. 10.12.1960).
7.	Substituted by S.R.O. 331 dated 15.01.1958 (w.e.f. 25.01.1958).

Paragraph 1[26- **Classes of employees entitled and required to join the Fund** –

(1) (a) Every employee employed in or in connection with the work of a factory or other establishment to which this Scheme applies, other than an excluded employee, shall be entitled and required to become a member of the Fund from the day this paragraph comes into force in such factory or other establishment.

(b) Every employee employed in or in connection with the work of a factory or other establishment to which this Scheme applies, other than an excluded employee, shall be entitled and required to become a member of the fund from the day this paragraph comes into force in such factory or other establishment if on the date of such coming into force, such employee is a subscriber to a provident fund maintained in respect of the factory or other establishment or in respect of any other factory or establishment (to which the Act applies) under the same employer:

Provided that where the Scheme applies to a factory o other establishment on the expiry or cancellation of an order of exemption under section 17 of the Act, every employee who but for the exemption would have become and continued as a member of the fund, shall become a member of the Fund forthwith.

(2) After this paragraph comes into force in a factory or other establishment, every employee employed in or in connection with the work of that factory or establishment, other than an excluded employee, who has not become a member already shall be entitled and required to become a member of the Fund from the date of joining the factory or establishment.

(3) An excluded employee employed in or in connection with the work of a factory or other establishment to which this Scheme applies shall, on ceasing to be such an employee, be entitled and required to become a member of the Fund from the date he ceased to be such employee.

(4) On re-election of an employee or a class of employees exempted under paragraph 27 or paragraph 27A to join the Fund or on the expiry or cancellation of an order under that paragraph, every employee, shall forthwith become a member thereof.

(5) Every employee who is a member of a private provident fund maintained in respect of an exempted factory or other establishment and who but for exemption would have become and

continued as a member of the fund shall, on joining a factory or other establishment to which this Scheme applies, become a member of the Fund forthwith.

(6) Notwithstanding anything contained in this paragraph, an officer not below the rank of an Assistant Provident Fund Commissioner may, on the joint request in writing of any employee of a factory or other establishment to which this Scheme applies and his employer, enroll such employee as a member or allow his to contribute more than rupees [2][fifteen thousand] of his pay per month if he is already a member of the Fund and thereupon such employee shall be entitled to the benefits and shall be subject to the conditions of the Fund provided that the employer gives an undertaking in writing that he shall pay the administrative charges payable and shall comply with all statutory provisions in respect of such employee.]

1.	Substituted by GSR 689 dated 19.10.1990 (w.e.f. 1.11.1990).
2.	Substituted by GSR 326 (E) dated 4.5.2001 (w.e.f. 1.9.2014).

Paragraph [1][26 A – Retention of membership – (1) A member of the Fund shall continue to be member until he withdraws under paragraph 69 of the amount standing to his credit in the Fund or is covered by a notification of exemption under section 17 of the Act or an order of exemption under paragraph 27 or paragraph 27A.

Explanation – In the case of claim for refund by a member under sub-paragraph (2) of paragraph 69, the membership of the Fund shall deemed to have been terminated from the date the payment is authorized to him by the authority specified in this behalf by Commissioner irrespective of the date of claim.

(2) Every member employed as an employee other than an excluded employee, in a factory or other establishment to which this Scheme applies shall contribute to the Fund, and the contribution shall also be payable to the Fund in respect of him by the employer. Such contribution shall be in accordance with the rate specified in paragraph 29:

Provided that subject to the provisions contained in sub-paragraph (6) of paragraph 26 and [2][in paragraph 27], or sub-paragraph (1) of paragraph 27A, where the monthly pay of such a member exceeds [3][fifteen thousand], the contribution payable by him, and in respect of him by the employer, shall be limited to the amounts payable on a monthly pay of [3][fifteen thousand rupees] including [4][dearness allowance, retaining allowance (if any) and cash value of food concession.]

1.	Added by GSR 584 dated 11.5.1959.
2.	Substituted by GSR 1522 dated 16.12.1960.
3.	Substituted by GSR 326 (E) dated 4.5.2001 (w.e.f. 1.6.2001).
4.	Substituted by GSR 201 dated 8.2.1961.

Paragraph [1][26 B – Resolution of doubts- If any question arises whether an employee is entitled or required to become or continue as a member, or as regards the date from which he is so entitled or required to become a member, the decision, thereon of the Regional Commissioner [2][xxx] shall be final:

Provided that no decision shall be given unless both the employer and the employee have been heard.]

1.	Added by GSR 584 dated 11.5.1959
2.	Deleted by GSR 1845 dated 28.11.1963 (w.e.f. 30.11.1963)

I. Eligibility for Membership:

The Act and the Schemes are meant for the industrial and other workers for the old age and for their family members in the event of death of the main earning member, therefore, it is root seeding to identify who could be a member of this scheme. Specific and wide spelled provisions have been incorporated both in the Act and the Schemes. Unlike the position prevailing prior to 01.11.1990 for P.F. membership, every employee, as defined in Section 2(f) is now eligible to become a member subject to that he is not an excluded employee as defined in paragraph 2 (f) of the EPF Scheme. Prior to 01.11.1990, there was a supplementary provision for membership. Despite an employee other than the excluded employee, was eligible to become member if he completed a certain period of service. It was called the qualifying period. The qualifying period was 60 days with in a period of three months or three months service, whichever is earlier. It is a statutory mandate for the employer to require his employees to become members and for the employees to obey it- *[Provident Fund Inspector vs. Ram Kumar- 1983 Lab.IC 717 (P&H); also Nazeena Traders (P) Ltd vs. R.P.F. Commissioner- AIR 1965 AP 200; (1966) 1 LLJ 334].*

But, it is relevant to mention that the qualifying period of 60 days within three months or three months is still there in respect of employees in Newspaper establishments as the rider in paragraph 26 as given in paragraph 80 has not been amended simultaneously in November, 1990 till date. Similarly, in paragraph 81 in relation to cine Workers and Cinema Theatre Workers (Regulation of Employment) Act, 1981, the rider to paragraph 26 has also not been amended so far.

The under lying idea behind the provision of day even membership is to bring all kind of employees within its fold as and when the Central Government might think fit after reviewing the circumstances of each class of establishment *[Mohmadali Vs. Union of India- AIR 1964 SC 980; (1963) 1 LLJ 536.].*

In **the membership** provisions under paragraph 26, the sub-paragraph (6) provides for membership of an excluded employee as defined under paragraph 2(f). it is also to keep in mind that a member remains a member until he ceases to be member under paragraph 69 or 70. Provision for retention of membership is given in paragraph 26 A. In case a member joins another establishment in which EPF Scheme or a private PF Scheme is applicable, he has to disclose about his previous membership in form No. 11.

At present, the only point of dispute which may come fore is that "whether an employee is an excluded employee or not, and whether he or she is entitle to become PF member or not." This is to be decided under paragraph 26 B.

II. Resolution of Dispute Regarding Membership of an Employee:

Before taking up the issue of excluded employee, it is important and relevant to see that which authority can resolve the dispute regarding membership of an employee. Paragraph 26 B of the Scheme contains the remedy to this. Under that paragraph, a Regional Commissioner has been authorized to resolve a dispute regarding membership and his decision on that dispute shall be final. While giving finality to the order passed under that paragraph, it has been made mandatory that before giving any decision, the Regional Commissioner is required to hear the disputing employer and the employee concerned. However, despite the finality of the order, a remedy is there under Section 7-I which, of-course, was inserted in 1988.

The points of dispute on which a Regional Commissioner can give his decision are-
- # entitled or required to become a member,
- # to continue as member, and
- # date from which he becomes a member.

It is obvious that first two points relate to the excluded employees, whether one is an excluded employee or not. The third point has now lost its relevancy as the counting of days as qualifying period has been done away, however, it may be relevant in respect of casual employees and the employees employed by or through a contractor.

In the context of the Act, the words used in paragraph 26 "entitled" means that the employee has got an absolute right to get benefits of the Act, and the word "required" implies an obligation on the employer to treat all the employees who are qualified and who are not exempted, as member of the Fund-*[R.P.F.Commissioner vs. K.R Subbaier Tape Factory- (1966) 2 LLJ 676; AIR 1967 Mad.129 (DB)].*

The controversy envisaged by this paragraph relates to a dispute between the employers and employees and in respect of a particular employee in an establishment, which is admittedly governed by the Scheme of the Act. This paragraph has no reference to the dispute between the Provident Fund Commissioner and the employer with regard to the direction of the Commissioner to the employer to pay the amount due under the Act-*['Glamour'- Proprietors Seth Hassaram and Sons (India) (P) Ltd. Vs. R.P.F. Commissioner – 1975 Lab.IC 954; (1975) 1 LLJ 514].* Further, the Commissioner has the right to decide whether an employee is eligible for membership or not. But this is a question which has to be decided after hearing the employee and his employer. Simply because the employer happens to remain ex-parte in a particular case, it cannot be said that no notice to the employee is necessary before taking a decision under paragraph 26-B. It is obligatory for the Commissioner to hear the employee-*[Sasidharan vs. R.P.F. Commissioner- 1982 Lab.IC 597 (Ker); South India Research Institute vs. R.P.F. Commissioner- (1981) 59 FJR 160 (AP) and Mysore State Coop. Printing Works Ltd. Vs. R.P.F. Commissioner- 1976 Lab.IC 1307 (Kant)].*

III. Excluded Employee:

For the time being, this area of excluded employee has become a grey-area which has provided grounds for evasion, subterfuge for the employers and abuse for the authorities, hence, the intelligence and the skillfulness could be seen in dealing with this matter of excluded employees.

In paragraph 2(f), an excluded employee has been defined, But, for certain categories of employees and classes of establishment, the excluded employee has been defined on slightly different footings. **Those classes of establishments are- the Newspaper establishments and the Cine and**

Cinema theatre employees as referred to in paragraph 80 and 81 respectively; and, the **categories are- Disabled employees taking up employment on or after 01.4.2008 and the International Workers** as mentioned in paragraph 82 and 83 respectively.

IV. Member who has withdrawn his P.F. amount in full:

Under this category that employee is covered who is re-employed in a factory or in an establishment after getting his full Provident fund accumulations on attaining the age of superannuation as per the establishment's or the factory's standing orders or rules or where such orders or rules does not exist, on attaining the age of 55 years covered under paragraph 69 (1) (a). The another category is covered under clause (c) where a member gets his full provident fund accumulation withdrawn on the ground of illness. Obviosly, incapacity should be certified by an authorized medical officer. The logic behind it may be that the member has attained the age of superannuation and if he is re-employed, it is for a very limited period or so and when the provision was drafted, the qualifying period was one year, hence such person, on getting re-employment is not considered for membership.

Certain employees of a company, who had retired on superannuation and withdrawn the full amounts of their provident funds, are re-employed by that company with a view to accommodate dedicated employees. They are allowed to work as per their convenience subject to their health. In view of paragraph 69 of the Scheme, it was held that Provident Fund authorities has no right to call upon the management to remit provident fund dues in respect of such employees from the date of their re-employment-*[Bombay Printers Ltd. Vs. Union of India- (1991) 63 FLR 106; (1991) 1 CLR 772].*

This condition is also applicable in to-to in respect of the employees taking up employment in a Newspaper Establishment and also taking up employment as a cine-worker in an establishment governed by the Cine-Workers and Cinema Theatre Workers (Regulation of Employment) Act, 1981.

V. Pay exceeding Rs. 15,000 P.M., the statutory Limit:

This reason, being connected with the direct liability and financial burden on the employer, has been the basis of many disputes. This condition of pay limit is considered in two ways, both to benefit the employer, Firstly, on appointment of a new employee, the gross pay being more than Rs. 15,000/- (prior to 01.09.2014, it was Rs. 6,500) per month, is taken with a view to keep the employee away from the PF membership. In such a case, in most of the cases, it is not taken on record whether the employee previously, was a member of provident fund and has not withdrawn the PF deposits, thus, his membership continues under paragraph 26 A . Secondly, after being enrolled a PF member, the pay of such employee is divided or bifurcated into different heads of pay with a view to reduce the liability of the employer. Obviously, such bifurcation is nothing but a subterfuge and it may attract section 12 of the Act.

To over-come such situations, an in-built remedy is available in the Scheme under paragraph 34 which requires every employer to obtain a declaration in form No 11 about his previous employment and his previous membership of provident fund whether he was a membership of a private provident fund or of the statutory Scheme. But, it has been mis-spelt after the qualifying period was removed for PF membership, as there is need to count the period between the date of employment and the date of becoming member. Form No. 11 still has its importance and it has to be obtained invariably in all the cases.

However, there is no exclusion on the basis of pay limit in respect of Newspaper Establishments. Every employee of a Newspaper Establishment has to become PF member irrespective of his pay. However, the ceiling of pay may be Rs. 6500/- (now Rs. 15,000 w.e.f. 01.09.2014) for the purpose of contribution. So in respect of the International Workers is also.

But, in respect of disabled persons, it is 25,000/- per month.

And, in respect of Cine-Workers, it is Rs. 1600/- per month or Rs. 15,000/- per year. Employee receiving pay more than the above mentioned limit is an excluded employee for the purpose of paragraph 2(f) of the Scheme.

VI. Membership continues even after pay exceeding Rs. 15,000/- P.M.:

Over a period of time, if the pay of a PF member exceeds Rs. 6500/- (now Rs. 15,000 w.e.f. 01.09.2014) per month, he will retain his membership and continue to be a PF member. In case a member leave an establishment, and joins another establishment with a pay more than Ra. 6500/- (now Rs. 15,000 w.e.f. 01.09.2014) per month, still he will not be an excluded employee in the new establishment, but he will require to continue as PF member. A mis-conception in this regard is prevailing by and large now a days that such employee will not require to become member. This could happen only, when declaration in form No. 11 is not obtained at the time of appointment of, or engaging a person.

VII. The Apprentices or the Trainees or the Learners:

Who is an apprentice, is clear that one, who has been engaged as an apprentice under the Apprentices Act, 1961 in a plain case. However, the term "apprentice" has been clarified in the explanation given under clause (iv) of paragraph 2 (f). It is explained that a person, who is engaged as an apprentice as per the Standing Orders of the Factory or the establishment duly certified by the competent authority, and other, who has been declared to be an apprentice by the authority specified by the appropriate Government.

In respect of Cine Workers, there is no provision for an apprentice, hence no exclusion on account of an apprentice; however, in Newspaper Establishments, apprentices are available and are excluded to become provident fund members.

Thus, in this regard, the most important is the Standing Orders approved by the competent authority in respect of the factory or the establishment. This is a requirement under the Industrial Employment (Standing Orders) Act, 1946 (XX of 1946).

In the Standing Orders of an establishment classification and condition of service of the workers and staff are mentioned. If, in the classification of workers, there is a mention of Apprentices and Learners or Trainees, than, apart from the Government sponsored Apprentices, such persons known as learners or/and trainees are eligible to get status of and excluded employee, provided that there must be a defined and designed scheme for training which also provide for timely tests and evaluation to upgrade the trainee to the next higher stage of training. During the training, the person is paid stipend and not a regular salary or pay. Person engaged so, can only be treated as a trainee or a learner otherwise not.

A trainee appointed to learn a trade for the prescribed period without any guarantee of future employment and paid not Wages, but stipend, had been held an apprentice within the meaning of the Act. Hence the company engaging him is not liable to make contribution on his behalf. –*[Sunderam Industries Ltd vs. R.P.F. Commissioner-(1996) 88 FJR 13; (1996)72 FLR 461 (Kant)].*

Once an apprentice got employment, and completed the requisite period of continuous service, his membership of the Fund became compulsory- *[Andhra Coop. Spg. Mills vs. R.P.F. Commissioner, - 1973 Lab.I.C. 325 (AP-DB).*

VIII. Membership to an "Excluded Employee":

No employer is under obligation to pay contributions etc. in respect of an excluded employee, however, if any such employee is willing to become a member and his employer is also agrees for his enrollment as PF membership, the employee may give a application in writing to the Commissioner through his employer and the employer agrees to pay administration charges on the pay such employee contributes to the Fund, than, the Assistant Provident Fund Commissioner may permit such employee to become a member of the Fund. On becoming such member, he is required to contribute to the Pension Fund also. W.e.f. 01.09.2014, a provision has been made in the Employees' Pension Scheme, 1995 that, and excluded employee seeks membership under paragraph 26 (6) of the EPF Scheme, 1952, whose pay exceeds Rs. 15,000 P.M. will not become member of the pension scheme.

IX. Declaration on Getting Employment:

Paragraph 34 of the Scheme requires every employer that he will ask every person before taking into employment to furnish in writing whether he is a member of the Fund or any exempted fund or not. If he is not a member of the Fund, the employee has to make a declaration to that effect, and if is a member, than, the employer is to ask for his/her PF account number, so that that may be intimated to the Commissioner for the record and initiate action for transfer of his accumulations in his past account through form No. 13 or 13A meant for inter-regional and intra-regional transfer respectively (at present, format has been changed compatible for online/networking.

For the purpose of this declaration, Form 11 (revised) has been prescribed by the Commissioner, in which information about membership of the Employees' Pension Scheme, 1995 have also been incorporated including whether or not he has obtained the Scheme Certificate or not and also whether he has taken a retiring or an early pension or not, so that continuation of the pension membership can be determined. If the employee has taken the Scheme Certificate, and he is below the age of superannuation (58 years), the Scheme Certificate is required to be surrendered and sent to the Commissioner along with Form NO. 5 (Revised) to add his previous pension membership to his new employment/membership.

X. Nomination and Declaration:

Paragraph. **61 provides for filing a Nomination by each** member. It the duty of every employer under paragraph 33 that on becoming a member of the Fund, he is required to obtain certain information about the employee him-self, about his family and the person whom the employee want to nominate as nominee under paragraph 61. On getting such information, the employer is to fill it up in form No. 2, statutorily prescribed under the Scheme.

Form No. 2 has 4 parts for practical purposes.

Part I of Form No. 2 relates to the member him-self, in which information about him-self, his father's name, permanent address, present address and **the most important, his date of birth** is mentioned. Information in this part is of permanent nature. The date of birth is the base for deciding the date of commencement of pension, on time. It is the duty of the employer to determine the date of birth of an employee as per the rules or standing orders applicable to the factory or establishment and also under various enactments governing the service conditions of the employees of his establishment. Any dispute about the date of birth of an employee is to be resolved by the employer only – *[General Manager, Bharat Coking Coal Ltd vs. Shib Kumar Dusad & others – 2001 LLR 74 SC]*.

Part II of Form No. 2 relates to the nomination for Provident Fund which is made as per provisions of paragraph 61. One or more persons can be nominated out-from the family members only. The *family* has been defined in paragraph 2 (g) of the Scheme. The nomination can be changed at any time during the employment by filing a fresh Form No. 2. Some important points for filling up Form No. 2 are given here under-

1. If the member is having family at the time of making nomination then the nominee can only be one or more members of the family clearly specifying the share of each nominee.

2. In case of "Male members" "Family" includes:-

a) *his wife;*

b) *his children whether married or unmarried;*

c) *his dependant parents;*

d) *his deceased son's widow and children.*

In case of "Female members" "Family" includes:-

a) *her husband;*

b) *her children whether married or unmarried;*

c) *her dependant parents;*

d) *her husband's dependant parents;*

e) *her deceased son's widow and children.*

3. In case a member is having a family as mentioned above and nominates a person outside the family, the said nomination is invalid.

4. In case a member is not having any member in a family as mentioned above, then he can nominate anybody, he chooses to nominate.

After nominating any person if the member acquires a family, the earlier nomination becomes invalid and he is to submit a fresh nomination form in favour of member(s) of the family.

5. In case the member was unmarried at the time of filing nomination form and subsequently gets married then he is required to file a fresh nomination form.

*6. If the nomination is made by the member in favour of a "**Minor**" the member is also required to mention any one major member of the family as guardian. In case, there is no major member in a family, then member at his discretion can nominate any other major person as guardian.*

Part III of Form No. 2 is for **declaration of family members** for the purpose of Employees' Pension Scheme, 1995. In this part spouse and children of any age, including legally adopted by the member are the family members as per paragraph 2 (vii) of the Pension Scheme.

And, the **Part IV** of Form No. 2 is the **nomination for Nominee Pension**. In case there is no family member to receive family pension in the event of death of a member before attaining the age of superannuation, whether while in service or away from service (subject to that the member should have rendered such period of service which entitled him for member pension i.e. 10 years membership). Therefore, it is advisable that in this part, spouse should not be nominated, because, spouse is, automatically entitled for family pension in case of death of a member under any condition, whether while in service or away from service or after commencement of pension.

Instruction for filling the form

*1. No abbreviation is to be used with respect to name of employee and father's name. For ex. **AMIT KUMAR VERMA** should not be written as **A.K. VERMA.***

2. Date of Birth (DOB) is important information and as such due care should be taken to fill up the correct date of birth.

Pension benefits is related to DOB, and once filled this will not be allowed to change under normal circumstances.

The Date of Birth given in this form should not vary with the Date of Birth as mentioned in Form No. 5 and 9.

3. To fill up Part "A" (Nomination for PF), the instructions as given from Sr. No. 3 to 9 may to adhered to.

4. If there are more than one nominee the percentage (%) share of each nominee should be mentioned clearly and the total percentage of all nominees should be equal to 100.

5. In part "B" relating to family details for the EPS' 95 the details of the spouse and children including legally adopted child should be mentioned, special care should be taken in filling up the date of birth.

6. While filling up the details of nominee for EPS, 95 the instruction at Sr. No. 10 should be observed.

XI. Membership of Employees' Pension Scheme, 1995:

The membership of pension scheme is linked with the membership of the PF membership, and in certain cases it was given effect from 01.03.1993, hence relevant paragraphs of the EPS have to be referred-

Paragraph [1][6. Membership of the Employees' Pension Scheme.

Paragraph [1][7. Option for joining the Scheme.

Paragraph 8. Resolution of doubts.

Paragraph [1][17. Payments on Exercise of Option.

Membership of the Pension Scheme is simultaneous with the membership of the Employees' Provident Fund. If an excluded employee on account of receipt of pay of Rs. 6,500 p.m. (Rs. 15,000 p.m. w.e.f. 01.09.2014) opts for P.F. membership, he was required to become member of the pension scheme compulsorily, prior to 01.09.2014 . But, if a person has attained the age of superannuation, i.e. 58 years, he is not require to become member of the Pension Scheme. On the other hand, if a person has taken early or retiring pension after 50 years of age, he is also not required to join pension scheme.

Due to a commitment given to the Parliament that the Employees' Pension Scheme would be applicable w.e.f. 1.4.1993; but it took two half year to get a nod of Parliament, a relaxation has been provided in the Scheme to the effect that any member of the ceased Employees' Family Pension Scheme, 1971 retired, superannuated or died between 01.4.1993 and 15.11.1995, he would be entitled to the benefits under the new pension scheme, any benefit withdrawn by such members is required to be deposited with interest @ 8.5 % p.a. The intention was not to allow membership to all EFPS, 1971 members, who were out of employment prior to 01.4.1993 and those who left the employment and were not entitled to pension benefits due being below the age of 50 years or having service less than 10 years; however, it is there as an interpretation and clarification about.

Another case of such PF members, who did not join EFPS in 1971, and now they want to join the pension scheme, have been allowed to give option to join the new pension scheme, but their membership would be commenced w.e.f. 01.3.1971 and such persons are required to pay contribution from March, 1971 with interest @ 8.5% P.A.

Initially, there was a time limit of six months for exercising option for membership as above except death cases as per paragraph 7 of the scheme, which was removed in February, 1996. But, after a long period even after retirement, many persons claimed for the option for membership of the pension scheme end pension accordingly. The Honorable Madras High Court has settled this issue while dismissing the writ petition in the case of ***Kappusaney G. Vs. R.P.F. Commissioner, Triuchirapalli and another [2010-111-LLJ-733 (Mad)].*** In that case, the High Court has observed that the petitioner got 37 years of services and he was supposed to know each and every regulation, laws, notification as he was serving in the personnel department and retired as personnel officer. Even it any right as accrued to the petitioner under the scheme, the court has to see the tenure of the scheme. The petitioner, after retirement from service on 30-4-1994 and after lapse of 4 years he made a claim to include his name in the family pension scheme. If an employee joins family pension scheme, the contribution would be deducted to the scheme from his salary, Therefore, petitioner's claim to become member of scheme without contribution cannot be sustained. The court further stated that person who is aware of right moves the writ to the court for the said right is not entitled to the relief. The petitioner slop over the matter and makes hire and cry after a very long delay. Delay defeats the rights. No doubt, the scheme is beneficial to the weaker section, namely workers. However the claim is belated one, and if any relief is given, it will open flood gate for many other similar placed persons like the petitioner. On that serve also, the petitioner is not entitled to any relief. Accordingly the petition was dismissed.

XII. Membership Employees' Deposit-Linked Insurance Scheme, 1976:

Membership of the Insurance Scheme is also simultaneous with the membership of the Provident Fund and remains as member till he is an employee. As soon as a person ceases to be an employee, he ceases to be member of the EDLI Scheme, irrespective of the fact that he continues to be a member of the provident fund.

XIII. Retention of Membership:

Under all the three Schemes, there is a provision of retaining the membership. In the Employees' Provident Funds Scheme, 1952, it under paragraph 26A which provides that until a member becomes entitled to receive his PF accumulation under paragraph 69 or dies entitling his family to receive PF accumulations under paragraph 70, he continues to be a member of provident fund.

In Employees' Pension Scheme, 1995, it is under paragraph 6A which was inserted in 1999 by GSR 66 dated 22.02.1999 which provides that a member shall continue to be a member until he or she attains
the age of 58 years or avails withdrawal benefit or dies or pension is vested in him under paragraph 12 whichever is earlier.

In the EDLI Scheme, there is no express provision for retention of membership, but as soon as a person becomes an employee and retains his PF membership, he becomes or retains his membership simultaneously.

Chapter 11

Benefits

> *Brief badinage-*
>
> *The ultimate aim of the Schemes is to provide a social security cover to the employees of establishments covered under the Act, which is meant for the old age and for family members in case death of a member, hence the provident fund cannot and should not be taken as savings in a saving bank account. Initially, an additional object was also worked behind it to retain the workers in the establishment or in a factory. But after withdrawing forfeiture clause in 1990, the provident fund account is being treated as a saving bank account attached to a particular employment which resulted in many irregularities and omissions in reporting or seeking compliance and obtaining declaration etc. which has been discussed in appropriate chapters. Thanks to the Income Tax authorities, who, with a view to generate additional source of revenue, compelled the PF authorities to deduct and deposit tax at source on premature closure of PF accounts before 5 years. Even then, the Provident Fund Scheme and the other schemes have not lost their importance, rather the need of these have been proved within the thunders and blunders of globalization.*

Employees' Provident Funds Scheme, 1952

I. The Provident Fund –

It is true that there is no defined benefit under the Employees' Provident Funds Scheme, 1952, however, whatever has been deposited into the provident fund by the employer and the member himself is paid out for different purposes, occasions and circumstances with a higher rate of interest declared by the Central Government from time to time, calculated on monthly running balances. Finally, it is fully secured and payable only to the member or to the beneficiaries of it.

II. Transfer of PF Account-

It is common feature that a person gets his employment changed for betterment and require his provident fund account transferred to his new account. The Act has taken care of it by making it mandatory that account of a member has to be transferred to his new account. Such provision is mentioned in section 17- A.

Transfer of account can only be processed when the employer comes to know that the member previously employed somewhere and he was a member of provident fund and of the pension fund. To give this information, there is a mandate that employer has to obtain a declaration in From No. 11 (paragraph 34) from the employee as soon as he is engaged by him. If, such a declaration is obtained, then, no fault of the employer for any lapse that may occur in absence of such a declaration or information.

Section [1][17A. **Transfer of accounts** – (1) Where an employee employed in an establishment to which this Act applies leaves his employment and obtains re-employment in another establishment to which this Act does not apply, the amount of accumulations to the credit of such employee in the fund, or as the case may be, in the provident fund of the establishment left by him shall be transferred, within such time as may be specified by the Central Government in this behalf, to the credit of his account in the provident fund of the establishment in which he is re-employed, if the employee so desires and the rules in relation to that provident fund permit such transfer.

(2) Where an employee employed in an establishment to which this Act does not apply leaves his employment and obtains re-employment in another establishment to which this Act applies, the amount of accumulations to the credit of such employee in the provident fund of the establishment left by him may, if the employee so desires and the rules in relation to such provident fund permit, be transferred to the credit of his account in the Fund or as the case may be, in the provident fund of the establishment in which he is re-employed.]

1.	Inserted by Act 28 of 1963, Sec. 2.

Related provisions have been made under paragraph 57 of the Scheme.

With the introduction of networking and computerization, a major shift to accounting system has taken place, and accordingly, in the transfer of PF accumulations in the present account. Now an initiative has been taken to issue an Unique Account Number (UAN) to every P.F. member which will facilitate single account number for life and every time, on change of employer or establishment, the contribution paid will be credited to that UAN only. Thus the problem of delayed transfer of P.F. accumulations will not arise.

III. Rate interest applicable year-wise:

Paragraph 60 provides for credit of interest to the members P.F. Account every year on monthly balances and compounded every year. Recently, it has been provided in that paragraph that if a member is not contributing for 36 months continuously, then the account will cease to earn interest until it is credited with the contribution and renewed from being it a dormant account.

The rate of interest declared under paragraph 60 is given hereunder from 1975-76 to 2014-15:-

1975-76	07.00 %	1989-90 to 4/2000	12.00 %
1976-77	07.50 %	7/2000 to 3/2001	11.00 %
1977-78	08.25 % + 0.50 % *	2001-02 to 2002-03	09.50 %
1978-79 to 1980-81	08.25 %	2003-04	09.50 % + 0.50 % *
1981-82	08.50 %	2004-05	09.50 %
1982-83	08.75 %	2005-06 to 2009-10	08.50 %
1983-84	09.15 %	2010-11	09.50 %

1984-85	09.90 %	2011-12	08.25 %
1985-86	10.15 %	2012-13	08.50 %
1986-87	11.00 %	2013-14 to 2014-15	08.75 %
1987-88	11.50 %		
1988-89	11.80 %		
• Silver jubilee and Golden jubilee bonus in addition to normal rate of interest.			

IV. Advance payments from P.F. Account (as withdrawal):

By the time passed, the ne eds and requirements were considered to provide financial assistance out from the provident fund account of a member. Originally, there stood a provision in paragraph 62 for financing of Life Insurance Policies obtained by the P.F. Member him-self and supporting provisions there for were duly incorporated in paragraph 63 to 67. Then, in early sixties, paragraph 68-B, 68-H, 68-J were added and thereafter, Paragraph 68-k, 68-L were inserted, and then rest of the provisions for advances related to other purposes were added which, after further corrections as required by the time, the provisions came into existence as available today.

(1) Payment to Life Insurance Policies (paragraph 62) –

There is a provision of financing of life insurance policies on the life of the P.F. member him-self and which is not an endowment policy. The payment can be made on yearly or half-yearly terms only. On maturity, the payment is received by the Commissioner and credited to the account of the member. But, due to various reasons, this facility is not being availed by the members.

Related provisions are incorporated in paragraph 62 to 67.

(2) Advance withdrawal for a dwelling House/Building (para 68-B & 68 BB) –

There are 2 types of withdrawals known as Housing Loan have been provided in paragraph 68-B and 68-BB. Paragraph 68-B provides for purchase of a dwelling site, a ready built house from an individual or from an agency, and the other, to repay housing loan taken from a financing agency under paragraph 68-BB.

For purchase of a residential plot or a ready built house, either in the name of the member or spouse or in the joint name, the amount is paid in one lump-sum. For construction of a house, the amount is paid in two installments. If the ready built house is purchased from an agency, the amount is paid to the agency directly.

Since, the clause (8) of paragraph 68-B has been deleted, no document is required to be submitted for such advance or withdrawal, but a declaration is required to be given by the member him-self along with the application in Form 31 presently in force.

The eligibility is 5 years' membership and requirement of minimum balance in the account is Rs. 1000/-. The amount payable is equal to 36 months pay or the cost or balance available in the member account including the employer's share with interest, whichever is less.

As per clause (10), the Commissioner may ask for a utilization certificate.

For the purpose of repayment of a housing loan, the eligibility is 10 years and the amount entitle is the same as above. It is paid directly to the financing agency.

(3) Advance for medical treatment (para 68-J) –

The provisions of para 68-J are clear. It is not available to such members who are enjoying the benefits under Employees' State Insurance Act, 1948.

The amount as advance is an amount equal to six months pay of the member or amount at the credit in the member's account of his own share only.

(4) Advance for marriage and post matriculation education (para 68-K) –

Advance under this provision is available for marriage-

= of self, sons, daughters, brother or sister, and

= post matriculation education of children.

It is available three times during membership. Seven years membership is required and the amount sanctioned is 50 % of his own share available in his account.

No document is required for this purpose too, only a declaration printed in the Form 31 it-self is to be given.

(5) Advance in case of closure of an establishment (para 68-H) –

Advance payment out of the PF account of member is sanctioned and paid in case the establishment has been closed and the member is not in receipt of pay for 2 months or more.

Amount available in his account of his own share can be sanctioned in one or more occasions.

If, the closure is for more than six months, further amount can be sanctioned out of the employer's share also.

If, a **member is dismissed** and the member has challenged it in the court of law, he is not entitled to final withdrawal under paragraph 69, but can avail advance payment from his account which is sanctioned by the Assistant Commissioner only. Many cases have been noticed, where a dismissed member withdraws his PF accumulation under paragraph 69, and after some time, when he is taken back in service, his membership starts a fresh. That renders the member and the department in a situation which puts question mark on either end, especially in pension matters.

(6) Part final payment (para 68-NN) –

In 1996, a provision has been inserted by which a member, within one year of his retirement, may withdraw 90 % of amount at his credit in the PF account for planning the post-retirement settlement.

(7) Other advances –

Paragraph 68L. Grant of advances in abnormal conditions.

Paragraph 68M. Grant of advance to members affected by cut in the supply of electricity.

68N. Grant of advance to members who are physically handicapped.

Paragraph **68NNN. Option for withdrawal at the age of 55 years for investment in Varishtha Pension Bima Yojana.**

V. Final Payment to the Member him-self:

Final payment of provident fund accumulations is made to the member him-self in the conditions laid down in paragraph 69. Basically, the conditions laid down in paragraph 69 have lost their utility because, the intention of the provident fund was to retain the person in employment, there for there was a provision for forfeiture of employers share of contribution as certain percentage for certain period of service in cases other than the cases of retirement either on attaining the age of superannuation or at the age of 55 year or on medical ground. Now, the provision stands removed w.e.f. 1.11.1990, hence, the deferent conditions of final payment of P.F. accumulations have lost the importance. The conditions are-

1. on getting the age of superannuation as prescribed in the rules governing the service conditions of the employees or 55 years, whichever is later [paragraph 69 (1) (a)]
2. on incapacitating to work on medical ground, retired from employment. [paragraph 69 (1) (b)]
3. on migration from India for permanent settlement [paragraph 69 (1) (c)]
4. on retrenchment from service, individual or mass, [paragraph 69 (1) (d)]
5. on voluntary retirement under a voluntary retirement scheme of the establishment [paragraph 69 (1) (dd)]
6. on leaving the service or resignation from service or the cases other than those specified at point 1 to 5 above [paragraph 69 (2)].

The cases falling under point 1 to 5 above are settled immediately on receipt of the claim application, but in other cases, the member has to wait for two months period. However, an un-married female member may be allowed to withdraw her full amount without any waiting period of two month if, she leaves her employment on account of her marriage.

VI. Final Payment on Death of a Member:

It is the duty of an employer to assist the E.P.F. department to make correct payment to the right claimant. In the event of death of a member either while in service or out of employment, the provident fund accumulations are paid to the family members as provided for in paragraph 70. In this paragraph, entitlement of family members has been mentioned that who will get the P.F. amounts lying with the P.F. Commissioner. The sequence of entitlement is as under-

1. The nominee or nominees nominated by the employee and a valid nomination is on record with the authorities, is/are entitled to receive the PF accumulations. If more than one person is nominated, all will get share as mentioned in the nomination form. If no share has been mentioned, than, all will get share in equal proportion *[Para 70(i)]*.
2. If, there is no valid nomination, the PF amount is paid to family members, but major son (s) and married daughter(s) are not entitled to get the share. In case, there is no spouse alive and/or dependent parents and also the minor son (s) and/or un-married daughter(s) is not there, than the amount is to be distributed among the remaining family members whether major son or married daughter *[Para 70 (ii)]*.
3. If, no valid nomination exist and no family member is alive to receive the P.F. amounts, than it is to be paid to the succession holder *[Para 70(iii)]*.

For claiming the P.F. accumulation of a deceased member, every major claimant is required to apply separately in the prescribed form. In case of a minor claimant, the claim is to be preferred through his/her guardian, whether natural or appointed.

As Guardians and Wards Act, 1880, in case of a Hindu minor, father or mother is the natural guardian. In case of a Muslim minor, father or the grand-father is the natural guardian; but, up to the age of 7 years of a male minor, and up to 14 years (the age of puberty) of a female minor, the mother is considered to be custodian. And, in the Christian law, there is no concept of natural guardian, hence an appointed guardian can only apply for PF amount of a deceased member, payable to a Christian minor.

However, in deserving cases the Commissioner or the Chairman, CBT may permit to be guardian, whom the authority considers to be the proper person representing the minor and the receipt of such person for the amount paid shall be a sufficient discharge of the amount paid *[Paragraph 72 (3)]*.

If, the claimant is a lunatic, then the payment is made through his appointed Estate Manager as per provisions of Indian Lunacy Act, 1912.

It is also relevant to remind here that the above mentioned persons are recipient of the PF amount only. After receipt of the amount, he or she is required to distribute the amount amongst all other heirs of the deceased member. Paragraph 61 of the E.P.F. Scheme, 1952 does not confer an absolute right on the nominee to receive the amount to the exclusion of the other heirs whether testamentary or otherwise - **[Smt. Om Wati vs. Delhi Transport Corpn. New Delhi and others- 1988 Lab,IC 500 (Delhi)]**. The Madras High Court has further clarified it in the case of **Narammal and another vs. Kanthani and others- [1992 (2) MLJ 538 (Mad)]** that if, there is any conflict between the Scheme and the Act, the Scheme must be read subject to the main provisions of the Act. Reading of paragraph 61 and 70 and also Form 2 mean that they provide a different line of succession. Such meaning cannot be given, if due regard is given to the main provision, namely, item No. 10 of Schedule II. Unless the main section clearly and unequivocally prescribes a different line of succession, it cannot be presumed that a different line of succession is prescribed by reading paragraph 61 and 70 of the Scheme alone. These paragraphs have to be read down to be in conformity with item No. 10 of Schedule II and with section 5 of the Act and by so reading, the nominee gets only a right to receive the amount to distribute the same to the heirs of the deceased in accordance with the law of succession governing them.

Where the **claimant is charged with the charge of murder of the member,** the P.F. amount is not paid to him, until he or she is acquitted from the charge. If, he or she is convicted for such charge including that of abetting the murder, he or she will be debarred to receive the amount, and that amount will be paid to other family members, if no other family member is available, to the succession holder *[Para 70 A]*.

VII. Modes of Payments:

In paragraph 72, the procedure has been laid down how the claim for PF accumulations is to be processed. It is the prime duty of every employer to assist the CBT in making correct payment to the right claimant, therefore, the employer is under obligation to fill up the claim form and verify all of it contents under his seal and signature and forward it to the Commissioner along with the required documents, returns and information. In case a claim is submitted direct to the Commissioner without attestation by the employer, the commissioner shall forward the same to the employer, and the employer is to return it with attestation and required information/returns to the commissioner within five days under the mandate of paragraph 72 (5). The failure may lead to action as provided for in paragraph 76.

It is not for the employer only to follow the instruction, but the Commissioner has also been made responsible for timely settlement and payment of the provident fund amounts. If the settlement is made beyond 30 days of the receipt of the claim duly completed in all respect, the Commissioner is liable to pay interest for the period beyond 30 days @ 12 % per annum to the claimant.

The payment may be made to the claimant as the claimant desires either through Money Order, Cheque or through core-banking system of the Bank now available all-over the country.

The Commissioner is liable to pay the amount standing to his credit. Taking into consideration the phraseology used in clause 72 of E.P.F. Scheme, 1952, the Commissioner should pay the amount standing to the credit of the member in his P.F. Account, such appears the intention of the legislature. In the present case, admittedly, the employer did not credit (paid) the amount of P.F. due from him to the P.F. account of the employee. This being the position on the strict interpretation of paragraph 72 of the Scheme, there is no liability on the part of the Commissioner to pay it to the employee which the employer has failed to credit it to his account - *[Rashtriya Mill Mazdoor Sangh and others vs. R.P.F.C. Bombay and others – 1991 Lab.IC 1572 (Bom); and Varadakkal vs. the RPFC and another- 2001 (1) CLR 770; 2002 (1) LLJ 1018].*

Employees' Pension Scheme, 1995

Prelude-

A social security scheme, when considered to be a welfare scheme, it is messed and becomes a tool for everybody connected with it to get something any how out of it. And, when it is bound to work under political pressure, not under social pressure, it is interpreted in the way, it losses its legal sanctity and the character of model social security scheme. The same thing happened with the Employee' Pension Scheme, 1995 right from its introduction in 1995 and even before, whence it was under consideration. Therefore, the provisions are not discussed here deeply, *but it is suggested that another book on the Pension Scheme entitled "Employees' Pension Scheme, 1995 – Know About It!" may be referred. However,* for the pension products given in the E.P.S., 1995, the following paragraphs to be seen-

Paragraph **9. Determination of eligible service.**

Paragraph **10. Determination of pensionable service.**

Paragraph **11. Determination of pensionable** salary.

Paragraph **12. Monthly Member's Pension.**

Paragraph **15. Benefits on permanent and total disablement during the service.**

Paragraph **16. Benefits to the family on the death of a member.**

Paragraph **16A. Guarantee of Pensionary Benefits.**

Paragraph **17A. Payment of pension.**

VIII. Pensions-

Under the Employee' Pension Scheme, 1995, two types of pension is available- One, pension to the member himself, which is called **Monthly Member Pension** which has further been classified as-

1. Superannuation Pension, payable on attaining the age of 58 years,
2. Retiring or Reduced Pension, payable after 50 years of age, if the member is not in employment. And
3. Disablement Pension.

and the other, the **Family Pension**, which has further been classified according to the person entitle to it. These are –

1. Widow Pension to spouse,
2. Children Pension to children up to two (till 25 years of age) at a time payable with widow pension only,
3. Orphan Pension to children up to two (till 25 years of age) at a time in lieu of the widow and children pension,
4. Nominee Pension to nominee nominated through Form No. 2, payable in absence of all above three,
5. Parents Pension to dependent father first than to mother, in absence of all above four.

The Family Pension is payable in case of death of a member whether while in service or away from service or death after commencement of Monthly Member Pension.

In case of death while in service, at any stage of age, but before attaining the age of 58 years.

IX. Eligibility-

For getting pension, the eligibility criterion is of prime importance, without which, no pension may become payable.

Eligibility for Monthly Member Pension- under the Employees' Pension Scheme, 1995, the eligibility for Member Pension is ten years' service. This includes membership under the Employees' Family Pension Scheme, 1971, which has been termed as **"Past Service"** and the service after 16.11.1995, which is known as **"Actual Service,"** the aggregate of both periods should be 10 years which is called the '**Eligible Service**,' and

The age should be 58 years for superannuation pension; 50 years of age for Reduced or Retiring Pension.

In the eligible service, if the Actual Service i.e. the service after 16.11.1995 is 20 years, a weightage of 2 years is given that is to say, 20 years' actual service will be taken as 22 years for the purpose of calculation of pension. Un-fortunately, the Karnataka State Commission under Consumer Act upheld mis-interpretation of the District Forum that the two years' weightage be given to those pensioners who have completed 20 years' membership including the Past service. The term 'actual service' used for this purpose has, thus been diluted and the department could not plead it and thought it proper to appeal before the Supreme Court. Hence, pensioners claiming this benefit is being given by revising the

PPOs, which attracts the cases in which pension sanctioned right from 16.11.1995. Otherwise, it will be available to the pensioners becoming entitled w.e.f. 16.11.1995.

For **Disablement Pension**, one month's contribution should have been paid, there is no limit of age, but the employee must be total and permanent disable which is to be certified by a competent medical board.

Similarly, for family pension, one month's contribution should have been paid by a member to entitle his family members, nominee or parents, if death occurs while in service, otherwise, 10 years service is required for nominee pension or parents pension. In case of death after commencement of monthly Member Pension, no nominee or parents are entitled to get family pension.

X. Pensionable Salary:

An important factor for calculation of pension is the pensionable salary. With the amendments given effect from 01.09.2014, including enhancement of pay limit for contribution, the pensionable salary is calculated in two parts; one, for the period up to 31.08.2014 and, the another, w.e.f. 01.09.2014. But, it will attract the cases which are payable between 01.09.2014 to 31.08.2015 to give effect of the enhanced salary.

However, it is calculated in the following manner-

$$\text{Pensionable salary} = \frac{\text{pay for 12 months}}{365 - \text{NCP days}} \times 30 \text{ or}$$

Average pay for 12 month as usually calculated.

For the purpose of widow pension, and for the disablement pension, the last pay is taken for calculation. If the last pay is for a broken period of a month, the pay is divided by the days if represent and than multiply the one day's pay by 30, the result will be the pay for the family pension and the disablement pension.

XI. Amount of Pension–

Member Pension:-

(1) In respect of new entrants i.e. the persons, who joined the Scheme after 16.11.1995 and were not members of the EFP Scheme, 1971-

The pension is calculated on the basis of the following formula as mentioned in para 12 (3) –

$$\text{Monthly Member Pension} = \frac{\text{pensionable salary} \times \text{pensionable service}}{70}$$

There is no provision for any minimum pension in such cases.

(2) In cases, where the person is a member of the ceased EFP Scheme, 1971 i.e. an existing member, prior to 16.11.1995; those have been put in 3 categories –

(i) who retired or superannuated before 16.11.2000,

(ii) who retired or superannuated between 16.11.2000 and 15.11.2005, and

(iii) who will retire or superannuate after 16.11.2005.

In all such cases, the pension is calculated in two parts, one, for the past service which known as the **Past Service Benefits** and the other, for the new service or the actual service, which is known as the **Formula Pension.**

The Formula Pension is the same as mentioned in paragraph 12 (3) and mentioned here in above.

(3) Past Service Benefits-

The Past Service Benefit is based on a table as below-

The past service benefit payable on completion of 58 years of age on 16.11.95

	Years of past Service	Salary upto than Rs. 2500/- per month	Salary more Rs. 2500/- per month
	(1)	(2)	(3)
(i)	Upto 11 years	Rs. 80	Rs. 85
(ii)	More than 11 years but upto 15 years	Rs. 95	Rs.105
(iii)	More than 15 years but less than 20 year	Rs. 120	Rs.135
(iv)	Beyond 20 year	Rs.150	Rs.170

(4) For member falling in category (iii) above-

Past Service Benefits <u>multiply by</u> corresponding factor of Table 'B'

Plus-formula pension(minimum Rs. 635/-) = payable **MMP**

Subject to minimum pension Rs. 800/-

After proportionate reduction, minimum pension shall be Rs. 450/-.

(5) For members falling in category (ii) above-

Past Service Benefits multiply by corresponding factor of Table 'B'

Plus-formula pension (minimum Rs. 438/-) = Payable **MMP**

Subject to minimum pension Rs. 600/-

After proportionate reduction, minimum pension shall be Rs.325/-.

(6) For member falling in category (i) above-

Past Service Benefits <u>multiply by</u> Corresponding factor Table 'B'

Plus- formula pension (Minimum Rs. 335/-) = payable **MMP**

Subject to minimum pension of Rs. 500/-

After proportionate reduction, minimum pension shall be Rs. 265/-.

(7) The pattern of calculation of pension is a combination of past service benefit and formula pension. For different categories, as above, different scales/minimum pensions have been defined and those are subject to completion of eligible service of 24 years.

Benefits

In cases, where the eligible service is less then 24 years, the pension is proportionately reduced. The factor is –

$$\frac{\text{M.M.P. X No. of years of eligible service}}{24}$$

A ready reckoner is given here under –

Years of membership	Factor of Proportionate reduction	Years of membership	Factor of Proportionate reduction
24	1000	16	0.667
23	0.958	15	0.625
22	0.917	14	0.583
21	0.875	13	0.542
20	0.833	12	0.500
19	0.792	11	0.458
18	0.750	10	0.417
17	0.708	00	0000

The Past Service Benefit is payable as on 16.11.1995, the date on which the EFP Scheme was ceased, thereafter it is enhanced by applying factor as mentioned in Table 'B.' The Table 'B' stands revised w.e.f. 10.6.2008. After all these calculations, if the aggregate member pension is less than Rs. 1000/-, then the minimum pension of Rs. 1000/- is payable.

(8) Early or retiring pension –

Normally, monthly member pension is payable on attaining the age of 58 year, however, looking to the employment conditions, perhaps, it was considered that an employee may cease to be in employment before he attains the age of 58 years. Therefore, on ceasation prior to the age of 58 years, the employee is allowed to get pension by option.

To get pension before superannuation, an employee must be at least of 50 years . In such cases, there shall be a reduction in the admissible pension at 58 years of ages at the rate of 3 % for each year falling short of 58 years. The maximum reduction shall be 25% of the admissible pension. Now, w.e.f. 26.9.2008, the rate of reduction has been enhance from 3 % to 4 % per year with maximum reduction in pension of 25 %, the same. **A ready-reckoner of such reduction on early pension is given here under:**

Age at which, pension is opted to draw	Factor of reduction Upto w.e.f. 25.9.2008 @ 3%	w.e.f. 26.9.2008 @ 4%
58	1.000	1.0000
57	0.970	0.9600
56	0.941	0.9216
55	0.913	0.8847
54	0.885	0.8493
53	0.859	0.8154

52	0.833	0.7828
51	0.808	0.7514
50	0.784	0.7500

XII. *WIDOW PENSION:*

The basis of calculation of family pension is the '**widow pension.**' Two way calculation of widow pension has been given in the scheme, namely-

(i) in case of death in service, and also death away from service, but before the age of 58 years in both the cases, the widow pension shall be – equal to the member pension as calculated above or the amount as per table 'C' corresponding to the pay of the member at time of his death, whichever is higher. (Table 'C' is given here-under).

(ii) in case of death after commencement of monthly member pension, the widow pension shall be 50 % of the member pension, subject to a minimum of Rs. 450/- per month.

If, the payable widow pension is less than Rs. 1000/-, the minimum pension of Rs. 1000/- will be paid.

Children pension – Amount of Children pension is 25 % of the widow pension calculated as above, but a minimum of Rs. 150/- per month per child, payable upto 2 children at time, if eligible. It is attached to the widow pension. If, recipient of widow pension is not there, than it will convert into Orphan pension.

If, the payable widow pension is less than Rs. 250/-, the minimum pension of Rs. 250/- will be paid.

Orphan Pension – The value of orphan pension is 75 % of the widow pension subject to a minimum of Rs. 175/- per month per child, payable up to 2 children at a time, if eligible. It is payable where the recipient of widow pension is not there.

If, the payable widow pension is less than Rs. 750/-, the minimum pension of Rs. 750/- will be paid.

Nominee pension - It is paid where no family member is to receive either the widow pension or the orphan pension. For nominee pension, there must be a valid nomination on record. The value is the same as of widow pension. It is not payable in the case of death after the member pension commenced or vested.

Parent pension – In absence above all, the widow pension is paid first to the dependant father, than to the dependant mother with same value of widow pension. It is also not payable in the case of death after the member pension commenced or vested.

XIII. Scheme Certificate:

If a member ceases to be in employment before attaining the age of 58 years, at which he can get pension, he may get a Membership Certificate, which is called "**Scheme Certificate.**"

The Scheme Certificate can be availed even being the membership of one month.

The advantages of the Scheme Certificate are-

= The member may continue his membership.

= He can get added his present membership to the new, which will benefit him in getting more pension as the Pension able Service shall be more. And he will qualify for pension, if, service fall short.

= By obtaining Scheme Certificate, E.P.S. membership is retained by retaining the membership, 2 years weight age is earned for the purpose of calculation of pension as per formula.

In the event of any mis-happening with the life of the member before the age of 58 years; the Scheme Certificate happens to be a guarantee note for the family, to receive family pension i.e. the Widow Pension *plus* children pension or the Orphan Pension and the Nominee Pension or Widow Pension to dependant father/dependant mother, if, the member has rendered eligible service of 10 years, as the case may be.

XIV. Withdrawal Benefit:

Under paragraph 14, where a member is not entitled to member pension, may claim for withdrawal benefit. The intention of the scheme is not to allow pre-matured ceasation of pension membership before attaining the age of 58 years. If a member has attained the age of 58 years and his eligible service is less than 10 years, than withdrawal benefit is only the way, but, if a member is below 58 years and his eligible service is less than 10 years, and he may further add to his eligible service, he should not be allowed withdrawal benefit. But, it has become a fashion to get withdrawal benefit as soon as a member leaves his service and his eligible service is less than 10 years service. Such practice is nothing but an effort to defeat the vary purpose of a social security scheme, which is entirely against the family in its finality.

Withdrawal benefit is calculated in two phases- one for the past service, which is based on table 'A' enhance by application of a factor in Table 'B' relevant to the period after 16.11.1995- plus – the other, an amount arrived at by application of a factor in Table 'D.'

XV. Commutation and Return of Capital:

The facility or the provisions for Commutation of member pension and option for Return of Capital which were available in para 12-A and 13 respectively, have been deleted with effect from 26.9.2008, therefore, these are not available thereafter.

XVI. Payment of Monthly Pensions:

Monthly pension is paid through certain designated Banks only, which have been authorized for at state levels separately. However, HDFC BANK, ICICI BANK AND AXIS BANK have been authorized at national level. Pensioners may choose any of the banks out of these or any other authorize at regional level.

Employees' Deposit-Linked Insurance Scheme, 1976

XVII. Insurance Benefit:

The Insurance benefit is payable to the family members, generally, the who receive the Provident Fund amount of a deceased member. When, death occurs while in service, the insurance benefit is paid, otherwise not.

The pattern of calculation the Insurance Benefit is given ink paragraph 22 of the Scheme.

The amount of insurance is calculated in the following manner-

Equal to 12 months (preceding the month in which the member died) or during the period of membership, whichever is less average P.F. balance in his account is paid if it is upto Rs. 50,000 in full.

If the average balance exceeds rupees fifty, it will be added by 40 % of the amount in excess of Rs. 50,000.

That total sum is payable as the Insurance benefit not exceeding Rs. One lakh.

W.e.f. 08.01.2011, an alternate calculation is also provided by substituting sub-paragraph (3) of paragraph 22. If a member is continuously in employment for 12 months, his 12 months average pay (subject to the ceiling of pay- which at present 15,000 p.m.) is multiplied by 20. The amount so arrived is payable, if it higher then the amount calculated as above – the maximum limit is 1,00,000/. Nautally, it will be more than the maximum limit, hence the main calculation is only to multiply the 12 months average pay, by 20.

W.e.f. 01.09.2014, a further addition is given by sub-paragraph (4) which 20 % of the amount of insurance payable as above. Thus, now the maximum insurance benefit payable is

$$15,000 \times 20 = 3,00,000 + 20 \% \text{ of } 3,00,000 = 3,60,000.$$

It is paid in the same manner in which the P.F. amount is paid except the mode of money order.

Chapter 12

Safeguards

Safeguard that has been provided by the Act is its section 10 which gives protection to all the benefits payable under any of the Schemes framed under this Act.

I. Protection against attachment-

Section 10. Protection against attachment.- (1) amount standing to the credit of any member in Fund [1][or of any exempted employee in a provident fund] shall not in any way be capable of being assigned or charged and shall not be liable to attachment under any decree or order of any court in respect of any debt or liability incurred by the member [1][or the exempted employee,] and neither the official assignee appointed under the Presidency Towns Insolvency Act, 1909 (3 of 1909) nor any receiver appointed under the Provincial Insolvency Act, 1920 (5 of 1920), shall be entitled to have any claim on, any such amount.

[2][(2) Any amount standing to the credit of a member in the fund or of an exempted employee in a provident fund at the time of his death and payable to his nominee under the Scheme or the rules of the provident fund shall, subject to any deduction authorised by the said Scheme or rules, vest in the nominee and shall be free from any debt or other liability incurred by the deceased or the nominee before the death of the member or of exempted employee [3][and shall also not be liable to attachment under any decree or order of any court.]]

[4][(3) The provisions of sub-section 1 and sub-section 2 shall, so far as may be, apply in relation to the [5][pension] or any other amount, payable under the [5][Pension] Scheme [6][and also in relation to any amount payable under the Insurance Scheme] as they apply in relation to any amount payable out of the Fund.]

---

1. Inserted by Act 37 of 1953, s. 8.
2. Substituted by Act 37, of s. 8.
3. Added by Act 33 of 1988, s. 15.
4. Inserted by Act 16 of 1971, s. 22.
5. Substituted by Act 25 of 1996, s. 4.
6. Inserted by Act 99 of 1976, s. 26.

No court can pass a decree against or order attachment of the benefits under the Act under any condition. As such, the Provident Fund Authorities cannot be compelled by any court of law to part with the money lying with them to any authority other than the beneficiary under the Scheme under which the benefit is to be paid. One of the purposes of provident fund is to make some provision for the families of the employees. The legislature, therefore, appears to have provided by Section 10 that the amount standing to the credit of a subscriber in the provident fund shall not be available to his creditors - *[Pearly Andrew Franz vs. Official Assignee- AIR 1966 Bom. 121; (1965) 2 LLJ 478].*

The protection against attachment granted under Section 10 shall continue to be available even after an employee leaves service till he withdraws the amount standing to his credit. So long as the amount does not cease to have the character of provident fund either by payment of the same to employee or by removing it from credit in his provident fund ledger, the immunity against attachment continues. Section 10 gives immunity to a retired employee also so long as the amount continues to lie in deposit with the employer and has not been paid over to the employee- *[A. Subbiah vs. Thiruvenkataswami- 1971 Lab.I.C. 1595 (Mad.) relying on Union of India vs. Hira Devi- AIR 1952 SC 227; Mettur Industries vs. Velayutha Mudaliar- (1961) 1 LLJ 279 and Syed Abdul Azeez Khan vs. Flower- (1967) 1 LLJ 796; 1968 LabIC 441 (Mad).]*

*In the case of **Vallabhaneni Ratnakumari vs. Katta Subbarvamma- [(1994) 2 LLJ 81]*** a question arose whether the amount standing to the credit of the deceased employee of Andhra Scientific Company, taken over by Bharat Electronics, could be attached. The amount was general insurance amount arising out of a group insurance scheme (in lieu of EDLI). The Andhra Pradesh High Court answered the question in negative and observed that a combined reading of sub-section (1) and (2) of Section 10 made it abundantly clear that the amount in question was not liable to be attached whatever might be the extent of debt or liability incurred by the deceased employee.

Order of attachment by a court- The R.P.F.C. Karnataka challenged the order of a Magistrate by which the provident fund amount of respondents 2 had been attached to recover the arrears of maintenance awarded to respondents 1 (a) to 1(f) under Section 125, Cr.P.C. However, by the time the case came up before the High Court, respondent 2 had retired and the amount of the provident fund, having become payable to him, was deposited in the court. In these peculiar circumstances of the case, the Karnataka High Court, although found the order of attachment to be contrary to Section 10 (1) of the Act, did not quash the same. Rather observing that its order in the instant case should not be taken as a precedent in any case, the High Court directed the amount deposited in the court to be paid to respondents 1(a) to 1(f) according to the order passed by the court. The High Court further directed that the court should not issue any further FLW in respect of the amount, if any, available on the provident fund account in respect of respondent 2 for any claim of maintenance- *[R.P.F. Commissioner Vs. Puttamma, (1999) 1 LLJ 377; (1999) 1 CLR 820 (Kant)].*

A scheme of provident fund prepared by an establishment exempted under Section 17 (1) of the Act is very much a scheme under the Act and the benefits conferred by the Act on the members of the fund under the scheme drawn up by the appropriate government will also be available to the members covered under the scheme framed by the exempted establishment and approved by the appropriate authority. Such a scheme has the same statutory force as a scheme under the Act. It, therefore, follows that the protection against attachment as laid down under Section 10 of the Act applies to such a scheme also. Such protection extends to all the components which go to make up the fund established under the scheme - *[Tata Iron & Steel Co. Ltd. Vs. Bir Singh- (1983) 63 FJR 32 (Pat)].*

II. Employer not to reduce wages:

Section 12 prohibits the employer from reducing wages etc. with a view to reduce his own liability under the Act. It includes paying employer share of contribution at a higher rate or on higher wages,

Safeguards

but it does not cover the higher rate of contribution being paid under the notification issued under proviso to section 6 or proviso to pare 29 of the EPF Scheme, 1952.

Section **12. Employer not to reduce wages, etc.** - *No employer in relation to an establishment to which any Scheme or the Insurance Scheme applies shall, by reason only of his liability for the payment of any contribution to the Fund or the Insurance Fund or any charges under this Act or the Scheme or the Insurance Scheme reduce whether directly or indirectly, the wages of any employee to whom the Scheme or the Insurance Scheme applies or the total quantum of benefits in the nature of old age pension, gratuity, provident fund or life insurance to which the employee is entitled under the terms of his employment, express or implied.*

Section 12 prevails over any trust deed or regulations there under which provide for deductions from the amount of pension on account of payment of provident fund amount. Even assuming that the parties had by private treaty agreed to the deductions before the coming into force of these beneficial provisions, they cannot now be deprivatory. Even if the regulations acquire a statutory flavour, they must be held to be invalid as they operate contrary to Section 12 of the EPF Act, 1952 and the Payment o Gratuity Act, 1972- *[Som Prakash Rekhi vs. UOI- (1981) 1 SCC 449; 1981 SCC (L&S) 200; (1981) 1 LLJ 79.]*

The scheme framed by an establishment prior to its coverage by the Act required contribution at the rate of 10 percent. After the coverage the rate of contribution was reduced to the statutory minimum of 8 percent. The Karnataka High court held that merely because the Act said that the contribution would be a 8 percent such a reduction was not warranted. The High Court rejected the employer's contention that Section 12 would apply only to a case where originally the unit was covered by the Act but for some reason or the other ceased to be so covered- *[R.P.F.Commissioner vs. Harihar Polyfibres – (1991) 2 LLN 948; 1992 LabIC 202; (1992) 1 CLR 517 (Kat-DB) reversing Harihar Polyfibres vs. RPFC- (1990) 1 CLR 342; 60 FLR 195; (1991) 2 LLJ 477].*

Also see the Supreme Court case of *Marathwada Gramin Bank Karmachari sanghathan* as discussed in chapter - 9.

Step by Step Into EPF

> *Exemptions from the Schemes*

Chapter 13

Exemptions

> ### Brief badinage–
>
> *Apart from the exclusions allowed to the establishments to enjoy in section 16, there had been certain establishments, which used to manage provident fund schemes at their own guided by the Provident Funds Act, 1925 and to keep that as per their suitability. Those funds were neither registered nor recognized by any law and supervision thereof by any authority. However, the efforts of those employers have been recognized by the EPF Act. They were given opportunity to get their schemes, funds recognized under the EPF Act and registered under the Trust Act so as to ensure the safeguard of the employees funds to keep secured and answerable to the authority under the E.P.F. & M.P. Act, 1952. This opportunity is initially available under section 15 to an establishment. But where a group of companies, or having various factories or establishments under one umbrella of an employer, whether, it is enjoyable by all the employees of all such establishments or not? The problem lies in the interpretation of section 2A under which the authorities used to find nexus between and club two or more establishments together to make the Act applicable, with a view to snatch away the infancy period that the employer use to claim to avail, whereas, the employers do insist for. Now, the infancy period stand withdrawn, there is hardly any cases to contest for clubbing or so, but, this doctrine has provided a green field for the employers to show unified group of establishments and make them participant in a provident fund trust as a single establishment instead of individual establishment participating in common provident fund, which make possible to leakage, decays in implantation of the Act and management of the fund. Un-earthed scams of different provident funds have alarmed the authorities to adopt a correct and vigilant go. However, the law allows to avail exemptions.*

Section - 15:- **Special provisions relating to existing provident funds-**

(1) [1][Subject to the provisions of section 17, every employee who is a subscriber to any provident fund or [2][an establishment] to which this Act applies shall, pending the application of a Scheme to] the [2][establishment] in which he is employed, continue to be entitled to the benefits accruing to him under the provident fund, and the provident fund shall continue to be maintained in the same manner and subject to the same conditions as it would have been if this Act had not been passed.

(2) [1][On the application of any Scheme to [2][an establishment], the accumulations in any provident fund of the [2][establishment], standing to the credit of the employees who become members of the Fund established under the Scheme] shall, notwithstanding anything to the contrary contained in any law for the time being in force or in any deed or other instrument establishing the provident fund but subject to the provisions, if any, contained in the Scheme, be transferred to the fund established under the Scheme, and shall be credited to the accounts of the employees entitled thereto in the Fund.

---
1. Substituted by Sec. 14 of Act 37 of 1953.
2. Substituted by Sec. 3 of Act 94 of 1956.

[Section - **16A. Authorising certain employers to maintain provident fund accounts** - (1) The Central Government may, on an application made to it in this behalf by the employer and the majority of employees in relation to an establishment employing one hundred or more persons, authorise the employer by an order in writing, to maintain a provident fund account in relation to the establishment, subject to such terms and conditions as may be specified in the Scheme:

Provided that no authorisation shall be made under this sub-section if the employer of such establishment had committed any default in the payment of provident fund contribution or had committed any other offence under this Act during the three years immediately preceding the date of such authorisation.

(2) Where an establishment is authorised to maintain a provident fund account under sub-section (1), the employer in relation to such establishment shall maintain such account, submit such return, deposit the contribution in such manner, provide for such facilities for inspection, pay such administrative charges, and abide by such other terms and conditions, as may be specified in the Scheme.

(3) Any authorisation made under this section may be cancelled by the Central Government by order in writing if the employer fails to comply with any of the terms and conditions of the authorisation or where he commits any offence under any provision of this Act:

Provided that before cancelling the authorisation, the Central Government shall give the employer a reasonable opportunity of being heard.]

---

1. Inserted by Act 33 of 1988 S. 22. (This section has not so far been notified hence no effect).

Section–1[**17:- Power to exempt-** (1) The appropriate Government may, by notification in the Official Gazette, and subject to such conditions as may be specified in the notification, 2[exempt, whether prospectively or retrospectively, from the operation] of all or any of the provisions of any Scheme -

(a) any 3[establishment] to which this Act applies, if, in the opinion of the appropriate Government, the rules of its provident fund with respect to the rates of contribution are not less favourable than those specified in section 6 and the employees are also in enjoyment of other provident fund benefits which on the whole are not less favourable to the employees than the benefits provided under this Act or any Scheme in relation to the employees in any other 3[establishment] of a similar character; or

(b) any 3[establishment] if the employees of such 3[establishment] are in enjoyment of benefits in the nature of provident fund, pension or gratuity and the appropriate Government is of opinion that such benefits, separately or jointly, are on the whole not less favourable to such employees than the benefits provided under this Act or any Scheme in relation to employees in any other 3[establishment] of a similar character.

4[Provided that no such exemption shall be made except after consultation with the Central Board which on such consultation shall forward its views on exemption to the appropriate Government within such time limit as may be specified in the Scheme.]

5[XXX]

2[(1A). Where an exemption has been granted to an establishment under clause (a) of sub-section 1,

(a) the provisions of sections 6, 7A, 8 and 14B shall, so far as may be, apply to the employer of the exempted establishment in addition to such other conditions as may be specified in the notification granting such exemption, and where such employer contravenes, or makes default in complying with any of the said provision or conditions or any other provision of this Act, he shall be punishable under section 14 as if the said establishment had not been exempted under the said clause a;

(b) the employer shall establish a Board of Trustees for the administration of the provident fund consisting of such number of members as may be specified in the Scheme;

(c) the terms and conditions of service of members of the Board of Trustees shall be such as may be specified in the Scheme;

(d) the Board of Trustees constituted under clause (b) shall –

(i) maintain detailed accounts to show the contributions credited, withdrawals made and interest accrued in respect of each employee;

(ii) submit such returns to the Regional Provident Fund Commissioner or any other officer as the Central Government may direct from time to time;

(iii) invest the provident fund monies in accordance with the directions issued by the Central Government from time to time;

(iv) transfer, where necessary, the provident fund account of any employee; and

(v) perform such other duties as may be specified in the Scheme.

(IB) Where the Board of Trustees established under clause (b) of sub-section (1A) contravenes, or makes default in complying with, any provisions of clause (d) of that sub-section, the Trustees of the said Board shall be deemed to have committed an offence under sub-section (2A) of section 14 and shall be punishable with the penalties provided in that sub-section.]

[6][(IC) The appropriate Government may, by notification in the Official Gazette, and subject to the condition on the pattern of investment of pension fund and such other conditions as may be specified therein, exempt any establishment or class of establishments from the operation of the Pension Scheme if the employees of such establishment or class of establishments are either members of any other pension scheme or propose to be members of such pension scheme, where the pensionary benefits are at par or more favourable than the Pension Scheme under this Act.]

(2) Any Scheme may make provision for exemption of any person or class of persons employed in any [3][establishment] to which the Scheme applies from the operation of all or any of the provisions of the Scheme, if such person or class of persons is entitled to benefits in the nature of provident fund, gratuity or old age pension and such benefits, separately or jointly, are on the whole not less favourable than the benefits provided under this Act or the Scheme:

Provided that no such exemption shall be granted in respect of a class of persons unless the appropriate Government is of opinion that the majority of persons constituting such class desire to continue to be entitled to such benefits.

[7][(2A) [2][The Central Provident Fund Commissioner may, if requested so to do by the employer, by notification in the Official Gazette, and subject to such conditions as may be specified in the notification, exempt, whether prospectively or retrospectively, any establishment from the operation of all or any of the provisions of the Insurance Scheme, if he is satisfied that the employees of such

establishment are, without making any separate contribution or payment of premium, in enjoyment of benefits in the nature of life insurance, whether linked to their deposits in provident fund or not, and such benefits are more favourable to such employees than the benefits admissible under the Insurance Scheme.]

(2B) Without prejudice to the provisions of sub-section 2A, the Insurance Scheme may provide for the exemption of any person or class of persons employed in any establishment and covered by that scheme from the operation of all or any of the provisions thereof, if the benefits in the nature of life insurance admissible to such person or class of persons are more favourable than the benefits provided under the Insurance Scheme.]

8[(3) Where in respect of any person or class of persons employed in an establishment an exemption is granted under this section from the operation of all or any of the provisions of any Scheme whether such exemption has been granted to the establishment wherein such person or class of persons is employed, or to the person or class of persons as such, the employer in relation to such establishment -

(a) shall, in relation to the provident fund, pension and gratuity to which any such person or class of persons is entitled, maintain such accounts, submit such returns, make such investment, provide for such facilities for inspection and pay such inspection charges, as the Central Government may direct.

(b) shall not, at any time after the exemption, without the leave of the Central Government, reduce the total quantum of benefits in the nature of pension, gratuity or provident fund to which any such person or class of persons was entitled at the time of exemption; and

(c) shall, where any such person leaves his employment and obtains re-employment in another establishment to which this Act applies, transfer within such time as may be specified in this behalf by the Central Government, the amount of accumulations to the credit of that person in the provident fund of the establishment left by him to the credit of that person's account in the provident fund of the establishment in which he is re-employed or, as the case may be, in the Fund established under the Scheme applicable to the establishment.]

7[(3A) Where, in respect of any person or class of persons employed in any establishment, an exemption is granted under sub-section (2A) or sub-section (2B) or from the operation of all or any of the provisions of the Insurance Scheme whether such exemption is granted to the establishment wherein such person or class of persons is employed or to the person or class of persons as such, the employer in relation to such establishment –

(a) shall, in relation to the benefits in the nature of life insurance, to which any such person or class of persons is entitled, or any insurance fund, maintain such accounts, submit such returns, make such investments, provide for such facilities for inspection and pay such inspection charges, as the Central Government may direct;

(b) shall not, at any time after the exemption without the leave of the Central Government, reduce the total quantum of benefits in the nature of life insurance to which any such person or class of persons was entitled immediately before the date of the exemption.

9[XXX]

9[(c) XXX]]

Exemptions

[10][(4) Any exemption granted under this section may be cancelled by the authority which granted it, by order in writing, if an employer fails to comply, -

(a) in the case of an exemption granted under sub-section 1, with any of the conditions imposed under that sub-section [11][or sub-section (1A)] or with any of the provisions of sub-section 3; [12][XXX]

[11][(aa) in the case of an exemption granted under sub-section 2 [(1C)], with any of the conditions imposed under that sub-section; and]

[13][(b) in the case of an exemption granted under sub-section (2), with any of the provisions of sub-section (3);]

[7][(c) in the case of an exemption granted under sub-section (2A), with any of the conditions imposed under that sub-section or with any of the provisions of sub-section (3A);

(d) in the case of an exemption granted under sub-section (2B), with any of the provisions of sub-section (3A).]

[10][(5) Where any exemption granted under sub-section (1), sub-section 2[(1C)], [14][sub-section (2), sub-section (2A) or sub-section (2B)] is cancelled, the amount of accumulations to the credit of every employee to whom such exemption applied, in the provident fund, 14[the [6][Pension] Fund or the Insurance Fund] of the establishment in which he is employed together with any amount forfeited from the employer's share of contribution to the credit of the employee who leaves the employment before the completion of the full period of service shall be transferred within such time and in such manner as may be specified in the Scheme or the [6][Pension] Scheme [14][or the Insurance Scheme] to the credit of his account in the Fund or the [6][Pension] Fund [14][or the Insurance Fund], as the case may be.

[10][(6) Subject to the provisions of sub-section 2[(1C)], the employer of an exempted establishment or of an exempted employee of an establishment to which the provisions of the [6][Pension] Scheme apply, shall, notwithstanding any exemption granted under sub-section (1) or sub-section (2), pay to the 6[Pension] Fund such portion of the employer's contribution [20][XXX] to its provident fund within such time and in such manner as may be specified in the [6][Pension] Scheme.]

1.	Substituted by Sec. 16 of Act 37 of 1953 in place of original section.
2.	Substituted by Sec. 23 of Act 33 of 1988 (w.e.f. 1.8.1988).
3.	Substituted by Sec. 3 of Act 94 of 1956.
4.	Inserted by Sec.23 of Act 33 of 1988 (w.e.f. 1.8.1988).
5.	Explanation deleted by Sec.11 of Act 28 of 1963.
6.	Substituted by Sec. 25 of Act 25 of 1996 (w.e.f. 16.11.1995).
7.	Inserted by Sec.34 of Act 99 of 1976 (w.e.f. 1.8.1976).
8.	Substituted by Sec.11 of Act 28 of 1963.
9.	Deleted by Sec.23 of Act 33 of 1988 (w.e.f. 1.8.1988).
10.	Inserted by Sec. 27 of Act 16 of 1971 (w.e.f. 23.4.1971).
11.	Inserted by Sec.23 of Act 33 of 1988 (w.e.f. 1.8.1988).
12.	Deleted by Sec. 27 of Act 16 of 1971 (w.e.f. 23.4.1971).
13.	Substituted by Sec.11 of Act 28 of 1963.
14.	Substituted by Sec.34 of Act 99 of 1976 (w.e.f. 1.8.1976).
15.	Deleted by Sec. 25 of Act 25 of 1996 (w.e.f. 16.11.1995).

Legislative reference:

The original section ran as follows-

Section 17- *"The appropriate government may, by notification in the Official Gazette, and subject to such conditions as may be specified in the notification, exempt from the operation of this Act, or of any scheme-*

(a) Any factory to which it applies if the rules of provident fund with respect to contributions are in conformity with, or are more favourable to the employees therein than those specified in this Act, and, if in the opinion of the appropriate government, the employees are otherwise in enjoyment of provident fund benefits generally which are on the whole not less favourable to the employees than the benefits provided under this Act or under any scheme in relation to employees un any factory of a similar character;

Explanation.- The following condition shall be deemed to be always included in the conditions which may be specified in a notification under clause (a), namely:

(i) The amount of accumulation in the provident fund shall be invested in such manner as the Central Government may direct;

(ii) The amount of accumulations to the credit of an employee in the provident fund shall, where he leaves is employment and obtains re-employment in another factory to which this Act applies within such time as may be specified in this behalf by the Central Government, be transferred to the credit of his account in the Fund established under the Scheme applicable to the factory;

(b) Any class of persons employed in any factory, if the Central Government is of the opinion that such class of persons is entitled to benefits in the nature of old age pension or gratuity or both, benefits which are on the whole not less favourable to such persons than the benefits provided under this Act or under any scheme in relation to persons employed un any factory of similar character:

Provided that no notification under clause (b) shall be issued unless the Central Government is satisfied that the majority of persons so employed desire to continue to be entitled to such benefits:

Provided further that it shall not apply to any person who has been employed in the factory for not less than ten year and who by a declaration in writing opts for the benefits to which he was entitled before the date of the notification."

Thereafter, the section was replace by the Act 37 of 1953 which is at present in force with the amendments brought-in in the section replacing the word 'factory' by 'establishment (by the Act 94 of 1956); inserting sub-sections (2A) and (2B) and (3A) (by Act 99 of 1976) providing for exemption from EDLI Scheme, 1976 which has further been replaced by Act 33 of 1988. By that amending Act of 1988, sub-sections (1A), (1B) were inserted, and by the Act 16 of 1971, sub-sections (1A), and (3A) were inserted. Similarly, other amendments were brought in as exist at present.

Related provisions in the **Employees' Provident Funds Scheme, 1952:-**

Para. [1][*27. Exemption of an employee* — *(1) A Commissioner may by order I and subject to such conditions as may be specified in the order exempt from the operation of all or any of the provisions of this Scheme an employee to whom the Scheme applies on receipt of application in Form-I from such an employee.*

Provided that such an employee is entitled to benefits in the nature of Provident Fund, gratuity or old age pension according to the rules of the factory or other establishment and such benefits separately or jointly are on the whole not less favourable than the benefits provided under the Act and the Scheme. 1

(2) Where an employee is exempted as aforesaid, the employer shall in respect of such employee maintain such account, submit such returns, provide such facilities for inspection, pay such inspection charges and invest provident fund collections in such manner as the Central Government may direct.

(3) An employee exempted under sub-paragraph (1) may by an application to the Commissioner make a declaration that he shall become a member of the Fund.

(4) No employee shall be granted exemption or permitted to apply out of exemption more than once on each account.]

1.	Subs. by G.S.R. 852, dated 6.5.1963.

Para. [1][27A. Exemption of a class of employees — *(1) [2][The appropriate Government] may by order and subject to such conditions as may be specified in the order exempt from the operation of all or any of the provisions of this Scheme any class of employees to whom the Scheme applies:*

Provided that such class of employees is entitled to benefits in the nature of provident fund, gratuity or old age pension according to the rules of the [3][factory or other establishment] and such benefits separately or jointly are on the whole not less favourable than the benefits provided under the Act and this Scheme.

(2) Where any class of employees is exempted as aforesaid, the employer shall in respect of such class of employees maintain such account, submit such returns, provide such facilities for inspection, pay such inspection charges and invest provident fund collections in such manner as the Central Government may direct.

(3) A class of employees exempted under sub-paragraph (1) or the majority of employees constituting such class may by an application to the Commissioner make a declaration that the class of employees shall become member of the Fund.

(4) No class of employees shall be granted exemption or permitted to apply out of exemption more than once on each account.

(5) The provisions of this paragraph shall be deemed to have come into force with effect from the 14th of October, 1953.]

1.	Added by S.R.O. 2035, dated 31.10.1953.
2.	Subs. by G.S.R. 1286, dated 13.10.1961.
3.	Subs. by S.R.O. 1363, dated 26.4.1957.

Para-27AA:-Terms and conditions of exemption, *(text is available in under foregoing paragraphs)*

Para-28:- Transfer of accumulations from existing Provident Funds, *(text is available in under going para)*

Para-79:- Special provisions relating to factories and other establishments in respect of which applications for exemption are received *(text is available in under going para)*

Para-79B:- Time limit for communicating the views of the Central Board to the appropriate government on a proposal for grant of exemption to an establishment. *(text is available in under going para)*

I. Exclusion and exemption, *difference between*:

A misconception is commonly working now-a-days among the employers and the officers also after various High Courts and many Supreme Court judgements on the issue of exclusion under section 16 of the Act. This has led into making a mess of the social security enactment, like the EPF & MP Act, 1952. **One should not forget that provisions of section 16 are invokable before the Act is applied. After application of the Act, section 16 should not and cannot be invoked.** If, such circumstances invites that an establishment is to be excluded, than there is a separate remedy provided for that and that is available under section 17 only. The provisions of clause (b) of sub-section (1) of the section 17 have provided for an exemption to an establishment, employees of which are in enjoyment of benefits in the nature of provident fund, pension or gratuity and the appropriate government is of the opinion that such benefits, separately or jointly, are on the whole not less favourable to such employees than those provided under the Act or any Scheme.

To be more specific, the wordings of section 16 are to be re-traveled. The opening words of the section are **'The Act shall not apply'** which have a perpetual nexus with the wordings and provisions of section 1(3), which opens with the words **'Subject to the provisions contained in section 16, it applies'**. Undoubtedly, the legislation has taken care of the situation which may warrant invocation of provision of section 16 after the Act has been applied to an establishment, and sufficient care has been taken by providing for exemption to such an establishment.

On this matter, a particular case may through light, which can be discussed here.

The Act was extended to certain establishments under the following categories, popularly known as the **'educational institutes'** vide notification No. SO 986 dated 19.2.1982 (w.e.f. 6.3.1982). Those are-

(i) **Any university,**

(ii) **Any college whether or not affiliated to a university,**

(iii) **Any school, whether or not recognized or aided by the central or a state government,**

(iv) **Any scientific institution**

(v) **Any institution in which research in respect of any matter is carried on,**

(vi) **Any other institution in which the activity of imparting knowledge or training is systematically carried on.**

The Schemes were made applicable to such institution w.e.f. 6.7.1982. Some institutions challenged the validity of the notification and the Supreme Court upheld the validity of the notification by an order dated 8.1.1988.

Owners of some aided schools in Rajasthan did not feel comfortable with the application of the Act and willing to continue to follow the arrangement made by the state government under Local Fund Audit Rules. In 1989, the state government enacted an Act known as The Rajasthan Non-Government Educational Institutions (Recognition and other Conditions) Act, 1989 which provided framing of provident fund in the Rules to be framed, which, were notified and made applicable w.e.f. 1.1.1993. In the state Act and in the Rules also, there was a provision of exempting any institution from any of the provision(s) of the said Rules. Accordingly, the state government issued a notification exempting all aided educational institutes from the operation of the provisions related to the provident fund with a view to continue to apply the EPF & MP Act, 1952. Aggrieved by this, some (more than 20) schools filed writ before the Rajasthan High Court which was disposed off in 2000 declaring that –

(1) the power to exempt was un-constitutional;

(2) since the power to grant recognition and cancel the recognition to any institution is with the state government, such institutions are under the **control of the state government,** as required under clause (b) of sub-section (1) of section 16 of the PF Act;

(3) the state Act has provided for establishment of a provident fund for the employees of the educational institutions, and they are getting (or supposed to get) benefit of the provident fund;

(4) being the social security area in the Concurrent List of the Constitution, and the state Act covering same area has been give accent by the President of India, in 1989 under **Article 35...**, it has to prevail over the central Act of 1952;

(5) the amount deposited with Regional PF Commissioner was to be refunded to the institutions in a time-bound manner to deposit the same with state government treasury in a Personal Account.

The order was challenged before the Division Bench which upheld it vide order dated 12.2.2002, then appealed before the Supreme Court, which did not grant stay, but admitted it and finally disposed of on 31.10.2006. During this period, on seeking advice about the effect of the order in 2002, the standing counsel advised to exclude all the educational institutes in Rajasthan, without any advice of taking other related provisions of section 16(1) (b) or (c) or section 17 (1) (b) or section 1(5) of the Act into consideration. After the order of the Supreme Court, the PF Commissioner started refund of the contributions received even since 1982. Neither the counsel nor the court spoke of the position prior to the notification of the state Rules or the date of the pronouncement of the order by the Division Bench, whether the applicability of the PF Act would remain or it would nullify the application of the Act since March, 1982.

In fact, in such a situation, the interpretation was required to be made in the light of the Supreme court's view taken initially in various cases, where it has emphasized that the PF Act is a piece of social legislation, and in the interpretation, its elasticity should cover the interests of the employees. No rigid view should be taken which deprives the beneficiaries/employees.

Therefore, there should be a clear demarcation between the *exclusion* **and the** *exemption.*

Exclusion is available from the Act itself, whereas the exemption is granted from the operation of a scheme. Exemption is not available from all the three Schemes, simultaneously, whereas the exclusion confers non-application of the Act.

Exemption does not mean that an exempted establishment will enjoy liberty not to consider the statutory schemes. As a matter of principle, the exemption for the operation of any scheme is the exemption from the provisions of the statutory scheme which cover the part of benefits such as—

Chapter Four – except paragraphs 26B, 27, 27A, 27AA and 28.

Chapter Five - except paragraphs 31, 32, 32A and 32B.

Chapter Six - except paragraphs 45 and 46.

Chapter Seven -except paragraph 60.

Chapter Eight – except paragraph 61.

Chapter Nine – except paragraphs 76, 78, 79, 79A, 79B, and 79 C.

All other provisions of the Scheme including those mentioned above as exceptions will continue to apply on the establishment granted exemption.

II. Pre-requisite for the exemption:

Not much harder requirements have been put for grant of exemption either to an establishment or a class of employees, as the case may be. For both types of exemption, condition is that the benefits available under the scheme of the establishment should not be less favourable than those are available under the Act and the schemes framed there-under. This is the general measurement. Beyond that, to be specific in respect of a particular case, specific provisions to be referred.

There separate provisions for separate scheme are made in the Act. Accordingly, the exemptions available are:-

From the Employees' Provident Funds Scheme, 1952

1: Exemption to the whole of the establishment from the operation of the Scheme,
2: Exemption to class of employees from the operation of the Scheme,
3: Exemption to an employees from the operation of the Scheme.

From the Employees' Pension Scheme, 1995

1: Exemption to the whole of the establishment from the operation of the Scheme,
2: Exemption to class of employees from the operation of the Scheme.

From the Employees' Deposit-linked Insurance Scheme, 1976

1: Exemption to an employee from the operation of the Scheme.

For the exemption to an establishment from the operation of the Scheme, provisions have been made in the Act itself under section 17(1) and for the rest, the Act contains enabling provision in section 17(2) deriving powers where from, provisions for exemptions have been made in the respective schemes.

Accordingly, in Employees' Provident Funds Scheme, 1952, under paragraph 27-A exemption to a class of employees is available, and under paragraph 27, an individual employee can be granted exemption.

In employees' Pension Scheme, 1995, provisions for **whole of the establishment as well as for a class of employees** have been provided under paragraph 39.

In the Employees' Deposit-linked Scheme, 1976, the available provisions under paragraph 28 are **for individual** exemption only.

III. Exemption to an establishment:

The power to grant exemption to an establishment is vested in the appropriate government. Hence the application is to be addressed to the appropriate government through the Secretary to Government of India (or state), Ministry of Labour. Section 17 (1) of the Act provides for exemption to an establishment.

The first and foremost requirement is that there must be a provident fund scheme in existence, only then the question of exemption under which provision is available can be considered.

1. **The first category of establishments seeking exemption is** – the provident fund rules of the establishment provides for a **higher rate of contribution** than it is provided in section 6

of the Act; and also the other provident fund benefits provided in the rules, on the whole are not less favourable than those which are available in the statutory scheme.

2. And, **the second category of the establishments seeking exemption is** – the employees of which are in enjoyment of **benefits in the nature of provident fund, pension or gratuity** and such benefits, separately or jointly are, on the whole not less favourable to such employees than the benefits provided under the Act i.e. in the Scheme.

It is also relevant to mention that when the provision was initially drafted, there was intention to implement the Employees' Provident Fund Scheme, 1952 only; hence, the requirement of benefits under the private schemes were compared to the available provident fund benefits only. But, at present, over a period of time, and as per requirement of the time, new schemes have been introduced under the Act with a view to provide more benefits of different nature, like the Pensions, the Insurance - linked with the deposits in the provident fund account of a member etc.. Therefore, the requirement for exemption as found in the statute always found to be less beneficial in the private provident fund schemes or rules than those are available under the Act, and the exemption under clause (b) does not attract attention or eyes, usually.

There were, and now also may be some cases, where an establishment may be having its own provident fund scheme or rules and on application of the Act, the establishment may want to continue with their existing arrangement of provident fund therefore, may choose to get exemption. But, immediately, it may not be possible for the establishment to move application for exemption to the appropriate government. To counter such a situation, the statute has taken care of and sufficient provisions have been made in section 15. This section gives automatic relaxation to such an establishment to continue with their own scheme, with the inherent direction that 'subject to the provisions of section 17' under which the employer is required to submit application for exemption to the appropriate government following the other mandatory provisions.

IV. Exemption to a person or a class of employees:

Sub-section (2) of section 17 provides for exemption to a person or a class of employees as per the provisions made in the Scheme. Accordingly, for exemption for an employee is available under paragraph 27 and for a class of employees, it is available under paragraph 27A of the Scheme. For individual exemption, the employee may choose to contribute to a provident fund of the same employer otherwise it is not permitted. However, for exemption to a class of employees, the provident fund must be of the establishment it-self or of the group of establishments under the same employer. If it is not there, the employer has to constitute a board of trustees and make rules for the maintenance of the provident fund in respect of the class of employees. Other procedure is the same as in respect of establishment seeking exemption under section 17 (1). On receipt of an application for exemption under under section 17 (1) or under paragraph 27A of the Scheme, the Regional Commissioner is required to invoke paragraph 79 and give relaxation to work with their PF and go on to finalize the request.

While granting exemption under paragraph 27 of the Scheme, the Commissioner can impose additional conditions to protect the private Fund from risk factors – *[Rhone Poulenc Employees' Union vs. R.P.F. Commissioner –(1996) 2 LLJ 1001; (1996) 3 LLN 709 (Bom.)].*

V. Relaxation pending exemption and the terms and conditions:

Further, beyond the above statutory requirement for exemption, with a view to bring uniformity, some mandatory provisions have been made in the scheme which are reproduced here -

Para-79:- Special provisions relating to factories and other establishments in respect of which applications for exemption are received – Notwithstanding anything contained in this Scheme, the Commissioner may, in relation to a factory or other establishment in respect of which an application for exemption under section 17 of the Act has been received, relax pending the disposal of the application the provisions of the Scheme in such manner as he may direct.

Here, the commissioner has been given exclusive power to put conditions, but with a view to bring uniformity in the process and practices, the conditions have been drafted and made mandatory by putting those under paragraph 27AA. Those are reproduced here-under-

Para-27AA:- Terms and conditions of exemption- All exemptions already granted or to be granted hereafter under section 17 of the Act or under paragraph 27-A of the Scheme shall be subject to the terms and conditions as given in the Appendix A.

Appendix A

Revised Condition for Grant of Exemption under Section 17 of the Employees' Provident Funds and Miscellaneous Act, 1952:

The following are the revised conditions for grant of exemption under section 17 of the Act, 1952:

1. The employer shall establish a Board of Trustees under his Chairmanship for the management of the Provident Fund according to such directions as may be given by the Central Government of the Central Provident Fund Commissioner, as the case may be, from time to time. The Provident Fund shall vest in the Board of Trustees who will be responsible for and accountable to the Employees' Provident Fund Organisation, inter alia, for proper accounts of the receipts into and payment from the Provident Fund and the balance in their custody. For this purpose, the 'employer' shall mean:

(i) in relation to an establishment, which is a factory, the owner or occupier of the factory; and

(ii) in relation to an establishment, the person who, or the authority, that has the ultimate control over the affairs of the establishment.

2. The Board of Trustees shall meet at least once in every three months and shall function in accordance with the guidelines that may be issued form time to time by the Central Government/ Central Provident Fund Commissioner (CPFC) or an officer authorized by him.

3. All employees, as defined in section 2(f) of the Act, who have been eligible to become members of the Provident Fund, had the establishment not been granted exemption, shall be enrolled as members.

4. Where an employee who is already a member of Employees' Provident Fund or a provident fund of any other exempted establishment is employed in his establishment, the employer shall immediately enroll his as a member of the fund. The employer should also arrange to have the accumulations in the provident fund account of such employee with his previous employer transferred and credited into his account.

5. The employer shall transfer to the Board of Trustees the contributions payable to the provident fund by himself and employees at the rate prescribed under the Act from time to time by the 15th of each month following the month for which the contributions are payable. The employer shall be liable to pay simple interest in terms of the provisions of section 7Q of the Act for any delay in payment of any dues towards the Board of Trustees.

6. The employer shall bear all the expenses of the administration of the Provident Fund and also make good may other loss that may be caused to the Provident Fund due to theft, burglary, defalcation, misappropriation or any other reason.

7. Any deficiency in the interest declared by the Board of Trustees is to be made good by the employer to bring it up to the statutory limit.

8. The employer shall display on the notice board of the establishment, a copy of the rules of the funds as approved by the appropriate authority and as and when amended thereto along with a translation in the language of the majority of the employees.

9. The rate of contribution payable, the conditions and quantum of advances and other matters laid down under the provident fund rules of the establishment and the interest credited to the account of each member, calculated on the monthly running balance of the member and declared by the Board of Trustees shall not be lower than those declared by the Central Government under the various provisions prescribed in the Act and the Scheme framed there under.

10. Any amendment in the Scheme, which is more beneficial to the employee than the existing rules of the establishment, shall be made applicable to them automatically pending formal amendment of the Rules of the Trust.

11. No amendment in the rules shall be made by the employer whithout the prior approval of the Regional Provident Fund Commissioner (referred to as RPFC hereafter). The RPFC shall before giving his approval give a reasonable opportunity to the employees to explain their point of view.

12. All claims for withdrawal, advances and transfers should be settled expeditiously, with in the maximum time prescribed by the Employees' Provident Funds Organisation.

13. The Board of Trustees shall maintain detailed accounts to show the contributions credited, withdrawals and interest in respect of each employee. The maintenance of such records should preferably be done electronically. The establishment should periodically transmit the details of members' accounts electronically as and when directed by the CPFC/RPFC.

14. The Board of Trustees shall issue an annual statement of accounts or pass-book to every employee within six months of the close of financial/accounting year free of cost once in the year. Addition printouts can be made available as and when the members want, subject to nominal charges. In case of passbook, the same shall remain in custody of employee to be updated periodically by the Trustees when presented to them.

15. The employer shall make necessary provisions to enable all the members to be able to see their account balance from the computer terminals as and when required by them.

16. The Board of Trustees and the employer shall file such returns monthly/ annually as may be prescribed by the Employees' Provident Fund Organisation within the specified time-limit, failing which it will be deemed as a default and the Board of Trustees and employer will jointly and separately be liable for suitable penal action by the Employees' Provident Fund Organisation.

17. The Board of Trustees shall invest the monies of the provident fund as per the directions of the Government from time to time. Failure to make investments as per directions of the Government shall make the Board of Trustees (and the employer) separately ad jointly liable to surcharge as may be imposed by the CPFC or his representative.

18. (a) The securities shall be obtained in the name of Trust. The securities so obtained should be in dematerialized (DEMAT) form and in case the required facility is not available in the area where the trust operates, the Board of Trustees shall inform the RPFC concerned about the same.

(b) The Board of Trustees shall maintain a script wise register and ensure timely realization of interest.

(c) The DEMAT Account should be opened through depository participants approved by Reserve Bank Of India and Central Government in this regard.

(d) The cost of maintaining DEMAT account should be treated as incidental cost of investment by the trust. Also all types of cost of investment like brokerage for purchase of securities etc. shall be treated as incidental cost of investment by the Trust.

19. All such investments made, like purchase of securities and bonds, should be lodged in the safe custody of depository participants, approved by Reserve Bank of India and Central Government, who shall be the custodian of the same. On closure of establishment or liquidation or cancellation of exemption from EPF Scheme, 1952, such custodian shall transfer the investment obtained in the name of the Trust and standing in its credit to the RPFC concerned directly on receipt of request from the RPFC concerned to that effect.

20. The exempted establishment shall intimate to the RPFC concerned the details of depository participants (approved by Reserve Bank of India and Central Government), with whom and in whose safe custody, the investments made in the name of trust, viz. Investments made in securities, bonds etc. have been lodged. However, the Board of Trustees may raise such sum or sums of money as may be required for meeting obligatory expenses such as settlement of claims, grant of advances as per rules and transfer of member's P.F. accumulations in the event of his/her leaving service of the employer and any other receipts by sale of the securities or other investments standing in the name of the Fund subject to the prior approval of the RPFC.

21. Any commission, incentive, bonus, or other pecuniary rewards given by any financial or other institutions for the investments made by the Trust should be credited to its account.

22. The employer and the members of the Board of Trustees, at the time of grant of exemption, shall furnish a written undertaking to the RPFC in such format as may be prescribed from time to time, inertalia, agreeing to abide by the conditions which are specified and this shall be legally binding on the employer and the Board of Trustees, including their successors and assignees, or such conditions as may be specified later for continuation of exemption.

23. The employer and the Board of Trustees shall also give an under-taking to transfer the funds promptly within the time limit prescribed by the concerned RPFC in the event of cancellation of exemption. This shall be legally binding on them and will make them liable for prosecution in the event of any delay in the transfer of funds.

24. (a) The account of the Provident Fund maintained by the Board of Trustees shall be subject to audit by a qualified independent chartered accountant annually. Where considered necessary, the CPFC or the RPFC in –charge of the Region shall have the right to have accounts re-audited by any other qualified auditor and the expenses so incurred shall be borne by the employer.

(b) A copy of the Auditor's report alongwith the audited balance sheet should be submitted to the RPFC concerned by the Auditors directly within six months after the closing of the financial year from 1st April to 31st March. The format of the balance sheet and the information ot be furnished in the report shall be as prescribed by the Employee' Provident Fund Organisation and made available with the RPFC Office in electronic format as well as a signed hard copy.

(c) The same auditors should not be appointed for two consecutive years and not more than two years in a block of six years.

25. A company reporting loss for three consecutive financial years or erosion in their capital base shall have their exmption withdrawn from the first day of the next / succeeding financial year.

26. The employer in relation to the exempted establishment shall provide for such facilities for inspection and pay such inspection charges as the Central Government may, form time to time direct under the close of every month.

27. In the event of any violation of the conditions for grant of exemption, by the employer or the Board of Trustees, the exemption granted may be cancelled after issuing a show cause notice in this regard to the concerned persons.

28. In the event of any loss to the trust as a result of any fraud, defalcation, wrong investment decisions etc. the employer shall be liable to make good the loss.

29. In case of any change of legal status of the establishment, which has been granted exemption, as a result of merger, demerger, acquisition, sale, amalgamation, formation of a subsidiary, whether wholly owned or not, etc., the exemption granted shall stand revoked and the establishment should promptly report the matter to the RPFC concerned for grant of fresh exemption.

30. In case, there are more than one unit/ establishment participating in the common Provident Fund Trust which has been granted exemption, all the trustees shall be jointly and sepsrately lliable/ responsible for any default committed by any of the trustees/ employer of any of the participating units and the RPFC shall take suitable legal action against all the trustees of the common Provident Fund Trust.

31. The Central Government may lay down any further conditions for continuation of exemption of the establishment.

Among these conditions, one related to formation of and re-constitution of the Board of Trustees on an interval, is most important as the responsibility to manage the private fund and keep it in secured hand so that no fraud may take place, a system to constitute or reconstitute the Board of Trustees has been defined under paragraph 79-C of the Scheme, which is mandatory to follow:-

[1]**[Para-79C:- Composition of the Board of Trustees of the exempted establishments and the terms and conditions of service of the trustees** -(1) The Board of Trustees of the establishment granted exemption under clause (a) of sub-section (2) of section 17 of the Act shall consist of not less than two and not more than six representatives each of the employers and emplpoyees. The number of trustees shall be so fixed, as to afford, as far as possible, representation to employees of each branch or department of the establishment. In the case of common provident fund for a group of two or more establishments, there will be at least one representative each from the participating establishment:*

[2]*[xxx]*

(2) The employer shall nominate his representatives on the Board of Trustees from amongst the officers employed in managerial or administrative capacity in the establishment.

(3) The representatives of the employees, on the Board of Trustees shall be nominated or elected in the following manner, namely:

- *(a) Wherever there is a union recognized by the employer under the Code of Discipline in industry or under any Act, such union shall nominate the representatives of the employees;*
- *(b) where there are more than on trade union recognized by the employer, the representatives of employees shall be elected by the members of the union in an election to be held for the purpose on any working day;*
- *(c) where there is no union recognized by the employer under the Code of Discipline in industry or under any Act but there are more than one registered union functioning in the*

establishment, the union having the largest number of members, subject to a minimum of 15 percent membership, shall have the right to nominate employees' representatives; and in case there is only one registered union, it shall have the right to nominate the employees' representative, provided it has a minimum of 15 percent membership.

[3][(4) *The employer shall be the Chairman of the Board of Trustees. In the event of equality of votes, the Chairman may exercise a casting vote.*]

[4][(5) *The term of office of the trustees shall be five years from the date of election or nomination. An outgoing Trustee shall be eligible for re-election or re-nomination. A Trustee elected or nominated to fill the casual vacancy shall hold office for the remaining period of the term of the trustee in whose place he is elected or nominated.*]

(6) *A person shall be disqualified form being a trustee if he:-*

  (a) *is declared to be of unsound mind by a competent court; or*

  (b) *has been convicted of an offence involving moral turpitude; or*

  (c) *is an undischarged insolvent; or*

  (d) *is an employer of an exempted or un-exempted establishment which has defaulted in payment of any dues under the Act.*

(7) *A person shall cease to be a Trustee of the Board if:-*

  (a) *he ceases to be an employee of the establishment; or*

  (b) *he cease to be a member of the provident fund of the establishment; or*

  (c) *the union on whose behalf he was elected or nominated, ceases to be recognized by the employer; or*

  (d) *he fails to attend three consecutive meetings of the Board without obtaining leave of absence from the Chairman of the Board of Trustees. The Chairman may, however, condone the absence of a trustee if he is satisfied that there were reasonable grounds for such absence.*

(8) *The procedure foe election or nomination of trustees, the quorum at the meeting of the board, records to be kept of the transaction of business and all other matters not specifically provided for in the Scheme shall be regulated as per the provisions of the approved provident fund rules of the establishment and the guidelines for the functioning of the Board of Trustees of the exempted establishments which the Commissioner may specify from time to time.*

(9) *In case of any dispute or doubt, the matter shall be referred to the Regional Provident Fund Commissioner in whose jurisdiction the head office of the establishment is located. The decision of the Commissioner in the matter shall be final and binding.*]

---

1. Inserted vide GSR 341 dated 9.7.1992 (w.e.f. 25.7.1992).
2. Provisio deleted vide GSR 658 (E) dated 10.11.2005 (w.e.f. 10.11.2005).
3. Substituted vide GSR 868 (E) dated 3.11.2003 (w.e.f. 6.11.2003).
4. Substituted vide GSR 18 dated 22.12.2000 (w.e.f. 6.1.2001)

Some-times back, there was a provision in this paragraph that not more than six establishments may participate in a trust, but, now that limitation has been removed w.e.f. 10-11-2005. For the present any number of establishments can participate in a common provident fund trust.

VI. Scope of Section 17:

Provisions of section 17 are not merely provisions dealing with a situation only, but, as the Bombay High Court has taken it, it is a complete Code. The Court has observed that the scheme of the Act and the Schemes clearly indicate that section 17 read on a whole constitute one complete ode dealing with exemptions and it is not possible to bifurcate the parameter of Section 17 (1) vis-à-vis Section 17 (2) of the Act, because, it will defeat the very object of the Act and it will defeat the entire scheme of the Provident Fund Act- *[Rhone-Poulene Employees' Union vs. R.P.F.C. and others- 1996 (2) LLJ. 1001 (Bom.)].*

After inserting supplementary provision in the Scheme, the effect of the exemption provisions have, become comprehensive. Even then, many employers take it as un-controlled powers with them to run the exempted funds as they wish. The rules of the P.F. of the Trust are subject to approval of the P.F. Authorities. Once those approved, it is tough to amend, if the directions of Supreme Court is followed that the P.F. Scheme of the appellant is not amended by the state government and as such the appellant was not legally bound to credit the accounts of respondent No. 1 to 9 with higher rate of interest declared by the Central Government – **[Jiyajeerao Cotton Mills Ltd. Vs. Dev Kumar Holani- 1998 (II) CLR 630 (SC)]**. Of-course, this judgement has prompted the Central Government to insert detailed conditions for exempted establishments in paragraph 27AA in the Scheme, inter-alia, making it mandatory that any inferior benefit or provision in the rules of the trust has to be prevailed-over by the statutory provisions, until suitable amendment is made in the rules through a due process. Thus, the above judgements stands taken care of by making it mandatory provisions. However, the Supreme Court has underlined the importance of the rules of a P.F. Trust.

The Division Bench of Karnataka High Court has also put an embargo on the employer who want to run the trust in his own fashion. In the case of **Binny Ltd. Bangalore vs. R.P.F.C. – [1999 (I) LLN.998 (Karn.DB)]**, it has been ruled that the rate of interest cannot be reduced in respect of exempted establishment merely because the yield from interest of P.F. moneys made in accordance with the pattern of investment prescribed by Central Government is insufficient to pay at statutory rate. As such, permission sought by the exempted establishment to pay at the rate below the statutory interest cannot be granted.

VII. Formation P.F. Trust and Application for exemption:

Prior to introduction of the E.P.F. & Misc. Provisions Act, 1952, some private provident funds existed and were working under the Provident Fund Act, 1925, and those were not even registered. After the Act of 1952 was passed, any establishment, which want to go with exemption has, first of all to get it's P.F. Trust registered under the Indian Trust Act, then make Rules of P.F. to regulate the fund entrusted to the Trust. At present, the E.P.F. Organisation has prepared Model Rules for such Trusts. Thereafter, an application, addressed to the Appropriate Government is to be submitted along with certain documents as detailed below-

1. Application for exemption duly signed by the employer addressed to the Appropriate Government.
2. Undertaking by employer to abide by the revised conditions governing the grant of exemption as provided in Appendix A under para 27 AA as amended form time to time.
3. Undertaking that all the eligible employees have been enrolled as members.

Exemptions

4. Consent of majority of employees/ or that of the Representative Union in favour of securing exemption.
5. Names and addresses of all the members of the Board of Trustees.
6. Two copies of the PF Trust Rules (as per Revised Model Rules) duly signed by all the Board of Trustees indicating their status in the Trust.
7. Copy of the Income Tax Recognition order.
8. Copy of objection, if any received from the employees for grant of exemption.
9. Certificate regarding enrolment of contract employees, if any, alongwith the name(s), code Nos., if any, already allotted to them.
10. Certificates of undertakings to abide by condition No. 22 and 23 of Appendix A to para 27AA as per prescribed proforma.
11. Copy of Audited Balance Sheet of the Trust for the last two years.
12. Copy of the Relaxation Order, if any, granted.
13. Comparison of benefits under the rules of the Trust (with statutory).
14. Whether the investment is made as per the Pattern of Investment prescribed from time to time.
15. Undertaking to maintain the accounts electronically.
16. Specific recommendation of the RPFC-I in Charge of the region for grant of exemption.
17. Mechanism proposed by the region to ensure that establishment is complying with the provisions of conditions of grant of exemption.
18. The payment/due which are to be paid by the establishment to EPFO even after grant of exemption viz. Employees' Pension Fund, Employees' Deposit Linked Insurance Fund (if not granted exemption), Administrative charges on inspection of EPS or EDLIS are to be shown.
19. Furnishing the ten check points in Annexure as prescribed by Ministry of Labour.
20. Any other additional information/documents, if any.

Submission of application:- It is the practice at present that the application is submitted to the concerned Regional P.F. Commissioner, and on examination of the same, he invokes the provisions of paragraph 79 grants relaxation to the establishment and thereafter, the employer, resubmits the application along with the copy of the relaxation order.

In the past, in many cases, it happened that the appropriate government received the application from an establishment and granted exemption without any notice or knowledge of the Commissioner or the Central Board of Trustees. Such action of the appropriate government put the Commissioner or the C.B.T. in an embracing position being the administrator of the Schemes. To over-come such a situation, a provision has been inserted in section 17 (1) itself as a *Provisio* which has made it a statutory requirement for the appropriate government to get the Central Board consulted on the issue of exemption, within a time-limit. The Central Board cannot be allowed to keep the matter pending for an indefinite period just to avoid or delay the notification. The time-limit has been fixed in paragraph 79-B, which reads as under-

Para-79B:- Time limit for communicating the views of the Central Board to the appropriate government on a proposal for grant of exemption to an establishment-

When an appropriate Government consults the Central Board with regard to its proposal for grant of exemption to an establishment under section 17 of the Act, the Board shall give its views

on the proposal within a period of three months from the date on which such proposal is received by it.

What does this provision mean with regard to the processing of an application exemption? The simplest version is, in the first instance, the application is to be submitted to the Appropriate Government completed in all respect, along with all the required documents and a copy of the same to be endorsed to the concerned Regional P.F. Commissioner for simultaneous scrutiny of the application. In this way, the Appropriate Government will initiate action for seeking opinion of the Central Board i.e. the Central P.F. Commissioner as per the above mentioned mandatory provisions. This process than will start counting the period laid down in paragraph 79 B.

VIII. Functions of the Board of Trustees:

All the functions with regard to maintenance of the funds and record of individual members' record, have been detailed in the 31 point conditions under paragraph 27AA, however, there are certain other matters and procedures on which suitable guidance is afforded by the **Inspector** or the Regional Commissioner concerned. Since, the employer is made fully responsible for the exempted fund management, even, it is obvious that default may take place and the fund of the employees may be in trouble. By the experience, in 1988, by the Act 33, Sub-section (1A) has been inserted in section 17, the provisions of section 6, 7A, 8 and 14B have been made applicable, which, by the interpretation, those are meant for un-exempted establishments, Now, the PF authorities are empowered to initiate action to (i) enforce the rate of contribution, (ii) determine the dues if not transferred to the Board of Trustees by the employer, (iii) go for enforcing recovery of any due by drawing a recovery certificate by the Recovery Officer, (iv) damages for the delayed transfer of PF dues to the Board of Trustees, and (v) and initiate penal action under section 14. Where an establishment has made an application for exemption from the Scheme under Section 17, till any decision is taken on the application, the employer is bound to comply with the provisions of the Act.-*[H.P. Agro Industries Corpn. Ltd. Vs. R.P.F.C. – 1994 Lab.IC 1286 (HP)].*

P.F. Commissioner has power to direct in terms of statutory provisions to transfer P.F. accumulations from one trust to another- *[Krishna Kumar Agarwala vs. Kelvin Jute Co. Ltd.- 2002 Lab.I.C. 3006 Cal.)].* Para 27AA refers to exemptions under section 17 of the Act and paragraph 27- A of the EPF Scheme. Reference to Sec. 17 of the Act to paragraph 27-AA would take into its compass the application made and exemption granted under paragraph 27-A also. The purpose of insertion of paragraph 27-AA was to impose certain terms and conditions on the employer in relation to the establishment, whom exemption has been granted. The Central Government found hat imposition of such conditions was necessary to safeguard the interests of the employees and greater control on the private provident fund schemes. In view of insertion of paragraph 27-AA, any doubts about the power of the commissioner to impose conditions for grant of exemption under paragraph 27- A and insistence on compliance with those conditions, also for continuance of the exemption already granted had vanished and the commissioner does have powers to impose conditions which were mentioned in Appendix A to paragraph 27 AA.-*[Pfizer Employees' Union and other vs. R.P.F,C. and others – 2000 (103) FJR 120].*

IX. Cancellation of Exemption:

In sub-section (4) of section 17, the general conditions have been laid down under which the exemption can be cancelled. The first and foremost condition is that the exemption can be cancelled by the authority who granted the exemption. Thus it is the appropriate government which can cancel the exemption. The power of cancellation of exemption is confined to the authority which granted it. The mere fact that the power of granting exemption was subsequently made exercisable by a State Government also would not empower it to cancel an exemption granted by another authority-*[R.K.L. Gupta vs. Ram Babu Lal- 1970 (I) LLJ.390].*

However, there are certain other conditions, under which the exemption stands cancelled automatically, if it is not re-processed a fresh. That is that, if the legal status of the establishment is changed, i.e. merger, demerger, acquisition, sale, amalgamation, formation of a subsidiary, whether wholly owned or not etc. as mentioned under the condition 29 under paragraph 27AA.

In case exemption is cancelled or stand cancelled, the employer has to transfer all the moneys lying in the trust as per balance sheet at the last day of such event. Such mandatory provisions are there under paragraph 28 of the Scheme in consonance of section 15. The purpose of the exemption is only to ensure a better scheme than Section 6 of the Act. It must be noted that notwithstanding, the exemption granted under section 17 of the Act, the appropriate Government does not lose its hold over the scheme framed by the establishment and there are built in safeguards in Section 17 itself to protect the interest of the employees and Section 17 is one such safeguard. Invoking this sub-section is not a penalty-*[N.K. Jain and other vs. C.K. Shah and others – 1991 Lab.I.C. 1013 (SC)].*

On cancellation of exemption of an establishment or otherwise, on transfer of an exempted employee to another exempted establishment or on becoming member of the statutory Scheme, the employer of the exempted establishment is under legal obligation to transfer the fund. In paragraph 28 of the Scheme which reads as under, the provision has been made –

Para-28:-Transfer of accumulations from existing Provident Funds- (1) Every authority in charge of, or entrusted with the management of, any Provident Fund in existence, the accumulations wherein are to be transferred to the Fund under sub-section (2) of section 15 of the Act, or sub-section (5) of section 17 thereof, as the case may be, shall

(i) send to the Commissioner, a statement showing the amount standing to the credit of each subscriber on the date of the transfer the total accumulations to the credit of the subscribers generally on that date and the advances, if any, taken by the subscriber within twenty five days of the application of the Scheme, or cancellation of exemption, as the case may be;

(ii) transfer to the Fund in the manner specified in sub-paragraph (2) the total accumulations standing to the credit of he subscribers in relation to each factory within ten days of the application of the Scheme, or cancellation of the exemption, as the case may be, in case of liquid cash in bank and within thirty days in case of securities; and

(iii) Transfer to the Central Board all pass books of account and other documents relating to the said accumulations.

(2) All accumulation standing to the credit of the subscribers, howsoever, invested, shall be transferred to the Fund by the authority aforesaid in cahs:

Provided that where the whole or any part of such accumulations consists of investments in Government securities, or in securities guaranteed by appropriate Government as regards repayment of principal and payment of interest or in both, the authority making the transfer to the Fund shall transfer those securities at the price for which they were actually purchased or transfer a sum equivalent to such price. In case, however, the whole or any part of such accumulations is invested in National Savings Certificates or National Plan Savings Certificates, the appreciated value of such certificates at the time of the transfer will be taken into account in determining the amount of the accumulations to be transferred, provided that the difference between the face value of such certificate and their appreciated value at the time of transfer has already been credited to the accounts of the subscribers;

Provided further that where the whole or any part of such accumulations consists of investments in securities bearing no guarantee of an appropriate Government as regards repayment of principal and payment of interest, the Central Government may, in exceptional cases, allow acceptance of the transfer of such securities from the authority making the transfer to the Fund at the price for which they were actually purchased.

Explanation- The total amount of provident fund accumulations includes interest thereon and the authority in charge of the Fund shall transfer in cash any balance of interest on investment which happens to be undistributed on the date of transfer, or realized or realizable for the period prior to the registration of the securities in the name of the Central Board of Trustees, Employees' Provident Fund.

(3) Any cash transferred under sub-section (2) shall be deposited in any office or branch of the Reserve Bank of India or the State Bank of India to the credit of the Central Board and the receipt obtained in respect thereof shall be forwarded to the Commissioner:

Provided that where there is no office or branch of either of the two Banks at the place where the factory or other establishment is situated, the amount shall be credited to the Central Board by means of a Reserve Bank of India Governmental draft at par.

(4) The accumulations transferred to the Fund in accordance with this paragraph shall be credited to the account of each of the members of the Fund, to the extent to which he may be entitled thereto having regard to the statement furnished by the authority aforesaid.

(5) When the accumulations in any such Provident Fund as is referred to in sub-paragraph (1) have been so transferred to the Fund, the Commissioner may, by notification in the Gazette of India, declare that the subscribers of such Provident Fund have now become members of the Fund and that the accumulations aforesaid have now become vested in the Central Board.

In these provisions, on cancellation of exemption or on application of the Scheme, and transfer of the accumulations to the Statutory Fund, rather a notification with regard to becoming member of the Fund is mandatory, but it is nowhere in practice. However the Central PF Commissioner, vide No. Exem/6(20) 08/DL/NZ/Vol. I/30327-477 dated 30.7.2009 has issued certain guide-lines for process of cancellation of exemptions is reproduced here under–

Central PF Commissioner, vide No. Exem/6(20) 08/DL/NZ/Vol. I/30327-477 dated 30.7.2009.

Sub.: - Procedure for the cancellation of examption-reg.

It is observed in the recent past that ROs/SROs are not submitting the requisite documents while forwarding proposals for cancellation of exemption. In order to ensure standardized procedure in such cases the following guidelines are enumerated for your guidance:–

2. In cases of surrender of exemption by the employer on its own volition, the following documents are required to be submitted to the Head Office while recommending any proposal for cancellation of exemption:-

(i) An application from the employer addressed to the Appropriate Govt. requesting for surrender of exemption.

(ii) A copy of resolution of the BOT.

(iii) A report of the concerned RPFC, regarding up to date compliance status.

(iv) A copy of the notification wherein exemption was originally granted by the appropriate Government.

3. In Cases where violation of conditions of exemption have been detected, the exemption can be cancelled u/s 17(4) of the EPF act, duly following the procedure which includes issue of a show cause notice to the establishment by the appropriate government/authority detailing the violation of the conditions of exemption. In this regard, RPFC shall forward the following:-

(i) A draft Show Cause Notice to Head Office mentioning the violation of the conditions of exemption & other defaults committed by the establishment. Head Office shall forward the same to the appropriate Govt. after approval of the competent authority.

(ii) Details of the period up to which establishment has remitted the dues to the P.F. Trust & EPFQ, status of audit of accounts of the Trust, period up to which the account slips have been issued to the employees, assessment made u/s 7A/14B if any, status of recovery of dues, and submission of returns & punitive actions if any initiated against the establishment along with status etc.

(iii) In case an establishment is not complying with any of the conditions governing grant of exemption and if the employer is willing to surrender exemption, consent of the majority of employees need not be insisted.

4. In this context your reference is also invited to Head Office circular No. Co-ord/11(24)05/Admn. Inst/Cir./25000 dated 16/05/05 wherein detailed procedure was stipulated in the light of the judgment of the Division Bench of the Hon'ble Kolkata High Court in the matter of *M/s. Delta Ltd. Vs. RPFC-II, West Bengal – [2005 (3) LLJ. 258: 2005 (106) FLR 16: 2005 (3) Lab.I.C. 2307:2005 LLR 788].* It is also be reiterated that besides cancellation of exemption, RPFCs may initiate all other actions as stipulated under sections 7A, 14B, 8, 14 against the defaulting exempted establishments as per the prescribed procedure.

It is requested to follow the above procedure scrupulously in all cases in future.

Central PF Commissioner, Letter No. Invst. I/1(76) 2001/Demat/1272 dated 13.4.2004.

Sub.: Transfer of securities in Demat form in favour of CBT, EPF-Reg.

Ref: - Invest.1/1(76)/2001/Demat/Dated:- 20-1-2003

Sir,

In suppression of earlier instructions following procedure should be followed for acceptance of securities in D-Mat form after cancellation of exemption. It may not be desirable that anybody and everybody should be able to transfer securities in favour of the CBT, EPF without any knowledge and/or permission from EPFO. Permission for transfer needs to be granted on case to case basis.

(i) On cancellation of exemption, there may be some securities not permitted in the investment pattern or may be going to mature shortly. As per existing manual provisions, exempted establishments basked to deposit cash/cheque (like deposit of usual provident fund dues in State Bank of India) in such cases by RPFCs and the same practice may continue.

(ii) Whenever a trust is wound up & surrenders its holding to RPFC Call securities are handed over to concerned RPFC. However, when the securities are held in dematerialized form, the trust should give written intimation to RPFC providing all the details such as DP Id No., DP Name etc. in advance.

(iii) After examining the details of securities, which the trust intends to transfer to CBT, EPF, if RPFC finds it fit, he can transfer these details to SSB for issuing 'receipt instructions,' so that SBI can incorporate the securities in the holding of CBT, EPF and mark a Copy of the same to the concerned exempted trust indicating following DP ID No. of CBT, EPF:

DPIDC No. IN 300351

Client ID No. 10040624

(iv) After receipt or above details at SBI, trust will give instructions to their DF to transfer the securities in the Demat a/c of CBT, EPF and intimate Security Service Branch by Fax/Telephonically. (Phone No. 022-22621528, Fax No. is 022-22611924). At present concerned officials in SSB are Shri G.R. Aiyer/Shri Ketan Joshi. Please note that instructions to DP by Trust for transfer of securities and acceptance of securities by the Securities Service Branch must be completed on the same day as per rules of NSDL. Hence Trust may be advised to contact Securities Service Branch by Fax and on telephone so that transaction can be affected.

(v) Once these securities are received in Demat a/c of SBI, SBI will incorporate these securities in the holding of CBT, EPF and issue credit confirmation to RPFC concerned. For crediting the account of exempted establishment, credit confirmation by SBI is must.

(vi) Trust should be intimated that CBT, EPF is holding all the Govt. Securities in C SGL account. Hence if the trusts are holding Govt. Securities in Demat Form, these are required to be rematerialized by transfer of securities from NSDL, SGL II to SBI CSGL A/C No. 2 for crediting the securities in the account of CBT, EPF.

In case of any doubt, the trusts may consult their Depository participants for this purpose.

(This issues with the approval of FA & CAO)

Central PF Commissioner, Letter No. Invst. II/6/Accep. with/46/05-06/4484 dated 24.4.2006.

Sub.: Acceptances and withdrawals of securities, upon transfer of Past Accumulations from/to the Central Board of Trustees, Employees' Provident Fund Account & credit confirmation regarding the same.

Sir,

Upon every cancellation of exemption of exemption or extension of coverage to an establishment, the past accumulations are to be transferred to the account of CBT, EPF. Regarding transfer in the form of securities, provisions are given in Para 28 of the EPF Scheme, 1952 and the MAP -I (Chapter 8 - Investment). However, it has been noted that the practice has been in aberration of the stated instructions. The problems noted in this regard and the requests for necessary actions in respect of them are stated below:

1. Delay in transfer of Securities:

At the time of cancellation of exemption, securities are supposed to be transferred from exempted establishment's trusts to the account of CBT, EPF. As per the MAP, It should be affected within 30 days from the date of order However, it is noticed that undue time is consumed in the transfer of securities. The securities are forwarded by the ROs/ SROs to the SSB, SB) for being transferred in the name of CBT and being credited to its account. However, due to certain deficiencies or lacunas these are returned to the field offices for removal of the deficiencies or rectification of the pointed errors or lacunas, and again forwarded thereof to the SBI, SSB for further action at their end. Letters are also written to the field offices for taking necessary action as per the advice of SBI. It is however, noted that in many a cases there occurs a lot of delay and resultant pendency in the transfers, due to laxity on the part of field offices.

It is also noticed that in many a cases the matter stretches so long that during the meanwhile securities become due for maturity before the transfer could take place. In such cases, the whole exercise goes down the drain and the securities are again returned to the Pvt. Provident Fund Trusts through the RPFCs concerned, for seeking the redemption proceeds and depositing funds with RPFCs.

It is urged that the matter may be given due consideration and efforts may be made to complete the work of transfer of securities within the reasonable time.

2. Confirmation of the transfer and credit of securities:-

EPFO follows the cash based system of accounting. Any income/assets are recognised only after the same are realised and not just on the basis of their accrual. In view of this, it is proper to reflect the "Acceptances' upon transfer and credit of securities to the account of CBT, EPF only after the same are confirmed by the SSB of SBI. After each transfer and credit of securities to the account of CBT, EPF, SSB of SSI sends a letter of confirmation to the concerned RPFC. At the end of each month, reports called 'Acceptances and Withdrawals' of securities is generated upon all the cases of securities which are transferred and credited to the account of CBT. EPF during that month. The same is forwarded to the EPFO, Head Office for our records. These reports are sent by Head Office on half yearly and annual basis to all the ROs to seek confirmation of the figures, from the respective ROs. along with the detailed report containing particulars about each transaction, a summary statement is also prepared by Head Office, which contains the aggregate amount of Acceptances in each category viz. CTG, STG, SDL, SDS etc. in respect of ail the ROs. At the end of each year, these figures are got verified and confirmed by the ROs and then finally they are incorporated in the final Annual Statement of Accounts for-the investment Wing. The corresponding figures of annual acceptances are also required to be reflected in the Annual Balance Sheets of the respective ROs The total value of acceptance shown in the Balance Sheet of the Organisation is the consolidated figure contained in the Balance Sheets of all the ROs. These figures should tally with the figure contained in the annual statement of accounts of the Investment Wing of Head Office. However, amazingly enough, it is noticed that the figures are rarely found to be tallying with each other The only reason noticed is the difference in the figures shown by the field offices in their Balance Sheets and the figures confirmed by them to the Investment Wing of Head Office.

It may be noticed that the figures of investment shown in the final accounts of the organisation do not tally with the actual figures as contained in the verifiable records of investment. It results in making the figures of final accounts of the organisation as highly misrepresentative, dubious, unreflective of true and fair picture of the state of affairs and unverifiable.

It is thus reiterated that the figures of Acceptances of securities as confirmed to the Investment Wing, should only be reflected In the annual Balance Sheets of the ROs.

X. Exemption from Employees' Pension Scheme, 1995:

Although, there are provision for grant of exemption from the operation of the Employees' Pension Scheme, 1995, but it is very tough to compare the benefits of the private pension scheme and the statutory one. The payment of pension is a long term, recurring payment, no establishment can sustain for such a long period with a sustainable corpus, and the authorities may continue to postpone the decision for an indefinite period on the application for exemption, that is why in the early days of the Scheme, the original paragraph 39 was replaced providing therein the condition, akin to that of paragraph 79B of the P.F. Scheme, that the appropriate Government has to take decision on the application with a period six month. On expiry of the six months period, the exemption shall be deemed granted. Of course, in the case of pension, the consultation is also required of the Central Provident Fund Commissioner, not of the C.B.T. as required in the cases of exemption from the E.P.F. Scheme, 1952.

The related provisions for exemption under the **Employees' Pension Scheme, 1995** (read with section 17 (1C):-

[1][39. Exemption from the operation of the Pension Scheme.

The appropriate Government may grant exemption to any establishment or class of establishments from the operation of this Scheme, if the employees of the establishments are either members of any other pension scheme or proposed to be members of a pension scheme wherein the pensionary benefits are at par or more favourable than the benefits provided under this Scheme. Where exemption is granted to any establishment or class of establishments under this paragraph, withdrawal benefits available to the credit of the employees of such establishment(s) under the ceased Family Pension Scheme, 1971, shall be paid, subject to the consent of the employees, to the pension fund of the establishment(s) so exempted. An application for exemption under this paragraph shall be presented to the Regional Provident Fund Commissioner having jurisdiction by the establishment or class of establishments, together with a copy of the pension scheme of the establishment (s) and other relevant documents, as may be called for by him. On receipt of such an application, the Regional Provident Fund Commissioner shall scrutinise it, obtain the recommendations of the Central Provident Fund Commissioner and submit the same to the appropriate Government for decision, pending disposal of application for exemption under this paragraph employers' share of the contribution shall not be remitted to the pension fund as envisaged in sub-paragraph (1) of paragraph 3. An application for exemption presented under this paragraph shall be disposed of within a period of six months from the date of its receipt or such further time as may be extended for reasons to be recorded in writing. If the

application for exemption is not disposed of within the period so specified, the exemption applied for shall be deemed to have been granted.

Explanation. - For the purpose of this paragraph, the period of six months will count from the date on which the application for exemption is given in compete form to the satisfaction of the Regional Provident Fund Commissioner.]

---
1. Subs. by G.S.R. 134, dated the 28th February, 1996 (w.e.f 16th March 1996).
---

[1][39A. Submission of return.–The employer of the exempted establishment or class of establishments and/or the Board of Trustees of the exempted establishment or class of establishments shall submit a monthly return to the Commissioner in Form 1.]

[2][39B. Transfer value.–In case exemption is granted to any establishment or in the case of a member being transferred from pension fund of one exempted establishment to another pension fund of exempted establishment or statutory pension fund or *vice-versa,* a transfer value payment will be made which will consist of the following:-

(a) Withdrawal benefit relating to past service period upto 15-11-1995 as per Table-A multiplied by Table-B factor for the period between 16-11-1995 to the date of exemption/transfer, and

(b) Transfer value for pensionable service as per Table E for the service rendered from 16-11-1995 or from the date of joining the establishment to the date of exemption/transfer as the case may be.

(c) In the event of cancellation of exemption granted under Para 39, transfer of fund will be made as per the conditions mentioned in the exemption notification.]

---
1. Ins. by Notification No. F. 650/2/1/2000-SS-II, dated 27th September, 2001 (w.e.f. 27-9-2001).
2. Ins. by G.S.R. 430 (E), dated 19th May, 2003 (w.e.f. 23-5-2003).

In case of cancellation of exemption, or transfer of an employee to such a establishment which is enjoying exemption, the transfer of value of the pension from the statutory or vice-versa, as per provisions of paragraph 39-B which is calculated on the basis of the factors corresponding to the period of membership mentioned in the Table 'E.' The Table 'E' is given here-under–

TABLE - E

(See Paragraph 39-B)

(Transfer of Contribution from Employees' Pension Scheme, 1995 to Exempted or Other Pension Fund or vice-versa)

Number of full year's contribution period	Proportion of pay payable on last contribution month
1	0.978
2	1.979
3	3.003
4	4.051
5	5.124
6	6.221

7	7.345
8	8.494
9	9.671

This table has been revised w.e.f. 10.8.2008 which is also given here take Table 'E.'

Number of full years' contribution paid	Proportion of pay on last contribution month	Number of full years' contribution paid	Proportion of pay on last contribution month
1	0.987	13	14.841
2	1.998	14	16.182
3	3.033	15	17.554
4	4.093	16	18.960
5	5.178	17	20.399
6	6.289	18	21.872
7	7.426	19	23.380
8	8.590	20	24.924
9	9.782	21	26.505
10	11.003	22	28.123
11	12.252	23	29.780
12	13.531	24	31.4771

Susbs. by G.S.R. 514(E), dated 10-7-2009. (w.e.f. 10.7.2009)

XI. Exemption from Employees' Deposit Linked Insurance Scheme, 1976:

Exemption form the EDLI Scheme is also available and relevant provisions have been made in paragraph 28 of that Scheme. Being the insurance scheme a scheme which provides insurance benefits based on a average balance of 12 months preceding the death of an employee (PF member), that too while in service, hence, it's a schemes which gives death insurance premium to which is counted for a year. That is why, such group insurance schemes are available with various insurance companies, and on making arrangement such a company, the exemption is granted for a period of three years only. And, being the exemption for a short period, the power to grant exemption from the EDLI Scheme has been given to the Central P.F. Commissioner, and until the notification is issued, the Regional P.F. Commissioner has been empowered to grant relaxation.

For the purpose of exemption from EDLI Scheme, an Insurance Fund is required to be constituted by the employer of the establishment in the same lines the provident fund rules and trust is formed; but, many Insurance companies have provided substitute of a private Insurance fund to be established by the employer, it is considered suitable to accept the group Insurance policies in lieu of a private insurance fund, Since, the group insurance policy is renewable every year and it covers all the employee of an establishment, it has been made compulsory that all the employees/PF members to be covered under the Insurance policy, as every employee is required to become PF member, and the renewal of the policy every year, it is considered proper to allow exemption for three years.

The exemption granted from this scheme is for three years every time, it is not granted once for all, it is because just to ensure that the insurance policy is renewed every year and the benefits are available every year in currency.

The related provisions for exemption under the **Employees' Deposit-linked Insurance Scheme, 1976** (read with section 17 (2A) and (2B):-

28. Special provisions relating to establishments in respect of which applications are received for exemption from the provisions of this Scheme. – (1) (i) A Commissioner may be order and subject to such conditions as may be specified in this order exempt from the operation of all or any of the provisions of this Scheme an employee to whom this Scheme applies on receipt of application from such an employee:

Provided that such an employee is without making any separate contribution or payment of premium, in enjoyment of benefits in the nature of life assurance, whether linked to their deposits in provident funds or not, according to the rules of the factory or other establishment and such benefits are more favourable than the benefits provided under this Scheme.

(ii) Where an employee is exempted, as aforesaid, the employer shall in respect of such employee maintain such accounts, submit such returns, provide such facilities for inspection as the Commissioner may direct and pay such inspection charges and make such investments as the Central Government may direct.

(2) An employee exempted under sub-paragraph 1 may, by an application to the Commissioner, make a request that the benefits of this Scheme be extended to him.

(3) No employee shall be granted exemption or permitted to apply out of exemption more than once on each account.

(4) (i) The Central Provident Fund Commissioner may by order and subject to such conditions as may be specified in the order exempt from the operation of all or any of the provisions of this Scheme any class of employees to whom this Scheme applies, on receipt of an application therefore, in such form as the Commissioner may specify:

Provided that such class of employees is, without making any separate contribution on payment of premium, in enjoyment of benefits in the nature of life assurance, whether linked to their deposits in provident fund or not, according to the rules of the factory or other establishment and such benefits are more favourable than the benefits provided under this Scheme.

(ii) Where any class of employees is exempted as aforesaid, the employer shall in respect of such class of employees maintain such accounts, submit such returns, provide such facilities for inspection, pay such inspection charges and make investments in such manner as the Central Government may direct.

(5) A class of employees exempted under sub-paragraph 4 or the majority of employees constituting such class may, by an application to the Commissioner, make a request that the benefits of this Scheme be extended to them.

(6) No class of employees or the majority of employees constituting such class shall be granted exemption or permitted to apply out of exemption more than once on each account.

(7) Notwithstanding anything contained in this Scheme the Commissioner may in relation to a factory or other establishment in respect of which an application for exemption under section 17 (2A) of the Act has been received, relax pending the disposal of the application, the provisions of this Scheme in such manner as he may direct.

Under this Scheme, the exemption is available for whole of the establishment or a class of employees also under sub-paragraph (5).

The exemption granted under the EDLI Scheme is automatically cancelled when the annual group insurance policy is not renewed. As such, there is no question of transfer of any value of the premium on transfer of an employee from the statutory to exempted fund or vice-versa.

XII. Investment pattern w.e.f. 01.4.2015:-

Vide Notification No. S.O. 1433 (E) dated 29.5.2015, following pattern has been notified-

1. Government Securities and related investments: Minimum 45 % to 50 %
   Includes- Govet. Securities; other securities and units
   Of Mutual funds for Govt. securities regulated by SEBI.
2. Debt Instruments and related investments: Minimum 35 % to 45 %
   Includes- Listed debt securities of bodies corporate
   With minimu 3 years maturity; Basel III tier Bonds of
   Banks and Rupee Bonds of minimu 3 years maturity.
   Term deposits for not less than one year & liste
   Insfrastrure bonds.
3. Short term debt instruments: up to 5 %
   units of liquid mutual Funds, & term deposits upto
   one year duration
4. Equities related Investment: Minimum 5 % to 15 %
5. Asset backed Trust structured and Misc. Investments: up to 5%

For details of the different instruments of investment, please refer to the Notification.

Step by Step Into EPF

> *Default Management*

Chapter 14

Determination of dues

> *Brief badinage-*
>
> Originally, Section 8 was placed in the statute book to provide for a Recovery Machinery in case any default by an employer is occurred and the payment of contribution is threatened depriving of the due social security benefits to the employees/members. In some cases, some employers challenged the process of recovery of provident fund dues as found not paid according to the monthly P.F. returns filed by the employer him-self, on the ground that there was no quantum of amount in default was determined by any authority, hence enforcing the recovery was not valid. The Allahabad High Court (DB), in the case of **Loon Karan Sethia vs. Additional Collector [(1964)_2 LLJ 331; AIR 1965 All. 373 (DB)]** held that in absence of any provision in the Act, as it stood at the relevant time, for ascertainment and determination of the amount due by any authority, it could not be said that the amount due had been ascertained. In this case, the employer did submit the statement and returns required by the Commissioner on the basis of which the amount could be determined by the Commissioner. Without determination of amount in default, recovery cannot be enforced. The Central Government, by that time, proposed insertion of the provision for determination of dues by putting Section 7A in the statute book in 1963. By the Act No 28 of 1963, Section 7A was inserted.
>
> There was no remedy to the finality of an order passed under section 7A except that a reference could be made to the Central Government under section 19A which could not give the results up to the mark, that a Social Security legislation could expect. In a large number of cases, the employers knocked the doors of High Courts. Simultaneously, the enforcement of recovery could also not render expected results under the procedure of recovery of P.F. dues as an arrear of land revenue. Thus, it was the demand of the time that a further review of the situation was under-taken and in 1988, comprehensive amendments were brought in, in the statute book, which relate to- **(i) delegating powers to other subordinate officers for determination of P.F. dues and also to resolve the dispute with regard to applicability of the Act, (ii) making provisions for review of the orders passed under section 7A, (iii) providing for legal remedies by setting-up E.P.F. Appellate Tribunal, (iv) setting up of an independent internal Recovery Machinery.**

Section-[1][7A. Determination of moneys due from employers.– [2][(1) The Central Provident Fund Commissioner, any Additional Central Provident Fund Commissioner, any Deputy Provident Fund Commissioner, any Regional Provident Fund Commissioner, or any Assistant Provident Fund Commissioner may, by order, -

    a.   in a case where a dispute arises regarding the applicability of this Act to an establishment, decide such dispute; and

b. determine the amount due from any employer under any provision of this Act, the Scheme or the 3[Pension] Scheme or the Insurance Scheme, as the case may be, and for any of the aforesaid purposes may conduct such inquiry as he may deem necessary.]

(2) The officer conducting the inquiry under sub-section (1) shall, for the purposes of such inquiry have the same powers as are vested in a court under the Code of Civil Procedure, 1908 (5 of 1908), for trying a suit in respect of the following matters, namely:-

(a) enforcing the attendance of any person or examining him on oath ;

(b) requiring the discovery and production of documents;

(c) receiving evidence on affidavit;

(d) issuing commissions for the examination of witnesses, and any such inquiry shall be deemed to be a judicial proceeding within the meaning of sections 193 and 228, and for the purpose of section 196 of the Indian Penal Code (45 of 1860).

(3) No order 4[* * *] shall be made under sub-section (1), unless 5[the employer concerned] is given a reasonable opportunity of representing his case.

6[(3A) Where the employer, employee or any other person required to attend the inquiry under sub-section (1) fails to attend such inquiry without assigning any valid reason or fails to produce any document or to file any report or return when called upon to do so, the officer conducting the inquiry may decide the applicability of The Act or determine the amount due from any employer, as the case may be, on the basis of the evidence adduced during such inquiry and other documents available on record.]

7[(4) Where an order under sub-section (1) is passed against an employer ex-parte, he may, within three months from the date of communication of such order, apply to the officer for setting aside such order and if he satisfies the officer that the show cause notice was not duly served or that he was prevented by any sufficient cause from appearing when the inquiry was held, the officer shall make an order setting aside his earlier order and shall appoint a date for proceeding with the inquiry:

Provided that no such order shall be set aside merely on the ground that there has been an irregularity in the service of the show cause notice if the officer is satisfied that the employer had notice of the date of hearing and had sufficient time to appear before the officer.

Explanation. – Where an appeal has been preferred under this Act against an order passed ex-parte and such appeal has been disposed of otherwise than on the ground that the appellant has withdrawn the appeal, no application shall lie under this sub-section for setting aside the ex-parte order.

(5) No order passed under this section shall be set aside on any application under sub-section (4) unless notice thereof has been served on the opposite party.].

1.	Inserted by Act 28 of 1963, s. 6.
2.	Inserted by At 33 of 1988, s. 10 (w.e.f. 1.8.1988).
3.	Substituted by Act 25 of 1996, s.4, for the words "Family Pension" (w.e.f. 16.11.1995).
4.	The words "determining the amount due from any employer" omitted by Act 33 of 1988, s.10 (w.e.f. 1.8.1988).
5.	Substituted by Act 33 of 1988, s.10, for the words "employer" (w.e.f. 1.8.1988).

6.	Inserted by Act 33 of 1988, s. 10, for the words "employer" (w.e.f. 1.8.1988).
7.	Substituted by Act 33 of 1988, s.10 (w.e.f. 1.8.1988).

Legislative reference–

The section was inserted in 1963 vide sec.6 of the Act No.28 of 1963 which was further amended by the Act 33 of 1988 by which officers down up to the level of Assistant P.F. Commissioners have been authorized to determine dues payable under the Act. Prior to the amendment, only the Regional Commissioner was authorized under Section 7A. There was also a clause (4) declaring the finality of the order passed under that Section was not questionable in any court of law, but aggrieved parties, by invoking Article 226 of the Constitution, raised dispute in various High Courts, where by the utility of the than Section 19-A was became not rendering the desired results, and need of a remedy of appeal was considered and it was brought- in on the statute book.

Section [1][**7B. Review of orders passed under Section 7A.** – (1) Any person aggrieved by an order made under sub-section (1) of section 7A, but from which no appeal has been preferred under this Act, and who, from the discovery of new and important matters or evidence which, after the exercise of due diligence was not within his knowledge or could not be produced by him at the time when the order was made, or on account of some mistake or error apparent on the face of record or for any other sufficient reason, desires to obtain a review of such order may apply for a review of that order to the officer who passed the order:

Provided that such officer may also on his own motion review his order if he is satisfied that it is necessary so to do on any such ground.

(2) Every application for review under sub-section (1) shall be filed in such form and manner and within such time as may be specified in the Scheme.

(3) Where it appears to the officer receiving an application for review that there is no sufficient ground for a review, he shall reject the application.

(4) Where the officer is of opinion that the application for review should be granted, be shall grant the same:

Provided that, -

(a) no such application shall be granted without previous notice to all the parties before him to enable them to appear and be heard in support of the order in respect of which a review is applied for, and

(b) no such application shall be granted on the ground of discovery of new matter or evidence which the applicant alleges was not within his knowledge or could not be produced by him when the order was made, without proof of such allegation.

(5) No appeal shall lie against the order of the officer rejecting an application for review, but an appeal under this Act shall lie against an order passed under review as if the order passed under review were the original order passed by him under section 7A.

1.	Secs. 7B to 7Q inserted by Act 33 of 1988, Sec. 11 (w.e.f. 1.7.1997).

Legislative reference:-

This section was added in the Act in 1988. Prior to this, there was a provision in sub-section (4) of Section 7A declaring the order passed under section 7A would be final and could not be challenged in any court of law. However, those were used to brought before the High Courts through writs under Article 226 of the Constitution, and various courts under lined the necessity of making review provisions and/or appeal. Hence this section was added.

Section- [1]**[7C. Determination of escaped amount. – Where an order determining the amount due from an employer under section 7A or section 7B has been passed and if the officer who passed the orders-**

- (a) **has reason to believe that by reason of the omission or failure on the part of the employer to make any document or report available, or to disclose, fully and truly, all material facts necessary for determining the correct amount due from the employer, any amount so due from such employer for any period has escaped his notice ;**

- (b) **has, in consequence of information in his possession, reason to believe that any amount to be determined under section 7A or section 7B has escaped from his determination for any period notwithstanding that there has been no omission or failure as mentioned in clause (a) on the part of the employer, he may within a period five years from the date of communication of the order passed under section 7A or section 7B, re-open the case and pass appropriate orders re-determining the amount due from the employer in accordance with the provisions of this Act:**

Provided that no order re-determining the amount due from the employer shall be passed under this section unless the employer is given a reasonable opportunity of representing his case.]

1. Secs. 7B to 7Q inserted by Act 33 of 1988, s. 11 (w.e.f. 1.7.1997).

I. Authorities under, and Scope of section 7A:-

This section involves exercise of quasi-judicial powers to the extent the section permits, thus it considered that the person exercising the powers will follow the principles of natural justice and pass a *speaking order*. Accordingly, in 1988, the powers were given to the officers down to the level of Assistant Provident Fund Commissioners with a view to curb the number of cases those likely to arise in future. It is also pertinent to emphasis only on the matters the law permits. Going beyond the scope may attract views otherwise. The Madras High Court decided such a case, which speaks of the scope of the section while deciding the case of *Commissioner, Office of Regional P.F. vs. Ariyamala & anr. [2002 II LLJ.627 (Mad.)]*-

"Respondent widow of deceased employee, filed civil suit, when family pension that was being paid to her, was stopped on the ground of her re-marriage. In this appeal, serious contention is raised that Civil Court has no jurisdiction in the matter in view of section 7A (4) of the Act."

"The contention is rejected. The issue raised in suit is not with regard to determination of money dues from employer which is governed under section 7A of the Act, but the one as to the status of the respondent-plaintiff as the widow of deceased employee Subramanium that entitles her to claim the family pension under EFP Scheme, 1971 clause 21 of the Scheme admittedly, applies to the widow and dis-qualifies the widow in the event of her re-marriage. But what is pertinent to be decided is whether the respondent – plaintiff had re-married. The suit was thus one as to the status of the respondent as widow of deceased employee." Obviously, an authority exercising powers of a Quasi-Judicial authority is required to be confined to the expressed barriers of law and should not allow both, the administrative capacity and the judicial capacity overlap.

However in the case of Group 4 Security services Ltd. Vs R.P.F.C. Karnataka, [unreported], the Supreme Court upheld the view taken by the Karnataka High Court, D.B. *[M/s. Group 4 Securities Guarding Ltd. Banglore vs. R.P.F.C. and others- 2004 Lab. I.C. 2075: 2004 (2) LLJ. 1142: 2004 LLR 540: 2004 (102) FLR 374]* that the Regional P.F. Commissioner has powers to enter into inquiry about the wage structure and nomenclature of the wage elements to ensure whether there is a subterfuge in the name of deferent types of allowances in the pay and whether any evasion is taking place by paying contribution on the pay less than the declared minimum wages.

Therefore, the scope of this section can be wider enough, however, the matters to be decided under these provisions can be summarized into two categories; namely-

(i) in case, where a dispute arises regarding the applicability of this Act to an establishment, decide such dispute; and

(ii) determine the amount due from any employer under any provision of this Act, the Scheme or the Pension Scheme or the Insurance Scheme as the case may be.

(iii) determination of escaped dues.

All the three types of matters have different footings and scope to go for into the investigations and *modus-oprendie*.

The Provident Fund Commissioner is an authority envisaged by the Act to objectively decide as to whether, in the given facts, a particular establishment or concern is to be brought within the purview of the Act and the Schemes framed there under. He him-self is not a party, as such to the issue that the statute calls upon him to decide and while deciding such issue, he himself does not act as a judge in his own cause. Thus, while determining the question of applicability of the Act to a particular establishment under Section 7A, the Provident Fund Commissioner does not act as a judge in his own cause- *[Khushi Ram Raghunath Rai vs. R.P.F.C.- ILR (19756)2 Punj 481]*.

The **purposes for which the** provisions of this section can be invoked, are clearly defined in the Section it-self. However, some interesting instances take place where the provisions of the section 7A have been invoked, which, in no way fall under any of the purposes mentioned in Section 7A. The Madras High Court encountered such a case, where the respondent widow of a deceased employee filed a civil suit, when family pension that was being paid to her, was stopped on the ground of her re-marriage. In this appeal, serious contention is raised that Civil Court has no jurisdiction in the matter in view of Section 7A of the Act. The High Court held that it was not a matter to be decided under Section 7A whether the widow got remarried or not. *[Commissionr, Office of Regional P.F. vs. Ariyamala & anr. 2002 II LLJ 627 (Mad)]*.

II. Role of a Provident Fund Inspector:

What is the role of an inspector in the disposal of a cases under section 7A ? Administratively, an inspector is a subordinate officer to the authority conducting enquiry under section 7A, hence, he has to work as per directions of the authority. It is on the part of the authority whether the report of the inspector to be accepted or not for the conclusion of the enquiry. Administratively, one may have different opinion in this regard, but in certain cases, the judicial authorities have expressed their views otherwise taking into account the judicial frame work and scope.

In the case of **Glamour vs. R.P.F.C.- [1975 Lab.I.C. 954; 1975 (I) LLJ. 514]**, the Court have observed that the investigation made by the Inspector or the report submitted by him was no substitute for a quasi-judicial enquiry envisaged by section 7A. The employer was entitled to show to the appropriate officer that the report of the Inspector was not correct and the establishment in dispute was not a part of his establishment or for any other reason was not covered by the Act. In the appeal of this case *[R.P.F.C. vs. Glamour Prop. S.H. & Sons.- 1982 Lab.I.C. 1787]*, the same view has been taken adding further that non-supply of the Inspector's report to the employer, the employer would be denied of opportunity to show that the report was not based on facts and the establishment is not covered by the Act. Further, determination of dues on the basis of the report of the provident fund Inspector is not in accordance with the provisions of section 7A. An independent enquiry by the competent authority is necessary, *[Minerva Stores vs. R.P.F.C. – 1978 Lab.I.C. 1160]*.

A different view has been expressed by the Calcutta High Court in the case of **Sree Gopikrishan Engineering (P) Ltd. Vs. R.P.F.C., W.B.- [1986 Lab.I.C. 2066 (Cal.)]** that having directed the Inspector to submit a report in response to the application filed by the petitioner, the Commissioner should have considered the report and should have disposed off the application on the basis of the same. An order passed against the petitioner ignoring the report of the inspector cannot be allowed to stand.

Among these different views, one thing mentioned in the provisions of the section is being ignored. That is, sub-section (2) has given the powers to the officer conducting the inquiry as the powers of a Civil Court for trying a suit in respect of the matters, namely—

(a) enforcing the attendance of any person or examining him on oath;

(b) requiring the discovery and production of documents;

(c) receiving evidence on affidavit;

(d) issuing commission for the examination of witnesses.

By invoking the (d) above, the courts use to issue commissions not only for examination of witnesses, but to give report on a particular given matter, which is, oftenly, taken as a valid document. Accordingly, if an inspector is directed to submit his report on a particular matter or topic, it must be treated as Commission issued by the authority conducting inquiry under section 7A. The intention of Calcutta High court in the above case of **Sree Gopikrishan Engineering (P) Ltd. Vs. R.P.F.C., W.B.-** seems to be on the same lines when it under-lined non-acceptance of the report of Inspector, and hence declared the order illegal.

Besides, the inherited powers of Inspector as mentioned in Section 13 (2) and the purposes for which those powers may be invoked have also been mentioned therein. Those are the basis on which the department may enter into investigation for the purpose of the inquiry under Section 7A.

III. Speaking Order:

Among administrative circles, when they discuss about a Speaking Order, it is defined in different ways by different persons. Some may insist for a better linguistic form, some may insist for a model format of the Speaking Order, some may prefer to give exhaustive details, some may express their egos and concepts through the Speaking Order. Many authorities use to draft it in a way as if it is for a competitive examination in which the facts and retrospect of the case is found absent. In a good Speaking Order, besides all the grammatical, linguistic excellence, the details of facts and their relevance with the historical legislative references is seen and those facts are discussed in a way those are expected as explained in the Evidence Act. In the Evidence Act, it is expected from a judicial or quasi-judicial authority that material facts or evidences or witnesses are discussed to establish whether those are relevant to the case under consideration and those lead to a judicious conclusion. If it is not found in an order, that order cannot be said to be a Speaking Order.

The concept of a Speaking Order is found in-build in the provisions related to different type of inquiries. When the words 'no order shall be passed unless the employer is given a reasonable opportunity to represent his case' require the order has to be a speaking order. If, the order does not speak of what the employer has represented, the order cannot be said to be a speaking order.

The need of passing a Speaking Order is required u/s 7-A, 7-B, 7-C, 14-B, and 7-Q, of the Act and Paragraph 26-B of the Scheme by the authorities upon whom the powers have been conferred to take any decision under those provisions, and if it is not found judicious and self contained order the higher Judicial Authority may take a different view some times and may pass comments on the authorities accordingly. Patna High Court has underlined his state of affairs in the case of *Inter-state Transport Agency, Sitamarhi Vs. R.P.F.C. Patna-[1993 Lab I.C. 940 (Pat.)]*, that Section 7A comes into play only when someone, who should have himself come forward, does not do so. Then the sums payable is determined under section 7A and if he commits default in making the contribution, he is subjected to imposition of penal damages under Section 14-B of the Act. Under both the provisions, there must be an enquiry for determining the amount due by providing "reasonable opportunity." As a matter of fact, the authorities under this Section are vested with the powers conferred under the Civil Procedure Code and particularly, they have to conduct the enquiry in a fair and reasonable manner. It cannot be said that no proper and effective hearing has been provided under Section 7A of the Act, as is expected from a judicial or quasi-judicial authority. Section 7A ensures just fair enquiry.

Any abuse of power and act of mala-fide is justiciable before the High Court and the Supreme Court.

Further, to protect the interest of the employees, the authority is vested with the powers to summon any record for evidence, examine any witness in person or on oath, admit any affidavit or issue commission for examination of a witness, as he deems proper and reasonable. Further, the employer is bound to be given a reasonable opportunity or representing his case. Thus the provisions of this Section prescribe a wholesome procedure for conducting enquiry for the purpose of determining the amount dues from the employer under any provision of the Act and Schemes.

Sometimes, it may happen that on a particular point, different opinions of different courts lead to so many administrative inconveniences. To remedy such situation, certain mandatory provisions have been made which are taken as an authority as the mandatory provision on that particular point. Such provision is available in section 20 and also the corresponding provision in paragraph 78 of the Employees' Provident Funds Scheme, 1952, under which the Central Government may issue direction and such directions will have status of a mandatory provision. This fact is always to be kept in mind while passing an order.

Different authorities take interpretation of the "speaking orders" as per their own sweet will and suitability. Sometimes, linguistically and grammatically well drafted order is taken as the best speaking order, in which points of merit are found absent, some authorities include all the facts of the case, but in the ultimate synthesis, the decision is found pre-conceived or pr-concepted one. In both the situations, the order cannot be said to be a speaking order. **An example** is given here under, by which it can be judged easily, what is a speaking order, in fact-

That is the case of a group of schools, facts of which are-

The Act was made applicable to the Schools w.e.f. 6.3.1982 and the Schemes w.e.f. 3.7.1982.

There was a stay on the notification published on 6.3.1982 and it was vacated on 8.1.1988 by passing an order by the Supreme Court upholding the validity of the notification, with a relief giving directions that if the employees share was not deducted from the pay of the employees, it need not be recovered now and only the employers' share was to be deposited, the Regional Commissioner would assess the past dues and fix installments thereof and for such delayed payments no damages would be demanded and no interest on the contribution paid as such was to be given.

Main school is in existence prior to March, 1982, which was coverable from March, 1982. After 1982, five branch-schools were started at different point of time and the last branch was opened in 1999. Proceedings under section 7A were initiated in 2003.

Being not satisfied by the information supplied by the employer, the authority summoned the Income Tax Authorities with the records related to the employer. The Income Tax Authority did not attend, but the information was collected through P.F. Inspector.

On the basis of the latest information and the number of employees employed by the employer the authority proceeded for determination of the dues and it were assessed w.e.f. 1st April, 1982 by a mechanical calculation applying the number of employees and the salary determined, as the amount due amounting to more than Rs.1.5 crores.

The expression "natural justice" is a term which summarises certain minimum standards of fairness upon the observance of which there can be insistence by court of law on administrative bodies and tribunals. One of the principle of natural justice is that the party is entitled to show the reason for a decision taken against him. It cannot be contended that the demand was not an order but a mere communication and that the commissioner was bound to disclose the basis of his calculation under Section 7A- **[Delhi Iron and Steel Stockists (C.S.) Association (P) Ltd. Vs. R.P.F.C. New Delhi - 1977 Lab.IC 1018; 1977 (2) LLJ 217].**

The Section itself provides for acting in accordance with the principle of natural justice. Sub-section (3) of Section 7A is mandatory. In that provision, no order determining the amount shall be made unless the employer is given a reasonable opportunity to represent his case. It will be fallacious to contend that the party concerned cannot invoke the provisions referred to in Sub-section 2(a) to 2(d). There is nothing in the Section which violates the principle of natural justice. The procedure prescribed in the Section is sufficient to make the hearing effectively. There is no infirmity in the Section as such.- *[T. Marimuthu Handloom Factory, Madurai vs. R.P.F.C. Madras- 1990 Lab.IC 2030 (Mad)]*.

Even an executive order has to be communicated to the person against whom it was passed, if it has to have any effect – *[Bachhittar Singh vs. State of Punjab – AIR 1963 S.C. 395 – was quoted in the case of Jagdish Prasad Nirmal Das (India wire Netting Factory) vs. R.P.F.C. Delhi]*.

The right of representation by a lawyer is not considered to be a part of natural justice and it cannot be claimed as of right, unless the said right is conferred by the statute- *[Kalindi vs. Tata Locomotives- AIR 1960 SC 914; H.C. Sarin s. Union of India- (1976) 4 SCC 765]*. The Section 30 of the Advocates Act, 1961 confers an absolute right on every advocate to practice in all courts including the Supreme Court, before any tribunal or person legally authorized to take evidence and before any authority or person before whom such advocate is or under any law for the time being in force entitled to practice, but the provisions of Section 30 of the Act have not so far been brought in force.

However, if the matter is very simple, e.g. whether the amount in question is paid or not, or whether the assessment orders were correct, the request for legal representation can be rejected. On the other hand, if the oral evidence produced at the inquiry requires services of a lawyer for cross-examination of witnesses, **or legal complexity is involved therein, or where** complicated questions of fact and law arise, or where the evidence is voluminous and the party concerned may not be in a position to meet with the situation effectively or where he is pitted against a trained prosecutor, he should be allowed to engage a legal practitioner to defend him "lest the scales should be weighed against him" These are all relevant grounds and in these circumstances, refusal to permit legal assistance may cause serious prejudice to the person concerned and may amount to a denial of reasonable opportunity of being heard- *[Krishna Chandra vs. UOI- (1974) 4 SCC 374; C.L. Subramaniam vs. Collector of Customs- (1972) 3 SCC 542 and other various cases.]*.

Basic requirements of a Speaking Order –

To protect the interest of the employee, the authority is vested with the powers to summon any evidence, examine any record, admit any affidavit or issue commission for examination of a witness, as he deems proper and reasonable. Further, the employer is bound to be given a reasonable opportunity of representing his case. Thus the provisions of this Section prescribe a wholesome procedure for conducting enquiry for the purpose of determining the amount due from the employer under any provision of the Act and Schemes- *[Sukchain & Co. Vs. F.C.I. – 1985 (65) FJR 337]*.

There was no mention about the **pinning of the beneficiaries** in the light of the Supreme Court observations in the case of *Food Corporation of India vs. R.P.F.C. and others- [1990 (I) SCC 68]* wherein, it has been observed that in respect whom the determination of dues is to done, is necessary by invoking powers given by sub section (2) of section 7A of the Act by summoning the contractors through whom the employees were engaged. Denying such request of the appellant the authority does not appear acted judiciously as the F.C.I. has expressed their difficulty in collecting the list of all workers engaged in depots scattered at different places. And, also, in old and stale period for P.F. contribution determination, it will be only for the employees who are identifiable, as ruled in the case of **Himachal Pradesh State Forest Corporation vs. R.P.F.C.- [2008 LLR. 980 (SC)].**

When Liability is disputed on the ground that the establishment is not governed by the Act, the authority under Section 7A has to make an enquiry and determine if the Act is applicable to the establishment under the circumstances of the case. Under sub-section (3), a reasonable opportunity is to be given to the employer for his representation in that enquiry. The competent authority is not preclude under section 7A of the Act from making his own estimate of an amount payable by an employer before issue a notice in terms of sub-section (3). Giving of notice to the employer amounts to giving his a reasonable opportunity to represent his case before passing of the final order- *[Younus Mohammed vs. R.P.F.C. and others – 1987 Lab.IC 1089 (MP); also see Radha Krishan vs. R.P.F.C.- AIR 1967 MP 157; Gunvantrai vs. R.P.F.C. – AIR 1970 MP 221; 1970 Lab.IC 1383 and Balasore Motor Association vs. R.P.F.C. AIR 1970 Orissa 199; 1970 Lab.IC 1393.].*

IV. Onus:

One of the areas which plays major and decisive role in passing an order is who is to prove the case on the material facts? As per the Evidence Act, and in the criminal cases, it is the prosecution or the complainant, who is to prove the case. But, case under the EPF Act, it cannot be the prosecution or the department, who is able to prove the case which are initiated under the Act other than the section 14 or under section 14AA. In the early days of implementation of this Act, this point came up before Patna High Court wherein it has been held that to prove that the establishment does not employ fifty (now twenty) of more persons lies on the petitioner who challenged the applicability of the EPF Act to his establishment. It was for the petitioner to have brought on the record materials on which they wanted to base their prayer for an issue in writ, and if they failed to do so, it may be presumed that there must have been fifty or more employees engaged in the company-*[Bnkim Chandra Chakraworty vs. R.P.F.C. – AIR 1958 Pat. 314].* This does not mean that the authority under section 7A has powers to decide a case on the basis of its own conclusions or presumptions. The authority has to follow certain principles of natural justice and quasi-judicial procedures. That is why the Supreme Court has desired that the beneficiary is to be identified *[Food Corporation of India vs. R.P.F.C. and others- 1990 (I) SCC 68].* Therefore, this has further been clarified in the case of *Laxmi Restaurant vs. R.P.F.C.- [1975 Lab.I.C. 1186]* that there is no presumption of law that every establishment employs more than twenty persons and so anybody who alleges to the contrary must establish it. Where the number of employees is disputed, it must be decided, as any other facts, according to law, on relevant material in accordance with the well established principles and not merely on surmises or conjunctions or onus of proof. However, in the eyes of law, there always remains a model situation which is in conformity of law, as explained in the case of *Tin Plate Co. of India Ltd. Vs. Presiding Officer, E.P.F. Appellate Tribunal, New Delhi –[2003(2) LLJ.997; 2003 (79) FLR 923]* that the provisions of the Act would not apply when employees are less than 20 persons and the employer is a part and parcel of a larger establishment. To decide the employment of persons, the most important parameters determining that status and nature of employment and the source of appointment with reference to their appointment orders and the drawl of emoluments by them.

But, in the field scenario, specially, when the employment is switched over to out-sourcing in sophisticated term, and through contractors in a contemporary term which leads to a subterfuge, how the facts to be proved and on whom the onus lies, is the situation, to which the authority is to encounter. Thus, it becomes relevant that in whose possession the record is! In fact, no government department is creating information and record, it is always collected or to say, supplied by various related sources, so happens with the EPF authorities who is fed with the information and records by the employers under various provisions of the Act and the Schemes, also, it the employer, on whose records and information the administration of the Act is based. Therefore, it is the employer, who is to submit records and prove the facts he relies upon, and allow to verify the correctness of the facts, information, evidences he is advancing. Undoubtedly, it is also the crux of the judicial process in which the evidences are testified whether those are relative and correct thus acceptable or not.

Non-Cooperation by the principal employer also becomes a crucial point while conducting an inquiry under Section 7A of the Act. A writ before the High Court of Delhi came up challenging the order of the Commissioner holding that the petitioner was liable to pay provident fund dues to an extent over Rs. 32 lakhs. The ground of challenge was failure on the part of the Commissioner to summon contractors engaged by the petitioner and that vitiated the enquiry under Section 7A of the Act. It has been held that an examination of the order of the Commissioner passed under Sec. 7A shows that he had dealt with petitioner's request for summoning the contractors and had repeatedly asked it to submit the relevant record to facilitate the determination of his liability. But petitioner had failed to comply with this raising that it had either withheld the record or avoided to produce it for some reason doubt. It was in that context that the Commissioner had fallen back upon other source to collect the requisite data for determination of liability. In this conspectus, it becomes difficult to hold that the Commissioner's determination suffered from any lack of basis or want of jurisdiction. Therefore, the petition failed-*[Food Corpn. Of India vs. R.P.F. Commissioner- 2003 (2) LLJ 376 (Del-DB)].*

For a judicious inquiry, the authorities have been given the certain powers as mentioned in the **Civil Procedure Code for specific purposes,** namely-

enforcing the attendance of any person or examining him on oath;
requiring the discovery and production of documents;
receiving evidence on affidavit;
issuing commission for the examination of witnesses.

The related provisions of **Civil Procedure Code** have been mentioned under **Sections 27, 30, 31 and Section 32** read with the Order V, Rule 9 to 13 and 15 to 30 (which relates to service of summons), Order XI (which relates to discovery of documents, Order XVI (relating to attendance of witnesses), Order XXVI (relating to issue commissions to examine witness). The Section referred above are reproduced here-under-

Section 27- Summons to defendants *– Where a suit has been duly instituted, a summons may be issued to the defendants to appear and answer the claim and may be served in manner prescribed.*

Section – 30 – Power to order discovery and the like – Subject to such conditions and limitations as may be prescribed, the Court may, at any time, either of its own motion or on the application of any party,-

(a) make such orders as may be necessary or reasonable in all matters relating to the delivery and answering of interrogatories, the admission of documents and facts, and the discovery, inspection, production, impounding and return of documents or other material objects producible as evidence;

(b) issue summons to persons whose attendance is required either to give evidence or to produce or to produce documents or such other objects as aforesaid;

(c) order any fact to be proved by affidavit.

Section – 31 – Summons to witness – The provisions in Section 27, 28 and 29 shall apply to summons to give evidence or to produce documents or other material objects.

Section – 32 – Penalty for default – The Court may compel the attendance of any person to whom a summons has been issued under Section 30 and for that purpose may –

(a) issue a warrant for his arrest;

(b) attach and sell his property;

(c) impose a fine upon him not exceeding five hundred rupees;

(d) order him to furnish security for his appearance and in default commit him to the civil prison.

Further, the proceeding have been given the status of judicial proceeding for the purpose of **Section 196 of Indian Penal Code**, and also, within the meaning of **Sections 193 and 228 of the Indian Penal Code.** Those are reproduced here-under-

Section – 196. punishment for false evidence – Whoever intentionally gives false evidence in any stage of a judicial proceedings, or fabricates false evidence for the purpose of being used in any stage of a judicial proceedings, shall be punished with imprisonment of either description for a term which may extend to seven years and shall also be liable to fine;

And whoever intentionally gives or fabricates false evidence in any other case, shall be punished with imprisonment of either description for a term which may extend to three years, and shall also be liable to fine.

Explanation 1.- a trial before a Court-material is a judicial proceeding.

Explanation 2.- An investigation directed by law preliminary to a proceeding before a Court of Justice, is a stage of a judicial proceeding, though that investigation may not take place before a Court of Justice.

Section -193 – Using evidence to be false. – Whoever corruptly uses or attempts to use as true or genuine evidence any evidence which he knows to be false or fabricated, shall be punished in the same manner as if he gave or fabricated false evidence.

Section – 228 – Intentional insult or interruption to public servant sitting in judicial proceeding. – Whoever intentionally offers any insult, or causes any interruption to any public servant, while such *public servant is sitting in any stage of a judicial simple imprisonment for a term which may extend to six months, or with fine which may extend to one thousand rupees, or with both.*

It is true that in case documents are not produced by the employer, the authorities are competent under Section 7A (3A) to determine the amount on the basis of other evidence. But it does not mean the sub-section (3A) absolves the authorities from the responsibility of making effective determination of the amount. The authorities are bound to force the person to appear in exercise of power under sec. 7A (2) as the authorities have to collect material for the purpose of discharging their statutory duties and responsibilities imposed under law- *[National Thermal Power Corp. Ltd. Vs. R.P.F.C.- 1998 (2) CLR 561 (Cal.-DB)].*

As far directing by the authority under Section 7A is concerned, the Andhra Pradesh High Court ruled that in the instant case, the petitioner employer was issued a warrant of arrest by the Commissioner under Section 7A, the High Court observed that the Commissioner under Section 7A could not direct arrest of the petitioner-employer merely for his failure to respond to show cause notice. At most he could have an ex-parte order. It is a gross misuse of power and so the warrant of arrest was set aside-

V. Time limit for disposal of an inquiry:

Instances have been there where the inquiry under Section 7-A is continuing for years together and those have not been concluded. Many of them are continuing for more than 10–15 years and the authorities could not take decision except to prolong further under the circumstances of probable questioning the decision. Such abnormal delay cruelly and criminally defeat the vary purpose of the social security scheme where beneficiary is absolved in the time set to the un-written history of the society, and the employer could be able to get what was not suppose to retain. The very same position came before the Bombay High Court which traveled to the Supreme Court also, where in their lordship have commented the words which are akin to stricture. The case was of levy of damages, which relevant to refer here, in which the establishment challenged the order under Section 14-B. In that case, it has been observed that 'If, it needed 17 years to issue a notice which only required turning the pages of a register with a view to seeing the date of payment, it is difficult to under-stand what sort of administration of this social welfare legislation is being done by the authorities concerned in the stat of Maharashtra. This case is a glaring example of the way the social welfare legislations are being dealt with and administered. It is high time the appropriate Government look into these matters and if it finds that those entrusted with the task of administering these social welfare legislation are not doing their duty, to deal with them sternly. If any loss is caused to the employees by their inaction, negligence or remissness, responsibility may be fixed and the amounts recovered from the persons so responsible. That will be the real deterrent and thereby the cases of default may go down. ...Any unreasonable delay in exercise of the power may affect its validity'- *[K.T. Rolling Mills (P) Ltd. Vs. R.M. Gandhi and others – 1993 Lab.IC 1466 (Bom); 1994 (I) LLJ 66 (Bom)].*

On the other hand, if an employer, by a writ petition restrains an enquiry under Section 7A is not maintainable. A writ will not lie or restraining from conducting an enquiry under Section 7A of the Act. In the present case, no final order about the applicability of the Act to the petitioner has been passed. Rather, just an enquiry was in progress and the records were being summoned from the petitioner, which was being avoided on one pretext or the other. The conduct of the petitioner in this respect cannot be appreciated. Whenever, any record was required with a view to reach a conclusion about applicability of the Act, the petitioner must have been candid enough to furnish details of all documents so that correct decision could be arrived at. It is open to the petitioner to lead any evidence of his choice on the date fixed. The petitioner must cooperate in the enquiry and furnish all the documents required on the date fixed. There is no justification to issue the writ as prayed for- *[Midlands (P) Ltd. Vs. R.P.F.C. and another- 1994 (I) LLJ 1230 (All)]*.

The insertion of sub-section (3A) in Section 7A is also aimed to that intention.

VI. Dispute regarding applicability:

Dispute regarding applicability of the Act mainly arises out of the immune provided under Section 16. Thereafter, provisions of Section 2A give rise to the disputes relating to clubbing of an establishment with another already existing and covered under the Act, and then the dispute regarding the number of persons employed in an establishment and , of course, the industry in which the establishment is engaged i.e. the dispute related to the Schedule head.

All the matters which may lead to dispute regarding applicability have been dealt with in Chapter - 2 hence, those are not discussed here again. However, important case-laws on the subject-matter, in the light of a quasi-judicial enquiry, are discussed here under.

The Commissioner ought to have given the document on the basis of which he has come to the conclusion that about 46 establishments in Bombay were nothing but branches and/or departments belonging to the petitioner formed only with object of subterfuge of the laws meant for the purpose of social security of various employees under the Act. Since, he failed to do so, it has definitely, affected the petitioners vital right to defend prejudicially and therefore, the impugned order is illegal and liable to be set aside- *[Damji L. Shah vs. R.P.F.C.- 1992 (1) LLJ 224 (Bom.)]*.

Where after receiving the notice of an enquiry under Section 7-A. the employer filed an objection claiming protection under Section 16, it was held that the authority under Section 7-A must decide the dispute relating to the applicability of the Act before determining the amount due from the employer- *[Mayur Biscuit Co. (P) Ltd. Vs. R.P.F.C.- (1999) 81 FLR 581 (Ori.DB)]*.

In *A.V.C. Investment and trading (P) ltd. Vs. R.P.F.C. [(1996) 2 LLJ 473; (1996) 73 FJR 1385 (Bom.DB)]* the petitioner company claimed it-self to be independent of the other company for the purpose of the Act, but the Regional PF Commissioner, by an order held otherwise. The Bombay High Court held it to be violative of the principle of natural justice by observing that the R.P.F. Commissioner ought to have held a proper inquiry and investigated all the factual questions after disclosing the material, if any, in his possession on the basis of which he had reached the said conclusion.

VII. Determination of dues:

The main purpose of this Section is to authorize certain officer to determine the dues payable by an employer in respect of his employee. The word "determination of dues" used in this section should not be taken similar to the word "assessment" as has been used in other taxation laws. The assessment denotes the sums not exactly defined in terms of quantum, whereas in the EPF & MP Act, 1952, it is determination of dues which are required to be paid by an employer in respect of his employees which stands quantified in term of pay or wages of the employees. There is no scope of investigations with a view to increase the revenue. However, to overcome any subterfuge on the part of an employer, as has been taken care of by the statute itself under Section 12, the authority may invoke the provisions as provided in sub-section (2) of Section 7A. Therefore, the rise in the disputes. These can be categorized as below-

- (i) determination involving resolution of dispute regarding applicability;
- (ii) determination involving entitlement of an employee for the membership;
- (iii) determination involving volume of pay; and
- (iv) determination involving non-payment of regular dues.

It may be noted that the (i) above can be a *bona-fide* dispute, with the exceptions like the case of **Midlands (P) Ltd. Vs. R.P.F.C. and another- [1994 (I) LLJ 1230 (All)]** where the employer avoided conclusion by the authority by prolonging it by one or the other pretext.

The (ii) and (iii) above in some cases may be *bona-fide*, but in most of the cases, it showed subterfuge and avoidance of payment of liability. For determination of the dues in the cases falling in the category (ii) above, the case is first decided under paragraph 26-B of the Employee' Provident Funds Scheme, 1952 by the Regional Commissioner only, then, the authority may determine the dues under Section 7A.

The cases falling under category (iii) above, by and large, have been discussed in Chapter – 9, and the ingredients of an assessment order have been discussed here in above. With a view to make the determination through a speaking order, it is relevant that the law regarding payment of wages, terms and conditions of service and the contract of appointment or the engaging a person are taken into consideration while passing an order determining the dues.

As for the determination of dues of regular nature which could not be paid for one or the other reason, is concerned, it does not involve any dispute or a point of law. Such dues can easily be determined on the basis of the information given by the employer, or collected by an Inspector or so. Such determination is, simply, for the purpose of initiating further legal action, which is required to be taken for a prolonged default.

VIII. Ex-parte order determining the dues:

Sub-section (3A) has been added in Section 7-A in 1988 to over-come the situation where the employer do not cooperate in the enquiry and also the records for determination of dues not produced, or so. In fact, by the insertion of this provision, the authority has been obliged to complete the enquiry without any delay and pass an order determining the dues even if the employer do no tern. That is why, the determination of dues is not a process of assessment of revenue, but dues under a social security scheme which is linked to certain class of people and that cannot be postponed for a long time or for indefinitely. However, it does not mean the sub-section (3A) absolves the authorities from the responsibility of making effective determination of the amount. The authorities are bound to force the person to appear in exercise of powers given under sec. 7A (2) as the authorities have to collect material for the purpose of discharging their statutory duties and responsibilities imposed under law-*[National Thermal Power Corp. Ltd. Vs. R.P.F.C.- 1998 (2) CLR 561 (Cal.-DB)]*.

IX. Setting aside the ex-parte order:

Sub-section (4) of Section 7-A has provided that if an ex-parte order under sub-section (1) read with sub-section (3A), has been passed, the employer aggrieved by it, may apply to the same authority, within 3 months from the date of the order, detailing the reason that he was prevented to attend the inquiry on the date, requesting for setting aside the order and the officer may set-aside the order and appoint a fresh date for hearing. In the proviso to this sub-section, it has been clarified that if, the service of the show-cause notice was irregular and the employer had notice of the date of hearing, the request for setting aside the order may be rejected.

X. Determination of escaped dues:

Occasions may arise when while determining the dues under Section 7A or under Section 7B while passing an order under review of the order passed under Section 7A, certain section, or certain part of dues could not be determined for the reasons that the sector could not be noticed hence escaped from the determination of the dues. Prior to amendments in 1988, there was a lacuna that once dues have been determined for a particular period, no dues can be determined for the same period again although, that may not be a double jeopardy, but is termed so in the eyes of the law. The anomaly has been removed by inserting Section 7-C.

However, the sub-section does not confer an absolute power on the authority to initiate action for determination of escaped dues for any period. There is limitation of time of five years from the date of order under Section 7-A or under Section 7-B, as the case may be, for the period for which the determination of escaped dues in intended. Beyond the period of five years, no determination of escaped dues can be initiated or done.

XI. Review of the orders:

(i) Grounds for Review:

It is not open for all in all cases where a review application can be preferred. The grounds have been mentioned in sub-section (1)-

(1) discovery of new and important matters or evidence which, after the exercise of due diligence was not within his knowledge or could not be produced by him at the time when the order was made, or

(2) on account of some mistake or error apparent on the face of record, or

(3) for any other sufficient reason.

Here, beyond the grounds mentioned at (1) and (2) above, a full discretion to the authority has been given to accept any ground mentioned in the application as provided, and the ground mentioned at (3) above however, the authority may on his own motion, review the order.

The authority to the review is the **same authority, who passed** the order under Section 7A of the Act, and not any other authority, whether superior of inferior, as usually provided in other taxation laws. Here, same authority does not mean the same person, but the authority.

(ii) Admission of a Review Application:

If, on examination, it is found that there are not sufficient grounds for the review, the authority may reject the application by passing a speaking order, disclosing the reasons for the rejection.

If, the application is found in order and grounds are justifiable, the authority has to summon the parties and hear them before admission of the review application.

If, any new matter or evidence is noticed after the order is passed, the applicant has to produce proof in support of his contention that the matter or the evidence was not within his knowledge at the time of the order.

For review of order passed under Section 7A the time limit has been fixed as 45 days whereas, for setting aside of an *ex-partie* order is fixed as 3 months. Is there any conflict in these two go? If an appeal is preferred against an order passed *ex-partie*, it denotes that the employer does not take it as an *ex-partie* order, and as such the opportunity to get *ex-partie* order set-aside is forgone by him. But, it is requested to be setting-aside, an opportunity is, further available to the employer to file an application for review under Section 7-B. As such, these are not conflicting one, but opportunity available in a series, i.e. 3 months and 45 days.

There may be some other situations which may lead to writ petitions. Importance of the application for Review has been underlined by High Court of Jharkhand in the case of Laxmi Devi Shroff Adarsh Sanskrit College, Deodhar vs. R.P.F.C. Ranchi and others-*[2009 LLR. 934 (Jhar.)]* that a review petition under Section 7-B of the EPF & MP Act against the ex-parte order should not have been brushed aside by the authority without deciding it and the steps as taken by the P.F Authorities in freezing the bank account of the employer during pendency of the review petition, deserve to be deprecated keeping petition aside and moving further in the matter is illegal.

Hyper Technical approach shown in the present case the review application was rejected only on the ground of not complying with the format or procedure prescribed by department. The High Cout held that the delay works to the detriment of the ultimate beneficiary for whom the enactment is being implemented. Hence, such hyper-technical approach defeats the purpose of the Act itself. The review application, hence stands restored- ***American Express Bakery vs. Regional P.F. Commissioner- 2011 (131) FLR 1093 (Bom H.C.)]***.

Review petition by a negligent defaulting employer has been rightly prceeded ex-parte by the Assistant P.F. Commissioner for determination of money when sufficient opportunity was given to him- [***M/s. Durga Body Builders vs. U.O.I. and another- 2009 LLR. 84 (Jhar.)]***.

(iii) Application and admission thereof:

In paragraph 79–A, the time limit of filing the review application is 45 days from the date of the order against which the appeal is being preferred, has been fixed and a form has also been prescribed for preferring the appeal. The Form 9 has been appended to the Scheme for this purpose.

The relevant provisions of para 79-A and Form No. 9 are re-produced here-under–

Para 79A. Filing application for review. – Any person aggrieved by an order made under sub-section (1) of section 7A and who desires to obtain a review of such order may apply for a review of that order, as provided in sub-section (1) of section 7B of the Act in Form 9 to the officer who passed such order:

Provided, that no application for review of an order will be entertained by the concerned officer, unless the application for review is submitted within 45 days from the date of making such order.]

FORM 9

Application for review filed under sub-section (1) of section 7B of the Employees' Provident Funds and Miscellaneous Provisions Act, 1952

(Paragraph 79A)

For use in Commissioner's Office

Date of filing or

Date of receipt by post Registration No.

                                                  Signature

                                                  for Commissioner

1. Name of the Applicant ………………………………..
2. Designation of the applicant or his ……………………………….. relationship with the factory/establishment (whether owner/partner/ director/manager, etc., to be indicated)
3. Name and complete address of the ……………………………….. factory/establishment
4. Address of the employer for service of……………………………….. notice/summons.
5. Particulars of the order against which……………………………….. the review application is filed –
    - (i) Order No. ………………………………..
    - (ii) Date of order ………………………………..
    - (iii) Passed by ………………………………..
    - (iv) Subject in brief ………………………………..
6. Main ground(s) on which the application for review has been made and the relief (s) sought. (If necessary, attach a duly signed statement with copies of the documents relied upon marked as A1, A2, A3 and so on.)………………………………..

Verification

I……………. (name of the applicant) s/o, d/o, w/o……………. age …………….. working as …………….. resident of ……………….. do hereby verify that the contents of particulars given at Sl. Nos. 1 to 6 above are true to the best of my knowledge and belief and I have not suppressed any material fact. I further declare that–

(i) I am filing the application within 45 days from the date of the original order.

(ii) I have not preferred any appeal against the original order under the Employees' Provident Funds and Miscellaneous Provisions Act, 1952.

(iii) I am filing with this application, the original document authorising me to represent the aggrieved person (applicable only in cases where the application is filed by agent, advocate or other representative).

Place …………….   Signature.

Date …………….

(iv). **Review and setting aside an *ex-parte* order, difference between:**

Chapter 15

Levy of Damages and Interest

Section 14-B was added in 1953 along with Section 14-A for managing default. In the original provision, the appropriate Government was authorized to exercise powers under this section. In 1973, the powers under this section were given to the Central P.F. Commissioner and such other officers as may be authorized by the Central Government. At present, the officers of the rank of Assistant P.F. Commissioners and above have been authorized to exercise the powers under this section.

With this amendment in 1973, it was mandatory that the employer shall be given a reasonable opportunity of **being heard, not to represent his case, as provided in section 7A,** with a view to pass a speaking order for recovery of damages.

Section- [1][14B. Power to recover damages.– Where an employer makes default in the payment of any contribution to the Fund [2][the [3][pension] Fund or the Insurance Fund] or in the transfer of accumulations required to be transferred by him under sub-section (2) of Section 15 [4][or sub-section (5) of Section 17] or in payment of any charges payable under any other provision of this Act or any [5][Scheme or Insurance Scheme] or under any of the conditions specified under Section 17, [6][the Central Provident Fund Commissioner or such other officer as may be authorized by the Central Government, by notification in the Official gazette, in the this behalf] may recover [7][from the employer by way of penalty such damages, not exceeding the amount of arrears, as may be specified in the Scheme:]

[8][Provided that before levying and recovering such damages, the employer shall be given a reasonable opportunity of being heard:]

[9][Provided further that the Central Board may reduce or waive the damages levied under this section in relation to an establishment which is a sick industrial company and in respect of which a scheme for rehabilitation has been sanctioned by the Board for Industrial and Financial Reconstruction established under Section 4 of the Sick Industrial Companies (Special Provisions) Act, 1985 (1 of 1986), subject to such terms and conditions as may be specified in the Scheme.]]

1.	Inserted by Act 37 of 1953, Sec. 13.
2.	Subs. By Act 99 of 1976 . (w.e.f. 1.8.1976).
3.	Subs. By Act 25 of 1996, sec. 4 for 'Family Pension . (w.e.f. 16.11.1995).
4.	Inserted by Act 28 of 1963 Sec. 10 (w.e.f. 30.11.1963).
5.	Subs. By Act 99 of 1976 . (w.e.f. 1.8.1976).
6.	Subs. By Act 40 of 1973 . (w.e.f. 1.11.1973).
7.	Subs. By Act 33 of 1988 . (w.e.f. 1.9.1991).
8.	Inserted by Act 40 of 1973 (w.e.f. 1.11.1973).
9.	Inserted by Act 33 of 1988 Sec. 20 (w.e.f. 1.9.1991).

By the amendments of 1988, which, of course, have been made effective from 01.9.1991, the nomenclature has been defined as penalty; simultaneously, provision for waiver, either full or in part, have been made in the section through a proviso under certain conditions as may be provided in the Scheme. All the Schemes have such provisions, reproduced here under:-

Provision in Employees' Provident Funds Scheme, 1952–

Paragraph **32A. Recovery of damages for default in payment of any contribution.**–[1][(1) Where an employer makes default in the payment of any contribution to the fund, or in the transfer of accumulations required to be transferred by him under sub-section (2) of section 15 or sub-section (5) of section 17 of the Act or in the payment of any charges payable under any other provisions of the Act or Scheme or under any of the conditions specified under section 17 of the Act, the Central Provident Fund Commissioner or such officer as may be authorised by the Central Government, by notification in the Official Gazette in this behalf, may recover from the employer by way of penalty, damages at the rates given below:–

Period of Default Rate of damages (% of arrears per annum)

(a)	Less than two months	Five
(b)	Two months and above but less than four months	Ten
(c)	Four months and above but less than six months	Fifteen
(d)	Six months and above	Twenty Five

The damages shall be calculated to the nearest rupees, 50 paise or more to be counted as the nearest higher rupee and fraction of a rupee less than 50 paise to be ignored.]

1. Ins. by G.S.R. 521, dated 16th August, 1991 (w.e.f. 1-9-1991).

Paragraph [1][**32B. Terms and conditions for reduction or waiver of damages.**–The Central Board may reduce or waive the damages levied under section 14B of the Act in relation to an establishment specified in the second proviso to section 14B, subject to the following terms and conditions, namely:–

- (a) in case of a change of management including transfer of the undertaking to workers' co-operative and in case of merger or amalgamation of the sick industrial company with any other industrial company, complete waiver of damages may be allowed;
- (b) in cases where the Board for Industrial and Financial Reconstruction, for reasons to be recorded in its schemes, in this behalf recommends, waiver of damages up to 100 per cent may be allowed;
- (c) in other cases, depending on merits, reduction of damages up to 50 per cent may be allowed.]

1. Ins. by G.S.R. 521, dated 16th August, 1991 (w.e.f. 1-9-1991).

The corresponding provision in Employees' Pension Scheme, 1995-

Paragraph [1][5. Recovery of damages for default in payment of any contribution.

The corresponding provision in Employees' Deposit-Linked Insurance Scheme, 1976–

Paragraph [1][8A. Recovery of damages for default in payment of any contribution –

Paragraph [1][8B. Terms and conditions for reduction or waiver of damages.

I. 1988 amendments = effects with regard to the powers of authority and previous defaults, proceedings initiated there after:

To levy damages, Additional Central PF Commissioners, all Regional P.F.

Commissioners and all Assistant PF Commissioners have been authorized to levy demages by notification No S.O. 1553 dated 19.4.2002

The default on the part of the writ petitioner occurred prior to, but the proceedings under section 14-B in respect of defaults were initiated by a show-cause notice after 1988 amendments and insertion of Paragraph 32-A in the Scheme. The Calcutta High Court held that the case was to be governed by the amended provisions and not by the pre-amendment provisions, and observed – "The intention of the legislature in amending Section 14-B and introducing the relevant Schemes…was to curtail the discretionary power of the levying authority. The amendment thus affects both, substantive right as well as procedural law and the authority enforcing the right or liability which had already accrued prior to the amendment has been divested to a great extent of the discretionary power which he earlier had. As such, in the instant case the levy of damages is to be governed by the amended provision of Section 14-B read with Para 32-A of the Scheme…"

"Thus the power of the Regional P.F. Commissioner to levy damages upto 100% stood curtail. He is now to follow the sliding table incorporated in Paragraph 32-A of the EPF Scheme, 1952 for applying the rates of damages according to the periods of default specified therein" – *[Atal Tea Co. Ltd. Vs. R.P.F. Commissioner- 1997 Lab.IC 1207; (1998) 79 FLR 372; (1998) 2 CLR 34 (Cal)].*

But, while disposing the issue, whether a case enjoying certain benefits prior to an amendment, would be curtailed after the amendment, the Supreme Court under lined the principle of "Promised estoppels" in the case of *Sangam Spinners vs. R.P.F.C.-I- [2008(I)CLR424 (SC); 2008-I-LLJ.661(SC)]* which related to infancy protection under Section 16 (1) (d) and which was deleted w.e.f. 22.9.1997, the establishment did not complete 3 years which it was claimed to enjoy till the completion of 3 years. The Supreme Court allowed 3 years infancy period to enjoy.

II. One answer to many questions:

Like the proceedings under Section 7A, so many points have also been raised on the issue of levy of damages under section 14-B also, but, fortunately, a case, which was decided by the Supreme Court, gave answer to all such questions and that has been a guide and throwing light on almost all the cases relating to levy of damages under section 14-B. The case is "*Organo Chemical Industries vs. Union of India- [(1979) 4 SCC 573; 1980 SCC (L&S) 92; (1979) 2 LLJ 416].* The back-ground of that case was also very interesting.

The establishment M/s. Organo Chemical Industries was situated in the state of Haryana, but was served by the Regional Office of EPF in Chandigarh, single for the two states Sub-Regional Office at Faridabad was opened. The powers for levy of damages were given to the Regional P.F. Commissioners only at that time. There was no Regional P.F. Commissioner posted in the Regional Office at Chandigarh for quite sometime. One Assistant Provident Fund Commissioner (Shri K.L. Lamba), recruited in 1975 was asked to head that office until a Regional Commissioner was posted. Administratively, that posting was made, but, the statutory work under section 7-A and 14-B was held-up. Hence a special notification in the name of that Assistant Commissioner was issued by the Central Government under section 14-B, and the case of levy of damages came up before him. Being a new officer, he was rather cautious then enjoying the powers, and passed the order dealing with all the points raised by the employer.

It was not the end. By the 42nd Constitution amendment, the writ jurisdiction of High Courts in respect of the Central Legislations was withdrawn and given it exclusively to the Supreme Court, hence, the writ filed in the Punjab and Haryana High Court was transferred to the Supreme Court, and the Supreme Court heard and decided the case in its original writ jurisdiction which has become a mile-stone judgement in the matter of levy of damages under Section 14-B of the Act. That judgement dealt so many question raised at that time and in subsequent cases, being relied upon by all the High Courts and the Supreme Court it-self, even being it a case prior to the amendments of 1988.

(a) **Damages- whether includes penal element-** Prior to 1988 amendments, there was a conflict of opinion among the High Courts on the question as to whether the damages levyable under Section 14-B included an element of penal payment. The controversy was ultimately settled when the Supreme Court answered the question in the affirmative. The damages under Section 14-B of the Act are penal in nature and not merely co-related with the loss of interest entailed by the delayed payments of contribution to the Fund.

(b) **Object of section 14-B -** "It is meant to penalise defaulting employer as also to provide reparation for the amount of loss suffered by the employees. It is not only a warning to employers in general not to commit a breach of the statutory requirements of Section 6, but at the same time it is meant to provide compensation or redress to the beneficiaries, i.e. to recompense the employees for the loss sustained by them. There is nothing in the section to show that the damages must bear relationship to the loss which is caused to the beneficiaries under the Scheme."

(c) **Not violative of the Constitution –** "The power of the Regional P.F. Commissioner to impose damages under Section 14-B is a quasi-judicial function. It must be exercised after notice to the defaulter and after giving him a reasonable opportunity of being heard. The discretion to award damages could be exercised within the limits fixed by the statute. Having regard to the punitive nature of the power exercisable under Section 14-B and the consequences that ensue there from, an order under Section 14-B must be a 'speaking order' containing the reasons in support of it. The guidelines are provided in the Act and its various provisions, particularly in the word 'damages', the liability for which in Section 14-B arises on the 'making of default'. While fixing the amount of damages, the Regional P.F. Commissioner usually takes into consideration......various factors, viz. the number of defaults, the period of delay, the frequency of default and the amounts involved. The word 'damages' in Section 14-B lays down sufficient guidelines for him to levy damages"

(d) **Meaning of the word 'damages'-** The word 'damages' in Section 14-B is related to the word 'default.' The words used in Section 14-B are 'default in the payment of contribution' and, therefore, the word 'default' must be construed in the light of Paragraph 38 of the E.P.F. Scheme which provides that the payment of contribution has got to be made by the 15th of the following month and, therefore, the word 'default' in Section 14-B must mean 'failure in performance' or 'failure to act'. At the same time, the imposition of damages under Section 14-B is to provide reparation for the amount of loss suffered by the employees."

(e) **Damages belong to Fund: Not general revenue of State-** It is wrong to credit the damages into the general revenue. The entire sum belongs to the Fund except perhaps the administrative charges which are usually separately indicated. If any State is diverting damages under the Act into its own coffers, it is improper.

(f) Section 14B of the Act does not envisage mandatory levy of damages. It does not contemplate computation of quantum of damages in a manner prescribed under paragraph 32A of the EPF Scheme. Though the statutory liability of the employer cannot be in dispute, but levy of damages in all circumstances is not imperative. The Appellate Tribunal has given its anxious consideration over the plea advanced by the respondent, who is a charitable trust, run by donations and grants from government, regarding the delay in payment of contributions–
[R.P.F.C. Manalore Vs. Jamiyyatul Falsh, Mangalore and Another–2010-LLJ-652 (Mad.)].

Similar, and many more questions have been dealt with by various courts subsequently, out of which many case-law dealing with such matters, which have been resolved by the amendments of 1988, such as fixing the rate of damages in a sliding scale, waiver of damages in deserving cases, and finally, remedy to finality by setting-up of an Appellate Tribunal.

III. Levy of damages: a quasi-judicial process:

Like the determination proceedings under Section 7A, the proceedings under Section 14-B for levy of damages is also a quasi-judicial proceedings in which the principle of natural justice is to be followed. In the case of Organo Chemical Industries, the Supreme Court held that "the conferral of power to award damages under Section 14-B is to ensure the success of the measure. It is dependent on existence of certain fats, there has to be an objective determination and not subjective. The R.P.F. Commissioner has not only to apply his mind to the requirement of Section 14-B, but is cast with the duty of making a speaking order, after conforming to the rule of natural justice.

The Supreme Court has repeatedly laid-down that where the discretion to apply the provisions of a particular statute is left with the Government or one of the highest officers, it will be presumed that the discretion vested in such higher authority will not be abused. The Government or such authority is in a position to have all the relevant and necessary information in relation to each kind of establishment, the nature of default made by the employer. It is an imperative of Section 14-B that the Commissioner shall give reason for his order imposing damages on the employer such a guarantee ensures rational action by the officer, because reasons imply relevant reasons, not capricious ink and the need for cogency rivets the officer's mind to the pertinent material on record. Moreover, once reasons are set down the order readily exposes itself to the writ jurisdiction of the court under Article 226 of the Constitution so that perversity, illiteracy, extraneous influence, mala-fides and other blatant infirmities straight get caught and corrected.

An appeal is a desirable corrective but not an indispensable imperative and while its presence is an extra check on way ward orders, its absence is not a sure index of arbitrary potential.

Not only the orders under this Act, but in all other administrative orders, it is required to be speaking order base on the principle of natural justice. If, the power to decide and determine to the prejudice of a person, duty to act judicially is implication in the exercise of such power. If, the essentials of justice be ignored, such an order is a nullity. That is a basic concept of the Rule of law and importance thereof transcends the significance of a decision in any particular case.-*[State of Orissa vs. Dr. (Miss) Bina Pani Dei – AIR 1967 SC 1269].*

For the purpose of natural justice, personal hearing is considered to be necessary. It is true, but, in individual cases only. The position in the case of levy of damages is rather different. In the case of *Vishwa*

Bharati Welfare Printing Press vs. R,P,F,C, Hyderabad – [1979 Lab.IC 269], it has been observed that personal hearing is not a principle of natural justice. If a case involves complicated questions of fact and law, and if the employer asks for a personal hearing, the authority shall have to consider the said request and grant the same, if the circumstances warrant it. The opportunity given for submitting an explanation, in the circumstances, was sufficient compliance with the proviso.

IV. Default leading to damages:

Default under Section 14-B is made whenever there is a delay in payment. Failure to make the payment within the stipulated time results in default in payment as enjoined by the Act-*[Bharat Heavy Electricals Ltd vs. R.P.F.C. – 1985 Lab.IC 282 (MP)]*. Failure to make payments within the stipulated period results in 'default' in payment of contribution as provided by the Act. 'Default in payment' is not limited to failure to pay.-*[Murarka Paints and Varnish Work Ltd. Vs. U.O.I. – 1976 Lab.IC 1953]*.

Where an establishment has made an application for exemption from the Scheme under Section 17, till any decision is taken on the application, the employer is bound to comply with the provisions of the Act.-*[H.P. Agro Industries Corporation Ltd. Vs. R.P.F.C. – 1994 Lab.IC 1286 (HP)]. Hence, so the damages.*

Liability to pay damages arises as soon as a default is committed by an employer in payment of the contribution to the fund. The mere fact that no action was initiated immediately after occurrence of default, would not take away the jurisdiction of the competent authority to enforce the provisions of Section 14-B and recover damages from the employer. –*[APSEB Hyderabad vs. R.P.F.C.- 1979 (1) An W.R. 66]*.

Damages also levyable on amalgamation. Where a scheme of amalgamation is sanctioned by the court, the transferee establishment becomes jointly and severally liable along with the transfer to pay the dues under Section 14-B of the Act, whether or not the scheme of amalgamation provides for the taking of such liabilities- *[R.N.T. Estates Ltd. Vs. U.O.I. -1989 Lab.IC N.O.C. 177 (Cal.)]*.

V. Limitation for levy of Damages:

It is clear that no time limit to initiate action under Section 14-B has been fixed, but, how much time is the reasonable to initiate the proceedings. In a large number of cases, this issue came up before various High Courts, and every time this question has been answered with the comment 'there should be a reasonable time limit'. Finally, the Bombay High Court, in the case of *K.T. Rolling Mills (P) Ltd. Vs. R.M. Gandhi and others-[1993 Lab.IC 1466 (Bom.); (1994) (i) LLJ 66 (Bom)]*, became critical on this issue and expressed that, "If, it needed 17 years to issue a notice which only required turning the pages of a register with a view to seeing the date of payment, it is difficult to under-stand what sort of administration of this social welfare legislation is being done by the authorities concerned in the State of Maharashtra. This case is a glaring example of the way the social welfare legislations are being dealt with and administered. It is high time the appropriate Government to look into these matters and if it finds that those entrusted with the task of administering these social welfare legislation are not doing their duty, to deal with them sternly. If any loss is caused to the employees by their inaction, negligence or remissness, responsibility may be fixed and the amounts recovered from the persons so responsible. That will be the deterrent and thereby the cases of default may go down.

Where no period of limitation is prescribed by the Act for exercise of any power, it must be exercised within a reasonable time. Any un-reasonable delay in exercise of the power may affect its validity. In fact, the initiation of proceedings after such long lapse of time amounts to abuse of the power. The initiation of proceedings and the impugned order passed in pursuance thereof are liable to be quashed.

And, the observation of the Supreme Court in its appeal is- The EPF and MP Act, 1952 was enacted to serve the beneficent purpose and it does constitute a welfare measure as it seeks to create a fund which could be drawn upon by certain categories of employees working in factories and some establishments to meet pressing demands, so also provide pension after the employees have ceased to be in service. So the Act has to be construed in such a way, in case two views can be possible, which advances the object. This has been the outlook of the court for three decades by now.

Though the general period of delay in the instant case is quite long, un-reasonably long but, if it is borne in mind that in view of the larger number of establishments in the State of Maharashtra, default at hand came to notice only in April, 1985, the killing effect of delay gets eroded. We do not, therefore, think if the order of merits to be struck down on the ground of delay when it is also kept in mind that the delay in default related even to the contribution of employers, which money the respondent, after deducting the same from wages of the employees, must have used for its own purpose and that too without paying any interest at the cost of those for whose benefit, it was meant. Any different stand would encourage the employees thwart the object of the Act, which cannot be permitted. We, therefore set aside the impugned judgement of the High Court - *[R.P.F.C vs. K.T. Rolling Mills Ltd. -1995(1) LLJ 882 (SC)].*

VI. Damages- whether for loss:

Over a period of time, how the change in translation of a provision takes place, the matter of levy of Damages is the best example. In 1979, in the case of *Atlantic Engineering Services (P) Ltd. Vs. U.O.I. [(1979) 54 FJR 331]* the version was "since the loss is presumed by the legislature and only the quantum of the loss has to be determined by the Govt., no evidence of loss is necessary before the order of levy of damages is passed. Whereas, in 2002, deciding a writ petition by the learned Single Judge set-aside the order levying damages on the ground that there was delay in issuing show cause notice and no loss was sustained by the department. In the writ appeal, the Division Bench disagreed with the single Judge and held that delay in issuing show-cause notice cannot be taken as ground for setting aside penalty for non-payment of contribution amount on due date - *[R.P.F.C. T.N. vs. Snap Top Machines Accessories India (P) Ltd. – 2002 (1) CLR 437 (Mad-DB)].* One step forward to this, in another case, it has been held that the damages have to be found and ascertained and then something more should be added to it by way of penalty.- *[Aditya Agro Industries (Pvt.) Ltd. And another vs. R,P,F.C. – 1997 (2) LLN 271].* Perhaps, it was underlining the introduction of Section 7Q w.e.f. 01.07.1997 in addition to the provisions of section 14-B.

VII. Contribution not deducted or wages not paid:

It was contended on behalf of the employer in the case of *Calicut Modern Spinning & Weaving Mills Ltd. Vs. R.P.F.C. [1982 Lab.IC 1422; (1982) 1 LLJ 440 (Ker)];* that the mode of payment was provided in Para 38 of the Scheme and Paragraph 30 only provided as to who should make the contributions, that the obligation on the employer to pay contribution arose only when wages in respect of the relevant period were paid and that Section 14-B would not be attracted in cases where the employer was disabled from paying wages to the employees in time for reasons beyond his control, e.g. a lock out, strike, etc. These contentions were not accepted by the Kerala High Court. It was held that paragraph 38 of the Scheme obliged the employer to make the payment within 15 days of the close of every month and paragraph 30 cast an obligation on the employer to pay the contributions payable by himself and on behalf of the member employed by him in the first instance. The word 'in the first instance' did not mean only for the first time. They meant payment of contribution voluntarily by the employer for every month irrespective of the fact whether wages have been paid or not.

Relying on the case of *Organo Chemical Industries vs. U.O.I - [supra]*, the High Court observed: "To allow the employer to make the contribution only when he pays the wages would be to stultify the project. To accept the petitioner's contention in this case would be to enable the employer to divert remittances to the Fund to suit his convenience putting forward sometimes reasonable grounds, sometimes justifiable grounds and most often unjustifiable grounds. The authority under the Act has discretion to mitigate damages depending upon the circumstances of the case but never a discretion to condone the delay; damages in rare cases can be nil percentage but failure to pay will always attract Section 14-B. A combined reading of paragraphs 30 and 32 shows that in cases where due payment of wages is made impracticable for certain reasons, the obligation of the employer to pay both the contribution payable by him and on behalf of the member continues… even in cases of a lock-out, strike, etc, failure to make the contribution resulting in default will have to be visited by damages under Section 14-B. The only question that can be considered by the authority is mitigation of damages having regard to the attendant circumstances that had resulted in the delay.

VIII. Damages for pre-discovery period:

The provisions of the Act were applied to the colleges and other educational institutions by a notification in 1982. The Supreme Court, while upholding the notification, directed the colleges etc. to deposit the entire arrears under the Act and the schemes within the time granted by the Regional P.F. Commissioner. It was also directed by the Supreme Court that in case the colleges complied with the said direction, the Commissioner should not levy any damages for the delay in payment of the arrears. The respondent in the case of *R.P.F. Commissioner vs. S. D. College [(1997) 1 SCC 241; 1997 SCC (L&S) 449; 1997 Lab.IC 910]*, who has been depositing the amounts of provident fund with the University under a scheme framed by the University, however, despite the directions, it continued to deposit the amounts with the University, and it was only about two and half long years later that the respondent withdrew the same with the University's permission and re-deposited with the P.F. Commissioner. Consequently, the Commissioner levied damages @ 25 % of the amount payable by the respondent. In such circumstance, upholding the levy of damages, the Supreme Court observed that the re-depositing of the amount with the University's permission could not afford protection against the consequences of non-deposit of the amount in the Fund.

In the case of *Navnit Lal K Shah (Dr.) vs. Union of India- [2003 (III) CLR 904 (Bom.)]*, the Bombay High Court has answered 4 questions. Those are –

(1) Damages for pre-discovery period,

(2) Compound interest,

(3) Meaning of damages in Sec. 14-B, and

(4) no power to waive damages.

The observations were-"By an order dated 20.10.2000, the respondent No. 2 Regional P.F. Commissioner passed an order imposing damages for the period prior to February, 1992 as also compound interest for pre-discovery period. This order is under challenge in this writ petition.

The Act was made applicable to the undertaking of the petitioner in August, 1979. Petitioner was through-out contending that at no point of time employees in his establishment exceeded 19. Inquiry under Section 7A of the Act and respondent No. 2 passed an order in February, 1992 that besides 19 employees, there were 3 trainees and establishment of petitioner was covered under the Act. It is therefore held in this case that period from August, 1979 till February, 1992 is pre-discovery period.

Relying on the decision of the Supreme Court in the case of *Organo Chemical Industries [suprs]*, it is observed that word "damages" in Section 14-B means in substance penalty imposed on the employer. The object of imposing damages is to penalize the employer who is a defaulter.

Imposing damages on a defaulter is by a statutory provision. In the absence of any power, imposing of penalty cannot be waived. Same has to be imposed even for pre-discovery period.

Respondent No. 2 has levied 10% compound interest to recover loss occurred to the Organisation. There is no provision in Section 14-B which would empower the authorities to claim compound interest. The imposition of interest should have been at simple interest even for pre-discovery period for the simple reason that dispute as to applicability was not on account of point of law but, on account of contention of number of employees. The fact that the establishment availed of services of 20 persons was within the knowledge of petitioner.

And, in the concusion, the court passed an order to modify the impugned order as follows-

(1) Period of August, 1979 to February, 1992 is pre-discovery period,

(2) Interest payable for pre-discovery period shall be simple and not compound interest @10% per annum,

(3) Damages at 10% per annum shall stand imposed for the period from August, 1979 to July, 1988 and at 17 % per annum for the period from August, 1988 to August, 1991.

Where, delay is committed by the P.F. Department, the levy of damages for late deposit of provident funds contributions by an employer will amount to high handedness and *malafide* since the employer has been, persistedly seeking allotment of Code number from the Commissioner for depositing contributions which has been delayed and as such the Provident Fund Authorities could not levy damages for the lapses on their part. – *[Poona Shims Pvt. Ltd. Vs. V.P, Ramaiah, Regional P.F. Commissioner and another- 2007 LLR 488 (Bom)].*

An object of Section 14-B of the E.P.F. & M.P. Act, 1952 is to act as a deterent measure on the employers to prevent them from not carrying out their statutory obligations to make payment to the provident fund. If the defaulter employer is permitted to escape his liability on the ground that the demand under the Act was raised belatedly, it would amount to allowing a defaulter to take benefit of his own wrong which is not justified.

Under Section 14-B of the Act, the liability of the defaulter arises because of his delay in depositing the contribution in time and using the same for his own gains.

Damages under Section 14-B of the Act are penal in nature.

Employer is duty bound to make the provident fund contribution in time. Any default on the part of the employer will attract provisions of the Act. It is not mandatory on the date of computation of damages under Section 14-B of the Act that provident fund dues must still be in 'arrears'. Paragraph 32-A of the EPF Scheme mentioning limit of damages to 25% of the arrears, shall not prevail onver amended section 14-B of the Act providing damages to the extent of 10%.

Section 7-Q of the Act stands on its own independent footing making a defaulter employer liable to pay simple interest as may be specified in the Scheme on any amount due from him till the date of actual payment.

An appeal for its maintainability must have the clear authority of law i.e. why the right of appeal is described as a creature of statute.

An appeal against the order under Section 7-Q of the Act would not lie under Section 7-I of the Act since there is no express provision of appeal against the order under the statute.

Delay caused due to delay in receiving the amount from the Government Agencies is not a justifiable ground for delayed deposit of the contribution.- *[Apex security and Detective Force Pvt. Ltd. Vs. Central Board of Trustees, EPF Irganisation- 2015 LLR. 900 (Delhi H.C.)].*

IX. Establishment registered with B.I.F.R. - levy of damages:

Section 22 of the Sick Industrial Companies (Special Provisions) Act, 1985 provides certain immunes to the companies registered under Section 4 of that Act. In such a case, **whether the P.F. Commissioner can proceed to levy damages or not!** In *Bakshi Steels Ltd. Vs. Regional P.F. Commissioner [(1994) 2 LLN 283; (1994) 69 FLR 549],* a notice was issued to the petitioner calling upon the petitioner to show cause as to why damages be not imposed on it for its failure to comply with the provisions of the Act. The petitioner replied that the unit had been declared sick by the B.I.F.R. It also stated that on account of closure of the unit and subsequent financial difficulties payment of dues could not be made in time. The petitioner made a request for condonation of delay in payment of dues. Thereafter, a notice of hearing was given to the petitioner. Finally, the impugned order was issued for levy of damages to the tune of Rs. 73,317, which amount represented 100% damages on the petitioner. The Rajasthan High Court, set-aside the said order on the ground that the Commissioner had not properly appreciated the ambit and scope of the provisions of the Act of 1985. Further, he had, in the impugned order made reference to the arguments of the petitioner about proceedings pending before the B.I.F.R. but had brushed the same aside by observing that the B.I.F.R. had not recommended suspension of the Provident Fund dues/damages.

Here, it may be noted that the second proviso to the Section 14-B provides for waiver of damages upto 100%, if it is recommended in the rehabilitation scheme approved by the B.I.F.R., than, how the B.I.F.R. could know the liability of the company as damages payable by it, if the quantum is not quantified under section 14-B. As such, the setting aside the order of the Commissioner does not lay-down a good law, the quantification was not disputed by the petitioner.

It must be clear that the B.I.F.R. does not have any power to waive damages or P.F. contribution in default, but being a statutory body for considering the Industrial and Financial Reconstruction, it works on a rehabilitation scheme in the first instance, and if it fails, than orders for winding up of the company and refers the matter to the judicial authority under the Companies Act. In case a rehabilitation scheme is approved, it proposes in the scheme how the amount of contribution in default would be liquidated, for which generally easy installments are proposed and the authority concerned facilitated for the same. And, in case of any fine or damages in case of P.F., it recommends for waiver of all or the part of such damages, which is hounored by the competent authority under the relevant Act.

X. Waiver of, or reduction in damages:

The Central Board of Trustees has been empowered under the second proviso to Section 14-B for waiver of, or reduction in the damages levied. To claim the waiver is the right of an employer, but it is not the right of him to get it form the Central Board. A scheme has been made for this purpose by putting paragraph 32-B in the EPF Scheme, 1952. There are three conditions, under which, the C.B.T. may consider a request for waiver of damages upto 100%. Those are-

(1) Change of management including transfer of the undertaking to the Workers' Cooperative society,

(2) Merger or amalgamation of a sick industrial company with any other company

(3) As recommended in a rehabilitation scheme approved by the B.I.F.R duly recorded reason therein.

And, in any other case, depending on the merits of the case, the C.B.T. may waive the damages upto 50 % at its discretion.

The Madras High Court in the case of *Kancheepuram Kamakshiamman Crop. Spg. Mills Ltd., Kancheepuram Vs. CBT, EPF and others–[2010-III-LLT-740 (Mad.)]* has observed that it could not know how the notification under Tamilnadu Act would ensure to the benefit of the petitioner. It was a state enactment and no exemption there is could be made by the state legislature from central statute (namely the EPF Act, 1952), Neither the State Act provided for grant of exemption is respect of EPF & M.P. Act, 1952, nor such legislature also be made by the state legislature, since the EPF & M.P. Act, 1952 is enacted by the parliament.

It may further be noted that the interest chargeable under Section 7Q of the Act, cannot be waived in any condition as there is no provision to that effect any-where in the Act.

XI. Interest on belated remittances:

Section [1][7Q*. **The employer shall be liable to pay simple interest at the rate of twelve per cent. Per annum or at such higher rate as may be specified in the Scheme on any amount due from him under this Act from the date on which the amount has become so due till the date of its actual payment:**

Provided that higher rate of interest specified in the Scheme shall not exceed the lending rate of interest charged by any scheduled bank.]

| * | Note: Marginal heading for Sec. 7Q not given in the official gazette. |
| 1. | Inserted by Act 33 of 1988 Sec. 11 (w.e.f. 1.7.1997). |

By amendments of 1988, one more provision has been added under Section 7Q which empowers the CBT to recover interest on belated remittances @ 12 % per annum. This provision, in fact, is the way out of various court decisions in which the damages levyable, were comprising elements of penalty as well as interest to meat the loss caused by delayed payments. Now, the damages are entirely become a measure of penalty as has been drafted in Section 14-B, and the interest is recoverable under Section 7Q for which no excuse for non-payment or waiver is avalable. However, despite a mechanical calculation of it, and the provision under the Act does not provide for show-cause notice, such an opportunity is necessary- *[Engser Ltd. & another vs. E.P.F. Organisation & Others -2007 III CLR 550 (Cal)].*

Similar views have been taken by the Punjab & Haryana High Court in the case of **Pathankot Janta Cooperative Labour & Construction society Ltd. and another vs. State of Punjab Through Secretary, Irrigation, Punjab, Chandigarh & other – [2011 LLr. 1162 (P & H H.C.)]** wherein it was held that EOF authority before passing any order of PF contribution, determination of amount has to be ensured that notice on the person/establishment on whom liability is proposed to be is fixed, is served and opportunity of hearing is provided. Contractor Society being exempted from EPF Act, not liable to pay contribution.

Before passing and order fro imposing any penalty or fixing liability of a person / party, non-service of show cause notice and not giving an opportunity of hearing to the concerned person/party by the Authority concerned will be against the principles of natural justice and liable to be quashed.

Any strict construction would adversely affect legislative objects as well as hamper proceedings before appropriate forum, hence provision providing for appeal should either be construed strictly nor liberally- *[Arcot Textile Mills Ltd. vs. The Riginal P.F. Commissioner and others- 2014 LLr. 89: 2014 (140) FLR 233 (S.C.)].*

Petitioners who were contract workers, due to late coverage under the Act were denied interest on their amounts due on the ground that employer had not paid the amount of interest. Hence this writ petition.

It is held that there is no interdiction from the court in the matter of realilsation of interest under Section 7Q and interdiction in only with regard to the realization of damages. Therefore, it is for the first respondent to take steps to realize interest under Section 7Q from the second respondent in case the same was not paid or otherwise held not liable. The first respondent is not justified in denying interest to the member on the ground that the employer has not paid interest. Petition is allowed.- *[Joseph K.V. vs. R.P.F.C., Ernakullam- 2003 II CLR 96 (Ker.)].*

Also see the case of ***Apex security and Detective Force Pvt. Ltd. Vs. Central Board of Trustees, EPF Irganisation- [2015 LLR. 900 (Delhi H.C.)] referred to herein above in this chapter.***

So far as the imposition of amount of interest is concerned, it is definitely governed by Section and P.F. Authority cannot impose over and above the rate given therein- *[Jyoti Cements (P) Ltd. and others vs. Commissioner and others – 2011 (131) FLR. 557 (Raj. H.C.)].*

Chapter 16

E.P.F. Appellate Tribunal

> ***Brief badinage:-***
>
> *Judicial process in our democracy is like the heart in the body, which, every moment, cleans the blood of belief and supplies it to the whole structure of the democracy, despite the un-healthy food habits both inherited and created by ourselves and nourished by the bureaucracy. That is why a chain of judicial process right from the chair of wisdom of an administrator to the highest forum, works for the satisfaction of them-selves instead of the shelter seekers under an umbrella of a social security. No doubt, still the faith is there.*

Legislative reference:-

Prior to amendments of 1988, the finality of the order under Section 7A and un-satisfactory out-come of the references, any, made under Section 19-Athen existed, a forum for appeal was under consideration and it was provided by the amendments of 1988, which were given effect as late as 01.7.1997 with set-up of an appellate-Tribunal, with the only bench in New-Delhi. Any body, who is aggrieved by any of the above notification or order, may prefer appeal, he may be a worker, he may be an employer or any officer of the department it-self, but, the language of the provisions is so that it is all intended towards the employer only, and only the employer will be aggrieved and prefer an appeal. It is also an inherent provision that the department (the EPFO) may also prefer an appeal against an order, no doubt, under Section 7A or 7-B or 7-C or 14-B. Unfortunately, instead of adopting this go, administrative action is taken against that authority, which, in the words of judiciary, is an abuse, which ultimately, renders un-pleasant and adverse results in administration of social security schemes.

*****

Section [1][7D. Employees' Provident Funds Appellate Tribunal.– (1) The Central Government may, by notification in the Official Gazette, constitute one or more Appellate Tribunals to be known as the Employees' Provident Funds Appellate Tribunals to be known as the powers and discharge the functions conferred on such Tribunal by this Act and every such Tribunal shall have jurisdiction in respect of establishments situated in such area as may be specified in the notification constituting the Tribunal.

(2) A Tribunal shall consist of one person only to be appointed by the Central Government.

(3) [2][A person shall not be qualified for appointment as the Presiding Officer of a Tribunal (hereinafter referred to as the Presiding Officer), unless he is, or has been, or is qualified to be,

(i) a judge of a High Court; or

(ii) A District Judge.]

1.	Secs. 7B to 7Q inserted by Act 33 of 1988, s. 11 (w.e.f. 1.7.1997).
2.	Substituted by Act 10 of 1998, s.3(w.e.f. 22.9.1997).

Section [1][7E. Term of office. – The Presiding Officer of a Tribunal shall hold office for a term of five years from the date on which he enters upon his office or until he attains the age of sixty-two years, whichever is earlier.]

1. Secs. 7B to 7Q inserted by Act 33 of 1988, s. 11 (w.e.f. 1.7.1997).

Section [1][7F. Resignation. – 1[(1) The Presiding Officer may, by notice in writing under his hand addressed to the Central Government, resign his office:

Provided that the presiding Officer shall, unless he is permitted by the Central Government to relinquish his officer sooner, continue to hold office until the expiry of three months from the date of receipt of such notice or until a person duly appointed as his successor enters upon his office or until the expiry of his term of office, whichever is the earliest.

[2][(2) The Presiding Officer shall not be removed from his office except by an order by the President on the ground of proved misbehavior or incapacity after an inquiry made by a Judge of the High Court in which such Presiding Officer had been informed of the charges against him and given a reasonable opportunity of being heard in respect of those charges.

(3) The Central Government may, by rules, regulate the procedure for the investigation of misbehaviors or incapacity of the Presiding Officer.]

1.	Re-numbered by Act 10 of 1998, s. 4 (w.e.f. 22.11.1997).
2.	Inserted by Act 10 of 1998, s.3 (w.e.f. 22.11.1997).

Section [1][7G. Salary and allowances and other terms and conditions of service of Presiding Officer.– The salary and allowances payable to, and the other terms and conditions of service (including pension, gratuity and other retirement benefits) of, the Presiding Officer shall be such as may be prescribed:

Provided that neither the salary and allowances nor the other terms and conditions of service of the Presiding Officer shall be varied to him disadvantage after his appointment.

Section [1][7H. Staff of the Tribunal.– (1) The Central Government shall determine the nature and categories of the officers and other employees required to assist a Tribunal in the discharge of its functions and provide the Tribunal with such officers and other employees as it may think fit.

(2) The officers and other employees of a Tribunal shall discharge their functions under the general superintendence of the Presiding Officer.

(3) The salaries and all allowances and other conditions of service of the officers and other employees of a Tribunal shall be such as may be prescribed.]

1. Secs. 7B to 7Q inserted by Act 33 of 1988, s. 11 (w.e.f. 1.7.1997).

Section [1][7-I. Appeals to the Tribunal.- (1) Any person aggrieved by a notification issued by the Central Government, or an order passed by the Central Government, or any authority, under the proviso to sub-section (3), or sub-section (4), of section 1, or section 3, or sub-section (1) of section 7A, or section 7B [except an order rejecting an application for review referred to in sub-section (5) thereof], or section 7C, or section 14B, may prefer an appeal to a Tribunal against such order.

(2) Every appeal under sub-section (1) shall be filed in such form and manner, within such time and be accompanied by such fees, as may be prescribed.]

---
1. Secs. 7B to 7Q inserted by Act 33 of 1988, s. 11 (w.e.f. 1.7.1997).

Section [1][7-J. Procedure of Tribunals. – (1) A Tribunal shall have power to regulate its own procedure in all matters arising out of the exercise of its powers or of the discharge of its functions including the places at which the Tribunal shall have its sittings.

(2) A Tribunal shall, for the purpose of discharging is functions, have all the powers which are vested in the officers referred to in section 7A and any proceeding before the Tribunal shall be 193 and 228, and for the purpose of section 196, of the Indian Penal Code (45 of 1860) and the Tribunal shall be deemed to be a civil court for all the purposes of section 195 and Chapter XXVI of the Code of Criminal Procedure, 1973 (2 of 1974).]

---
1. Secs. 7B to 7Q inserted by Act 33 of 1988, s. 11 (w.e.f. 1.7.1997).

Section [1][7K. Right of appellant to take assistant of legal practitioner and of Government, etc., to appoint presenting officers.- (1) A person preferring an appeal to a Tribunal under this Act may either appear in person or take the assistance of a legal practitioner of his choice to present his case before the Tribunal.

(2) The Central Government or a State Government or any other authority under this Act may authorised one may present the case with respect to any appeal before a Tribunal.]

---
1. Secs. 7B to 7Q inserted by Act 33 of 1988, s. 11 (w.e.f. 1.7.1997).

Section [1][7L. Orders of Tribunal. – (1) A Tribunal may, after giving the parties to the appeal, an opportunity of being heard, pass such orders thereon as it thinks fit, confirming, modifying or annulling the order appealed against or may refer the case back to the authority which passed such order with such directions as the Tribunal may think fit, for a fresh adjudication or order, as the case may be after taking additional evidence, if necessary.

(2) A Tribunal may, at any time within five years from the date of its order, with a view to rectifying any mistaken apparent from the records, amend any order passed by it under sub-section (1) and shall make such amendment in the order if the mistake is brought to its notice by the parties to the appeal:

Provided that an amendment which has the effect of enhancing the amount due from, or otherwise increasing the liability of, the employer shall not be made under this sub-section, unless the Tribunal has given notice to him of its intention to do so and has allowed him a reasonable opportunity of being heard.

(3) A Tribunal shall send a copy of every order passed under this section to the parties to the appeal.

(3) Any order made by a Tribunal finally disposing of an appeal shall not be questioned in any court of law.]

---
1. Secs. 7B to 7Q inserted by Act 33 of 1988, s. 11 (w.e.f. 1.7.1997).

Section [7M. Filling up of vacancies. – If, for any reason, a vacancy occurs in the office of the Presiding Officer, the Central Government shall appoint another person in accordance with the provisions of this Act, to fill the vacancy and the proceedings may be continued before a Tribunal from the stage at which the vacancy is filled.]

---
1. Secs. 7B to 7Q inserted by Act 33 of 1988, s. 11 (w.e.f. 1.7.1997).

Section [7N. Finality of orders constituting a Tribunal. – No order of the Central Government appointing any person as the Presiding Officer shall be called in question in any manner, and no act or proceeding before a Tribunal shall be called in question in any manner on the ground merely of any defect in the constitution of such Tribunal.]

---
1. Secs. 7B to 7Q inserted by Act 33 of 1988, s. 11 (w.e.f. 1.7.1997).

Section [7-O. Deposit of amount due, on filing appeal. - No. appeal by the employer shall be entertained by a Tribunal unless he has deposited with it seventy-five per cent. Of the amount due from him as determined by an officer referred to in section 7A:

Provided that the Tribunal may, for reasons to be recorded in writing, waive or reduce the amount to be deposited under this section.]

---
1. Secs. 7B to 7Q inserted by Act 33 of 1988, s. 11 (w.e.f. 1.7.1997).

Section [7P. Transfer of certain applications to tribunals. – All applications which are pending before the Central Government under section 19A, shall stand transferred to a Tribunal exercising jurisdiction in respect of establishments in relation to which such applications had been made as if such applications were appeals preferred to the Tribunal.]

---
1. Secs. 7B to 7Q inserted by Act 33 of 1988, s. 11 (w.e.f. 1.7.1997).

I. Matters which can be appealed against:

An appeal is made under Section 7-I of the Act. The matters in which or the orders against which appeal can be preferred are –

(i) a notification issued by the Central Government;

(ii) an order passed by the Central Government or any authority

\# under proviso to sub-section (3) or sub-section (4) of Section 1, or

\# under sub-section (1) of Section 7-A, or

\# under Section 7-B (except the order rejecting the review application), or

\#   under Section 7-C, or

\#   under Section 14-B.

No other matter can be undertaken by the Tribunal.

Anybody aggrieved by such order or notification can prefer an appeal for a suitable order or direction from the Tribunal.

An appeal against under Section 7-Q of the Act would not lie under Section 7-I of the Act since there is no express provision of appeal against the order under Section 7-Q – *[Apex Security and Detective force Pvt. Ltd. Vs. Cental Board of Trustees, EPFO -2015 LLr. 900 (delhi H.C.)].*

II. Application for appeal:

The procedure and other conditions of appeal have been prescribed in the **Employees' Provident Funds Appellate Tribunal (Procedure) Rules, 1997.** The appeal can be submitted within 60 days of the making of such order against which appeal if being preferred. The Tribunal may extend the period on his satisfaction of the reasons for delay.

Fee payable with the appeal is Rs.500 through a demand draft drawn on a Nationalized Bank and payable at the station where the Tribunal is situated.

75% of the amount due as determined under Section 7-A is also required to be deposited, but the tribunal may waive or reduce the amount with the reason to be recorded in writing.

In an appeal under Section 7-I of the Act, Appellate Tribunal directed pre-deposit amount determined under Section 7-A of the Act and disallowed exemption or waiver of the same. In writ petition against the said order, learned single judge refused to interfere with the said order of the appellate Tribunal, Hence this writ appeal.

Conduct of the appellant-company in procrastinating and prolonging proceedings and coming out with version of destruction of records due to fire demonstrates its lack of *bona-fides.* Learned Single Judge rightly refused to exercise jurisdiction at interim stage. There is no infirmity in the order of Learned Single Judge - *[Girdhar Silk Mills vs. P.O. EPF Appellate Tribunal- 2003 (1) LLN 172 (Del. DB)].*

III. Finality of the order of the Tribunal:

In sub-section (4) of Section 7-L provides that the order of the Tribunal disposing of an appeal shall not be questionable in court of law. But, Article 226 and 227 of the Constitution keep doors opened for a writ as the **jurisdiction of the High Courts.** Though, appeal is available under the Act and is definitely an adequate alternative remedy not preclude the writ jurisdiction altogether. When it does not involve any amount of determination of fact, it is purely a simple question of law. High Court cannot refuse to exercise jurisdiction on account of existence of alternative remedy - *[Om Roller Flour Mills vs. U.O.I. – 2002 (3) LLJ 228; 2002 Lab.IC 1221; 2002 (94) FLR 908; 2002 LLR 683].*

Order demanding contribution for petitioner's canteen employees was challenged in the writ and contrary argument was advanced that there is remedy of appeal under Section 7-I of the Act, hence writ petition is not maintainable.

There is some substance in the contention of petitioner that the authority, while passing the order has not addressed itself to the preposition of law which ought to have done while considering the question having regard to law that is settled by Supreme Court. The imposition of liability is founded on such finding and such it is a question which goes to the root of the case. When it is dependent on the root and relates to a fact which gives jurisdiction to the authority, it is a jurisdictional fact and in that event, High Court can very well enter into the question despite remedy of appeal being available. If it is found that there has been a violation of fundamental principal of law or that fundamental principal of law has not been addressed to, in that event. High Court, despite alternative remedy, can interfere - **[Standard Chartered Bank vs. U.O.I – 2002 (II) LLJ 754 (Cal.)].**

IV. Procedure of Appeal and Tribunal:

Tribunal is a substitute of an intermediatory to the High Courts, and empower to deliver as if a court hence procedure for that purpose and to maintain dignity of the court, Separate rules have been framed, which contains everything relating to the court-procedure. The Rules are given below-

The Employees' Provident Funds Appellate Tribunal (Procedure) Rules, 1997

NOTIFICATION

[11]**G.S.R. 268.—** In exercise of the powers conferred by sub-section (1) of Section 21 of the Employees' Provident Funds and Miscellaneous Provisions Act, 1952 (19 of 1952), the Central Government hereby makes the following rules namely:—

1. Short title and Commencement. — (1) These rules may be called the Employees' Provident Funds Appellate Tribunal (Procedure) Rules, 1997.

(2) They shall come into force from the date of their publication in the Official Gazette.

2. Definitions. — In these rules unless the context otherwise requires:—

(a) 'Act' means the Employees' Provident Funds and Miscellaneous Provisions Act, 1952 (19 of 1952);

(b) 'Agent' means a person duly authorised by a party to present as appeal or a written reply on its behalf before the Tribunal;

(c) 'Appellant' means a person or the establishment making an appeal to the Tribunal under Section 7-1;

(d) 'Form' means a form specified in Appendix;

[2][(dd) 'Fund' means Provident Fund, Pension Fund and Insurance Fund established under the Act;]

(e) 'Legal Practitioner' shall have the same meaning as is assigned to it in the Advocates Act, 1961 (25 of 1961);

(f) 'Legal Representative' means a person who in law represents the estate of the deceased;

(g) 'Registrar' means the Registrar appointed for the Tribunal and includes any officer to whom the powers and functions of the Registrar may be delegated under these rules,

(h) 'Registry' means the Registry of the Tribunal;

(i) 'Tribunal' means the Employees' Provident Funds Appellate Tribunal established under sub-section (1) of section 7(D) of the Act;

(j) The words and expressions used and not defined in these rules but defined in the Act shall have the same meanings respectively assigned to them in the Act.

3. Language of the Tribunal– The language of the Tribunal shall be English;

Provided that the parties proceeding before the Tribunal may, file documents drawn up in Hindi, if they so desire;

Provided further that: (a) The Tribunal may in its discretion permit the use of Hindi in the proceedings but the final order shall be in English;

(b) The Tribunal hearing the matter, may in its discretion, direct English translation of pleadings and documents to be filed.

4. Procedure for Filing Appeals — (1) An appeal to this Tribunal shall be presented in Form-I by the appellant in person or by an agent or by a duly authorised legal practitioner to the Registrar or any other officer authorised in writing by the Registrar to receive the same or be sent by registered post with acknowledgement due addressed to the Registrar of the Tribunal.

(2) The appeal under sub-rule (1) shall be presented in triplicate in a paper-book form alongwith one unused file size envelope bearing full address of the respondent.

(3) Where the number of respondents is more than one, as many extra copies of the appeal in paper-book form as there are respondents together with unused file size envelopes bearing the full address of each respondent shall be furnished by the appellant:

Provided that where the number of respondents is more than five, the Registrar may permit the appellant to file the extra copies of the appeal at the time of issue of notice to the respondents.

(4) The appellant may attach to and present with his appeal a receipt slip in Form-II which shall be signed by the Registrar or the Officer receiving the appeal on behalf of the Registrar in acknowledgement of the receipt of the appeal.

5. Presentation and Scrutiny of Appeals. — (1) The Registrar, or the officer authorised by him under Rule 4, shall endorse on every appeal the date on which it is presented or deemed to have been presented under that rule and shall sign the endorsement.

(2) If, on scrutiny, the appeal is found to be in order it shall be duly registered and given a serial number.

(3) If the appeal, on scrutiny, is found to be defective and the defect noticed is formal in nature, the Registrar may allow the party to rectify the same in his presence, and if the said defect is not formal in nature, the Registrar may allow the appellant such time to rectify the defect as he may deem fit.

(4) If the appellant fails to rectify the defect within the time allowed under sub-rule (3), the Registrar may by order and for reasons to be recorded in writing, decline to registrar the appeal and inform the appellant accordingly.

6. Place of Filing Appeals.— The appeal shall ordinarily be filed by the appellant with the Registrar of the Tribunal within whose jurisdiction:— (i) the appellant is residing for the time being, or

(ii) the cause of action has arisen, or (iii) the respondent or any of the respondents against whom relief is sought, ordinarily resides.

7. Fee, Time for Filing Appeal, Deposit of Amount Due on Filing Appeal. — [1][(1) Every appeal filed with the Registrar shall be accompanied by a fee of rupees five hundred to be remitted in the form of Crossed Demand Draft on a nationalised bank in favour of the Registrar of the Tribunal and payable at the main Branch of the bank at the station where the seat of the said Tribunal is situate].

(2) Any person aggrieved by a notification issued by the Central Government or an Order passed by the Central Government or any other authority under the Act, may within 60 days from the date of issue of the notification/order, prefer an appeal to the Tribunal:

Provided that the Tribunal may if it is satisfied that the appellant was prevented by sufficient cause from preferring the appeal within the prescribed period, extend the said period by a further period of 60 days:

Provided further that no appeal by the employer shall be entertained by a Tribunal unless he has [1][deposited with the tribunal a Demand Draft payable in the Fund and bearing] 75% of the amount due from him as determined under section 7-A:

Provided also that the Tribunal may for reasons to be recorded in writing, waive or reduce the amount to be deposited under section 7-O.

8. Content of The Appeal. — Every appeal filed under rule 4 shall set forth concisely under distinct heads the grounds for such appeal. Such grounds shall be numbered consecutively. Every appeal, including any miscellaneous appeal shall be typed in double space on one side on thick paper of good quality.

9. Documents to Accompany the Appeal — (1) Every appeal shall be accompanied by a paper-book containing —

(i) an attested true copy of the order against which the appeal is filed;

(ii) copies of the documents relied upon by the appellant and referred to in the appeal;

(iii) an index of the documents.

(2) The documents referred to in sub-rule (1) may be attested by a legal practitioner or by a gazetted officer and each document shall be marked serially as Annexure A1, A2, A3 and so on.

(3) Where an appeal is filed by an agent, document authorising him to act as such agent shall also be appended to the appeal:

Provided that where an appeal is filed by a legal practitioner, it shall be accompanied by a duly executed 'Vakalatnama.'

10. Plural Remedies. — An appeal shall be based upon a single cause of action and may seek one or more reliefs provided that they are consequential to one another.

11. Service of Notices and Processes Issued by the Tribunal. — (1) Notices or process to be jissued by the Tribunal may be served by any of the following modes directed by the Tribunal:

(i) service by the party itself;

(ii) by hand delivery (Dasti) through process server;

(iii) by registered post with acknowledgement due.

(2) Where notice issued by the Tribunal is served by the party himself by 'Hand delivery' (Dasti), he shall file with the Registry of the Tribunal, the acknowledgement, together with an affidavit of service.

(3) Notwithstanding anything contained in Sub-rule (1) the Tribunal may, taking into account the number of respondents and their places of residence or work and other circumstances, direct that notice of the appeal shall be served upon the respondents in any other manner including any manner of substituted service, as it appears to the Tribunal just and convenient.

(4) Notwithstanding anything done under sub-rule (1) the Tribunal may in its discretion, having regard to the nature and urgency of the case, direct the service of the notice on the Standing Counsels appointed as such by the Central Government or any State Government or any other authority under the Act.

(5) Every notice issued by the Tribunal shall, unless otherwise ordered, be accompanied by a copy of the appeal along with a copy of the paper-book.

(6) Every appellant shall pay a fee for the service or execution of processes in such manner as the Tribunal may direct under sub-rule (3) such a sum, not exceeding the actual charges incurred in effecting the service, as may be determined by the Tribunal.

(7) The fee for the service or execution of processes under sub-rule (3) shall be remitted in the manner prescribed in Rule *1* within one week of the date of the order determining the fee or within such extended time as the Registrar may permit.

(8) Notwithstanding anything contained in sub-rules (1) to (4), if the Tribunal is satisfied that it is not reasonably practicable to serve notice of appeal upon all the respondents, it may, for reasons to be recorded in writing, direct that the appeal shall be heard notwithstanding that some of the respondents have not been served with notice of the application; provided that no appeal shall be heard unless: —

(i) Notice of the appeal has been served on the Central Government or the State Government or the Central Board or if such Government or Board is a respondent;

(ii) Notice of the appeal has been served on the authority which passed the order against which the appeal has been filed; and

(iii) the Tribunal is satisfied that the interests of the respondents on whom notice of the appeal has not been served are adequately and sufficiently represented by the respondents on whom notice of the appeal has been served

12. Filing of Reply and other Documents by The Respondents.— (1) Each respondent intending to contest the appeal, shall file in triplicate the reply to the appeal and the documents relied upon in paper-book form with the Registry within one month of the service of notice of the appeal on him.

(2) In the reply filed under sub-rule (1), respondent shall specifically, admit, deny or explain the facts stated by the appellant in his appeal and may also state such additional facts as may be found necessary for the just decision of the case. It shall be signed and verified as a written statement by the respondent or any other person duly authorised by him in writing in the same manner as provided for in order VI, Rule 15 of the Code of Civil Procedure, 1908 (5 of 1908).

(3) The documents referred to in sub-rule (2) shall also be filed alongwith the reply and the same shall be marked as R1 , R2, R3 and so on.

(4) The respondent shall also serve a copy of the reply alongwith documents as mentioned in sub-rule (1) on the appellant or his legal practitioner, if any, and file proof of such service in the Registry.

(5) The Tribunal may allow filing of the reply after the expiry of the prescribed period.

13. Date and Place of Hearing to be Notified.— The Tribunal shall notify to the parties the date and the place of hearing of the appeal in such manner as the Presiding Officer may by general or special order direct.

14. Calendar of Cases. — (1) The Tribunal shall draw up a calendar for the hearing of cases and, as far as possible, hear and decide cases according to the calendar.

(2) Every appeal shall be heard and decided, as far as possible within six months from the date of its registration.

(3) The Tribunal shall have the power to decline an adjournment and also to limit the time for oral arguments.

15. Action on Appeal for Appellant's Default. — (1) Where on the date fixed for hearing of the appeal or on any other date to which such hearing may be adjourned, the appellant does not appear when the appeal is called for hearing, the Tribunal may, in its discretion either dismiss the appeal for default or hearing and decide it on merit.

(2) Where an appeal has been dismissed for default and the appellant files an appeal within thirty days from the date of dismissal and satisfies the Tribunal that there was sufficient cause for his non-appearance when the appeal was called for hearing, the Tribunal shall make an order setting aside the order dismissing the appeal and restore the same:

Provided, however where the case was disposed of on merits the decision shall not be reopened except by way of review.

16. Ex-parte Hearing and Disposal of Appeal. — (1) Where on the date fixed for hearing the appeal or on any other date to which such hearing may be adjourned, the appellant appears and the respondent does not appear when the appeal is called for hearing, the Tribunal may, in its discretion adjourn the hearing or hear and decide the appeal ex-parte.

(2) Where an appeal has been heard ex-parte against a respondent or respondents, such respondent or respondents may apply to the Tribunal for an order to set it aside and if such respondent or respondents satisfy the Tribunal that the notice was not duly served or that he or they were prevented by any sufficient cause from appearing when the appeal was called for hearing the Tribunal may make an order setting aside the ex-parte hearing as against him or them upon such terms as it thinks fit, and shall appoint a day for proceeding with the appeal:

Provided that where the ex-parte order the appeal is of such nature that it cannot be set aside as against one respondent only, it may be set aside as against all or any of the other respondents also:

Provided further that in cases covered by sub-rule (8) of rule 11, the Tribunal shall not set aside ex-parte order of an appeal merely on the ground that it was not served upon a respondent or respondents.

17. Substitution of Legal Representatives. — (1) In the case of death of a party during the pendency of the proceedings before the Tribunal, the legal representatives of the deceased party may apply within thirty days of the date of such death for being brought on record as necessary parties.

(2) Where no application is received from the legal representatives within the period specified in sub-rule (1), the proceedings against the deceased party shall abate:

Provided that on good and sufficient reasons the Tribunal, on an application, may set aside the order of abatement and substitute the legal representatives.

18. Adjournment of Hearing. — The Tribunal may if sufficient cause is shown at any stage of proceedings grant time to the parties or any of them, and adjourn the hearing of the appeal.

19. Order to be Signed and Dated. — (1) Every order of the Tribunal shall be in writing and shall be signed by the Presiding Officer who pronounced the order.

(2) The order shall be pronounced in open Court.

20. Communication of Orders to Parties.— (1) Every final order passed on any appeal shall be communicated to the appellant and to the respondent concerned either by hand delivery or by registered post free of cost.

(2) If the appellant or the respondent to any proceeding requires a copy of any document or proceeding the same shall be supplied to him on such terms and conditions on payment of such fees as may be fixed by the Presiding Officer by general or special order.

21. Orders and Directions in Certain Cases. — The Tribunal may make such orders or give such directions as may be necessary or expedient to give effect to its orders or to prevent abuse of its process or to secure the ends of justice.

22. Working Hours of the Tribunal. — Except on Saturday, Sundays and other public holidays, the office of the Tribunal shall, subject to any order made by the Presiding Officer remain open from 9.30 A.M. to 6.00 P.M.

23. Sitting Hours of the Tribunal. — The silting hours of the Tribunal shall ordinarily be from 10.30 A.M. to 1.30 P.M. and 2.30 P.M. to 5.00 P.M. subject to any general or special order made by the Presiding Officer.

24. Orders and Functions of The Registrar.— (1) The Registrar shall have the custody of the records of the Tribunal and shall exercise such other functions as are assigned to him under these rule or by the Presiding Officer by separate order.

(2) The Official seal shall be kept in the custody of the Registrar.

(3) Subject to any general or special direction by the Presiding Officer, the l of the Tribunal shall not be affixed to any order, summons or other process save under the authority in writing of the Registrar.

(4) The seal of the Tribunal shall not be affixed to any certified copy issued by the Tribunal save under the authority in writing of the Registrar.

25. Additional Powers and Duties of Registrar.— In addition to the powers conferred elsewhere in these rules, the Registrar shall have the following powers and duties subject to any general or special order of the Presiding Officer namely —

(i) to receive all appeals and other documents;

(ii) to decide all questions arising out of the scrutiny of the appeals before they are registered;

(iii) to require any appeal presented to the Tribunal to be amended in accordance with the Act and the rules;

(iv) subject to the direction of the Tribunal, to fix the date of first hearing of the appeals or other proceedings and issue notices thereof;

(v) to direct any formal amendment of records;

(vi) to order grant of copies of documents to parties to the proceedings;

(vii) to grant leave to inspect the records of the Tribunal;

(viii) to dispose of all matters relating to the service of notices or other processes for the issue of fresh notices and for extending the time for filing such appeals and to grant time not exceeding

15 days for filing a reply or rejoinder if any and to place the matter before the Tribunal for appropriate order after the expiry of the aforesaid period;

(ix) to requisition records from the custody of any court or other authority;

(x) to receive appeals within thirty days from the date of death for substitution of legal representatives of the deceased parties during the pendency of the appeals;

(xi) to receive and dispose of appeals for substitution, except where the substitution would involve setting aside of order of abatement;

(xii) to receive and dispose of applications by parties for return of documents.

26. Seal and Emblem.— The official seal and emblem of the Tribunal shall be in a round shape bearing name of the Tribunal in capital letters with Ashoka Pillar in the Centre.

27. Dress of the Presiding Officer and Staff of the Tribunal.— The dress for the Presiding Officer of the Tribunal and members of the staff of the Tribunal shall be such as the Presiding Officer may specify.

28. Dress of the Parties.— A legal practitioner or, as the case may be, a Presenting officer shall appear before the Tribunal in his professional dress, if any, and if there is no such dress —

(i) if a male, in a closed collared coat and trousers or in a lounge suit;

(ii) if a female, in a saree or any other customary dress of a sober colour.

29. Expenses of the Tribunals. — The entire administrative expenses of the Tribunal shall be borne by the Central Board of Trustees, Employees' Provident Fund:[and the fee or any other money received by the Tribunal shall form a part of the administrative fund of the Central Board].

E.P.F. Appellate Tribunal

APPENDIX

FORM I
(See Rule 4)

APPEAL UNDER SECTION 7-1 OF THE EMPLOYEES' PROVIDENT FUNDS AND MISCELLANEOUS PROVISIONS ACT, 1952

Title of the Case:

INDEX

Serial No.   Description of documents relied   Page No.

1.
2.
3.
4.

Signature of the Applicant

For use in Tribunal Office.

Dale of Filing

or

Date of Receipt by post.   *Signature for*
Registrar

Registration No.

IN THE EMPLOYEES' PROVIDENT FUNDS APPELLATE TRIBUNAL

BETWEEN

A.   B.   APPELLANT

         Versus

C.   D.   RESPONDENT

Details of Appeal

  1. Particulars of the appellant:

    (i) Name of the appellant

    (ii) Office address

    (iii) Address for service of notices

  2. Particulars of the respondent:

    (i) Name of the respondent:

    (ii) Office address

(iii) Address for service of notices:

3. Particulars of the order/notification against which appeal is made. The appeal is against the following order/notification:—

(i) Order/Notification No. with reference to Annexure

(ii) Date

(iii) Passed by

(iv) Subject in brief

4. Jurisdiction of the Tribunal.— The appellant declares that the subject-matter of the order against which he wants redressal is within the jurisdiction of the Tribunal.

5. Limitation.— The appellant further declares that the appeal is within the limitation prescribed in section 7-1 of the Employees' Provident Funds and Miscellaneous Provisions Act, 1952.

6. Facts of the case.— The facts of the case are given below:

(Give here a concise statement of facts in a chronological order, each paragraph containing as nearly as possible a separate issue, fact or otherwise).

7. Details of the remedies exhausted.— The appellant declares that he has availed of all the remedies available to him under the Act.

(Give here chronologically the details of representations made and the outcome of such representation with reference to the Annexure numbers).

8. Matters not previously filed or pending with any other Court.— The appellant further declares that he had not previously filed any appeal, writ petition or suit regarding the matter in respect of which this appeal has been made, before any court of law or any other authority or any other bench of the Tribunal and nor any such appeal, writ petition or suit is pending before any of them.

In case the appellant had previously filed any appeal, writ petition or suit, the stage at which it is pending and if decided, the gist of the decision should be given with reference to the Annexure.

9. Relief(s) sought.— In view of the facts mentioned in para 6 above the appellant prays for the following relief(s):—

[Specify below the relief(s) sought explaining the ground for relief(s) and the legal provisions (if any) relied upon.]

10. Interim order, if any prayed for.— Pending final decision on the appeal the appellant seeks issue of the following interim order:—

(Give here the nature of the interim order prayed for with reasons).

11. In the event of appeal being sent by Registered post. It may be stated whether the appellant desires to have oral hearing at the admission stage and if so, he shall attach a self-addressed post card/inland letter, at which intimation regarding the date of hearing could be sent to him.

12. Particulars of bank draft/postal order in respect of the appeal fee:

1. Name of the bank on which drawn.

2. Demand Draft No.

or

1. Number of Indian Postal Order(s)
2. Name of the issuing Post Office
3. Date of issue of Postal Order(s)
4. Post Office at which payable

13. **List of enclosures:**
    1.
    2.
    3.
    4.
    5.
    6.

VERIFICATION

I, ………………….. (Name of the appellant) S/o, D/o, W/o. ……………….. age ……………. working as ………………………………………………… in the office of ………………………,…………………………….. resident of ……………………….. do hereby verify that the contents of paras ……….. to …………………….. are true to my personal knowledge and para ……………….. to ………………… believed to be true on legal advice and that I have not suppressed any material fact.

Date: *Signature of the appellant*

Place:

To, The Registrar,

FORM-II

[See Rule 4(4)]
RECEIPT SLIP

Receipt of the appeal filed in the Employees' Provident Funds Appellate Tribunal by Shri/Kum,/Smt./ ……………………………………………………… working in/for ………………………………………………………………….. of ……………………… residing at ………………….. in hereby acknowledged.

Date: For Registrar

Seal: EPF Appellate Tribunal

The Employees' Provident Funds Appellate Tribunal (Conditions of Service) Rules, 1997[1]

In exercise of the powers conferred by sub-section (1) of section 21 of the Employees' Provident Funds and Miscellaneous Provisions Act, 1952 (19 of 1952), the Central Government hereby makes the following rules, namely —

1. Short title and commencement— (1) These rules may be called the **Employees' Provident Funds Appellate Tribunal (Conditions of Service) Rules, 1997.**

(2) They shall come into force on the date of their publication in the Official Gazette.

2. Definitions — In these rules, unless the context otherwise requires,—

(a) "Act" means the Employees' Provident Funds and Miscellaneous Provisions Act, 1952 (19 of 1952);

(b) "Tribunal" means the Employees' Provident Funds Appellate Tribunal constituted under section 70 of the Act.

3. Pay— The Presiding Officer shall receive pay in the scale -of (Rs. 7300-7600) per mensem:

Provided that in the case of an appointment as a Presiding Officer of a person who has retired as a judge of a High Court and who is in receipt of or has received or has become entitled to receive any retirement benefits by way of pension and/or gratuity, employer's contribution to the contributory Provident Fund or other forms of retirement benefits, the pay shall be reduced by the gross amount of pension equivalent of service gratuity or employer's contribution to Contributory Provident Fund or any other form of retirement benefits, if any, but excluding pension equivalent of retirement gratuity, drawn or to be drawn by him.

4. Dearness Allowance— The Presiding Officer shall receive dearness allowance appropriate to his pay at the rates admissible to Group 'A' Officers of the Central Government drawing pay in the scale of Rs. 7300-7600.

5. City Compensatory Allowance— The Presiding Officer shall receive City Compensatory Allowance appropriate to his pay at the rates admissible to a Group 'A' Officer of the Central Government drawing pay in the scale of Rs. 7300–7600.]

6. Leave— (1) A person, on appointment in the Tribunal as a Presiding Officer shall be entitled to leave as follows —

(i) Earned Leave at the rate of fifteen days for every completed calendar year of service;

(ii) Half pay leave on medical certificate or on private affairs at the rate of twenty days in respect of each completed year of service and the leave salary for half pay leave shall be equivalent to half of the leave salary admissible during the earned leave;

(iii) Leave on half pay can be commuted to full pay leave at the discretion of the Presiding Officer, provided it is taken on medical grounds and is supported by a medical certificate from the competent medical authority;

(iv) Extraordinary leave without pay and allowances up to a maximum period of 180 days in one term of Office.

(2) If the Presiding Officer is unable to enjoy full vacation on account of his occupation with the Tribunal, he shall be entitled to add the unenjoyed period of vacation to the leave account.

Explanation — For the purpose of this sub-rule, "Vacation" means vacation of 30 days in each calendar year observed by the Tribunal.

(3) On the expiry of the term of his office in the Tribunal, the Presiding Officer shall be entitled to receive cash equivalent of leave salary in respect of the earned leave standing to his credit subject to the conditions that the maximum of leave encashed under this sub-rule or at the time of retirement from previous service, as the case may be, or taken together shall not in any case exceed 240 days.

(4) The Presiding Officer shall be entitled to receive the dearness allowance as admissible on the leave salary under sub-rule (2) at the rates in force on the date of the relinquishment of the Office in the Tribunal:

Provided that he shall no be entitled for the city compensatory allowance or any other allowance on such leave.

7. Leave sanctioning authority— That Central Government shall be the authority competent to sanction leave to the Presiding Officer.

8. Pension— The Presiding Officer on deputation with the Tribunal shall be entitled to pension under rules of the parent employer.

9. Provident Fund— The Presiding Officer shall be entitled to subscribe to the General Provident Fund at his option and in case of his so opting shall be governed by the provisions of the Central Provident Fund (Central Services) Rules:

Provided that if the Presiding Officer is already a member of any other Provident Fund he shall be governed by the rules which were applicable to him immediately before joining the Tribunal.

10. Travelling Allowance— The Presiding Officer while on tour or on transfer (including the journey undertaken to join the Tribunal or on the expiry of his term with the Tribunal to proceed to his home town) shall be entitled to the travelling allowances, daily allowance, transportation of personal effects and other similar matters at the same scales and the same rates as are prescribed in the rule applicable to officers holding equivalent post in the Central Government.

11. Leave Travel Concession— The Presiding Officer shall be entitled to the leave travel concession at the same rates and at the same scales and on the same conditions as are applicable to a Group 'A' Officer of the Central Government drawing pay in the scale of Rs. 7300-7600.

12. Accommodation— (1) The Presiding Officer shall be entitled to residential accommodation on the terms and conditions as are made available to officers of the Central Government drawing pay in the scale of Rs. 7300-7600.

(2) When a Presiding Officer is not provided with or does not avail himself of the accommodation referred to in sub-rule (1) he may be paid every month an allowance at the rate admissible to officers of the Central Government drawing pay in the scale of Rs. 7300-7600.

(3) Where the Presiding Officer occupies an official residence beyond the permissible period he shall be liable to pay additional licence fee or penal rent, as the case may be, and liable to eviction in

accordance with the rule applicable to officers of the Central Government drawing pay in the scale of Rs. 7300-7600.

13. Facilities for Medical treatment— The Presiding Officer shall be entitled to medical treatment and hospital facilities as provided in the Contributory Health Service Scheme Rules, 1954 and in places where the Central Health Services Scheme is not in operation, the Presiding Officer shall be entitled to the facilities as provided in the Central Service Medical Attendance Rules.

14. Conditions of service of sitting Judges of the High Court appointed as Presiding Officers— Notwithstanding anything contained in these rules, where a sitting Judge of a High Court is appointed as the Presiding Officer of the Tribunal the service conditions as contained in the High Court Judges (Conditions of Service) Act, 28 of 1954 and the rules made there under shall apply to him.

15. Residuary Provision— The conditions of service of the Presiding Officer for which no express provision is available in these rules shall be determined by the rules and orders for the time being applicable to officers of the Central Government drawing pay in the scale of Rs. 7300-7600.

16. Staff of the Tribunal — The nature and categories of the officers and other employees of the Tribunal and the scale of pay attached thereto shall be as specified in the Schedule appended of these rules.

17. Conditions of Service — The conditions of service of the officers and other employees of the Tribunal in the matters of pay, allowance, leave, provident fund, age of superannuation, pension and retirement benefits, medical facilities and other conditions of service, shall be regulated in accordance with such rules and regulations as are for the time being applicable to officers and employees belonging to Group 'A,' Group 'B,' Group 'C' and Group 'D'], as the case may be, corresponding posts in the Central Government/Central Board.

18. Power to relax— The Central Government shall have power to relax the provisions of any of these rules with respect to any class or category of persons.

SCHEDULE

S. No.	Name of the post	No. of Post	Scale of Pay
1	2	3	4
1.	Registrar	One	Rs. 3000–4500
2.	Sr. PA (for Presiding Officer)	One	Rs. 2000–3200
3.	Steno, Gr. D. (for Registrar)	One	Rs. 1200–2040
4.	UDC	One	Rs. 1200–2040
5.	LDC	One	Rs. 950–1500
6.	Driver	One	Rs. 950–1500
7.	Daftry	One	Rs. 775–1150
8.	Peon	One	Rs. 750–940

Chapter 17

Recovery of the Dues

> **Brief Badinage:-**
>
> *Prior to the amendments of 1988, the recovery of the PF due was being made as an arrear of land revenue through the state revenue authorities for which a certificate was to be issued to them. That procedure accumulated a lot of arrears, hence in-house machinery was created by the amending Act of 1988. But it took three years to come into being when sections 8-B to 8-G inserted for this purpose were notified w.e.f. 1.7.1991.*
>
> *In the new mechanism, two-way system of recovery has been made as has been existed under the Income Tax Act, 1961. The one is, through a Recovery Officer who gets authority to recover any amount by a Recovery Certificate issued by an Authorised Officer. And the another is, by the Authorized Officer him-self as defined the 'other modes of recovery' as detailed in Section 8-F. Recovery Officer is not authorized to invoke the powers mentioned under Section 8-F.*

Section [1][8. Mode of recovery of moneys due from employers.– Any amount due–

(a) from the employer in relation to [2][an establishment] to which any [3][Scheme or the Insurance Scheme] applies in respect of any contribution payable to [4][the Fund or, as the case may be, the Insurance Fund,] damages recoverable under section 14B, accumulations required to be transferred under sub-section (2) of section 15 [5][or under sub-section (5) of section 17] or any charges payable by him under any other provisions of this Act or of any provision of the [3][Scheme or the Insurance Scheme]; or

(b) from the employer in relation to an exempted [2][establishment] in respect of any damages recoverable under section 14B or any charges payable by him the appropriate Government under any provision of this Act or under any of the conditions specified 6[under section 17 or in respect of the contribution payable by him towards the [7][Pension] Scheme under the said section 17], may, if the amount is in arrear, be recovered 8[in the manner specified in section 8B to 8G.]

---

1. Substituted by Act 37 of 1953, s.6, for original section.
2. Substituted by Act 94 of 1956, s.3.
3. Substituted by Act 99 of 1976, s.24, for "Scheme" (deemed to have come into force w.e.f. 1.8.1976).
4. Substituted by Act 99 of 1976, s.24, for "the Fund" (deemed to have come into force w.e.f. 1.8.1976).
5. Inserted by Act 28 of 1963 s.7.
6. Substituted by Act 1971, s. 21.
7. Substituted by Act 25 of 1996, s.4 (w.e.f. 16.11.1995).
8. Substituted by Act 33 of 1988, s. 12 (w.e.f. 1.7.1990).

Section [1][8B. Issue of certificate to the Recovery Officer.– (1) Where any amount is in arrear under section8, the authorised officer may issue, to the Recovery Officer, a certificate under his signature specifying the amount of arrears and the Recovery Officer, on receipt of such certificate, shall proceed to recover the amount specified therein from the establishment or, as the case may be, the employer by one or more of the modes mentioned below:-

(a) attachment and sale of the movable or immovable property of the establishment or, as the case may be, the employer;

(b) arrest of the employer and his detention in prison;

(c) appointing a receiver for the management of the movable or immovable properties of the establishment or, as the case may be, the employer:

Provided that the attachment and sale of any property under this section shall first be effected against the properties of the establishment and where such attachment and sale is insufficient for recovery the whole of the amount of arrears specified in the certificate, the Recovery Officer may take such proceedings against the property of the employer for recovery of the whole or any part of such arrears.

(2) The authorised officer may issue a certificate under sub-section 1, notwithstanding that proceedings for recovery of the arrears by any other mode have been taken.]

1. Ins. by Act 33 of 1988, sec. 14 (w.e.f. 1-7-1990).

Section [1][8C. Recovery officer to whom certificate is to be forwarded.

(1) The authorised officer may forward the certificate referred to in section 8B to the Recovery Officer within whose jurisdiction the employer –

(a) carries on his business or profession or within whose jurisdiction the principal place of his establishment is situated; or

(b) resides or any movable or immovable property of the establishment or the employer is situated.

(2) Where an establishment or the employer has property within the jurisdiction of more than one Recovery Officers and the Recovery Officer to whom a certificate is sent by the authorised officer -

(a) is not able to recover the entire amount by the sale of the property movable or immovable, within his jurisdiction; or

(b) is of the opinion that, for the purpose of expediting or securing the recovery of the whole or any part of the amount, it is necessary so to do,

he may send the certificate or, where only a part of the amount is to be recovered, a copy of the certificate certified in the prescribed manner and specifying the amount to be recovered to the Recovery Officer within whose jurisdiction the establishment or the employer has property or the employer resides, and thereupon that Recovery Officer shall also proceed to recover the amount due under this section as if the certificate or the copy thereof had been the certificate sent to him by the authorised officer.]

1. Ins. by Act 33 of 1988, sec. 14 (w.e.f. 1-7-1990).

Section ¹[8D. Validity of certificate, and amendment thereof.- (1) When the authorised officer issues a certificate to a Recovery Officer under section 8B, it shall not be open to the employer to dispute before the Recovery Officer the correctness of the amount, and no objection to the certificate on any other ground shall also be entertained by the Recovery Officer.

(2) Notwithstanding the issue of a certificate to a Recovery Officer, the authorised officer shall have power to withdraw the certificate or correct any clerical or arithmetical mistake in the certificate by sending an intimation to the Recovery Officer.

(3) The authorised officer shall intimate to the Recovery Officer any orders withdrawing or canceling a certificate or any correction made by him under sub-section 2 or any amendment made under sub-section 4 of section 8E.]

---
1. Ins. by Act 33 of 1988, sec. 14 (w.e.f. 1-7-1990).

Section ¹[8E. Stay of proceedings under certificate and amendment or withdrawal thereof.

(1) Notwithstanding that a certificate has been issued to the Recovery Officer for the recovery of any amount, the authorised officer may grant time for the payment of the amount, and thereupon the Recovery Officer shall stay the proceedings until the expiry of the time so granted.

(2) Where a certificate for the recovery of amount has been issued, the authorised officer shall keep the Recovery Officer informed of any amount paid or time granted for payment, subsequent to the issue of such certificate.

(3) Where the order giving rise to a demand of amount for which a certificate for recovery has been issued has been modified in appeal or other proceeding under this Act, and, as a consequence thereof, the demand is reduced but the order is the subject-matter of further proceeding under this Act, the authorised officer shall stay the recovery of such part of the amount of the certificate as pertains to the said reduction for the period for which the appeal or other proceeding remains pending.

(4) Where a certificate for the recovery of amount has been issued and subsequently the amount of the outstanding demand is reduced as a result of an appeal or other proceeding under this Act, the authorised officer shall, when the order which was the subject-matter of such appeal or other proceeding has become final and conclusive, amend the certificate or withdraw it, as the case may be.]

---
1. Ins. by Act 33 of 1988, sec. 14 (w.e.f. 1-7-1990).

Legislative reference:

Section 8 is the original section providing for recovery of P.F. contribution and other dues which were provided to be recovered as 'arrears of land revenue.' The increasing work of recovery could not be managed by the revenue authorities of the States which compelled to switch over to another mechanism. Finally, by the amendments of 1988, Section 8 was amended and the provision of "arrears of land revenue" replaced by the words "in the manner as provided in Section 8-B to 8-G" The provisions of these sections authorizes the department itself to enforce the recovery. For this purpose, two new definitions have been added in Section 2 as clauses (aa) and (kb) the Authorised Officer, and the Recovery Officer, respectively.

Section 11. Priority of payment of contributions over other debts.- ¹[(1)] ²[Where any employer is adjudicated insolvent or, being a company, an order for winding up is made, the amount due–

(a) from the employer in relation to ³[an establishment] to which any ⁴[Scheme or the Insurance Scheme] applies in respect of any contribution payable to the Fund ⁵[or, as the case may be, the Insurance Fund], damages recoverable under section 14B, accumulations required to be transferred under sub-section (2) of section 15 or any charges payable by him under any other provision of this Act or of any provision of the ³[Scheme or the Insurance Scheme]; or

(b) from the employer in relation to an exempted ³[establishment] in report of any contribution to ⁶[the provident fund or any insurance fund] (in so far it relates to exempted employees), under the rules of ⁶[the provident fund or any insurance fund], ⁷[any contribution payable by him towards the ⁸[Pension] Fund under sub-section (6) of section 17,] damages recoverable under section 14B or any charges payable by him to the appropriate Government under any provision of this Act or under any of the conditions specified under section 17, shall, where the liability there for has accrued before the order of adjudication or winding up is made, be deemed to be included] among the debts which under section 49 of the Presidency-towns Insolvency Act, 1909 (3 of 1909), or under section 61 of the Provincial Insolvency Act, 1920 (5 of 1920), or under ⁹[section 530 of the Companies Act, 1956 (1 of 1956)] are to be paid in priority to all other debts in the distribution of the property of the insolvent or the assets of the company being wound up, as the case may be.

¹⁰[*Explanation.*–In this sub-section and in section 17, "insurance fund" means any fund established by an employer under any scheme for providing benefits in the nature of life insurance to employees, whether linked to their deposits in provident fund or not, without payment by the employees of any separate contribution or premium in that behalf.]

¹¹[(2) Without prejudice to the provisions of sub-section (1), if any amount is due from an employer ¹²[whether in respect of the employee's contribution (deducted from the wages of the employee) or the employer's contribution], the amount so due shall be deemed to be the first charge on the assets of the establishment, and shall, notwithstanding anything contained in any other law for the time being force, be paid in priority to all other debts.]

---

1. Section 11 re-numbered as sub-section (1) of that section by Act 40 of 1973, sec. 3 (w.e.f. 1-11-1973).
2. Subs. by Act 37 of 1953, sec. 9, for certain words.
3. Subs. by Act 94 of 1956, sec. 3, for "a factory."
4. Subs. by Act 99 of 1976, sec. 27, for "Scheme" (w.r.e.f. 1-8-1976).
5. Ins. by Act 99 of 1976, sec. 27 (w.r.e.f. 1-8-1976).
6. Subs. by Act 99 of 1976, sec. 27, for "the provident fund" (w.r.e.f. 1-8-1976).
7. Ins. by Act 16 of 1971, sec. 23 (w.e.f. 23-4-1971).
8. Subs. by Act 25 of 1996, sec. 4, for "Family Pension" (w.r.e.f. 16-11-1995).
9. Subs. by Act 40 of 1973, sec. 3, for certain words (w.e.f. 1-11-1973).
10. Ins. by Act 99 of 1976, sec. 27 (w.e.f. 1-8-1976).
11. Ins. by Act 40 of 1973, sec. 3 (w.e.f. 1-11-1973).
12. Subs. by Act 33 of 1988, sec. 16, for certain words (w.e.f. 1-8-1988).

---

¹[**17B. Liability in case of transfer of establishment.**–Where an employer, in relation to an establishment, transfers that establishment in whole or in part, by sale, gift, lease or licence or in any other manner whatsoever, the employer and the person to whom the establishment is so transferred shall jointly and severally be liable to pay the contribution and other sums due from the employer under

any provision of this Act or the Scheme or ²[the ³[Pension] Scheme or the Insurance Scheme], as the case may be, in respect of the period up to the date of such transfer:

Provided that the liability of the transferee shall be limited to the value of the assets obtained by him by such transfer.]

1. Ins. by Act 40 of 1973, sec. 8 (w.e.f. 1-11-1973).
2. Subs. by Act 99 of 1976, sec. 31, for "the Family Pension Scheme" (w.e.f. 7-9-1976).
3. Subs. by Act 25 of 1996, sec. 4, for "Family Pension" (w.r.e.f. 16-11-1995).

I. Amounts Due for which Recovery is enforced:

In Section 8, various types of the amount due have been mentioned recovery of which can be enforced under this Act. Those are –

(i) contributions,

(ii) damages,

(iii) amounts required to be transferred from a private P.F. Trust before the Act is applied to such establishment [Section 15(2)],

(iv) amounts required to be transferred from an exempted P.F. Trust on cancellation of exemption of such establishment [Section 17(5)],

(v) damages recoverable from an exempted establishment or other contribution and/or any other charges payable by the establishment,

(vi) and any other charges payable by an employer, which includes the amount of interest chargeable under Section 7-Q.

Before asking the establishment to deposit any amount, the commissioner was required to determine the liability and it was to be done by initiating proceedings under Section 7-A of the EPF Act *[or Section 14-B]* without determining the liability, if any the establishment can not be called upon to deposit any unspecified amount– *[Tapan Kumar Battacharyya Vs. Asstt. P.F. Commissioner and Others– 2010-III-LLJ-700 (Cal.)]*.

Is there any time limit to enforce recovery after the due are determined? Yes, Gujrat High Court gave an affirmative answer to it while deciding the case of *Mahindra Gears and Transmission Pvt. Ltd vs. Assistant P.F. Commissioner, EPF- [2011 LLR. 602 (Guj. H.C.)]*. As and when any order under Section 7-A is passed by the Provident Fund Authority and the amount is determined to be recovered, such recovery is to be made after expiry of 60 days' period i.e. prescribed for filing of an appeal before the EPF appellate Tribunal hence in the present case, the Provident Fund Authorities having recovered the amount before expiry of the statutory period for filing of appeal, the petitioner can file an appeal asking for condonation of delay, but the High Court observed that such hasty steps for recovery will not be repeated by the provident Fund Authorities.

Provision of EPF Act do not prohibit the authorities to proceed for recovery of amount even during the period of appeal provided to the employer. When an order under Section 7-A of the Act is passed by the determining authority, it is not imperative on the part of EPFO to wait for the period as provided for filing of an appeal by the aggrieved employer for making recovery of the contribution – *[Employees' Provident Fund Organisation vs. Rollwell Forge Ltd. & others – 2011 LLR. 1006 (Guj. H.C.)]*.

II. Priority of payment of contributions over other debts:

In case of an order of the competent court for winding up of a company, and in case of adjudication insolvent of an employer, the provident fund dues have been given priority over other dues under Section 530 of the Companies Act, 1956 and Section 49 of the Presidency Towns Insolvency Act, 1909 or Section 61 of the Provincial Insolvency Act, 1920 respectively. But, as per sub-section (2) of Section 11, the provident fund contribution deducted from the salary of the employees and also the employer's share not deposited with the PF authorities, will have the first charge on all other debts. Here, it is to be noted that the priority to all other debts and first charge are the two different things, therefore, while filing the claim, a clear mention of contribution and other charges is must to ensure the recovery of the contribution creditable to the employees provident fund accounts.

It may also be noted that in the Companies Act, a new Section 529-A has been added subsequently splitting the original Section 530 and the envisaged priority in Section 11 require a reference to Section 529-A, absence which leads so many legal adversities. However, in the case of *P.V. Joseph vs. Official Liquidator and Others- [2002 (100) FJR 197]*, it has been held that a beneficial interpretation considering the purpose of Section 529-A (3) (b) of the Companies Act, 1956 has to be adopted. When salary was payable during the respective wage-period, contribution also should have been remitted and contribution payable to EPF is a workmen's due as defined under Section 529 (3) (b) and is entitled to be claimed as preferential claim under Section 529-A *pari-passu* with the secured creditors. The Official Liquidator has correctly included P.F. claim on behalf of the workers under Section 529-A as workmen's dues.

This issue of interpretation has finally been cleared by the Supreme Court in the case of *EPF Commissioner vs. Official Liquidator of Eskay Pharmaceuticals Ltd. – 2011 (10) SCC. 727: 2011 (5) LLN. 1: 2012 (1) LLJ. 1: 2012 (132) FLR. 98: 2012 LLR. 23 (S.C.)]. As a back-gound of the provision of the Companies Act, In Section 11 of EPF Act, priority of P.F. dues has been given under Section 530 of the companies Act, 1956. In 1985, this section was amended and a new section 529-A was inserted. By this amendment, the priority available under section 530 was shifted in Section 529-A which was not referred in Section 11 of P.F. Act, hence, in cases of winding-up P.F. dues have not been considered as first charge or priority. First time, the Supreme Court interpreted the amended provision.*

The Supreme Court observed that while inserting Section 529-A in the Companies Act by Act No. 35 of 1985, Parliament, in its wisdom, did not declare the workmen's dues as first charge. The effect of amendment in the Companies Act in 1985 is only to expend the scope of the dues of workmen and place them at par with the debts due to the secured creditors and there is no reason to interpret this amendment as giving priority to the debts due to the secured creditors over the dues of Provident Fund payable by an employer. Of course, after the amount due from an employer under the P.F. Act is paid, the other dues of workers will be treated at par with the debts due to secured creditors and payment thereof will be regulated by the provisions contained in Section 529 (1) read with sections 529 (3), 529-A and 530 of the Companies Act.

Now, the Companies Act, 1956 has been replaced by the Companies Act, 2013 and the corresponding provisions have been resettled in Sections are 325, 326 and Section 327 respectively.

In another case of *Recovery Officer and APFC vs. Kerala Financial Corpn. –[2002 III CLR 191 (Ker.DB)]*, the Division Bench of Kerala High Court had occasion to discuss a priority case in conflict with the SFC Act. In that case, the appellant has issued notices to the respondent company for recovery of P. F. dues. Respondent No. 1, the Finance Corporation Challenged the same alleging that it has first charge in view of Section 46-B of SFC Act. The learned single Judge allowed the same and hence this appeal. No doubt, both Section 46-B of SFC Act and Section 11(2) of EPF & MP Act declare their intent by usage of non-obstante clause. But, since Section 11(2) has been enacted later, one must abscribe to the parliament the intention to override the earlier legislation also. It is, therefore, clear that Section 11(2) of EPF Act overrides all the provisions of other enactments, including Section 46-B of SFC Act. It is, therefore, held that the appellant shall be entitled to exercise his powers as a Recovery Officer for recovering PF dues.

III. Liability in case of transfer of establishment:

Scope of Section 17-B: Under Section 17-B of the Act, the transferee is the other person. So there is a distinction between the "employer" and "the other person." The later comes only after the transfer of the establishment either in whole or in part. Section 14-B contemplates in its proviso, notice upon "the employer" and not upon "the other persons." Notice under Section 14-B, for the purpose of hearing of the employer is to be given upon "the employer" and not upon the person to whom the establishment is so transferred, hence notice cannot be served on the petitioner who is transferee of the establishment. Unless and until such sum due is ascertained and quantified which liability of the transferee shall be limited to the value of the estate obtained by him by such transferee, no demand can be raised on the transferee, in the instant case the petitioner - *[Darjeeling Doors Plantation Ltd. and another Vs. R.P.F.C.. W.B.-1995 (1) LLJ 939 (Cal.)]*.

Sale by a court is not a transfer: If transfer other than a transfer by the employer had been contemplated, the language employed in Section 17-B would have been different. A court sale takes place by operation of law and not by any transaction *inter-vivas*. In that sense, it is an involuntary sale against the wishes of the person whose property is sold. That can hardly be called a transfer. Hence, the provisions of Section 17-B are not attracted - *[Sri Angappa Spinning Mills and others Vs. R.P.F.C. TN- 1986 Lab.I.C. 458]*.

Damages levyable on amalgamation: Where a scheme of amalgamation is sanctioned by the court, the transferee establishment becomes jointly and severally liable along with the transfer or to pay the due under Section 14-B of the Act, whether or not the scheme of amalgamation provides for the taking of such liabilities - *[R.N.T. Estates Ltd. Vs. U.O.I. 1989 Lab I.C. N.O.C. 177 (Cal.)]*.

Liability of the Transferee: After transfer has legally been effected, liability is upon the transferee and not upon the petitioner. The P.F. authorities have to proceed against second respondent and not against the petitioner. *[Neyveli Lignite Corpn. Ltd. Vs. R.P.F.C. Madras and others -1997 (i) CLR-699. (Mad.)]*. Section 17-B cannot be interpreted to mean that the transferee employer would be liable also to pay penalty for the default committed by the previous employer during the period anterior to the transfer. Penalty cannot be saddled on somebody who is not guilty - *[R.P.F.C. Mangalore Vs. Karnataka Forest Plantation Corps. Ltd. Bangalore. 2000 Lab I. C. 1268.]*. It was not correct that as a purchaser of establishment, the petitioner who not liable and only the vendors were liable to pay the contribution due for period before the purchase having regard to section 17-B of the Act - *[Mohammed Ali Jinnah, Prop. M.A.J. Cins Part, Trichy Vs. APFC– 2010-III-LLJ-765-(Mad.)]*.

The petitioner purchasing an undertaking from the Financial Corporation will not be liable to pay the arrears of the provident fund which were payable by the earlier owner since the petitioner has not purchased the establishment from the owner but from the Financial Corporation- *[Alico Rubber Reclamation (Private) Limited vs. Employees' Provident Funds Organisation and another- 2011 LLR. 1032 (H.P. H.C.)]*.

In the case of *A. L. Subramanian vs. E.P.F. Appellate Tribunal, New delhi & others- [2011 LLR. 1074 (Mad. H.C.)]* the Madras High Court has taken a view that on transfer of property of one establishment to the other, the vendee will be liable for arrears of the provident fund dues as per the provisions of Section 170B of the E.P.F. & M.P. Act, 1952.

As soon as a workman ceases to be in employment, the liability of the employer to contribute to the fund of such workman also comes to an end Similarly, if all the workmen cease to be in employment, the liability of the employer would also come to an end. If the establishment is purchased by a new person, he cannot be burdened with the past liabilities and obligations - *[Pragati Metal Works Vs. The RPFC-2001 (89) FLR 981]*.

IV. Modes of Recovery and Authorities to Enforce Recovery:

A two way recovery procedure has been provided in the Act; one is, by the Central Provident Fund Commissioner or any other officer authorized by the Central Board by a notification in the official Gazette under Section 8-F (1) and Section 8-F (5), and the other is, the Recovery Officer authorized by the Central Government in the official gazette. It is not necessary that the Recovery Officer has to be authourised out from the officers of the E.P.F.O. Any officer of the Central Government or of a State Government or of the C.B.T. i.e. the EPFO, who is authorized to exercise the powers of a Recovery Officer as mentioned in Section 8-B and 8-C.

V. Recovery by an authority other than Recovery Officer:

[1][8F. **Other modes of recovery.**– (1) Notwithstanding the issue of a certificate to the Recovery Officer under section 8B, the Central Provident Fund Commissioner or any other officer authorised by the Central Board may recover the amount by any one or more of the modes provided in this section.

(2) If any amount is due from any person to any employer who is in arrears, the Central Provident Fund Commissioner or any other officer authorised by the Central Board in this behalf may require such person to deduct from the said amount the arrears due from such employer under this Act, and such person shall comply with any such requisition and shall pay the sum so deducted to the credit of the Central Provident Fund Commissioner or the officer so authorised, as the case may be:

Provided that nothing in this sub-section shall apply to any part of the amount exempt from attachment in execution of a decree of a civil court under section 60 of the Code of Civil Procedure, 1908 (5 of 1908).

(3) (i) The Central Provident Fund Commissioner or any other officer authorised by the Central Board in this behalf may, at any time or from time to time, by notice in writing, require any person from whom money is due or may become due to the employer or, as the case may be, the establishment

or any person who holds or may subsequently hold money for or on account of the employer or as the case may be, the establishment, to pay to the Central Provident Fund Commissioner either forthwith upon

the money becoming due or being held or at or within the time specified in the notice not being before the money becomes due or is held so much of the money as is sufficient to pay the amount due from the employer in respect of arrears or the whole of the money when it is equal to or less than that amount.

(ii) A notice under this sub-section may be issued to any person who holds or may subsequently hold any money for or on account of the employer jointly with any other person and for the purposes of this sub-section, the shares of the joint holders in such account shall be presumed, until the contrary is proved, to be equal.

(iii) A copy of the notice shall be forwarded to the employer at his last address known to the Central Provident Fund Commissioner or as the case may be, the officer so authorised and in the case of a joint account to all the joint holders at their last addresses known to the Central Provident Fund Commissioner or the officer so authorised.

(iv) Save as otherwise provided in this sub-section, every person to whom a notice is issued under this sub-section shall be bound to comply with such notice, and, in particular, where any such notice is issued to a post office, bank or an insurer, it shall not be necessary for any pass book, deposit receipt, policy or any other document to be produced for the purpose of any entry, endorsement or the like being made before payment is made notwithstanding any rule, practice or requirement to the contrary.

(v) Any claim respecting any property in relation to which a notice under this sub-section has been issued arising after the date of the notice shall be void as against any demand contained in the notice.

(vi) Where a person to whom a notice under this sub-section is sent objects to it by a statement on oath that the sum demanded or any part thereof is not due to the employer or that he does not hold any money for or on account of the employer, then nothing contained in this sub-section shall be deemed to require such person to pay any such sum or part thereof, as the case may be, but if it is discovered that such statement was false in any material particular, such person shall be personally liable to the Central Provident Fund Commissioner or the officer so authorised to extent of his own liability to the employer on the date of the notice, or to the extent of the employer's liability for any sum due under this Act, whichever is less.

(vii) The Central Provident Fund Commissioner or the officer so authorised may, at any time or from time to time, amend or revoke any notice issued under this sub-section or extend the time for making any payment in pursuance of such notice.

(viii) The Central Provident Fund Commissioner or the officer so authorised shall grant a receipt for any amount paid in compliance with a notice issued under this sub-section, and the person so paying shall be fully discharged from his liability to the employer to the extent of the amount so paid.

(ix) Any person discharging any liability to the employer after the receipt of a notice under this sub-section shall be personally liable to the Central Provident Fund Commissioner or the officer so authorised to the extent of his own liability to the employer so discharged or to the extent of the employer's liability for any sum due under this Act, whichever is less.

(x) If the person to whom a notice under this sub-section is sent fails to make payment in pursuance thereof to the Central Provident Fund Commissioner or the officer so authorised he shall be deemed to be an employer in default in respect of the amount specified in the notice and further proceedings may be taken against him for the realisation of the amount as if it were an arrear due from him, in the manner provided in sections 8B to 8E and the notice shall have the same effect as an attachment of a debt by the Recovery Officer in exercise of his powers under section 8B.

(4) The Central Provident Fund Commissioner or the officer authorised by the Central Board in this behalf may apply to the court in whose custody there is money belonging to the employer for payment to him of the entire amount of such money, or if it is more than the amount due, an amount sufficient to discharge the amount due.

(5) The Central Provident Fund Commissioner or any officer not below the rank of Assistant Provident Fund Commissioner may, if so authorised by the Central Government by general or special order, recover any arrears of amount due from an employer or, as the case may be, from the establishment by distraint and sale of his or its movable property in the manner laid down in the Third Schedule to the Income-Tax Act, 1961 (43 of 1961).]

1. Ins. by Act 33 of 1988, sec. 14 (w.e.f. 1-7-1990).

Recovery by an officer other than a Recovery Officer have been incorporated in section 8-F, in which 4 way means have been provided for recovery from a person other than the employer, who has to pay any amount to such defaulting employer –

(1) any person from whom any amount is due to the employer, provided that the amount is not attached for execution of a decree of a civil court under the Civil Procedure Code, 1908, which is exempted from any other attachment;

(2) any other person, who holds any sums for the employer or subsequently may hold, by prohibiting that person not to pay the same or any part of that which may satisfy the due amount, and pay forthwith to the authority;

(3) Where a court is having custody of any money is lying belonging to the employer, by making a request to the court to pay the entire or such amount which may sufficient to discharge the amount due;

(4) Distraint and sale of the movable property of the employer or the establishment, as the case may be, in the manner specified in the Third Schedule attached to the In-come Tax Act, 1961. Here, it may be noted that no officer has been notified under this section, hence, the provisions of the sub-section (5) are not evocable except by the Central P.F. Commissioner.

In case of (3) above, the person who fails to obey the prohibitory orders of the authority, the person shall be deemed defaulter personally and the amount asked to be paid may be recovered under Section 8-B by issuing a certificate to the Recovery Officer.

The Recovery Officer is not notified or authorised to invoke the provisions of Section 8-F in any case.

Besides, the competent authority may grant installment facility to the employer with a view to facilitate employer to pay the dues according to the sustainability of the financial condition of the establishment.

Inquiry under Section 8F (3) (vi) is mandatory. Such is the view of the M.P. High Court in the case of *Ferro Concrete Construction (I) Pvt. Ltd. Vs. RPFC Indore and others – [2002 Lab.IC 412; 2002 (I) LLJ 986; 2002 (2) LLN 269 (MP)]* where it has been held that holding of an inquiry for the person concerned by the Recovery Officer into the requirement of Section 8-F (3) (vi) is mandatory and any deviation from this will result in vitiating the order.

The appellant Bank filed writ petition challenging demand of Rs. 30,000/- and the prohibitory order of the first respondent made under Section 8-F (3) of the Act. That petition having been dismissed hence this appeal filed.

While allowing the appeal it is observed that Section 8-F (3) (i) and Section 11 (2) should be read harmoniously and reasonably. The construction, which the employer is obliged to make under the Act could not be fathered on the third party except as directed by the Act. Demand can be raised against the third party only when the Commissioner found the money of the employer is in the hand of such third party, or in course of time required money would become due to the employer. It is held that in so far as this case is concerned the money demanded from the Bank was not due to the employer.- *[Manager, Vijaya Bank vs. RPFC – 2003 (III) LLJ 419 (Karn.DB)].*

VI. Recovery by a Recovery Officer:

The recovery is the main function of the Recovery Officer, whose function starts with the receipt of a certificate which issued by an Authorized Officer. The certificate can be issued despite the recovery has initiated recovery under Section 8-F of the Act. There are three modes by which the Recovery Officer may recover the amount due as per the certificate. No amount except mentioned in the certificate, a Recovery Officer is not authorized to recovery any additional amount by adding as interest or so, but he is authorized to recover the cost as the rules permit for. In the case of **Indian Drilling and Mining (Pvt.) Ltd. An another vs. R.P.F.C., EPFO and others- [2001 (2) LLN 306],** it has been held that the Recovery Officer can recover only the amount specified in the certificate. The provision contained in Section 7-Q of the Act merely enable the authorized officer under Section 7-A to impose interest, but if such interest is not included in the certificate, it is beyond the competence of the Recovery Officer to demand such amount.

The three modes are-

(1) attachment and sale of the movable or immovable property of the establishment or of the employer;

(2) arrest of the employer and his detention in prison,

(3) appointing a receiver for the management of the movable or immovable property of the establishment or, of the employer.

The procedure and other modalities are as prescribed by the In-come Tax Act, 1961 in the Second Schedule and the Income Tax (Certificate Proceedings) Rules, 1962. The Schedule II and the Rules are reproduced here under item NO. XII.

VII. Attachment and sale of the property of:

(1) the establishment:-

(2) the employer:-

In Section 8, the recovery of dues is intended to be recovered from the 'employer' only. That might be for the reason that the 'arrears of land revenue' are collected from a person and not from an incorporated person. But later-on, it might have been found proper that the recovery of the provident fund dues could be affected from the property of the establishment and the establishment covered under the Act has a considerable property. Therefore, now, the recovery can be affected by attachment and sale of the property of the establishment as well as of the employer.

In the first instance, the property of the establishment is to be attached and sold, thereafter, the property of the employer to be considered.

While attaching a property, an inventory of the property so attached should be made with descriptions in the presence of a local person and of-course in the presence of the owner employer of the property, and a copy of the inventory be handed over to the owner of the property. It is also a requirement that either the property be taken away by the Recovery Officer him-self or by his representative, who should not be below the rank of an Inspector or the property should be handed over to a custodian whom the Recovery may consider fit, who can be the owner or he employer also.

Any officer entrusted with the work of executing the order of the Recovery Officer, who is generally the Inspector, is also deemed a Recovery Officer under Rule 19-A of II Schedule.

Property hypothecated to Vijaya Bank for credits was destroyed in fire and Insurance Company paid Rs. 9,49,168.60 to the Bank on which R.P.F.C. issued prohibitory orders for Rs. 30,217.75 due as employer's contribution on the Bank. The R.P.F.C., having priority, by virtue of Section 11 of the Act over hypothecated property, can recover the sums from the said property. Bank is directed to remit Rs. 30,217.75 to the Regional P.F. Commissioner - *[Manager, Vijaya Bank vs. R.P.F.C.- 1999 (83) FLR 738 (Kern.)]*.

Goods (Sugar Bags) pledged by the employer with the petitioner Bank caused to be the property of the employer and as such Recovery Officer could not have proceeded to attach them under Section 8-B of the Act terming them as the property of the employer- *[State Bank of Mysore vs, R.P.F. Commissioner, Bangalore = 1999 (I) 316 (Karn.)]*. Here, it may be noted that where property is pledged to any financial or other institution, and if the right of disposal of that property is, still vested in the employer, than the Recovery Officer should have right to attach that property or recover from that property.

Where the property is mortgaged, refusal to entertain and investigate the objection filed by the Bank with whom the property was mortgaged and public notice was issued by the authorities under the Act for recovery of dues was improper and amounts to refusal to exercise jurisdiction vested by law. In view of huge amount of decretal dues and in view of the fat that property is already mortgaged, the Bank have right to be heard before sale of the property. Hence, direction given to Respondent NO. 1 to investigate objections filed by Bank- *[Allahabad Bank vs. S.K. Bhattacharya- 1999 (3) LLN 140 (Cal)]*.

Cases under B.I.F.R, the proceeding under the Act for recovery of P.F. Dues by way of execution distress etc. could not be taken against a company which is declared sick industry by BIFR in view of Section 22 (1) of Sick Industrial Companies (Special Provisions) Act, 1985. The proceedings remain suspended- *[SLM Manek Lal Industries vs. RPFC -1997 (2) LLJ 283 (Guj.)]*.

In another case, a different view has been taken in the case of **Universal Paper Mills Ltd. And others vs. RPFC and others -*[2001 (2) LLJ 1193; 2001 (91) FLR 591; 2002 LLR 41; 2001 (99) FJR 199]*** where it has been held that the company has no right to take shelter under Section 22 of the SICA, 1985 in respect of statutory liabilities and the employees are entitled to have their statutory benefits under the EPF Act and thereby, any default on the part of the employer under the said Act cannot attract the said section 22 or can get away taking an advantage of the Section. The provisions of Section 22 of the SICA would not apply to statutory dues of an employee covered under the PF Scheme- *[Industrial Development Corp. of Orrissa Ltd. And another vs. RPFC II and another- 2002 (I) LLJ 774; 2002 (92) FLR 945]*. Also see the case of **Digpal Singh vs. U.O.I.- *[2002 Lab.IC 3547; 2003 (I) LLJ 876]***.

Property under attachment cannot be attached by a civil court. The Recovery Officer objected the order of attachment of the cabin room of the Cinema, issued by the Addl. Munsif Magistrate by virtue of

Rule 16 (1) of schedule II to the Income Tax Act, 1961 by way of filling application under Section 151 and Rule 58 o order 21 of the Civil Procedure Code, which was rejected.

It has been held by Kerala High Court that the court should have considered the objection under Section 151 of C.P.C. regarding jurisdiction of the civil court and should have lifted the attachment effected on the property already under attachment by the department as the civil court has no jurisdiction to attach the projector cabin of the cinema- *[N. Sathisan Enforcement Officer (Recovery) vs. P. Velappan Nair and Others- CRP NO. 504/1992 F. pronounced on 17.9.1992 – unreported judgement].*

VIII. Arrest of employer and his detention in prison:

The Recovery Officer may issue a show-cause notice to a defaulter that why he should not be arrested. This action is invoked under certain conditions which are enumerated in the Second Schedule. Ladies cannot be arrested. Arrest can be made only after sun-rises and before sun-sets. The reasons are required to be recorded in writing for making arrest.

For the purpose of recovering any amount determined in Section 7A of the Act, Rule 73 of the Second Schedule attached to the In-come Tax Act should, strictly be followed. According to the said Rule 73, warrant of arrest cannot be issued unless Tax Recovery Officer, for the reason recorded in writing, is satisfied that the defaulter, with the object or effect of obstructing, the execution of the certificate, has, after the drawing up of the certificate by the Tax Recovery Officer, dishonestly transferred, concealed to removed any part of property, or that the defaulter has or has had since the drawing up of the certificate by the Tax Recovery Officer, the means to pay the arrears or some substantial part thereof and refuses or neglects or has refused or neglected to pay the same- *[Vikram Poddar vs. RPFC and others – 2001 (2) LLJ 518; 2001 (2) LLN 78].*

Therefore, the P.F. authorities are competent to proceed against defaulting establishment including arrest when the dues of PF, as payable have not been deposited in time– *[Khushiram Agarwal vs. EPFO and others – 2008 LLR 474 (Cal.)].*

IX. Appointment of Receiver for management of property of the establishment or the employer:

The Recovery Officer, after attachment of a property, may appoint any person as receiver for management of the property and the Receiver is paid sum or remuneration for the work. The Receiver is responsible for keeping all the accounts of the property and the income, if any, after payment of legal and other dues, to be paid to the Recovery Officer.

X. Transfer of certificate of other Recovery Officer:

It may happen that the property of the establishment or the employer is situated in a place which does fall under the jurisdiction of the Recovery Officer to whom the certificate has been issued. In such a case a certificate is sent to the Recovery Officer having jurisdiction over the property. Section 8C contains provisions to this effect and the procedure has been laid down in the II Schedule and the CP Rules.

XI. Corrections in and/or stay on the Recovery Certificate:

It may happen that any clerical mistake occur in the certificate, Section 8-D provides necessary directions to correct the same by the Authorised Officer.

Similarly, the defaulter employer is not authorized to raise any question before the Recovery Officer about the correctness of the amount hence the Recovery Officer is not authorized to entertain any objection raised by the employer on the certificate.

Whenever the certificate is intended to cancel or withdraw under for any reason, the Authorized Officer is to inform the Recovery Officer immediately, so that any action by him that may lead to any legal complication may be avoided. The reason for withdrawal of the certificate may be review under relevant provisions for review or remitting back the case by a competent court for re-hearing.

Further, Section 8-E provides for immediate communication to the Recovery Officer about any amount paid by the employer or realized by the authorized officer under Section 8-F so that the Recovery Officer may re-plan his action accordingly.

XII. The Recovery Rules-

Although, by Section 21 of the Act, the Central Government has been given powers to frame Rules, but as far as the Recovery procedure is concern, these was nothing like to frame new Rules. The century old Civil Procedure Code contains Rules relating to recovery of Land revenue. In this country, nothing is model taxation like Land Revenue, hence those rules are treated as mother rules. The Income Tax payer, as an individual tax payer, is treated at par the land-tiller, hence adopted those rules with modifying as tax-payer and tax collector. Those are in Schedule II and III and Income-Tax (Certificate Proceedings) Rules, 1962. Instead of making separate set of Rules, the Rules as made under the Income Tax Act, have been adopted by virtue of section 8-G.

In Provident Funds, an individual – the owner or the employer – is the secondary, the establishment, an incorporated person, is the first person as defaulter; therefore, the recovery is to be enforced against the property of the establishment first. Accordingly, the those Rules, in their application in the matters of Recovery of Provident Fund Dues, stands modified as mentioned in the proviso to Section 8-G.

Section [1][**8G. Application of certain provisions of Income-tax Act.– The provisions of the Second and Third Schedules to the Income-tax Act, 1961 (43 of 1961) and the Income-tax (Certificate Proceedings) rules, 1962, as in force from time to time, shall apply with necessary modifications as if the said provisions and the rules referred to the arrears of the amount mentioned in section 8 of this Act instead of to the income-tax:**

Provided, that any reference in the said provisions and the rules to the "assessee" shall be construed as a reference to an employer as defined in this Act.]

---
1. Ins. by Act 33 of 1988, sec. 14 (w.e.f. 1-7-1990).

Adoption of Second and Third Schedule to the Income Tax Act, 1961 and The Income-Tax (Certificate Proceedings) Rules, 1961:

Second Schedule to the Income Tax Act, 1961

See Sections 222 and 276 of I.T. Act

(See Section 8-G of EPF & M.P. Act, 1952)

Procedure for Recovery of Tax

Part-I

General Provisions

Definitions:

1. In this Schedule, unless the context otherwise requires:

   (a) "certificate" except in rules 7, 44, 65 and sub-rule (2) of rule 66, means the certificate drawn up by the Tax Recovery Officer under section 222 in respect of any assessee referred to in that section;

   (b) "defaulter" means the assessee mentioned in the certificate;

   (c) "execution," in relation to a certificate, means recovery of arrears in pursuance of the certificate;

   (d) "movable property" includes growing crops;

   (e) "officer" means a person authorised to make an attachment or sale under this Schedule;

   (f) "rule" means a rule contained in this Schedule; and

   (g) "share in a corporation" includes stock, debenture-stock, debentures or bonds.

Issue of notice:

2. When a certificate has been drawn up by the Tax Recovery Officer for the recovery of arrears under this Schedule, the Tax Recovery Officer shall cause to be served upon the defaulter a notice requiring the defaulter to pay the amount specified in the certificate within fifteen days from the date of service of the notice and intimating that in default steps would be taken to realise the amount under this Schedule.

When Certificate may be Executed:

3. No step in execution of a certificate shall be taken until the period of fifteen days has elapsed since the date of the service of the notice required by the preceding rule:

Provided that, if the Tax Recovery Officer is satisfied that the defaulter is likely to conceal, remove or dispose of the whole or any part of such of his movable property as would be liable to attachment in execution of a decree of a civil court and that the realisation of the amount of the certificate would in consequence be delayed or obstructed, he may at any time direct, for reasons to be recorded in writing, an attachment of the whole or any part of such property:

Provided further that if the defaulter whose property has been so attached furnishes security to the satisfaction of the Tax Recovery Officer, such attachment shall be cancelled from the date on which such security is accepted by the Tax Recovery Officer.

Mode of recovery:

4. If the amount mentioned in the notice is not paid within the time specified therein or within such further time as the Tax Recovery Officer may grant in his discretion, the Tax Recovery Officer shall proceed to realise the amount by one or more of the following modes:

(a) by attachment and sale of the defaulter's movable property;

(b) by attachment and sale of the defaulter's immovable property;

(c) by arrest of the defaulter and his detention in prison;

(d) by appointing a receiver for the management of the defaulter's movable and immovable properties.

Interest, costs and charges recoverable:

5. There shall be recoverable, in the proceedings in execution of every certificate:

(a) such interest upon the amount of tax or penalty or other sum to which the certificate relates as is payable in accordance with sub-section (2) of section 220, and

(b) all charges incurred in respect of:

   (i) the service of notice upon the defaulter to pay the arrears, and of warrants and other processes, and

   (ii) all other proceedings taken for realising the arrears.

Purchaser's title:

6. (1) Where property is sold in execution of a certificate, there shall vest in the purchaser merely the right, title and interest of the defaulter at the time of the sale, even though the property itself be specified.

(2) Where immovable property is sold in execution of a certificate, and such sale has become absolute, the purchaser's right, title and interest shall be deemed to have vested in him from the time when the property is sold, and not from the time when the sale becomes absolute.

Suit against purchaser not maintainable on ground of purchase being made on behalf of plaintiff.

7. (1) No suit shall be maintained against any person claiming title under a purchase certified by the Tax Recovery Officer in the manner laid down in this Schedule, on the ground that the purchase was made on behalf of the plaintiff or on behalf of some one through whom the plaintiff claims.

(2) Nothing in this section shall bar a suit to obtain a declaration that the name of any purchaser certified as aforesaid was inserted in the certificate fraudulently or without the consent of the real purchaser, or interfere with the right of a third person to proceed against that property, though ostesibly sold to the certified purchaser, on the ground that it is liable to satisfy a claim of such third person against the real owner.

Disposal of proceeds of execution:

8. (1) Whenever assets are realised by sale or otherwise in execution of certificate, the proceeds shall be disposed of in the following manner, namely:

(a) they shall first be adjusted towards the amount due under the certificate in execution of which the assets were realised and the costs incurred in the course of such execution;

(b) if there remains a balance after the adjustment referred to in clause (a), the same shall be utilised for satisfaction of any other amount recoverable from the assessee under this Act which may be due on the date on winch the assets were realised; and

(c) the balance, if any, remaining after the adjustments under clauses (a) and (b) shall be paid to the defaulter.

(2) If the defaulter disputes any adjustment under clause (b) of sub-rule (1), the Tax Recovery Officer shall determine the dispute.

General bar to jurisdiction of civil courts, save where fraud alleged:

9. Except as otherwise expressly provided in this Act, every question arising between the Tax Recovery Officer and the defaulter or their representatives, relating to the execution, discharge or satisfaction of a certificate or relating to the confirmation or setting aside by an order under this Act of a sale held in execution of such certificate, shall be determined, not by suit, but by order of the Tax Recovery Officer before whom such question arises:

Provided that a suit may be brought in a civil court in respect of any such question upon the ground of fraud.

Property exempt from attachment:

10. (1) All such property as is by the Code of Civil Procedure, 1908 (5 of 1908), exempted from attachment and sale in execution of a decree of a civil court shall be exempt from attachment and sale under this Schedule.

(2) The Tax Recovery Officer's decision as to what property is so entitled to exemption shall be conclusive.

Recovery Officer:

11. (1) Where any claim is preferred to, or any objection is made to the attachment or sale of, any property in execution of a certificate, on the ground that such property is not liable to such attachment or sale, the Tax Recovery Officer shall proceed to investigate the claim or objection:

Provided that no such investigation shall be made where the Tax Recovery Officer considers that the claim or objection was designedly or unnecessarily delayed.

(2) Where the property to which the claim or objection applies has been advertised for sale, the Tax Recovery Officer ordering the sale may postpone it pending the investigation of the claim or objection, upon such terms as to security or otherwise as the Tax Recovery Officer shall deem fit.

(3) The claimant or objector must adduce evidence to show that -

(a) (in the case of immovable property) at the date of the service of the notice issued under this Schedule to pay the arrears, or

(b) (in the case of movable property) at the date of the attachment, he had some interest in, or was possessed of, the property in question.

(4) Where, upon the said investigation, the Tax Recovery Officer is satisfied that, for the reason stated in the claim or objection, such property was not, at the said date, in the possession of the defaulter or of some person in trust for him or in the occupancy of a tenant or other person paying rent to him, or that, being in the possession of the defaulter at the said date, it was so in his possession, not

on his own account or as his own property, but on account of or in trust for some other person, or partly on his own account and partly on account of some other person, the T Recovery Officer shall make an order releasing the property, wholly or to such extent as he thinks fit, from attachment or sale.

(5) Where the Tax Recovery Officer is satisfied that the property was, at the said date, in the possession of the defaulter as his own property and not on account of any other person, or was in the possession of some other person in trust for him, or in the occupancy of a tenant or other person paying rent to him, the Tax Recovery Officer shall disallow the claim.

(6) Where a claim or an objection is preferred, the party against whom an order is made may institute a suit in a civil court to establish the right which he claims to the property in dispute; but, subject to the result of such suit (if any), the order of the Tax Recovery Officer shall be conclusive.

Removal of attachment on satisfaction or cancellation of certificate:

12. Where -

(a) the amount due, with costs and all charges and expenses resulting from the attachment of any property or incurred in order to hold a sale, are paid to the Tax Recovery Officer, or

(b) the certificate is cancelled, the attachment shall be deemed to be withdrawn and, in the case of immovable property, the withdrawal shall, if the defaulter so desires, be proclaimed at his expense and a copy of the proclamation shall be affixed in the manner provided by this Schedule for a proclamation of sale of immovable property.

Officer entitled to attach and sell:

13. The attachment and sale of movable property and the attachment and sale of immovable property may be made by such persons as the Tax Recovery Officer may from time to rime direct.

Defaulting purchaser answerable for loss on resale:

14. Any deficiency of price which may happen on a resale by reason of the purchaser's default, and all expenses attending such resale, shall be certified to the Tax Recovery Officer by the officer holding the sale, and shall, at the instance of either the Tax Recovery Officer or the defaulter, be recoverable from the defaulting purchaser under the procedure provided by this Schedule:

Provided that no such application shall be entertained unless filed within fifteen days from the date of resale.

Adjournment or stoppage of sale:

15. (1) The Tax Recovery Officer may, in his discretion, adjourn any sale hereunder to a specified day and hour; and the officer conducting any such sale may, in his discretion, adjourn the sale, recording his reasons for such adjournment:

Provided that, where the sale is made in, or within the precincts of, the office of the Tax Recovery Officer, no such adjournment shall be made without the leave of the Tax Recovery Officer.

(2) Where a sale of immovable property is adjourned under sub-rule (1) for a longer period than one calendar month, a fresh proclamation of sale under this Schedule shall be made unless the defaulter consents to waive it.

(3) Every sale shall be stopped if, before the lot is knocked down, the arrears and costs (including the costs of the sale) are tendered to the officer conducting the sale, or proof is given to his satisfaction that the amount of such arrears and costs has been paid to the Tax Recovery Officer who ordered the sale.

Private alienation to be void in certain cases:

16. (1) Where a notice has been served on a defaulter under rule 2, the defaulter or his representative in interest shall not be competent to mortgage, charge, lease or otherwise deal with any property belonging to him except with the permission of the Tax Recovery Officer, nor shall any civil court issue any process against such property m execution of a decree for the payment of money.

(2) Where an attachment has been made under this Schedule, any private transfer or delivery of the property attached or of any interest therein and any payment to the dafaulter of any debt, dividend or other moneys contrary to such attachment, shall be void as against all claims enforceable under the attachment.

Prohibition against bidding or purchase by officer:

17. No officer or other person having any duty to perform in connection with any sale under this Schedule shall, either directly or indirectly, bid for, acquire or attempt to acquire any interest in the property sold.

Prohibition against sale on holidays:

18. No sale under this Schedule shall take place on a Sunday or other general holiday recognised by the State Government or on any day which has been notified by the State Government to be a local holiday for the area in which the sale is to take place.

Assistance by police:

19. Any officer authorised to attach or sell any property or to arrest the defaulter or charged with any duty to be performed under this Schedule, may apply to the officer-in-charge of the nearest police station for such assistance as may be necessary in the discharge of his duties, and the authority to whom such application is made shall depute a sufficient number of police officers for furnishing such assistance.

Entrustment of certain functions by Tax Recovery Officer:

19-A. A Tax Recovery Officer may, with the previous approval of the Joint Commissioner, entrust any of this functions as the Tax Recovery Officer to any other officer lower than him in rank (not being lower in rank than an Inspector of Income tax) and such officer shall, in relation to the functions so entrusted to him, be deemed.

Part II
Attachment and sale of movable property
Attachment

Warrant:

20. Except as otherwise provided in this Schedule, when any movable property is to be attached, the officer shall be furnished by the Tax Recovery Officer (or other officer empowered by him in that behalf) a warrant in writing and signed with his name specifying the name of the defaulter and the amount to be realised.

Service of copy of warrant:

21. The officer shall cause a copy of the warrant to be served on the defaulter.

Attachment:

22. If, after service of the copy of the warrant, the amount is not paid forthwith, the officer shall proceed to attach the movable property of the dafaulter.

Property in defaulter's possession:

23. Where the property to be attached is movable property (other than agricultural produce) in the possession of the defaulter, the attachment shall be made by actual seizure, and the officer shall keep the property in his own custody or the custody of one of his subordinates and shall be responsible for due custody thereof:

Provided that when the property seized is subject to speedy and natural decay or when the expense of keeping it in custody is likely to exceed its value, the officer may sell it at once.

Agricultural produce:

24. (Not Printed)

Provisions as to agricultural produce under attachment

25. (Not Printed)

Debts and shares, etc.:

26. (1) In the case of-

(a) A debt not secured by a negotiable instrument,

(b) a share in a corporation, or

(c) other movable property not in the possession of the defaulter except property deposited in, or in the custody of, any court,

the attachment shall be made by a written order prohibiring,-

(i) in the case of the debt- the creditor from recovering the debt and the debtor from making payment thereof until the further order of the Tax Recovery Officer;

(ii) in the case of the share- the person in whose name the share may be standing from transferring the same or receiving any dividend thereon;

(iii) in the case of the other movable property (except as aforesaid)- the person in possession of the same from giving it over to the defaulter.

(2) A copy of such order shall be affixed on some conspicuous part of the office of the Tax Recovery Officer, and another copy shall be sent, in the case of the debt, to the debtor, in the case of the share, to the proper officer of the corporation, and in the case of the other movable property (except as aforesaid), to the person in possession of the same.

(3) A debtor prohibited under clause (i) of sub-rule (1) may pay the amount of his debt to the Tax Recovery Officer, and such payment shall discharge him as effectually as payment to the party entitled to receive the same.

Attachment of decree:

27. (1) The attachment of a decree of a civil court for the payment of money or for sale in enforcement of a mortgage or charge shall be made by the issue to the civil court of a notice requesting the civil court to stay the execution of the decree unless and until:

(i) the Tax Recovery Officer cancels the notice, or

(ii) the Tax Recovery Officer or the defaulter applies to the court receiving such notice to execute, the decree.

(2) Where a civil court receives an application under clause (ii) of sub-rule (1), it shall, on the application of the Tax Recovery Officer or the defaulter and subject to the provisions of the Code of Civil Procedure, 1908 (5 of 1908), proceed to execute the attached decree and apply the net proceeds in satisfaction of the certificate.

(3) The Tax Recovery Officer shall be deemed to be the representative of the holder of the attached decree, and to be entitled to execute such attached decree in any manner lawful for the holder thereof.

Share in movable property:

28. Where the property to be attached consists of the share or interest of the defaulter in movable property belonging to him and another as co-owners, the attachment shall be made by a notice to the defaulter prohibiting him from transferring the share or interest or charging it in any way.

Salary of Government servants:

29. Attachment of the salary or allowances of servants of the Government or a local authority may be made in the manner provided by rule 48 of Order 21 of the First Schedule to the Code of Civil Procedure, 1908 (5 of 1908), and the provisions of the said rule shall, for the purposes of this rule, apply subject to such modifications as may be necessary.

Attachment of negotiable instrument:

30. Where the property is a negotiable instrument not deposited in a court nor in the custody of a public officer, the attachment shall be made by actual seizure, and the instalment shall be brought before the Tax Recovery Officer and held subject to his orders.

Attachment of property in custody of court or public officer:

31. Where the property to be attached is in the custody of any court or public officer, the attachment shall be made by a notice to such court or officer, requesting that such property, and any interest or dividend becoming payable thereon, may be held subject to the further orders of the Tax Recovery Officer by whom the notice is issued:

Provided that, where such property is in the custody of a court, any question of title or priority arising between the Tax Recovery Officer and any other person, not being the defaulter, claiming to be interested in such property by virtue of any assignment, attachment or otherwise, shall be determined by such court.

Attachment of partnership property:

32. (1) Where the property to be attached consists of an interest of the defaulter, being a partner, in the partnership property, the Tax Recovery Officer may make an order charging the share of such partner in the partnership property and profits with payment of the amount due under the certificate, and may, by the same or subsequent order, appoint a receiver of the share of such partner in the profits, whether already declared or accruing and of any other money which may become due to him in respect of the partnership, and direct accounts and inquiries and make an order for the sale of such interest or such other order as the circumstances of the case may require.

(2) The other persons shall be at liberty at any time to redeem the interest charged or, in the case of a sale being directed, to purchase the same.

Inventory:

33. In the case of attachment of movable property by actual seizure, the officer shall, after attachment of the property, prepare an inventory of all the property attachment, specifying in it the place where it is lodged or kept, and shall forward the same to the Tax Recovery Officer and a copy of the inventory shall be delivered by the officer to the defaulter.

Attachment not to be excessive:

34. The attachment by seizure shall not be excessive, that is to say, the property attached shall be as nearly as possible proportionate to the amount specified in the warrant.

Seizure between sunrise and sunset:

35. Attachment by seizure shall be made after sunrise and before sunset and not otherwise.

Power to break open doors, etc.:

36. The officer may break open any inner or outer door or window of any building and enter any building in order to seize any movable property if the officer has reasonable grounds to believe that such building contains movable property liable to seizure under the warrant and the officer has notified his authority and intention of breaking open if admission in not given. He shall, however, give all reasonable opportunity of women to withdraw.

Sale

Sale:

37. The Tax Recovery Officer may direct that any movable property attached under this Schedule or such portion thereof as may seem necessary to satisfy the certificate shall be sold.

Issue of proclamation:

38. When any sale of movable property is ordered by the Tax Recovery Officer, the Tax Recovery Officer shall issue a proclamation, in the language of the district, of the intended sale, specifying the time and place of sale and whether the sale is subject to confirmation or not.

Proclamation how made:

39. (1) Such proclamation shall be made by beat of drum or other customary mode,-

(a) in the case of property attached by actual seizure-

  (i) in the village in which the property was seized, or, if the property was seized in a town or city, then, in the locality in which it was seized; and

  (ii) at such other places as the Tax Recovery Officer may direct;

(b) in the case of property attached otherwise than by actual seizure, in such places, if any, as the Tax Recovery Officer may direct.

(2) A copy of the proclamation shall also be affixed in a conspicuous part of the office of the Tax Recovery Officer.

Sale after fifteen days:

40. Except where the property is subject to speedy and natural decay or when the expense of keeping it in custody is likely to exceed its value, no sale of movable property under this Schedule shall, without the consent in writing of the defaulter, take place until after the expiry of at least fifteen days calculated from the date on which a copy of the sale proclamation was affixed in the office of the Tax Recovery Officer.

Sale of agricultural produce:

41. (Not printed)

Special provisions relating to growing crops

42. (Not printed)

Sale to be by auction:

43. The property shall be sold by public auction in one or more lots as the officer may consider advisable, and if the amount to be realised by sale is satisfied by the sale of a portion of the property, the sale shall be immediately stopped with respect to the remainder of the lots.

Sale by public auction:

44. (1) Where movable property is sold by public auction, the price of each lot shall be paid at the time of sale or as soon after as the officer holding the sale directs and in default of payment, the property shall forthwith be resold.

(2) On payment of the purchase-money, the officer holding the sale shall grant a certificate specifying the property purchased, the price paid and the name of the purchaser, and the sale shall become absolute.

(3) Where the movable property to be sold is a share in goods belonging to the defaulter and a co-owner, and two or more persons, of whom one is such co-owner, respectively bid the same sum for such property or for any lot, the bidding shall be deemed to be the bidding of the co-owner

Irregularity not to vitiate sale, but any person injured may sue:

45. No irregularity in publishing or conducting the sale of movable property vitiate the sale, but any person sustaining substantial injury by reason of such irregularity at the hand of any other person may institute a suit in a civil court against him for compensation, or (if such other person is the purchaser) for the recovery of the specific property and for compensation in default of such recovery.

Negotiable instruments and shares in a corporation:

46. Notwithstanding anything contained in this Schedule, where the property to be sold is a negotiable instrument or a share in a corporation, the Tax Recovery Officer may, instead of directing the sale to be made by public auction, authorise the sale of such instrument or share through a broker.

Order for payment of coin or currency notes to the Assessing Officer:

47. Where the property attached in current coin or currency notes, the Tax Recovery Officer may, at any time during the continuance of the attachment direct that such coins or notes shall be credited to the Central Government and the amount so credited shall be dealt with in the manner specified in rule 8.

Part III
Attachment and sale of immovable Property
Attachment

Attachment:

48. Attachment of the immovable property of the dafaulter shall be made by an order prohibiting the defaulter from transferring or charging the property in any way and prohibiting all persons from taking any benefit under such transfer or charge.

Service of notice of attachment:

49. A copy of the order of attachment shall be served on the defaulter.

Proclamation of attachment:

50. The order of attachment shall be proclaimed at some place on or adjacent to the property attached by beat of drum or other customary mode, and a copy of the order shall be affixed on a conspicuous part of the property and on the notice board of the office of the Tax Recovery Officer.

Attachment to relate back from the date of service of notice:

51. Where any immovable property is attached under this Schedule, the attachment shall relate back to, and take effect from, the date on which the notice to pay the arrears, issued under this Schedule, was served upon the defaulter.

Sale

Sale and proclamation of sale:

52. (1) The Tax Recovery Officer may direct that any immovable property which has been attached, or such portion thereof as may seem necessary to satisfy the certificate, shall be sold.

(2) Where any immovable property is ordered to be sold, the Tax Recovery Officer shall cause a proclamation of the intended sale to be made in the language of the district.

Contents of proclamation:

53. A proclamation of sale of immovable property shall be drawn up after notice to the defaulter, and shall state the time and place of sale, and shall specify, as fairly and accurately as possible,-

(a) the property to be sold;

(b) the revenue, if any, assessed upon the property or any part thereof;

(c) the amount for the recovery of which the sale is ordered;

(cc) the reserve price, if any, below which the property may not be sold; and

(d) any other tiling which the Tax Recovery Officer considers it material for a purchaser to know, in order to judge the nature and value of the property.

Mode of making proclamation:

54. (1) Every proclamation for the sale of immovable property shall be made at some place on or near such property by beat of drum or other customary mode, and a copy of the proclamation shall be affixed on a conspicuous part of the property and also upon a conspicuous part of the office of the Tax Recovery Officer.

(2) Where the Tax Recovery Officer so directs, such proclamation shall also be published in the Official Gazette or in a local newspaper, or in both; and the cost of such publication shall be deemed to be costs of the sale.

(3) Where the property is divided into lots for the purpose of being sold separately, it shall not be necessary to make a separate proclamation for each lot, unless proper notice of the sale cannot, in the opinion of the Tax Recovery Officer, otherwise be given.

Time of sale:

55. No sale of immovable property under this Schedule shall, without the consent in writing of the defaulter, take place until after the expiration of at least thirty days calculated from the date on which a copy of the proclamation of sale has been affixed on the property or in the office of the Tax Recovery Officer, whichever is later.

Sale to be by auction:

56. The sale shall be by public auction to the highest bidder and shall be subject to confirmation by the Tax Recovery Officer:

Provided that no sale under this rule shall be made if the amount bid by the highest bidder is less than the reserve price, if any, specified under clause (cc) of rule 53.

Deposit by purchaser and resale in default:

57. (1) On every sale of immovable property, the person declared to be the purchaser shall pay, immediately after such declaration, a deposit of twenty five per cent on the amount of his purchase money, to the officer conducting the sale; and, in default of such deposit, the property shall forthwith be resold.

(2) The full amount of purchase money payable shall be paid, by the purchaser to the Tax Recovery Officer on or before the fifteenth day from the date of the sale of the property.

Procedure in default of payment:

58. In default of payment within the period mentioned in the preceding rule, the deposit may, if the Tax Recovery Officer thinks fit, after defraying the expenses of the sale, be forfeited to the Government, and the property shall be resold, and the defaulting purchaser shall forfeit all claims to the property or to any part of the sum for which it may subsequently be sold.

Authority to bid:

59. (1) Where the sale of a property, for which a reserve price has been specified under clause (cc) of rule 53, has been postponed for want of a bid of an amount not less than such reserve price, it shall be lawful for an Assessing Officer, if so authorised by the Chief Commissioner or Commissioner in this behalf, to bid for the property on behalf of the Central Government at any subsequent sale.

(2) All persons bidding at the sale shall be required to declare, if they are bidding on their own behalf or on behalf of their principals. In the latter case, they shall be required to deposit their authority, and in default their bids shall be rejected.

(3) Where the Assessing Officer referred to in sub-rule (1) is declared to be the purchaser of the property at any subsequent sale, nothing contained in rule 57 shall apply to the case and the amount of the purchase price shall be adjusted towards the amount specified in the certificate.

Application to set aside sale of immovable property on deposit:

60. (1) Where immovable property has been sold in execution of a certificate, the defaulter, or any person whose interests are affected by the sale, may, at any time within thirty days from the date of the sale, apply to the Tax Recovery Officer to set aside the sale, on his depositing -

- (a) the amount specified in the proclamation of sale as that for the recovery of which the sale was ordered, with interest thereon at the rate of fifteen per cent per annum, calculated from date of the proclamation of sale to the date when the deposit is made; and

(b) for payment to the purchaser, as penalty, a sum equal to five per cent of the purchase money, but not less than one rupee.

(2) Where a person makes an application under rule 61 for setting aside the sale of his immovable property, he shall not, unless he withdraws that application, be entitled to make or prosecute an application under this rule.

Application to set aside sale of immovable property on ground of non-service of notice or irregularity:

61. Where immovable property has been sold in execution of a certificate, such Income-tax Officer as may be authorised by the Chief Commissioner or Commissioner in this behalf, the defaulter, or any person whose interests are affected by the sale, may, at any time within thirty days from the date of the sale, apply to the Tax Recovery Officer to set aside the sale of the immovable property on the ground that notice was not served on the defaulter to pay the arrears as required by this Schedule or on the ground of a material irregularity in publishing or conducting the sale ,

Provided that:

(a) no sale shall be set aside on any such ground unless the Tax Recovery Officer is satisfied that the applicant has sustained substantial injury by reason of the non-service or irregularity; and

(b) an application made by a defaulter under this rule shall be disallowed unless the applicant deposits the amount recoverable from him in the execution of the certificate.

Setting aside sale where defaulter has no saleable interest:

62. At any time within thirty days of the sale, the purchaser may apply to the Tax Recovery Officer to set aside the sale on the ground that the defaulter had no saleable interest in the property sold.

Confirmation of sale:

63. (1) Where no application is made for setting aside the sale under the foregoing rules or where such an application is made and disallowed by the Tax Recovery Officer, the Tax Recovery Officer shall (if the full amount of the purchase money has been paid) make an order confirming the sale, and, thereupon, the sale shall become absolute.

(2) Where such application is made and allowed, and where, in the case of an application made to set aside the sale on deposit of the amount and penalty and charges, the deposit is made within thirty days from the date of the sale, the Tax Recovery Officer shall make an order setting aside the sale:

Provided that no order shall be made unless notice of the application has been given to the persons affected thereby.

Return of purchase money in certain cases:

64. Where a sale of immovable property is set aside, any money paid or deposited by the purchaser on account of the purchase, together with the penalty, if any, deposited for payment to the purchaser, and such interest as the Tax Recovery Officer may allow, shall be paid to the purchaser.

Sale certificate:

65. (1) Where a sale of immovable property has become absolute, the Tax Recovery Officer shall grant a certificate specifying the property sold, and the name of the person who at the time of sale is declared to be the purchaser.

(2) Such certificate shall state the date on which the sale became absolute.

Postponement of sale to enable defaulter to raise amount due under certificate:

66. (1) Where an order for the sale of immovable property has been made, if the defaulter can satisfy the Tax Recovery Officer that there is reason to believe that the amount of the certificate may be raised by the mortgage or lease or private sale of such property, or some part thereof, or of any other immovable property of the defaulter, the Tax Recovery Officer may, on his application, postpone the sale of the property comprised in the order for sale, on such terms, and for such period as he thinks proper, to enable him to raise the amount.

(2) In such case, the Tax Recovery Officer shall grant a certificate to the defaulter, authorising him, within a period to be mentioned therein, and notwithstanding anything contained in this Schedule, to make the proposed mortgage, lease or sale:

Provided that all moneys payable under such mortgage, lease or sale shall be paid, not to the defaulter, but to the Tax Recovery Officer:

Provided also that no mortgage, lease or sale under this rule shall become absolute until it has been confirmed by the Tax Recovery Officer.

Fresh proclamation before re-sale:

67. Every re-sale of immovable property, in default of payment of the purchase money within the period allowed for such payment, shall be made after the issue of a fresh proclamation in the manner and for the period hereinbefore provided for the sale.

Bid of co-sharer to have preference:

68. Where the property sold is a share of undivided immovable property, and two or more persons, of whom one is a co-sharer, respectively bid the same sum for such property or for any lot, the bid shall be deemed to be the bid of the co-sharer.

Acceptance of property in satisfaction of amount due from the defaulter:

68A. (1) Without prejudice to the provisions contained in this part, an Assessing Officer, duly authorised by the Chief Commissioner or Commissioner in this behalf, may accept in satisfaction of the whole or any part of the amount due from the defaulter the property, the sale of which has been postponed for the reason mentioned in sub-rule (1) of rule 59, at such price as may be agreed upon between the Assessing Officer and the defaulter.

(2) Where any property is accepted under sub-rule (1), the defaulter shall deliver possession of such property to the Assessing Officer and on the date the possession of the property is delivered to the Assessing Officer, the property shall vest in the Central Government and the Central Government shall, where necessary, intimate the concerned Registering Officer appointed under the Registration Act, 1908 (16 of 1908), accordingly.

(3) Where the price of the property agreed upon under sub-rule (1) exceeds the amount due from the defaulter, such excess shall be paid by the Assessing Officer to the defaulter within a period of three months

from the date of delivery of possession of the property and where the Assessing Officer fails to pay such excess within the period aforesaid, the Central Government shall, for the period commencing on the expiry of such period and ending with the date of payment of the amount remaining unpaid, pay simple interest at [1][six] percent per annum to the defaulter on such amount.

[2][**Time limit for sale of attached immovable property:**

68B. (1) No sale of immovable property shall be made under this part after the expiry of three[3] years from the end of the financial year in which the order giving rise to a demand of any tax, interest, fine, penalty or any other sum, for the recovery of which the immovable property has been attached, has become conclusive under the provisions of section 245-1 or, as the case may be, final in terms of the provisions of Chapter XX:

Provided that where the immovable property is required to be re-sold due to the amount of highest bid being less than the reserve price or under the circumstances mentioned in rule 57 or rule 58 or where the sale is set aside under rule 61, the aforesaid period of limitation for the sale of the immovable property shall stand extended by one year.

(2) In computing the period of limitation under sub-rule (1), the period:

(i) during which the levy of the aforesaid tax, interest, fine, penalty or any other sum is stayed by an order or injunction of any court; or

(ii) during which the proceedings of attachment or sale of the immovable property are stayed by an order or injunction of any court; or

(iii) commencing from the date of the presentation of any appeal against the order passed by the Tax Recovery Officer under this Schedule and ending on the day the appeal is decided, shall be excluded:

Provided that where immediately after the exclusion of the aforesaid period, the period of limitation for the sale of the immovable property is less than 180 days, such remaining period shall be extended to 180 days and the aforesaid period of limitation shall be deemed to be extended accordingly.

(3) Where any immovable property has been attached under this part before the 1st day of June, 1 992, and the order giving rise to a demand of any tax, interest, fine, penalty or any other sum, for the recovery of which the immovable property has been attached, has also become conclusive or final before the said date, that date shall be deemed to be the date on which the said order has become conclusive or, as the case may be, final.

(4) Where the sale of immovable property is not made in accordance with the provisions of sub-rule (1), the attachment order in relation to the said property shall be deemed to have been vacated on the expiry of the time of limitation specified under this rule.

Part-V
Appointment of Receiver

Appointment of Receiver for business:

69. (1) Where the property of a defaulter consists of a business, the Tax Recovery Officer may attach the business and appoint a person as receiver to manage the business.

(2) Attachment of a business under this rule shall be made by an order prohibiting the defaulter from transferring or charging the business in any way and prohibiting all persons from taking any benefit under such transfer or charge, and intimating that the business has been attached under this rule. A copy of the order of attachment shall be served on the defaulter, and another copy shall be affixed on a conspicuous part of the premises in which the business is carried on and on the notice board of the office of the Tax Recovery Officer.

Appointment of receiver for immovable property:

70. Where immovable property is attached, the Tax Recovery Officer may, instead of directing a sale of the property, appoint a person as receiver to manage such property.

Powers of Receiver:

71. (1) Where any business or other property is attached and taken under management under the foregoing rules, the receiver shall, subject to the control of the Tax Recovery Officer, have such powers as may be necessary for the proper management of the property and the realisation of the profits, or rents and profits, thereof.

(2) The profits, or rents and profits, of such business or other property, shall, after defraying the expenses of management, be adjusted towards discharge of the arrears, and the balance, if any, shall be paid to the defaulter.

Withdrawal of management:

72. The attachment and management under the foregoing rules may be withdrawn at any time at the discretion of the Tax Recovery Officer, or if the arrears are discharged by receipt of such profits and rents or are otherwise paid.

Part-V
Arrest and detention of the defaulter

Notice to show cause:

73. (1) No order for the arrest and detention in civil prison of a defaulter shall be made unless the Tax Recovery Officer has issued and served a notice upon the defaulter calling upon him to appear before him on the date specified in the notice and to show cause why he should not be committed to the civil prison, and unless the Tax Recovery Officer, for reasons recorded in writing is satisfied:

(a) that the defaulter, with the object or effect of obstructing the execution of the certificate, has, after the drawing up of the certificate by the Tax Recovery Officer, dishonestly transferred, concealed, or removed any part of his property, or

(b) that the defaulter has, or has had since the drawing up of the certificate by the Tax Recovery Officer, the means to pay the arrears or some substantial part thereof and refuses or neglects or has refused or neglected to pay the same.

(2) Notwithstanding anything contained in sub-rule (1), a warrant for the arrest of the defaulter may be issued by the Tax Recovery Officer if the Tax Recovery Officer is satisfied, by affidavit or otherwise, that with the object or effect of delaying the execution of the certificate, the defaulter is likely to abscond or leave the local limits of the jurisdiction of the Tax Recovery Officer.

(3) Where appearance is not made in obedience to a notice issued and served under sub-rule (1), the Tax Recovery Officer may issue a warrant for the arrest of the defaulter.

(3A) A warrant of arrest issued by a Tax Recovery Officer under sub-rule (2) or sub-rule (3) may also be executed by any other Tax Recovery Officer within whose jurisdiction the defaulter may for the time being be found.

(4) Every person arrested in pursuance of a warrant or arrest under this rule shall be brought before the Tax Recovery Officer issuing the warrant as soon as practicable and in any event within twenty-four hours of his arrest (exclusive of the time required for the journey):

Provided that, if the defaulter pays the amount entered in the warrant of arrest as due and the costs of the arrest to the officer arresting him, such officer shall at once release him.

Explanation: For the purposes of this rule, where the defaulter is a Hindu undivided family, the karta thereof shall be deemed to be the defaulter.

Hearing:

74. When a defaulter appears before the Tax Recovery Officer in obedience to a notice to show cause or is brought before the Tax Recovery Officer under rule 73, the Tax Recovery Officer shall give the defaulter an opportunity of showing cause why he should not be committed to the civil prison.

Custody pending hearing:

75. Pending the conclusion of the inquiry, the Tax Recovery Officer may, in his discretion, order the defaulter to be detained in the custody of such officer as the Tax Recovery Officer may think fit or release him on his furnishing security to the satisfaction of the Tax Recovery Officer for his appearance when required.

Order of detention:

76. (1) Upon the conclusion of the inquiry, the Tax Recovery Officer may make an order for the detention of the defaulter in the civil prison and shall in that event cause him to be arrested if he is not already under arrest:

Provided that in order to give the defaulter an opportunity of satisfying the arrears, the Tax Recovery Officer may, before making the order of detention, leave the defaulter in the custody of the officer arresting him or of any other officer for a specified period not exceeding 15 days, or release him on his furnishing security to the satisfaction of the Tax Recovery Officer for his appearance at the expiration of the specified period if the arrears are not so satisfied.

(2) When the Tax Recovery Officer does not make an order of detention under sub-rule (1) he shall, if the defaulter is under arrest, direct his release.

Detention in and release from prison:

77. (1) Every person detained in the civil prison in execution of a certificate may be so detained:

(a) where the certificate is for a demand of an amount exceeding two hundred and fifty rupees - for a period of six months, and

(b) in any other case — for a period of six weeks; Provided that he shall be released from such detention:

(i) on the amount mentioned in the warrant for his detention being paid to the officer-in-charge of the civil prison, or

(ii) on the request of the Tax Recovery Officer on any ground other than the grounds mentioned in rules 78 and 79,

(2) A defaulter released from detention under this rule shall not, merely by reason of his release, be discharged from his liability for the arrears; but he shall not be liable to be rearrested under the certificate in execution of which he was detained in the civil prison.

Release:

78. (1) The Tax Recovery Officer may order the release of a defaulter who has been arrested in execution of a certificate upon being satisfied that he has disclosed the whole of his property and has placed it at the disposal of the Tax Recovery Officer and that he has not committed any act of bad faith.

(2) If the Tax Recovery Officer has ground for believing the disclosure made by a defaulter under sub-rule (1) to have been untrue, he may order the rearrest of the defaulter in execution of the certificate, but the period of his detention in the civil prison shall not in the aggregate exceed that authorised by rule 77.

Release on ground of illness:

79. (1) At any time after a warrant for the arrest of a defaulter has been issued, the Tax Recovery Officer may cancel it on the ground of 1 ,*; serious illness;

(2) Where a defaulter has been arrested, the Tax Recovery Officer may release him if, in the opinion of the Tax Recovery Officer, he is not in a fit state of health to be detained in the civil prison.

(3) Where a defaulter has been committed to the civil prison, he may be released therefrom by the Tax Recovery Officer on the ground of the existence of any infectious or contagious disease, or on the ground of his suffering from any serious illness.

(4) A defaulter released under this rule may be rearrested, but the period of his detention in the civil prison shall not in the aggregate exceed that authorised by rule 77.

Entry into dwelling house:

80. For the purpose of making an arrest under this Schedule:

(a) no dwelling house shall be entered after sunset and before sunrise;

(b) no outer door of a dwelling house shall be broken open unless such dwelling house or a portion thereof is in the occupancy of the defaulter and he or other occupant of the house refuses or in any way prevents access thereto; but, when the person executing any such warrant has duly gained access to any dwelling house, he may break open the door of any room or apartment if he has reason to believe that the defaulter is likely to be found there;

(c) no room, which is in the actual occupancy of a woman who, according to the customs of the country, does not appear in public, shall be entered into unless the officer authorised to make the arrest has given notice to her that she is at liberty to withdraw and has given her reasonable time and facility for withdrawing.

Prohibition against arrest of women or minors, etc.:

81. The Tax Recovery Officer shall not order the arrest and detention in the civil prison of:

(a) a woman, or

(b) any person who, in his opinion, is a minor or of unsound mind.

Part –VI
Miscellaneous

Officers deemed to be acting judicially:

82. Every Chief Commissioner ,or Commissioner, Tax Recovery Officer or other officer acting under this Schedule shall, in the discharge of his functions under this Schedule, be deemed to be acting judicially within the meaning of the Judicial Officers Protection Act, 1850 (18 of 1850).

Power to take evidence:

83. Every Chief Commissioner or Commissioner, Tax Recovery Officer or other officer acting under the provisions of this Schedule shall have the powers of a civil court while trying a suit for the purpose of receiving evidence, administering oaths, enforcing the attendance of witnesses and compelling the production of documents.

Continuance of certificate:

84. No certificate shall cease to be in force by reason of the death of the defaulter.

Procedure on death of defaulter:

85. If at any time after the certificate is drawn up by the Tax Recovery Officer the defaulter dies, the proceedings under this Schedule (except arrest and detention) may be continued against the legal representative of the defaulter, and the provisions of this Schedule shall apply as if the legal representative were the defaulter.

Appeals:

86. (1) An appeal from any original order passed by the Tax Recovery Officer under this Schedule, not being an order which is conclusive, shall lie to the Chief Commissioner or Commissioner.

(2) Every appeal under this aile must be presented within thirty days from the date of the order appealed against.

(3) Pending the decision of any appeal, execution of the certificate may be stayed if the appellate authority so directs, but not otherwise.

(4) Notwithstanding anything contained in sub-rule (1), where a Chief Commissioner or Commissioner is authorised to exercise powers as such in respect of any area, then, all appeals against the orders passed before the date of such authorisation by any Tax Recovery Officer authorised to exercise powers as such in respect of that area, or an area which is included in that area, shall lie to such Chief Commissioner or Commissioner.

Review:

87. Any order passed under this Schedule may, after notice to all persons interested, be reviewed by the Chief Commissioner or Commissioner, Tax Recovery Officer or other officer who made the order, or by his successor in office, on account of any mistake apparent from the record.

Recovery from surety:

88. Where any person has under this Schedule become surety for the amount due by the defaulter, he may be proceeded against under this Schedule as if he were the defaulter.

[1][**Penalties:**

89. x x x]

Subsistence allowance:

90. (1) When a defaulter is arrested or detained in the civil prison, the sum payable for the subsistence of the defaulter from the time of arrest until he is released shall be borne by the Tax Recovery Officer.

(2) Such sum shall be calculated on the scale fixed by the State Government for the subsistence of judgment-debtors arrested in execution of a decree of a civil court.

(3) Sums payable under this rule shall be deemed to be costs in the proceeding: Provided that the defaulter shall not be detained in the civil prison or arrested on account of any sum so payable.

Forms:

91. The Board may prescribe the form to be used for any order, notice, warrant, or certificate to be issued under this Schedule.

Power to make rules

92. (Not printed)

Saving regarding charge:

93. Nothing in this Schedule shall affect any provision of this Act whereunder 'he tax is a first charge upon any asset.'

Continuance of certain pending proceedings and power to remove difficulties

94. (Not printed)

D

Third Schedule to the In-come Tax Act, 1961
The Third Schedule
Procedure for distraint by Assessing Officer or Tax Recovery Officer

Distraint and sale:

Where any distraint and sale of movable property are to be effected by any Assessing Officer or Tax Recovery Officer authorised for the purpose, such distraint and sale shall be made, as far as may be, in the same manner as attachment and sale of any movable property attachable by actual seizure, and the provisions of the Second Schedule relating to attachment and sale shall, so far as may be, apply in respect of such distraint and sale.

Income-Tax (Certificate Proceedings) Rules, 1962

S.O. 955, Dated 26.3.1962: *In exercise of the powers conferred by sub-section (1) of section 295 of the Income-tax Act, 1961 (43 of 1961), and rules 91 and 92 of the Second Schedule to that Act, the Central Board of Revenue hereby makes the following rules, namely:*

Part-1
Preliminary

Short title and commencement:

1. (1) These rules may be called the "Income-tax (Certificate Proceedings) Rules, 1962."

(2) They shall come into force on the 1st day of April, 1962.

Definitions:

2. In these rules, unless the context otherwise requires:

(1) "Act" means the Income-tax Act, 1961 (43 of 1961);

(1A) "authorised bank" shall have the same meaning as in clause *(aa)* of sub-rule (1) of rule 2 of the Income-Tax Rules, 1962;

(2) "public officer" shall have the same meaning as in the Code of Civil Procedure, 1908 (5 of 1908);

(3) "principal rules" means the rules contained in the Second Schedule to the Act; and

(4) "section" and "Schedule" mean respectively section of, and Schedule to, the Act.

Forms:

3. All references to "Forms" in these rules shall be construed as references to the forms set out in the Appendix hereto.

Tax Recovery Commissioners appointed by the Central Government:

4. [Omitted for dt. 1.1.1972]

Jurisdiction of Tax Recovery Commissioners:

5. [Omitted by Amendment Rules, 1990]

Jurisdiction of Tax Recovery Officers authorised to function as such by the Central Government:

6. [Omitted for dt. 12.9.1990]

Jurisdiction of other Tax Recovery Officers:

7. [Omitted by Amendment Rules, 1990]

Transfer of proceedings from one Tax Recovery Officer to another:

8. Where any proceeding for execution of a certificate pending before a Tax Recovery Officer stands transferred or is transferred to any other Tax Recovery Office the Tax Recovery Officer to whom

the proceeding stands transferred or is transferred may continue the proceedings from the stage at which it stood immediately before such transfer and such transfer shall not render necessary the re-issue of any notice warrant, proclamation, order, or certificate already issued.

Part – II
General Procedure

Procedure to be followed while sending certificate to another Tax Recovery Officer:

9. When a certificate is sent by a Tax Recovery Officer to another Tax Recovery Officer under sub-section 223, he shall:

(i) keep a copy of the certificate in his office; and

(ii) inform the Assessing Officer of his having sent the certificate.

Procedure to be followed while sending a certified copy of certificate to another Tax Recovery Officer:

9A. (1) Where only a part of the amount in respect of which certificate has been drawn up by a Tax Recovery Officer is to be recovered by any other Tax Recovery Officer under sub-section (2) of section 223, the Tax Recovery Officer shall, before sending a copy of the certificate to the other Tax Recovery Officer, endorse on such copy a certificate in the following form -

Form of Certificate

1, ... (Name), Tax Recovery Officer, ..., do hereby certify that the document bearing this endorsement is a true copy of certificate No. .... date .... drawn up by the Tax Recovery Officer .... against .... [name of defaulter] for the recovery of an amount of Rs.. ....

I do hereby specify that out of the aforesaid amount, an amount of Rs. .... as noted below, is to be recovered from the defaulter, by the Tax Recovery Officer

Rs. P.

Part of certificate amount
Costs and charges
Interest

Total

(2) When a copy of the certificate is sent by a Tax Recovery Officer to another Tax Recovery Officer under sub-section (2) of section 223, he shall,:

(i) keep the certificate in his office; and

(ii) inform the Assessing Officer of his having sent a copy of the certificate.

Procedure to be followed on receipt of a certificate from a Tax Recovery Officer:

10. When a certificate or the certified copy of a certificate is sent by a Tax Recovery Officer to another Tax Recovery Officer under sub-section (2) of section 223, such other Tax Recovery Officer

shall follow the same procedure as is laid down in the principal ailes and these rules including the issue of the notice under aile 2 of the principal ailes.

Intimation by the first Tax Recovery Officer:

11. The Tax Recovery Officer shall intimate the details of all amounts recovered in respect of a certificate, from time to time to the Assessing Officer, and, also, to any Tax Recovery Officer to whom the certificate or a certified copy of the Certificate has been sent by him under sub-section (2) of section 223.

Intimation by the other Tax Recovery Officer:

12. When a certificate or the certified copy of a certificate is sent by a Tax Recovery Officer to another Tax Recovery Officer under sub-section (2) of section 223, such other Tax Recovery Officer shall communicate to the first-mentioned Tax Recovery Officer and to the Assessing Officer the details of all amounts recovered by him in respect of such certificate from time to time.

Intimation by the Income-tax Officer

13. [Omitted by Amendment Rules, 1990]

Form of notice of demand:

14. The notice of demand under rule 2 of the principal rules shall be issued in Form No. I.T.C.P. 1 which shall be in Form No. 57 of the Income-tax Rules, 1962 which may be so varied as the circumstances of each case may require.

Part - III
Attachment and sale of property

Continuance of attachment subject to claim of encumbrancer:

15. Where, in the course of investigation made under rule 11 of the principal rules, the Tax Recovery Officer is satisfied that the property is subject to a mortgage or charge (other than a mortgage or charge referred to in section 281* or rule 16 of the said rules) in favour of some person not in possession, and thinks fit to continue the attachment, he may do so, subject to such mortgage or charge.

Proclamation of sale:

16. For the purpose of ascertaining the matters to be specified in a of sale, the Tax Recovery Officer may summon any person whom he thinks proclamation necessary to summon and may examine him in respect of any matters relevant to the proclamation and require him to produce any document in his possession or power relating thereto.

Sale to be held by whom and his remuneration:

17. If the Tax Recovery Officer is of the opinion that it will be more advantageous to appoint a person other than an official subordinate to him to sell a property, he may appoint a fit person for the purpose and fix the remuneration to be allowed to him for rendering such services; and the remuneration payable to such person shall be deemed to be costs of the sale.

Reserve price:

18. It shall be competent for the Tax Recovery Officer to fix a reserve price in respect of any property, other than agricultural produce, to be sold and order that any bid shall be accepted only on condition that it is not less than the said reserve price.

Report of sale:

19. The officer conducting a sale shall forthwith pay the entire amount received by him from the purchaser of the property into the Government treasury and shall submit a full report of the sale to the Tax Recovery Officer.

Sale proceeds not to be disbursed till sale confirmed:

20. The proceeds of the sale of immovable property shall not be disbursed until the sale is confirmed by the Tax Recovery Officer or, where an appeal has been filed against the order confirming the sale, until the disposal of the appeal.

Registration of sale:

21. Every Tax Recovery Officer granting a certificate of sale to the purchaser of immovable property sold under the Second Schedule shall send a copy of such certificate to the registering officer concerned under the Indian Registration Act, 1 908 (16 of 1908), within the local limits of whose jurisdiction the whole or any part of the immovable property comprised in the certificate is situate.

Forms:

22. The following forms, which may be so varied as the circumstances of each case may require, shall be used for the purpose mentioned against each:

(i) Form No. I.T.C.P. 2, for issuing a warrant of attachment of movable property under rule 20 of the principal rules;

(ii) Form No. I.T.C.P. 3, for issuing a prohibitory order in the case of a debt not secured by a negotiable instrument under rule 26 (1) *(i)* of the principal rules;

(iii) Form No. I.T.C.P. 4, for issuing a prohibitory order in the case of a share in a corporation under rule 26 (1) *(ii)* of the principal rules;

(iv) Form No. I.T.C.P. 5, for issuing a prohibitory order in case of other movable property under rule 26 (1) *(iii)* of the principal rules;

(v) Form No. I.T.C.P. 6, for issuing a notice of attachment of a decree of a civil court under rule 27 of the principal rules;

(vi) Form No. I.T.C.P. 7, for issuing a notice of attachment where the property consists of a share or interest in movable property under rule 28 of the principal rules;

(vii) Form No. I.T.C.P. 8, for issuing an order of attachment of salary or allowances under rule 29 of the principal rules;

(viii) Form No. I.T.C.P. 9, for issuing an order of attachment of a negotiable instrument under aile 30 of the principal rules;

(ix) Form No. I.T.C.P. 10, for issuing a notice of attachment of movable property in the custody of any court or public officer under rule 31 of the principal rules;

(x) Form No. I.T.C.P. 11, for issuing an order of attachment of property consisting of an interest in partnership property under rule 32 of the principal rules;

(xi) Form No. I.T.C.P.12, for issuing a warrant of sale of property under rule 37 or rule 52 (1) of the principal rules;

(xii) Form No. l.T.C.P. 13, for issuing a proclamation of sale of movable or immovable property under rule 38 or rule 52 (2) of the principal rules;

(xiii) Form No. l.T.C.P. 14, for issuing a certificate of sale of movable property under sub-rule (2) of rule 44 of the principal rules;

(xiv) Form No. I.T.C.P. 15, for issuing an order for payment under rule 47 of the principal rules;

(xv) Form No. I.T.C.P. 16, for issuing an order of attachment of immovable property under rule 48 of principal rules;

(xvi) Form No. I.T.C.P. 17, for issuing a notice to the defaulter for settling a proclamation of sale under rule 53 of the principal rules;

(xvii) Form No. I.T.C.P.18, for making an order of confirmation of sale of immovable property under sub-rule (1) of rule 63 of the principal ailes;

(xviii) Form No. I.T.C.P. 19, for issuing a notice to interested parties under the proviso to sub-rule (2) of rule 63 of the principal rules;

(xix) Form No. I.T.C.P. 20, for issuing *a* certificate of sale of immovable property under rule 65 *of* the principal rules;

(xx) Form No. I.T.C.P. 21, for issuing a certificate to defaulter authorising him to mortgage, lease or sell immovable property under sub-rule (2) of rule 66 of the principal rules;

(xxi) Form No. I.T.C.P. 22, for issuing an order of attachment of a business under rule 69 of the principal rules.

Part - IV

Maintenance and custody, while under attachment of livestock or other Movable Property, fees for such Maintenance and Custody, sale thereof and disposal of sale proceeds

Property to which rules apply:

23. The rules in this part relate to movable property (other than agricultural produce) attached by actual seizure under the Second Schedule.

Custody at place of attachment:

24. (1) Where the properly attached is of such a nature that its removal from the place of attachment is impracticable or its removal involves expenditure out of proportion to the value of the property, the attaching officer shall, subject to any directions which the Tax Recovery Officer may issue in this behalf, arrange for the proper maintenance and custody of property at the place of attachment. The attaching officer shall forthwith send a report of having done so to the Tax Recovery Officer.

(2) On receipt of a report from the attaching officer under sub-rule (1), the Tax Recovery Officer may either order the removal of the property to a place which he shall specify or sanction its maintenance and custody at the place of attachment under such conditions as he may think fit.

Removal and custody of property in other cases:

25. Where the attached property is not kept at the place of attachment, it shall be kept in the custody of an officer (hereinafter in this part referred to as the "custody officer") subordinate to the Tax Recovery Officer and authorised by the Tax Recovery Officer for this purpose. The custody officer may remove the property to the office of the Tax Recovery Officer for custody under his own supervision or, with the approval of the Tax Recovery Officer, may make such arrangements as may be convenient and economical for its safe custody with any other fit person under his own supervision and the Tax Recovery Officer may fix the remuneration to be allowed to such person.

Property may be handed over to the defaulter:

26. Notwithstanding anything contained in rule 24 or rule 25, the attaching officer or the custody officer may, with the previous approval of the Tax Recovery Officer, entrust, subject to his right of supervision, the attached property to the defaulter on his executing a duly stamped bond *(sapurdnama)* in Form No. I.T.C.P. 23, which may be so varied as the circumstances of each case may require.

Explanation: Where the Tax Recovery Officer proceeds to recover any arrears due from the defaulter by attachment and sale of, or by appointing a receiver for the management of, any movable or immovable property which is held by or stands in the name of, any of the persons referred to in the *Explanation* to sub-section (1) of Action 222 and which is included in the defaulter's movable or immovable property by virtue of that *Explanation,* the reference to "defaulter" in this rule and in rules 28 to 32 (both inclusive), rules 39 and 40 and rules 42 to 47 (both inclusive) shall, in relation to such movable or immovable property, be construed as a reference to the person referred to in said Explanation.

Custody of attached cash, securities, etc.:

27. If the property attached consists of cash, Government or other securities, bullion, jewellery or other valuables, the attaching officer shall send them for safe custody to the nearest Government treasury or a branch of the Reserve Bank of India or State Bank of India or of its subsidiaries or of any authorised bank.

Claim of any person other than the defaulter to the property under attachment:

28. When the property remains at the place where it is attached in the custody of the attaching officer, and any person other than the defaulter claims the same, or any part thereof the officer shall nevertheless remain in possession and shall direct the claimant to prefer his claim to the Tax Recovery Officer.

Return of property on cancellation or withdrawal of attachment:

29. (1) If in consequence of withdrawal or cancellation of the attachment, the defaulter becomes entitled to receive back the movable property attached, the possession thereof shall be given to him on payment of costs, charges and expenses due, if any in respect of the execution of the certificate against such property.

(2) For the purpose of giving possession under sub-rule (1), the attaching officer shall inform the defaulter that the property is at his disposal.

(3) In the absence of any person to take charge of the property the officer shall if the property has been moved from the premises in which it was seized, replace it where it was found at the time of seizure.

Property may be sold if costs, etc., not paid:

30. In default of the payment of costs, charges and expenses referred to in sub-rule (1) of rule 29, the movable property or such portion thereof as may be necessary shall be sold by auction and after defraying the expenses of such sale and the costs charges and expenses aforesaid, the balance, if any, of the movable property as has not been sold shall be handed over to the defaulter.

Feeding and tending of livestock under attachment:

31. Whenever livestock is kept at the place where it has been attached, the defaulter shall be at liberty to undertake the due feeding and tending of it, under the supervision of the attaching officer.

Removal of livestock:

32. In the event of the defaulter failing to feed attached livestock, the livestock may be placed in the custody of the custody officer or in the circumstances mentioned in rule 33 may be placed in a pound maintained by the Government or a local authority.

Custody of livestock in pound:

33. If there be any such pound near the office of the Tax Recovery Officer, the attaching officer or the custody officer may place in it such attached livestock as can properly be kept there in which case the pound-keeper shall be responsible for the livestock and shall receive the same rates for accommodation and maintenance thereof as are payable in respect of impounded cattle of the same description.

Custody with a person other than custody officer:

34. Notwithstanding anything contained in rule 33, the custody officer may, with the approval of the Tax Recovery Officer, entrust the attached livestock to any other fit person under his own supervision and the Tax Recovery Officer may fix the remuneration to be allowed to such person after taking into account the local circumstances and the charges which such person may have to incur for the maintenance and custody of such livestock.

Expenses of custody, maintenance, etc.:

35. The expenses of maintenance and custody of movable property including the Enumeration payable to the person concerned under rule 25 or rule 34 shall be deemed to be costs of the sale.

Part-V
Delivery of property sold and execution of document or Endorsement of Negotiable instrument or share in a Corporation

Delivery of movable property, debts and shares:

36. (1) Where the property sold is movable property of which actual seizure has been made, it shall be delivered to the purchaser.

(2) (a) Where the property sold is movable property in the possession of some person other than the defaulter, the delivery thereof to the purchaser shall be made by giving notice to the person in possession prohibiting him from delivering possession of the property to any person except the purchaser and requiring him to deliver possession of the property to the purchaser within the time stipulated by the Tax Recovery Officer.

(b) Where such person in possession of the property fails without reasonable cause to deliver possession of the property to the purchaser within the time stipulated by the Tax Recovery Officer, or within such further time as may be allowed by him, the Tax Recovery Officer shall cause the property to be seized and delivered to the purchaser and the provisions or rules 35 and 36 of the principal rules shall, as far as may be, apply to such seizure.

(3) (a) Where the property sold is a debt not secured by a negotiable instrument, the delivery thereof to the purchaser shall be made by a written order of the Tax Recovery Officer prohibiting the creditor from receiving the debt or any interest thereon and the debtor from making payment thereof to any person except the purchaser and requiring the debtor to make payment thereof to the purchaser within the time stipulated by the Tax Recovery Officer.

(b) Where the debtor fails to make such payment to the purchaser within the time stipulated by the Tax Recovery Officer, or within such further time as may be allowed by him, the Tax Recovery Officer may take further proceedings to recover the amount due from the debtor as if the debtor were a defaulter in respect of whom the Tax Recovery Officer had drawn up a certificate under section 222 for the recovery of arrears of tax equal to the amount or the debt

(4) (a) Where the property sold is a share in a corporation, the delivery thereof to the purchaser shall be made by a written order of Tax Recovery Officer prohibiting the person in whose name the share may be standing from making any transfer of the share to any person except the purchaser, or receiving payment of any dividend or interest thereon and requiring him to deliver the share certificate or other document of title along with the instrument of transfer duly completed by him to the Tax Recovery Officer within the time stipulated by the Tax Recovery Officer and prohibiting the manager, secretary or other proper officer of the corporation from , permitting any such transfer or making any such payment to any person except the purchaser.

(b) Where the person in whose name the share may be standing fails to deliver the share certificate or other document of title to the Tax Recovery Officer within the time stipulated by him, or within such further time as may be allowed by him, the Tax Recovery Officer may take steps to obtain a duplicate of the share certificate or other document of title as if the share certificate or other document of title had been lost or destroyed.

Transfer of negotiable instruments and shares:

37. (1) Where the execution of a document or the endorsement of the party in whose name a negotiable instrument or a share in corporation is standing is required to transfer such negotiable instrument or share to a person who has purchased it under 3 sale under the Second Schedule, the Tax Recovery Officer may execute such Document or make such endorsement as may be necessary and such execution or endorsement shall have the same effect as an execution or endorsement by the party.

(2) Such execution or endorsement may be in the following form, namely:

"..........by................ Tax Recovery Officer .... in the proceedings for the recovery of arrears under the Income-tax Act, 1961, against ...."

(3) The Tax Recovery Officer may cause the document to be executed on proper stamp paper and to be registered if its registration is required by any law for the time being in force and the expenses of such execution and registration shall be borne by the purchaser.

(4) Until the transfer of such negotiable instrument or share, the Tax Recovery Officer may, by order, appoint some person to receive any interest or dividend due thereon and to sign a receipt for the same; and any receipt so signed shall be as valid and effectual for all purposes as if the same had been signed by the party himself.

Vesting order in case of other property:

38. In the case of any movable property not hereinbefore provided for, the Tax Recovery Officer may make an order vesting such property in the purchaser or as the purchaser may direct; and such property shall vest accordingly.

Delivery of immovable property in occupancy of defaulter:

39. (1) Where the immovable property sold is in the occupancy of the defaulter or of some person on his behalf or of some person claiming under a title created by the defaulter subsequently to the attachment of such property and a certificate in respect thereof has been granted under rule 65 of the principal rules, the Tax Recovery Officer shall, on the application of the purchaser, order delivery to be made by putting such purchaser on any person whom the purchaser may appoint to receive delivery on his behalf in possession of the property, and if need be, by removing any person who refuses to vacate the same.

(2) For the purposes of sub-rule (1), if the person in possession does not afford free access, the Tax Recovery Officer may, after giving reasonable warning and facility to any woman not appearing in public according to the customs of the country to withdraw, remove or open any lock or bolt or break open any door or do any other act necessary for putting the purchaser, or any person whom the purchaser may appoint to receive delivery on his behalf, in possession.

Delivery of immovable property in occupancy of tenant:

40. Where the immovable property sold is in the occupancy of a tenant or other person entitled to occupy the same and a certificate in respect thereof has been granted under rule 65 of the principal rules, the Tax Recovery Officer shall, on the application of the purchaser, order delivery to be made by affixing a copy of the certificate of sale in some conspicuous place on the property, and proclaiming to the occupant by beat of drum or other customary mode, at some convenient place, that the interest of the defaulter has been transferred to the purchaser.

Part - VI

Resistance or Obstruction to delivery of Possession to Purchaser

Resistance or obstruction to possession of immovable property:

41. (1) Where the purchaser of immovable property sold in execution of a certificate is resisted or obstructed by any person in obtaining possession of the property, he may make an application to the

Tax Recovery Officer complaining of such resistance or obstruction within thirty days of the date of such resistance obstruction.

(2) The Tax Recovery Officer shall fix a day for investigating the matter and shall summon the party against whom the application is made to appear and answer the same.

Resistance or obstruction by defaulter:

42. Where the Tax Recovery Officer is satisfied that the resistance or obstruction was occasioned without any just cause by the defaulter or by some other person at his instigation, he shall direct that applicant be put into possession of the property, and where the applicant is still resisted or obstructed in obtaining possession, the Tax Recovery Officer may also, at the instance of the applicant, take steps to put the applicant into possession of the property by removing the defaulter or any person acting at his instigation.

Resistance or obstruction by bonafide claimant:

43. Where the Tax Recovery Officer is satisfied that the resistance or obstruction was occasioned by any person (other than the defaulter) claiming in good faith to be in possession of the property on his own account or on account of some person other than the defaulter, the Tax Recovery Officer shall make an order dismissing the application.

Dispossession by purchaser:

44. (1) Where any person other than the defaulter is dispossessed of immovable property sold in execution of a certificate by the purchaser thereof, he may make an application to the Tax Recovery Officer complaining of such dipossession within thirty days of such dispossession.

(2) That Tax Recovery Officer shall fix a day for investigating the matter and shall summon the party against whom the application is made to appear and answer the same.

Bona fide claimant to be restored to possession:

45. Where the Tax Recovery Officer is satisfied that the applicant was in possession of the property on his own account or on account of some person other than the defaulter, he shall direct that the applicant be put into possession of the property.

Rules not applicable to transferee lite pendente:

46. Nothing in rules 43 and 45 shall apply to resistance or obstruction by a person to whom the defaulter has transferred the property after the service of a notice under rule 2 of the principal rules or to the dispossession of any such person.

Right to file a suit:

47. Any party not being a defaulter against whom an order is made under rule 42 or rule 43 or rule 45 may institute a suit in a civil court to establish the right which he claims to the present possession of the property.

Part-VII
Appointment, Powers and Duties of a Receiver

Powers of a Receiver:

48. A receiver appointed under the Second Schedule shall have all such powers, as to bringing in and defending suits and for the realisation, management, protection and preservation of the property, the collection of the rents and profits thereof, the application and disposal of such rents and profits, and the

execution of document as the owner himself has, or such of those powers as the Tax Recovery Officer thinks fit.

Remuneration of a receiver:

49. The Tax Recovery Officer may, by general or special order, fix the amount to be paid as remuneration for the services of the receiver.

Duties of a receiver:

50. (1) Every receiver so appointed shall:

(a) furnish such security (if any) as the Tax Recovery Officer thinks fit, duly to account for what he shall receive in respect of the property;

(b) submit his accounts at such periods and in such form as the Tax Recovery Officer directs;

(c) pay the amount due from him as the Tax Recovery Officer directs; and

(d) be responsible for any loss occasioned to the property by his wilful default or gross negligence.

(2) The receiver shall maintain true and regular accounts of the receivership and shall in particular maintain a cash book in which shall be entered from day to day all receipts and payments and also a ledger. He shall also maintain a counterfoil receipt book with the leaves numbered serially in print, from winch shall be given, as far as possible, all receipts for payments made to the receiver.

(3) Unless the Tax Recovery Officer otherwise directs, the receiver shall, as soon as may be after his appointment, open an account in the name of the receivership in such bank as the Tax Recovery Officer may direct and shall deposit therein all moneys received in the course of the receivership immediately on receipt thereof save any minimum sums that may be required for meeting day to day current expenses. All payments by the receiver shall, as far as possible, be made by cheques drawn on the bank account.

(4) Unless otherwise ordered, a receiver shall submit his accounts once in every three months. The first of such accounts commencing from the date of his appointment and ending with the expiry of three months therefrom shall be submitted within fifteen days of the expiry of the said period of three months and the subsequent accounts brought down to the end of each succeeding period of three months, within fifteen days of the expiry of each such period of three months.

Enforcement of receiver's duties:

51. (1) Where a receiver fails to submit his accounts at such periods and in such form as the Tax Recovery Officer directs, the Tax Recovery Officer may direct his property to be attached until such time as such accounts are submitted to him.

(2) The Tax Recovery Officer may at any time make an enquiry as to the amount, if any, due from the receiver, as shown by his accounts or otherwise, or an enquiry as to any loss to the property occasioned by his wilful default or gross negligence and may order the amount found due, if not already paid by the receiver under rule 50, or the amount of the loss so occasioned, to be paid by the receiver within a period to be fixed by the Tax Recovery Officer.

(3) Where the receiver fails to pay any amount which he has been ordered to pay under sub-rule (2) within the period specified, the Tax Recovery Officer may direct such amount to be recovered from the security (if any) furnished by the receiver or by attachment and sale of his property or, if his property has been attached under sub-rule (1), by the sale of such property, and may direct the sale proceeds to be applied in making good any amount found due from the receiver or any such loss occasioned by him and the balance (if any) of the sale proceeds shall be paid to the receiver.

(4) If a receiver fails to submit his accounts at such periods and in such form as directed by the Tax Recovery Officer without reasonable cause or improperly retains any cash in his hands, the Tax Recovery Officer may disallow the whole or any portion of the remuneration due to him for the period of the accounts with reference to which the default is committed and may also charge interest at a rate not exceeding 12 per cent per annum on the moneys improperly retained by him for the period of such retention without prejudice to any other proceedings which might be taken against the receiver.

Form of order of appointment of a receiver:

52. An order of appointment of a receiver under rule 69 or rule 70 of the principal rules, shall be made in Form No. I.T.C.P. 24 which may be so varied as the circumstances of each case may require.

Part - VIII
Arrest and Detention

Prison in which defaulter may be detained:

53. A person against whom an order of detention has been passed under Part V of the Second Schedule may be detained in the civil prison of the district in which the office of the Tax Recovery Officer ordering the detention is situate, or, where such civil prison does not afford suitable accommodation, in any other place which the State Government may appoint for the detention of persons ordered by the civil courts of such district to be detained.

Subsistence allowance:

54. (1) The subsistence allowance shall be supplied by the Tax Recovery Officer by monthly instalments in advance before the first day of each month.

(2) The first payment shall be made to the Tax Recovery Officer for such portion of the current month as remains unexpired before the defaulter is committed to the civil prison, and the subsequent payment (if any) shall be made to the officer in charge of the civil prison.

Forms:

55. The following forms, which may be so varied as the circumstances of each case may require, shall be used for the purpose mentioned against each:

(i) Form No. I.T.C.P. 25, for issuing a notice to show cause why a warrant of arrest should not issue under rule 73 of the principal rules;

(ii) Form No. I.T.C.P. 26, for issuing a warrant of arrest under Part V of the principal rules;

(iii) Form No. I.T.C.P. 27, for issuing a warrant of detention under Part V of the principal rules;

(iv) Form No. I.T.C.P. 28, for issuing an order of release under rule 77 or rule 78 or rule 79 of the principal rules.

Part-V
Appeals to a Chief Commissioner or Commissioner

Form of appeal:

55A. (1) Every appeal under sub-rule (1) of rule 86 of the principal rules, shall be made in Form No. I.T.C.P. 29A which shall be verified in the manner indicated therein and shall be accompanied by a copy of the order appealed against.

(2) The form of appeal prescribed by sub-rule (1), the grounds of appeal and the form of verification appended thereto shall be signed:

- (a) in the case of an individual, by the individual himself; where the individual is absent from India, by the individual concerned or by some person duly authorised by him in this behalf; and where the individual is mentally incapacitated from attending to his affairs, by his guardian or by any other person competent to act on his behalf;
- (b) in the case of a Hindu undivided family, by the karta, and where the karta is absent from India or is mentally incapacitated from attending to his affairs by any other adult member of such family;
- (c) in the case of a company or local authority, by the principal officer thereof
- (d) in the case of a firm, by any partner thereof, not being a minor;
- (e) in the case of any other association, by any member of the association or the principal officer thereof; and
- (f) in the case of any other person, by that person, or by some person competent to act on his behalf.

Procedure in appeal:

55B. (1) The Chief Commissioner or Commissioner shall fix a day and place for the hearing of the appeal and shall give notice of the same to the appellant and the Chief Commissioner or Commissioner against whose order the appeal is preferred.

(2) The following shall have the right to be heard at the time of appeal:

- (a) the appellant, either in person or by an authorised representative referred to in rule 62 of these rules;
- (b) the Tax Recovery Officer, either in person or by a representative.

(3) The Chief Commissioner or Commissioner may, if sufficient cause is shown, at any stage of the appeal, grant time to the parties or to any of them, and may, for reasons to be recorded in writing, adjourn from time to time the hearing of the appeal.

(4) The Chief Commissioner or Commissioner may, before disposing of any appeal, make such further inquiry as he thinks fit, or may direct the Tax Recovery Officer to make further inquiry and report the result of the same to the Chief Commissioner or Commissioner.

(5) The Chief Commissioner or Commissioner may, at the hearing of an appeal, allow the appellant to go into any ground of appeal not specified in the grounds of appeal, if the Chief Commissioner or Commissioner is satisfied that the omission of that ground from the form of appeal was not wilful or unreasonable.

(6) The order of the Chief Commissioner or Commissioner disposing of the appeal shall be in writing and shall state the points for determination, the decision thereon and the reason for the decision.

(7) On the disposal of the appeal, the Chief Commissioner or Commissioner shall communicate the order passed by him to the appellant, the defaulter (if he is not the appellant) and the Tax Recovery Officer.

(8) Every appeal shall be disposed of by the Chief Commissioner or Commissioner as expeditiously as possible and endeavour shall be made to dispose of the appeal within six months from the date on which it is presented.

Part-IX
Scale of fees for processes, charges for other Proceedings and Poundage fees, etc.

Process fees:

56. The following scale of fees shall be charged for service and execution of processes issued under the Second Schedule and these rules:

		exceeds Rs. 1,000	Where the amount mentioned in the certificate is Rs. 1,000 or under
		Rs.	Rs.
(a)	Notice of demand	1.50	1.00
(b)	Warrant of attachment	3.00	2.00
(c)	Warrant of arrest	3.00	2.00
(d)	Warrant of delivery	3.00	2.00
(e)	Proclamation of sale	5.00	3.00
(f)	Any process not provided for hereinabove	1.50	1.00

Levy and scale of poundage fees:

57. (1) In respect of any sale made in the execution of a certificate, there shall be levied a fee by way of poundage on the gross amount realised by the sale, calculated at the rate of 2 percent on such gross amount up to Rs. 1,000 and at the rate of 1 per cent on the excess of such gross amount over Rs. 1,000.

(2) The poundage fee leviable under sub-rule (1) shall be calculated on multiples of Rs. 25, that is to say, a poundage fee of 50 paise shall be levied for every Rs 25, or part of Rs. 25, realised by the sale up to Rs. 1,000 and in the case of the proceeds of the sale exceeding Rs. 1,000, an additional fee of 25 paise for every Rs. 25 or part thereof on the excess of such amount over Rs. 1000, shall be levied.

(3) Where the sale is in more than one lot, the poundage fee shall be calculated with reference to the sale proceeds of each lot separately.

(4) The poundage fee under sub-rule (1) shall be paid by the purchaser of the property as soon as the sale is completed.

(5) When a sale of immovable property is set aside under sub-rule (2) of rule 63 of the principal rules, the Tax Recovery Officer may make an order for payment, by the defaulter or by the person at whose instance the sale is set aside, of the poundage fees paid by the purchaser of the property under sub-rule (1) read with sub-rule (4).

Copying fees:

58. (1) Except in cases where copies are supplied free under rules or instruction in force, copying fees shall be charged for supplying a copy of any document at the rate or Re. 1 for each page of such document.

(2) Copying fees shall be payable in advance.

(3) The fees to be charged for the supply of a copy of any document urgently shall be Rs. 4 for each document, in addition to the fees payable under sub-rule (1).

Inspection fees:

59. (1) Fees for inspecting records of proceedings before the Chief Commissioner or Commissioner or Tax Recovery Officer under the Second Schedule shall, where such inspection is permitted, be charged as follows:

(a) for the first hour or part thereof Rs. 2

(b) for every additional hour or part thereof 50 Paise. (2) Fees for inspection shall be payable in advance.

Part - X
Miscellaneous

Proceedings against legal representative of a deceased defaulter:

60. A notice to the legal representative of a deceased defaulter under rule 65 of the principal rules read with rule 2 of those rules shall be issued in Form No. I.T. C. P. 29 which may be so varied as the circumstances of each case may require.

Recovery from surety:

61. A notice to a surety under rule 88 of the principal rules read with rule 2 of those rules shall be issued in Form No. I.T.C.P. 30 which may be so varied as the circumstances of each case may require.

Appearance before Tax Recovery Officer:

62. (1) Any person who is entitled or required to attend before any Chief Commissioner or Commissioner or Tax Recovery Officer in connection with any proceeding under the Second Schedule or these rules, otherwise than when required under rule 83 of the principal rules to attend personally for examination on oath or affirmation, may attend either in person or by an authorised representative.

Explanation: For the purposes of this sub-rule, "authorised representative" shall have the meaning assigned to it in clauses (iii) to (vii) of sub-section (2) of section 288.

(2) In any proceeding before the Tax Recovery Officer, referred to in sub-rule (1), the Assessing Officer concerned shall have the right to be heard either in person or by a representative.

Chapter 18

Penalties

Section 14. Penalties.–(1) Whoever, for the purpose of avoiding any payment to be made by himself under this Act [1][the Scheme [2][the [3][Pension] Scheme or the Insurance Scheme]] or of enabling any other person to avoid such payment, knowingly makes or causes to be made any false statement or false representation shall be punishable with imprisonment for a term which may extend to [4][one year, or with fine of five thousand rupees, or with both].

[5][(1A) An employer who contravenes, or makes default in complying with, the provisions of section 6 or clause (a) of sub-section (3) of section 17 in so far as it relates to the payment of inspection charges, or paragraph 38 of the Scheme in so far as it relates to the payment of administrative charges, shall be punishable with imprisonment for a term which may extend to [6][three years], but–

(a) which shall not be less than [7][one year and fine of ten thousand rupees] in case of default in payment of the employees' contribution which has been deducted by the employer from the employees' wages;

[8][(b) which shall not be less than six months and a fine of five thousand rupees, in any other case]:

[9][***]

Provided that the court may, for any adequate and special reasons to be recorded in the judgment, impose a sentence of imprisonment for a lesser term [10][***]

[11][(1B) An employer who contravenes, or makes default in complying with, the provisions of section 6C, or clause (a) of sub-section (3A) of section 17 in so far as it relates to the payment of inspection charges, shall be punishable with imprisonment for a term which may extend to [12][one year] but which shall not be less than [13][six months] and shall also be liable to fine which may extend to [14][five thousand rupees]:

Provided that the court may, for any adequate and special reasons to be recorded in the judgment, impose a sentence of imprisonment for a lesser term [10][***].

(2) [15][Subject to the provisions of this Act, the Scheme] [16][, the [10][Pension] Scheme or the Insurance Scheme] may provide that any person who contravenes, or makes default in complying with, any of the provisions thereof shall be punishable with imprisonment for a term which may extend to [18][one year, or with fine which may extend to four thousand rupees, or with both].

[19][(2A) Whoever, contravenes or makes default in complying with any provision of this Act or of any condition subject to which exemption was granted under section 17 shall, if no other penalty is elsewhere provided by or under this Act for such contravention or non-compliance, be punishable with imprisonment which may extend to [18][six months, but which shall not be less than one month, and shall be liable to fine which may extend to five thousand rupees].]

[20][***]

1. Subs. by Act 16 of 1971, sec. 25, for "or under any Scheme."
2. Subs. by Act 99 of 1976, sec. 30, for "or the Family Pension Scheme" (w.e.f. 7-9-1976).
3. Subs. by Act 25 of 1996, sec. 4, for "Family Pension" (w.r.e.f. 16-11-1995).
4. Subs. by Act 33 of 1988, sec. 18, for certain words (w.e.f. 1-8-1988).
5. Ins. by Act 40 of 1973, sec. 4 (w.e.f. 1-11-1973).
6. Subs. by Act 33 of 1988, sec. 18, for "six months" (w.e.f. 1-8-1988).
7. Subs. by Act 33 of 1988, sec. 18, for "three months" (w.e.f. 1-8-1988).
8. Subs. by Act 33 of 1988, sec. 18, for clause (b) (w.e.f. 1-8-1988).
9. Certain words omitted by Act 33 of 1988, sec. 18 (w.e.f 1-8-1988).
10. The words "or of fine only in lieu of imprisonment" omitted by Act 33 of 1988, sec. 18 (w.e.f. 1-8-1988).
11. Ins. by Act 99 of 1976, sec. 30 (w.e.f. 7-9-1976).
12. Subs. by Act 33 of 1988, sec. 18, for "six months" (w.e.f. 1-8-1988).
13. Subs. by Act 33 of 1988, sec. 18, for "one month" (w.e.f. 1-8-1988).
14. Subs. By Act 33 of 1988, sec. 18, for "two thousand rupees" (w.e.f.1-8-1988).
15. Subs. by Act 40 of 1973, sec. 4, for "the Scheme" (w.e.f 1-11-1973).
16. Subs. by Act 99 of 1976, sec. 30, for "or the Family Pension Scheme" (w.e.f. 7-9-1976).
17. Subs. By Act 25 of 1996, sec. 4, for "Family Pension" (w.r.e.f.16-11-1995).
18. Subs. by Act 33 of 1988, sec. 18, for certain words (w.e.f. 1-8-1988).
19. Ins. by Act 37 of 1953, sec. 12.
20. Sub-section (3) omitted by Act 40 of 1973, sec. 4 (w.e.f. 1-11-1973).

Legislative reference–

The initial provisions in Section 14 have been amended from time to time as the time demanded and new offences and penalties have been added. By the feedback from the field and outcome of various court orders in awarding penalty under this section, new sections have been inserted in accordance with the provisions of the Criminal Procedure Code to the effect that who will be responsible in case the offence is committed by a company, to make it a non-cognizable offence, if the contribution is not paid, who will be responsible for filing complaint in the court and empowering the court to make order regarding payment of the dues and providing penalty per day in case of failure and finally, in 1973, making provision for enhanced punishment in case of repeated offence by adding Section 14-AA.

[1][14A. Offences by companies.–(1) If the person committing an offence under this Act [2][the Scheme or [3][the [4][Pension] Scheme or the Insurance Scheme]] is a company, every person, who at the time the offence was committed was in charge of, and was responsible to, the company for the conduct of the business of the company, as well as the company, shall be deemed to be guilty of the offence and shall be liable to be proceeded against and punished accordingly:

Provided that nothing contained in this sub-section shall render any such person liable to any punishment, if he proves that the offence was committed without his knowledge or that he exercised all due diligence to prevent the commission of such offence.

(2) Notwithstanding anything contained in sub-section (1), where an offence under the Act [5][the Scheme or [6][the [4][Pension] Scheme or the Insurance Scheme]] has been committed by a company and it is proved that the offence has been committed with the consent or connivance of, or is attributable to, any neglect on the part of, any director or manager, secretary or other officer of the company, such director, manager, secretary or other officer shall be deemed to be guilty of that offence and shall be liable to be proceeded against and punished accordingly.

Explanation.–For the purposes of this section,-

(a) "company" means any body corporate and includes a firm and other association of individuals; and

(b) "director," in relation to a firm, means a partner in the firm.]

1.	Ins. by Act 37 of 1953, sec. 13.
2.	Subs. by Act 33 of 1988, sec. 19, for certain words (w.e.f. 1-8-1988).
3.	Subs. by Act 99 of 1976, sec. 31, for "the Family Pension Scheme" (w.e.f 7-9-1976).
4.	Subs. by Act 25 of 1996, sec. 4, for "Family Pension" (w.r.e.f. 16-11-1995).
5.	Subs. by Act 16 of 1971, sec. 26, for "or the Scheme made thereunder" (w.r.e.f. 23-4-1971).
6.	Subs. by Act 99 of 1976, sec. 31, for "the Family Pension Scheme" (w.e.f 7-9-1976).

[1][**14-AA. Enhanced punishment in certain cases after previous conviction.**- Whoever, having been convicted by a court of an offence punishable under this Act, the Scheme or [2][the [3][Pension] Scheme or the Insurance Scheme], commits the same offence shall be subject for every such subsequent offence to imprisonment for a term which may extend to [4][five years, but which shall not be less than two years, and shall also be liable to a fine of twenty-five thousand rupees].

1.	Ins. by Act 40 of 1973, sec. 5 (w.e.f. 1-11-1973).
2.	Subs. by Act 99 of 1976, sec. 31, for "the Family Pension Scheme" (w.e.f 7-9-1976).
3.	Subs. by Act 25 of 1996, sec. 4, for "Family Pension" (w.r.e.f. 16-11-1995).
4.	Subs. by Act 33 of 1988, sec. 19, for certain words (w.e.f. 1-8-1988).

[1][**14AB. Certain offences to be cognizable.**–Notwithstanding anything contained in the Code of Criminal Procedure, 1898 (5 of 1898) an offence relating to default in payment of contribution by the employer punishable under this Act shall be cognizable.

14AC. Cognizance and trial of offences.–(1) No court shall take cognizance of any offence punishable under this Act, the Scheme or [2][the [3][Pension] Scheme or the Insurance Scheme] except on a report in writing of the facts constituting such offence made with the previous sanction of the Central Provident Fund Commissioner or such other officer as may be authorised by the Central Government, by notification in the Official Gazette, in this behalf, by an Inspector appointed under section 13.

(2) No court inferior to that of a Presidency Magistrate or a Magistrate of the first class shall try any offence under this Act or Scheme or [2][the [3][Pension] Scheme or the Insurance Scheme.]]

1.	Inserted by Act 40 of 1973, sec. 5.
2.	Subs. by Act 99 of 1976, sec. 31, for "the Family Pension Scheme" (w.e.f. 7-9-1976).
3.	Subs. by Act 25 of 1996, sec. 4, for "Family Pension" (w.r.e.f. 16-11-1995).

[1][**14C. Power of court to make orders.**- (1) Where an employer is convicted of an offence of making default in the payment of any contribution to the Fund [2][the [3][Pension] Fund or the Insurance Fund] or in the transfer of accumulations required to be transferred by him under sub-section (2) of section 15 or sub-section (5) of section 17, the court may, in addition to awarding any punishment, by order in writing require him within a period specified in the order (which the court may, if it think fit and on application in that behalf, from time to time, extend), to pay the amount of contribution or transfer the accumulations, as the case may be, in respect of which the offence was committed.

(2) Where an order is made under sub-section (1), the employer shall not be liable under this Act in respect of the continuation of the offence during the period or extended period, if any, allowed by the court, but if, on the expiry of such period or extended period, as the case may be, the order of the court has not been fully complied with, the employer shall be deemed to have committed a further offence and shall be punished with imprisonment in respect thereof under section 14 and shall also be liable to pay fine which may extend to one hundred rupees for every day after such expiry on which the order has not been complied with.]

1. Ins. by Act 40 of 1973, sec. 7 (w.e.f. 1-11-1973).
2. Subs. by Act 99 of 1976, sec. 33, for "or the Family Pension Fund" (w.e.f. 1-8-1976).
3. Subs. by Act 25 of 1996, sec. 4, for "Family Pension" (w.r.e.f. 16-11-1995).

I. Offences under the Act and penalties:

Under the social security Act, there cannot be a single compliance. The compliance involves various way of compliance, hence for every nature, default leads to different offences. Therefore, in Section 14, different offences have been defined and punishment for each has been prescribed. Five type offences have been defined in the Act-

(1) Non-payment of contribution by employer and by any other person,

(2) Non-payment of employees' contribution deducted from their wages,

(3) Non-submission of returns and non compliance of any of the provisions of the Schemes,

(4) Non-compliance of any of the condition of exemption by an exempted establishment,

(5) Repeated conviction for the same offence.

And the penalties prescribed for each offence is as under-

(1) For the offence at (1) above, up to 3 years' imprisonment, which shall not be less than six months and fine of Rs. five thousand or both, in case of employer; and imprisonment for one year or fine of Rs. Five thousand or both in case of offence is committed by a person other than the employer.

(2) For offence at (2) above, up to 3 years' imprisonment, which shall not be less than one year and fine of Rs. ten thousand.

(3) For offence at (3) above, up to one year's imprisonment or fine of Rs. 4,000/- or both.

(4) For offence at (4) above, six months,' but not less than one month's imprisonment and a fine up to Rs. five thousand.

(5) For offence at (5) above, up to five years' imprisonment but not less than for two years, and a fine of Rs. 25,000/- .

As far the default is related to non-payment of contribution, the offence has been made "cognizable offence."

For prosecution, Coverage must, not Code No. Mere allotment of Code No. by P.F. authorities will not mean that the establishment stands covered under the E.P.F. Act. Unless, EPF Act is applicable, no prosecution is maintainable under the Act, no matter if the Code No. issued to the establishment-
[Provident Fund Inspector, Kota vs. Smt Bhogi Bai and Others – 2008 (118) FLR 687 (Raj.)].

By insertion of sub-section (1-A) in Section 17, some more provisions, legal and penal, are also made applicable to **exempted establishments** with the view to make the penal provision more stringent for the exempted establishments with a view to check the growing arrears. Therefore, it cannot be contended that Section14 (1-A) and 14 (2-A) are inapplicable to exempted establishments. If, no other penalty is, elsewhere, provided by or under the Act, then the contravention or non-compliance is punishable. Cancellation of exemption is not a penalty - *[N.K. Jain and other vs. C.K. Shah – 1991 Lab.IC 1013 (SC); 1991 (2) SCJ 323].*

The expression "employer" as defined in Section 2 (e) and expression "person in charge of and responsible to, the company for the conduct of business" in Section 14-A are distinct and the person cannot be prosecuted for non-compliance of Section 17 (3) (a) merely because he has been described as a person in charge of, and responsible to, the company for the conduct of its business. Without any specific averment that they had ultimate control over the affairs of the establishment do not clearly, make out an offence punishable under Section 14 (2-A) or contravention of the provisions of Section 17 (3) (a) of the Act- *[K.L. Jalan and others vs. Stat of W.B. and others – 1994 (I)LLJ 224 (Cal.)].*

By now, there has no reason been left that the offence under the EPF Act is not a **continuing offence**. The Supreme Court has ruled in the case of *State of Bihar vs. Deokaran Menshi – [AIR 1973 SC 908]* that the question whether a particular offence is a continuing offence, must necessarily depend upon the language of the statute which creates that offence, the nature of the offence and above all, the purpose which is intended to be achieved by continuing the particular act as an offence. The respondents were unquestionably liable to pay their contribution to the provident fund before due date had expired as they willed. The late payment could not have absolved them of their original guilt, but it could have snapped the recurrence. Each day that they failed to comply with the obligation to pay their contribution to the fund, they committed a fresh offence. Hence, the offence which is alleged against the appellants will be governed by Section 472 of the Code of Criminal Procedure according to which a fresh period of limitation begins to run every moment of the time during which the offence continues. Section 468 of the Cr.P.C. cannot have any application to such a case.

Again, in the case of *Bhagirath Kanoria vs. State of M.P. – [AIR 1984 SC 1688; 1984 (2) SCC 222],* the Apex Court observed that in case of such nature, which are confronted with the provisions which lay down a rule of limitation governing prosecution, the courts should give due weight and consideration to the provisions contained in Section 473 of the Cr.P.C. The hair splitting argument as to whether the offence alleged against the appellant is of a continuing or non-continuing nature, could have been averted by holding that considering the object and purpose of the Act, the magistrate ought to take cognizance of the offence after the expiry of the period of limitation, if any such period is applicable, because the interest of justice so requires.

Further, the failure to pay contribution or to submit any return or statement continues from the day to day, and from day to day, a fresh offence is committed by the accused so long as he continues in his failure to pay contribution or to submit the return or statements. It is not mere failure to obey an order or to comply with the direction. It is not as if once he fails to pay the contribution or to submit returns on the due date, the employer is relieved of his duties and that there is nothing more to be done. Therefore, such failure if a continuing breach of duty which continues till it is performed and non-performance of such duty from day to day a continuing wrong and as such a fresh period of limitation for prosecution would begin to run at every moment of time during which the offence continues - *[Premier Stud and Chaplets Co. vs. State – (1980) 56 FJR 611]*. The disputed issue of limitation under Section 468 to 473 of the Cr.P.C. cannot be appropriately raised directly in the High Court for quashing of proceedings under Section 482 of the Cr.P.C. - *[Ram Kripal Prasad and Others vs. State of Bihar and Others – AIR 1986 Patna 254 (F.B.); 1986 Lab.I.C. 571]*.

A writ petition to quash the proceedings of prosecution for non-payment of dues was dismissed hence appeal before D.B. During the pendency of his appeal, under order of court, P.F. dues have been paid. However, facts remains that as soon default was committed, it constituted an offence under Section 14 of the Act. Notwithstanding the above position, following the decision of the Supreme Court in the case of **Aadonoy Cotton Mills [1995 (4) SCC 550]**, direction is given to the Magistrate before whom complaints are pending that if he is satisfied that payments are made, he shall take steps to drop proceedings- *[Josolda Glass and Sillicate vs. R.P.f.C.- 2002 (3) LLN 1146 (Cal.DB)]*.

Non-submission of return is not a continuing offence, the Bombay High Court observed in the case of **Transport Corporation of India Ltd. Vs. R.M. Gandhi and others- *[1991 Lab.I.C. 2017 (Bom); (1992) 64 FLR 697]*** that there is vital distinction between an offence of failure to pay the contribution and an offence of failure to file the statutory returns by the due date. The Supreme Court, in the case of **State of Bihar vs. Deo Karan Menshi (supra)** considered a situation and pointed out that the failure to file statutory returns would be a breach or an offence which occurs once for all and would not be a continuing offence.

II. Persons liable to be charged for offence:

This area of identifying a person against whom the charges to be framed for the offence, is the most important area and requires an intelligent working. Hence, the wording for the particular offence applied in the section is to be under-stood properly.

In sub-section (1) of Section 14, the words are "'whoever' for the purpose of avoiding any payment, by him-self or by any other person," covers any person, may be the employer, may be the responsible person for the affairs of the establishment, may be part-timer, advisor including a professional one.

In sub-section (1-A), the word is "'an employer' for the purpose of payment of contribution either his share or employees' share whether deducted or not." If, the employees' share is deducted and not paid, than there is a rider provision in clause (a) of this sub-section.

Again, in sub-section (1-B), which relates to payment of contribution under E.D.L.I. Scheme, 1976 and inspection charges payable under that Scheme, it is the 'employer.'

In sub-section (2-A), which relates to the exempted establishment, it is 'whoever' which intend to include the employer and the members of the board of trustees of the exempted fund and also any other person, who is responsible for the affairs of the exempted establishment and PF Trust, it is included.

In sub-section (2), it is not the 'employer' alone, but 'any person' for the offences for contravention or non-compliance of any provision of any Scheme, as provided in paragraph 76 of the

Employees' P.F. Scheme, 1952; paragraph 42 of the Employees' Pension Scheme, 1995 and paragraph 29 of the E.D.L.I. Scheme, 1976, which are re-produced here-under -

*Paragraph 76. **Punishment for failure to pay contribution, etc.**–If any person–*

(a) deducts or attempts to deduct from the wages or other remuneration of a member the whole or any part of the employer's contribution, or

(b) fails or refuses to submit any return, statement or other document required by this Scheme or submits a false return, statement or other document, or makes a false declaration, or

(c) obstructs any Inspector or other official appointed under the Act or this Scheme in the discharge of his duties or fails to produce any record for inspection by such Inspector or other official, or

(d) is guilty of contravention of or non-compliance with any other requirement of this Scheme.

he shall be punishable with imprisonment which may extend to one year, or with fine which may extend to four thousand rupees or with both.

*Paragraph 42. **Punishment for failure to submit return, etc.**–If any person–*

(a) deducts or attempts to deduct from the wages or other remuneration of the member, the whole or any part of the employer's contribution, or

(b) fails or refuses to submit any return, statement or other documents required by this Scheme or submits a false return, statement or other documents, or makes a false declaration, or

(c) obstructs any Inspector or other official appointed under the Act or this Scheme in the discharge of his duties or fails to produce any record for inspection by such Inspector or other officials, or

(d) is guilty of contravention of or non-compliance with any other requirement of this Scheme,

he shall be punishable with imprisonment, which may extend to one year, or with fine which, may extend to five thousand rupees, or with both.

*Paragraph 29. **Punishment for failure to submit returns, etc.**–If any person,–*

(a) deducts or attempts to deduct from the wages or other remuneration of a member the whole or any part of the employer's contribution; or

(b) fails or refuses to submit any return, statement or other documents required by this Scheme or submits a false return, statement or other documents, or makes a false declaration; or

(c) obstructs any Inspector or other official appointed under the Act or this Scheme in the discharge of his duties or fails to produce any record for inspection by such Inspector or other official; or

(d) is guilty of contravention of or non-compliance with any other requirements of this Scheme,

he shall be punishable with imprisonment which may extend to one year or with fine which may extend to four thousand rupees, or with both.

Employer has been defined in section 2 (e), but for the purpose of penalties, by Section 14-A, the scope has been enlarged by defining that 'every person, who was in charge at the time offence was committed, and was responsible for the conduct of the business of the company. The word 'responsible' has led to many disputes before the superior courts and they have interpreted this word from various angles. The language of Section 14-A has the word 'ultimate control' which has provided a lot discuss and consider the employer in a different way and ultimately, only such employer can be prosecuted, who has ultimate control over the affairs of the establishment. The expression "was in-charge of, and was responsible to the company for the conduct of business" are very wide in their import. It cannot, therefore, be confined to the employer only. It includes even directors. Therefore, every such person, who has ultimate control over the affairs of the company, becomes employer. The declaration in Form 5-A, including the appellant director as one of the person in-charge of and responsible for affairs of the company was in accordance with law. Therefore, his prosecution for violations of the Scheme does not suffer from any error of jurisdiction – *[Shrikanta Datta Narsimharaja Wodiyar vs. Enforcement Officer, Mysore, 1993 Lab.I.C. 1359; 1993 (2) LLJ 531 (SC)]*.

The Rajasthan High Court has correctly defined the position of the Managing Director in the case of ***Sampat Mal Lodha vs. State of Rajasthan – [1988 (72) FJR 11 (Raj.)]*** that the Managing Director of the company happens to be mind and brain of the company without whose direction no other officer or the manager or authorized to make payment to meet any obligation by signing cheques, can perform his duties. Non-payment of P.F. contribution by the authorised officer, definitely cannot happen without the direction of the Managing Director. Hence, the Managing Director is liable for action under Section 406/409 of the Indian Penal Code for non-payment of P.F. Contribution.

The appeal and other cases show how some establishments can behave in an outrageous manner and violate the provisions of the Act from time to time with impunity. Not only that they do not pay their share of contribution, they do not also deposit the employees' share which they have deducted from the wages of their employees. On behalf of the Regional P.F. Commissioner, it has been stated that about a sum of Rs. 113 crores is due on account of arrears of P.F. dues in respect of different establishments in the state alone. This is possible because of laches and gross negligence on the part of the R. P. F. Commissioners in the performance of their statutory duties, if not something more. In view of the same, the establishment concerned has been able to obtain an interim order or another, in one writ petition after another, sometimes in respect of the very same period, obtaining orders of injunction against prosecution pending or impending against the directors and other officers, thereafter, making default after paying one or two installments granted by court. Thereafter, moving a fresh writ petition again and getting a fresh order of injunction or some fresh order of installment and the repetition of the same following the same cycle *adinfinitum*.

It is crystal clear that the respondent company which is an habitual defaulter, is in the practice of obtaining orders from the courts granting installments not with the intention of paying the installments but with the intention to obtain an interim order in order to prevent any action which may be taken by the Regional P.F. Commissioner for such default. In the facts and circumstances of the case, the learned judge acted arbitrarily and improperly varying the earlier order which was a final order. The application made by the company did not justify any such order particularly having regard to the background of this case and the conduct of the respondent company as stated above. The Regional P.F. Commissioner shall be entitled to take appropriate steps including criminal proceedings as they are entitled in accordance with law and they are directed accordingly - *[R.P.F.C. W.B. vs. the Gauripore Co. Ltd.- 1992 Lab.IC 1515 (Cal.)]*.

Employer having ultimate control over the affairs of the establishment deducting P.F. contribution from employees nd not remitting the same to the Provident Fund is liable for penal action - *[Aniruddh Kumar Dhote vs. State of Maharashtra – 2002 (3) LLJ 400; 2002 (94) FLR 914].*

Protection provided under various Acts under certain conditions, whether available in the case of offence under the EPF Act, has been under consideration before various high Courts and the rulings there for have been of great importance.

First of all, **protection under Section 633 of the Companies Act**, availability of which has been denied by the Supreme Court in the case of *Rabindra Chamaria and others vs. Registrar of Companies, W.B. [AIR 1992 SC 398; 1992 (I) LLJ 313 (SC)].* In that case, it has been held that the expression "any proceedings" occurring under Section 633 of the Companies Act, 1956 cannot be read out of context and treated in isolation. It must be construed in the light of penal provisions, otherwise what will happen is that the penal clauses under the various other Acts would be rendered ineffective by application of Section 633. It is a sound rule of construction to confine the provisions of a statute to itself.

While referring to "any proceeding" under sub-section (2) of Section 633 of the Companies Act, the Parliament intended to restrict it only to the proceedings arising out of negligence, default, breach of trust, misfeasance or breach of duty in respect of duties prescribed under the provisions of the Companies Act. Further examining the sub-section with reference to the contest and the placement of sub-section, the only conclusion that is possible, is that the proceedings for which relief under this section could be claimed are the proceedings against the officer of the company for breach of the provisions of the Companies Act. Sub-section (2) can not apply to proceedings instituted against the officer of the company to enforce the liability arising out of violation of the provisions of other statutes. If the interpretation suggested is accepted, it would cover not only the existing laws, but all legislations to be enacted in future. Thus relief under Section 633 cannot be extended to offences committed under the EPF 7 MP Act, 1952.

Similarly, **suspension of PF liabilities to Relief Under-takings** is not allowed. Declaration of an establishment a Relief Under-taking, cannot, in any way go to help the Directors or other officers of the undertaking from discharging their obligations and liabilities under the P.F. Act. The liabilities under the P.F. Act are the personal liabilities of the employer. The notification issued under the Relief Undertaking Act will not, in any way, suspect the liabilities incurred by the employer. In this view, persons who had ultimate control over the affairs of the establishment cannot take refuge under the notification declaring the establishment as a relief undertaking - *[Travencore Rayons Ltd. Vs. Provident Fund Officer and others – 1989 (I) LLJ 414(Ker.)].* The Madras High Court has also taken a similar view in the case of *S. Ganpathy vs. Mahalaxmi Textile Mills Ltd. And others – 1989 Lab,IC (NOC) 200 (Mad.)]* that notification issued under Tamil Nadu Relief Undertakings (Special Provisions) Act. 1969 cannot have the effect of staying prosecution for offences committed under the P.F. Act, 1952, either by the company or by those in-charge of, or responsible for the affairs of the Company.

A **contrary view** has been taken by the Rajasthan High Court that during the pendency of prosecution proceedings against a company and its officers, if the company is declared a relief undertaking under the state law, no proceedings under any law before any court could be proceeded with during the period the company remains a relief undertaking. Hence, the prosecution against the officers of the company also remains suspended - *[Jaipur Udyog Ltd. Sawai Madhopur vs. Inspector, Kota- (1979) 55 FJR 161].*

And, the **Supreme Court again held** that in fact, responsibility of the Directors and/or Officers of an establishment are not those of the Relief Undertaking. If, such persons have accumulated the liabilities and responsibilities other than those of the establishment, they should be proceeded against for such commission. If they are protected by the notification, it will be a reward for their commission. **To pay the contribution into the fund was the responsibility of the appellants (the directors) and they** have committed default, they are liable to be prosecuted under paragraph 76 (a) of the E.P.F. Scheme. The Magistrate was directed to take cognizance of the offence - *[Indrajit C. Parikh vs. V.K. Bhatt & others- AIR 1974 SC 1183]*.

The Patna High Court has observed in the case of *State of Bihar vs. Bhadani [AIR 1959 Pat. 9; (1959) 1 LLJ 157]*, wherein it was contended by the employer that Section 14 (1) was subject to Section 14 (2) and no officer of a company could be held guilty of any violation of the provisions of the Scheme or the Act unless the prosecution had established that the offence had been committed with the consent or connivance of or is attributable to any neglect on the part of any director, manager, secretary or other such officer of the company, that "on a true construction of the provisions of sub-section (1) and sub-section (2) there is no doubt that the legislature was providing for officers with varying degrees of responsibility. The defaulting company is always liable for the commission of any offence under the Act or the Scheme, and there is nothing is Section 14-A to excuse the company from the penalties imposed by law, but under sub-section (1) of Section 14-A, apart from the company which has committed an offence under the Act and the Scheme, every person, who at the time of the offence was committed, was in charge of and was responsible to the company for the conduct of the business, shall also be deemed to be guilty of the offence and shall be liable to be proceeded against and punished accordingly. All the officers of the company do not come within the mischief of sub-section (1). The application of this sub-section is confined only to the officers in the immediate charge of the management of the company. If, the officer concerned is not entrusted with the management of the business of the company and owes no responsibility to the company either for good or bad management, he is not covered by sub-section (1). If, however, where the offence under the Act or the Scheme is committed by a company, every person in charge and responsible to the company for the conduct of its business shall be deemed to be guilty of the offence, and such officer may avoid conviction as enacted by the proviso to sub-section (1), namely, by showing that the offence was committed without his knowledge or in spite of all due diligence exercised by his to prevent the commission of the offence. There may, however, be several other officers of the company. They have different duties assigned to them. When they are not in charge of the management they cannot possibly be indicted for failure to make the necessary contributions for the simple reason that the payment of the contribution was beyond the scope of their duty. When they were not responsible for making the requisite contributions, it is pain they cannot be held guilty of the contravention of the provisions of paragraph 38. They may, however, be guilty, if the conditions laid down in sub-section (2) are fulfilled. It is for such officers that sub-section (2) has been enacted. Where an officer has been committed by a company, such officers of the company will be deemed to be liable for its commission as have consented to or connived at the commission of the offence or its commission is attributable to any neglect on their part. It is manifest, therefore, that all the officers of the company not in direct charge of the management of the business are immune from the liability for the offence unless they have contributed to its commissions by consent, connivance or neglect. Thus, sub-sections (1) and (2) classify the officers of the company in two different categories and fix the degree of their responsibility for the offences. The opening word of sub-section (2), namely, 'notwithstanding anything contained in sub-section (1) do not make sub-section (1) subject to sub-section (2). It only means that the provisions of sub-section (2) will have application independent of what has been laid down in sub-section (1). The officer of the company envisaged in sub-section (1) is the one who is in direct management of the affairs of the company. Wherever any offence has been committed by the company under the Act or the

Scheme, such officer will also be deemed to be guilty of the offence and in his case it will not be necessary for the prosecution to prove consent, connivance, or neglect on his part. Since he is in-charge of the management and thus directly responsible for the remittance of the contributions to the fund, both the company and he have been made liable under sub-section (1) without proof of consent, connivance or neglect on their part. The other officers covered by sub-section (2) cannot be deemed to be guilty of the offence committed by the company unless the prosecution further establishes that the offence was committed with the consent or connivance of such officer, be he the director, manager or secretary or any other officer of the company. Therefore, in cases falling under sub-section (2), the prosecution must fail if it is not proved that the commission of the offence was due to consent, connivance or neglect of the officer concerned.'

III. Authority to file complaint in the Court:

As a matter of bringing uniformity in the practice and process, Section 14-AC has been added in which it has been made mandatory that-

(i) the complaint has to be made by an Inspector appointed under Section 13. The complaint should be supported by a reference of the notification under Section 13, a copy can be attached.

(ii) previous sanction of the Central P.F. Commissioner or such officer as may be authorized by the Central Government for initiating the prosecution is necessary. For this purpose, all Regional P.F. Commissioners have been authorized to sanction prosecution within their jurisdiction vide Notification No. S.O. 549 (E) dated 17.10.1973. The sanction should bear a reference of such authorization.

(iii) cognizance on the complaint can be taken by a magistrate equal to the Presidency Magistrate or of a First Class Magistrate.

(iv) in the complaint, a request can be made with reference to Section 14-C for making an order, if the offence relates to non-payment of contribution.

It is for the **prosecution to establish contravention** of provisions of the Act by the accused by production of acceptable evidence. It is not for the employer to establish that he had not contravened any provisions of the Act. It is no doubt, true that a duty is cast on the employer to remit his part of the contribution, but any contravention of the provisions of the Act, the provident fund authorities have to establish the same by the production of the relevant materials, - *[P.F. Inspector, Vijaywada vs. Sivarama Krishna Industries and others- 1992 (I) LLN 248 (AP)]*. On a plain language of Section 14 (1) it is seen that there is an element of *mens-rea* and therefore, the burden is on the authority prosecuting the person to prove the offence - *[S.H. Salve Kadam & Co. vs. R.P.F.C.- 1981 Lab.IC 568 (Kar.)]*. For an offence under Section 14 (1-A), *mens-rea* is not an essential element - *[P.F. Inspector vs. Ram Kumar – 1983 Lab. IC 717 (P&H)]*.

The cases in which no evidence at all is led in support of the allegation are bound to end in acquittal of the person against whom cases are file. No Court of Law can take the allegation as Gospel truth for want of the evidence in support of the same. There is no question for holding the judgement of the court allow to suffer from any kind of perversity in law - *[G.D. Singh, E.O. vs. M/s. Koshi Refinary and others – 2003 (2) LLJ 671; 2003 (97) FLR 289; 2003 LLR 577]*.

Here, it may be noted that the proviso under section 14 (1) says that the accused has to prove that the offence was committed without his knowledge or that he exercise all due diligence to prevent the commissions of such offence, where is under sub-section (2), it is for the prosecutions to prove that the offence has been committed with consent or connivance of, or is attributable to, any neglect on the part of, any director, manager, secretary or other officer, shall be deemed to be guilty. Therefore, it cannot be taken as rule that it the prosecution to prove all the way, but it depends under which sub-section, the accused is defined while filing a complaint.

The **use of printed forms for filing complaint,** in fact, may well focus the attention of the authorities below on the material ingredients of the offence with regard to which the facts have to be pointedly specified and pleaded and later established in the course of the trial. It is difficult to see how the use of a form by itself would be something of an anathema to the law which would vitiate the prosecution - *[Ram Kripal Prasad and others vs. State of Bihar – AIR 1986 Patna 254 (F.B.)]*. When the complaints were worded in practically identical terms, the Supreme Court in *Delhi Municipality vs. Purshottam Das - [1983 Cr. LJ 172]* had upheld the complaint stating that the rest was for evidence. Thus, in the instant case. There is no legal infirmity at all and the complaint is in order, with the necessary averments against all accused and it will only be during trial that further details are required to be given - *[Shanti Vihar Hotels Ltd. And other vs. P.F. Inspector, Madras – 1992 MLJ (Cr.) 59 (Mad)]*.

IV. Cognizable Offence, Scope of:

Section 14-AB declares non-payment of contribution by the employer shall be cognizable offence. By putting is provision, the defaulting employer in making payment of contribution can be complained against and an FIR can be file against him with the Police. The police, then may proceed against such employer and arrest him. For filing FIR, neither sanction of the Regional P.F. Commissioner is required nor any prerequisite is there. Only Inspector, who detects the default, at his wisdom, can file FIR. Both the requirements are needed only when a prosecution in filed in the court before an appropriate Magistrate.

V. Power of court to make order:

Where the employer has been convicted for non-payment of contribution, the court may make order that the within a specified period the dues to be deposited failing which, a fine of one hundred rupees per day shall be imposed until the payment is not made. Having regard to the Parliamentary mandate, good and adequate reasons must exist before the discretion to impose a sentence of mere fine, is exercised by a court. The matter must receive anxious consideration at the hands of the court. In the matter relating to contravention of the provisions of such an act, imposing of a sentence of imprisonment must be rule and imposing of a sentence of mere fine an exception. A rich man, who commits an economic offence out of avarice or, in order to enlarge his economic empire and to maintain his privileged position arising out of his influence, cannot be treated on at par with a poor man who commits a property offence for his bread or sustenance. A person, who robs a poor man of even the rags on his person deserves a very deterrent punishment and, if a lenient view of such offence is taken by the court, the administration of justice would lose the respect which it enjoys at the hands of the society at large - *[C.K. Shah, P.F. Inspector vs. Natson Mfg. Co. Pvt. Ltd. – (1976) 17 GLR 419]*. Of course, the court has discretion to impose a lesser term of imprisonment or a sentence of fine only in view of the proviso, but then the condition precedent to the exercise of the power under the proviso to impose a lesser sentence or sentence of fine only was that special and adequate reason existed in his opinion and reasons were recorded in his judgement - *[State of Gujrat vs. Indequip Engineering Ltd. –(1979) 2 GLR 784]*.

Chapter 19

Suppliments

Schedule I:

Cement,

Cigarettes,

Electrical, mechanical or general engineering products,

Iron an steel,

Paper,

Textiles (made wholly or in part of cotton or wool or jute or silk, whether natural or artificial).

[1. Matches,
2. Edible oils and fats,
3. Sugar,
4. Rubber and rubber products,
5. Electricity, including the generation, transmission and distribution thereof,
6. Tea,
7. Printing [other than printing industry relating to newspaper establishments as defined in the Working Journalists (Conditions of Service) and Miscellaneous Provisions Act, 1955, including the process of composing types for printing, printing by letterpress, lithography, photogravure or other similar process of book-binding.],
8. Glass,
9. Stone-ware pipes,
10. Sanitary wares,
11. Electrical porcelain insulators of high and low tension,
12. Refractories,
13. Tiles.] *[Added by S.R.O. 1566 dated 04.07.1956 w.e.f. 31.07.1956]*

[1. Heavy and fine chemicals, including-
    (i) Fertilizers,
    (ii) Turpentine,
    (iii) Resin,
    (iv) Medical and pharmaceutical preparations,
    (v) Toilet preparations,
    (vi) Soaps,
    (vii) Inks,

(viii) Intermediates, dyes, colour lacs and toners,

(ix) Fatty acids, {and

(x) Oxygen, acetylene and carbon-dioxide gases industry}

[Added by S.R.O. 1976 dated 08.06.1957 w.e.f. 31.07.1957]

2. Indigo
3. Lac, including shellac,
4. Non-edible vegetable and animal oils and fats]

[Added by S.R.O. 2026 dated 03.09.1956 w.e.f. 30.09.1956]

[Mineral oil refining industry]

[Added by S.R.O. 218 dated 12.01.1957 w.e.f. 31.01.1957]

[Industrial and Power Alcohol industry; and Asbestos Cement Sheet industry]

[Added by S.R.O.3067 dated 19.09.1957 w.e.f. 30.11.1957]

Biscuit making industry including composite unit making biscuit and producing such as bread, confectionery and Milk and milk powder]

[Added byG. S.R. 170 dated 12.03.1958 w.e.f. 30.04.1958]

[Mica industry] *[Added by G.S.R.312 dated 05.03.1960 w.e.f. 31.05.1960]*

[Plywood industry] *[Added by G.S.R.632 dated 30.05.1960 w.e.f. 30.06.1960]*

[Automobile repairing and servicing industry]

[Added by G.S.R. 683 dated 09.06.1960 w.e.f. 30.06.1960]

[Rice milling

Flour milling

Dal milling] *[Added by G.S.R. 1443 dated 14.11.1960 w.e.f. 31.12.1960]*

[Starch industry] *[Added by G.S.R. 535 dated 10.04.1961 w.e.f. 31.05.1961]*

[Petroleum or natural gas exploration, prospecting, drilling or production,

Petroleum or natural gas refining.] *[Added by G.S.R. 705 dated 16.05.1961 w.e.f. 30.06.1961]*

[Leather and leather products industry] *[Added by G.S.R. 993 dated 29.07.1961 w.e.f. 31.08.1961]*

[Stone-ware jars, Crockery.] *[Added by G.S.R. 1382 dated 4.11.1961 w.e.f. 30.11.1961]*

[Fruit and vegetable preservation industry, (that is to say any industry which is engaged in the preparation or production of any of the following articles, namely-

(i) canned and bottled fruits, juices and pulps,

(ii) canned and bottled vegetables,

Suppliments

- (iii) frozen fruits and vegetables,
- (iv) Jams, jellies and marmalades,
- (v) tomato products, ketchup and sauces,
- (vi) squashes, crushes, cordials and ready-to-serve beverages or any other beverages containing fruit juice or fruit pulp,
- (vii) preserved, candied and crystallized fruits and peels,
- (viii) Chutneys,
- (ix) any other unspecified item relating to the preservation or canning of fruits and vegetables.)

[Added by G.S.R. 786 dated 06.06.1962 w.e.f. 30.06.1962]
[Further added by G.S.R.1460 dated 29.08.1963]

[Cashewnut industry] *[Added by G,S.R. 1125 dated 18.08.192 w.e.f. 30.09.1962]*

[Confectionery products]

[Added by G.S.R. 786 dated 06.06.1962 w.e.f. 30.06.1962]

[(1) Buttons,
(2) Brushes,
(3) Plastic and Plastic products,
(4) Stationery products.]

[Added by G.S.R. 591 dated 27.03.1963 w.e.f. 30.04.1963s]

[Aerated water industry, that is to say may industry engaged in the manufacture of aerated water, soft drinks or carbonated water.]

[Added by G.S.R. 1432 dated 03.08.1963 w.e.f. 31.08.1963]

[Distilling and rectifying of spirits (not falling under industrial and power alcohol) and blending of spirits industry.]

[Added by G.S.R. 1605 dated 26.09.1963 w.e.f. 31.10.1963]

[Paints and Varnish industry.]

[Added by G.S.R.1983 dated 21.12.1963 w.e.f. 31.01.1964]

[Bone Crushing industry.]

[Added by G.S.R. 67 dated 31.12.1963 w.e.f. 31.01.1964]

[Pickers industry.] *[Added by G.S.R. 822 dated 22.05.1964 w.e.f. 30.06.1964]*

[Milk and milk products industry.]

[Added by G.S.R. 1723 dated 27.11.1964 w.e.f. 31.12.1964]

[Non-ferrous metals and alloys in the form of ingots industry.]

[Added by G.S.R. 1795 dated 09.12.1964 w.e.f. 31.01.1965]

[Bread Industry.] *[Added by G.S.R. 402 dated 02.03.1965 w.e.f. 31.03.1965]*

[Stemming or re-drying of tobacco leaf industry, that is to say, any industry engaged in the stemming, re-drying, handling, sorting, grading or packing of tobacco leaf.]

[Added by G.S.R. 1768 dated 18.05.1965 w.e.f. 30.06.1965]

[Agarbatti (including Dhoop and Dhoopbatti) industry.]

[Added by G.S.R. 910 dated 23.06.1965 w.e.f. 31.07.1965]

[Coir (excluding the spinning sector) industry.]

[Added by G.S.R. 952 dated 03.07.1965 w.e.f. 30.09.1965]

[Tobacco industry, that is to say any industry engaged in the manufacture of cigars, zarda, snuff, quivam and guraku from tobacco.]

[Added by G.S.R. 895 dated 01.06.1966 w.e.f. 30.06.1966]

[Paper products industry.]

[Added by G.S.R. 1119 dated 11.07.1966 w.e.f. 31.07.1966]

[Licenced salt industry, that is to say any industry engaged in the manufacture of salt for which a licence is necessary and which has land not less than (4.05 hectares -*substituted by G.S.R. 1945 dated 16.12.1966 for ten acres*).

[Added by G.S.R. 1362 dated 30.08.1966 w.e.f. 30.09.1966]

[Linoleum Industry and Indoleum Industry.]

[Added by G.S.R. 437 dated 27.03.1967 w.e.f. 30.04.1967]

[Explosive Industry.]

[Added by G.S.R. 1019 dated 01.07.1967 w.e.f. 31.07.1967]

[Jute balling or pressing industry.]

[Added by G.S.R. 1226 dated 05.08.1967 w.e.f. 31.08.1967]

[Fireworks and percussion cap works industry.]

[Added by G.S.R. 1530 dated 05.10.1967 w.e.f. 31.10.1967]

[Tent making industry.]

[Added by G.S.R. 1716 dated 03.11.1967 w.e.f. 30.11.1967]

[Ferro-manganese industry.]

[Added by G.S.R. 1018 dated 22.04.1969 w.e.f. 30.04.1969]

[Ice or ice-cream industry.]

[Added by G.S.R. 1506 dated 11.06.1969 w.e.f. 30.06.1969]

[Winding of thread and yarn reeling industry.]

[Added by G.S.R. 1988 dated 22.11.1971 w.e.f. 30.11.1971]

[Cotton Ginning, Bailing and pressing industry

[Added by G.S.R. 1251 dated 23.09.1972 w.e.f. 30.09.1972]

[Katha making industry.]

[Added by G.S.R. 503 dated 02.05.1973 w.e.f. 31.05.1973]

[Beer manufacturing industry, that is to say, any industry engaged in the manufacture of the product of alcoholic fermentation of a mash in potable water of malted barley and hops, or of hops concentrated with or without the addition of other malted or unmalted cereals or other carbohydrate preparations.]

[Added by G.S.R. 428 dated 15.04.1974 w.e.f. 30.04.1974]

[Beedi Industry, that is to say, any industry engaged in manufacture of beedis *[Added by G.S.R. 660 dated 17.05.1977 w.e.f. 31.05.1977]*

[Ferro-Chrome industry.]

[Added by G.S.R. 938 dated 25.06.1979 w.e.f. 31.07.1979]

[Dimond cutting industry.]

[Added by G.S.R. 564 dated 05.05.1980 w.e.f. 31.05.1980]

[Myrobalan Extract Powder, Myrobalan Extract Solid and vegetable Tannin Blended Extract industry.]

[Added by G.S.R. 613 (E) dated 30.10.1980 w.e.f. 31.10.1980]

[Bricks industry.] *[Added by G.S.R. 662(E) dated 27.11.1980 w.e.f. 30.11.1980]*

[All industries based on asbestos as principal raw material.]

[Added by S.O. 2459 dated 20.05.1983 w.e.f. 01.06.1983]

[Industries manufacturing iron ore pellets.]

[Added by S.O. 2276 dated 30.08.1989 w.e.f. 01.09.1989]

[Explanation- In this Schedule, without prejudice to the ordinary meaning of expressions used therein, - *Inserted by Act 37 of 1953]*.

(a) The expression "Electrical, mechanical or general engineering products" includes-

   (1) machinery and equipment for the generation, transmission, distribution or measurement of electrical energy and motors including cables and wires,
   (2) telephones, telegraph and wireless communication apparatus,
   (3) electric lamps (not including glass bulbs),
   (4) electric fans and electrical domestic appliances,
   (5) storage and dry batteries,
   (6) radio receivers and sound reproducing instruments,
   (7) machinery used in industry (including textile machinery) other than electrical machinery and machine tools,
   (8) boilers and prime movers, including internal comnstion engines, marine engines and locomotives,
   (9) machine tools, that is to say metal and wood working machinery,
   (10) grinding wheels,
   (11) ships.
   (12) automobiles and tractors,
   (13) bolts, nuts and rivets.
   (14) power-driven pumps,

(15) bicycles,
(16) hurricane lanterns,
(17) sewing and knitting machines,
(18) mathematical and scientific instruments,
(19) product of metal rolling and re-rolling,
(20) wires, pipes, tubes and fittings,
(21) ferrous and non-ferrous castings,
(22) safes, vaults and furniture made of iron or steel or steel alloy,
(23) cutlery and surgical instruments,
(24) drums and containers,
(25) parts and accessories of products specified in items 1 to 24;

(b) The expression "Iron and Steel" includes pig iron, ingots, blooms, billets and rolled or re-rolled products into basic forms and tool and alloy steel;

(c) the expression "Paper" includes pulp, paperboard and straw-board;

(d) the expression "textiles" includes the products of carding, spinning, weaving, finishing and dyeing yarn and fabrics, printing, knitting and embroidering.]

List of other establishments Notified undersection 1(3) (b) of the Act:

Class of other establishments	Notification No. & date	W.e.f.
1. Newspaper establishments	Act 45 of 1955	31.12.1956
2. Tea plantations (other than the tea plantation in the State of Assam), Coffee plantations, Rubber plantations, Cardamom plantations, Pepper plantations.	SRO 529 dated 13.02.1957	30.04.1957
3. Iron-ore mines, manganese mines, Lime-stone mines, Gold mines.	SRO 2708 dated 17.08.1957	30.11.1957
4. Coffee curring establishments.	SRO 3411 dated 16.10.1957	30.11.1957
5. Road motor transport establishments.	GSR 399 dated 24.03.1959	30.04.1959
6. Mica mines	GSR 313 dated 05.03.1960	31.05.1960
7. Cane farms owned by sugar factories.	GSR 1274 dated 21.10.1960	30.11.1960
8. 1. Hotels 2. Restaurants	GSR 704 dated 16.05.1961	30.06.1961
9. Establishments engaged in the storage or transport or distribution of petroleum or natural gas or products of either petroleum or natural gas.	GSR 706 dated 16.05.1961	30.06.1961
10. 1. Cinemas including pre-view theatres,	GSR 827 dated 19.06.1961	31.07.1961

2. Film studios, 3. Film production concerns, 4. Distribution concerns dealing exposed film 5. Film processing laboratories.		
11. 1. Tea plantations (other than the tea plantation in the State of Assam), Coffee plantations, Rubber plantations, Cardamom plantations, Pepper plantations. 2. Iron-ore mines, manganese mines, Lime- stone mines, Gold mines. 3. Coffee curring establishments. 4. Road motor transport establishments. 5. Cane farms owned by sugar factories.	GSR 1013 dated 29.07.1961	31.07.1961
12. Every cane farm owned by the owner or occupier of a sugar factory or cultivated by such owner or occupier or any person on his behalf.	GSR 1458 dated 02.12.1961	31.12.1961
13. Every trading and commercial establishment engaged in the purchase, sale or storage of any goods, including establishment of export, import, advertisers, commission agents and brokers and commodity and stack exchange but not including banks or warehouses establishment under the Central or State Act.	GSR 346 dated 07.03.1962	31.04.1962
14. Establishments engaged in the processing or treatment of wood including manufacture of hard board, or chip-board, jute or textile wooden accessories, cork products, wooden furniture, wooden sports goods, cane or bamboo products, wooden battery separators, Saw mills, Wood seasoning kilns, Wood preservation plants, Wood workshops.	GSR 1232 dated 07.09.1962	31.10.1962

15. Bauxite mines.	GSR 1625 dated 23.11.1962	31.12.1962
16. Laundry and laundry services.	GSR 561 dated 23.03.1963	31.04.1963
17. 1. Theatres where dramatic performances or other forms of entertainment are held and where payment is required to be made for admission as audience or spectators; 2. Societies, clubs or associations which provide board or lodging or both or facility for amusement or any other members or to any of their guests on payment. 3. Companies, societies, associations, clubs or troupes which give any exhibition of acrobatic or other performances or both, in any arena, circular or otherwise, or perform or permit any other form of entertainment in any plae, other than a theatre, and require payment for admission into such exhibition or entertainment as spectators or audience.	GSR 728 dated 20.04.1963	31.05.1963
18. Canteens.	GSR 1285 dated 29.07.1963	31.08.1963
19. China clay mines.	GSR 823 dated 22.05.1964	30.06.1964
20. 1. Attorneys, as defined in the Advocates Act, 1961 (25 of 1961), 2. Chartered or registered Accountants, as defined in the Chartered Accountants Act 1949 (38 of1949), 3. Cost and Works Accountants within the meaning of the Cost and Works Accountants Act, 1959 (23 of 1959), 4. Engineers and engineering contractors, not being exclusively engaged in building and construction industry, 5. Architects, 6. Medical practitioners and medical specialists.	GSR 1398 dated 17.09.1964	31.10.1964

21. Travel agencies engaged in
  (i) booking of International Air and Sea passengers and other travel arrangements.
  (ii) booking of internal air and mail passengers and other travel arrangements, and
  (iii) forwarding and clearing of cargo from and to overseas and within India.
	GSR 1796 dated 07.12.1964	31.01.1965

22. Forwarding agencies engaged in the collecting, packing, forwarding or delivery of any goods including car loading, break-bulk service and foreign freight service.	GSR 1796 dated 07.12.1964	31.01.1965
23. Magnesite Mines.	GSR 1166 dated 09.08.1965	31.08.1965
24. Stone quarries producing roof and floor slabs, dimension stones, monumental stones and mosaic chips.	GSR 1779 dated 27.11.1965	31.12.1965
25. Banks [other than the nationalized Banks established under any Central or state Act.]	GSR 2 dated 18.12.1965	31.01.1966
26. Barytes, dolomite, fireclay, gypsum, kyanite, siliminate and steatite mines.	GSR 1560 dated 07.08.1968	31.08.1968
27. Cinchona plantations.	GSR 2084 dated 22.11.1968	31.12.1968
28. Diamond mines.	GSR 1508 dated 28.05.1969	30.06.1969
29. Establishments which are exclusively or particularly engaged in general insurance business.	GSR 14 dated 23.01.1970	01.07.1970
30. Establishments rendering expert services, such as supply of personnel, advice on domestic or departmental enquiries, special services in rectifying pilferage, thefts and pay rolls irregularities, to factories and establishments.	GSR 805 dated 17.05.1971	31.05.1971
31. Railway booking agencies run by contractors or other private establishments on commission basis.	GSR 505 dated 17.03.1972	31.03.1972
32. Messes other than Military messes.	GSR 299 dated 15.03.1973	31.03.1973
33. Hospitals, run by private establishments or associations not covered under Notification	GSR 1082 dated 15.09.1973	31.08.1973

No. GSR 1398 dated 17.9.1964.		
34. Establishments engaged in sorting, cleaning and teasing of cotton waste industry.	GSR 1094 dated 26.09.1974	30.09.1974
35. Societies, clubs and associations which render service to their members without charging any fee and over and above the subscription fee or membership fee.	GSR 1294 dated 16.11.1974	30.11.1974
36. Garment making factories.	GSR 1295 dated 23.11.1974	30.11.1974
37. Agricultural farms, Fruit Orchards, Botanical gardens, Zoological gardens.	GSR 1315 dated 27.11.1974	31.12.1974
38. Soapstone mines and establishments engaged in the grinding of soapstone.	SO 1955 dated 21.06.1975	30.06.1975
39. Apatite mines, Asbestos mines, Calcite mines, Ball clay mines, Corundum mines, Emerald mines, Feldspar mines, Silica (sand) mines, Quartz mines, Ochre mines, Chromites mines, Graphite mines, Fluorite mines.	GSR 1102 dated 06.07.1976	31.07.1976
40. 1. Glue and gelatin factories, 2. Stone quarries producing stone hips, stone sets, stone boulders and ballasts, 3. Establishments engaged in fish processing and non-vegetable food preservation industry including bacon factories and pork processing plats.	GSR 204 dated 31.01.1977	28.02.1977
41. Financing establishments (other than banks) not being the Unit Trust of India established under the Unit Trust of India Act, 1963 (52 of 1963), the Industrial Development Bank of India established under the Industrial Development Bank of India Act, 1964 (18 of 1964), the Industrial Finance Corporation of India	GSR 1458 dated 18.11.1978	31.12.1978

established under the Industrial Finance Corporation of India Act, 1948 (15 of 1948) the State Finance Corporations.		
42. Lignite mines.		
43. Quartzite mines.	GSR 31 dated 16.12.1978	06.11.1979
44. Inland water transport establishments.	GSR 563 dated 05.05.1980	31.05.1980
	GSR 565 dated 05.05.1980	31.05.1980
45. Establishments engaged in building and construction industry.	GSR 1069 dated 23.09.1980	31.10.1980
46. Establishments engaged in stevedoring, loading and unloading of ships.	GSR 611(E) dated 23.11.1981	23.11.1981
47. Establishments engaged in poultry farming.		
48. Establishments engaged in 'cattle feed' industry.	GSR 643(E) dated 07.12.1981	07.12.1981
49. (i) Any university,	GSR 644(E) dated 07.12.1981	07.12.1981
(ii) Any college whether or not affiliated to a university,	SO 986 dated 19.02.1982	06.03.1982
(iii) Any school. Whether or not recognized or aided by the Central or a State Government,		
(iv) Any scientific institution,		
(v) Any institution in which research in respect of any matter is carried on.		
(vi) Any other institution in which the activity of imparting knowledge or training is systematically carried on.		
50. Cinema theatres employing five or more workers as specified in section 24 of the Cine Workers and Cinema theatre Workers (Regulation of Employment) Act, 1981.	GSR 347 dated 30.04.1986	01.10.1984
51. Guar gum Factories, Marble mines, Diamond saw mills.	GSR 170 dated 25.03.1992	01.04.1992
52. 1. An establishment engaged in rendering Courier Services, 2. An establishment of aircraft or airlines other than the aircraft or airlines owned or controlled by the Central or	SO 746 dated 22.03.2001	01.04.2001

State Government, 3. An establishment engaged in rendering cleaning and sweeping services.		
53. Establishments engaged in Railways for construction, maintenance, operation and commercial activities of Railways excluding Indian Railways exclusively managed by Government of India.	GSR 401 dated 10.11.2005	19.11.2005
54. Establishments engaged in manufacturing and usage of a computer [as defined in clause (i) of Sub-section (1) of Section 2 of the Information Technology Act, 2000 (21 of 2000) / or deriving any form of output there from/or employing it for any type of processing services including – Software product companies, Internet and E-Commerce companies, Information technology Services and Remote maintenance companies, Research and development companies, System integrators, On-site Service companies, and Off-shore Software development companies etc.	SO 1190 (E) dated 27.07.2006	27.07.2006
55. (i) Companies offering life insurance, annuities etc. other than Life Insurance Corporation of India, (ii) Private airports and joint venture airports, (iii) Electronic media companies in private sector, and (i) Lodging houses, service apartments and condominiums.	SO 3456 dated 16.11.2007	08.12.2007
56. Municipal Councils and Municipal Corporations constituted under sub-clauses (b) and (c) of Article 243Q of the Constitution of India.	SO 30 (E) dated 08.01.2011	08.01.2011

Schedule II

[1][See Section 5 (1B)]

MATTERS FOR WHICH PROVISION MAY BE MADE IN A SCHEME-

1. The employees or class of employees who shall join the Fund, and the conditions under which employees may be exempted from joining the Fund or from making any contribution.

2. The time and manner in which contribution shall be made in the Fund by the employers and by, or behalf of employees, [2][(whether employed by him directly or by or through a contractor)], the contribution which an employee may, if he so desires, make under [3][xxx] section 6, and the manner in which such contribution may be recovered.

[2][2A. The manner in which employees' contribution may be recovered by contractors from employees employed by or through such contractors.]

3. The payment by the employer of such sums of money as may be necessary to meet the cost of administering the Fund and the rate at which and the manner in which the payment shall be made.

[1][4. The constitution of any committee for assisting any Board of Trustees.]

[1][5. The opening of regional and other offices of any Board of Trustees.]

6. The manner in which accounts shall be kept, the investment of moneys belonging to the Fund in accordance with any directions issued or conditions specified by the Central Government, the preparation of the budget, the audit of accounts and the submission of reports to the Central Government.

7. The conditions under which withdrawal from the Fund may be permitted and any deduction or forfeiture may be made and the maximum amount of such deduction or forfeiture.

8. The fixation by the Central Government in consultation with Board of Trustees concerned of the rate of interest payable to members.

9. The form in which an employee shall furnish particulars about himself and his family whenever required.

10. The nomination of a person to receive the amount standing to the credit of a member after his death and the cancellation or variation of such nomination.

11. The registers and records to be maintained with respect to employees and the returns to be furnished by employers [2][or contractors].

12. The form or design of any identity card, token or disc for the purpose of identifying any employee, and for the issue, custody and replacement thereof.

13. The fee to be levied for any of the purposes specified in this Schedule.

14. The contraventions or defaults which shall be punishable under sub-section (2) of section 14.

15. The further powers, if any, which may be exercised by an Inspector.

16. The manner in which accumulation in any existing provident fund shall be transferred to the Fund under section 15, and the mode of valuation of any assets which may be transferred by the employers in this behalf.

17. The conditions under which a member may be permitted to pay premium on life insurance from the Fund.

18. Any other matter ²[which is to be provided for in the Scheme or] which may be necessary or proper for the purpose of implementing the Scheme.

1.	Substituted by Act 28 of 1963, Sec. 13. (w.e.f. 30.11.1963)
2.	Inserted by Act 28 of 1963, Sec. 13. (w.e.f. 30.11.1963)
3.	Omitted by Act 28 of 1963, Sec. 13. (w.e.f. 30.11.1963).

¹[SCHEDULE III
[See Section 6A (5)]
MATTERS FOR WHICH PROVISION MAY BE MADE IN THE PENSION SCHEME-

1. The employees or class of employees to whom the Pension Scheme shall apply.

2. The time within which the employees who are not members of the Family Pension Scheme under section 6A as it stood before the commencement of the Employees' Provident Funds and Miscellaneous Provisions Act, 1996 (hereafter in this Schedule referred to as the amending Act) shall opt for the Pension Scheme.

3. The portion of employer's contribution to the Provident Fund which shall be credited to the Pension Fund and the manner in which it is credited.

4. The minimum qualifying service for being eligible for pension and the manner in which the employees may be granted the benefits of their past service under Section 6A as it stood before the commencement of the amending Act.

5. The regulation of the manner in which and the period of service for which, no contribution is received.

6. The manner in which employees' interest will be protected against default in payment is received.

7. The manner in which the accounts of the Pension Fund shall be kept and investment of moneys belonging to Pension Fund to be made subject to such pattern of investment as my be determined by the Central Government.

8. The form in which an employee shall furnish particulars about himself and the members of his family whenever required.

9. the forms, registers and records to be maintained in respect of employees, required for the administration of t he Pension Scheme.

10. The scale of pension and pensionary benefits and the conditions relating to grant of such benefits to the employees.

11. The manner in which the exempted establishments have to pay contribution towards the Pension Scheme and the submission of returns relating thereto.

12. The mode of disbursement of pension and arrangements to be entered in to with such disbursing agencies as may be specified for the purpose.

13. The manner in which the expenses for administering the Pension Scheme will be met from the income of the Pension Fund.

14. Any other matter which is to be provided for in the Pension Scheme or which may be necessary for the purpose of implementation of the Pension Scheme.

1. Schedule Substituted by Act 25 of 1996, Sec. 4. (w.e.f. 16.11.1995)

This scheme, un-like the Family Pension Scheme, it was made compulsory for all the existing members of the old Family Pension Scheme, with a rider provision for the members of family pension scheme who ceased their membership between 1st April, 1993 and 16th November, 1995 and who were entitled to the benefits under the new scheme, to join it and get benefit available under the new scheme. But, an exclusion provision has been added in paragraph 6 w.e.f. 01.9.2014 barring new entrants with a pay more than 15,000 rupees p.m.

[1][Schedule IV]
[See Section 6C]
MATTERS TO BE PROVIDED FOR IN THE EMPLOYEES' DEPOSIT-LINKED INSURANCE SCHEME-

1. The employees or class of employees who shall be covered by the Insurance Scheme.

2. The manner in which the accounts of the Insurance Fund shall be kept and the investment of moneys belonging to the Insurance Fund subject to such pattern of investment as may be determined, by order, by the Central Government.

3. The form in which an employee shall furnish particulars about himself and the members of his family whenever required.

4. The nomination of a person to receive the insurance amount due to the employee after his death and the cancellation or variation of such nomination.

5. The registers and records to be maintained in respet of employees, the form or design of any identity card, token or disc for the purpose of identifying any employee or his nominee or member of his family entitled to receive the insurance amount.

[2]*[6. The scale of insurance benefits and conditions relating to the grant of such benefits to the employees.]*

7. [3]*[xxx]*

8. The manner in which the amount due to the nominee or the member of the family of the employee under the scheme is to be paid including a provision that the amount shall not be paid otherwise than in the form of a deposit in a savings bank account, in the name of such nominee or member of family, in any corresponding new bank specified in the First Schedule to the Banking Companies (Acquisition and Transfer of Undertakings) Act, 1970 (5 of 1970).

9. Any other matter which is to be provided for in the Employees' Deposit-Linked Insurance Scheme or which may be necessary or proper for the purpose of implementing that Scheme.]

1.	Inserted by Act 99 of 1976, Sec. 38 (w.e.f. 1.8.1976).
2.	Substituted by Act 33 of 1988 Sec. 26 (w.e.f. 1.8.1988)
3.	Omitted by Act 33 of 1988 Sec. 26 (w.e.f. 1.8.1988)

The Employees' Provident Funds Scheme, 1952

New Delhi, 2nd September, 1952.

S.R.O. 1509- In exercise of the powers conferred by section 5 of the Employees' Providend Fund Act, 1952 (19 of 1952), the Central Government hereby frames the following Employees' Provident Funds Scheme, 1952, namely-

Chapter-I
PRELIMINARY

1. Short title and application.–(1) This Scheme may be called the Employees' Provident Fund Scheme, 1952.

(2) [1][Save as otherwise provided in the Scheme, this Chapter] and Chapters II and III shall come into force at once and the remaining provisions shall come into force on such date or dates as the Central Government may by notification in the Official Gazette appoint and different dates may be appointed for different provisions.

[2][(3) (a) Subject to provisions of sections 16 and 17 of the Act, this Scheme shall apply to all factories [3][and other establishments] to which the Act applies or is applied under sub-section (3) [4][or sub-section (4)] of section 1 or section 3 thereof:]

[5][Provided that the provisions of this scheme shall not apply to–

[6][(i) ***]

[6][(ii) ***]

(iii) Tea factories in the State of Assam.]

1.	Subs. by S.R.O. 2035, dated 28th October, 1953.
2.	Added by S.R.O. 2035, dated 28th October, 1953.
3.	Ins. by S.R.O. 1363, dated 26th April, 1957.
4.	Ins. by S.R.O. 488, dated 4th February, 1958 (w.e.f. 12-12-1958).
5.	Added by S.R.O. 1567, dated 4th July, 1956.
6.	Sub-clauses (i) and (ii) omitted by Notification No. 417, dated 19th March, 1962 (w.e.f. 31-3-1962).

(b) Provisions of this Scheme shall-

(i) as respects every establishment which is a factory engaged in any industry mentioned herein, namely, cement, cigarettes, electrical, mechanical or general engineering products, iron and steel, paper and textiles (made wholly or in part of cotton or wool or jute or silk, whether natural or artificial) be deemed to have come into force, with effect from 2nd day of September, 1952;

Inserted by GSR 571 dated 12.4.1977 and re-numbered.

(ia) as respects factories relating to the industries added to Schedule I of the Act, by notification of the Government of India in the Ministry of Labour, No. S.R.O. 1566, dated 4th July, 1956, come into force on the 31st day of July, 1956;

> Inserted by GSR 571 dated 12.4.1977 and re-numbered.

(ii) as respects factories relating to the industries added to Schedule I of the Act, by notification of the Government of India in the Ministry of Labour, No. S.R.O. 2026, dated 3rd September, 1956, come into force on the 30th day of September, 1956;

> Added vide SRO 2027 dated 03.09.1956.

(iii) as respects factories relating to the mineral oil refining industry added to Schedule I of the Act by notification of the Government of India in the Ministry of Labour, No. S.R.O. 218, dated the 19th January, 1957, come into force on the 31st day of January, 1957;

> Added vide SRO 815 dated 9.03.1957.

(iv) as respects plantations of tea (other than tea plantations in the State of Assam, coffee, rubber, cardamom and pepper, covered by the notification of the Government of India in the Ministry of Labour, No. S.R.O. 529, dated the 16th February, 1957, come into force on the 30th day of April, 1957;

> Added vide SRO 1363 dated 26.04.1957.

(v) as respects factories relating to the oxygen, acetylene and carbon dioxide gases in industry added to Schedule I of the Act as item (x) under the head "Heavy and Fine Chemicals" by the notification of the Government of India in the Ministry of Labour and Employment, No. S.R.O. 1976, dated the 15th June, 1957, come into force on the 31st day of July, 1957;

> Added vide SRO 2146 dated 21.06.1957.

(vi) as respects iron ore, limestone, manganese and gold mines, covered by the notification of the Government of India in the Ministry of Labour and Employment, No. S.R.O. 2705, dated the 24th August, 1957, come into force on the 30th day of November, 1957;

> Added vide SRO 3376 dated 10.10.1957.

(vii) as respects factories relating to the Industrial and Power Alcohol and Asbestos Cement Sheets Industries added to Schedule I of the Act by the notification of the Government of India in the Ministry of Labour and Employment, No. S.R.O. 3067, dated the 28th September, 1957, come into force on the 30th day of November, 1957;

> Added vide SRO 3565 dated 31.10.1957.

(viii) as respects coffee curing establishments covered by the notification of the Government of India in the Ministry of Labour and Employment, No. S.R.O. 3411, dated the 26th October, 1957, come into force on the 30th day of November, 1957;

> Added vide SRO 3972 dated 4.12.1957.

(ix) as respects factories relating to the biscuit making industry including composite units making biscuits and products such as bread, confectionery and milk and milk powder, added to Schedule I of the Act, vide Government of India, Ministry of Labour and Employment, Notification No. G.S.R. 170, dated the 12th March, 1958, come into force on the 30th day of April, 1958;

> Added vide GSR 261 dated 10.04.1958.

(x) as respects motor roads transport establishments covered by the notification of the Government of India in the Ministry of Labour and Employment, No. G.S.R. 399, dated the 24th March, 1959, come into force on the 30th day of April, 1959;

> Added vide GSR 583 dated 8.05.1959.

(xi) as respects mica mines and mica industry covered by the notifications of the Government of India in the Ministry of Labour and Employment, Nos. G.S.R.312 and 313, dated the 5th March, 1960, respectively, come into force on the 31st day of May, 1960;

> Added vide GSR 362 dated 16.03.1960.

(xii) as respects factories relating to the plywood industry covered by the notification of the Government of India in the Ministry of Labour and Employment, No. G.S.R. 632, dated the 30th May, 1960, come into force on the 30th day of June, 1960;

> Added vide GSR 718 dated 17.06.1960.

(xiii) as respects factories relating to the automobile repairing and servicing industry covered by the notification of the Government of India in the Ministry of Labour and Employment, No. G.S.R. 683, dated the 9th June, 1960, come into force on the 30th day of June, 1960;

> Added vide GSR 748 dated 27.06.1960.

(xiv) as respects any cane farm owned by a sugar factory covered by the notification of the Government of India in the Ministry of Labour and Employment, No. G.S.R. 1274, dated the 21st October, 1960, come into force on the 30th day of November, 1960;

> Added vide GSR 1444 dated 24.11.1960.

(xv) as respects factories relating to rice, flour and Dal milling industries covered by the notification of the Government of India in the Ministry of Labour and Employment, No. G.S.R. 1443, dated the 24th November, 1960, come into force on the 31st December, 1960;

> Added vide GSR 1548 dated 24.12.1960.

(xvi) as respects factories relating to the starch industry covered by the notification of the Government of India in the Ministry of Labour and Employment, No. G.S.R. 535, dated the 10th April, 1961, come into force on the 31st May, 1961;

> Added vide GSR 680 dated 5.5.1961.

(xvii) as respects hotels and restaurants covered by the notification of the Government of India in the Ministry of Labour and Employment, No. G.S.R. 704, dated the 19th May, 1961, come into force on the 30th day of June, 1961;

> Added vide GSR 783 dated 5.6.1961.

(xviii) as respects factories relating to petroleum or natural gas exploration, prospecting, drilling or production and petroleum or natural gas refining and establishments engaged in the storage or transport or distribution of petroleum or natural gas or products of either petroleum or natural gas covered by the notifications of the Government of India in the

Ministry of Labour and Employment Nos. G.S.R. 705 and 706, dated the 16th May, 1961, respectively, come into force on the 30th day of June, 1961;

> Added vide GSR 783 dated 5.6.1961.

(xix) as respects the establishments covered by the notification of the Government of India in the Ministry of Labour and Employment, No. G.S.R. 827, dated the 19th June, 1961, come into force on the 31st day of July, 1961;

> Added vide GSR 992 dated 24.7.1961.

(xx) as respects the establishments covered by the notification of the Government of India in the Ministry of Labour and Employment, No. G.S.R. 1013, dated the 29th July, 1961, come into force on the 31st day of July, 1961;

> Added vide GSR 1033 dated 8.8.1961.

(xxi) as respects the factories relating to the leather and leather products industry covered by the notification of the Government of India in the Ministry of Labour and Employment, No. G.S.R. 993, dated the 29th July, 1961, come into force on the 31st day of August, 1961;

> Added vide GSR 1033 dated 8.8.1961.

(xxii) as respects the factories relating to the stoneware jars and crockery industries covered by the notification of the Government of India in the Ministry of Labour and Employment, No. G.S.R. 1382, dated the 4th November, 1961, come into force on the 30th day of November, 1961;

> Added vide GSR 1456 dated 29.11.1961.

(xxiii) as respects the establishments covered by the notification of the Government of India in the Ministry of Labour and Employment, No. G.S.R. 1458, dated the 2nd December, 1961, but not including the establishments referred to in sub-clause (xiv), come into force on the 31st December, 1961;

> Added vide GSR 3087 dated 20.12.1961.

(xxiv) as respects every trading and commercial establishment engaged in the purchase, sale or storage of any goods including establishments of exporters, importers, advertisers, commission agents and brokers, and commodity and stock exchanges, but not including banks or warehouses established under any Central or State Act, covered by the notification of the Government of India in the Ministry of Labour and Employment, No. G.S.R. 346, dated the 7th March, 1962, come into force on the 30th day of April, 1962;

> Added vide GSR 460 dated 3.4.1962.

(xxv) as respects the factories relating to fruit and vegetable preservation industry covered by the notification of the Government of India, in the Ministry of Labour and Employment, No. G.S.R. 786, dated the 6th June, 1962 @[as amended by the notification No. G.S.R. 1461, dated the 29th August, 1963], come into force on the 30th June, 1962;

> Added vide GSR 887 dated 23.6.1962.
> @ Inserted by GSR 1982 dated 18.12.1963.

(xxvi) as respects the factories relating to cashew nut industry covered by the notification of the Government of India in the Ministry of Labour and Employment, No. G.S.R. 1125, dated the 18th August, 1962, come into force on the 30th September, 1962;

Added vide GSR 1299 dated 19.9.1962.

(xxvii) as respects the establishment specified in the notification of the Government of India in the Ministry of Labour and Employment, No. G.S.R. 1232, dated the 7th September, 1962, come into force on the 31st October, 1962;

Added vide GSR 1321 dated 27.9.1962.

(xxviii) as respects bauxite mines covered by the notification of the Government of India in the Ministry of Labour and Employment, No. G.S.R. 1625, dated the 23rd November, 1962, come into force on the 31st December, 1962;

Added vide GSR 1757 dated 12.12.1962.

(xxix) as respects the confectionery industry come into force on the 31st March, 1963;

Added vide GSR 504 dated 18.3.1963.

(xxx) as respects establishment engaged in laundry and laundry services referred to in the notification of the Government of India in the Ministry of Labour and Employment, No. G.S.R. 561, dated the 23rd March, 1963, come into force on the 30th April, 1963;

Added vide GSR 663 dated 10.4.1963.

(xxxi) as respects the industries engaged in the manufacture of buttons, brushes, plastic and plastic products and stationery products, come into force on the 30th day of April, 1963;

Added vide GSR 666 dated 15.4.1963.

(xxxii) as respects the establishments covered by the notification of the Government of India in the Ministry of Labour and Employment, No. G.S.R. 728, dated the 20th April, 1963, come into force on the 31st day of May, 1963;

Added vide GSR 853 dated 10.5.1963.

(xxxiii) as respects canteens covered by the notification of the Government of India in the Ministry of Labour and Employment, No. G.S.R. 1285, dated the 29th July, 1963, come into force on 31st day of August, 1963;

Added vide GSR 1401 dated 9.8.1963.

(xxxiv) as respects aerated water industry, that is to say, any industry, engaged in the manufacture of aerated water, soft drinks, carbonated water, [1][***] come into force on 31st day of August, 1963;

Added vide GSR 1433 dated 22.8.1963 and corrigendum issued by GSR 1606 dated 27.09.1963.
1. Words 'industry' deleted by SRO 164 dated 22 01.1964.

(xxxv) as respects distilling and rectifying of spirits (not falling under industrial and power alcohol) and blending of spirits industry, come into force on the 31st day of October, 1963;

Added vide GSR 1688 dated 15.10.1963.

(xxxvi) as respects the establishments in Pondicherry territory covered under the Employees' Provident Funds Act, 1952 (19 of 1952), by virtue of the Pondicherry (Laws) Regulation, 1963 (7 of 1963), come into force on the 31st day of October, 1963;

Added vide GSR 1873 dated 23.11.1963.

(xxxvii) as respects the paint and varnish industry come into force on the 31st day of January, 1964;

Added vide GSR 93 dated 8.01.1964.

(xxxviii) as respects bone crushing industry come into force on the 31st day of January, 1964;

Added vide GSR 127 dated 20.01.1964.

(xxxix) as respects china clay mines come into force on the 30th day of June, 1964;

Added vide GSR 864 dated 6.6.1964.

(xl) as respects pickers industry come into force on the 30th day of June, 1964;

Added vide GSR 863 dated 6.06.1964.

(xli) as respects the establishments in the Union territory of Goa, Daman and Diu in which territory the Employees' Provident Funds Act, 1952 (19 of 1952), has been enforced from the 1st July, 1964 by the notification of the Government of Goa, Daman and Diu, Industries and Labour Department No. LC/6/64, dated the 24th June, 1964, come into force on the 31st day of July, 1964;

Added vide GSR 1288 dated 01.09.1964.

(xlii) as respects the establishments specified in the notification of the Government of India in the Department of Social Security, No. G.S.R. 1398, dated the 17th September, 1964, come into force on the 31st day of October, 1964;

Added vide GSR 1500 dated 8.10.1964.

(xliii) as respects milk and milk products industry specified in the notification of the Government of India in the Department of Social Security, No. G.S.R.1723, dated the 27th November, 1964, come into force on the 31st day of December, 1964;

Added vide GSR 1845 dated 21.12.1964.

(xliv) as respects (1) travel agencies engaged in the (i) booking of international air and sea passages and other travel arrangements, (ii) booking of internal air and mail passages and other travel arrangements, and (iii) forwarding and clearing of cargo from and to overseas and within India; and (2) forwarding agencies engaged in the collection, packing, forwarding or delivery of any goods including, carloading, break-bulk service and foreign freight service specified in the notification of the Government of India in the Department of Social Security, No. G.S.R. 1796, dated the 9th December, 1964, come into force on the 31st day of January, 1965;

Added vide GSR 71 dated 1.01.1965.

(xlv) as respects non-ferrous metals and alloys in the form of ingots industry specified in the notification of the Government of India in the Department of Social Security, No. G.S.R. 1795, dated the 9th December, 1964, come into force on the 31st day of January, 1965;

> Added vide GSR 106 dated 2.01.1965.

(xlvi) as respects bread industry specified in the notification of the Government of India in the Department of Social Security, No. G.S.R. 402, dated the 2nd March, 1965, come into force on the 31st day of March, 1965;

> Added vide GSR 475 dated 19.03.1965.

(xlvii) as respects the stemming or re-drying of tobacco leaf industry, that is to say, any industry engaged in the stemming, re-drying, handling, sorting, grading or packing of tobacco leaf specified in the notification of the Government of India in the Department of Social Security, No. G.S.R. 768, dated the 18th May, 1965, come into force on the 30th day of June, 1965;

> Added vide GSR 823 dated 1.06.1965.

(xlviii) as respects agarbatee (including dhoop and dhoop-batee) industry specified in the notification of the Government of India in the Department of Social Security, No. G.S.R. 910, dated the 23rd June, 1965, come into force on the 31st day of July, 1965;

> Added vide GSR 969 dated 6.07.1965.

(xlix) as respects coir (excluding the spinning sector) industry specified in the notification of the Government of India in the Department of Social Security, No. G.S.R. 952, dated the 3rd July, 1965, come into force on the 30th day of September, 1965;

> Added vide GSR 997 dated 15.07.1965.

(l) as respects magnesite mines covered by the notification of the Government of India in the Department of Social Security, No. G.S.R. 1166, dated the 9th August, 1965, come into force on the 31st day of August, 1965;

> Added vide GSR 1241 dated 18.08.1965.

(li) as respects stone quarries producing roof and floor slabs, dimension stones, monumental stones and mosaic chips covered by the notification of the Government of India in the Department of Social Security, No. G.S.R. 1779, dated the 27th November, 1965, come into force on the 31st day of December, 1965;

> Added vide GSR 1837 dated 9.12.1965.

(lii) as respects @[banks other than the nationalised banks established under any Central or State Act] covered by the notification of the Government of India in the Department of Social Security, No. G.S.R. 2, dated the 18th December, 1965, come into force on the 31st day of January, 1966;

> Added vide GSR 170 dated 20.01.1966.
> @ Substituted by GSR 79 dated 25.02.2000 (w.e.f. 04.03.2000).

(liii) as respects the tobacco industry, that is to say, any industry engaged in the manufacture of cigars, zarda, snuff, quivam and guraku from tobacco covered by the notification of the Government of India in the Ministry of Labour, Employment and Rehabilitation

(Department of Labour and Employment), No. G.S.R. 895, dated the 1st June, 1966, come into force on the 30th day of June, 1966;

Added vide GSR 997 dated 17.06.1966.

(liv) as respects paper products industry covered by the notification of the Government of India in the Ministry of Labour, Employment and Rehabilitation (Department of Labour and Employment), No. G.S.R. 1119, dated the 11th July, 1966, come into force on the 31st day of July, 1966;

Added vide GSR 1187 dated 21.07.1966.

(lv) as respects licensed salt industry covered by the notification of the Government of India in the Ministry of Labour, Employment and Rehabilitation (Department of Labour and Employment), No. G.S.R. 1362, dated 30th August, 1966, come into force on the 30th day of September, 1966;

Added vide GSR 1412 dated 12.09.1966.

(lvi) as respects linoleum and indoleum industries specified in the notification of the Government of India in the Ministry of Labour, Employment and Rehabilitation (Department of Labour and Employment), No. G.S.R. 437, dated the 27th March, 1967, come into force on the 30th day of April, 1967;

Added vide GSR 533 dated 11.04.1967.

(lvii) as respects explosives industry, come into force on the 31st day of July, 1967;

Added vide GSR 1103 dated 17.07.1967.

(lviii) as respects Jute bailing or pressing industry specified in the notification of the Government of India in the Ministry of Labour, Employment and Rehabilitation (Department of Labour and Employment), No. G.S.R. 1226, dated the 5th August, 1967, come into force on the 31st day of August, 1967;

Added vide GSR 1268 dated 21.08.1967.

(lix) as respects fireworks and percussion cap works industry specified in the notification of the Government of India in the Ministry of Labour, Employment and Rehabilitation (Department of Labour and Employment), No. G.S.R. 1530, dated the 5th October, 1967, come into force on the 31st day of October, 1967;

Added vide GSR 1645 dated 23.10.1967.

(lx) as respects tent making industry specified in the notification of the Government of India in the Ministry of Labour, Employment and Rehabilitation (Department of Labour and Employment), No. G.S.R. 1716, dated the 3rd November, 1967, come into force on the 30th day of November, 1967;

Added vide GSR 1795 dated 20.11.1967. (see also GSR 1857 dated 20.11.1967).

(lxi) as respects the barytes, dolomite, fireclay, gypsum, kyanite, siliminite and steatite mines, come into force on the 31st day of August, 1968;

Added vide GSR 1592 dated 24.08.1968.

(lxii) as respects Chinchona plantations, come into force on the 31st day of December, 1968;

Added vide GSR 2083 dated 22.11.1968.

(lxiii) as respects ferro-manganese industry, come into force on the 30th day of April, 1969;

Added vide GSR 1017 dated 22.04.1969.

(lxiv) as respect ice or ice-cream industry, come into force on the 30th day of June, 1969;

Added vide GSR 1510 dated .06.1969.

(lxv) as respects diamond mines come into force on the 30th day of June, 1969;

Added vide GSR 1512 dated 11.06.1969.

(lxvi) as respects establishments which are exclusively or principally engaged in general insurance business, come into force on the 31st day of January, 1970;

Added vide GSR 14 dated 23.12.1969.

(lxvii) as respects establishments rendering expert services, come into force on the 31st day of May, 1971;

Added vide GSR 731 dated 17.05.1971.

(lxviii) as respects factories engaged in the winding of thread and yarn reeling covered by the notification of the Government of India in the Ministry of Labour, Employment and Rehabilitation (Department of Labour and Employment), No. G.S.R. 1988, dated the 22nd November, 1971, come into force on the 30th day of November, 1971;

Added vide GSR 263 dated 7.02.1972.

(lxix) as respects Railway Booking Agencies run by the contractors or by other private establishments on commission basis specified in the notification of the Government of India in the Department of Labour and Employment, No. 4/3/65-P.F.11.(i) dated the 17th March, 1972, come into force on the 31st day of March, 1972;

Added vide GSR 506 dated 18.03.1972.

(lxx) as respects cotton ginning, bailing and pressing industry specified in the notification of the Government of India in the Ministry of Labour, Employment and Rehabilitation (Department of Labour and Employment), No. G.S.R. 1251, dated the 23rd September, 1972, come into force on the 30th day of September, 1972;

Added vide GSR 1490 dated 15.11.1972.

(lxxi) as respects messes other than military messes covered by the notification of the Government of India in the Ministry of Labour, Employment and Rehabilitation (Department of Labour and Employment), No. G.S.R. 299, dated the 24th March, 1973, come into force on the 31st March, 1973;

Added vide S.O. 1219 dated 17.04.1973. (also see GSR 1039 dated 17.04.1973.)

(lxxii) [***]

Omitted vide GSR 571 dated 12.04.1977.

(lxxiii) as respects factories relating to "Katha" making industry covered by the notification of the Government of India in the Ministry of Labour, Employment and Rehabilitation

Suppliments

(Department of Labour and Employment), No. G.S.R.503, dated the 2nd May, 1973, come into force on 31st day of May, 1973;

> Added vide GSR 843 dated 19.07.1973.

(lxxiv) as respects the establishments known as hospitals specified in the notification of the Government of India in the Ministry of Labour, Employment and Rehabilitation (Department of Labour and Employment), No. G.S.R. 1082, dated the 29th September, 1973, come into force on the 31st August, 1973;

> Added vide GSR 1249 dated 02.11.1973.

(lxxv) as respects the employees of the beer manufacturing industry, that is to say, any industry engaged in the manufacture of the product www.epfindia.gov.in 13 of alcoholic fermentation of a mash in potable water of malted barley and hops, or of hops concentrated with or without the addition of other malted or unmalted cereals or other carbohydrate preparations, specified in the notification of the Government of India in the Ministry of Labour, No. G.S.R. 428, dated the 27th April, 1974, come into force on the 30th April, 1974;

> Added vide GSR 321 dated 15.05.1974.

(lxxvi) as respects the establishments engaged in sorting, cleaning and teasing of cotton waste specified in the notification of the Government of India, in the Ministry of Labour, No. G.S.R. 1094, dated the 26th September, 1974, come into force on the 30th day of September, 1974;

> Added vide GSR 1255 dated 12.11.1974.

(lxxvii) as respect societies, clubs, or associations which render service to their members without charging any fee over and above the subscription fee or membership fee specified in the notification of the Government of India in the Ministry of Labour, No. G.S.R. 1294, dated 16th November, 1974, come into force on the 30th day of November, 1974;

> Added vide GSR 1401 dated 21.12.1974.

(lxxviii) as respects every garments making factory specified in the notification of the Government of India in the Ministry of Labour No. G.S.R. 1295, dated 23rd November, 1974, come into force on the 30th day of November, 1974;

> Added vide GSR 1400 dated 21.12.1974.

(lxxix) as respects the Agricultural Farms, Fruit, Orchards, Botanical gardens, and Zoological Gardens specified in the notification of the Government of India in the Ministry of Labour No. G.S.R. 1315, dated 27th November, 1974, come into force on the 31st day of December, 1974;

> Added vide GSR 268 dated 26.12.1974.

(lxxx) as respects soap stone mines and establishment engaged in the grinding of soap stone covered by the notification of the Government of India in the Ministry of Labour, S.O. 1955, dated the 21st June, 1975, come into force on the 30th June, 1975;

> Added vide GSR 984 dated 26.07.1975.

(lxxxi) as respects the apatite, asbestos, calcite, ball clay, corundum, emerald, feldspar, silica (sand), quartz, ochre, Chromite, graphite and flourite mines covered by the notification of the Government of India in the Ministry of Labour, No. G.S.R. 1102, dated the 24th July, 1976, come into force on the 30th September, 1976;

Added vide GSR 1355 dated 03.09.1976.

(lxxxii) as respects,—
(1) establishments which are factories engaged in the manufacture of glue and gelatine,
(2) stone quarries producing stone chips, stone sets, stone boulders, and ballasts, and
(3) establishments engaged in fish processing and nonvegetable food preservation industry including bacon factories and pork preservation plants, covered by the notification of the Government of India in the Ministry of Labour, No. G.S.R. 204, dated the 31st January, 1977, come into force on the 28th February, 1977;

Added vide GSR 305 dated 19.02.1977.

(lxxxiii) as respects the beedi industry, that is to say, any industry engaged in the manufacture of beedies, specified in the notification of the Government of India in the Ministry of Labour, No. G.S.R. 660, dated the 17th May, 1977, come into force on the 31st May, 1977;

Added vide GSR 677 dated 23.05.1977.

(lxxxiv) as respects the financial establishment (other than banks) engaged in the activities of borrowing, lending, advancing of money and dealing with other monetary transactions with a view to earn interest not being the Unit Trust of India established under the Unit Trust of India Act, 1963 (52 of 1963), the Agricultural Refinance Corporation established under the Agricultural Refinance Corporation Act, 1963 (10 of 1963), the Industrial Development Bank of India established under the Industrial Development Bank of India Act, 1964 (18 of 1964), the Industrial Finance Corporation of India established under the Industrial Finance Corporation Act, 1948 (15 of 1948) and State Finance Corporations established under the State Finance Corporation Acts specified in the notification of the Government of India in the Ministry of Labour No. G.S.R. 1458, dated the 18th November, 1978, come into force on the day of 31st day of December, 1978;

Added vide GSR 1523 dated 12.12.1978.

(lxxxv) as respects lignite mines specified in the notification of the Government of India in the Ministry of Labour, No. G.S.R. 31, dated the 16th December, 1978, come into force on the 6th January, 1979;

Added vide GSR 462 dated 09.03.1979.

(lxxxvi) as respects the Ferro Chrome Industry, that is to say, any industry engaged in the manufacture of Ferro Chrome, specified in the notification of the Government of India in the Ministry of Labour No. G.S.R. 938, dated the 25th June, 1978, come into force on the 31st July, 1979;

Added vide GSR 982 dated 13.07.1979.

Suppliments

(lxxxvii) as respects the Diamond Cutting Industry, that is to say, any industry engaged in the cutting of diamond, specified in the notification of the Government of India in the Ministry of Labour, No. G.S.R. 564, dated the 17th May, 1980, come into force on the 31st May, 1980;

Added vide GSR 605 dated 24.05.1980.

(lxxxviii) as respects the quartzite mines covered by the notification of the Government of India in the Ministry of Labour, No. G.S.R. 563, dated the 17th May, 1980, come into force on the 31st May, 1980;

Added vide GSR 605 dated 24.05.1980.

(lxxxix) as respects the inland water transport establishments, that is to say, any establishment engaged in the activities of inland water transport specified in the notification of the Government of India in the Ministry of Labour, No. G.S.R. 565, dated the 17th May, 1980, come into force on the 31st May, 1980;

Added vide GSR 605 dated 24.05.1980.

(xc) as respects the establishments engaged in Building and Construction Industry specified in the notification of the Government of India in the Ministry of Labour, No. G.S.R. 1069, dated the 11th October, 1980, come into force on the 31st October, 1980;

Added vide GSR 592 (E) dated 22.10.1980.

(xci) as respects factories relating to the Myrobalan Extract Power, Myrobalan Extract Solid, and Vegetable Tannin Blended Extract Industries, specified in the notification of the Government of India in the Ministry of Labour No. G.S.R. 613(E), dated the 30th October, 1980, come into force on the 31st October, 1980;

Added vide GSR 614 (E) dated 31.10.1980.

(xcii) as respects the Brick Industry, that is to say, any industry engaged in the manufacture of bricks, specified in the notification of the Government of India in the Ministry of Labour, No. G.S.R. 662(E), dated the 27th November, 1980, come into force on the 30th November, 1980;

Added vide GSR 665 dated 29.11.1980.

(xciii) as respects the establishments engaged in stevedoring, loading and unloading of ships specified in the notification of the Government of India in the Ministry of Labour, No. G.S.R. 611(E), dated the 23rd November, 1981, published in Part II, Section 3, sub-section (i) of the Gazette of India, Extraordinary, dated the 23rd November, 1981;

Added vide GSR 642 (E) dated 05.12.1981.

(xciv) as respects establishments engaged in poultry farming specified in the notification of the Government of India in the Ministry of Labour, No. G.S.R.643(E), dated the 7th December, 1981 published at page 1834 in Part II, Section 3, sub-section (i) of the Gazette of India, Extraordinary, dated the 7th December, 1981;

Added vide GSR 437 dated 23.04.1982.

(xcv) as respects the establishments engaged in Cattle Feed Industry specified in the notification of the Government of India in the Ministry of Labour, No. G.S.R. 644(E), dated the 7th December, 1981, published at page 1834 in Part II, Section 3, sub-section (i) of the Gazette of India, Extraordinary, dated the 7th December, 1981;

> Added vide GSR 437 dated 23.04.1982.

(xcvi) as respects the educational, scientific, research and training institutions specified in the notification of the Government of India in the Ministry of Labour, No. S.O. 986, dated the 19th February, 1981, www.epfindia.gov.in 16 published in Part II, Section 3, sub-section (ii) of the Gazette of India, dated 6th March, 1982;

> Added vide GSR 591 dated 21.06.1982.

(xcvii) as respects the industries based on asbestos as principal raw material, specified in the notification of the Government of India in the Ministry of Labour and Rehabilitation No. S.O. 2459, dated the 21st May, 1983, published in Part II, Section 3, sub-section (ii) of the Gazette of India, dated the 4th June, 1983;

> Added vide GSR 13 dated 17.12.1983. (w.e.f. 01.01.1984).

(xcviii) as respect the cinema theatres employing 5 or more workers as specified in section 24 of the Cine-Workers and Cinema Theatre Workers (Regulations of Employment) Act, 1981 (50 of 1981) be deemed to have come into force with effect from the 1st day of October, 1984;

> Added vide GSR 347 dated 30.04.1986.

(xcix) as respects the Iron Ore pellets industry as specified in the notification of the Government of India in the Ministry of Labour, No. S.O. 2276, dated 30th August, 1989, published in Part II, Section 3, sub-section (ii) of the Gazette of India, dated 16th September, 1989;

> Added vide GSR 112 dated 02.02.1993. (w.e.f. 20.02.1993).

(c) as respects the establishments engaged in Guar Gum Factories, Marble Mines and Diamond Saw Mills specified in the notification of the Government of India, in the Ministry of Labour, No. G.S.R. 170, dated 25th March, 1992, published in Part II, Section 3, sub-section (ii) of the Gazette of India, dated 11th April, 1992;

> Added vide GSR 112 dated 02.02.1993. (w.e.f. 20.02.1993).

(ci) as respects the establishments engaged in rendering—

(i) courier services,

(ii) aircraft or airlines other than the aircrafts or air-lines owned or controlled by the Central or State Government, and

(iii) cleaning and sweeping services, specified in the notification of Government of India in the Ministry of Labour, No. S.O. 746, dated 22nd March, 2001, published in Part II, Section 3, sub-section (ii) of the Gazette of India dated 7th April, 2001; come into force with effect from 1st April, 2001;

> Added vide GSR 296 dated 22.07.2002. (w.e.f. 01.04.2001). Serial No. against the entries has not been mentioned in the notification, to show distinct entries, sub-serial Nos. have been marked.

Suppliments

(cii) with respect to the establishments engaged in Railways for construction, maintenance, operation and commercial activities of Railways, excluding Indian Railways exclusively managed by Government of India whose employees are in enjoyment of the Provident Fund, Pension and other retiral (sic it may be retairal) benefits under the rules made by the Central Government; specified in notification of the Government of India in the Ministry of Labour and employment, G.S.R. 401, dated 10.11.2005 published in Part II of Section 3, sub-section (i) of the Gazette of India dated 19.11.2005 comes into force from the date of publication.

> Added vide S.O. 45 dated 17.01.2006. (w.e.f. 17.01.2006). Serial No. against this entry has been shown as (xxiv) which may intend to show it as (civ) treating entries at serial No. (ci) the sub-entries as (ci), (cii), and (ciii) respectively. Hence this entry be treated as (civ).

[Note: Following notification are also given for the benefit of readers.]

(ciii) With respect to the establishment engaged in manufacture, marketing, servicing and usage of a computer as defined in clause (i) of sub-section (1) of Section 2 of the Information Technology Act (21 of 2000)/or deriving any form of output there from/or employing it for any type of processing services including software product companies, Internet and E-commerce Companies, Information Technology Services and Remote Maintenance Companies, Research and Development Companies, Systems Intergrators, On-site Services Companies and Off-shore Software Development Companies etc. specified in the notification S.O.1190(E) of Ministry of Labour and Employment New Delhi dated 27th July 2006.

> Notification to this effect has not so far been issued.

(civ) With respect to the class of establishment to which the Act shall apply, with effect from 28 December 2008 the date of publication of this notification in the official Gazette, namely:- i) companies offering life insurance, annuities etc. other than life Insurance Corporation of India; ii) private airports and joint venture airports; iii) electronic media companies in private sector; and iv) lodging houses, service apartments and condominiums. as specified in S.O.3456 notification dated 16 November 2007.

> Notification to this effect has not so far been issued.

2.- Definitions – In this Scheme, unless the context otherwise requires, -

(a) "Act" means the 'The Employees' Provident Funds [1][and Family Pension Fund] Act, 1952 (19 of 1952);

(b) [2][xxx]

---

1. Substituted by GSR 320 dated 16.02.1972 (w.e.f. 13.2.1971)
2. Deleted by GSR 1845 dated 28.11.1963

(c) "children" means legitimate children and includes adopted children if the Commissioner is satisfies that under the personal law of the member adoption of a child is legally recognized;

[3][(d) "Commissioner" means a Commissioner of Employees' Provident Fund appointed under section 5D of the Act and includes a Deputy Provident Fund Commissioner and a Regional Provident Fund Commissioner;]

---
3. Substituted by GSR 1845 dated 28.11.1963

(e) "continuous service" means uninterrupted service and includes service which is interrupted by sickness, accident, authorized leave, strike which is not illegal, or cessation of work not due to the employee's fault;

(f) "excluded employee" means-

[4][(i) an employee who, having been a member of the Fund, withdrew the full amount of his accumulations in the Fund under clause (a) or (c) of paragraph 69;]

[5][(ii) an employee whose pay at the time he is otherwise entitled to become a member of the Fund, exceeds [6][fifteen thousand rupees] per month;

Explanation- "Pay" includes basic wages with dearness allowance, [7][retaining allowance (if any)] and cash value of food concessions admissible thereon;]

[8][(iii) xxx]

[9][(iv) an apprentice;

Explanation – An apprentice means a person who, according to the certified standing orders applicable to the factory or establishment, is an apprentice, or who is declared to be an apprentice by the authority specified in this behalf by the appropriate Government;]

---
4. Substituted by GSR 1122 dated 19.9.1960
5. Added by GSR 1337 dated 16.4.1957
6. Substituted by GSR 608 (E) dated 22.8.2014 for Rs. 6,500/- (w.e.f. 01.9.2014).
7. Added by GSR 201 dated 08.02.1961
8. Omitted by GSR 1467 dated 02.12.1960
9. Substituted by GSR 331 dated 15.01.1958

Note:- The definition of 'excluded employee' stands modified/ amended in relation to –

1. *The Newspaper establishments vide paragraph 80;*

(2) For paragraph 2(f), the following shall be substituted, namely-

(i) an employee who, having been a member of the Fund, has withdrawn the full amount of his accumulations in the Fund under clause (a) or (c) of sub-paragraph (1) of paragraph 69;

(ii) an apprentice.

Explanation.-'Apprentice' means a person who, according to the standing order applicable to the newspaper establishment concerned, is an apprentice or who is declared to be an apprentice by the authority specified in this behalf by the appropriate Government.

2. the Cine-workers, including cinema theatres, under para 81;

(f) "Excluded employee" means-

(i) a cine-worker, who having been a member of the Fund had withdrawn the full amount of accumulations in the Fund under clause (a) or (c) of sub-paragraph (1) of paragraph 69;

(ii) a "cine-worker," whose wages at the time hs is otherwise entitled to become a member of the Fund exceeds on thousand and six hundred rupees per month and where such remuneration is by way of a lump-sum exceeding fifteen thousand rupees.

Explanation.-"wages" means "wages" as defined in clause (k) of section 2 of the Cine Workers and Cinema Theatre Workers (Regulation of Employment) Act, 1981 (50 of 1981).

3. the disabled employees employed by the establishment, under para 82,

(f) "Excluded employee" means-

(i) a person with disability, who having been a member of the Fund has withdrawn the full amount of his accumulation under clause (a) or clause (c) of sub-paragraph (1) of paragraph 69;

(ii) a person with disability, whose pay at the time he is otherwise entitled to become a member of the Fund, exceeds twenty-five thousand rupees per month ;

(iii) an apprentice.

[10][4. in respect of International Workers, under paragraph 83-

(f) "Excluded employee" means (i) an International Worker, who is contributing to a social security programme of his country of origin, either as a citizen or resident, with whom India has entered into a social security agreement on reciprocity basis and enjoying the status of detached worker for the period and terms, as specified in such an agreement; or

(ii) an International Worker, who is contributing to a social security programme of his country of origin, either as a citizen or resident, with whom Inda has entered into a bilateral comprehensive economic agreement conataining a clause on social security prior to 1st October, 2008, which specifically exempts natural person of either country to contribute to the social security fund of the host country.]

10. Subs. By GSR 148 dated 3.9.2010 (w.e.f. 11.9.2010) in place of originally Added by GSR 706 (E) dated 01.10.2008 (w.e.f. 01.10.2008)

(g) "family means –

[11][(i) in the case of a male member, his wife, his children, whether married or unmarried, his dependant parents and his deceased son's widow and children:]

Provided that if a member proves that his wife has ceased, under the personal law governing him or the customary law of the community to which the spouses belong, to be entitled to maintenance she shall no longer be deemed to be a part of the member's family for the purpose of this Scheme, unless the member subsequently intimates by express notice in writing to the Commissioner that she shall continue to be so regarded, and

[11][(ii) in the case of a female member, her husband, her children, whether married or unmarried, her dependant parents, her husband's dependent parents and her deceased son's wife and children:]

Provided that if a member by notice in writing to the Commissioner expresses her desire to exclude her husband from the family, the husband and his dependant parents shall no longer be deemed to be a part of the member's family for the purpose of this Scheme, unless the member subsequently cancels in writing any such notice.

Explanation- In either of the above two cases, if the child of a member [of, as the case may be, the child of a deceased son of the member] has been adopted by another person and if, uner personal law of the adopter, adoption is legally recognized, such a child shall be considered as excluded from the family of the member;

---
11. Substituted by GSR 351 dated 03.03.1966

(h) "financial year" means the year commencing on the first day of April;

(i) "Government Security" shall have the meaning assigned to it in the Public Debt "Act, 1944 (18 of 1944);

(j) "Inspector" means a person appointed as such under section 13 of the Act;

(k) "quarter" means a period of three months commencing on the first day of January, the first day of April, the first day of July and the first day of October of each year;

[11][(kk) "seasonal factory" means a factory which is exclusively engaged in the manufacturing of [13][tea, sugar, rubber, turpentine, rosin, indigo, lac, fruit and vegetable preservation industry, rice milling industry, dal milling industry, cashew nut industry, stemming or re-drying of tobacco leaf industry, tiles industry ,hosiery industry, oil milling industry, licensed salt industry, jute bailing or pressing industry, fireworks and percussion cap industry, ice or ice-cream industry or cotton ginning and pressing industry];

[14][(kkk) "seasonal establishment" means a plantation of tea, coffee, rubber, cardamom or pepper, [15][a coffee curing establishment, a fire clay mine or a gypsum mine;]]

(l) "trustee" means a member if a Board of Trustees; and

(m) All other words and expressions shall have the meaning respectively assigned to them in the Act.

---
12. Added by GSR 1660 dated 21.7.1956
13. Added by different notifications from 1956 to 1972
14. Added by SRO 1363 dated 26.4.1957
15. Substituted by GSR 12 dated 22.12.1969

Suppliments

CHAPTER – II

[1][BOARD OF TRUSTEES, EXECUTIVE COMMITTEE AND REGIONAL COMMITTEES]

[2][**3.- Election of certain members of the Executive Committee–** (1) The Chairman of the Central Board shall call a meeting of the Board for the purpose of election to the Executive Committee of the members representing the employer ,as the case may be, the employees referred to in clauses (d) and (e) of sub-section (2) of section 5AA of the Act.

(2) In the meeting referred to in sub-paragraph (1), the Chairman of the Central Board may invite the members to propose the names of those members who represent the employers or, as the case may be, the employees and every such proposal shall be duly seconded by another member of the board.

(3) If the number of persons proposed and seconded for election under sub-paragraph (2) does not exceed the number of vacancies to be filled up from amongst the persons representing the employers, as the case maybe, the employees, the persons whose names have been so proposed and seconded in relation to the category of employers or employees, shall be declared elected to the Executive Committee.

(4) If the number of persons proposed and seconded for election under sub-paragraph (2) exceeds the number of vacancies to be filled up from amongst the persons representing the employers or, as the case may be, the employees, each member of the Board present at the meeting shall be given a ballot paper containing the names of all the candidates so proposed and seconded and he may record his votes thereon for as many candidates belonging to the categories o employers or employees, as there are vacancies to be filled up in relation to each such category, but not more than one vote shall be given in favour of any one candidate. If any member votes for more candidates than the number of vacancies in relation to the categories of employers or employees or gives more than one vote in favour of any one candidate, all his votes shall be deemed to be invalid.

(5) The person getting the highest number of votes shall be declared by the Chairman as duly elected to the Executive Committee at the same meeting or as soon thereafter as possible:

Provided that where there is an equality of votes between any candidates, and the addition of one vote will entitle any of the candidates to be declared elected, such candidate shall be elected by lot to be drawn in the presence of the Chairman.

(6) If any question arises as to the validity of any election, it shall be referred the Central Government, who shall decide the same.]

---
1. Subs. by GSR 690 (E) dated 30.6.1989 (w.e.f. 1.7.1989).
2. Inserted by GSR 690 (E) dated 30.9.1989 (w.e.f. 1.7.1989).

4.- Regional Committee - (1) Until such time as a State board is constituted for a State, the [1][Chairman of the Central Board] may, [2][by notification in the Official Gazette], set up a Regional Committee for the State, which will function under the control of the Central Board. The Regional Committee shall consist of the following persons, namely-

(a)   a Chairman [3][appointed] by the [1][Chairman of the Central Board];

(b) Two persons ³[appointed] by the ¹[Chairman of the Central Board] on the recommendation of the State Government;

(c) ¹[two persons] representing employers in the ⁴[industries or other establishments] to which this Scheme applies in the State ⁵[appointed by the Chairman of the Central Board] in consultation with such organisations of employers in the State as may be recognised for the purpose by the Central Government;

(d) ¹[two persons] representing employees in the ⁴[industries or other establishments] to which this Scheme applies in the State ⁵[appointed by the Chairman of the Central Board] in consultation with such organisations of employees in the State as may be recognised for the purpose by the Central Government; ⁶[and

(e) the non-official members of the Central board ordinarily resident in the State;]

⁷[Provided that where the Chairman of the Central Board considers it expedient so to do, he may appoint up to ⁸[five] addition representatives of the employers or, as the case may be the employees.]

⁹[(2) A Regional Committee shall advise the Central Board-

(i) on such matters as the Central Board may refer to it from time to time;

(ii) generally, on all matters connected with the administration of th Scheme in the State and, in particular, on -

(a) progress of recovery of provident fund contributions and other charges,

(b) expeditious disposal of prosecutions,

(c) speedy settlement of claims,

(d) annual rendering of accounts to members of the Fund, and

(e) speedy sanction of advances.]

(3) As soon as a State Board is constituted for any State, the Regional Committee constituted for that State under this paragraph shall stand dissolved.

---

1. Subs. by GSR 690 (E) dated 30.6.1989 (w.e.f. 1.7.1989).
2. Added by GSR 401 dated 1.3.1965
3. Inserted by GSR 690 (E) dated 30.9.1989 (w.e.f. 1.7.1989).
4. Subs. By GSR 1363 dated 26.4.1957.
5. Subs. by GSR 690 (E) dated 30.6.1989 (w.e.f. 1.7.1989).
6. Subs. By GSR 502 dated 14.3.1953.
7. added by GSR 690 (E) dated 30.6.1989 (w.e.f. 1.7.1989).
8. Subs. By GSR 85 (E) dated 28.1.2004 (w.e.f. 29.1.2004).
9. Subs. by GSR 297 dated 11.2.1963.

---

¹[**5 – Term of office-** ¹[(1)The term of office of the Chairman, Vice-Chairman and every Trustee of the Central Board referred to in clauses 9B0, (c), (d) and (e) of sub-section (1) of section 5A of the Act shall be five years commencing on and from the date on which their appointment is notified in the Official Gazette.

(2) The term of office of the Chairman and every Member of the Executive Committee referred to in clauses (b), (c), (d) and (e) of sub-section (2) of Section 5AA shall be two years and six months commencing on and from the date on which their appointment is notified in the Official Gazette.

(2A) The term of office of the Chairman and every member of a Regional Committee referred to in clauses (b), (c), (d) and (e) of sub-paragraph (1) of paragraph 4 shall be three years commencing on and from the date on which their appointment is notified in the Official Gazette.

(2B) Notwithstanding anything contained in sub-paragraph (1), (2) and (2A) every trustee or member shall continue to hold office until the appointment of his successor is notified in the Official Gazette.

Provided that a member of the Executive Committee shall cease to hold office when he ceases to be a member of the Central Board.]]

(3) A trustee or a member referred to in ²[sub-paragraph (1), (2), and (2A)] appointed to fill a casual vacancy shall hold office for the remaining period of the term of office of the trustee or member in whose place he is appointed and shall continue to hold office on the expiry of the term of office until the appointment of his successor is notified in the Official Gazette.

³[(4) All out going trustee or members shall be eligible for reappointment.]

---

1. Subs. by GSR 1298 dated 27.9.1972.
2. Subs. by GSR 690 (E) dated 30.6.1989 (w.e.f. 1.7.1989).
3. Subs. By GSR 18 dated 22.12.2000. (w.e.f. 6.1.2001).

---

6 - Resignation – ¹[xxxx] A trustee of the Central Board or a member of ²[the Executive Committee may resign his office by letter in writing addressed to the Central Government and his office shall fall vacant from the date on which his resignation is accepted by the Central Government. ³[A member of the Regional Committee may resign his office by a letter in writing addressed to the Chairman, Central Board, and his office shall fall vacant from the date on which his resignation is accepted by the Chairman, Central Board.]

¹[xxx]

---

1. Sr. No. 1 & (2) deleted by GSR 1845 dated 28.11.1963.
2. Subs. by GSR 690 (E) dated 30.6.1989 (w.e.f. 1.7.1989).
3. Added By GSR 690 (E) dated 30.6.1989 (w.e.f. 1.7.1989).

---

7 - Cessation and restoration of trusteeship- If a trustee or a member of ¹[the Executive Committee or a Regional Committee] fails to attend three consecutive meetings of the Board or Committee, as the case may be, without obtaining leave of absence from the Chairman of the Board or Committee, he shall cease to be a trustee or member of the Committee:

²[Provided that the Central Government in the case of the Central Board ¹[or the Executive Committee may restore him to trusteeship or membership of the Executive Committee or of] the Regional Committee, as the case may be, if it is satisfied that there were reasonable grounds for the absence.]

1. Subs. by GSR 690 (E) dated 30.6.1989 (w.e.f. 1.7.1989).
2. Added By GSR 1845 dated 28.11.1963.

8 - Dis-qualification for trusteeship or membership of a Regional Committee – (1) person shall be disqualified for being appointed as, or for being a trustee or member of a Regional Committee,-

(i) if he is declared to be for unsound mind by a competent court; or

(ii) if he is a un-discharged insolvent; or

(iii) if before or after the commencement of the Act he has been convicted of an offence involving moral turpitude; [1][or

(iv) if he as an employer in relation to an exempted establishment or an establishment to which the Scheme applies has defaulted in the payment of any dues to the Central Board or the Fund recoverable from him under the Act or the Scheme, as the case may be.]

[2][(2) If any question arises whether any person is disqualified under sub-paragraph (1), it shall be referred to the Central Government and the decision of the Central Government on any such question shall be final.]

1. Added by GSR 1488 dated 01.9.1971.
2. Subs. by GSR 1845 dated 28.11.1963.

[1][**9 - Removal from trusteeship or membership of a Regional Committee** – [2][The Central Government may remove from office any trustee of the Central Board, or the Chairman, Central Board may remove from office any member of a Regional Committee-

(i) if, in the opinion of the Central Government or the Chairman, Central Board, such trustee or member has ceased to represent the interest which he purports to represent on the Board or Committee, as the case may be; or]

(ii) if he as an employer in relation to an exempted establishment or an establishment to which the Scheme applies has defaulted in the payment of any dues to the Board or the Fund recoverable from him under the Act or the Scheme, as the case may be:

Provided that no such trustee or member shall be removed from office unless a reasonable opportunity is given to such trustee or member and the body whom he represents, of making any representation against the proposed action.]

1. Subs. by GSR 1488 dated 01.9.1971.
3. Subs. by GSR 690 (E) dated 30.6.1989.

10 – Absence from India – (1) Before a non-official trustee or a member of a Regional Committee leaves India-

(a) he shall intimate to the Chairman of the [1][Central Board] or of the Committee, as the case may be, of the dates of his departure from and expected return to India, or

(b) if he intends to absent himself or a period longer than six months, he shall tender his resignation.

(2) If any trustee or a member of a Regional Committee leaves India for a period of six months or more without intimation to the Chairman of the ¹[Central Board] or of the Regional Committee, as the case may be, he shall be deemed to have resigned from the ¹[Central Board] or the Committee.

---
1. Subs. by GSR 1845 dated 28.11.1963.

---

11 – Meetings – (1) ¹[The Central Board] of Trustees ²[or the Executive Committee] or Regional Committee shall, subject to the provisions of paragraph 12, meet at such place and time as may be appointed by the Chairman:

³[Provided that the Central Board or the Regional Committee shall meet at least twice in each financial year and the Executive Committee shall meet at least four times in each financial year.]

(2) The Chairman may, whenever he thinks fir, and shall within fifteen days of the receipt of a requisition in writing from not less than one third of the members in the case of the ¹[Central Board] ²[or the Executive Committee] and not less than three excluding the Chairman in the case of ²[a Regional Committee], call a meeting thereof.

---
1. Subs. by GSR 1845 dated 28.11.1963.
2. Added. by GSR 690 (E) dated 30.6.1989.
3. Subs. By GSR 690 (E) dated 30.6.1989.

---

12 – Notice of meeting and list of business – Notice of not less than 15 days from the date of posting, containing the date, time and place of every ordinary meeting together with a list of business to be conducted at the meeting shall be dispatched by registered post or by special messenger to each Trustee or a member of the Executive Committee or the Regional Committee, as the case may be, present in India:

Provided that when the Chairman calls a meeting or considering any matter which in his opinion is urgent, a notice giving such reasonable time as he may consider necessary, shall be deemed sufficient.

¹[**13 - Chairman to preside at meetings –** The Chairman of the Central Board or the Executive Committee or a Regional Committee shall preside at every meeting of the Central Board or the Executive Committee or the Regional Committee, as the case may be, at which he is present. If the Chairman of the Central Board is absent at any time, the Vice-Chairman thereof shall preside over the meeting of the Central Board and exercise all the powers of the Chairman at the meeting. If the Vice-Chairman of the Central Board or the Chairman of the Executive Committee or of a Regional Committee is absent at any time, the trustees or members present shall elect one of the trustees or, as the case may be, the members to preside over the meeting and the trustee or member so elected, shall exercise all the powers of the Chairman at the meeting.]

---
1. Subs. by GSR 690 (E) dated 30.6.1989.

---

¹[**14 – Quorum –** (1) No business shall be transacted at a meeting of the Central Board ²[or the Executive Committee or a Regional Committee unless at least eleven trustees or four members of the Executive Committee or a Regional Committee, as the case may be,] are present, of whom-

(a) in the case of the Central Board at least on each shall be from among those appointed under clauses (d) and (e) respectively of sub-section (1) of Section 5A of the Act;

³[(aa) in the case of the Executive Committee at least one each shall be from among those elected under clause (d) and (e) of sub-section (2) of Section 5AA of the Act;]

(b) in the case of a Regional Committee, at least one shall be from among those ⁴[appointed] under clause (c) and at least one from among those ⁴[appointed under clause (d) of sub-paragraph (1) of paragraph 4.

(2) If at any meeting the number of trustees or members of ³[the Executive Committee or] a Regional Committee is less than the required quorum, the Chairman shall adjourn the meeting to a date not later than seven days from the date of the original meeting informing the trustees or members of ³[the Executive Committee or the Regional Committee, as the case may be, of the date, time and place of the adjourned meeting and it shall thereupon be lawful to dispose of the business at such adjourned meeting irrespective of the number of trustees or members of ³[the Executive Committee] or the Regional Committee present.]

---

1. Subs. by GSR 1845 dated 28.11.1963.
2. Added. by GSR 690 (E) dated 30.6.1989.
3. Subs. By GSR 690 (E) dated 30.6.1989.
4. Subs. By GSR 401 dated 1.3.1965.

---

¹[**14A – Nomination of a substitute during the absence of a trustee/member of the ²[Central Board/Regional] Committee** – (1) If a trustee of a member is unable to attend any meeting of the ²[Central Board] or the Regional Committee as the case may be, he may , by a written instrument signed by him, addressed to the Chairman of the ²[Central Board] or the Regional Committee, as the case may be, and explaining the reasons for the inability to attend the meeting, appoint any representative of the Organisation, which he represents on the ²[Central Board] or th Regional Committee, as his substitute for attending that meeting of the ¹[Central Board] or the Regional Committee in his place:

Provided that no such appointment shall be valid unless-

(i) such appointment has been approved by the Chairman of the ²[Central Board] or the Regional Committee, and

(ii) the instrument making such appointment has been received by the Chairman of the ²[Central Board] or the Regional Committee, as the case may be, ³[***] before the date fixed for the meeting.

(2) A substitute validly appointed under sub-paragraph (1) shall have all the rights and powers of a trustee or a member, in relation to the meeting of the ²[Central Board] or the Regional Committee, in respect of which he is appointed and shall receive allowances, and be under obligations as if he were a trustee or a member appointed under the Act and the Scheme respectively.

(3) A trustee or a member appointed a substitute for attending any meeting of the ²[Central Board] or the Regional Committee, as the case may be, shall notwithstanding anything contained in this paragraph, continue to be liable for the misappropriation or misapplication of the Fund by the

substitute and shall also be liable for any act of misfeasance or non-feasance committed in relation to the Fund by the substitute appointed by him.]

---
1. Added. by GSR 1666 dated 10.10.1963.
2. Subs. by GSR 1845 dated 28.11.1963.
3. Certain words deleted by GSR 363 dated 25.3.1985.

---

15 – Disposal of business – Every question considered at a meeting of the ¹[Central Board] ²[or the Executive Committee] or a Regional Committee shall be decided by a majority of the votes of the trustees or ³[members of the Executive Committee or a Regional Committee] present and voting. In the event of an equality of votes, the Chairman shall exercise a casting vote:

Provided that the Chairman may, if he thinks fit, direct that any question shall be decided by circulation of necessary papers of trustees or ³[members of the Executive Committee or a Regional Committee] present in India and by securing their opinions in writing. Any such question shall be decided in accordance with the opinion of the majority of trustees or members received within the time limit allowed and if the opinions are equally divided, the opinion of the Chairman shall prevail:

Provided further that any trustee or member of the ²[Executive Committee or] a Regional Committee may request that the question referred to trustees ²[or members of the Executive Committee or] a Regional Committee, as the case may be, for written opinion be considered at a meeting of the ¹[Central Board] ²[or the Executive Committee] or a Regional Committee and thereupon the Chairman may and if the request is made by not less than three trustees or ³[members of the Executive Committee of a Regional Committee] shall direct that it shall be so considered.

---
1. Subs. by GSR 1845 dated 28.11.1963.
2. Added. by GSR 690 (E) dated 30.6.1989.
3. Subs. By GSR 690 (E) dated 30.6.1989.

---

16 – Minutes of meetings –(1) The minutes of a meeting of the ¹[Central Board] ²[or the Executive Committee] or a Regional Committee showing *inter alia* the names of the trustees or members of ³[Executive Committee or a Regional Committee] present thereat shall be circulated to all trustees or members of ³[Executive Committee or a Regional Committee] present in India not later than one month from the date of the meeting. The minutes shall thereafter be recorded in minute book as a permanent record:

Provided that if another meeting is held within a period of one month and ten days, the minutes shall be circulated so as to reach the trustees or members at least ten days before such meeting.

(2) The records of the minutes of each meeting shall be signed by the Chairman after confirmation with such modifications, if any, as may be considered necessary at the next meeting.

---
1. Subs. by GSR 1845 dated 28.11.1963.
2. Added. by GSR 690 (E) dated 30.6.1989.
3. Subs. By GSR 690 (E) dated 30.6.1989.

¹[17 – **Acts of** ²[****] **a Regional Committee not invalid by reason merely of any vacancy in, or defect in the Constitution, etc.**- No act or proceeding of ¹²[****] a Regional Committee shall be deemed to be invalid by reason merely of any vacancy in or any defect in the constitution of ²[***] the Regional Committee ²[***].

---

1. Subs. by GSR 1845 dated 28.11.1963.
2. Certain words deleted by GSR 690 (E) dated 30.6.1989.

---

18 – Fees and allowances – (1) The ¹[travelling allowance and daily allowance of an official trustee or official member of the Executive Committee or a Regional Committee] shall be governed by the rules applicable to him for journeys performed on official duties and shall be paid by the authority paying his salary.

¹[(2) Subject to the provisions of sub-paragraphs (3) and (4), every non-official trustee or non-official member of the Executive Committee or a Regional Committee shall be allowed travelling and daily allowances for attending the meeting of the Central Board or the Executive Committee or the Regional Committee, as the case may be, at the following rates, namely:

(i) Travelling allowance:

(A) a non-official trustee or member residing at the place where a meeting is held shall be allowed the actual expenditure incurred by him on conveyance, subject to the maximum of ²[rupees one hundred and fifty for each day for travel within the city];

(B) a non-official trustee or member not residing at the place where a meeting is held, shall be allowed–

   (a) actual expenditure incurred by him on air journey by economy ³[** ** **] class;

   (b) actual expenditure incurred by him on single return journey fare by rail by first air-conditioned class or by 2ⁿᵈ A.C., two tier sleeper or first class, as the case may be;

   (c) actual fare or expenditure incurred by him on road journey by taxi or own car or auto-rickshaw or bus (other than an air-conditioned bus) but not exceeding the rates notified by the concerned Director of Transport for journey by taxi or auto-rickshaw. When the journey is performed between places connected by rail, the fare will be limited to what would have been admissible to the trustee or member under clause (b) of this item.

(ii) Daily allowance:

(A) a non-official trustee or member residing at a place where a meeting is held shall not be entitled to any daily allowance;

²[(B) a non-official trustee or a member not residing at the place where a meeting is held shall be paid Rs. 1500 per day if the member stays in a hotel, and not exceeding Rs. 200 per day as expenses towards food.]

(3) Where such trustee or member being a member of a State Legislature attends a meeting of the ⁴[Central Board] or ²[the Executive Committee or] the Regional Committee, as the case may be, he shall be entitled–

(i) when the State Legislature is not in session, to such travelling and daily allowances as are admissible to Grade I Officers of the State Government; and

(ii) when the State Legislature is in session, to such travelling and daily allowances as are admissible to the members of that Legislature for attending meetings of the Legislature.

(4) Where such trustee or member being a member of either House of Parliament attends a meeting of the [4][Central Board] or [2][the Executive Committee or] the Regional Committee, as the case may be, he shall be entitled to such travelling and daily allowances as may be admissible to him under the rules laid down by the Central Government on the subject from time to time:

[5][Provided that when a Minister is appointed as Chairman or member of the Board or of [2][the Executive Committee or of the Regional Committee], and attends a meeting of such Central Board or [2][the Executive Committee or] Regional Committee, as the case may be, his travelling and daily allowance shall be governed by the rules applicable to him for journeys performed on official duties and shall be paid by the authority paying his salary.]

[6][(5) xxx]

Explanation I.– No daily or travelling allowance in respect of any day journey, as the case may be, shall be claimed under this paragraph by a trustee or member of [2][the Executive Committee or] a Regional Committee if he has drawn or will draw allowance for the same from his employer or as a member of any Legislature or of any Committee or Conference constituted or convened by Government and no travelling allowance shall be claimed if he uses a means of transport provided at the expense of Government or his employer.

[7][*Explanation II. xxx*]

---

1. Subs. by GSR 609 (E) dated 30.6.1989.
2. Subs. by GSR 744 (E) dated 9.9.2010.
3. Certain words deleted By GSR 744 (E) dated 9.9.2010.
4. Subs. by GSR 1845 dated 28.11.1963.
5. Added by GSR 1427 dated 16.6.1976.
6. Sub-para deleted by GSR 690 (E) dated 30.6.1989.
7. Explanation II deleted by 690 (E) dated 30.6.1989.

CHAPTER – III

APPOINTMENT AND POWERS OF COMMISSIONER AND OTHER STAFF OF BOARD OF TRUSTEES

[1][**19 – Central Provident Fund Commissioner and Financial Advisor and Chief Accounts Officer** – The central Provident Fund Commissioner and the Financial Adviser and Chief Accounts Officer shall not undertake any work unconnected with their office without the previous sanction of the Central Government.]

1.	Substituted by GSR 690(E) dated 30.6.1989 (w.e.f. 1.7.1989).

20. [1][xxxx]

[2][**21 – Opening of regional and other offices** –The Central Board may, [1][xxx] open such regional and local offices as it may consider desirable for the proper implementation of the Scheme. It may also define the functions and duties of the regional and local offices.]

1.	Deleted by GSR 690(E) dated 30.6.1989 (w.e.f. 1.7.1989)
2.	Substituted by GSR 1845 dated 28.11.1963 (w.e.f. 30.11.1963)

22 – Secretary of the Central Board or Regional Committee– [1][(1) The Central Provident Fund Commissioner shall be the Secretary of the Central Board and the Executive Committee. The Regional Provident Fund Commissioner –in-charge of the region shall be the Secretary of the Regional Committee of the State/Union Territory within his jurisdiction.]

(2) The Secretary to the Central Board or [2][the Executive Committee or] a Regional Committee shall; in consultation with the Chairman, convene meetings of the Central Board or [2][the Executive Committee or] the Regional Committee, as the case may be, keep a record of its minutes and shall take the necessary steps for carrying out the decisions of the Central Board or [2][the Executive Committee or] the Regional Committee, as the case may be.]

1.	Substituted by GSR 154 dated 24.1.2012 (w.e.f. 24.1.2012).
2.	Substituted by GSR 690(E) dated 30.6.1989 (w.e.f. 1.7.1989)

[1][**22A – Appointment of Officers and Employee of the Central Board** – The power of appointment vests in the Central Board under sub-section (3) of section 5D of the Act shall be exercised by the Board in relation to posts [2][equivalent to Joint Secretary to the Government of India].

1.	Inserted by GSR 609 (E) dated 30.6.1989 (w.e.f. 1.7.1989).
2.	Substituted by GSR 93 (E) dated 20.01.2016 (w.e.f. 20.01.2016).

[1][**23 – Information of appointments to the Central Board**- Reference relating to all appointments of officers of the [2][level of the Regional Provident Fund Commissioners and above made by the Chairman, Central Board] shall be placed before the next meeting of the Central Board for information.]

1.	Substituted by GSR 1845 dated 28.11.1963.
2.	Substituted by GSR 521 dated 16.8.1991 (w.e.f. 1.9.1991).

[1][24 – **Administrative and Financial Powers of the Commissioner** – (1) A Commissioner may, without reference to the [2] [Central Board] sanction expenditure on contingencies, supplies and services and purchase of articles required for administering the Fund subject to financial provision in the budget and subject to the limits up to which a Commissioner may be authorized to sanction expenditure on any single item from time to time by the Central Board [3][xxx].

(2) A Commissioner may also exercise such administrative and financial powers other then those specified in sub-paragraph (1) above, as may be delegated to him from time to time by the Central Board [3][xxx].

(3) A Commissioner may delegate from time to time th administrative and financial powers delegated to him by the Central Board to any officer under his control or superintendence to the extent considered suitable by him for the administration of the Scheme. A statement of such delegation shall be placed before the next meeting of the Central Board for information.]

1.	Substituted by GSR 147 dated 29.1.1960
2.	Substituted by GSR 1845 dated 28.11.1963
3.	deleted by GSR 690(E) dated 30.6.1991

[1][**24A. Delegation of power by the Central Board.**– [2][(1) The Central Board [3][***] may, by a resolution, empower its Chairman to sanction expenditure on any item, whether in the nature of capital expenditure or revenue expenditure, as it may deem necessary for the efficient administration of the Fund, subject to financial provisions in the Budget, where such expenditure is beyond the limits up to, which the Commissioner is authorized to sanction expenditure on any single item.]

(2) The Central Board may also, by a resolution, empower its Chairman to appoint such officers and employees other than those mentioned in subsections (1) and (2) of section 5D of the Act, as he may consider necessary for the efficient administration of the Scheme.

(3) All sanctions of expenditure made by the Chairman in pursuance of sub-paragraph (1) shall be reported to the Central Board as soon as possible after the sanction of the expenditure.]

1.	Subs. By G.S.R. 1845, dated 28th November, 1963 (w.e.f. 30-11-1963).
2.	Subs. By G.S.R. 421, dated 12th May, 1988 (w.e.f. 21-5-1988).
3.	Omitted by G.S.R. 690 (E), dated 30th June, 1989 (w.e.f. 1-7-1989).

25. Powers of the Central Government until the Central Board is constituted.–Until the Central Board is constituted, the Central Government shall administer the Fund and may exercise any of the powers and discharge any of the functions of the Board:

Provided that on the constitution of the Central Board, the Central Government shall transfer amounts standing to the credit of the Fund to the Central Board.

CHAPTER – IV

MEMBERSHIP OF THE FUND

[1][**26- Classes of employees entitled and required to join the Fund –**

(1) (a) Every employee employed in or in connection with the work of a factory or other establishment to which this Scheme applies, other than an excluded employee, shall be entitled and required to become a member of the Fund from the day this paragraph comes into force in such factory or other establishment.

(b) Every employee employed in or in connection with the work of a factory or other establishment to which this Scheme applies, other than an excluded employee, shall be entitled and required to become a member of the fund from the day this paragraph comes into force in such factory or other establishment if on the date of such coming into force, such employee is a subscriber to a provident fund maintained in respect of the factory or other establishment or in respect of any other factory or establishment (to which the Act applies) under the same employer:

Provided that where the Scheme applies to a factory o other establishment on the expiry or cancellation of an order of exemption under section 17 of the Act, every employee who but for the exemption would have become and continued as a member of the fund, shall become a member of the Fund forthwith.

(2) After this paragraph comes into force in a factory or other establishment, every employee employed in or in connection with the work of that factory or establishment, other than an excluded employee, who has not become a member already shall be entitled and required to become a member of the Fund from the date of joining the factory or establishment.

(3) An excluded employee employed in or in connection with the work of a factory or other establishment to which this Scheme applies shall, on ceasing to be such an employee, be entitled and required to become a member of the Fund from the date he ceased to be such employee.

(4) On re-election of an employee or a class of employees exempted under paragraph 27 or paragraph 27A to join the Fund or on the expiry or cancellation of an order under that paragraph, every employee, shall forthwith become a member thereof.

(5) Every employee who is a member of a private provident fund maintained in respect of an exempted factory or other establishment and who but for exemption would have become and continued as a member of the fund shall, on joining a factory or other establishment to which this Scheme applies, become a member of the Fund forthwith.

(6) Notwithstanding anything contained in this paragraph, an officer not below the rank of an Assistant Provident Fund Commissioner may, on the joint request in writing of any employee of a factory or other establishment to which this Scheme applies and his employer, enroll such employee as a member or allow his to contribute more than [2][fifteen thousand rupees] of his pay per month if he is already a member of the Fund and thereupon such employee shall be entitled to the benefits and shall be subject to the conditions of the Fund provided that the employer gives an undertaking in writing that he shall pay the administrative charges payable and shall comply with all statutory provisions in respect of such employee.]

---

1. Substituted by GSR 689 dated 19.10.1990 (w.e.f. 1.11.1990).

2.	Substituted by GSR 608 (E) dated 22.8.2014 (w.e.f. 1.9.2014).

¹[**26 A – Retention of membership** – (1) A member of the Fund shall continue to be member until he withdraws under paragraph 69 of the amount standing to his credit in the Fund or is covered by a notification of exemption under section 17 of the Act or an order of exemption under paragraph 27 or paragraph 27A.

Explanation – In the case of claim for refund by a member under sub-paragraph (2) of paragraph 69, the membership of the Fund shall deemed to have been terminated from the date the payment is authorized to him by the authority specified in this behalf by Commissioner irrespective of the date of claim.

(2) Every member employed as an employee other than an excluded employee, in a factory or other establishment to which this Scheme applies shall contribute to the Fund, and the contribution shall also be payable to the Fund in respect of him by the employer. Such contribution shall be in accordance with the rate specified in paragraph 29:

Provided that subject to the provisions contained in sub-paragraph (6) of paragraph 26 and ²[in paragraph 27], or sub-paragraph (1) of paragraph 27A, where the monthly pay of such a member exceeds ³[six thousand five hundred rupees], the contribution payable by him, and in respect of him by the employer, shall be limited to the amounts payable on a monthly pay of ³[six thousand five hundred rupees] including ⁴[dearness allowance, retaining allowance (if any) and cash value of food concession.]

1.	Added by GSR 584 dated 11.5.1959.
2.	Substituted by GSR 1522 dated 16.12.1960.
3.	Substituted by GSR 608 (E) dated 22.8.2014 (w.e.f. 1.9.2014).
4.	Substituted by GSR 201 dated 8.2.1961.

¹[**26 B – Resolution of doubts-** If any question arises whether an employee is entitled to or required to become, or continue as, a member, or as regards the date from which he is so entitled or required to become a member, the same shall be referred to the Regional Commissioner who shall decide the same:

Provided that both the employer and the employee shall be heard before passing any order in the matter.]

1.	Subs. by GSR 320 (E) dated 06.5.2014 (w.e.f. 07.5.2014).

¹[***27. Exemption of an employee*** — (1) A Commissioner may by order I and subject to such conditions as may be specified in the order exempt from the operation of all or any of the provisions of this Scheme an employee to whom the Scheme applies on receipt of application in Form-I from such an employee.

Provided that such an employee is entitled to benefits in the nature of Provident Fund, gratuity or old age pension according to the rules of the factory or other establishment and such benefits separately or jointly are on the whole not less favourable than the benefits provided under the Act and the Scheme. 1

(2) Where an employee is exempted as aforesaid, the employer shall in respect of such employee maintain such account, submit such returns, provide such facilities for inspection, pay such inspection charges and invest provident fund collections in such manner as the Central Government may direct.

²[Provided that above mentioned return shall be submitted by the employer in electronic format also, in such form and manner as may be specified by the Commissioner.]

(3) An employee exempted under sub-paragraph (1) may by an application to the Commissioner make a declaration that he shall become a member of the Fund.

(4) No employee shall be granted exemption or permitted to apply out of exemption more than once on each account.]

1.	Subs. by G.S.R. 852, dated 6.5.1963.
2.	Inserted by GSR 336 (E) dated 4.5.2012 (w.e.f. 4.5.2012).

¹[**27A. Exemption of a class of employees** — (1) ²[The appropriate Government] may by order and subject to such conditions as may be specified in the order exempt from the operation of all or any of the provisions of this Scheme any class of employees to whom the Scheme applies:

Provided that such class of employees is entitled to benefits in the nature of provident fund, gratuity or old age pension according to the rules of the ³[factory or other establishment] and such benefits separately or jointly are on the whole not less favourable than the benefits provided under the Act and this Scheme.

(2) Where any class of employees is exempted as aforesaid, the employer shall in respect of such class of employees maintain such account, submit such returns, provide such facilities for inspection, pay such inspection charges and invest provident fund collections in such manner as the Central Government may direct.

⁴[Provided that above mentioned return shall be submitted by the employer in electronic format also, in such form and manner as may be specified by the Commissioner.]

(3) A class of employees exempted under sub-paragraph (1) or the majority of employees constituting such class may by an application to the Commissioner make a declaration that the class of employees shall become member of the Fund.

(4) No class of employees shall be granted exemption or permitted to apply out of exemption more than once on each account.

(5) The provisions of this paragraph shall be deemed to have come into force with effect from the 14th of October, 1953.]

1.	Added by S.R.O. 2035, dated 31.10.1953.
2.	Subs. by G.S.R. 1286, dated 13.10.1961.
3.	Subs. by S.R.O. 1363, dated 26.4.1957.
4.	Proviso inserted by GSR 336 (E) dated 4.5.2012 (w.e.f. 4.5.2012).

¹[**Para-27AA:- Terms and conditions of exemption-** All exemptions already granted or to be granted hereafter under section 17 of the Act or under paragraph 27-A of the Scheme shall be subject to the terms and conditions as given in the Appendix A.

²[Appendix A

Revised Condition for Grant of Exemption under Section 17 of the Employees' Provident Funds and Miscellaneous Act, 1952:

The following are the revised conditions for grant of exemption under section 17 of the Act, 1952:

1. The employer shall establish a Board of Trustees under his Chairmanship for the management of the Provident Fund according to such directions as may be given by the Central Government of the Central Provident Fund Commissioner, as the case may be, from time to time. The Provident Fund shall vest in the Board of Trustees who will be responsible for and accountable to the Employees' Provident Fund Organisation, inter alia, for proper accounts of the receipts into and payment from the Provident Fund and the balance in their custody. For this purpose, the 'employer' shall mean:

    (i) in relation to an establishment, which is a factory, the owner or occupier of the factory; and

    (ii) in relation to an establishment, the person who, or the authority, that has the ultimate control over the affairs of the establishment.

2. The Board of Trustees shall meet at least once in every three months and shall function in accordance with the guidelines that may be issued form time to time by the Central Government/Central Provident Fund Commissioner (CPFC) or an officer authorized by him.

3. All employees, as defined in section 2(f) of the Act, who have been eligible to become members of the Provident Fund, had the establishment not been granted exemption, shall be enrolled as members.

4. Where an employee who is already a member of Employees' Provident Fund or a provident fund of any other exempted establishment is employed in his establishment, the employer shall immediately enroll his as a member of the fund. The employer should also arrange to have the accumulations in the provident fund account of such employee with his previous employer transferred and credited into his account.

5. The employer shall transfer to the Board of Trustees the contributions payable to the provident fund by himself and employees at the rate prescribed under the Act from time to time by the 15th of each month following the month for which the contributions are payable. The employer shall be liable to pay simple interest in terms of the provisions of section 7Q of the Act for any delay in payment of any dues towards the Board of Trustees.

6. The employer shall bear all the expenses of the administration of the Provident Fund and also make good may other loss that may be caused to the Provident Fund due to theft, burglary, defalcation, misappropriation or any other reason.

7. Any deficiency in the interest declared by the Board of Trustees is to be made good by the employer to bring it up to the statutory limit.

8. The employer shall display on the notice board of the establishment, a copy of the rules of the funds as approved by the appropriate authority and as and when amended thereto along with a translation in the language of the majority of the employees.

9. The rate of contribution payable, the conditions and quantum of advances and other matters laid down under the provident fund rules of the establishment and the interest credited to the account

of each member, calculated on the monthly running balance of the member and declared by the Board of Trustees shall not be lower than those declared by the Central Government under the various provisions prescribed in the Act and the Scheme framed thereunder.

10. Any amendment in the Scheme, which is more beneficial to the employee than the existing rules of the establishment, shall be made applicable to them automatically pending formal amendment of the Rules of the Trust.

11. No amendment in the rules shall be made by the employer whithout the prior approval of the Regional Provident Fund Commissioner (referred to as RPFC hereafter). The RPFC shall before giving his approval give a reasonable opportunity to the employees to explain their point of view.

12. All claims for withdrawal, advances and transfers should be settled expeditiously, with in the maximum time prescribed by the Employees' Provident Funds Organisation.

13. The Board of Trustees shall maintain detailed accounts to show the contributions credited, withdrawals and interest in respect of each employee. The maintenance of such records should preferably be done elcctronically. The establishment should periodically transmit the details of members' accounts electronically as and when directed by the CPFC/RPFC.

14. The Board of Trustees shall issue an annual statement of accounts or pass-book to every employee within six months of the close of financial/accounting year free of cost once in the year. Addition printouts can be made available as and when the members want, subject to nominal charges. In case of passbook, the same shall remain in custody of employee to be updated periodically by the Trustees when presented to them.

15. The employer shall make necessary provisions to enable all the members to be able to see their account balance from the computer terminals as and when required by them.

16. The Board of Trustees and the employer shall file such returns monthly/annually as may be prescribed by the Employees' Provident Fund Organisation within the specified time-limit, failing which it will be deemed as a default and the Board of Trustees and employer will jointly and separately be liable for suitable penal action by the Employees' Provident Fund Organisation.

[3][Provided that above mentioned return shall be submitted by the employer in electronic format also, in such form and manner as may be specified by the Commissioner.]

17. The Board of Trustees shall invest the monies of the provident fund as per the directions of the Government from time to time. Failure to make investments as per directions of the Government shall make the Board of Trustees (and the employer) separately ad jointly liable to surcharge as may be imposed by the CPFC or his representative.

18. (a) The securities shall be obtained in the name of Trust. The securities so obtained should be in dematerialized (DEMAT) form and in case the required facility is not available in the area where the trust operates, the Board of Trustees shall inform the RPFC concerned about the same.

(b) The Board of Trustees shall maintain a script wise register and ensure timely realization of interest.

(c) The DEMAT Account should be opened through depository participants approved by Reserve Bank of India and Central Government in this regard.

(d) The cost of maintaining DEMAT account should be treated as incidental cost of investment by the trust. Also all types of cost of investment like brokerage for purchase of securities etc. shall be treated as incidental cost of investment by the Trust.

19. All such investments made, like purchase of securities and bonds, should be lodged in the safe custody of depository participants, approved by Reserve Bank of India and Central Government, who shall be the custodian of the same. On closure of establishment or liquidation or cancellation of exemption from EPF Scheme, 1952, such custodian shall transfer the investment obtained in the name of the Trust and standing in its credit to the RPFC concerned directly on receipt of request from the RPFC concerned to that effect.

20. The exempted establishment shall intimate to the RPFC concerned the details of depository participants (approved by Reserve Bank of India and Central Government), with whom and in whose safe custody, the investments made in the name of trust, viz. Investments made in securities, bonds etc. have been lodged. However, the Board of Trustees may raise such sum or sums of money as may be required for meeting obligatory expenses such as settlement of claims, grant of advances as per rules and transfer of member's P.F. accumulations in the event of his/her leaving service of the employer and any other receipts by sale of the securities or other investments standing in the name of the Fund subject to the prior approval of the RPFC.

21. Any commission, incentive, bonus, or other pecuniary rewards given by any financial or other institutions for the investments made by the Trust should be credited to its account.

22. The employer and the members of the Board of Trustees, at the time of grant of exemption, shall furnish a written undertaking to the RPFC in such format as may be prescribed from time to time, inert-alia, agreeing to abide by the conditions which are specified and this shall be legally binding on the employer and the Board of Trustees, including their successors and assignees, or such conditions as may be specified later for continuation of exemption.

23. The employer and the Board of Trustees shall also give an under-taking to transfer the funds promptly within the time limit prescribed by the concerned RPFC in the event of cancellation of exemption. This shall be legally binding on them and will make them liable for prosecution in the event of any delay in the transfer of funds.

24. (a) The account of the Provident Fund maintained by the Board of Trustees shall be subject to audit by a qualified independent chartered accountant annually. Where considered necessary, the CPFC or the RPFC in –charge of the Region shall have the right to have accounts re-audited by any other qualified auditor and the expenses so incurred shall be borne by the employer.

(b) A copy of the Auditor's report alongwith the audited balance sheet should be submitted to the RPFC concerned by the Auditors directly within six months after the closing of the financial year from 1st April to 31st March. The format of the balance sheet and the information ot be furnished in the report shall be as prescribed by the Employee' Provident Fund Organisation and made available with the RPFC Office in electronic format as well as a signed hard copy.

(c) The same auditors should not be appointed for two consecutive years and not more than two years in a block of six years.

25. A company reporting loss for three consecutive financial years or erosion in their capital base shall have their exmption withdrawn from the first day of the next / succeeding financial year.

26. The employer in relation to the exempted establishment shall provide for such facilities for inspection and pay such inspection charges as the Central Government may, form time to time direct under the close of every month.

27. In the event of any violation of the conditions for grant of exemption, by the employer or the Board of Trustees, the exemption granted may be cancelled after issuing a show cause notice in this regard to the concerned persons.

28. In the event of any loss to the trust as a result of any fraud, defalcation, wrong investment decisions etc. the employer shall be liable to make good the loss.

29. In case of any change of legal status of the establishment, which has been granted exemption, as a result of merger, demerger, acquisition, sale, amalgamation, formation of a subsidiary, whether wholly owned or not, etc., the exemption granted shall stand revoked and the establishment should promptly report the matter to the RPFC concerned for grant of fresh exemption.

30. In case, there are more than one unit/ establishment participating in the common Provident Fund Trust which has been granted exemption, all the trustees shall be jointly and sepsrately lliable/ responsible for any default committed by any of the trustees/ employer of any of the participating units and the RPFC shall take suitable legal action against all the trustees of the common Provident Fund Trust.

31. The Central Government may lay down any further conditions for continuation of exemption of the establishment.]]

1.	Added by GSR. 18, dated 22.12.2000.
2.	Subs. by G.S.R. 853, dated 29.10.2003 (w.e.f. 30.10.2003).
3.	Proviso inserted by GSR 336 (E) dated 4.5.2012 (w.e.f. 4.5.2012).

28. **Transfer of accumulations from existing Provident Funds-** (1) Every authority in charge of, or entrusted with the management of, any Provident Fund in existence [1][xxx], the accumulations wherein are to be transferred to the Fund under sub-section (2) of section 15 of the Act, [2][or sub-section (5) of section 17 thereof, as the case may be], shall [1][xxx]

(i) send to the [1][xxx] Commissioner, a statement showing the amount standing to the credit of each subscriber on the date of the transfer the total accumulations to the credit of the subscribers generally on that date and the advances, if any, taken by the subscriber [2][within twenty five days of the application of the Scheme, or cancellation of exemption, as the case may be];

(ii) transfer to the Fund in the manner specified in sub-paragraph (2) the total accumulations standing to the credit of the subscribers in relation to each factory [2][within ten days of the application of the Scheme, or cancellation of the exemption, as the case may be, in case of liquid cash in bank and within thirty days in case of securities]; and

(iii) Transfer to the [4][Central Board] all pass books of account and other documents relating to the said accumulations.

(2) All accumulation standing to the credit of the subscribers, howsoever, invested, shall be transferred to the Fund by the authority aforesaid in cash:

[5][Provided that where the whole or any part of such accumulations consists of investments in Government securities, [6][or in securities guaranteed by appropriate Government as regards repayment of principal and payment of interest or in both], the authority making the transfer to the Fund shall transfer those securities at the price for which they were actually purchased or transfer a sum equivalent to such price. In case, however, the whole or any part of such accumulations is invested in National Savings Certificates or National Plan Savings Certificates, the appreciated value of such certificates at the time of the transfer will be taken into account in determining the amount of the accumulations to be transferred, provided that the difference between the face value of such certificate and their appreciated value at the time of transfer has already been credited to the accounts of the subscribers:]

[7][Provided further that where the whole or any part of such accumulations consists of investments in [6][securities bearing no guarantee of an appropriate Government as regards repayment of principal and payment of interest], the Central Government may, in exceptional cases, allow acceptance of the transfer of such securities from the authority making the transfer to the Fund at the price for which they were actually purchased.]

[5][**Explanation**- The total amount of provident fund accumulations includes interest thereon and the authority in charge of the Fund shall transfer in cash any balance of interest on investment which happens to be undistributed on the date of transfer, or realized or realizable for the period prior to the registration of the securities in the name of the Central Board of Trustees, Employees' Provident Fund.]

(3) Any cash transferred under sub-section (2) shall be deposited in any office or branch of the Reserve Bank of India or the [8][State Bank of India] to the credit of the [4][Central Board] and the receipt obtained in respect thereof shall be forwarded to the [1][xxx] Commissioner:

Provided that where there is no office or branch of either of the two Banks at the place where the [9][factory or other establishment] is situated, the amount shall be credited to the Central Board by means of a Reserve Bank of India [10][Governmental draft at par].

(4) The accumulations transferred to the Fund in accordance with this paragraph shall be credited to the account of each of the members of the Fund, to the extent to which he may be entitled thereto having egard to the statement furnished by the authority aforesaid.

(5) When the accumulations in any such Provident Fund as is referred to in sub-paragraph (1) have been so transferred to the Fund, the [1][xxx] Commissioner may, by notification in the Gazette of India, declare that the subscribers of such Provident Fund have now become members of the Fund and that the accumulations aforesaid have now become vested in the Central Board.]

1.	Certain words deleted by GSR 897 dated 6.9.1985
2.	Added by GSR 897 dated 6.9.1985.
3	certain words deleted by GSR 1845 dated 28.11.1963.
4.	Subs. by GSR 1845 dated 28.11.1963.
5.	Inserted by GSR 970 dated 1.10.1958.
6.	Added by GSR 579 dated 12.4.1971.
7.	Inserted by GSR 86 dated 3.1.1963.
8.	Subs. by GSR 974 dated 10.8.1960 in place of Imperial Bank.
9.	Subs. by S.R.O. 1363 dated 26.4.1957.
10.	Subs. by SRO 270 dated 7.2.1953.

CHAPTER – V

CINTRIBUTIONS

¹[29. Contribution.– (1) The contributions payable by the employer under the Scheme shall be at the rate of ²[ten per cent.] of the ³[basic wages, dearness allowance (including the cash value of any food concession) and retaining allowance (if any)] payable to each employee to whom the Scheme applies:

⁴[Provided that the above rate of contribution shall be ²[twelve per cert.] in respect of any establishment or class of establishments which the Central Government may specify in the Official Gazette from time to time under the first proviso to sub-section (1) of section 6 of the Act.]

(2) The contribution payable by the employee under the Scheme shall be equal to the contribution payable by the employer in respect of such employee:

⁵[Provided that in respect of any employee to whom the Scheme applies, the contribution payable by him may, if he so desires, be an amount exceeding ²[ten per cent, or twelve per cent.], as the case may be, of his basic wages, dearness allowance and retaining allowance (if any) subject to the condition that the employer shall not be under an obligation to pay any contribution over and above his contribution payable under the Act.]

⁶[(3) The contributions shall be calculated on the basis of ³[basic wages, dearness allowance (including the cash value of any food concession) and retaining allowance (if any)] actually drawn during the whole month whether paid on daily, weekly, fortnightly or monthly basis.]

⁷[(4) Each contribution shall be calculated to ³[the nearest rupee, 50 paise or more to be counted as the next higher rupee and fraction of a rupee less than 50 paise to be ignored.]

1.	Subs. by S.R.O. 2387, dated 13th July, 1957.
2.	Subs. by G.S.R. 406, dated 27th October, 1997 (w.r.e.f. 22-9-1997).
3.	Subs. by G.S.R. 201, dated 8th February, 1961 (w.e.f. 31-12-1960).
4.	Ins. by G.S.R. 1756, dated 12th December, 1962.
5.	Subs. by G.S.R. 690 (E), dated 30th June, 1989 (w.e.f. 1-7-1989).
6.	Ins. by G.S.R. 164, dated 30th June, 1989 (w.e.f. 1-7-1989).
7.	Ins. by S.R.O. 3375, dated 10th October, 1957.
8.	Subs. by GSR 548 dated 27.10.1997 (w.e.f. 22.9.1997).

¹[30. Payment of contributions.–(1) The employer shall, in the first instance, pay both the contribution payable by himself (in this Scheme referred to as the employer's contribution) and also, on behalf of the member employed by him directly or by or through a contractor, the contribution payable by such member (in this Scheme referred to as the member's contribution).

(2) In respect of employees employed by or through a contractor, the contractor shall recover the contribution payable by such employee (in this Scheme referred to as the member's contribution) and shall pay to the principal employer the amount of member's contribution so deducted together with an equal amount of contribution (in this Scheme referred to as the employer's contribution) and also administrative charges ²[***].

(3) It shall be the responsibility of the principal employer to pay both the contribution payable by himself in respect of the employees directly employed by him and also in respect of the employees employed by or through a contractor and also administrative charges ²[***].]

³[*Explanation.*–For the purposes of this paragraph the expression "administrative charges" means such percentage of the pay (basic wages, dearness allowance, retaining allowance, if any, and cash value of food concessions admissible thereon) for the time being payable to the employees other than an excluded employee, as the Central Government may, in consultation with the Central Board and having regard to the resources of the Fund for meeting its normal administrative expenses, fix.]

1.	Subs. by G.S.R. 1845, dated 28th November, 1963 (w.e.f. 30-11-1963).
2.	Omitted by G.S.R. 1399, dated 18th September, 1964 (w.e.f. 1-10-1964).
3.	Ins. by G.S.R. 1845, dated 28th November, 1963 (w.e.f. 30-11-1963).

31. Employer's share not to be deducted from the members- Notwithstanding any contract to the contrary the employer shall nit be entitled to deduct the employer's contribution from the wages of a member or otherwise to recover in from him.

32. Recovery of a member's share of contribution.–(1) The amount of a member's contribution paid by the employer ¹[or a contractor] shall, notwithstanding the provisions in this Scheme or any law for the time being in force or any contract to the contrary, be recoverable by means of deduction from the wages of the member and not otherwise:

Provided that no such deduction may be made from any wage other than that which is paid in respect of the period or part of the period in respect of which the contribution is payable:

Provided further that the employer ¹[or a contractor] shall be entitled to recover the employee's share from a wage other than that which is paid in respect of the period for which the contribution has been paid or is payable where the employee has in writing given a false declaration at the time of joining service with the said employer ¹[or a contractor] that he was not already a member of the Fund:

Provided further that where no such deduction has been made on account of an accidental mistake or a clerical error, such deduction may, with the consent in writing of the Inspector be made from the ²[subsequent] wages.

(2) Deduction made from the wages of a member paid on daily, weekly or fortnightly basis should be totaled up to indicate the monthly deductions.

(3) Any sum deducted by an employer ¹[or the contractor] from the wages of an employee under this Scheme shall be deemed to have been entrusted to him for the purpose of paying the contribution in respect of which it was deducted.

1.	Ins. by G.S.R. 1845, dated 28th November, 1963 (w.e.f. 30-11-1963).
2.	Subs. by S.R.O. 500, dated 2nd March, 1953.

¹[**32A . Recovery of damages for default in payment of any contribution.**- ²[(1) Where an employer makes default in the payment of any contribution to the fund, or in the transfer of accumulations required to be transferred by him under sub-section (2) of section 15 or sub-section (5) of section 17 of the Act or in the payment of any charges payable under any other provisions of the Act

or Scheme or under any of the conditions specified under section 17 of the Act, the Central Provident Fund Commissioner or such officer as may be authorised by the Central Government, by notification in the Official Gazette in this behalf, may recover from the employer by way of penalty, damages at the rates given below:–

Period of Default Rate of damages (% of arrears per annum)

(a)	Less than two months	Five
(b)	Two months and above but less than four months	Ten
(c)	Four months and above but less than six months	Fifteen
(d)	Six months and above	Twenty Five]

(2) The damages shall be calculated to the nearest rupees, 50 paise or more to be counted as the nearest higher rupee and fraction of a rupee less than 50 paise to be ignored.]

1. Ins. by G.S.R. 521, dated 16th August, 1991 (w.e.f. 1-9-1991).
2. Subs. by GSR 689 (E) dated 26.9.2008 (w.e.f. 26.9.2008).

[1][**32B. Terms and conditions for reduction or waiver of damages.**–The Central Board may reduce or waive the damages levied under section 14B of the Act in relation to an establishment specified in the second proviso to section 14B, subject to the following terms and conditions, namely:–

(a) in case of a change of management including transfer of the undertaking to workers' co-operative and in case of merger or amalgamation of the sick industrial company with any other industrial company, complete waiver of damages may be allowed;

(b) in cases where the Board for Industrial and Financial Reconstruction, for reasons to be recorded in its schemes, in this behalf recommends, waiver of damages up to 100 per cent may be allowed;

(c) in other cases, depending on merits, reduction of damages up to 50 per cent may be allowed.]

1. Ins. by G.S.R. 521, dated 16th August, 1991 (w.e.f. 1-9-1991).

Suppliments

CHAPTER – VI
DECLARATION, CONTRIBUTION CARDS AND RETURNS

33. Declaration by persons already employed at the time of institution of the Fund.–Every person who is required or entitled to become a member of the Fund shall be asked forthwith by his employer to furnish and shall, on such demand, furnish to him, for communication to the Commissioner, particulars concerning himself and his nominee required for the declaration form in Form 2. Such employer shall enter the particulars in the declaration form and obtain the signature or thumb impression of the person concerned.

34. Declaration by persons taking up employment after the, Fund has been established.–The employer in relation to a [1][factory or other establishment] shall, before taking any person into employment, ask him to state in writing whether or not he is a member of the Fund and if he is, ask for the Account Number and/or the name and particulars of the last employer. If he is unable to furnish the Account Number, he shall, require such person to furnish and such person shall, on demand, furnish to him for communication to the Commissioner, particulars regarding himself and his nominee required for the Declaration Form. Such employer shall enter the particulars in the Declaration Form and obtain the signature or thumb impression of the person concerned:

[2][Provided that in the case of any such employee who has become a member of the Family Pension Fund under the Employees' Family Pension Scheme, 1971, the aforesaid Declaration Form shall also contain such particulars as are necessary to comply with the requirements of that Scheme.]

1. Subs. by S.R.O 1363, dated 26th April, 1957.
2. Ins. by G.S.R 320, dated 16th February, 1972 (w.e.f. 18-3-1972).

35. Preparation of contribution cards.–The employer shall prepare a contribution card [1][in Form 3] [2][or Form 3A] as may be appropriate, in respect of every employee in his employment at the commencement of the Scheme or who is taken into employment after that date and who is required or entitled to become or is a member of the Fund including those who produce an Account Number and in respect of whom no fresh Declaration Form is prepared:

[3][Provided that in the case of any such employee who has become a member of the Family Pension Fund under the Employees' Family Pension Scheme, 1971*, the aforesaid Forms shall also contain such particulars as are necessary to comply with the requirements of that Scheme.]

1. Subs. by G.S.R 1300, dated 19th September, 1962.
2. Ins. by G.S.R 1809, dated 28th September 1968.
3. Ins. by G.S.R 320, dated 16th February, 1972 (w.e.f. 18-3-1972).
* EPS, 1995 has replace the Scheme of 1971, but no correction to that effect has been done.

36. Duties of Employers.– (1) Every employer shall send to the Commissioner, within fifteen days of the commencement of this Scheme, a consolidated return in such form as the Commissioner may specify, [3][xxx] of the employees required or entitled to become members of the Fund showing the [1][basic wage, retaining allowance (if any) and dearness allowance including the cash value of any food concession] paid to each of such employee:

[2][Provided that if there is no employee who is required or entitled to become a member of the Fund, the employer shall send a 'NIL' return.]

(2) Every employer shall send to the Commissioner within fifteen days of the close of each month a return–

(a) [3][xxx] in Form 5, of the employees qualifying to become members of the Fund for the first time during the preceding month together with the declarations in Form 2 furnished by such qualifying employees, and

(b) [3][xxx] [8][in such form as the Commissioner may specify] of the employees leaving service of the employer during the preceding month:

[2][Provided that if there is no employee qualifying to become a member of the Fund for the first time or there is no employee leaving service of the employer during the preceding month, the employer shall send a 'NIL' return.]

[4][(c) *Provided further that a copy of the forms as mentioned in clause (a) and (b) above shall be provided by the employer to concerned employees immediatelt ater joining the service or at the time of leaving the service, as the case may be.]

[3][xxx]

[5][(4) Every employer shall maintain an inspection note book in such form as the Commissioner may specify, for an Inspector to record his observation on his visit to the establishment.]

[6][(5)] Every employer shall maintain such accounts in relation to the amounts contributed to the Fund by him and by his employees as the [7][Central Board] may, from time to time, direct, and it shall be the duty of every employer to assist the [7][Central Board] in making such payments from the Fund to his employees as are sanctioned by or under the authority of the [7][Central Board].

[6][(6)] Notwithstanding anything hereinbefore contained in this paragraph, the Central Board may issue such directions to employer generally as it may consider necessary or proper for the purpose of implementing the Scheme, and it shall be the duty of every employer to carry out such directions.

[4][(7) Every employer shall send to the Commissioner such returns in electronic format also, in such form and manner as may be specified by the Commissioner.]

---

1. Subs. by G.S.R. 201, dated 8th February, 1961 (w.r.e.f. 31-12-1960).
2. Ins. by G.S.R. 413, dated 11th March, 1966.
3. Certain words deleted by GSR 1300 dated 19.9.1962.
4. Ins. by G.S.R. 336, dated 4.5.2012. (*Before added proviso (c) has been put which is not correct as per format of legal notification).
5. Ins. by G.S.R. 1176, dated 17th August, 1964.
6. Sub-paragraphs (4) and (5) renumbered as sub-paragraphs (5) and (6) by G.S.R. 1176, dated 17th August, 1964.
7. Subs. by GSR 1845 dated 28.11.1964.
8. Subs. by G.S.R. 25, dated 31st December, 1996, for "in copy of the Wages Payment Register" (w.e.f. 11-1-1997). Earlier the words "in copy of the Wages Payment Register" were substituted by G.S.R. 294, dated 24th May, 1994, for the words "in such form as the Commissioner may specify" (w.r.e.f. 1-3-1994).

---

[1][**36A. Employer to furnish particulars of ownership**] - Every employer in relation to a factory or other establishment to which the Act applies on the date of coming into force of the Employees' Provident www.epfindia.gov.in 47 Funds (Tenth Amendment) Scheme, 1961, or is applied after that date, shall furnish [2][in duplicate] to the [3][Regional] Commissioner in Form No. 5A annexed hereto, [4][particulars of all the branches and departments, owners], occupiers, directors, partners, manager or any other person or persons who have the ultimate control over

the affairs of such factory or establishment and also send intimation of any change in such particulars, within fifteen days of such change, to the [3][Regional] Commissioner by registered post and in such other manner as may be specified by the[3] [Regional] Commissioner]:

[4][Provided that in the case of any employer of a factory or other establishment to which the Act and the Family Pension Scheme, 1971, shall apply the aforesaid Form may be deemed to satisfy the requirements of the Employees' Family Pension Scheme, 1971, for the purpose specified above.

1.	Added by G.S.R. 1457 dated 21st February, 1961 (w.r.e.f. 31-12-1960).
2.	Ins. by G.S.R. 1714 dated 1.6.1966.
3.	Subs. by GSR 1845 dated 28.11.1963.
4.	ubs. by G.S.R. 1836, dated 7.12.1965.
5.	Ins. by G.S.R. 336 (E) dated 4.5.2012.

[1][**36B. Duties of Contractors**— Every contractor shall, within seven days of the close of every month, submit to the principal employer a statement showing the recoveries of contributions in respect of employees employed by or through him and shall also furnish to him such information as the principal employer is required to furnish under the provisions of the Scheme to the Commissioner.]

1.	Subs. by G.S.R. 1845, dated 28th November, 1963.

37. Allotment of account numbers.–On receipt of the information referred in sub-paragraphs 33, 34 and 36, the Commissioner shall promptly allot an Account Number to each employee qualifying to become a member and shall communicate the Account Number to the member through the employer.

38. Mode of payment of contributions.–(1) The employer shall, before paying the member his wages in respect of any period or part of period for which contributions are payable, deduct the employee's contribution from his wages which together with his own contribution as well as an administrative charge of such percentage [1][of the pay (basic wages, dearness allowance, retaining allowance, if any, and cash value of food concessions admissible thereon) for the time being payable to the employees other than an excluded employee, as the Central Government may fix. He shall within fifteen days of the close of every month pay the same to the Fund [8][electronic through internet banking of the State Bank of India or any other Nationalised Bank authorized for collection] on account of contributions and administrative charge]:

[2][Provided that if the payment is made by a cheque, it should be drawn only on the local bank of the place in which deposits are made]:

Provided further that where there is no branch of the Reserve Bank or the [3][State] Bank of India at the station where the [4][factory or other establishment] is situated, the employer shall pay to the Fund the amount mentioned above by means of Reserve Bank of India [5][Governmental Drafts at par] separately on account of contributions and administrative charge.

[6][(2) The employer shall forward to the Commissioner within twenty-five days of close of the month, a monthly abstract in such form as the Commissioner may specify showing the aggregate amount of recoveries made from the wages of all the members and the aggregate amount contributed by the employer in respect of all such members for the month:

Provided that an employer shall send a Nil return, if no such recoveries have been made from the employees:

Provided further, that in the case of any such employee who has become a member of the Pension Funds under the Employees' Pension Scheme, 1995, the aforesaid Form shall also contain such particulars as are necessary to comply with the requirements of that Scheme.]

[6][(3) The employer shall send to the Commissioner within one month of the close of the period of currency, a consolidated Annual Contribution Statement in Form 6-A, showing the total amount of recoveries made during the period of currency from the wages of each member and the total amount contributed by the employer in respect of each such member for the said period. The employer shall maintain on his record duplicate copies of the aforesaid monthly abstract and consolidated annual contribution statement for production at the time of inspection by the Inspector.]

[7][Provided that the employer shall send to the commissioner returns or details as required under sub-paragraph (2) and (3) above, in electronic format also, in such form and manner as may be specified by the Commissioner.]

1.	Subs. by G.S.R. 1399, dated 18th September, 1964 (w.e.f. 1-10-1964).
2.	Subs. by G.S.R. 706, dated 9th September, 1983.
3.	Subs. by G.S.R. 794, dated 10th August, 1960.
4.	Subs. by S.R.O. 963, dated 26th April, 1957.
5.	Subs. by S.R.O. 270, dated 7th February, 1953.
6.	Subs. by G.S.R. 25, dated 31st December, 1996, for sub-paragraph (2) (w.e.f. 11-1-1997). Earlier sub-paragraph (2) was substituted by G.S.R. 294(E), dated 24th May, 1994 (w.r.e.f. 1-3-1994).
7.	Added by G.S.R. 336 (E), dated 4.5. 2012 (w.e.f. 4.5.2012).
8.	Added by GSR 360 (E) dated 5.5.2015 (w.e.f. 5.5.2015).

39. Fixation of administrative charges.–The Central Government may, in consultation with the Central Board and having regard to the resources of the Fund available for meeting its normal administrative expenses, fix the percentage of administrative charges payable under sub-paragraph (1) of paragraph 38 above.

40. Contributions to be entered in the contribution card.–The amount recovered every month from the wages of an employee as well as the contribution made by the employer in respect of each such employee shall be entered by the employer every month in the contribution card opened in the name of each member under this Scheme.

[1][**40A. Supply of pass books to the members.**– With effect from such date as the Commissioner may specify in this behalf, every employer shall, on an employee becoming a member of the fund, provide a pass book to every such member and maintain the same in such form and manner as the Commissioner may direct from time to lime:

Provided that different dates may be specified for different industries or classes of establishments or for different areas.]

1.	Ins. by G.S.R. 341, dated 9th July, 1992 (w.e.f. 25-7-1992).

41. Currency of contribution cards.–The contribution cards issued under this Scheme shall be current for one year:

Provided that the said period of one year may commence and terminate at such different times in different ¹[factories and other establishments] as may be decided by the Commissioner from time to time:

²[Provided further that the cards issued,-

(i) in respect of the first contribution period, or

(ii) in respect of the contribution period immediately preceding the date from which the establishment is notified as an annually posted establishment, may be for a period which may be less or more than a year.]

1.	Subs. by S.R.O. 1363, dated 26th April, 1957.	
2.	Subs. by G.S.R. 1809, dated 28th September, 1968.	

42. Renewal of contribution cards.-An employer shall, on or before the expiration of the period of currency of the contribution card prepare in respect of each member employed by him a card in Form 3 ¹[or Form 3A] as may be appropriate, for the next period of currency:

²[Provided that in the case of any such employee who has become a member of the Family Pension Fund under the Employees' Family Pension Scheme, 1971, the aforesaid Form shall also contain such particulars as are necessary to comply with the requirements of that Scheme.]

³[Provided further that above mentioned contribution card in respect of each employee shall be prepared by the employer in electronic format also, in such form an manner as may be specified by the Commissioner.]

1.	Ins. by G.S.R. 1809, dated 28th September, 1968.	
2..	Ins. by G.S.R. 320, dated 16th February, 1972 (w.e.f. 18-3-1972).	
3.	Proviso added by GSR 336 (E) dated 4.5.2012 (w.e.f. 4.5.2012).	

43. Submission of contribution cards to the Commissioner.-Every employer shall within one month from the date of expiration of the period of currency of the contribution cards in respect of members employed by him, send the contribution cards to the Commissioner together with a statement in Form 6:

¹[Provided that where a member leaves service, the employer shall send the contribution card in respect of such members before the twentieth day of the month following that in which the member left the service:]

²[Provided further that in the case of any such employee who has become a member of the Family Pension Fund under the Employees' Family Pension Scheme, 1971, the aforesaid Form shall also contain such particulars as are necessary to comply with the requirements of that Scheme.]

³[Provided further that above mentioned contribution card in respect of each employees together with statement in Form 6 shall be sent by the employer in electronic format also, in such form and manner as may be specified by the Commissioner.]

1.	Added by G.S.R. 348, dated 26th February, 1966.	
2.	Ins. by G.S.R. 320, dated 16th February, 1972 (w.e.f. 18-3-1972).	
3.	Proviso added by GSR 336 (E) dated 4.5.2012 (w.e.f. 4.5.2012).	

44. Custody of contribution cards.–The employer shall retain in his custody the contribution cards in respect of each member employed by him and shall take every precaution against loss or damage of the contribution cards.

45. Inspection of cards by members.–Any member making a request in this behalf to the employer shall be permitted to inspect his cards himself or to have the same inspected by any person duly authorised by him in writing to do so, within 72 hours of making such request provided that no such request shall be entertained fore than once in every two calendar months.

46. Production of cards and records for inspection by the Commissioner or Inspector.–Every employer shall, whenever the Commissioner or any other officer authorised by him in this behalf or an Inspector so requests, either in person or by notice in writing, produce before the Commissioner, Officer, or Inspector, as the case may be, the records of any member employed by him and any card then in his possession, and if so required, by the said Commissioner, Officer or Inspector shall deliver such record to the said Commissioner, Officer or Inspector, who may, if he thinks fit, retain the record provided that he shall grant a receipt for every record retained by him.

47. Supply of cards and forms to employers.–The Commissioner shall supply to employer, free of charge on demand contribution cards, [1][pass books,] declaration forms and other forms referred to in this Scheme:

Provided that if any employer desires to obtain any cards, [1][pass books], or forms in excess of the number which the Commissioner considers to be the requirements of the employer, the Commissioner may, if he thinks fit, supply such extra cards, [1][pass books], or forms and make such charge therefor as he considers reasonable.

1.	Ins. by G.S.R. 341, dated 9th July, 1992 (w.e.f. 25-7-1992).

[1][**48: Current Account** –The Commissioner shall deposit the contribution received from the employers electronically through internet banking or any other mode other than internet banking in the Reserve Bank of India or the State Bank of India or any other Nationalised Bank in the Current Account of the Fund.]

1.	Added by GSR 360 (E) dated 5.5.2015 (w.e.f. 5.5.2015).

Suppliments

CHAPTER – VII
ADMINISTRATION OF THE FUND, ACCOUNTS AND AUDIT

49: Administration Accounts – 1[xxx] A separate account shall be kept called the "Central Administration Account" for recording all administrative expenses of the Fund including such administrative charges as the Fund may be authorized to levy.

¹[xxx]

1.	Sub-paragraph (2) omitted by G.S.R. 1845, dated 28th November, 1963 (w.e.f. 30-11-1963).

50: Provident Fund Account – The aggregate amount received as the employers' and the employees' contribution to the Fund shall be credited to an account to be called the "Provident Fund Account."

¹[**51: Interest Suspense Account** – All interest, rent and other income realized, and net profits or losses, if any, from the sale or investments not including therein the transactions of the Administration Account, shall be credited or debited, as the case may be, to an account called the "Interest Account" and brokerage and commissions on the purchase and sale of securities and other investments shall be included in the purchase or sale price, as the case may be, and not separately charged to the "Interest Account."]

1.	Subs. by GSR 60 (E) dated 01.02.2013 (w.e.f. 1.2.2013).

52: Investment of moneys belonging to Employees' Provident Fund – (1) All moneys belonging to the Fund shall be deposited in the Reserve Bank of India or the ¹[State Bank of India] or in such other Scheduled Banks as maybe approved by the Central Government from time to time or shall be invested, subject to such direction as the Central Government may from time to time give, in the securities mentioned or referred to in ²[section 20 of the Indian Trust Act, 1882 (2 of 1882)]:

Provided that such securities are payable both in respect of capital and in respect of interest in India.

(2) All expenses incurred in respect of, and loss, if any, arising from, any investment shall be charged to the Fund.

³[(3) xxx]

1.	Subs. by G.S.R. 974, dated 10th August, 1960.
2.	Subs. By GSR 666 (E) dated 27.08.2015 (w.e.f. 27.08.2015).
3.	Deleted by GSR 499 dated 5.3.1968.

53: Disposal of Funds – ¹[(1) Subject to the provisions of the Act and of this Scheme, the Fund, not including therein the Administration Account, shall not, except with the previous sanction of the Central Government, be expended for any purpose other than the payment of the sums standing to the credit of individual members of the Fund or the their nominees or heirs or legal representatives in accordance with the provisions of this Scheme.]

(2) The Fund shall be operated upon by such officers as may be authorized in this behalf by the ²[Central Board.]

1.	Subs. by G.S.R. 1314, dated 16th August, 1960.
2.	Subs. by GSR 1845 dated 28.11.1963.

¹[**54: Expenses of Administration** – (1) All expenses relating to the administration of the Fund including those incurred on Regional Committee, shall be met from the Fund.

(2) All expenses of administration of the Fund, including the fees and allowances, of the Trustees of the Central Board and salaries, leave and joining time allowances, traveling and compensatory allowances, gratuities and compassionate allowances, pensions, contributions to Provident Fund and other benefit fund instituted for the officers and employees of the Central Board, the cost of audit of the accounts, legal

expenses and cost of all stationary and forms incurred in respect of the Central Board, cost and all expenses incurred in connection with the construction of office buildings and staff quarters shall be met from the Administration Account of the Fund.

(3) The expenses incurred by the Central Government in connection with the establishment of the Fund shall be treated as a loan and such loan shall be repaid from the Administration Account.]

1.	Subs. by G.S.R. 1845, dated 28th November, 1963.

[1][55: **Form and manner of maintenance of Accounts** – The Central Board shall maintain proper accounts of its income and expenditure, including its administrative accounts, in Form No, 10, and the balance sheet in Form No. 11. The accounts shall be prepared for the financial year and the books shall be balanced on the thirty first March each year.]

1.	Subs. by G.S.R. 11, dated 21st December, 1992 (w.e.f. 2-1-1993).

56: Audit – (1)The accounts of the Fund, including the Administration Accounts, shall be audited in accordance with the instruction issued by the Central Government in consultation with the Comptroller and Auditor-General of India.

(2) The charges on account of audit shall be paid out of the Administration Account.

[1][**57. Inter-State transfer of members.**–(1) Where a member of the Fund ceases to be employed in one region and secures employment in another region in an establishment to which this Scheme applies or which is an exempted establishment or which is not covered under the Act but has a provident funds scheme of its own, he may apply to the Commissioner within whose jurisdiction he was previously employed, in such form as the Commissioner may specify, for transfer of balance of the provident fund in his existing account to his account in the other region.

(2) Where a member of the Fund ceases to be employed in one establishment and secures employment in another establishment in the same region, he may apply to the Commissioner of the region, in such form as the Commissioner may specify for the transfer of balance of the Provident Fund in his previous account to his account in the new establishment where he takes up the employment.]

1.	Substituted by GSR 1770 dated 10.11.1966.

[1][**58: Budget**– (1) The Commissioner shall place before the Central Board each year before the first fortnight of February, a budget showing separately the probable receipts from the contributions and from the levy of administrative charges and the expenditure which it proposes to incur during the following financial year. The budget as approved by the Central Board shall be submitted for sanction to the Central Government within a month of its being placed before the Central Board.

(2) The Central Government may make such modifications in the budget as it considers desirable before sanctioning it.]

[2][(3) The Commissioner may, at any time during the year, make budgetary re-appropriation of funds sanctioned in the budget by the Central Government, provided that-

(i) the total amount sanctioned in the budget by the Central Government is not exceeded;

(ii) it is made only fro meeting such expenses of administration as are to be met from the Administration Account in accordance with paragraph 54, and

(ii) every re-appropriation so made shall be reported by him to the Central Board at the next meeting of such Board.]

³[(4) The Commissioner shall place before the Central Board a supplementary budget for a financial year, giving detailed estimates and reasons, of inescapable expenditure which are likely to be incurred during the year for which no provision has been made in the sanctioned budget and which cannot be covered under the provisions of sub-paragraph (3) of paragraph 58. The supplementary budget as approved by the Central Board shall be submitted for sanction to the Central Government within a month of its being placed before the Central Board.

(5) Any expenditure incurred by the Commissioner over and above the sanctioned budget of a financial year and not covered under the provisions of sub-paragraph (3) and (4) of paragraph 58 shall be reported to the Central Board at the earliest practicable moment after the excess is established for its consideration and for obtaining sanction of the Central Government.]

---

1. Subs. by G.S.R. 1845, dated 28th November, 1963 (w.e.f. 30-11-1963).
2. Added by G.S.R. 261, dated 14th February, 1964.
3. Ins. by G.S.R. 593, dated 2nd May, 1975 (w.e.f. 10-5-1975).

59: Members' Accounts – (1) An account shall be opened in the office of the Fund in the name of each member in which shall be credited –

(a) his contributions,

(b) the contribution made by the employer in respect of him, and

(c) interest as provided in paragraph 60.

¹[(2) All items of account shall be calculated to the ³[nearest rupee, 50 paise or more to be counted as the next higher rupee and fraction of a rupee less than 50 paise to be ignored.]]

(3) On receipt of the contribution card or cards of a member from the employer or employers at the end of the period of currency of the contribution card, the Commissioner shall compare the entries made in the contribution card or cards with those made in the member's individual account in the office of he Fund and shall be rectify any discrepancy found in these entries.

---

1. Subs. by S.R.O. 2387, dated 13th July, 1957 (w.e.f. 1-4-1957).

60: Interest – (1) The Commissioner shall credit to the account of each member interest at such rate as may be determined by the Central Government in consultation with the Central Board.

¹[(2) (a) Interest shall be credited to the member's account on monthly running balance basis with effect from the last day in each year in the following manner-

(i) on the amount at the credit of a member on the last day of the preceding year, less any sums withdrawn during the current year- interest for twelve months;

(ii) on sums withdrawn during the current year- interest from the beginning of the current year upto the last day of the month preceding the month of withdrawal;

(iii) on all the sums credited to the member's account after the last day of the preceding year- interest from the first day of the month succeeding the month credit to the end of the current year;

(iv) the total of interest shall be rounded to the nearest whole rupee (fifty paise counting as the next higher rupee.]

[2][(b) In the case of a claim for the refund under paragraph 69 or 70, interest shall be payable up to the end of the month preceding the date on which the final payment is authorized irrespective of the date of receipt of the claim from the claimant concerned:

[3][Provided that interest up to and for the current month shall be payable on the claims which are authorized on or after 25th day of a particular month along with actual payment after the end of the current month;

Provided further that the rate of interest to be allowed on claims for refund for the broken currency period shall be the rate fixed for the financial year in which the refund is authorized.]

[4][Provided also that the rate of interest to be allowed on claims for refund for the broken currency period shall be the last declared rate on Employees' Provident Fund and if the rate declared for the current year happens to be less than the previous year's declared rate, then it would accrue as bonus to the outgoing members and it shall be incorporated into calculation for deriving the current year's rate of interest at the end of the year and the claims settled under this proviso shall be final.]

[1][**Explanation**- If an establishment is covered for the first time under the Act/Scheme during the course of the currency period the interest shall be allowed on the sums credited to the member's account on and from the first day of the month succeeding the month of credit to the end of the current year.]

(3) The aggregate amount of interest credited to the accounts of the members shall be debited to [5]['Interest Account.']

(4) In determining the rate of interest, the Central Government shall satisfy itself that there is no over-drawl on the [5]["Interest Account"] as a result of the debit thereto of the interest credited to the accounts of members.

[6][(5) Interest shall not be credited to the account of a member if he informs the Commissioner in writing that he does not wish to receive it. If, however, the member subsequently asks for interest, it shall be credited to his account with effect from the first day of the period of currency in which he makes a request therefore.]

[7][(6) Interest shall not be credited to the account of a member from the date on which it has become Inoperative Account, under the provisions of sub-paragraph (6) of paragraph 72.]

[8][Provided that if the settlement of claim in respect of inoperative account is delayed for more than thirty days from the date of receipt of the application for settlement of claim, interest shall be credited to the account in accordance with sub-paragraph (2) for delay period excluding the period of thirty days.]

1.	Subs. by G.S.R. 222, dated 31st March, 1993 (w.e.f. 1-4-1993).
2.	Subs. by GSR 206 dated 30.1.1964.
3.	Subs. by G.S.R. 393, dated 31st March, 1982 (w.e.f. 17-4-1982).
4.	Added by S.O. 380(E), dated 15th March, 2007 (w.e.f. 15-3-2007).
5.	Subs. by GSR 60 (E) dated 01.2.2013 (w.e.f. 1.2.2013).
6.	Ins. by G.S.R. 412, dated 10th March, 1966.
7.	Inserted by GSR 25 (E) dated 15.1.2011 (w.e.f. 1.4.2011).
8.	Proviso substituted by GSR 891 (E) dated 12.12.2014 and given effect from 01.04.2011. Original proviso was added by GSR 321 (E) dated 6.5.2014 (w.e.f. 7.5.20140.

Suppliments

CHAPTER – VIII

NOMINATIONS, PAYMENTS AND WITHDRAWALS FROM THE FUND

61. Nomination— (1) Each member shall make in his declaration in Form 2, a nomination conferring the right to receive the amount that may stand to his credit in the Fund in the event of his death before the amount standing to his credit has become payable, or where the amount has become payable before payment has been made.

(2) A member may in his nomination distribute the amount that may stand to his credit in the fund amongst his nominees at his own discretion.

(3) If a member has a family at the time of making a nomination, the nomination shall be in favour of one or more persons belonging to his family. Any nomination made by such member in favour of a person not belonging to his family shall be invalid:

[1][Provided that a fresh nomination shall be made by the member on his marriage and any nomination made before such marriage shall be deemed to be invalid.]

(4) If at the time of making a nomination the member has no family, the nomination may be in favour of any person or persons but if the member subsequently acquires a family, such nomination shall forthwith be deemed to be invalid and the member shall make a fresh nomination in favour of one or more persons belonging to his family.

[2][(4-A) Where the nomination is wholly or partly in favour of a minor, the member may, for the purposes of this Scheme appoint a major person of his family, as defined in clause (g) of paragraph 2, to be the guardian of the minor nominee in the event of the member predeceasing the nominee and the guardian so appointed:

Provided that where there is no major person in the family, the member may, at his discretion, appoint any other person to be a guardian of the minor nominee.]

(5) A nomination made under sub-paragraph (1) may at any time be modified by a member after giving a written notice of his intention of doing so in Form [3][2] annexed thereto. If the nominee predeceases the member, the interest of the nominee shall revert to the member who may make a fresh nomination in respect of such interest.

(6) A nomination or its modification shall take effect to the extent that it is valid on the date on which it is received by the Commissioner.

1.	Added by GSR 2438 dated 25.8.1995.
2.	Added by 1707 dated 17.11.1965.
3.	Substituted by GSR 521 dated 16.8.1991. (w.e.f. 1.9.1991)

[1][**62. Financing of Members' Life Insurance Policies.**– (1) Where a member desires that premium due on a policy of Life Insurance taken by him on his own life should be financed from his Provided Fund Account, he may apply in such form and in such manner as may be prescribed by the Commissioner.

(2) On receipt of such application the Commissioner, or, where so authorised by the Commissioner, any other officer subordinate to him may make payment on behalf of the member to the Life Insurance Corporation of India towards premium due on his policy:

Provided that no such payment shall be made unless the premium is payable [2][xxx] yearly.

(3) Any payment made under sub-paragraph (2) shall be made out of and debited to the member's own contribution with interest thereon standing to his credit in the Fund.

(4) No payment shall be made under sub-paragraph (2) unless the member's own contribution in his Provident Fund Account with interest thereon is sufficient to pay the premium: and where the payment is to be made on the first premium, sufficient to pay the premium for two years.

(5) No payment shall be made towards a policy unless it is legally assignable by the member to the Central Board.

(6) The Commissioner shall before making payment in respect of existing policies, satisfy himself by reference to the Life Insurance Corporation that no prior assignment of the policy exists and the policy is free from all encumbrances.

(7) No education endowment policy or marriage endowment policy shall be financed from the Fund, if such policy is due for payment in whole or in part before the member attains the age of 55 years.]

1.	Substituted by GSR 1083, dated 30.6.1966.
2.	Deleted by GSR 1185 dated 26.8.1972.

[1][**63. Conversion of policy into a paid-up one and payment of late fee, etc.**–Where a policy of Life Insurance of a member is financed from his Provident Fund Account, the Commissioner may–

(a) convert the Insurance Policy into a paid-up one when the credit in his Provident Fund on account of his share becomes inadequate for the payment of any premium;

(b) pay late fee and interest out of the member's own contribution in his Provident Fund Account, if any, premium cannot be remitted to the Life Insurance Corporation in time because of delay in sending to the Commissioner the policy duly assigned to the Central Board or any other reasons for which the member or his employer may be responsible.]

1.	Substituted by GSR 1083, dated 30.6.1966.

64. Assignment of policies to the Fund.– [1][(1) The policy shall, within six months of the first payment under paragraph 62, be assigned by endorsement thereon, to the Central Board and shall be delivered to the Commissioner.

(2) Notice of the assignment of the policy shall be given by the member to the Life Insurance Corporation and the acknowledgement of the said notice by the Corporation shall be sent to the Commissioner within three months of the date of assignment.]

(3) The terms of the policy shall not be altered nor shall the policy be exchanged for another policy without the prior consent of the Commissioner to whom the details of the alteration or of the new policy shall be furnished in such form as he may specify.

[1][(4) If the policy is not assigned and delivered as required under sub-paragraph (1), or is assigned otherwise than to the Central Board, or is charged or encvimbered or lapses, any amount paid from the

Fund in respect of such policy shall, with interest thereon at the rate provided under paragraph 60 be repaid by the member forthwith to the Fund. In the event of default, the employer shall, on receipt of such directions as may be issued by the Commissioner in this behalf deduct the amount in lump sum or in such instalments as the Commissioner may determine from the emoluments of the member and pay it to the Fund within such time and in such manner as may be specified by the Commissioner. The amount so repaid or recovered shall be credited to the member's account in the Fund.]

1.	Substituted by GSR 1083, dated 30.6.1966.

¹[**65. Bonus on policy to be adjusted against payments made from the Fund.**–So long as the policy remains assigned to the Central Board, any bonus accruing on it may be drawn by the Central Board or where authorised by the Central Board by the Commissioner, and adjusted against the payments made on behalf of the member under paragraph 62.]

1.	Substituted by GSR 1083, dated 30.6.1966.

¹[**66. Reassignment of policies.**– (1) Where the accumulations standing to the credit of the member are withdrawn under paragraph 69 or when the member repays to the Fund the amounts of premium paid by the Board with interest thereon at the rate provided in paragraph 60, the Central Board or where authorised by the Central Board, the Commissioner shall reassign by endorsement thereon the policy to the member together with a signed notice of reassignment addressed to the Life Insurance Corporation.

(2) If the member dies before the policy has been reassigned under sub-paragraph (1), the Central Board or where authorised by the Central Board, the Commissioner, shall reassign by the endorsement thereon, the policy to the nominee of the member if a valid nomination subsists and if there be no such nominee, to such person as may be legally entitled to receive it together with a signed notice of reassignment addressed to the Life Insurance Corporation.]

1.	Substituted by GSR 1083, dated 30.6.1966.

¹[**67. Recovery of amounts paid towards Insurance Policies.**–If a policy matures or otherwise falls due for payment during the currency of its assignment, the Central Board or, where so authorised by the Central Board, the Commissioner shall realise the amount assured together with bonus, if any, accrued thereon place to the credit of the member the amount so realised, or the whole of the amount paid from the Fund in respect of the policy with interest thereon, whichever is less, and refund the balance, if any, to the member.]

²[68. Xxx]

³[68-A. xxx]

1.	Substituted by GSR 1083, dated 30.6.1966.
2.	Deleted by GSR 1083, dated 30.6.1966.
3.	Deleted by GSR 98 dated 15.1.1962.

¹[**68B.** ²[**Withdrawal**] **from the Fund for the purchase of a dwelling house/flat or for the construction of a dwelling house including the acquisition of a suitable site for the purpose.**– (1) The Commissioner, or where so authorised by the Commissioner, any officer subordinate to him, may on an application from a member in such form as may be prescribed and subject to the conditions

prescribed in this paragraph sanction from the amount standing to the credit of the member in the fund, an ²[withdrawal]–

(a) for purchasing a dwelling house/flat, including a flat in a building owned jointly with others (outright or on hire purchase basis), or for constructing dwelling house including the acquisition of a suitable site for the purpose from the Central Government, the State Government, a co-operative society, an institution, a trust, a local body or a Housing Finance Corporation (hereinafter referred to as the agency/agencies); or

(b) for purchasing a dwelling site for the purpose of construction of a dwelling house or a ready-built dwelling house/flat from any individual ³[***].

⁴[(bb) for purchasing dwelling house/flat on ownership basis from a promoter governed by the provisions of any Flats or Apartments Ownership Act or by any other analogous or similar law of the Central Government or the State Government as may be in force in any State or area for the time being and who intends to construct or constructs dwelling house or block of flats and the member is required to pay to the said promoter in advance for financing the said construction of the house/flat:

Provided that the member has entered into an agreement with the promoter as may be required under the Flat or Apartments Ownership Act or any other analogous or similar law of the Central Government or State Government which may be in force in any State or any area and the said agreement is registered under the Indian Registration Act, 1908.] or

(c) for the construction of a dwelling house on a site owned by the member or the spouse of the member or jointly by the member and the spouse, or for completing/continuing the construction of a dwelling house already commenced by the member or the spouse, on such site ¹⁵[or for purchase of a house/flat in the joint name of the member arid the spouse under clauses (a) and (b) above].

Explanation 1.– In this paragraph, the expression, 'co-operative society' means a society registered or deemed to be registered under the Co-operative Societies Act, 1912 (2 of 1912), or under any other law for the time being in force in any State relating to co-operative societies.

¹⁶[*Explanation 2.–* * * *]

⁷[(2) (a) For the purpose of purchase of a site for construction of house thereon, the amount of withdrawal shall not exceed the member's basic wages and clearness allowance for twenty-four months or the member's own share of contributions, together with the employer's share of contributions with interest thereon or the actual cost towards the acquisition of the dwelling site, whichever is the least.

(b) For the purpose of acquisition of a ready built house/flat or for construction of a house/flat, the withdrawal shall not exceed the member's basic wages and dearness allowance for thirty-six months or the member's own share of contributions, together with the employer's share of contributions, with interest thereon, or the total cost of construction, whichever is the least.]

⁶[*Explanation–* The actual cost towards the acquisition of the dwelling site or the purchase of dwelling house/flat shall include the charges payable to wards registration of such site, house or flat.]

(3) (a) No ²[withdrawal] under this paragraph shall be granted unless–

(i) the member has completed five year's membership of the Fund;

(ii) the member's own share of contributions with interest thereon in the amount standing to his credit in the Fund is not less than one thousand rupees;

⁷[(iii) a declaration from the member that the dwelling site or the dwelling house/flat or the house under construction is free from encumbrances and the same is under title of the member and/or the spouse:]

Provided that where a dwelling site or a dwelling house/flat is mortgaged to any of the agencies referred to in clause (a) of sub-paragraph (1), solely for having obtained funds for the purchase of a dwelling house/flat or for the construction of a dwelling house including the requisition of a suitable site for the purpose, such a dwelling site or a dwelling house/flat, as the case may be, shall not be deemed to be an encumbered property:

Provided further that a land acquired on a perpetual lease or on lease for a period of not less than 30 years for constructing a dwelling house/flat, or a house/flat, built on such a leased land, shall also not be deemed to be an encumbered property:

Provided also that where the site of the dwelling house/flat is held in the name of only agency, referred to in clause (a) of sub-paragraph (1) and the allottee is precluded from transferring or otherwise disposing of, the house/flat without the prior approval of such agency, the mere fact that the allottee does not have absolute right of ownership of the house/flat and the site is held in the name of the agency, shall not be a bar to the giving of an ²[withdrawal] under clause (a) of sub-paragraph (1), if the other conditions mentioned in this paragraph are satisfied.

(b) No ²[withdrawal] shall be granted for purchasing a share in a joint property or for constructing a house on a site owned jointly except on a site owned jointly with the spouse.

(4) Subject to the limitation prescribed in sub-paragraph (2)–

(a) where the ²[withdrawal] is for the purchase of a dwelling house/flat or a dwelling site from an agency referred to in clause (a) of sub-paragraph (1), the payment of ²[withdrawal] shall not be made to the member but shall be made direct to the agency in one or more installments, as may be authorised by the member;

(b) where the ²[withdrawal] is for the construction of a dwelling house, it may be sanctioned in such number of installments as the Commissioner or where so authorised by the Commissioner, any officer, subordinate to him, thinks fit;

⁸[(c) ***]

⁴[(d) where the withdrawal is for purchasing a dwelling house/flat on ownership basis from a promoter as referred to in clause (bb) of sub-paragraph (1), the payment or withdrawal shall be made to the member in one or more instalments as may be required to be paid by the said promoter and as authorised by the member.

Explanation.–"Promoter" includes a person who constructs or causes to be constructed a block or building of flats or apartments for the purpose of selling some or all of them to other persons or to a company, co-operative society or other association of persons and his assignees and where the person who builds and the person who sells are different persons, the term "promoter" includes both.]

(5) Where a ²[withdrawal] is sanctioned for the construction of a dwelling house, the construction shall commence within six months of the withdrawal of the first installment and shall be completed within twelve months of the withdrawal of the final installments. Where the ²[withdrawal] is sanctioned for the purchase of a dwelling house/flat or for the acquisition of a dwelling site, the purchase or acquisition, as the case may be, shall be completed within six months of the withdrawal of the amount:

Provided that this provision shall not be applicable in case of purchase of a dwelling house/flat or hire-purchase basis and in cases where a dwelling site is to be acquired or houses are to be constructed by a co-operative society on behalf of its members with a view to their allotment to the members.

(6) Except in the cases specified in sub-paragraphs (7) ²[and 7A] no further ²[withdrawal] shall be admissible to a member under this paragraph.

(7) An additional ²[withdrawal] up to ²[twelve months] basic wages and dearness allowance or the member's own share of contributions with interest thereon, in the amount standing to his credit in the Fund, whichever is less, may be granted ¹⁰[***] in one installment only, for additions, substantial alterations or improvements necessary to the dwelling house owned by the member or by the spouse or jointly by the member and the spouse:

Provided that the ²[withdrawal] shall be admissible only after a period of" five years from the date of completion of the dwelling house.

¹¹[(7A) A further withdrawal equivalent to the amount of difference between the amount of withdrawal admissible to a member under sub-paragraph (2) above as on the date of fresh application and the amount of withdrawal that was drawn by a member under this paragraph any time during 6 years preceding 3rd October, 1981, may be granted to such a member (i) who had availed of the earlier withdrawal for purchase of a dwelling site and has now proposed to construct a dwelling house on the land so purchased or (ii) who had availed of the earlier withdrawal for making initial payment towards the allotment/purchase of a house/flat from any agency as referred to in clause (a) of sub-paragraph (1) above and has now proposed to avail withdrawal for completing the transaction to get the sole ownership of the house/flat so purchased or (iii) who had availed of the earlier withdrawal for construction of a house but could not complete the construction in the time due to lack of funds.]

¹²[(7B) A further withdrawal up to twelve months' basic wages and dearness allowance or member's own share of contribution with interest thereon in his account, whichever is the least, may be granted for addition, alteration, improvement or repair of the dwelling house owned by the member or by the spouse or jointly by the member and the spouse after ten years of withdrawal, under sub-paragraph (7).]

¹³[(8) * * *]

(9) (a) If the ²[withdrawal] granted under this paragraph exceeds the amount actually spent for the purpose for which it was sanctioned, the excess amount shall be refunded by the member to the Fund in one lump sum within thirty days of the finalisation of the purchase, or the completion of the construction of, or necessary additions, alterations or improvements to a dwelling house, as the case

may be. The amount so refunded shall be credited to the employer's share of contributions in the member's account in the Fund to the extent of ²[withdrawal] granted out of the said share and the balance, if any, shall be credited to the member's share of contributions in his account.

(b) In the event of the member not having been allotted a dwelling site/ dwelling house/flat, or in the event of the cancellation of an allotment made to the member and of the refund of the amount by the agency, referred to in clause (a) of sub-paragraph (1) or in the event of the member not being able to acquire the dwelling site or to purchase the dwelling house/flat from any individual or to construct the dwelling house, the member shall be liable to refund to the Fund in one lump sum and in such manner as may be specified by the Commissioner, or where so authorised by the Commissioner, any officer subordinate to him, the amount of ²[withdrawal] remitted under this paragraph to him or, as the case may be, to the agency referred to in clause (a) of sub-paragraph (1).

The amount so refunded shall be credited to the employer's share of contributions in the member's account in the Fund, to the extent of ²[withdrawal] granted out of the said share, and the balance, if any, shall be credited to the member's own share of contributions in his account.

(10) If the Commissioner, or where so authorised by the Commissioner, any officer subordinate to him is satisfied that the ²[withdrawal] granted under this paragraph has been unutilised for a purpose other than that for which it was granted or that the member refused to accept an allotment or to acquire a dwelling site or that the conditions of ²[withdrawals] have not been fulfilled or that there is reasonable apprehension that they will not be fulfilled wholly or partly; or that the excess amount will not be refunded in terms of clause (a) of sub-paragraph (9) or that the amount remitted back to the member by any agency referred to in clause (a) of sub-paragraph (1), will not be refunded in terms of clause (b) of sub-paragraph (9), the Commissioner, or where so authorised by the Commissioner, any officer subordinate to him, shall forthwith take steps to recover the amount due with penal interest thereon at the rate of two per cent per annum from the wages of the member in such number of instalments as the Commissioner, or where so authorised by the Commissioner, any officer subordinate to him, may determine. For the purpose of such recovery Commissioner or where so authorised by the Commissioner, any officer subordinate to him may direct the employer to deduct such installment from the wages of the member and on receipt of such direction, the employer shall deduct accordingly. The amount so deducted; shall be remitted by the employer to the Commissioner, or where so authorised by the Commissioner, any officer subordinate to him within such time and in such manner as may be specified in the direction. The amount so refunded, excluding the penal interest, shall be credited to the employer's share of contributions in the member's account in the Fund to the extent of ²[withdrawal] granted out of the said share and the balance, if any, shall be credited to the member's own share of contributions in his account. The amount of penal interest shall, however, be credited to the ⁹[interest account]:

¹⁴[Provided that the recovery of withdrawal under sub-paragraph (10) shall be restricted to cases where the recovery has been ordered by the sanctioning authority while the member is in service.]

(11) Where any ²[withdrawal] granted under this paragraph has been misused by the member, no further ²[withdrawal] shall be granted to him under this paragraph within a period of three years from

the date of grant of the said ²[withdrawal] or till the fund recovery of the amount of the said ²[withdrawal] with penal interest thereon, whichever is later.]

1.	Subs. by G.S.R. 549 (E), dated 3rd October, 1981 (w.e.f. 8-10-1981).
2.	Subs. by G.S.R. 954, dated 22nd August, 1984 (w.e.f. 8-9-1984).
3.	Omitted by G.S.R. 954, dated 22nd August, 1984 (w.e.f. 8-9-1984).
4.	Ins. by G.S.R. 421, dated 12th May, 1988 (w.e.f. 21-5-1988).
5.	Subs. by G.S.R. 81, dated 20th January, 1993 (w.e.f. 6-2-1993).
6.	Added by G.S.R. 449, dated 31st May 1983.
7.	Subs. by GSR 79 dated 25.2.2000.
8.	Clause (c) omitted by G.S.R. 81, dated 20th January, 1993 (w.e.f. 6-2-1993).
9.	Subs. by GSR 60 (E) dated 01.02.2013 (w.e.f. 01.02.2013).
10.	Omitted by G.S.R. 341, dated 9th July, 1992 (w.e.f. 25-7-1992).
11.	Added by G.S.R. 954, dated 22nd August, 1984 (w.e.f. 8-9-1984).
12.	Subs. by GSR 341 dated 9.7.1992 (w.e.f. 25.7.1992).
13.	Sub-paragraph (8) omitted by G.S.R. 79, dated 25th February, 2000 (w.e.f. 4-3-2000).
14.	Ins. by G.S.R. 832, dated 23rd October, 1987 (w.e.f. 7-11-1987).
15.	Added by G.S.R. 954, dated 22nd August, 1984 (w.e.f. 8-9-1984).
16.	*Explanation II* omitted by G.S.R. 954, dated 22nd August, 1984 (w.e.f. 8-9-1984).

¹[**68BB.** ²[**Withdrawal**] **from the Fund for repayment of loans in special cases.**– (1)(a) The Commissioner or, where so authorised by the Commissioner, any officer subordinate to him, may on an application from a member sanction from the amount standing to the credit of the member in the Fund, ²[withdrawal] for the repayment, wholly or partly, of any outstanding principal and interest of a loan ³[obtained in the name of the member or spouse of the member or jointly by the member and spouse from a State Government, registered Co-operative Society, State Housing Board, Nationalised Banks, Public Financial Institutions], Municipal Corporation or anybody similar to the Delhi Development Authority solely for the purposes specified in sub-paragraph (i) of paragraph 68B.

(b) The amount of ²[withdrawal] shall not exceed the member's basic wages and dearness allowance for ⁴[thirty-six months] or his own share of contributions together with the employer's share of contributions, with interest thereon, in the member's account in the Fund or the amount of outstanding principal and interest of the said loan, whichever is least.

(2) No ²[withdrawal] shall be sanctioned under this paragraph unless–

(a) the member has completed ⁵[ten] years' membership of the Fund; and

(b) the member's own share of contributions, with interest thereon, in the amount standing to his credit in the Fund, is one thousand rupees or more; and

(c) the member produces a certificate to such other documents, as may be prescribed by the Commissioner or where so authorised by the Commissioner, any officer subordinate to him, from such agency, indicating the particulars of the members, the loan granted, the outstanding principal and interest of the loan and such other particulars as may be required.

(3) The payment of the ²[withdrawal] under this paragraph shall be made direct to such agency on receipt of an authorisation from the member in such manner as may be specified by the Commissioner,

or where so authorised by the Commissioner, any officer subordinate to him, and in no event the payment shall be made to the member.]

1.	Ins. by G.S.R. 507(E), dated 29th September, 1981 (w.e.f. 5-9-1981).
2.	Subs. by G.S.R. 954, dated 22nd August, 1984 (w.e.f. 8-9-1984).
3.	Subs. by G.S.R. 79, dated 25th February, 2000 (w.e.f. 4-3-2000).
4.	Subs. by G.S.R. 667, dated 27th June, 1985 (w.e.f. 13-7-1985).
5.	Subs. by G.S.R. 221, dated 15th March, 1990 (w.e.f. 1-7-1990).

[1]**[68BC. Withdrawal/financing from the Fund for the purchase of a dwelling house/flat or the construction of a dwelling house including the acquisition of a suitable site by the member.-** (1) Notwithstanding anything contained in paragraph 68B or 68BB, where a member desires to purchase a dwelling house/flat, including a flat in a building owned jointly with others (outright or on hire purchase basis), or for construction of a dwelling house including the acquisition of a suitable site for the purpose, from the Central Government, a State Government, or a Housing Agency under a Housing Scheme as notified by the Central Provident Fund Commissioner from time to time, may apply in such form and in such manner, as may be prescribed by the Commissioner, for withdrawal from the amount standing to the credit of the member in the Fund, and the commissioner, or where So authorized by the Commissioner, any officer subordinate to him, on receipt of such application may sanction such amount not exceeding the members own share of contributions with interest thereon (and the employers share of contributions with interest thereon to his credit) or the cost of the acquisition of the proposed property whichever is less by debiting to the members account:

Provided that no withdrawal under this paragraph shall be granted unless–

(i) the member has completed five years membership of the Fund; and

(ii) the share of contributions with interest thereon in the amount standing to the credit in the Fund of the member/or together with the spouse who is also a member, is not less than twenty thousand rupees.

Provided further that the Commissioner may, on sufficient grounds being shown through an application from a member in this regard, reduce the period as stipulated in (i) above to three years for withdrawal from the amount standing to the credit of the member in the Fund, for the repayment, wholly or partly, of any outstanding principal and/or interest of a loan obtained in the name of the member or spouse of the member or jointly by the member and spouse from any Government or a Housing Agency under Housing Scheme so notified, solely for the purposes specified in this proviso and the commissioner, or where so authorized by the Commissioner, any officer subordinate to him, on receipt of such application may sanction such amount not exceeding the member's own share of contributions with interest thereon alongwith with the employers share of contributions with interest thereon, or the amount requested by the member or the outstanding balance in the loan account, whichever is less, by debiting to the members account.

Provided also that, where a member desires that monthly installments for the repayment, wholly or partly, of any outstanding principal and/or interest of a loan obtained in the name of the member or spouse of the member or jointly by the member and spouse, solely for the purposes specified in this proviso, may be paid from the amount standing to the credit of the member in the Fund, he may apply in such form and in such manner, as may be prescribed by the Commissioner and on receipt of such an application, the Commissioner or where so authorized by the Commissioner, any other officer subordinate to him may make payment by the 15th of each month on behalf of the member to the government or a Housing Agency concerned, as the case may be.

Provided also that when the membership of the member ceases to exist, or, where the amount standing in the credit of the member's account is not sufficient to pay the monthly installment for any month, the Commissioner or where so authorized by the Commissioner any other officer subordinate to him shall not be liable to pay the monthly installment or any late fee and/or interest, if any monthly installment could not be remitted in time.

(2) The withdrawal or finance for the purchase of a dwelling house/flat or a dwelling site or construction of a dwelling house, under sub-paragraph (1) and proviso thereunder, shall not be made to the member in any event and shall be made direct to the Government or Housing Agency concerned only, as the case may be, in one or more installments, as may be authorizd by the member.

(3) No further withdrawal under sub-paragraph (1) above shall be admissible to a member unless he has discharged his liability towards the existing loan.

(4) (a) If the withdrawal or finance granted under this paragraph exceeds the amount actually spent for the purpose for which it was sanctioned, the excess amount shall be refunded by the member to the Fund in one lump sum within thirty days of the finalisation of the purchase, or the completion of the construction of, or necessary additions or alternations to a dwelling house/flat, as the case may be.

(b) The amount so refunded under sub-paragraph (a) shall be credited to the employer's share of contributions in the members account in the Fund to the extent of withdrawal granted out of the said share and the balance, if any, shall be credited to the member's share of contributions in his account.

(c) In the event of the member not having been allotted a dwelling site/ dwelling house/flat or in the event of the cancellation of an allotment made to the member by the Government or the Housing Agency, referred to in sub-paragraph (1) above, then the Government or the said Housing Agency, to which the amount so withdrawn has been given shall be liable to refund the amount to the Fund in one lump sum in such manner as may be specified by the Commissioner, within a period not exceeding fifteen days from the date of such cancellation or non-allotment.

(d) The amount so refunded under clause (c) shall be credited to the employer's share of contributions in the members account in the Fund, to the extent of withdrawal granted out of the said share, and the balance, if any, shall be credited to members own share of contributions in his account.

(5) The Commissioner or where so authorized by the commissioner any officer subordinate to him has reason to believe that the amount remitted to the Housing Agency under the Housing Scheme under this paragraph has been misutilized and will not be refunded, he shall forthwith take steps to recover the amount due with interest including penal interest thereon at the rate to be notified by the Commissioner from time to time and the amount so recovered shall be credited to member's account in the Fund to the extent of withdrawal granted out of the said account and interest thereon and the remaining amount, if any shall be credited to Administrative Account.

(6) The Commissioner may notify such Housing Agency be debarred from participation in the Housing Scheme.]

---

1. Ins. by G.S.R. 783 (E), dated 3rd October, 2003 (w.e.f. 6-10-2003).

[1][**68E. Computation of period of membership.**– In computing the period of membership of the Fund of a member under paragraphs 68B, 68BB and 68K, his total service exclusive of periods of breaks under the same employer of factory/establishment before this scheme applied to him, as well as the periods, of his membership, whether of the Fund or of private provident fund of exempted factories/establishments or as an employee exempted under paragraph 27 or 27A, as the case may be, immediately preceding the current membership of the Find, shall be included:

Provided that the member has not severed his membership by withdrawal of his provident fund during such period.]

[2][**68-F. xxxx**]

[2][**68-G. xxxx**]

[3][**68-GG. xxx**]

1.	Subs. by G.S.R. 549 (E), dated 3rd October, 1981 (w.e.f. 3-10-1981).
2.	Deleted by G.S.R. 549 (E), dated 3rd October, 1981 (w.e.f. 3-10-1981).
3.	Deleted by GSR 221 dated 15.3.1990 (w.e.f. 01.01.1990).

[1][**68-H Grant of advances in special cases.**- [2][(1) In case a factory or other establishment has been locked up or closed down for more than fifteen days and its employees are rendered unemployed without any compensation or in case an employee does not receive his wages for a continuous period of two months or more, these being for reasons other than a strike, the Commissioner or where so authorised by the Commissioner, any officer subordinate to him may on an application from an employee, who is a member of the Fund, in such form as may be prescribed, authorise payment to him, of one or more non-recoverable advances from his provident fund account not exceeding from his own total contribution including interest thereon up to the date the payment has been authorised.]]

[3][(1-A) In case a provident fund member is discharged or dismissed or retrenched by the employer and such discharge or dismissal or retrenchment is challenged by the member and the cases are pending in a Court of Law, an officer not below the rank of Assistant Provident Fund Commissioner may on an application from the member in such form as may be prescribed, authorise payment to him of one or more non-recoverable advance from his Provident Fund Account not exceeding fifty percent of his own share of contribution with interest thereon standing to his credit in the fund on the date of such authorisation.]

[4][(2) [5][(a) In case the factory or other establishment continues to remain locked up or closed down for more than six months, the Commissioner, or where so authorised by the Commissioner any officer subordinate to him, on being satisfied that a member who has already been granted one or more non-recoverable advances from his provident fund account under sub-paragraph (1) still continues to be unemployed and no compensation is likely to be paid to him at an early date, may, on receipt of an application therefor in such form as may be prescribed in this behalf, authorise payment to the member of one or more recoverable advances from his provident fund account up to the extent of 100% of the employers' total contribution including interest thereon upto the date on which the payment has been authorized:]

[6][Provided that if the factory or establishment in which the member is employed remains closed for more than five years for reasons other than strike, recoverable advance may be converted into non-recoverable advance on receipt of a request in writing from the member concerned.]

(b) The advance granted under clause (a) shall be interest-free.

(c) The advance granted under clause (a) shall be recovered by deductions from the wages of the member in such instalments [7][subject to a maximum of thirty-six instalments] as may be determined by the Commissioner [2][or where so authorised by the Commissioner, any officer subordinate to him]. The recovery shall commence from the first wages paid to the member immediately after the re-start of the factory or establishment.

(d) The employer shall remit the amount so deducted to the Fund within such time and in such manner as may be specified by the Commissioner [2][or where so authorised by the Commissioner, any officer subordinate to him]. The amount on receipt, shall be credited to the member's account in the Fund.]

[8][*Explanation:* For the purpose of grant of advance under this paragraph, the establishment may be closed legally, illegally, with permission or without permission, so long as the establishment is closed.]

[9][68-I. xxx]

1.	Inserted by G.S.R. 1501 dated 6. 10. 1962.
2.	Subs. by G.S.R. 321, dated 04.4 1983 (w.e.f. 16.4.1983).
3.	Ins. by G.S.R. 421, dated 12th May, 1988 (w.e.f. 21-5-1988).
4.	Added by G.S.R. 1900, dated 16th October, 1968.
5.	Subs. by G.S.R. 221, dated 15.3.1990 (w.e.f. 01.01.1990).
6.	Added by G.S.R. 341, dated 9th July, 1992 (w.e.f. 25-7-1992).
7.	Subs. by G.S.R. 341, dated 9th July, 1992 (w.e.f. 25-7-1992).
8	Added by GSR 221, dated 15.3.1990 (w.e.f. 01.01.1990)
9.	Deled by G.S.R. 1103, dated 6.7.1976.

[1][**68J. Advance from the Fund for illness in certain cases.**–[2][(1) A member may be allowed non-refundable advance from his account in the Fund in cases of (a) hospitalisation lasting for one month or more or (b) major surgical operation in a hospital, or (c) suffering from T.B., leprosy, [2][paralysis, cancer, mental derangement or heart ailment] and having been granted leave by his employer for treatment of the said illness.

(2) [3][The advance shall be granted if–

(a) the employer certifies that the Employees' State Insurance Scheme facility and benefits there under are not actually available to the member or the member produces a certificate from the Employees' State Insurance Corporation to the effect that he has ceased to be eligible for cash benefits under the Employees' State Insurance Scheme; and

(b) a doctor of the hospital certifies that a surgical operation or, as the case may be, hospitalisation for one month or more had or has become necessary [4][or a registered medical practitioner, or in the case of a mental derangement or heart ailment, a specialist certifies that the member is suffering from T.B., leprosy, paralysis, cancer, mental derangement or heart ailment]:

[8][***]]

[3][(3) A member may be allowed non-refundable advance from his account in the Fund for the treatment of a member of his family who has been hospitalised, or requires hospitalisation, for one month or more–

(a) for a major surgical operation, or

(b) for the treatment of T.B., Leprosy, ²[paralysis, cancer, mental derangement or heart ailment]:

Provided that no such advance shall be granted to a member unless he has produced–

(i) a certificate from a doctor of the hospital that the patient has been hospitalised or requires hospitalisation for one month or more, or that a major surgical operation had or has become necessary, and

(ii) a certificate from his employer that the Employees' State Insurance Scheme facility and benefits are not available to him for the treatment of the patient.]

⁵[(4) The amount advanced under this paragraph shall not exceed the member's basic wages ⁴[and dearness allowance] for ⁶[six] months or his own share of contribution with interest in the Fund, whichever is less.]

⁷[(5). ***]

(6) Where the Commissioner ³[or, where so authorised by the Commissioner any officer subordinate to him] is nof satisfied with a medical certificate furnished by the member under this paragraph, he may, before granting an advance under this paragraph, demand from the member another medical certificate to this satisfaction.]

1. Added by G.S.R. 126, dated 16th January, 1964.
2. Subs. by G.S.R. 496 (E), dated 27th August, 1981 (w.e.f. 27-8-1981).
3. Subs. by G.S.R. 48, dated 23rd December, 1968.
4. Ins. by G.S.R. 496 (E), dated 27th August, 1981 (w.e.f. 27-8-1981).
5. Proviso omitted by G.S.R. 1858, dated 30th November, 1968.
6. Subs. by G.S.R. 81, dated 20th January, 1993 (w.e.f. 6-2-1993).
7. Sub-paragraph (5) omitted by G.S.R. 496 (E), dated 27th August, 1981 (w.e.f. 27-8-1981). Earlier sub-paragraph (5) was inserted by G.S.R. 48(E), dated 23rd December, 1968.
8. Proviso removed by GSR 1858 dated 30.11.1966.

¹[68K. ²[**Advance from the Fund for marriages or post-matriculation education of children**].–
³[(1) The Commissioner or where so authorised by the Commissioner, an officer subordinate to him may on an application from a member, authorise payment to him or her of a non-refundable advance from his or her provident fund account not exceeding fifty per cent of his or her own share of contribution with interest thereon, standing to his or her credit in the Fund, on the date of such authorisation, for his or her own marriage, the marriage of his or her daughter, son, sister or brother or for the post-matriculation education of his or her son or daughter.]

⁴[(2) No advance under this paragraph shall be sanctioned to a member unless–

(a) he has completed seven year's membership of the Fund; and

(b) the amount of ³[his own share of contributions] with interest thereon standing to his credit in the Fund is rupees one thousand or more.]

(3) ⁵[Not more than ⁶[three] advances] shall be admissible to a member under this paragraph.]
⁷[***]

1. Ins. by G.S.R. 1922, dated 21st July, 1969.
2. Subs. by G.S.R. 1457, dated 16th November, 1978 (w.e.f. 2-12-1978).

3.	Subs. by G.S.R. 496 (E), dated 27th August, 1981 (w.e.f. 27-8-1981).
4.	Subs. by G.S.R. 1103, dated 6th July, 1976.
5.	Subs. by G.S.R. 1095, dated 27th September, 1974.
6.	Subs. by G.S.R. 449, dated 31st May, 1983 (w.e.f. 18-6-1983).
7.	Sub-paragraph (4) omitted by G.S.R. 832, dated 23rd October, 1987 (w.e.f. 7-11-1988). Earlier sub-paragraph (4) was substituted by G.S.R. 496(E), dated 27th August, 1981 (w.e.f. 27-8-1981).

68L. [1][**68L. Grant of advances in abnormal conditions.**– (1) The Commissioner [2][or where so authorised by the Commissioner, any officer subordinate to him] may on an application from a member whose property, movable or immovable, has been damaged by a calamity of exceptional nature, such as floods, earthquakes or riots, authorise payment to him from the provident fund account, a non-refundable advance, of [3][rupees five thousand] or fifty per cent of his own total contribution including interest thereon standing to his credit on the date of such authorisation, whichever is less to meet any unforeseen expenditure:

[4][***]

[5][(2) No advance under sub-paragraph (1) shall be paid unless–

(i) the State Government has declared that the calamity has affected the general public in the area: [7][xxx]

(ii) the member produces a certificate from an appropriate authority to the effect that his property (movable or immovable) has been damaged as a result of the calamity;]

[6][(iii) the application for advance is made within a period of 4 months from the date of declaration referred to in sub-para (i)].]

1.	Ins. by G.S.R. 2686, dated 20th November, 1969.
2.	Ins. by G.S.R. 496 (E), dated 27th August, 1981 (w.e.f. 27-8-1981).
3.	Subs. by G.S.R. 343, dated 8th May, 1991 (w.e.f. 1-4-1991).
4.	Proviso omitted by G.S.R. 1103, dated 6th July, 1976.
5.	Subs. by G.S.R. 1103, dated 6th July, 1976.
6.	Ins. by G.S.R. 1118, dated 21st August, 1979 (w.e.f. 1-9-1979).
7.	Word 'and' deleted by G.S.R. 1118, dated 21st August, 1979 (w.e.f. 1-9-1979).

[1][**68M. Grant of advance to members affected by cut in the supply of electricity.**– A member may be allowed a non-refundable advance from his account in the Fund, if there is a cut in the supply of electricity to a factory or establishment in which he is employed on the following conditions, namely:–

[2][(a) The advance may be granted only to a member whose total wages for any one month commencing from the month of January, 1973 were three-fourths or less than three-fourths of wages for a month.]

(b) The advance shall be restricted to the amount of wages for a month or [3][Rs. 300] or the amount standing to the credit of the member in the fund as his own share of contribution with interest thereon, whichever is less.

(c) No advance shall be paid unless the State Government certify that the cut in the supply of electricity was enforced in the area in which the factory or establishment is located and the employer certifies that the fall in the member's pay was due to cut in the supply of electricity.

(d) Only one advance shall be admissible under this paragraph.

Explanation.- 'Wages' means, for the purpose of this paragraph, basic wages and dearness allowance excluding lay-off compensation, if any.]

1.	Ins. by G.S.R. 552, dated 10th May, 1973 (w.e.f. 26-5-1973).
2.	Subs. by G.S.R. 1117, dated 21st September, 1973 (w.e.f. 22-9-1973).
3.	Subs. by G.S.R. 871, dated 7th July, 1975.

[1][**68N. Grant of advance to members who are physically handicapped.**– (1) A member, who is physically handicapped, may be allowed a non-refundable advance from his account in the Fund, for purchasing an equipment required to minimise the hardship on account of handicap.

(2) No advance under sub-paragraph (1) shall be paid unless the member produces a medical certificate from a competent medical practitioner to the satisfaction of the Commissioner or such other officer as may be authorised by him in this behalf to the effect that he is physically handicapped.

(3) The amount advanced under this paragraph shall not exceed the member's basic wages and dearness allowance for six months or his own share of contributions with interest thereon or the cost of the equipment, whichever is the least.

(4) No second advance under this paragraph shall be allowed within a period of three years from the date of payment of an advance allowed under this paragraph.]

1.	Ins. by G.S.R. 625 (E), dated 30th November, 1981 (w.e.f. 1-12-1981).

[1][**68NN. Withdrawal within one year before the retirement.**–The Commissioner, or, where so authorised by the Commissioner, any officer subordinate to him, may, on an application from a member in such form as may be prescribed, permit withdrawal of upto 90% of the amount standing at his credit, at any time after attainment of the age of [2][57 years] by the member or within one year before his actual retirement, or superannuation whichever is later.]

1.	Inserted by GSR 283 (E) dated 2.2.1996 (W.e.f. 6.7.1996).
2.	Substituted by G.S.R. 158 (E) dated 10.02.2016 (w.e.f. 10.02.2016).

[1][**68NNN. Option for withdrawal at the age of 55 years for investment in Varishtha Pension Bima Yojana.**–The Commissioner, or where so authorised by the Commissioner, any officer subordinate to him, may, on an application from a member in such form as may be prescribed, permit withdrawal of upto 90 per cent of the amount standing at his credit, at any time after attaining the age of 55 years by the member, to be transferred to the Life Insurance Corporation of India for investment in Varishtha Pension Bima Yojana.]

1.	Ins. by S.O. 304 (E), dated 4th March, 2004 (w.e.f. 4-3-2004).

[1][**68NNNN. Option for withdrawal on cessation of employment**- (1) The Central Board, o where so authorized by the Central Board, the Commissioner, or any officer subordinate to him, may, on an application made by a member in such form as may be specified, authorize payment to him from his provident fund account not exceeding his own total contribution including interest thereon up to the date the payment has been authorized on ceasing to be an employees in any establishment to which the Act applies.

(2) The member making an application for withdrawl under sub-paragraph (1) shall not be employed in any factory or other establishment, to which the Act applies, for a continuous period of not less than two months immediately preceding the date on which such application is made:

Provided that the requirement of two months' period referred to in sub-paragraph (2) shall not apply in cases of female members resigning from the services of the establishments for the purpose of getting married or on account of pregnancy or child birth.]

1.	Ins. by G.S.R 158 (E), dated 10th February, 2016 (w.e.f. 10.02.2016).

¹[**68-O. Payment of withdrawal or advance.**–The payment of withdrawal or advance under paragraphs 68B, ²[***] 68H, 68J, 68K, 68L, 68M ³[68-N, 68-NN, 68-NNN and 68-NNNN] of the Scheme may be made, at the option of the member–

(i) by postal money order, or

(ii) by deposit in the payee's bank account in any Scheduled Bank or in Co-operative Bank (including the Urban Co-operative Bank) or any post office, or

(iii) through the employer.]

1.	Ins. by G.S.R. 832, dated 23rd October, 1987 (w.e.f. 7-11-1987).
2.	Omitted by G.S.R. 690 (E), dated 30th June, 1989 (w.e.f. 1-7-1989).
3.	Subs. by G.S.R. 158 (E), dated 10th February, 2016 (w.e.f. 10-02-2016).

¹[**69. Circumstances in which accumulations in the Fund are payable to a member.** – (1) A member may withdraw the full amount standing to his credit in the Fund–

(a) on retirement from service after attaining the age of ¹⁷[58 years]:

²[Provided that a member, who has not attained the age of ¹⁷[58 years] at the time of termination of his service, shall also be entitled to withdraw the full amount standing to his credit in the Fund if he attains the age of ¹⁷[58 years] before the payment is authorised;]

³[(b) on retirement on account of permanent and total incapacity for work due to bodily or mental infirmity duly certified by the medical officer of the establishment or where an establishment has no regular medical officer, by a registered medical practitioner designated by the establishment;]

(c) immediately before migration from India for permanent settlement abroad ⁴[or for taking employment abroad];

⁵[(d) on termination of service in the case of mass or individual retrenchment:

⁶[* * *]]

⁷[(dd) on termination of service under a voluntary scheme of retirement framed by the employer and the employees under a mutual agreement specifying, *inter alia*, that notwithstanding the provisions contained in sub-clause (a) of clause (oo) of section 2 of the Industrial Disputes Act, 1947, excluding voluntary retirement from the scope of definition of "retrenchment" such voluntary retirements shall for the purpose be treated as retrenchments by mutual consent of the parties;]

¹²[(e) ****]

Suppliments

[9][(f) * * *]

[10][(1A) For the purpose of clause (b) of sub-paragraph (1)–

(i) where an establishment has been closed, the certificate of any registered medical practitioner may be accepted;

(ii) where there is no medical officer in the establishment, the employer shall designate a registered medical practitioner stationed in the vicinity of the establishment; or

(iii) where the establishment is covered by the Employees' State Insurance Scheme, medical certificate from a medical officer of the Employees' State Insurance Dispensary with which or from the Insurance Medical Practitioner with whom, the employee is registered under that Scheme, shall be produced:

Provided that where by mutual agreement of employers and employees, a Medical Board exists for any establishment or a group of establishments, certificate issued by such Medical Board may also be accepted for the purpose of this paragraph:

Provided further that it shall be open to the Regional Commissioner to demand from the member a fresh certificate from a Civil Surgeon or any doctor acting on his behalf where the original certificate produced by him gives rise to suspicion regarding its genuineness:

Provided further the entire fee of the Civil Surgeon or any doctor acting in his behalf shall be paid from the Fund in case the findings of the Civil Surgeon or any doctor acting on his behalf agree with the original certificate and that where such findings do not agree with the original certificate, only half of the fee shall be paid from the Fund and the remaining half shall be debited to the member's account;

(iv) A member suffering from tuberculosis or leprosy [11][or cancer even if contracted after leaving the service of an establishment on grounds of illness but before payment has been authorised, shall be deemed to have been permanently and totally incapacitated for work.]

[12][(2) ****]

[13][(3) ***]

[14][(4) ***]

[12][(5) ****]

[16][(6) ***]

---

1. Subs. by S.R.O. 2706, dated 17th August, 1957 (w.e.f. 24-8-1957).
2. Added by G.S.R 1044, dated 23rd October, 1958 (w.e.f. 1-11-1958).
3. Subs. by G.S.R. 350, dated 26th February, 1966.
4. Ins. by G.S.R. 832, dated 23rd October, 1987 (w.e.f. 7-11-1987).
5. Added by G.S.R. 1501, dated 6th November, 1962.
6. Proviso omitted by G.S.R. 1184, dated 16th October, 1974 (w.e.f. 2-11-1974).
7. Added by G.S.R. 63, dated 9th January, 1973.
8. Subs. by G.S.R. 496 (E), dated 27th August, 1981 (w.e.f. 27-8-1981).
9. Clause (f) omitted by GSR 341, dated 18th March, 1974.
10. Ins. by G.S.R. 350, dated 26th February, 1966.
11. Ins. by G.S.R. 1457, dated 16th November, 1978 (w.e.f. 2-12-1978).
12. Omitted by G.S.R. 158 (E), dated 10th February, 2016 (w.e.f. 10.02.2016).
13. Sub-paragraph (3) omitted by G.S.R. 221, dated 15th March, 1990 (w.e.f. 1-1-1990).

14.	Sub-paragraph (4) omitted by G.S.R. 1501, dated 6th November, 1962.
15.	*********
16.	Sub-paragraph (6) and *Explanation* omitted by G.S.R. 221, dated 15th March, 1990 (w.e.f. 7-4-1990).
17.	Subs. by G.S.R. 158 (E), dated 10th February, 2016 (w.e.f. 10.02.2016).

70. Accumulations of a deceased member–to whom payable.–On the death of a member before the amount standing to his credit has become payable, or where the amount has become payable before payment has been made–

(i) if a nomination made by the member in accordance with paragraph 61 subsists, the amount standing to his credit in the Fund or that part thereof to which the nomination relates, shall become payable to his nominee or nominees in accordance with such nomination; or

(ii) if no nomination subsists or if the nomination relates only to a part of the amount standing to his credit in the Fund, the whole amount or the part thereof to which the nomination does not relate, as the case may be, shall become payable to the members of his family in equal shares:

Provided that no share shall be payable to–

(a) sons who have attained majority;

(b) sons of a deceased son who has attained majority;

(c) married daughters whose husbands are alive;

(d) married daughters of a deceased son whose husbands are alive; if there is any member of the family other than those specified in clauses (a), (b), (c) and (d):

Provided further that the widow or widows, and the child or children of a deceased son shall receive between them in equal parts only the share which that son would have received if he had survived the member and had not attained the age of majority at the time of the member's death.

(iii) In any case to which the provisions of clauses (i) and (ii) do not apply the whole amount shall be payable to the person legally entitled to it.

Explanation.–For the purpose of this paragraph a member's posthumous child, if born alive, shall be treated in the same way as a surviving child born before the member's death.

[1][**70A. Payment of provident fund accumulations in the case of a person charged with the offence of murder.**– (1) If a person, who in the event of the death of a member of the fund is eligible to receive provident fund accumulations of the deceased member under paragraph 70, is charged with the offence of murdering the member or abetting in the commission of such an offence, his claim to receive the share of provident fund shall remain suspended till the conclusion of the criminal proceedings initiated against him for such offence.

(2) If on the conclusion of the criminal proceedings referred to in sub-paragraph (1), the person concerned is,–

(a) convicted for the murder of the member or abetting the murder of the member, he shall be debarred from receiving the share of provident fund accumulations which shall be payable to other eligible members, if any, of the deceased members; or

(b) acquitted of the murdering or abetting the murder of the member, his share of provident fund shall be payable to him.]

²[71. Xxx]

1. Ins. by G.S.R 341, dated 9th July, 1992 (w.e.f. 25-7-1992).
2. Deleted by GSR 707 dated 4.5.1976.

72. Payment of Provident Fund.–(1) When the amount standing to the credit of a member ¹[***] becomes payable, it shall be the duty of the Commissioner to make prompt payment as provided in this Scheme, ²[***]. In case there is no nominee in accordance with this Scheme ³[or there is no person entitled to receive such amount under sub-paragraph (ii) of paragraph 70], the Commissioner may, if the amount to the credit of the Fund does not exceed ⁴[Rs. 10,000] and if satisfied after enquiry about the title of the claimant, pay such amount to the claimant.

(2) If any portion of the amount, which has become payable, is in dispute or doubt, the Commissioner shall make prompt payment of that portion of the amount in regard to which there is no dispute or doubt, the balance being adjusted as soon as may be possible.

⁵[(3) If the person to whom any amount is to be paid under this Scheme is a minor for whose estate a guardian under the Guardians and Wards Act, 1890 (8 of 1890) has been appointed, the payment shall be made to such guardian. Where no guardian under the Guardians and Wards Act, 1890 (8 of 1890) has been appointed, the payment shall be made to the guardian, if any, appointed under the sub-paragraph (4A) of paragraph 61. Where no guardian under the Guardians and Wards Act, 1890 (8 of 1890) or under sub-paragraph 61 has been appointed, the payment shall be made to the natural guardian and in the absence of a natural guardian, to such person as the Commissioner ⁴[where the amount does not exceed ⁶[Rs. 20,000] or the Chairman of the Central Board, if the amount exceeds ⁶[Rs. 20,000], considers to be the proper person representing the minor and the receipt of such person for the amount paid shall be a sufficient discharge thereof ⁷[***].

(3A) If the person to whom any amount is to be paid under this Scheme is a lunatic for whose estate a manager under the Indian Lunacy Act, 1912 (4 of 1912), has been appointed, the payment shall be made to such manager. If no such manager has been appointed, the payment shall be made to the natural guardian of the lunatic and in the absence of any such natural guardian, to such person as the Commissioner ⁹[where the amount does not exceed ⁸[Rs. 20,000] or the Chairman of the Central Board, if the amount exceeds ⁸[Rs. 20,000], considers to be the proper person representing the lunatic and the receipt of such person for the amount paid shall be a sufficient discharge thereof ¹⁰[***].]

(4) If it is brought to the notice of the Commissioner that a posthumous child is to be born to the deceased member he shall retain the amount which will be due to the child in the event of its being born alive, and distribute the balance. If subsequently no child is born or the child is still born, the amount retained shall be distributed in accordance with the provisions of the paragraph 70.

¹¹[(5)(a) Every employer shall, at the time when a member of the Fund leaves the service, be required to get the claim application, for payment of provident fvmd in cases specified in clauses (a) to (dd) of sub-paragraph (1) ¹²[***] of paragraph 69, duly filled in and attested and to forward the said application ¹³[within five days of its receipt] to the Commissioner or any other officer authorised by him in this behalf.

(b) Every employer shall, at the time when a member of the Fund leaves the service, be required to get the claim application, for payment of provident fund in cases specified in clause (e) of sub-paragraph (1), and in ¹²[***] sub-paragraph (2) of paragraph 69, duly filled in and attested, and to give the said application to the member, for submission, on completion of the period specified in [12][***] sub-paragraph (2) of paragraph 69, [14][provided the member continues to remain unemployed in a factory or other establishment to which the Act applies], either through post or in person with proper identification, to the Commissioner or any other officer authorised by him in this behalf.

(c) Every employer shall, on the death of the member and on receipt of an application for receiving the amount standing to the credit of such member, forward forthwith, [6][but not later than five days of its receipt,] the said application to the Commissioner or any other officer authorised by him in this behalf.

(d) If the applicant is unable to send the claim application through the employer or duly attested by him, for any reason whatsoever, he may forward it to the Commissioner or any other officer authorised by him in this behalf and wherever necessary, the Commissioner or any other officer authorised by him in this behalf, may forward such application to the employer and the employer shall be required to return it within five days of its receipt.

[15][(e) The payment may be made, in the option of the person to whom payment is to be made, (i) by postal money order, or (ii) by deposit in the payee's bank account in any Scheduled Bank or any Co-operative Bank including the Urban Co-operative Banks or any post office, or (iii) by deposit in the payee's name the whole or part of the amount in the form of annuity term deposits scheme in any Nationalised Bank, or (iv) through the employer:]

[16][Provided that the Provident Fund amount payable by postal money order shall be to the extent of maximum Rs. 2000. Any payment of benefit above Rs. 2000 under the scheme shall be remitted through cheque only. Where the amount payable by postal money order exceeds Rs. 500 it shall be remitted at the cost of the payee.]

[20][(f) Every employer shall, at the time when an employee joins the service, be required to get the application for transfer of provident fund in cases specified in sub-paragraph (1) and (2) of paragraph 57, duly filled in and attested, and to forward the said applicaton within five days of its receipt to the Commissioner or any other officer authorized by him in this behalf.]

[23][Provided that notwithstanding anything contained in this sub-paragraph, the Central Provident Fund commissioner may permit a member to submit his claim, in such form and manner, and on such terms and conditions as may be specified by him in this regard, directly to the Commissioner.]

[17][(6) Any amount becoming due to a member as a result of (i) supplementary contribution from the employer in respect of leave wages, arrears of pay, instalment of arrear contribution received in respect of a member whose claim has been settled on account but which could not be remitted for want of latest address, or (ii) accumulation in respect of any member who has either ceased to be employed or died, [21][but no application for withdrawal under paragraph 69 or 70 or transfer as the case may be, has been preferred] within a period of [22][thirty six months] from the date it becomes payable, or if any amount remitted to a person is received back undelivered, and it is not claimed again within a period of three years from the date it becomes payable shall be transferred to an account to be called the [18][Inoperative Account]:

Provided that in the case of a claim for the payment of the said balance, the amount shall be paid by debiting the [18][Inoperative Account].]

Suppliments

[19][(7) The claims, complete in all respects submitted along with the requisite documents shall be settled and benefit amount paid to the beneficiaries within 30 days from the date of its receipt by the Commissioner. If there is any deficiency in the claim, the same shall be recorded in writing and communicated to the applicant within 30 days from the date of receipt of such application. In case the Commissioner fails without sufficient cause to settle a claim complete in all respects within 30 days, the Commissioner shall be liable for the delay beyond the said period and penal interest at the rate of 12% per annum may be charged on the benefit amount and the same may be deducted from the salary of the Commissioner.]

1.	Omitted by G.S.R. 221, dated 15th March, 1990 (w.e.f. 1-1-1990).
2.	Omitted by G.S.R. 1415, dated 24th September, 1964.
3.	Ins. by G.S.R. 473, dated 14th March, 1977 (w.e.f. 2-4-1977).
4.	Subs. by G.S.R. 473, dated 14th March, 1977 (w.e.f. 2-4-1977).
5.	Subs. by G.S.R. 1707, dated 17th November, 1965.
6.	Subs. by G.S.R. 832, dated 23rd October, 1987 (w.e.f. 17-11-1987).
7.	Omitted by G.S.R. 473, dated 14th March, 1977 (w.e.f. 2-4-1977).
8.	Subs. by G.S.R. 832, dated 23rd October, 1987 (w.e.f. 17-11-1987).
9.	Subs. by G.S.R. 473, dated 14th March, 1977 (w.e.f. 2-4-1977).
10.	Omitted by G.S.R. 473, dated 14th March, 1977 (w.e.f. 2-4-1977).
11.	Subs. by G.S.R. 141, dated 28th January, 1982 (w.e.f. 6-2-1982).
12.	Omitted by G.S.R. 221, dated 15th March, 1990 (w.e.f. 1-1-1990).
13.	Ins. by G.S.R. 521, dated 16th August, 1991 (w.e.f. 1-9-1991).
14.	Subs. by G.S.R. 421, dated 12th May, 1988 (w.e.f. 21-5-1988).
15.	Subs. by G.S.R. 188, dated 2nd February, 1985 (w.e.f. 16-2-1985).
16.	Subs. by G.S.R. 79, dated 25th February, 2000, for the proviso (w.e.f. 4-3-2000). Earlier the proviso was added by G.S.R. 449, dated 31st April, 1983 (w.e.f. 13-6-1983).
17.	Ins. by G.S.R. 1415, dated 24th September, 1964.
18.	Subs. by G.S.R. 228(E), dated 22nd March, 2007, for "Unclaimed Deposits Account" (w.e.f. 22-3-2007).
19.	Ins. by Notification No. H-11016/24/97-SS.II, dated 26th August, 1997.
20.	Inserted ny GSR 336 dated 4.5. 2012 (w.e.f. 4.5. 2012).
21	Subs. by GSR 25 (E) dated 15.1.2011 (W.e.f. 01.4.2011).
22.	Subs. by GSR 25 (E) dated 15.1.2011 for the words 'three years' (W.e.f. 01.4.2011).
23.	Ins. By G.S.R. 25 (E) dated 14th January, 2016 (w.e.f. 14.01.2016).

73. Annual statement of member's account.–(1) As soon as possible after the close of each period of currency of contribution card the Commissioner shall send to each member through the employer of the [1][factory or other establishment] in which he was last employed a statement of his account in the Fund showing the opening balance at the beginning of the period, amount contributed during the year, the total amount of interest credited at the end of the period or debited in the period and the closing balance at the end of the period.

(2) Members should satisfy themselves as to the correctness of the annual statement and any error should be brought to the notice of the Commissioner within six months of the receipt of the statement.

1.	Subs. by S.R.O. 1363, dated 26th April, 1957.

CHAPTER – IX
MISCELLANEOUS

[1][73A. Xxxx]

[2][**74. Annual report on the work and activities of the Board and its audited accounts.**–(1) The annual report on the work and activities of the Central Board and its audited accounts together with the report of Comptroller and Auditor-General of India shall be considered by the Executive Committee and shall be placed for adoption at a meeting of the Board to be held before the tenth of December following the close of the financial year concerned:

Provided that if the report of the Comptroller and Auditor-General is not received by the First of December following the close of the financial year to which it pertains, the audited accounts together with report of the Comptroller and Auditor-General may be placed before the Executive Committee/Board.

(2) The annual report on the work and activities of the Board and the audited accounts of the Board together with the report of the Comptroller and Auditor-General of India, as adopted by the Board, shall be authenticated by affixing the common seal of the Board and four copies thereof together with the comments of the Board on the report of the Comptroller and Auditor-General shall be submitted to the Central Government not later than twentieth of December following the close of the financial year concerned for being placed before Parliament:

Provided that if the report of the Comptroller and Auditor-General is not received by the First of December following the close of the financial year to which it pertains, the audited accounts together with the report of the Comptroller and Auditor-General and the comments of the Board thereon shall be submitted to the Central Government separately from the annual report on the work and activities of the Board.]

1.	Added by GSR 1467 dated 02.12.1960 and deleted by GSR 725 dated 16.4.1963.
2.	Subs. by G.S.R. 54, dated 12th January, 1990 (w.e.f. 27-1-1990).

75. Issue of copies of Member's Accounts, Annual Reports etc.–The Commissioner shall furnish copies of the member's account and of the annual reports of the Fund to employer or member on written application and on payment of such fees and subject to such conditions as may be specified by the [1][Central Board] in this behalf.

1.	Added by G.S.R. 1845, dated 28-11-1963 for "Board."

76. Punishment for failure to pay contribution, etc.–If any person–

[1][(a) xxxx]

[2][(a)] deducts or attempts to deduct from the wages or other remuneration of a member the whole or any part of the employer's contribution, or

[2][(b)] fails or refuses to submit any return, statement or other document required by this Scheme or submits a false return, statement or other document, or makes a false declaration, or

[2][(c)] obstructs any Inspector or other official appointed under the Act or this Scheme in the discharge of his duties or fails to produce any record for inspection by such Inspector or other official, or

²[(d)] is guilty of contravention of or non-compliance with any other requirement of this Scheme. he shall be punishable with imprisonment which may extend to ³[one year, or with fine which may extend to four thousand rupees] or with both.

1. Original clause (a) remove by GSR 305 dated 11.3. 1974.
2. Clauses re-numbered by GDR 305 dated 11.3.1974.
3. Subs. by GSR 690 (E) dated 30.6.1989 (w.e.f. 01.7.1989).

77- Conduct of business of the ¹[Central Board]- (1) All orders and other instruments shall be made and executed in the name of the ¹[Central Board] and shall be authenticated by such person and in such manner as the ¹[Central Board] may specify.

(2) All contracts and assurances of property shall be expressed to be made by the ¹[Central Board] and shall be executed on behalf of the ¹[Central Board] by the Commissioner.

1. Subs. by GSR 1845 dated 28.11.1963.

Para 78: Power to issue directions. – (1) The Central Government may, from time to time, issue such directions to State Governments, the Central Board or any other authority, under this Act or Scheme as it may consider necessary for the proper implementation of this Scheme or for the purpose of removing any difficulty which may arise in the administration thereof including difficulties in the matter of payment of accumulations in the Fund to members after they cease to be such members.

¹[* * *]

(3)The authority to whom any directions are issued under this paragraph shall comply with such directions.

1. Sub-paragraph (2) Omitted by G.S.R. 1845, dated the 28.11.1963.

¹[**79:- Special provisions relating to factories and other establishments in respect of which applications for exemption are received** – Notwithstanding anything contained in this Scheme, the Commissioner may, in relation to a ²[factory or other establishment] in respect of which an application for exemption under section 17 of the Act has been received, ³[xxx] relax pending the disposal of the application the provisions of the Scheme in such manner as he may direct.]

1. Added by SRO 1858 dated 8.11.1952.
2. Subs. by SRO 1363 dated 26.4. 1957.
3. The words "on 31ˢᵗ October, 1952 or prior" deleted by SRO 2057 dated 3.9.1956.

¹[**79A. Filing application for review.** – Any person aggrieved by an order made under sub-section (1) of section 7A and who desires to obtain a review of such order may apply for a review of that order, as provided in sub-section (1) of section 7B of the Act in Form 9 to the officer who passed such order:

Provided that no application for review of an order will be entertained by the concerned officer, unless the application for review is submitted within 45 days from the date of making such order.]

1. Added by GSR 690 (E) dated 30.6.1989 (w.e.f. 01.7.1990).

[1]**[79B:- Time limit for communicating the views of the Central Board to the appropriate government on a proposal for grant of exemption to an establishment-** When an appropriate Government consults the Central Board with regard to its proposal for grant of exemption to an establishment under section 17 of the Act, the Board shall give its views on the proposal within a period of three months from the date on which such proposal is received by it.]

> 1. Added by GSR 521 dated 16.8.1991 (w.e.f. 01.9.1991).

[1]**[Para-79C:- Composition of the Board of Trustees of the exempted establishments and the terms and conditions of service of the trustees** -(1) The Board of Trustees of the establishment granted exemption under clause (a) of sub-section (2) of section 17 of the Act shall consist of not less than two and not more than six representatives each of the employers and emplpoyees. The number of trustees shall be so fixed, as to afford, as far as possible, representation to employees of each branch or department of the establishment. In the case of common provident fund for a group of two or more establishments, there will be at least one representative each from the participating establishment:

[2][xxx]

(2) The employer shall nominate his representatives on the Board of Trustees from amongst the officers employed in managerial or administrative capacity in the establishment.

(3) The representatives of the employees, on the Board of Trustees shall be nominated or elected in the following manner, namely:

(a) Wherever there is a union recognized by the employer under the Code of Discipline in industry or under any Act, such union shall nominate the representatives of the employees;

(b) where there are more than on trade union recognized by the employer, the representatives of employees shall be elected by the members of the union in an election to be held for the purpose on any working day;

(c) where there is no union recognized by the employer under the Code of Discipline in industry or under any Act but there are more than one registered union functioning in the establishment, the union having the largest number of members, subject to a minimum of 15 percent membership, shall have the right to nominate employees' representatives; and in case there is only one registered union, it shall have the right to nominate the employees' representative, provided it has a minimum of 15 percent membership.

[3][(4) The employer shall be the Chairman of the Board of Trustees. In the event of equality of votes, the Chairman may exercise a casting vote.]

[4][(5) The term of office of the trustees shall be five years from the date of election or nomination. An outgoing Trustee shall be eligible for re-election or re-nomination. A Trustee elected or nominated to fill the casual vacancy shall hold office for the remaining period of the term of the trustee in whose place he is elected or nominated.]

(6) A person shall be disqualified form being a trustee if he:-

(a) is declared to be of unsound mind by a competent court; or

(b) has been convicted of an offence involving moral turpitude; or

(c) is an undischarged insolvent; or

(d) is an employer of an exempted or un-exempted establishment which has defaulted in payment of any dues under the Act.

(7) A person shall cease to be a Trustee of the Board if:-

(a) he ceases to be an employee of the establishment; or

(b) he cease to be a member of the provident fund of the establishment; or

(c) the union on whose behalf he was elected or nominated, ceases to be recognized by the employer; or

(d) he fails to attend three consecutive meetings of the Board without obtaining leave of absence from the Chairman of the Board of Trustees. The Chairman may, however, condone the absence of a trustee if he is satisfied that there were reasonable grounds for such absence.

(8) The procedure foe election or nomination of trustees, the quorum at the meeting of the board, records to be kept of the transaction of business and all other matters not specifically provided for in the Scheme shall be regulated as per the for of the functioning of the Board of Trustees of the exempted establishments which the Commissioner may specify from time to time.

(9) In case of any dispute or doubt, the matter shall be referred to the Regional Provident Fund Commissioner in whose jurisdiction the head office of the establishment is located. The decision of the Commissioner in the matter shall be final and binding.]

1.	Inserted vide GSR 341 dated 9.7.1992 (w.e.f. 25.7.1992).
2.	Provisio deleted vide GSR 658 (E) dated 10.11.2005 (w.e.f. 10.11.2005).
3.	Substituted vide GSR 868 (E) dated 3.11.2003 (w.e.f. 6.11.2003).
4.	Substituted vide GSR 18 dated 22.12.2000 (w.e.f. 6.1.2001)

CHAPTER - X

[Special provisions]*

¹[80. Special provisions in the case of newspaper establishments and newspaper employees.- The Scheme shall, in its application to newspaper establishments and newspaper employees, as defined in section 2 of the Working Journalists (Conditions of Service) and Miscellaneous Provisions Act, 1955, come into force on the 31st day of December, 1956 and be subject to the modifications mentioned below:

(1) In Chapters I to IX, references to 'industry,' 'factories' and 'employees' shall be construed as references to 'newspaper industry,' newspaper establishments' and newspaper employees,' respectively:

(2) For paragraph 2(f), the following shall be substituted, namely:-

(f) 'excluded employee' means,-

²[(i) an employee who, having been a member of the Fund, has withdrawn the full amount of his accumulations in the Fund under clause (a) or (c) of sub-paragraph (1) of paragraph 69;]

(ii) an apprentice. ³[****]

Explanation.-'Apprentice' ³[****] means a person who, according to the standing orders applicable to the newspaper establishment concerned, is an apprentice or who is declared to be an apprentice by the authority specified in this behalf by the appropriate Government.

(3) For paragraph 26 the following shall be substituted, namely:-

26. *Class of employees entitled and required to join the Fund.*- (1)(a) Every newspaper employee employed to do any work in, or in relation to, any newspaper establishment to which this Scheme applies, other than an excluded employee, shall be entitled and required to become a member of the Fund from the beginning of the months following that in which this paragraph comes into force in such establishment, if on the date of such coming into force he has completed ⁴[three months' continuous service] or has actually worked for not less than ⁴[60 days during a period of three months or less] in that newspaper establishment or in another such establishment ⁵[to which the Act applies] under the same employer or partly in one and partly in the other ⁶[or has been declared permanent in any such newspaper establishment, whichever is the earliest].

(b) Every newspaper employee employed to do any work, in or in relation to, any newspaper establishment to which this Scheme applies other than an excluded employee, shall be entitled and required to become a member of the Fund from the beginning of the month following that in which this paragraph comes into force in such newspaper establishment if on the date of such coming into force such employee is a subscriber to a provident fund maintained in respect of the establishment or in respect of another establishment ⁵[to which the Act applies] under the same employer.

(2) Where the Scheme applies to a newspaper establishment on the expiry or cancellation of an order of exemption under section 17 of the Act, every employee, who, but for the exemption would have become and continued as a member of the Fund, shall become a member of the Fund forthwith.

(3) After this paragraph comes into force in a newspaper establishment, every newspaper employee thereof other than an excluded employee, who has not become a member already shall also

be entitled and required to become a member from the beginning of the month following that in which he completes ⁴[three months' continuous service] or has actually worked for not less than ⁴[60 days during a period of three months or less] in that establishment or in another such establishment ¹[to which the Act applies] under the same employer or partly in one and partly in the other ⁶[or has been declared permanent in any such newspaper establishment, whichever is the earliest].

(4) An excluded employee referred to in clause (ii) or paragraph 2(f) of a newspaper establishment to which this Scheme applies shall, on ceasing to be such an employee be entitled and required to become a member of the Fund from the beginning of the month following that in which he ceases to be such employee, provided that on the date on which he ceases to be an excluded employee, he has completed ⁴[three months' continuous service] or has actually worked for not less than ⁴[60 days during a period of three months or less] in that newspaper establishment or in another such establishment ⁵[to which the Act applies] under the same employer or partly in one and partly in the other ⁶[or has been declared permanent in any such newspaper establishment, whichever is the earliest].

(5) On re-election of a class of newspaper employees exempted under paragraph 27A to join the Fund or on the expiry or cancellation of an order under that paragraph, every newspaper employee, who but for such exemption would have become and continued as a member of the Fund, shall forthwith become a member thereof.

(6) Every newspaper employee who is a member of a private provident fund maintained in respect of an exempted newspaper establishment and who, but for the exemption would have become and continued as a member of the Fund shall, on joining a newspaper establishment to which this Scheme applies, become a member of the Fund forthwith.

(7) Notwithstanding the other provisions of this paragraph, a commissioner may, on a joint request in writing of any newspaper employee of a newspaper establishment to which this Scheme applies and his employer, enrol such employee as a member who shall, thereafter, be entitled to the benefits and shall be subject to the conditions of the Fund:

Provided that the employer gives an undertaking, in writing, that he shall pay the administrative charges payable and comply with all statutory provisions of the Act and this Scheme in respect of such employee.

Explanation I.–For purposes of this paragraph the provision contained in clause (e) of paragraph 2 shall not apply and "continuous service" shall mean uninterrupted service and include service which is interrupted by sickness, accident, authorised leave, strike which is not illegal or involuntary unemployment.

Explanation II.–In computing the period of work for ⁴[60 days] under this paragraph–

(a) periods of involuntary unemployment caused by stoppage of work due to shortage of raw materials or fuel, changes in the line of production, breakdown of machinery or any other similar cause;

(b) periods of authorised leave; ⁷[****]

(c) in the case of female employees, periods of maternity leave for any number of days not exceeding twelve weeks; ⁸[and

(d) Sunday and holidays intervening the days of actual work.]

shall also be deemed to be days on which the employee has worked in the ⁹[establishment].

26A. *Retention of membership*.–A member of the Fund shall continue to be a member until he withdraws under paragraph 69 the amount standing to his credit in the Fund or is covered by a notification of exemption under section 17 of the Act or an order of exemption under paragraph 27 or 27A.

Explanation.–In the cases of a claim for refund by a member under sub-paragraph (2) of paragraph 69 the membership of the Fund shall be deemed to have been terminated from the date the payment is authorised to him by the authority specified in this behalf by the Commissioner irrespective of the date of claim.

¹[**26 B – Resolution of doubts- If any question arises whether an employee is entitled to or required to become, or continue as, a member, or as regards the date from which he is so entitled or required to become a member, the same shall be referred to the Regional Commissioner who shall decide the same:**

Provided that both the employer and the employee shall be heard before passing any order in the matter.]

1.	Ins. by S.R.O. 2981, dated 4th December, 195
2.	Subs. by G.S.R. 1513, dated 15th December, 1961.
3.	Omitted by G.S.R. 767, dated 18th May, 1965.
4.	Subs. by G.S.R. 130, dated 16th January, 1981 (w.e.f. 31-1-1981).
5.	Ins. by G.S.R. 1176, dated 14th September, 1961.
6.	Ins. by G.S.R. 1990, dated 3rd December, 1971.
7.	Omitted by G.S.R. 871, dated 31st July, 1974.
8.	Ins. by G.S.R. 871, dated 31st July, 1974.
9.	Subs. by G.S.R. 1307, dated 24th November, 1959 (w.e.f. 31-12-1959).
10.	Omitted by G.S.R. 1845, dated 28th November, 1963.
11.	Subs. by GSR 320 (E) dated 06.5.2014 (w.e.f. 07.5.2014).

¹[**81. Special provisions in the case of cine-workers.**–The Scheme shall, in its application to cine-workers as defined in clause (c) of section 2 of the Cine-Workers and Cinema Theatre Workers (Regulation of Employment) Act, 1981 (50 to 1981), be subject to the following modifications, namely:–

(1) In Chapters I to IX, references to 'industry' and 'employees' shall be construed as references to 'film production' and cine workers, respectively;

(2) for sub-paragraph (f) of paragraph 2, the following sub-paragraph shall be substituted namely:–

(f) "excluded employee" means–

(i) a cine-worker, who having been a member of the Fund has withdrawn the full amount of his accumulations in the fund under clause (a) or clause (c) of sub-paragraph (1) of paragraph 69;

(ii) a "cine-worker," whose wages at the time he is otherwise entitled to become a member of the Fund exceeds one thousand and six hundred rupees per month and where such remuneration is by way of a lump sum exceeding fifteen thousand rupees.

Explanation.–"Wages" means "wages" as defined in clause (k) of section 2 of the Cine-Workers and Cinema Theatre Workers (Regulation of Employment) Act, 1981 (50 of 1981)";

(3) For paragraph 26, the following paragraph shall be substituted, namely:–

26. *Class of employees entitled and required to join the fund.* –(1)(a) Every cine-worker to whom this scheme applies, other than an excluded employee, shall be entitled and required to become a member of the fund from the beginning of the month following that in which this paragraph comes into force, if on the date of such coming into force he had worked in not less than three feature films with one or more producers.

Explanation.–"Feature film" means "feature film" as defined in clause (f) of section 2 of the Cine-Workers and Cinema Theatre Workers (Regulation of Employment) Act, 1981 (50 of 1981).

(b) Every cine-worker employed to do any work, in or in relation to any feature film in a film production unit to which this Scheme applies other than an excluded employee, shall be entitled and required to become a member of the fund from the beginning of the month following that in which this paragraph comes into force in such film production unit, if on the date of such coming into force, such employee is a subscriber to a provident fund maintained in respect of the establishment or in respect of another establishment under the same employer.

(2) Where the scheme applies to a film production unit on the expiry or cancellation of an order of exemption under section 17 of the Act, every cine-worker who, but for the exemption would have become and continued as a member of the fund shall become a member of the fund forthwith.

(3) After this paragraph comes into force in a film production unit, every cine-worker thereof, other than an excluded employee, who has not become a member already shall also be entitled and required to become a member from the beginning of the month following that in which he completes work in three feature films in that production unit or in another such unit (to which the Act applies) under the same producer or partly in one and partly in the other.

(4) An excluded employee referred to in clause (ii) of paragraph 2 (f) of a film production unit to which this scheme applies shall, on ceasing to be such an employee be entitled and required to become a member of the fund from the beginning of the month following that on which he ceases to be such employee, provided that on the date on which he ceases to be an excluded employee, he had worked in not less than three feature films in that production unit to which the Act applies under the same producer or partly in one and partly in the other.

(5) On re-election of a class of cine-workers exempted under paragraph 27A to join the fund or on the expiry or cancellation of an order under that paragraph, every cine-worker, who but for such exemption would have become and continued as a member of the fund, shall forthwith become a member thereof.

(6) Every cine-worker who is a member of a private provident fund maintained in respect of an exempted film production unit and who, but for the exemption, would have become and continued as a member of the fund shall, on joining a film production unit to which this scheme applies, become a member of the Fund forthwith.

(7) Notwithstanding the other provisions of this paragraph, a Commissioner may, on a joint request in writing of any cine-worker of a film production unit to which this scheme applies and his

producer, enrol such cine-worker as a member who shall, thereafter, be entitled to the benefits and shall be subject to the conditions of the fund:

Provided that the producer gives an undertaking, in writing, that he shall pay the administrative charges payable and comply with all statutory provisions of the Act and this Scheme in respect of such cine-worker.

26A. *Retention of membership.* –A member of the fund shall continue to be a member until he withdraws under paragraph 69 the amount standing to his credit in the fund or is covered by a notification of exemption under section 17 of the Act or an order of exemption under paragraph 27 or 27A.

Explanation.–In the case of a claim for refund by a member under sub-paragraph (2) of paragraph 69, the membership of the fund shall be deemed to have been terminated from the date the payment is authorised to him by the authority specified in this behalf by the Commissioner irrespective of the date of claim.

[1]**[26 B – Resolution of doubts- If any question arises whether a Cine-worker is entitled to or required to become, or continue as, a member, or as regards the date from which he is so entitled or required to become a member, the same shall be referred to the Regional Commissioner who shall decide the same:]**

[2]**[Provided that both the producer and the Cine-worker shall be heard before passing any order in the matter.]**

1.	Subs. by GSR 320 (E) dated 06.5.2014 (w.e.f. 07.5.2014).
2.	Corrective provisions added by GSR 689 (E) dated 25.9.2014.

[1]**[82. Special provisions in respect of certain employees.**–The Scheme shall, in its application to an employee who is a person with disability under the Persons with Disabilities (Equal Opportunities, Protection of Right and Full Participation) Act, 1995 (1 of 1996) and under the National Trust for Welfare of Persons with Autism, Cerebral Palsy, Mental Retardation and Multiple Disabilities Act, 1999 (44 of 1999) respectively, be subject to the following modifications, namely:–

(1) For [2][clause (A) of] paragraph 2, the following clause shall be substituted, namely:–

[3][(f) "excluded employee"] means–

(i) a person with disability, who having been a member of the Fund has withdrawn the full amount of his accumulations in the Fund under clause (a) or clause (c) of sub-paragraph (1) of paragraph 69;

(ii) a person with disability, whose pay at the time he is otherwise entitled to become a member of the Fund, exceeds twenty-five thousand rupees per month,

(iii) an apprentice."

(2) In paragraph 30, after sub-paragraph (3), the following proviso shall be inserted, namely:–

"Provided that the Central Government shall contribute the employer's share of contribution up to a maximum period of three years from the date of commencement of membership of the Fund, in respect of an employee who is a person with disability, employed directly by the principal employer or through a contractor."

(3) In paragraph 34, after the first proviso, the following proviso shall be inserted, namely:–

"Provided further that in the case of any such employee who is a person with disability, the aforesaid Declaration Form shall further contain such particulars as are necessary for such employees."

(4) In paragraph 36, after sub-paragraph (1), the following sub-paragraph shall be inserted, namely:–

"(1A) Every employer shall send to the Commissioner, within fifteen days of every month commencing from the 1st day of April, 2008, in such form as the Commissioner may specify, the particulars as are necessary, of an employee who is a person with disability and is a member on or entitled to become a member after the 1st day of April, 2008."

[3][Provided that the particulars of disabled employee shall be sent by employer in electronic format also, in such form and manner, as may be specified by the Commissioner.]

(5) In paragraph 38, in sub-paragraph (1), after the second proviso, the following proviso shall be inserted, namely:–

"Provided also that the Central Government shall pay the employer's share of contribution in respect of an employee who is a person with disability, up to a maximum period of three years from the date of commencement of membership of the Fund."]

1. Ins. by G.S.R. 253(E), dated 31st March, 2008. (w.e.f. 1.4.2008)
2. Corrected by corrigendum No. F.No. 35012/1/2008-SS II, dated 30.4.2008.
3. Added by GSR 336 (E) dated 4.5.2012 (w.e.f. 4.5.2012).

[1][**83. Special provision in respect of International Workers:** The Scheme shall, in its application to International Workers as defined in clause (ff) of paragraph 2 of this scheme be subject to the following modifications, namely:-

1. For clause (f) of paragraph 2, the following clauses shall be substituted, namely:-

[2][(f) "Excluded employee" means (i) an International Worker, who is contributing to a social security programme of his country of origin, either as a citizen or resident, with whom India has entered into a social security agreement on reciprocity basis and enjoying the status of detached worker for the period and terms, as specified in such an agreement; or

(ii) an International Worker, who is contributing to a social security programme of his country of origin, either as a citizen or resident, with whom Inda has entered into a bilateral comprehensive economic agreement conataining a clause on social security prior to 1st October, 2008, which specifically exempts natural person of either country to contribute to the social security fund of the host country.]

2. After clause (j) of paragraph 2, the following clause shall be substituted, namely:-

(ja) "**International Worker**" means:-

(a) an Indian employee having worked or going to work in a foreign country with which India has entered into a social security agreement and being eligible to avail the benefits under a social security programme of that country, by virtue of the eligibility gained or going to gain, under the said agreement;

(b) an employee other than an Indian employee, holding other than an Indian passport, working for an establishment in India to which the Act applies;

3. For the paragraphs 26, 26 A and 26 B, the following paragraphs shall be substituted, namely:—

26. Class of employees of International Workers entitled and required to join the fund:- (1)(a) Every International Worker (other than an excluded employee), employed after 1st October, 2008 in an establishment to whom this Scheme applies, who has not become a member already, shall be entitled and required to become a member of the Fund with immediate effect from the 1st day of October, 2008.

(2) Every International Worker (other than an excluded employee), employed after 1st October, 2008 in an establishment to which this Scheme applies, who has not become a member already, shall be entitled and required to become a member of the Fund from the date of his joining the establishment.

(3) Where the Scheme applies to an establishment on the expiry or cancellation of an order of exemption under section 17 of the Act, every International Worker who, but for the exemption would have become and continued as a member of the Fund shall become a member of the Fund forthwith.

(4) An excluded employee of an establishment to which this Scheme applies shall, on ceasing to be such an employee, be entitled and required to become a member of the Fund from the date he ceases to be such employee.

(5) On re-election of a class of International Workers exempted under paragraph 27 A to join the fund or on the expiry or cancellation of an order under that paragraph, every International Worker, who but for such exemption would have become and continued as a member of the Fund, shall forthwith become a member thereof.

(6) Every International Worker who is a member of a private provident fund maintained in respect of an exempted establishment and who, but for the exemption, would have become and continued as a member of the Fund shall, on joining an establishment to which this Scheme applies, become a member of the Fund forthwith.

26A. Retention of membership: A member of the Fund shall continue to be a member until he withdraws under paragraph 69 the amount standing to his credit in the Fund or is covered by a notification of exemption under section 17 of the Act or an order of exemption under paragraph 27 or 27A or the benefits are settled in terms of the relevant provisions under the social security agreement entered into between India and his country or origin.

³[**26B. Resolution of doubts:** If any question arises as to whether an International Worker is entitled or required to become or continue as member, or as to the date from which he is entitled or required to become a member, the same shall be referred to the Regional Provident fund Commissioner who shall decide the same:

Provided that no decision shall be given unless both the employer and the International Worker shall be heard before passing any order in the matter and such hearing, if any, shall be in India.]

4. In paragraph 29, in sub-paragraph (1), after the points, the following proviso shall be inserted, namely:-

Provided further that where wages are paid in a currency other than in the Indian Rupee, the rate of conversion of that currency shall be the telegraphic transfer buying rate offered by the State Bank of India established under the State Bank of India Act, 1955 (23 of 1955) for buying such currency on the last working day of the month for which the wages are due.

5. For paragraph 36, the following paragraphs shall be substituted, namely:—

36. Duties of employers: (1) Every employer of an establishment to which this scheme applies shall send to the Commissioner, within fifteen days of the application of the Scheme to such establishment, a consolidated return in such form as the Commissioner may specify, of the International Workers (indicating distinctly the nationality of each and every International Worker) required or entitled to become members of the Fund showing the basic wage, retaining allowance (if any) and dearness allowance including the cash value of any food concession paid to each of such International Worker:

Provided that if there is no International Worker who is required or entitled to become a member of the Fund, the employer shall send a 'NIL return.

(2) Every employer shall send to the Commissioner within fifteen days of the close of each month a return -

(a) in Form 5, of the International Workers qualifying to become members of the Fund for the first time during the preceding month together with the declarations in Form 2 furnished by such qualifying International Workers (indicating distinctly the nationality of each and every International Worker), and

(b) in such form as the Commissioner may specify, of the International Workers (indicating distinctly the nationality of each and every International Worker) leaving service of the employer during the preceding month:

Provided that if there is no International Worker qualifying to become a member of the Fund for the first time or there is no International Worker leaving service of the employer during the preceding month, the employer shall send a 'Nil return.

[4][Provided further that a copy of the forms as mentioned in clauses (a) and (b) above shall be provided by the employer to concerned employees immediately after joining the service or at the time of leaving the service, as the case may be.]

6. For paragraph 69, the following paragraph shall be substituted, namely:-

69. Circumstances in which accumulations in the Fund are payable to an International Worker:-

(1) An International Worker may withdraw the full amount standing to his credit in the Fund-

(a) on retirement from service in the establishment at any time after the attainment of 58 years;

(b) On retirement on account of permanent and total in-capacity for work due to bodily or mental infirmity duly certified by the medical officer of the establishment, or where an establishment has no regular medical officer, by a registered medical practitioner designated by the establishment:

Provided that:-

(i) Where the establishment has been closed, the certificate of any registered medical practitioner may be accepted;

(ii) Where the establishment is covered by the Employees' State Insurance Scheme, medical certificate from a medical officer of the Employees' State Insurance Dispensary with which or from the Insurance Medical Practitioner with whom the employee is registered under the Scheme, shall be produced;

(iii) Where by mutual agreement of employers and employees, a Medical Board exists for any establishment or a group of establishments, a certificate issued by such Medical Board may also be accepted for the purpose of this sub-paragraph.

(2) It shall be open to the Regional Commissioner to demand from the member a fresh certificate from a Civil Surgeon or any doctor acting on his behalf where the original certificate produced by him under clause (b) of sub-paragraph (1) gives rise to suspicion regarding it genuineness:

Provided that the entire fee of the Civil Surgeon or any doctor acting in his behalf shall be paid from the Fund in case the findings of the Civil Surgeon or any doctor acting on his behalf agree with the original certificate, and that where such findings do not agree with the original certificate, only half of the fee shall be paid from the Fund and the remaining half shall be debited to the member's account.

(3) A member suffering from tuberculosis or leprosy or cancer, even if contracted after leaving the service of an establishment on grounds of illness but before payment has been authorized, shall be deemed to have been permanently and totally incapacitated for work.

[5][(4) In respect of a member covered under a social security agreement entered into between the Government of India and any other country, on ceasing to be an employee in an establishment covered under the Act.]

7. For paragraph 72, the following paragraph shall be substituted, namely:-

2. Payment of Provident Fund-

(1) When the amount standing to the credit of a member becomes payable, it shall be the duty of the Commissioner to make prompt payment as provided in the Scheme.

[5][(2) The due amount in respect of the member shall be payable in the payees bank account directly or through the employer.]

(3) In all other cases, the amount due shall be payable to the credit of the payee's bank account in India.

8. After paragraph 78, the following paragraph shall be inserted, namely:-

78-A. Performing certain special functions under social security agreements:-

The Commissioner shall perform all such functions as are assigned to the Employees' Provident Fund Organisation under a social security agreement entered into between by the Government of India and any other country, in the manner and as per the terms specified therein.]

1.	Ins. by G.S.R. 706 (E), dated 01.10. 2008. (w.e.f. 1.10.2008) and subs. by GSR 148 dated 3.9.2010 (w.e.f. 11.9.2010).
2.	Subs. by GSR 382 (E) dated 24.5.2012 (w.e.f 24.5.2012).
3.	subs. by GSR 320 (E) dated 6.5.2014 (w.e.f. 7.5.2014).
4.	Insered by GSR 336 (E) dated 4.5.2012 (w.e.f 4.5.2012).
5.	Subs. by GSR 744 (E) dated 5.10.2012 (w.e.f. 5.10.2012).

Suppliments

FORM 9
Application for review filed under sub-section (1) of section 7B of the Employees' Provident Funds and Miscellaneous Provisions Act, 1952
(Paragraph 79A)

For use in Commissioner's Office

Date of filing or

Date of receipt by post Registration No.

           Signature

           for Commissioner

1. Name of the Applicant   ………………………………..
2. Designation of the applicant or his ………………………………..
relationship with the factory/establishment
(whether owner/partner/ director/manager,
etc., to be indicated)
3. Name and complete address of the ………………………………..
factory/establishment
4. Address of the employer for service of………………………………..
notice/summons.
5. Particulars of the order against which………………………………..
the review application is filed –
 (i) Order No.   ………………………………..
 (ii) Date of order   ………………………………..
 (iii) Passed by   ………………………………..
 (iv) Subject in brief   ………………………………..
6. Main ground(s) on which the application
for review has been made and the relief
(s) sought. (If necessary, attach a duly signed
statement with copies of the documents relied
upon marked as A1, A2, A3 and so on.)………………………………..

Verification

I………….. (name of the applicant) s/o, d/o, w/o…………… age ………….. working as ……………. resident of ……………….. do hereby verify that the contents of particulars given at SI. Nos. 1 to 6 above are true to the best of my knowledge and belief and I have not suppressed any material fact. I further declare that–

(i) I am filing the application within 45 days from the date of the original order.

(ii) I have not preferred any appeal against the original order under the Employees' Provident Funds and Miscellaneous Provisions Act, 1952.

(iii) I am filing with this application, the original document authorising me to represent the aggrieved person (applicable only in cases where the application is filed by agent, advocate or other representative).

Place …………… Signature.

Date ……………

Suppliments

The Employees' Pension Scheme, 1995

1. Short title, commencement and application.–(1) This Scheme may be called the Employees' Pension Scheme, 1995.

(2) (a) This Scheme shall come into force on 16th day of November, 1995;

(b) Subject to the provisions of this Scheme the employees have an option to become the members of the Scheme with effect from the 1st April, 1993.

(3) Subject to the provisions of section 16 of the Employees' Provident Funds and Miscellaneous Provisions Act, 1952, this Scheme shall apply to the employees of all factories and other establishments to which the Employees' Provident Funds and Miscellaneous Provisions Act, 1952 applies or is applied under sub-section (3) or sub-section (4) of section 1 or section 3 thereof.

2 – Definitions- In this Scheme, unless the context otherwise requires-

(i) "Act" Means the Employees' Provident Funds and Miscellaneous Provisions Act, 1952 (19 of 1952);

(ii) "Actual service" means the aggregate of periods of service rendered from the 16th November, 1995 or from the date of joining any establishment, whichever is later, to the date of exit from the employment of the establishment covered under the Act;

(iii) "Commissioner" means a Commissioner for Employees' Provident Funds appointed under Section 5D of the Act;

(iv) "Contributory service" means the period of actual service rendered by a member for which contribution to the fund have been [1][received or are receivable];

(v) "Eligible member" means an employee who is eligible to join the Employees' Pension Scheme;

(vi) "Existing member" Means an existing employee who is a member of the Employees' Family Pension Scheme, 1971;

(vii) "Family" means:

(1) wife in the case of male member of the Employees Pension /fund;

(2) husband in the case of a female member of the Employees' Pension Fund; and

(3) sons and [2][xxx] daughters of a member of the Employees' pension Fund;

Explanation:- The expression 'sons' and 'daughters' shall include children [1][legally adopted by the member].

(viii) "Pension" means the pension payable under the Employees' pension Scheme and also includes the family pension admissible and payable under the Employees' Family Pension Scheme, 1971 immediately preceding the commencement of the Employees' Pension Scheme, 1995 with effect from 16th November, 1995;

(ix) "member" means an employee who becomes a member of Employees' Pension Fund in accordance with the provisions of this Scheme;

³[Explanation:- An employee shall cease to be the member of Pension Fund from the date of attaining 58 years of age or from the date of vesting admissible benefits under the Scheme, whichever is earlier.]

(x) "Non contributory service" is the period of 'actual service' rendered by a member for which no contribution to the Employees' Pension Fund has been ¹[received or are receivable];

(xi) "Orphan" means a person, none of whose parents is alive ²[xxx];

(xii) "Past service" means the period of service rendered by an existing member from the date of joining Employees' Family Pension Fund till 15th November, 1995;

(xiii) "Pay" means basic wages, with dearness allowance, retaining allowance and cash value of food concession admissible, if any;

(xiv) "Pension Fund" means the Employees' Pension Fund set up under sub-section (2) of section 6A of the Act;

(xv) "Pensionable service" means the service rendered by the member for which contributions have been ¹[received or are receivable];

¹[(xvi) "Permanent total disablement" means such disablement of permanent nature as incapacitates an employee for all work which he/she was capable of performing at the time of disablement, regardless whether such disablement is sustained in the course of employment or otherwise];

(xvii) "Table" means Table appended to this Scheme;

(xviii) The words and expression defined in the Act but not defined in this Scheme shall have the same meaning as assigned to them in the Act.

1. Substituted by GSR 134 dated 28.02.1996 (w.e.f. 16.03.1996).
2. Deleted by GSR 134 dated 28.02.1996 (w.e.f. 16.03.1996).
3. Added by GSR 66 dated 22.02.1999 (w.e.f. 06.03.1999).

3. Employees' Pension Fund.– (1) From and out of the contributions payable by the employer in each month under section 6 of the Act or under the rules of the Provident Fund of the establishment which is exempted either under clauses (a) and (b) of sub-section (1) of section 17 of the Act or whose employees are exempted under either paragraph 27 or paragraph 27A of the Employees' Provident Funds Scheme, 1952, a part of contribution representing 8.33 per cent, of the employees' pay shall be remitted by the employer to the Employees' Pension Fund within 15 days of the close of every month by a separate bank draft or cheque on account of the Employees' Pension Fund contribution in such manner as may be specified in this behalf by the Commissioner. The cost of the remittance, if any, shall be borne by the employer.

(2) The Central Government shall also contribute at the rate of 1.16 per cent. if the pay of the members of the Employees' Pension Scheme and credit the contribution to the Employees' Pension Fund:

Provided that where the pay of the member exceeds ¹[fifteen thousand rupees] per month the contribution payable by the employer and the Central Government be limited to the amount payable on his pay of ¹[fifteen thousand rupees] only.

(3) Each contribution payable under sub-paragraphs (1) and (2) shall be calculated to the nearest rupee, fifty paise or more to be counted as the next higher rupee and fraction of a rupee less than fifty paise to be ignored.

(4) The net assets of the Family Pension Scheme, 1971 shall vest in and land transferred to the Employees' Pension Fund.

---
1. Subs. by G.S.R. 609 (E), dated 22nd August, 2014 (w.e.f. 1-9-2014).

---

4. Payment of contribution.–(1) The employer shall pay the contribution payable to the Employees' Pension Fund in respect of the [1][each member] of he Employees' Pension Fund employed by him directly or by or through a contractor.

(2) It shall be the responsibility of the principal employer to pay the contributions payable to the Employees' Pension Fund by himself in respect of the employees directly employed by him and also in respect of the employees employed by or through a contractor:

[2][Provided that the Central Government shall pay the contribution payable to the Employees' Pension Fund in respect of an employee who is a person with disability under the Persons with Disabilities (Equal Opportunities, Protection of Rights and Full Participation) Act, 1995 (1 of 1996) and under the National Trust for Welfare of Persons with Autism, Cerebral Palsy, Mental Retardation and Multiple Disabilities Act, 1999 (44 of 1999) respectively, up to a maximum period of three years from the date of commencement of membership of the Fund.]

---
1. Subs. by G.S.R. 134, dated 28th February, 1996 (w.e.f. 16-3-1996).
2. Ins. by G.S.R. 252(E), dated 31st March, 2008 (w.e.f. 1-4-2008).

---

[1][**5. Recovery of damages for default in payment of any contribution.**– (1) Where an employer makes default in the payment of any contribution to the Employees' Pension Fund, or in the payment of any charges payable under any other provisions of the Act or the Scheme, the Central Provident Fund Commissioner or such officer as may be authorised by the Central Government, by notification in the Official Gazette, in this behalf, may recover from the employer by way of penalty, damages at the rates given below:

Period of default	Rate of damages (Percentage of arrears per annum)
(a) Less than two months	Five
(b) Two months and above but less than four months	Ten
(c) Four months and above but less than six months	Fifteen
(d) Six months and above	Twenty five

(2) The damages shall be calculated to the nearest rupee, fifty paise or more to be counted as the nearest higher rupee and fraction of a rupee less than fifty paise to be ignored.

---
1. Ins. by G.S.R. 521, dated 16th August, 1991 (w.e.f. 1-9-1991).

[1][6. Membership of the Employees' Pension Scheme—Subject to sub-paragraph (3) of paragraph 1, this Scheme shall apply to every employee:

(a) who on or after the 16th November, 1995 becomes a member of the Employees' Provident Fund Scheme, 1952 or of the Provident Funds of the Factories and other establishments exempted by the appropriate Government under section 17 of the Act, or in whose case exemption has been granted under paragraph 27 or 27A of the Employees' Provident Fund Scheme, 1952, from the date of such membership;

(b) who has been a member of the ceased Employees' Family Pension Scheme, 1971 before the commencement of this Scheme from 16th November, 1995;

(c) who ceased to be a member of the Employees' Family Pension Scheme, 1971 between 1st April, 1993 and 15th November, 1995 and opts to exercise his option under paragraph 7.

(d) who has been a member of the Employees' Provident Fund or of Provident Funds of Factories and other establishments exempted by the appropriate Government under section 17 of the Act or in whose case exemption has been granted under paragraph 27 or 27A of the Employees' Provident Fund Scheme, 1952, on 15th November, 1995 but not being a member of the ceased Employees' Family Pension Scheme, 1971 opts to exercise his option under paragraph 7].

1.	Substituted by GSR 134, dated 28.2.1996. (w.e.f. 16.3.1996).

[1][6A. Retention of membership.–A member of the Employees' Pension Fund shall continue to be such member till he attains the age of 58 years or he avails the withdrawal benefit to which he is entitled under para 14 of the Scheme, or dies, or the pension is vested in him in terms of para 12 of the Scheme, whichever is earlier.]

1.	Ins. by G.S.R. 66, dated 22.02.1999 (w.e.f. 6-3-1999).

[1][7. Option for joining the Scheme — (1) Members referred to under sub-paragraph (c) of paragraph 6 who have died between 1st April, 1993 am 15th November, 1995 shall be deemed to have exercised the option of joining the Scheme on the date of his death.

(2) Members referred to in sub-paragraph (c) of paragraph 6 who are alive shall have the option to join the Scheme as per the provisions of paragraph 11 from the date of exit from the employment.

(3) Members referred to in sub-paragraph (d) of paragraph 6 shall have the option to join the Scheme as per the provisions of paragraph 17 from 16th November, 1995.].

1.	Substituted by GSR 134, dated 28.2.1996. (w.e.f. 16.3.1996)

8. Resolution of doubts — If any doubt arises whether an employee is entitled to become a member of the Employees' Pension Fund, the same shall be referred to the Regional Provident Fund Commissioner who shall decide the same:

Provided that both the employer and the employee shall be heard before passing final order in the matter.

9. Determination of eligible service.– The eligible service shall be determined as follows:

(a) In the case of 'new entrant' the [1]['contributory service'] shall be treated as eligible service. The total [1][contributory service] shall be rounded off to the nearest year. The fraction of service for six months or more shall be treated as one year and the service less than six months shall be ignored.

Explanation: In the case of employees employed seasonally in any establishment, the period of [1]['contributory service'] in any year, notwithstanding that such service is less than a year shall be treated as a full year.

(b) In the case of the 'existing member' the aggregate of [1]['contributory service']and the 'past service' shall be treated as eligible service:

Provided that if there is any period in the 'past service' for which the contributions towards the Family Pension Scheme, 1971 has not been received, the said period shall count as eligible service only if the contributions thereof have been received in the Employees' Pension Fund.

[2][**Explanation:** For the purpose of this sub-paragraph, the aggregate of [1]['contributory service'] and past service for less than six months shall be ignored and six months and above shall be rounded off to a year.]

---
1. Substituted by GSR 226(E) dated 26.3.2015 in place of 'actual service.' (w.e.f. 26.3.2015).
2. Substituted by GSR 594(E) dated 21.8.2009. (w.e.f. 21.8.2009).
---

10. Determination of pensionable service - (1) The pensionable service of the member shall be determined with reference to the contributions [1][received or receivable] on his behalf in the Employees' Pension Fund.

(2) In the case of the member who superannuates on attaining the age of 58 years, [2][and] who has rendered 20 years pensionable service or more, his pensionable service shall be increased by adding a weightage of 2 years.

---
1. Substituted by GSR 134, dated 28.2.1996. (w.e.f. 16.3.1996)
2. Substituted by GSR 546(E) dated 23.7.2009. (w.e.f. 24.7.2009)
---

11. Determination of pensionable salary - [1][(1) The pensionable salary shall be the average monthly pay drawn in any manner including on piece-rate basis during the contributory period of service in the span of sixty months preceding the date of exit from the membership of the Pension Fund and the pensionable salary shall be determined on pro-rata basis for the pensionable service up to the 1st day of September, 2014, subject to a maximum of six thousand and five hundred rupees per month and for the period thereafter at the maximum of fifteen thousand rupees per month:

Provided that if a member was not in receipt of full pay during the period of sixty months preceding the day he ceased to be the member of Pension Fund, the average of previous sixty months full pay drawn by him during the period for which contribution to the Pension Fund was recovered, shall be taken into account as pensionable salary for calculating Pension.]

(2) If during the said span of [2][sixty months] there are non-contributory periods of service including cases where the member has drawn salary for a part of the month, the total wages during the 12 months span shall be divided by the actual number of days for which salary has been drawn and the amount so derived shall be multiplied by 30 to work out the average monthly pay.

(3) The maximum pensionable salary shall be limited to [3][fifteen thousand rupees] per month.

⁵[******]

{Note:- The proviso giving right to contribute on a higher salary than the ceiling has been removed w.e.f. 01.9.2014, however, anticipating litigation on this issue, this proviso is retained here for ready reference in future-

⁴*[Provided that if at the option of the employer and employee, contribution paid on salary exceeding Rs. 6,500 per month from the date of commencement of this Scheme or from the date salary exceeds Rs. 6,500 whichever is later, and 8.33% share of the employers thereof is remitted into the Pension Fund, pensionable salary shall be based on such higher salary].}*

⁶[(4) The existing members as on the 1ˢᵗ day of September, 2014, who at the option of the employer and employee, has been contributing on salary exceeding six thousand and five hundred rupees per month, may on a fresh option to be exercised jointly by the employer and employee continue to contribute on salary exceeding fifteen thousand rupees per month:

Provided that the aforesaid members have to contribute at the rate of 1.16 percent of salary exceeding fifteen thousand rupees as an additional contribution from and out of the contributions payable by the employee for each month under the provisions of the Act or the rules made there-under:

Provided further that the fresh option shall be exercised by the member within a period of six months from the 1ˢᵗ day of September, 2014:

Provided also that the period specified in the second proviso may, on sufficient cause being shown by the member, be extended by the Regional Provident Fund Commissioner for a further period not exceeding six months:

Provided also that if no option is exercised by the member within such period (excluding the extended period), it shall be deemed that the member has not opted for contribution over wage ceiling and the contribution to the Pension Fund made over the wage ceiling in respect of the member shall be diverted to the Provident Fund account of the member along with interest as declared under the Employees' Provident fund Scheme from time to time.]

1.	Subs. by GSR 609 (E) dated 22.8.2014. (w.e.f. 01.9.2014).
2.	Subs. by GSR 609 (E) dated 22.8.2014 in place of '12months' (w.e.f. 01.9.2014).
3.	Subs. by GSR 609 (E) dated 22.8.2014 in place of 'Rs. 6,500.' (w.e.f. 01.9.2014).
4.	Subs. by GSR 66 dated 22.2.1999. (w.e.f. 6.3.1999).
5.	Proviso deleted by GSR 609 (E) dated 22.8.2014. (w.e.f. 01.9.2014).
6.	Inserted by GSR 609 (E) dated 22.8.2014. (w.e.f. 01.9.2014).

¹[**12. Monthly Member's Pension** - (1) A member shall be entitled to:

(a) superannuation pension, if he has rendered eligible service of 10 years or more and retires on attaining the age of 58 years;

(b) early pension, if he has rendered eligible service of 10 years or more and retires or otherwise ceases to be in the employment before attaining the age of 58 years;

(2) In the case of a new entrant, the amount of monthly superannuation pension or early pension, as the case may be, shall be computed in accordance with the following factors, namely:

$$\text{Monthly Member's Pension} = \frac{\text{Pensionable Salary} \times \text{Pensionable Service}}{70}$$

Suppliments

[2][Provided that the members' monthly pension shall be determined on a pro-rata basis for the pensionable service up to the 1st day of September, 2014 at the maximum pensionable salary of six thousand and five hundred rupees per momnth and for the period thereafter at the maximum pensionable salary of fifteen thousand rupees per month.]

(3) In the case of an existing member in respect of whom the date of commencement of pension is after the 16th November, 2005,-

(i) superannuation or early pension shall be equal to the aggregate of:-

(a) pension as determined under sub-paragraph (2) for the period of pensionable service rendered from the 16th November, 1995 or Rs. 635/- per month whichever is more;

(b) past service pension shall be as given below:

The past service pension payable on completion of 58 years of age on the 16th November, 1995.

S. No.	Years of past service	Salary upto Rs. 2,500/- p.m.	Salary more than Rs. 2,500/- p.m.
(i)	Upto 11 years	80	85
(ii)	More than 11 years but upto 15 years	95	105
(iii)	More than 15 years but less than 20 years	120	135
(iv)	Beyond 20 years.	150	170

The amount under column (2) or column (3) above, as the case may be, shall be multiplied by the factor given in Table 'B' corresponding to the period between the 16th November, 1995 and the date of exit to arrive at past service pension payable.

(ii) The aggregate of (a) and (b) calculated as above shall be subject to a minimum of Rs. 8007- per month, provided the eligible service is 24 years. Provided further, if it is less than 24 years, the pension as computed above shall be reduced proportionately subject to a minimum of Rs. 4507- per month.

(4) In the case of an existing member and in respect of whom the date of commencement of pension is between the 16th November, 2000 and the 16th November, 2005,-

(i) superannuation or early pension shall be equal to the aggregate of:-

(a) pension as determined under sub-paragraph (2) for the period of service rendered from the 16th November, 1995 or Rs. 43 8/- per month whichever is more;

(b) past service pension as provided in sub-paragraph (3).

(ii) The aggregate of (a) and (b) calculated as above shall be subject to a minimum of Rs. 600/- per month, provided the eligible service is 24 years. Provided further, if it is less than 24 years the pension shall be proportionately less subject to the minimum of Rs. 325/- per month.

(5) In the case of an existing member and in respect of whom the date of commencement of pension is before the 16th November, 2000,-

(i) The superannuation or early pension shall be equal to the aggregate of:

(a) pension as determined under sub-paragraph (2) for the period of service rendered from the 16th November, 1995 or Rs. 335/- per month whichever is more,

(b) past service pension as provided in sub-paragraph (3).

(ii) The aggregate of (a) and (b) calculated as above shall be subject to the minimum of Rs. 500/- per month, provided the eligible service is 24 years. Provided further, if it is less than 24 years the pension shall be proportionately lesser but subject to the minimum of Rs. 265/- per month.

(6) Except as otherwise expressly provided hereinafter, the monthly member's pension under sub-paragraphs (2) to (5) mentioned hereinabove, as the case may be, shall be payable from a date immediately following the date of completion of 58 years of age notwithstanding that the member has retired or ceased to be in the employment before that date.

(7) A member, if he so desires, may be allowed to draw an early pension from a date earlier than 58 years of age but not earlier than 50 years of age. In such cases, the amount of pension shall be reduced at the rate of [3][four per cent], for every year the age falls short of 58 years.]

[4][(7-A) The monthly member's pension including the relief payable to any existing or future member under this paragraph shall not be less than one thousand rupees for the financial year 2014-15.]

(8) If a member ceases to be in the employment by way of retirement or otherwise earlier than the date of superannuation from which pension can be drawn, the member may, on his option, either be paid pension as admissible under this Scheme on attaining the age exceeding 50 years or he may be issued a scheme certificate by the Commissioner indicating the pensionable service, the pensionable salary and the amount of pension due on the date of exit from the employment. If he/she is subsequently employed in an establishment coverable under this Scheme, his/her earlier service as per the scheme certificate shall be reckoned for pension along with the fresh spell of pensionable service. The member postponing the commencement of payment of pension under this paragraph shall also be entitled to additional relief sanctioned under this Scheme from time to time:

Provided that if the member does not take up an employment coverable under this Scheme, but dies before attaining the age of 58 years, the amount of contributions received in his case shall be converted into a monthly widow pension/children pension. The widow pension in such cases shall be calculated at the scale laid down in Table "C," and the children pension at 25 per cent thereof for each child (up to two). If there is no widow, then the orphan pension shall be payable at the rate of 75 per cent of the amount which would have been payable as a widow pension subject to the provisions of paragraph 16.

1.	Subs. by GSR 431 (E) dated 15.6.2007 sub-para (1) to (7). (w.e.f. 16.11.1995).
2.	Added by GSR 609 (E) dated 22.8.2014 in place of '12months' (w.e.f. 01.9.2014).
3.	Subs. by GSR 688 (E) dated 26.9.2008 in place of 'three percent.' (w.e.f. 26.9.2008).
4.	Added by GSR 593 (E) dated 19.8.2014. (w.e.f. 1.9.2014).

[1][12-A. Option for commutation- *****]

1. Deleted by G.S.R. 688 (E) dated 26.8.2008 (w.e.f. 26.8.2008).

[1][13. Option for return of capital- *****]

> 1. Deleted by G.S.R. 688 (E) dated 26.8.2008 (w.e.f. 26.8.2008).

[1][**14. Benefits on leaving service before being eligible for monthly member's pension.**- (1) If a member has not rendered the eligible service prescribed in sub-paragraph (1) of paragraph 12 on the date of exit, or on attaining 58 years of age, whichever is earlier, such member shall be entitled to a withdrawal benefit as laid down in Table 'D' or may opt to receive the scheme certificate provided on the date he has not attained he 58 years of age:

Provided that for calculating such withdrawal benefit, the wages at exit shall be the weighed average of his wages at the end of every wage ceiling period:

Provided that an existing member shall receive additional return of contributions "of contribution for his past service under the Employees' Family Pension Scheme, 1971, computed as withdrawal-cum-retirement benefits as per Table 'A' multiplied by the factor given in Table 'B.']

> 1. Subs. by GSR 609 (E) dated 22.8.2014. (w.e.f. 1.9.2014).

15. Benefits on permanent and total disablement during the service.-

(1) A member, who is permanently and totally disabled during the employment shall be entitled to pension as admissible under [1][paragraphs 12], subject to a minimum of Rs. 250/- per month notwithstanding the fact that he/she has not rendered the pensionable service entitling him/her to pension under paragraph 12 provided that he/she has made at least one month's contribution to the Pension Fund.

(2) The monthly member's pension in such cases shall be payable from the date following the date of permanent total disablement and shall be tenable foi the life time of the member.

(3) A member applying for benefits under this paragraph shall be required to undergo such medical examination as may be prescribed by the Central Board to determine whether or not he or she is permanently and totally unfit for the employment which he or she was doing at the time of such disablement.

> 1. Subs. by GSR 593 (E) dated 19.8.2014. (w.e.f. 1.9.2014).

16. Benefits to the family on the death of a member.— (1) [1][Pension to the family] shall be admissible from the date following the date of death of the member if the member dies:

(a) while in service, provided that at least one month's contribution has been paid into the Employees' Pension Fund, or

(b) after the date of exit but before attaining the age of 58, from the employment having rendered service entitling him/her to monthly member's pension but [1][before the commencement of pension payment], or

(c) after commencement of payment of the monthly member's pension.

Note:— The cases where a member has rendered less than 10 years eligible service on the date of exit but has retained the membership of the Pension Fund, and dies before attaining the age of 58 years, shall be regulated under sub-paragraph (8) of paragraph 12.

(2) (a) The monthly widow pension shall be:

(i) in the cases covered by clause (a) of sub-paragraph (1) equal to the monthly member's pension which would have been admissible as the member had retired on the date of death or Rs. 450/- or the amount indicated in Table 'C' whichever is more;

(ii) in the cases covered by clause (b) of sub-paragraph (1) equal to the monthly members pension which would have been admissible as if the member had retired on the date of exit or [2][Rs. 450/- per month] or the amount indicated in Table 'C,' whichever is more;

(iii) in the cases covered by clause (c) of sub-paragraph (1), equal to 50 per cent of the monthly members' pension payable to the member on the date of his death subject to a minimum of [2][Rs. 450- per month].

[3][(iv) In all the cases, where the amount of family pension sanctioned under the ceased Family Pension Scheme, 1971 and is paid/payable under this scheme is less than Rs. 450/- per month, the amount of family pension in such cases shall be enhanced to Rs. 450/- per month.]

[4][(v) All the cases, where the monthly widow pension including relief, if any, is less than one thousand rupees per month, the amount of monthly widow pension in such cases shall be enhanced to one thousand rupees per month for the financial year 2014-15.]

(b) the monthly widow pension shall be payable up to the date of death of the widow or remarriage whichever is earlier.

Note:— In cases where there are two or more widows, family pension shall be payable to the eldest surviving widow. On her death, it shall be payable to the next surviving widow, if any. The term 'eldest' would mean seniority with reference to the date of marriage.

(3) Monthly children pension:

(a) If there are any surviving children of the deceased member falling within the definition of family, they shall be entitled to a monthly children pension in addition to the monthly widow/widower pension.

[5][(b) Monthly children pension for each child shall be equal to 25 per cent, of the amount admissible to the widow of the deceased member as monthly widow pension payable under clause (a) of sub-paragaph (2):

Provided that minimum monthly children pension including relief, if any, for each child of the deceased member shall not be less than two hundred and fifty rupees per month for the financial year 2014-15.]

[6][(c) Monthly children pension shall be payable until the child attains the age of 25 years.]

(d) The monthly children pension shall be admissible to maximum of two children at a time and will run from the oldest to the youngest child in that order.

[7][(e) If a member dies leaving behind a family having son or daughter who is permanently and totally disabled such son or daughter shall be entitled to payment of Monthly Children Pension or Orphan Pension, as the case may be, irrespective of age and number of children in the family in addition to the pension provided under Clause (d).]

(4) [8][(a) If the deceased member is not survived by any widow but is survived by children falling within the definition of family or if the widow pension is not payable, the children shall be entitled to a monthly orphan pension equal to 75 per cent, of the amount of the monthly widow pension as payable under clause (a) of sub-paragraph (2):

Provided that minimum monthly orphan pension including relief, if any, for each orphan shall not be less than seven hundred fifty rupees per month for the financial year 2014-15].

(b) In the event of death or remarriage of the widow/widower after sanctioning of widow/widower pension, the children shall be entitled, in lieu of the monthly children pension, to a monthly orphan pension from the date following the date of death/remarriage of the widow/widower.

[9][(c) The monthly orphan pension shall be admissible to a maximum of two orphans at a time and shall run in order from the oldest to the youngest orphan.]

(5) (a) A member who is not married or who does not have any living spouse and/or an eligible child may nominate a person to receive benefits as laid down hereinafter provided that in the event of his/her acquiring a family subsequently, the nomination so made shall become void. In the event of death of the member such a nominee shall be entitled to receive a monthly pension equal to the monthly widow pension as admissible under sub-clauses (i) and (ii) of clause (a) sub-paragraph (2).

[10][(aa) If a member dies leaving behind no spouse and/or an eligible child falling within the definition of family and no nomination by such deceased member exists, the widow pension shall be paid under sub clauses (i) and (ii) of clause (a) of sub paragraph 2 either to dependant father or dependant mother, as the case may be. On grant of Pension to such dependant father and in the event of death of the father Pensioner, the admissible pension shall be extended to the surviving mother life long.]

(b) If the deceased member had not rendered pensionable service on the date of exit from the employment which would have made him entitled to a monthly members pension under paragraph 12, but had opted to retain the membership of this scheme under sub-paragraph (8) of paragraph 12, the [11][nominee or the dependent father or the dependent mother as the case may be] shall be entitled to [12][a withdrqwal benefit as provided in paragraph 14.]

1.	Added by GSR 134 dated 28.2.1996. (w.e.f. 16.3.1996).
2.	Subs. by GSR 41, dated 12.1.2000 for "Rs. 250/-" (w.e.f. 29.1.2000).
3.	Added by GSR 41 dated 12.1.2000. (w.e.f. 29.1.2000).
4.	Added by GSR 593 (E) dated 19.8.2014 (w.e.f. 01.9.2014).
5.	Substituted by GSR 593 (E) dated 19.8.2014 (w.e.f. 01.9.2014).
6.	Subs. by GSR 134 dated 28.2.1996. (w.e.f. 16.3.1996).
7.	Substituted by GSR 66 dated 22.2.1999. (w.e.f. 6.3.1999).
8.	Substituted by GSR 593 (E) dated 19.8.2014 (w.e.f. 01.9.2014).
9.	Added by GSR 41 dated 12.1.2000. (w.e.f. 29.1.2000).
10.	Added by GSR 66 dated 22.2.1999. (w.e.f. 6.3.1999).
11.	Substituted by GSR 66 dated 22.2.1999. (w.e.f. 6.3.1999).
12.	Substituted by GSR 80 (E) dated 14.2.2013. (w.e.f. 26.9.2008).

[1][**16A. Guarantee of Pensionary Benefits.**— None of the pensionary benefits under this Scheme shall be denied to any member or beneficiary for want of compliance of the requirements by the employer under sub-paragraph (1) of paragraph 3 provided, however, that the employer shall not be absolved of his liabilities under the Scheme.]

1.	Added by GSR 134 dated 28.2.1996. (w.e.f. 16.3.1996).

[1][17. Payments on Exercise of Option.—

(1) Beneficiaries of the deceased members of Employee's Family Pension Scheme, referred to in sub-para (1) of paragraph 7, shall receive higher of the benefits available under the Employees' Family Pension Scheme, 1971 and under this Scheme.

(2) Members referred to in sub-paragraph (2) of paragraph 7, shall have the option to join this Scheme by returning the amount of withdrawal benefit received, if any, together with interest at the rate of 8.5 per cent per annum from the date of payment of such withdrawal benefit and date of exercise of the option, to receive monthly pension as per the provisions of this Scheme.

(3) Members referred to in sub-paragraph (3) of paragraph 7, shall be deemed to have joined the ceased Employees' Family Pension Scheme, 1971 with effect from 1.3.1971 on remittance of past period contribution with interest thereon].

| 1. | Substituted by GSR 134, dated 28.2.1996. (w.e.f. 16.3.1996). |

[1][17A. Payment of pension.— The claims, complete in all respects submitted along with the requisite documents shall be settled and benefit amount paid to the beneficiaries within [2][20 days] from the date of its receipt by the Commissioner. If there is any deficiency in the claim, the same shall be recorded in writing and communicated to the applicant within [2][20 days] from the date of receipt of such application. In case, the Commissioner fails without sufficient cause to settle a claim complete in all respects within [2][30 days], the Commissioner shall be liable for the delay beyond the said period and penal interest at the rate of 12 per cent, per annum may be charged on the benefit amount and the same may be deducted from the salary of the Commissioner.]

| 1. | Added by GSR 376 dated 27.10.1997. (w.e.f. 8.11.1997). |
| 2. | Subs. By GSR 526 (E) dated 02.7.2015 (w.e.f. 02.7.2015). |

18. Particulars to be supplied by the employees already employed at the time of commencement of the Employees' Pension Scheme.–Every person who is entitled to become a member of the Employees' Pension Fund shall be asked forthwith by his employer to furnish and that person shall, on such damand, furnish to him for communication to the Commissioner particulars concerning himself and his family in the form prescribed by the Central Provident Fund Commissioner.

19. Preparation of contribution cards.–The employer shall prepare an Employees' Pension Fund Contribution Card, in respect of each employee who has become a member of the Employees' Pension Fund.

20. Duties of employers.— (1) Every employer shall send to the Commissioner, within three months of the commencement of this Scheme, a consolidated return of the employees entitled to become members of the Employees' Pension Fund showing the basic wage; retaining allowance, if any, and dearness allowance including the cash value of any food concession paid to each of such employees:

Provided that if there is no employee who is entitled be become a member of Employees' Pension Fund, the employer shall send a 'Nil' return.

(2) Every employer shall send to the Commissioner within fifteen days ot the close of each month a return in respect of the employees leaving service of the employer during the preceding month:

Provided that if there is no employee leaving service of the employer during the preceding month the employer shall send a 'Nil' return.

(3) Every employer shall maintain such accounts in relation to the amounts contributed by him to the Employees' Pension Fund as the Central Board may, from time to time, direct and it shall be the duty of every employer to assist the Central Board in making such payments from the Employees' Pension Fund to his employees as are sanctioned by or under the authority of the Central Board.

(4) Notwithstanding anything contained in this paragraph, the Central Board may issue such directions to the employers generally, as it may consider necessary or expedient; for the purpose of implementing the Scheme; and it shall be the duty of every employer to carry out such directions.

[1][(5) Every employer shall send to the Commissioner, an electronic format of the returns referred to in sub-paragraph (1) and (2), in such form and manner as may be specified by the Commissioner.]

1. Added by GSR 1809 dated 5.8.2011 (w.e.f. 5.8.2011).

21. Employer to furnish particulars of ownership.— Every employer in relation to a factory or other establishment to which the Act applies or is applied hereafter shall furnish to the Commissioner particulars of all the branches and departments, owners, occupiers, directors, partners, managers or any other person or persons who have the ultimate control over the affairs of such factory or establishment and also send intimation of any change in such particulars, within fifteen days of such change, to the Commissioner by registered post.

22. Duties of contractors.–Every contractor shall, within seven days of the close of every month, submit to the principal employer a statement showing the particulars in respect of employees employed by or through him in respect of whom contributions to the Employees' Pension Fund are payable and shall also furnish to him such information as the principal employer is required to furnish under the provisions of this Scheme to the Commisioner.

23. Allotment of account [1][numbers].— (1) For purposes of this Scheme, where the member has already been allotted or is allotted hereafter an account number under the Employees' Provident Funds Scheme, 1952, he shall retain the same account number.

(2) In the case of employees of the establishments exempted from Employees' Provident Funds Scheme, 1952 under section 17 of the Act, who are members of the Employees' Family Pension Fund the account number already allotted shall be retained by them.

(3) In the case of employees of the establishment exempted from the Employees' Provident Funds Scheme, 1952 under section 17 of the Act, who are not members of the Employees' Family Pension Fund but opt to become members of Employees' Pension Fund and in case of new employees of such establishments, fresh account numbers shall be allotted by the Commissioner.

1. Subs. by G.S.R. 134, dated 28th February, 1996 (w.e.f. 16-3-1996).

24. Declaration by persons taking up employment after the fund has been established.–The employer shall before taking any person into employment, ask him/her to state in writing whether or not he/she is a member of the Employees' Pension Fund and, if he/she is, also ask him/her to furnish a copy of the scheme certificate issued by the Commissioner to him in respect of the past employment in terms of paragraph 12 as the case may be. If the person concerned was not in employment previously or had availed of return of contribution in respect of his/her previous employment, he/she shall, on demand by the employer, furnish to him, for communication to the Commissioner, particulars concerning him/her and his/her family in the Form prescribed by the Central Provident Fund Commissioner:

[Provided that if such person is a person with disability, the aforesaid Form shall further contain such particulars as are necessary for such person.][1]

---
1. Ins. by G.S.R. 252(E), dated 31st March, 2008 (w.e.f. 1-4-2008).
---

25. Employees' Pension Fund Account.–The account called the "Employees' Pension Fund Account" shall be opened by the Commissioner in such manner as may be specified by the Central Board with the approval of Central Government.

26. Investment of the Employees' Pension Fund.–(1) All moneys accruing to the Employees' Pension Fund Account except the contributions of the Central Government shall be invested in accordance with the provisions of paragraph 52 of the Employees' Provident Funds Scheme, 1952.

(2) Net assets of the Family Pension Fund as on the 16-11-1995 shall merge in the Pension Fund and remain invested in the Public Account of the Government of India. The future Central Government's contributions accruing to the Pension Fund from 17th November, 1995 onwards shall also be invested in the Public Account of the Government of India.

27. Disposal of the Fund.–(1) Subject to the provisions of the Act and this Scheme, the Fund shall not, except with the prior sanction of the Central Government, be expended for any purpose other than the payments envisaged in this Scheme; for continued payment of family pension, life assurance benefit and retirement-cum-withdrawal benefits sanctioned under the Employees' Family Pension Scheme, 1971 prior to the date of introduction of this Scheme or which may be sanctioned under that scheme after the 16th November, 1995 in respect of cases arising before the date.

[(2) All administrative expenses shall be met from the 'Central Administration Account' as specified in Paragraph 49 of the Employees' Provident Funds Scheme, 1952. However, the cost of remittance of Pension shall be charged on the Pension Fund.][1]

---
1. Subs. by G.S.R. 3, dated 29th December, 2006, for sub-paragraph (2) (w.e.f. 6-1-2007).

[28. **********][1]

---
1. Deleted by GSR 3 dated 29.12.2006 (w.e.f. 06.1.2007).
---

29. Forms of accounts.–The accounts of the Employees' Pension Fund, as also the Employees' Pension Administration Account shall be maintained by the Commissioner in such form and in such manner as may be specified by the Central Board with the approval of the Central Government.

30. Audit.–The accounts of the Employees' Pension Fund including the administrative expenses incurred in running this Scheme shall be audited in accordance with the instructions issued by the Central Government in consultation with Comptroller and Auditor-General of India.

31. Rounding up of the benefits.–All items of benefits shall be calculated to the nearest rupee, fifty paise or more to be counted as the next higher rupee and fraction of a rupee less than fifty paise shall be ignored.

32. Valuation of the Employees' Pension Fund and review of the rates of contributions and quantum of the pension and other benefits.–(1) [The Central Government shall have an annual valuation of the Employees Pension Fund made by a valuer appointed by it.][1]

Provided that it shall be open to the Central Government to direct a valuation to be made at such other times as it may consider necessary.

(2) At any time, when the Employees' Pension Fund so permits, the Central Goverment may alter the rate of contributions payable under this Scheme or the scale of any benefit admissible under this Scheme or the period for which such benefit may be given.

1.	Subs. by G.S.R. 134, dated 28th February, 1996 (w.e.f. 16-3-1996).

[1][**33. Disbursement of pension and other benefits.**–The Commissioner shall, with the approval of the Central Board, enter into arrangement for the disbursement of pension and other benefits under this Scheme with disbursing agencies like Post Office or Nationalised Banks or Treasuries or scheduled commercial banks including regional rural banks or cooperative banks. The Commission payable to the disbursing agencies and other charges incidental thereto shall be met as provided in paragraph 27 of this Scheme.]

1.	Modified by G.S.R. 746 (E), dated 27th September, 2001 (w.e.f. 27-9-2001).

34. Registers, records, etc.–The Commissioner shall, with the approval of the Central Board, prescribe the registers and records to be maintained in respect of the employees, the form or design of any identity card, token or disc for the purpose of identifying any employee or his nominee or a member of a family entitled to receive the pension and such other forms/formalities as have to be completed in connection with the grant of pension and other benefits or for the continuance thereof subject to such periodical verification as may be considered necessary.

35. Power to issue directions.–The Central Government may issue, such directions as may be deemed just and proper by it for resolving any difficulty in the disbursement of pension and other benefits or for resolving any difficulty in implementation of this Scheme.

36. Regional Committee.–The Regional Committee set up under paragraph 4 of the Employees' Provident Funds Scheme, 1952 shall advise the Central Board, on such matters, in relation to the administration of this Scheme as the Central Board may refer to it from time to time and in particular on–

(a) progress of recovery of contributions under this scheme both from factories and establishments exempted under section 17 of the Act and other factories and establishments covered under the Act,

(b) expeditious disposal of prosecutions,

(c) speedy settlement of claims relating to pension and other benefits under this Scheme.

37. Annual report.–The Central Board shall cause to be included in the annual report on the working of this Scheme prepared under paragraph 74 of the Employees' Provident Funds Scheme, 1952, a report on the working of this Scheme during the previous financial year.

38. Application of the provisions of the Employees' Provident Funds Scheme, 1952.–In regard to matters for which either there is no provision or there is inadequate provisions in this Scheme the corresponding provisions in the Employees' Provident Funds Scheme, 1952 shall apply.

[1][**39. Exemption from the operation of the Pension Scheme.** The appropriate Government may grant exemption to any establishment or class of establishments from the operation of this Scheme, if the employees of the establishments are either members of any other pension scheme or proposed to be members of a pension scheme wherein the pensionary benefits are at par or more favourable than the benefits provided under this Scheme. Where exemption is granted to any establishment or class of establishments under this paragraph, withdrawal benefits available to the credit of the employees of such

establishment(s) under the ceased Family Pension Scheme, 1971, shall be paid, subject to the consent of the employees, to the pension fund of the establishment(s) so exempted. An application for exemption under this paragraph shall be presented to the Regional Provident Fund Commissioner having jurisdiction by the establishment or class of establishments, together with a copy of the pension scheme of the establishment (s) and other relevant documents, as may be called for by him. On receipt of such an application, the Regional Provident Fund Commissioner shall scrutinise it, obtain the recommendations of the Central Provident Fund Commissioner and submit the same to the appropriate Government for decision, pending disposal of application for exemption under this paragraph employers' share of the contribution shall not be remitted to the pension fund as envisaged in sub-paragraph (1) of paragraph 3. An application for exemption presented under this paragraph shall be disposed of within a period of six months from the date of its receipt or such further time as may be extended for reasons to be recorded in writing. If the application for exemption is not disposed of within the period so specified, the exemption applied for shall be deemed to have been granted.

Explanation. - - For the purpose of this paragraph, the period of six months will count from the date on which the application for exemption is given in compete form to the satisfaction of the Regional Provident Fund Commissioner.]

1.	Subs. by G.S.R. 134, dated the 28th February, 1996 (w.e.f 16th March 1996).

¹[**39A. Submission of return.**–**The employer of the exempted establishment or class of establishments and/or the Board of Trustees of the exempted establishment or class of establishments shall submit a monthly return to the Commissioner in Form 1.**] ²[and such return shall balso be submitted in electronic format in such form and manner as may be specified by the Commissioner.]

1.	Ins. by GSR 747 dated 27th September, 2001 (w.e.f. 28-9-2001).
2.	Added by GSR 1809 dated 5.8.2011 (w.e.f. 5.8.2011).

¹[**39B. Transfer value.**–**In case exemption is granted to any establishment or in the case of a member being transferred from pension fund of one exempted establishment to another pension fund of exempted establishment or statutory pension fund or *vice-versa*, a transfer value payment will be made which will consist of the following:–**

- (a) **Withdrawal benefit relating to past service period upto 15-11-1995 as per Table-A multiplied by Table-B factor for the period between 16-11-1995 to the date of exemption/transfer, and**
- (b) **Transfer value for pensionable service as per Table E for the service rendered from 16-11-1995 or from the date of joining the establishment to the date of exemption/transfer as the case may be.**
- (c) **In the event of cancellation of exemption granted under Para 39, transfer of fund will be made as per the conditions mentioned in the exemption notification.**]

1.	Ins. by G.S.R. 430 (E), dated 19th May, 2003 (w.e.f. 23-5-2003).

40. Information to the Central Government.–The Central Board shall furnish such information to the Central Government from time to time in respect of the income and expenditure from the Employees' Pension Fund account in such manner as may be directed by the Central Government.

41. Interpretation.–Where any doubt arises with regard to the interpretation of the provisions of this Scheme, it shall be referred to the Central Government who shall decide the same.

Suppliments

42. Punishment for failure to submit return, etc.–If any person–

(a) deducts or attempts to deduct from the wages or other remuneration of the member, the whole or any part of the employer's contribution, or

(b) fails or refuses to submit any return, statement or other documents required by this Scheme or submits a false return, statement or other documents, or makes a false declaration, or

(c) obstructs any Inspector or other official appointed under the Act or this Scheme in the discharge of his duties or fails to produce any record for inspection by such Inspector or other officials, or

(d) is guilty of contravention of or non-compliance with any other requirement of this Scheme, he shall be punishable with imprisonment, which may extend to one year, or with fine which, may extend to five thousand rupees, or with both.

43. Payment of pension in the case of a person charged with the offence of murder.–(1) If a person, who in the event of the death of a member of the Pension Fund is eligible to receive pension of the deceased under paragraph 12 or paragraph 16, is charged with the offence of murdering the member or for abetting the commission of such an offence, his claims to receive pension shall remain suspended till the conclusion of the criminal proceedings instituted against him for such offence.

(2) If on the conclusion of the criminal proceedings referred to in sub-paragraph (1), the person concerned is–

(a) convicted for the murder or abetting in the murder of the member, he shall be debarred from receiving pension which shall be payable to other eligible members, if any, of the family of the member; or

(b) acquitted of the charge of murder or abetting the murder of the member, pension benefit shall be payable to him.

[1][**43A. Special provisions in respect of International Workers:** The Scheme shall, in its application to International Workers as defined in this paragraph, be subject to the following modifications, namely:

(1) After clause (vii) of paragraph 2, the following clause shall be inserted, namely:-

(vii a) "International Worker"means,-

(a) an Indian employee having worked or going to work in a foreign county with which India has entered into a social security agreement and being eleigible to avail the benefits under a social security program of that country, by virtue of the eligibility gained or going to gain, under the said agreement;

(b) an employee other than an India employee, holding other than an Indian passport, working for an establishment in India to the Act applies;

(2) For clause (xv) of paragraph 2, the following clause shall be substituted, namely:-

[2][(xv) *****]

2. Deleted by GSR 745 dated 5.10.2012 (w.e.f. 5.10.2012).

(3) Sub-paragraph (2), (3) and (4) of paragraph 3 shall be omitted.

(4) Sub-paragraph (2) of paragraph 4 shall be omitted.

[3][**(4 A) For paragraph 9 of the principal scheme, the following paragraph shall be substituted, namely:-**

9. Determination of eligible service in respect of International Worker:- The eligible service shall be determined as follows:-

(i) in case of the 'existing member' or the 'new entrant,' the "actual service" shall be treated as eligible service;

(ii) in case of the member covered by a social security agreement, the period of coverage under relevant social security program in another country shall be added to actual service and the aggregate thereof shall be treated as eligible service as may be provided in the social security agreement].

(5) For sub-paragraph (1) of paragraph 10, the following sub-paragraph shall be substituted, namely:—

2[*****]

(6) For paragraph 11, the following paragraph shall be substituted, namely:-

11. Determination of pensionable salary - The pensionable salary shall be the average monthly pay drawn in any manner including on piece-rate basis during the contributory period of service of the membership of the Employees' Pension Fund.

(7) For paragraph 14, the following paragraph shall be substituted, namely-

14. Benefits on leaving service before being eligible for monthly member's pension –An International Worker covered under a social security agreement entered into between India and another country who has not rendered the eligible service prescribed in paragraph 9 on the date of exit, or on attaining the 58 years of age, whichever is earlier, shall be entitled to a totalisation benefit as may be provided in the said social security agreement:

Provided that if the International Worker covered under the provisions of the said agreement has not rendered the eligible service even after including the totalisation benefit as may be provided in the said agreement, then, such International Worker shall be entitled to a withdrawal benefit as laid down under Table 'D.'

(8) After paragraph 33, the following paragraph shall be inserted, namely:-

Provided that if the beneficiary under the Scheme is covered under a social security agreement between India and another country, the pension and other benefits under the scheme shall be disbursed in the manner as per the terms and conditions specified in the said agreement.

(9) After paragraph 35, the following paragraph shall be inserted, namely:-

To 35-A. Performing certain functions under the social security agreement:- The Commissioner shall perform all such functions as are assigned to the Employees' Provident Fund Organisation under a social security agreement entered into between the Government of India and any other country, in a manner and as per the terms and conditions specified therein.]

1.	Subs. By GSR 149 dated 03.9.2010 in place of original paragraph inserted by G.S.R. 705(E), dated 1.10.2008. (w.e.f. 1.10.2008).
2.	Deleted by GSR 745 (E) dated 05.10.2012 (w.e.f. 5.10.2012).
3.	Added by GSR 745 (E) dated 5.10.2012 (w.e.f.5.10.2012).

Suppliments

44. Repeal and Savings.–(1) On commencement of this Scheme, the Employees' Family Pension Scheme, 1971 in force immediately before such commencement shall cease to operate with effect from the 16th November, 1995.

(2) Notwithstanding anything contained in sub-paragraph (1) every nomination made under the Employees' Family Pension Scheme, 1.971, and every form regarding the details of family of an employee for the purposes of the Employees' Family Pension Scheme, 1971, shall be deemed to have been made under the provisions of this Scheme.

(3) All orders/authorisations/Pension Payment Orders issued under the Family Pension Scheme, 1971 shall be deemed to have been made under this Scheme.

TABLE 'A'
(See Paragraph 14)
(WITHDRAWAL BENEFIT)

No of full years' proportion of pay paid cessation of membership	No. of full years' Proportion of pay paid cessation of membership	Contribution payable at	Contribution of payble at
1	2	1	2
01	0.20	21	5.21
02	0.41	22	5.52
03	0.62	23	5.83
04	0.84	24	6.14
05	1.06	25	6.46
06	1.29	26	6.79
07	1.51	27	7.12
08	1.75	28	7.46
09	1.98	29	7.81
10	2.23	30	8.16
11	2.47	31	8.52
12	2.72	32	8.89
13	2.98	33	9.26
14	3.24	34	9.64
15	3.51	35	x10.03
16	3.78	36	10.43
17	4.05	37	10.83
18	4.34	38	11.24
19	4.62	39	11.66
20	4.92	40	12.08

TABLE B

(See Paragraphs 12 and 14)

FACTOR FOR COMPUTATION OF PAST SERVICE BENEFIT UNDER THE CEASED FAMILY PENSION SCHEME FOR EXISTING MEMEBRES ON EXIT FROM THE EMPLOYMENT

Years Factor	Upto 09.6.2008	w.e.f. 10.6.2008*
Less than 1	1.049	1.039
Less than 2	1.154	1.122
Less than 3	1.269	1.212
Less than 4	1.396	1.309
Less than 5	1.536	1.413
Less than 6	1.689	1.526
Less than 7	1.858	1.649
Less than 8	2.044	1.781
Less than 9	2.248	1.923
Less than 10	2.473	2.077
Less than 11	2.720	2.243
Less than 12	2.992	2.423
Less than 13	3.292	2.616
Less than 14	3.621	2.826
Less than 15	3.983	3.052
Less than 16	4.381	3.296
Less than 17	4.819	3.560
Less than 18	5.301	3.845
Less than 19	5.810	4.152
Less than 20	6.414	4.485
Less than 21	7.056	4.843
Less than 22	7.761	5.231
Less than 23	8.537	5.649
Less than 24	9.390	6.101
Less than 25		6.589
Less than 26		7.117
Less than 27		7.686
Less than 28		8.301
Less than 29		8.965
Less than 30		9.682

Suppliments

Less than 31	10.457
Less than 32	11.294
Less than 33	12.197
Less than 34	13.173]

*Table 'B' substituted by GSR 438 (E) dated 09.06.2008 (w.e.f. 10.6.2008). Old Table is also given for reference for old cases.

TABLE 'C'

(See Paragraph 16)

EQUIVALENT WIDOW PENSION

Salary at day of Death not more than	Equivalent widow pension	Salary at day of death not more than	Equivalent widow pension
1	2	1	2
300	250	1700	797
350	327	1750	808
400	343	1800	826
450	359	1850	844
500	375	1900	862
550	391	1950	880
600	408	2000	898
650	425	2050	916
700	442	2100	935
750	459	2150	954
800	476	2200	973
850	493	2250	992
900	510	2300	1011
950	527	2350	1030
1000	544	2400	1049
1050	561	2450	1068
1100	578	2500	1087
1150	595	2550	1106
1200	612	2600	1125
1250	629	2650	1144
1300	646	2700	1163
1350	664	2750	1182
1400	682	2800	1201
1450	700	2850	1221
1500	718	2900	1241
1550	736	2950	1261
1600	754	3000	1281
1650	772	3050	1301

Suppliments

3100	1321	5100	1911
3150	1341	5150	1916
3200	1361	5200	1921
3250	1381	5250	1926
3300	1401	5300	1931
3350	1421	5350	1936
3400	1441	5400	1941
3450	1461	5450	1946
3500	1481	5500	1951
3550	1501	5550	1956
3600	1521	5600	1961
3650	1541	5650	1966
3700	1561	5700	1971
3750	1581	5750	1976
3800	1601	5800	1981
3850	1621	5850	1986
3900	1641	5900	1991
3950	1661	5950	1996
4000	1681	6000	2001
4050	1701	6050	2006
4100	1721	6100	2011
4150	1741	6150	2016
4200	1751	6200	2021
4250	1761	6250	2026
4300	1771	6300	2031
4350	1781	6350	2036
4400	1791	6400	2041
4450	1801	6450	2046
4500	1811	6500	2051
4550	1821	*[6550	2056
4600	1831	6600	2061
4650	1841	6650	2066
4700	1851	6700	2071
4750	1861	6750	2076
4800	1871	6800	2081
4850	1881	6850	2086
4900	1891	6900	2091
4950	1896	6950	2096
5000	1901	7000	2101
5050	1906	7050	2106

7100	2111	9050	2306
7150	2116	9100	2311
7200	2121	9150	2316
7250	2126	9200	2321
7300	2131	9250	2326
7350	2136	9300	2331
7400	2141	9350	2336
7450	2146	9400	2341
7500	2151	9450	2346
7550	2156	9500	2351
7600	2161	9550	2356
7650	2166	9600	2361
7700	2171	9650	2366
7750	2176	9700	2371
7800	2181	9750	2376
7850	2186	9800	2381
7900	2191	9850	2386
7950	2196	9900	2391
8000	2201	9950	2396
8050	2206	10000	2401
8100	2211	10050	2406
8150	2216	10100	2411
8200	2221	10150	2416
8250	2226	10200	2421
8300	2231	10250	2426
8350	2236	10300	2431
8400	2241	10350	2436
8450	2246	10400	2441
8500	2251	10450	2446
8550	2256	10500	2451
8600	2261	10550	2456
8650	2266	10600	2461
8700	2271	10650	2466
8750	2276	10700	2471
8800	2281	10750	2476
8850	2286	10800	2481
8900	2291	10850	2486
8950	2296	10900	2491
9000	2301	10950	2496
11000	2501	12900	2691

Suppliments

11050	2506	12950	2696
11100	2511	13000	2701
11150	2516	13050	2706
11200	2521	13100	2711
11250	2526	13150	2716
11300	2531	13200	2721
11350	2536	13250	2726
11400	2541	13300	2731
11450	2546	13350	2736
11500	2551	13400	2741
11550	2556	13450	2746
11600	2561	13500	2751
11650	2566	13550	2756
11700	2571	13600	2761
11750	2576	13650	2766
11800	2581	13700	2771
11850	2586	13750	2776
11900	2591	13800	2781
11950	2596	13850	2786
12000	2601	13900	2791
12050	2606	13950	2796
12100	2611	14000	2801
12150	2616	14050	2806
12200	2621	14100	2811
12250	2626	14150	2816
12300	2631	14200	2821
12350	2636	14250	2826
12400	2641	14300	2831
12450	2646	14350	2836
12500	2651	14400	2841
12550	2656	14450	2846
12600	2661	14500	2851
12650	2666	14550	2856
12700	2671	14600	2861
12750	2676	14650	2866
12800	2681	14700	2871
12850	2686	14750	2876
14800	2881	14950	2896

14850	2886	15000	29011
14900	2891		

- Additional benefits added by GSR 227 (E) dated 26.03.2015 (w.e.f. 01.9.2014).

TABLE-D
(Return of contribution on exit from the employment)
(See Paragraph 14)

Year of	Proportion Service Up to 10.8.2008	wages at exit w.e.f. 10.8.2008 *
1	1.02	1.02
2	2.05	1.99
3	3.10	2.98
4	4.18	3.99
5	5.28	5.02
6	6.40	6.07
7	7.54	7.13
8	8.70	8.22
9	9.88	9.33

- Table 'D' revised by GSR 438 (E) dated 9.6.2008 (w.e.f. 10.6.2008).

Suppliments

TABLE - E
(See Paragraph 39-B)
(Transfer of Contribution from Employees' Pension Scheme, 1995 to Exempted or Other Pension Fund or vice-versa)

Number of full year's contribution period	Proportion of pay payable on last contribution month
1	0.978
2	1.979
3	3.003
4	4.051
5	5.124
6	6.221
7	7.345
8	8.494
9	9.671

*This table has been revised w.e.f. 10.8.2008 which is also given here take Table 'E.'

Number of full years' contribution paid	Proportion of pay on last contribution month	Number of full years' contribution paid	Proportion of pay on last contribution month
1	0.987	13	14.841
2	1.998	14	16.182
3	3.033	15	17.554
4	4.093	16	18.960
5	5.178	17	20.399
6	6.289	18	21.872
7	7.426	19	23.380
8	8.590	20	24.924
9	9.782	21	26.505
10	11.003	22	28.123
11	12.252	23	29.780
12	13.531	24	31.4771

*Susbs. by G.S.R. 514(E), dated 10-7-2009. (w.e.f. 10.7.2009).

Employees' Deposit-Linked Insurance Scheme, 1976

1. Short title, commencement and application.–(1) This Scheme may be called the **Employees' Deposit-Linked Insurance Scheme, 1976.**

(2) The provisions of this Scheme shall come into force on the 1st day of August, 1976.

(3) Subject to the provisions of sub-section (2) of section 16 and section 17(2A) of the Employees' Provident Funds and Miscellaneous Provisions Act, 1952, this Scheme shall apply to the employees of all factories and other establishments [1][to which the said Act applies]:

Provided that the provisions of this scheme shall not apply to tea factories in the State of Assam.

---

1. Subs. by G.S.R. 1788, dated 7th December, 1976 (w.e.f. 1-8-1976).

---

2 – Definitions- In this Scheme, unless the context otherwise requires-

(a) "Act" Means the Employees' Provident Funds and Miscellaneous Provisions Act, 1952 (19 of 1952);

(b) "assurance benefit" means a payment linked to the average balance in the Provident Fund Account of an employee, payable to a person belonging to his family or otherwise entitled to it in the event of death of the employee while being a member of the Fund;

(c) all other words and expressions used herein but not defined shall have the meaning respectively assigned to them in the Act or the Employees' Provident Funds Scheme, 1952.

3. Administration of the Scheme.–This Scheme shall be administered by the Central Board constituted under section 5A of the Ac

4. Regional Committee.–The Regional Committee set up under paragraph 4 of the Employees' Provident Funds Scheme, 1952, shall advise the Central Board on such matters, in relation to the administration of this Scheme, as the Central Board may refer to it from time to time and in particular, on–

(a) progress of recovery of contributions, under this Scheme, both from factories and establishments exempted under section 17 of the Act and other factories and establishments covered under the Act; and

(b) expeditious disposal of prosecutions.

5. Delegation of power by the Central Board.–(1) The Central Board may, by a resolution, empower its Chairman or the Commissioner or both to sanction expenditure, subject to such limits .as may be specified in the resolution, on contingencies, supplies and purchases of articles required for administering the Insurance Fund subject to financial provision in the Budget, where such expenditure is beyond the limits upto which the Chairman or the Commissioner is authorised to sanction expenditure on any single item.

(2) The Central Board may also by a resolution empower its Chairman or the Commissioner or both, to appoint such officers and employees other than those mentioned in sub-sections (2) and (3) of section 5D of the Act, as the Chairman or the Commissioner may consider necessary for the efficient administration of this Scheme.

(3) All sanctions of expenditure made by the Chairman or Commissioner in pursuance of sub-paragraph (1) shall be reported to the Central Board as soon as possible after the sanction of the expenditure.

6. Administrative and financial powers of the Commissioner.–The Commissioner may, without reference to the Central Board, sanction expenditure on contingencies, supplies and services and purchase of articles required for administering the Insurance Fund, subject to financial provision in the budget and subject to the limits upto which he may be authorised to sanction expenditure on any single item from time to time by the Central Board.

7. Contribution.–(1) The contribution payable by the employer and the Central Government under sub-section (2) and sub-section (3) of section 6C of the Act, shall be calculated on the basis of basic wages, dearness allowance (including the cash value of any food concession) and retaining allowance, if any, actually drawn during the whole month whether paid on daily, weekly, fortnightly or monthly basis:

[1][Provided that where the monthly pay of an employee exceeds [2][fifteen thousand rupees], the contribution payable in respect of him by the employer and the Central Government shall be limited to the amounts payable on a monthly pay of [2][fifteen thousand rupees], dearness allowance, retaining allowance (if any) and cash value of food concession].

(2) Each contribution shall be calculated to the [3][nearest rupee, 50 paise or more to be counted as the next higher rupee and fraction of a rupee less than 50 paise to be ignored].

1.	Ins. by G.S.R. 969, dated 14th July, 1978 (w.e.f. 29-7-1978).
2.	Subs. by G.S.R. 576, dated 1st November, 1994 (w.e.f. 1-10-1994) and by G.S.R. 398 (E), dated 30th May, 2001 (w.e.f. 1-6-2001). Again by G.S.R.610 (E) dated 22.8.2014 substituted Rs.6500 w.e.f. 01.09.2014).
3.	Subs. by G.S.R. 547, dated 19th July, 1983 (w.e.f. 1-4-1983).

8. Mode of payment of contribution.–(1) The contribution by the employer shall be remitted by him together with administrative charges at such rate as the Central Government may fix from time to time under sub-section (4) of section 6C of the Act (at present the rate of contribution is @ 0.05% of Insurance Fund and its administrative charges @ 01.01%) to be deposited within fifteen days of the close of every month by a separate bank draft or cheque or by remittance in cash in such manner as may be specified in this behalf by the Commissioner. The cost of remittance, if any, shall be borne by the employer.

(2) It shall be the responsibility of the employer to pay the contribution payable by himself in respect of the employees directly employed by him and also in respect of the employees employed by or through a contractor.

(3) The Central Government shall credit its contribution to the Insurance Fund as soon as possible after the close of every financial year.

(4) The Commissioner shall deposit the bank draft or cheque received from the employers in the State Bank of India or any Bank specified in the First Schedule to the Banking Companies (Acquisition and Transfer of Undertakings) Act, 1970 (5 of 1970).

[1][**8A. Recovery of damages for default in payment of any contribution** – [2][(1) Where an employer makes default in the payment of any contribution to the Insurance Fund, or in the payment

of any charges payable under any other provisions of the Act or the Scheme, the Central Provident Fund Commissioner or such officer as may be authorised by the Central Government by notification in the Official Gazette in this behalf, may recover from the employer by way of penalty, damages at the rates given below:

	Period of default	Rate of damages (% of arrears per annum)
(a)	Less than two months	Five
(b)	Two months and above but less than four months	Ten
(c)	Four months and above but less than six months	Fifteen
(d)	Six months and above	Twenty Five]

(2) The damages shall be calculated to the nearest rupee, 50 paise or more to, be counted as the nearest higher rupee and fraction of a rupee less than 50 to be ignored.]

1. Added by G.S.R. 522, dated 16th August, 1991 (w.e.f. 1-9-1991).
2. Substituted by G.S.R. 690(E), dated 26.9.2008 (w.e.f. 26-8-2008).

[1][**8B. Terms and conditions for reduction or waiver of damages.**–The Central Board may reduce or waive the damages levied under section 14B oft Act in relation to an establishment specified in the second proviso to section 14B, subject to the following terms and conditions, namely:–

(a) in case of a change of management including transfer of the undertaking to workers' co-operative and in case of merger or amalgamation of I sick industrial company with any other industrial company, complete waiver of damages may be allowed;

(b) in cases, where the Board for Industrial and Financial Reconstruction, f reasons to be recorded in its scheme, in this behalf recommends waiver c damages up to 100 per cent may be allowed;

(c) in other cases, depending on merits, reduction of damages up to 50 per cent may be allowed].

1. Added by G.S.R. 522, dated 16th August, 1991 (w.e.f. 1-9-1991).

9. Employer's contribution not to be deducted from the wages of the employees.–Notwithstanding any contract to the contrary, the employer shall not be entitled to deduct the employer's contribution payable by him under this Scheme from the wages of the employees or to recover it from them in any other manner.

10. Duties of employers— [1](1) Every employer shall send to the Commissioner, within fifteen days of the commencement of the Scheme, a consolidated return in such form as he may specify, of the employees who arc entitled and required to become members of the Insurance Scheme showing, *inter alia*, the Insurance Scheme Number, name, accumulations in the Insurance Scheme as at the end of the financial or accounting year preceding the date on which this Scheme comes into force together with certified copies of nomination executed by each employee under the rules of the Provident Fund of the establishment.]

[2][(1A) Every employer shall send to the Commissioner, within fifteen days of the close of each month, a return [3][in Form 5 of the Employees' Providenl Fund Scheme] of the employees, —

(a) qualifying to become members of the Insurance Fund, for the first time during the preceding month together with the certified copies of nomination made by each such qualifying employee and

(b) leaving service of the employee during the preceding month
4[* * * *]

Provided that if there is no employee qualifying to become a member of the Insurance Fund for the first time or there is no employee leaving the service of the employer during the preceding month, the employer shall send a 'NIL' return.

2[(2B) Every employer shall send to the Commissioner, within twenty-five days of the close of the month, in such form as he may specify, a monthly abstract showing *inter alia,* the aggregate amount of wages of all the members on which contributions are payable and the employers' contribution in respect of all such members for the month.]

(2) Every employer shall maintain such accounts in relation to the amounts contributed to the Insurance Fund by him as the Central Board may, from time to time, direct, and it shall be the duty of every employer to assist the Central Board in making such payment from the Insurance Fund 5[XXX] as are sanctioned by or under the authority of the Central Board.

5[XXX].

6[XXX].

---

1. Subs. by G.S.R. 420, dated 31st Augest, 1992 (w.e.f. 19-9-1992).
2. Added by G.S.R. 420, dated 31st Augest, 1992 (w.e.f. 19-9-1992).
3. Subs. by G.S.R. 331, dated 24th May, 1994 (w.e.f. 1-3-1994).
4. Omitted by G.S.R. 24, dated 31st December, 1996.
5. Omitted by G.S.R. 329, dated 20th February, 1978. (w.e.f. 4.3.1978).
6. Omitted by G.S.R. 648, dated 4th May, 1977. (w.e.f. 21.5.1977).

---

11. Inspection of records and registers by the Commissioner or Inspector.– Every employer shall, whenever the Commissioner or any other offia authorised by him in this behalf or an inspector so requires, produce before hi: the records and other registers then in his possession, for inspection.

12. Supply of forms to employers.– The Commissioner shall supply to employer free of charge, on demand, forms referred to in this Scheme to the extent absolutely necessary.

13. Administration Account.– The contributions received from the employers and the Central Government under sub-section (4) of section 6C of the Act shall be credited to a separate account called "The Insurance Fund Central Administration Account" and all expenses in connection with the administration of this scheme, other than the cost of benefits provided by or under this Scheme, shall be met out of this account.

14. Deposit-linked Insurance Fund Account. – The amount received as the employer's contribution and also the Central Government's contribution to the Insurance Fund under sub-sections (2) and (3) of section 6C shall be credited to an account called the "Deposit-Linked Insurance Fund Account," and all expenses towards the cost of any benefits provided by or under the Scheme shall be met out of this account.

[15. **Investment of moneys belonging to the Insurance Fund.** – (1) All moneys standing to the credit of the Insurance Funds as on 31st March, 1997 shall be kept in deposit with the Central Government shall allow interest at a rate not less than 8½% per annum

(2) The moneys credited as contributions to the Insurance Fund on and from the 1st day of April, 1997 shall be invested as per the investment pattern notified under paragraph 52 of the Employees' Provident Funds Scheme, 1952].

---

1. Subs. by G.S.R. 24, dated 29th August, 1997.

---

16. Interest. – All interest, rent and other income realised and net profits or losses, if any, from the sale or investments, not including therein the transaction of the Insurance Fund Central Administration Account shall be credited or debited as the case may be to the Insurance Fund.

17. Disposal of the Insurance Fund. – (1) Subject to the provisions of the Act and of this Scheme, the Insurance Fund, not including therein the Insurance Fund Central Administration Account, shall not, except with the previous sanction of the Central Board, be expended for any purpose other than the payment of the benefits in accordance with the provisions of this Scheme.

(2) The Insurance Fund shall be operated upon by such officers as may be authorised in this behalf by the Central Board.

18. Expenses of Administration. – All expenses relating to the idministration of this Scheme including the expenses incurred on Regional Committee shall be met from the "Insurance Fund Central Administration Account."

[19. **Forms and manner of maintenance of accounts.** – The Central Board shall maintain the accounts of its income and expenditure including its administrative account in Form 1 and Form 2 and the balance-sheet in Form 3. The accounts shall be prepared for the financial year and the books shall be balanced on the thirty-first March each year].

---

1. Subs. by G.S.R. 12, dated 21st December, 1992 (w.e.f. 2-1-1993).

---

20. Audit. – (1) The accounts of the Insurance Fund, including the Insurance Fund Central Administration Account, shall be audited in accordance with the instructions issued by the Central Government in consultation with the Comptroller and Auditor General of India.

(2) The charges on account of audit shall be paid out of the Insurance Fund Central Administration Account.

21. Budget. – (1) The Commissioner shall place before the Central Board each year before the first fortnight of February a budget showing separately the probable receipts from the contributions and from the levy of administrative charges and the expenditure which is proposed to be incurred during the following financial year. The budget as approved by the Central Board shall be submitted for sanction to the Central Government within a month of its being placed before the Central Board.

(2) The Central Government may make such modification in the budget as it considers desirable before sanctioning it. .

(3) The Commissioner may at any time during the year make budgetary, reappropriation of funds sanctioned in the budget by the Central Government provided that–

(i) the total amount sanctioned in the budget by the Central Government is not exceeded;

(ii) it is made only for meeting such expenses of administration as are to be met from the Insurance Fund Central Administration Account in accordance with paragraph 18; and

(iii) every reappropriation so made shall be reported by him to the Central Board at its next meeting.

(4) The Commissioner shall place before the Central Board a supplementary budget for a financial year, giving detailed estimates and reasons of inescapable expenditure which is likely to be incurred during the year for which no provision has been made in the sanctioned budget and which cannot be covered under the provisions of sub-paragraph (3). The supplementary budget as approved by the Central Board shall be submitted for sanction to the Central Government within a month of its being placed before the Central Board.

(5) Any expenditure incurred by the Commissioner over and above the sanctioned budget of the financial year and not covered under the provisions of sub-paragraphs (3) and (4) shall be reported to the Central Board at the earliest practicable moment after the excess is established for its consideration and for obtaining sanction of the Central Government.

22. Scales of assurance benefit and the minimum average balance to be maintained by an employee.- [1][(1) [2][On the death of an employee, who is a member of the Fund or of a provident fund exempted under section 17 of the Act, as the case may be, the persons entitled to receive the provident fund accumulations of the deceased shall, in addition to such accumulations be paid an amount, equal to the average balance in the account of the deceased in the Fund or of a Provident Fund exempted under section 17 of the Act, as the case may be, during preceding twelve months or during the period of his membership, whichever is less, except where the average balance exceeds rupees fifty thousand, the amount payable shall be rupees fifty thousand plus 40 per cent of the amount in excess of [2][rupees thirty five thousand subject to a ceiling of one lakh rupees].

[3][***]

[4][*Explanation 1.*–For the purpose of determining the average balance in the Fund or in the provident fund exempted under section 17 of the Act, as the case may be, in relation to any employee, the sum total of contributions by the employee and the employer, due for and up to the relevant period, whether paid or unpaid in the Fund or in the provident fund exempted under section 17 of the Act, as the case may be, together with interest thereon, shall be included.

Explanation 2.–The period of [5][twelve months] for calculation of benefit! under this Scheme shall be computed backwards from the month preceding t month in which death of the member occurs.]

(2) In the case of a part-time employee who was a member of Fund [4][or of a Provident Fund exempted under section 17 of the Act, as the case may be,] while serving in more than one factory or establishment the quantum of benefit under this Scheme shall be determined with reference to the average of the aggregate balance in all his accounts in the Fund during the preceding [5][twelve months].

[6][[7][(3)] On death of an employee, who is a member of the Fund or of a provident fund exempted under Section 17 of the Act, as the case may be, who was in the employment of the same establishment for a continuous period of twelve months, preceding the month in which he died, the persons entitled

to receive the provident fund accumulations of the deceased shall, in addition to such accumulations be paid an amount equal to:-

- (i) the average monthly wages drawn (subject to a maximum of [8][fifteen thousand rupees)] during the twelve months preceding the month in which he died, multiplied by twenty times or;
- (ii) the amount of benefit under sub-paragraph (1), whichever is higher.

Explanation – In case of a part-time employee who is a member of the fund or of a provident fund exempted under Section 17 of the Act, as the case may be, who was serving in more than one factory or establishment for a continuous period of twelve months, preceding the month in which he died, the quantum of benefit under this scheme shall be determined with reference to the average of the aggregate of all the wages wherever he was continuously working for more than twelve months, subject to the wage ceiling of [8][fifteen thousand rupees].]

[9][(4) The benefit under this Scheme shall be further increased by twenty percent in addition to the benefits admissible under sub-paragraphs (1), (2), or (3) of paragraph 22, as the case may be.]

1.	Subs. by G.S.R. 153, dated 7th March, 1994 (w.e.f. 1-4-1993).
2.	Para (1) Subs by GSR 523(E) dated 18.6.2010 (w.e.f. 18.6.2010) in palace of old substitutions by G.S.R. 238, dated 7th June, 2000 (w.e.f. 24-6-2000).
3.	Proviso omitted by G.S.R. 153, dated 7th March, 1994 (w.e.f. 1-4-1993).
4.	Ins. by G.S.R. 329, dated 20th February, 1978 (w.e.f. 4-3-1978).
5.	Subs. by G.S.R. 354, dated 22nd May, 1990 (w.e.f. 1-3-1990).
6.	Ins. by G.S.R. 9 (E), dated 8th January, 2011 (w.e.f. 8-1-2011).
7.	Re-numbered by G.S.R. 83, dated 11th February, 2011 (w.e.f. 11-2-2011).
8.	Subs. by G.S.R. 610 (E), dated 22nd August, 2014 (w.e.f. 1-9-2014).
8.	Inserted by G.S.R. 610 (E), dated 22nd August, 2014 (w.e.f. 1-9-2014).

23. Assurance benefit to whom payable.–(1) The nomination made by an employee under the Employees' Provident Funds Scheme, 1952 [1][or under the provident fund exempted under section 17 of the Act, as the case may be] shall be treated as nominations under this Scheme and the assurance amount shall become payable to such nominee or nominees.

(2) If no nomination subsists or if the nomination relates only to part of the amount standing to his credit in the Fund [1][or of a provident fund exempted under section 17 of the Act, as the case may be] the whole amount or the part thereof to which the nomination does not relate, as the case may be, shall become payable to the members of his family in equal shares:

Provided that no share shall be payable to–

- (a) sons who have attained majority;
- (b) sons of a deceased son who have attained majority;
- (c) married daughters whose husbands are alive;
- (d) married daughters of a deceased son whose husbands are alive; if there is any member of the family other than those specified in clauses (a), (b), (c) and (d):

Provided further that the widow or widows, and the child or children of a deceased son shall receive between them in equal parts only the share which that son would have received if he had survived the employee and had not attained the age of majority at the time of his death.

(3) In any case to which the provisions of sub-paragraphs (1) and (2) do not apply the whole amount shall be payable to the person legally entitled to it.

²[(4) If a person who is eligible to receive Assurance Scheme benefit of the deceased member in terms of sub-paragraphs (1), (2) or (3) is charged with the offence of murdering the member or for abetting in the commission of such an offence, his claim to receive assurance benefit shall remain suspended till the conclusion of the criminal proceedings instituted against him. If on the conclusion of the criminal proceedings, the person concerned is–

(a) convicted for the murder or abetting in the murder of the member, he shall be debarred from receiving his share of deposit linked assurance benefit which shall be payable to any other eligible member of the family, or

(b) acquitted of the charge of murdering or abetting in the murder of the member, his share shall be payable to him.

Explanation.–For the purpose of this paragraph an employee's posthumous child, if born alive, shall be treated in the same way as a surviving child born before his death.

---

1. Ins. by G.S.R. 329, dated 20th February, 1978 (w.e.f. 4-3-1978).
2. Ins. by G..S.R. 420, dated 31st August, 1992 (w.e.f. 19-9-1992).

---

24. Assurance amount–How to be paid.–(1) The nominee or nominees or other claimants shall send a written application to the Commissioner through the employer in such form as the Commissioner may specify, to claim payment under this Scheme.

(2) If the person to whom any amount is to be paid under this Scheme is a minor or a lunatic, the payment shall be made in accordance with the provisions in the Employees' Provident Funds Scheme, 1952, relating to payment to such persons.

¹[(3) The payment may be made, at the option of the person to whom payment is to be made,

(i) by postal money order, or

(ii) by deposit in the payee's bank account in any Scheduled Bank or any Co-operative Bank (including the Urban Co-operative Banks or any post office, or

(iii) by deposit in the payee's name (the whole or part of the amount) in the form of annuity/term deposits scheme in any nationalised bank, or

(iv) through the employer.]

²[(4) The claims, complete in all respects submitted alongwith the requisite documents shall be settled and benefit amount paid to the beneficiary within ³[20 days] from the date of its receipt by the Commissioner. If there is any deficiency in the claim, the same shall be recorded in writing and communicated to the applicant within ³[20 days] from the date of receipt of such application. In case the Commissioner fails without sufficient cause to settle a claim complete in all respect within ³[20 days], the Commissioner shall be liable for the delay beyond the said period and penal interest @12%

per annum may be charged on the benefit amount and the same may be deducted from the salary of the Commissioner.]

1.	Subs. by G..S.R. 873, dated 25th September, 1986 (w.e.f. 11-10-1986).
2.	Ins. by G.S.R. 334, dated 29th August, 1997 (w.e.f. 13-9-1997).
3.	Subs. By G.S.R. 527 (E) dated 02.7.2015 for '30 days' (w.e.f. 02.7.2015).

25. Registers, Records, etc.–The Commissioner may with the approval of the Central Board specify the registers and records to be maintained in respect of the employees, the form or design of any identity card, token or disc for the purpose of identifying any employee or his nominee or nominees or a member of his family entitled to receive the benefit under this Scheme and such other formalities as have to be completed in connection with the payment of the said benefit, subject to such periodical verification as may be considered necessary.

26. Annual Report on the working of this Scheme.–The Central Board shall approve before the [1][tenth of December] and submit to the Central Government before the [1][twentieth of December] each year, a report on the working of the Scheme during the previous financial year.

1.	Subs. by G.S.R. 354, dated 22nd May, 1990 (w.e.f. 1-3-1990).

27. [*******]
[Deleted by G.S.R. 648 dated 4.5.1977 (w.e.f. 21.5.1977).]

28. Special provisions relating to establishments in respect of which applications are received for exemption from the provisions of this Scheme. – (1) (i) A Commissioner may be order and subject to such conditions as may be specified in this order exempt from the operation of all or any of the provisions of this Scheme an employee to whom this Scheme applies on receipt of application from such an employee:

Provided that such an employee is without making any separate contribution or payment of premium, in enjoyment of benefits in the nature of life assurance, whether linked to their deposits in provident funds or not, according to the rules of the factory or other establishment and such benefits are more favourable than the benefits provided under this Scheme.

(ii) Where an employee is exempted, as aforesaid, the employer shall in respect of such employee maintain such accounts, submit such returns, provide such facilities for inspection as the Commissioner may direct and pay such inspection charges and make such investments as the Central Government may direct.

(2) An employee exempted under sub-paragraph 1 may, by an application to the Commissioner, make a request that the benefits of this Scheme be extended to him.

(3) No employee shall be granted exemption or permitted to apply out of exemption more than once on each account.

(4) (i) The [1][Central Provident Fund Commissioner] may by order and subject to such conditions as may be specified in the order exempt from the operation of all or any of the provisions of this Scheme any class of employees to whom this Scheme applies, on receipt of an application therefore, in such form as the Commissioner may specify:

Provided that such class of employees is, without making any separate contribution on payment of premium, in enjoyment of benefits in the nature of life assurance, whether linked to their deposits in provident fund or not, according to the rules of the factory or other establishment and such benefits are more favourable than the benefits provided under this Scheme.

(ii) Where any class of employees is exempted as aforesaid, the employer shall in respect of such class of employees maintain such accounts, submit such returns, provide such facilities for inspection, pay such inspection charges and make investments in such manner as the Central Government may direct.

(5) A class of employees exempted under sub-paragraph 4 or the majority of employees constituting such class may, by an application to the Commissioner, make a request that the benefits of this Scheme be extended to them.

(6) No class of employees or the majority of employees constituting such class shall be granted exemption or permitted to apply out of exemption more than once on each account.

(7) Notwithstanding anything contained in this Scheme the Commissioner may in relation to a factory or other establishment in respect of which an application for exemption under section 17 (2A) of the Act has been received, relax pending the disposal of the application, the provisions of this Scheme in such manner as he may direct.

2[(8) Every employer shall sent to the Commissioner, an electronic format of the returns refered to in clause (ii) of sub-paragraph (1) and clause (ii) of sub-paragraph (4), in such form and manner as may be specified by the Commissioner.]

1. Subs. by G..S.R. 228 (E), dated 2nd March, 1989 (w.e.f. 25-3-1989).
2. Ins. by G..S.R. 1810 (E), dated 5th August, 2011 (w.e.f. 5-8-2011).

1[**29. Punishment for failure to submit returns, etc.**–If any person,–

(a) deducts or attempts to deduct from the wages or other remuneration of a member the whole or any part of the employer's contribution; or

(b) fails or refuses to submit any return, statement or other documents required by this Scheme or submits a false return, statement or other documents, or makes a false declaration; or

(c) obstructs any Inspector or other official appointed under the Act or this Scheme in the discharge of his duties or fails to produce any record for inspection by such Inspector or other official; or

(d) is guilty of contravention of or non-compliance with any other requirements of this Scheme,

he shall be punishable with imprisonment which may extend to one year or with fine which may extend to four thousand rupees, or with both.]

2. Ins. by G.S.R. 420, dated 31st August, 2011 (w.e.f. 19-9-1992).

Table of Cases

"A"

Aditya Agro Industries (Pvt.) Ltd. And another Vs. R,P,F.C.–1997 (2) LLN 271	213
Aadonoy Cotton Mills [1995 (4) SCC 550	290
Ahmedabad Cooperative Departmental Stores Ltd. Vs. U.O.I.- 1997 (II) CLR 123 (Guj)	37
Ajmeri Gold Fingers vs. Asstt. P.F. Commissioner and another-2013 LLR. 1127 (Bom. HC)	31
A. L. Subramanian vs. E.P.F. Appellate Tribunal, New delhi & others- 2011 LLR. 1074 (Mad. H.C.)	244
Alico Rubber Reclamation (Private) Limited vs. Employees' Provident Funds Organisation and another- 2011 LLR. 1032 (H.P. H.C.)	244
Allahabad Bank Vs. S.K. Bhattacharya- 1999 (3) LLN 140 (Cal)	248
Alliminium Corpn. Of India Ltd. Vs. RPF Commissioner- SIR 1958 Cal 570; (1959) 1 LLJ 249	117
Amal Kumar Ghatak Vs. R.P.F. Commissioner- (1980) 2 LLJ 308 (Cal)	110
American Express Bakery vs. Regional P.F. Commissioner-2011 (131) FLR 1093 (Bom H.C.)	202
Anantharamaih Woolen Factory Vs. State- 1981 Lab IC 538; (1981) 1 LLN 170 (Kant)	89
Andhra Cement Co. Ltd, Vijaywada Vs. R.P.F.C. and others-1988 (2) LLJ.453 (AP)	30
Andhra Coop. Spg. Mills Vs. R.P.F. Commissioner, - 1973 Lab.I.C. 325 (AP-DB)	129
Andhra University Vs. R.P.F.C. and other- AIR 1986 SC 463; 1986 Lab.I.C. 103	28, 42
Aniruddh Kumar Dhote Vs. State of Maharashtra – 2002 (3) LLJ 400; 2002 (94) FLR 914	292
APSEB Hyderabad Vs. R.P.F.C.- 1979 (1) An W.R. 66	212
Apex security and Detective Force Pvt. Ltd. Vs. Central Board of Trustees, EPF Irganisation-2015 LLR. 900 (Delhi H.C.)	216, 218, 223
Arcot Textile Mills Ltd. vs. The Riginal P.F. Commissioner and others- 2014 LLR. 89: 2014 (140) FLR 233 (S.C.)	218
Associated Cement Companies Ltd. Vs. their workmen - AIR. 1960 S.C. 56	30
Associated Cement Company Ltd. And other Vs. R.M. Gandhi, R.P.F.C. and others -1992 Lab.IC 2110 (Guj)	112
Associated Industries (P) Ltd. Vs. R.P.F.C. Kerala- AIR 1964 SC 314; 1963 (2) LLJ.652 (SC)]	42
A. Subbiah Vs. Thiruvenkataswami- 1971 Lab.I.C. 1595 (Mad.)	150
Atal Tea Co. Ltd. Vs. R.P.F. Commissioner- 1997 Lab.IC 1207; (1998) 79 FLR 372; (1998) 2 CLR 34 (Cal)	209
Atlantic Engineering Services (P) Ltd. Vs. U.O.I. - (1979) 54 FJR 331]	213
A.V.C. Investment and trading (P) ltd. Vs. R.P.F.C. -(1996) 2 LLJ 473; (1996) 73 FJR 1385 (Bom.DB)	199

"B"

Bachhittar Singh Vs. Stat of Punjab – AIR 1963 S.C. 395	194
Bajarang Lal Padia Vs. Stat of Orissa- 1975 Lab.I.C. 830	48
Bakshi Steels Ltd. Vs. Regional P.F. Commissioner -(1994) 2 LLN 283; (1994) 69 FLR 549	216
Balasore Motor Association Vs. R.P.F.C. AIR 1970 Orissa 199; 1970 Lab.IC 1393.	195
Balbari Vidya Mandir and others vs. State and others	24
Balveer Kaur & Others V/s Steel Authority of India & Others	5
Bhagirath Kanoria Vs. State of M.P. – AIR 1984 SC 1688; 1984 (2) SCC 222	289

General Manager, Bharat Coking Coal Ltd vs. Shib Kumar Dusad & others – 2001 LLR 74 SC	131
Bharat Heavy Electricals Ltd Vs. R.P.F.C. – 1985 Lab.IC 282 (MP)	212
Bhaskara Ceramic Industries Vs. R.P.F.C. A.P.- 1991 Lab. I.C. 1138 (A.P.)	9, 27, 52
Binny Ltd. Bangalore Vs. R.P.F.C. – 1999 (I) LLN.998 (Karn.DB)	172
Bankim Chandra Chakraworty Vs. R.P.F.C. – AIR 1958 Pat. 314	196
Bombay Printers Ltd. Vs. Union of India- (1991) 63 FLR 106; (1991) 1 CLR 772	128
Bridge and Roof Co Vs. Union of India –(1962) 2 LLJ 490; AIR 1963 SC 1474; (1963) 3 SCR 978	110
Builders' Association of India and others vs U.O.I. and others, decided on 16.10.2015	107

"C"

C.K. Shah, P.F. Inspector Vs. Natson Mfg. Co. Pvt. Ltd. – (1976) 17 GLR 419	296
C.L. Subramaniam vs. Collector of Customs- (1972) 3 SCC 542	195
M/s. Calcutta Construction Company vs. Regional P.F. Commissioner and others. – 2015 (146) FLR 579 (P & H H.C.)	42
Calicut Modern Spinning & Weaving Mills Ltd. Vs. R.P.F.C. [1982 Lab.IC 1422; (1982) 1 LLJ 440 (Ker)	120, 213
Can Bank Financial Services Ltd. Vs. R.P.F.C. – (1998) 1 LLJ.92; (1997) 3 LLN 575; (1997) 2 CLR 734 (Kant.DB)	48
Cemendia Co. Ltd. Vs. Bachu Bhai N. Rawal- [AIR 1987 SC 1956; 1987 Lab.IC. 1648; 1988 (I) LLJ.138	28
Central P.F. Commissioner Vs. S.K. Nasiruddin Beedi Merchant Ltd.–(1999) 1 LLJ 360 (Pat. DB)	116
Chennimalai Weavers' Coop. P. & S. Society Vs. Govt. of India- 1981 Lab.I.C. 203 (Mad)	46
Chetram Vs. R.P.F.C. Orissa 1972 (I) LLJ. 60 9SC).	33
Christian Association for Radio and Audio Visual Service (CURAVS), Jabalpur Vs. R.P.F.C. 1979 Lab.I.C. 283	42, 48
Christian Medical Collage and Brown Memorial Hospital, Ludhiana Vs. R.P.F.C. Chandigarh- 1982 Lab.I.C. 952; 1988 (2) LLJ. 379 (SC)	46
Commissioner, Office of Regional P.F. Vs. Ariyamala & anr. 2002 II LLJ. 627 (Mad.)	191

"D"

Daily Pratap Vs. R.P.F.C and others – 1999 LLR 1 (SC); 1999 (1) CLR 2; 1998 (80) FLR 894	111
Damji L. Shah Vs. R.P.F.C.- 1992 (1) LLJ 224 (Bom.)	199
Darjeeling Doors Plantation Ltd. and another Vs. R.P.F.C.. W.B.-1995 (1) LLJ 939 (Cal.)	243
Delhi Clothe & General Mills Company Ltd. Vs. RPFC UP – 1961 (2) LLJ-444	6, 30
Delhi Iron and Steel Stockists (C.S.) Association (P) Ltd. Vs. R.P.F.C. New Delhi – 1977 Lab.IC 1018; 1977 (2) LLJ 217	194
Delhi Municipality Vs. Purshottam Das -1983 Cr. LJ 172	296
M/s. Delta Ltd. Vs. RPFC-II, West Bengal – [2005 (3) LLJ. 258: 2005 (106) FLR 16: 2005 (3) Lab.I.C. 2307:2005 LLR 788	177
Digpal Singh Vs. U.O.I.- 2002 Lab.IC 3547; 2003 (I) LLJ 876	8, 249
District Exhibitors Association Vs. Union of India – (1991)3 SCC 119; 1991 SCC (L&S) 822; (1991) 2 LLJ 115	118
M/s. Durga Body Builders vs. U.O.I. and another- 2009 LLR. 84 (Jhar.)	202

"E"

EPF Commissioner vs. Official Liquidator of Eskay Pharmaceuticals Ltd. – 2011 (10) SCC. 727: 2011 (5) LLN. 1: 2012 (1) LLJ. 1: 2012 (132) FLR. 98: 2012 LLR. 23 (S.C.)	242
E.P.F. Inspector, Trichure Vs. The Poly Clinic (P) Ltd. -1989 Lab.I.C. 969; 1989 (2) LLJ 562 (Ker.)	47
Employees' Provident Fund Organisation vs. Rollwell Forge Ltd. & others – 2011 LLR. 1006 (Guj. H.C.)	241
Engser Ltd. & another Vs. E.P.F. Organisation & Others -2007 III CLR 550 (Cal)	218

"F"

Ferro Concrete Construction (I) Pvt. Ltd. Vs. RPFC Indore and others – 2002 Lab.IC 412; 2002 (I) LLJ 986; 2002 (2) LLN 269 (MP)	246
Food Corpn. Of India Vs. R.P.F. Commissioner- 2003 (2) LLJ 376 (Del-DB)	197
Food Corporation of India vs. Provident Fund Commissioner – (1990) 1 SCC. 68: 1990 (60) FLR. 15: 1990 1 CLR. 720: 1990 SCC (L & S) 1	31, 195, 196

"G"

G.D. Singh, E.O. Vs. M/s. Koshi Refinary and others – 2003 (2) LLJ 671; 2003 (97) FLR 289; 2003 LLR 577	295
G.M. ONGC Contractual Workers Union- CLR (II) 2008 P. 988 (SC)	37
G.V.V. Swamy Vs. R.P.F.C and others- 1987 Lab.I.C. 719 (AP)	36, 37
Gandhi Vanita Ashram Vs. Provident Fund Commissioner -(1996) 73 FLR 1612 (P&H)	35
George Issac, Managing Partner, Malabar Coast Products, Kottayam vs. Assistant Regional Provident Fund Commissioner and Others. 2015 LLR. 844 (Ker. HC)	18
Girdhar Silk Mills Vs. P.O. EPF Appellate Tribunal- 2003 (1) LLN 172 (Del. DB)	223
Gitaben Arvindkumar Sheth vs. Union of India -(1995) 2 LLN 226	101
Glamour Vs. R.P.F.C.- 1975 Lab.I.C. 954; 1975 (I) LLJ. 514	191
Gordon Woodroffe Ltd Vs. Regional Commissioner, EPF- 2002 Lab.IC 653 (Mad)	113
M/s. Group 4 Securities guarding Ltd, Bangalore vs. R.P.F.C. and others – 2004 Lab.I.C. 2075; 2004 (2) LLJ. 1142; 2004 LLR. 540; 2004 (102) FLR 374	111, 190
Gujrat Cypromet Ltd. Vs. A.P.F.C. – 2004 (3) CLR 485; 2004 (103) FLR. 908	112
Gunvantrai Vs. R.P.F.C. – AIR 1970 MP 221; 1970 Lab.IC 1383	195

"H"

H.C. Sarin Vs. Union of India- (1976) 4 SCC 765	194
H.P. Agro Industries Corpn. Ltd. Vs. R.P.F.C. – 1994 Lab.IC 1286 (HP)	174, 212
Heary Engg. Mazdoor Union Vs. State of Bihar" – AIR 1970 SC 82; 1969 (2) LLJ-549; 1969 (i) SCC 765	21
Himachal Pradesh Nagar Vikas Pradhikaran Vs. R.P.F.Commissioner-(1998) 2 LLJ 267 (HP-DB)	116
Himachal Pradesh State Forest Corporation Vs. R.P.F.C.- 2008 LLR. 980 (SC)	195
Hymavathi vs. Special By. Tehsildar. – 2008 (119) FLR 279 (Kerala HC)	25

Table of Cases

Hindustan Lever Employees' Union vs. Regional P.F. Commissioner, Maharashtra and Goa- 1995 Lab.IC 775 (777); (1995) 1 LLN 767; (1995) 2 LLJ 279; (1995) 71 FLR 46	109, 111

"I"

Imambhai Gulam Husein Shaikh Vs. R.P.F.C.- 23 CLR 581	33
India United Mills Vs. R.P.F.C. Bombay-AIR 1960 Bom. 203; 1959 (2) LLJ 733	112
Indian Drilling and Mining (Pvt.) Ltd. An another Vs. R.P.F.C., EPFO and others- 2001 (2) LLN 306	247
Indian Institute of Technology, Madras Vs. R.P.F.C. Madras- 1979-54 FJR 429	47
Indrajit C. Parikh Vs. V.K. Bhatt & others- AIR 1974 SC 1183	293
Industrial Development Corp. of Orrissa Ltd. and another Vs. R.P.F.C.II and another- 2002 (I) LLJ 774; 2002 (92) FLR 945	9, 248
Inspector, EPF Vs. Alwin Concrete Blocks and Tiles Mfg. Co.- AIR 1974 SC 337; (1974) 3-SCC. 717; 1974 Lab.I.C. 770; 1974 (I) LLH. 276	32
Inter-state Transport Agency, Sitamarhi Vs. R.P.F.C. Patna-[1993 Lab I.C. 940 (Pat.)	63

"J"

J & J Dechane Vs. R.P.F.Inspector – (1960) 1 LLJ 765 (AP) relying on State of Madras Vs. V.G. Row, AIR 1952 SC 196	85
J.G. Vakharia Vs. R.P.F.C. (1957) 1 LLJ 448	9, 27, 52
J.K. college of Nursing & Paramedicals vs. Union of India & Others- 2011 LLR. 1013 (Delhi HC)	31
Jagdish Prasad Nirmal Das (India wire Netting Factory) Vs. R.P.F.C. Delhi, AIR 1963 S.C. 395	194
Jaggi & Co. vs. E.P.F. Appellate Tribunal and another- FLR (116)2008 P. 326 (Delhi HC); 2008 LLR.126 (Delhi HC)	34
Jaipur Udyog Ltd. Sawai Madhopur Vs. Inspector, Kota- (1979) 55 FJR 161	293
Jamnabai PurshottamAsar Vs. State of Maharashtra [(1964) 2 LLJ 7; AIR 1964 Bom. 267	88
Jay Engineering Works Ltd. Vs. Union of India- (1963) 2 LLJ 72; AIR 1963 SC 1480	110, 111
Jayakar Rao N. Shetty Vs. R.P.F.C. (1993) 2 LLJ 78: 1993 Lab IC 561	10, 52
Jiyajeerao Cotton Mills Ltd. Vs. Dev Kumar Holani- 1998 (II) CLR 630 (SC)	172
Joseph K.V. Vs. R.P.F.C., Ernakullam- 2003 II CLR 96 (Ker.)	218
Josolda Glass and Sillicate Vs. R.P.f.C.- 2002 (3) LLN 1146 (Cal.DB)	290
Jyoti Cements (P) Ltd. and others vs. Commissioner and others – 2011 (131) FLR. 557 (Raj. H.C.)	218

"K"

K Gopalan Vs. U.O.I. – 1973 Lab.I.C. 287	18, 47

Table of Cases

Case	Page
K.B. Jacob Vs. R.P.F.C. – 1987 Lab.I.C. 1139 (Ker.)	46
K.L. Jalan and others Vs. Stat of W.B. and others – 1994 (I)LLJ 224 (Cal.)	289
K.R. Subbier Tape Factory Vs. RPF Commissioner- (1970) 2 LLJ 109	117
K.T. Rolling Mills (P) Ltd. Vs. R.M. Gandhi and others – 1993 Lab.IC 1466 (Bom); 1994 (I) LLJ 66 (Bom)	199, 212
Kalindi Vs. Tata Locomotives- AIR 1960 SC 914	194
Kancheepuram Kamakshiamman Crop. Spg. Mills Ltd., Kancheepuram Vs. CBT, EPF and others–2010-III-LLT-740 (Mad.)	217
Kappusaney G. Vs. R.P.F. Commissioner, Triuchirapalli and another 2010-111-LLJ-733 (Mad)	133
Kerala Automobiles Ltd. Vs. Naveetha P (Mrs) – 2008 (III) LLJ 530 (Del)	117
Kerala Sareeram Model School through its Trust-in-charge, A.P.R. Nair vs. U.O.I. and others-2006 LLR. 383 (Jharkhand H.C.)	41
Khemchand Motilal Tobacco Products Ltd. Vs. Union of India- (1995) 1 LLN 1002; (1995) 2 CLR 360 (MP-DB)	112
Khushiram Agarwal vs. EPFO and others – 2008 LLR 474 (Cal.)	249
Khushi Ram Raghunath Rai Vs. R.P.F.C.- ILR (19756)2 Punj 481	191
Kottathala Handloom Industrial Co-op. Society Vs. Enforcement Officer, 2008 III C.L.R. 464 (Kerala H.C.)	44
Krishna Chandra Vs. UOI- (1974) 4 SCC 374;	195
Krishna Kumar Agarwala Vs. Kelvin Jute Co. Ltd.- 2002 Lab.I.C. 3006 Cal.	174
Kumpur Textile Finishing Mills Vs. R.P.F.C., AIR 1955 Punjab 130	9, 51

"L"

Case	Page
Laxmi Bai K. Vs. RPFC A.P. – 2006 (I) LLJ. 27	25
Laxmi Restaurant Vs. R.P.F.C.- 1975 Lab.I.C. 1186	196
Leo Mercantile Corporation, Madras Vs. The Secretary, Ministry of Labour, G.O.I.- 1987Lab.I.C. 557 (Mad.)	44
Loon Karan Sethia Vs. Additional Collector -(1964) 2 LLJ 331; AIR 1965 All. 373 (DB)	187

"M"

Case	Page
M.G.Poddar Vs. R.P.F.C.- 1971 (1) LLJ. 381 (Cal)	47
Madathnpath Weavers' Co-oriduction & Sales Society Ltd. Vs. R.P.F.C.- 1997 Lab.I.C. 2957(Mad.); 1998 (I) LLJ. 824 (Mad.)	35
Mahalaxmi Cotton Mills Ltd (in Liquidation), AIR 1960 Cal. 199	89
Mahindra Gears and Transmission Pvt. Ltd vs. Assistant P.F. Commissioner, EPF- 2011 LLR. 602 (Guj. H.C.)	241
Manager, Vijaya Bank Vs. R.P.F.C.- 1999 (83) FLR 738 (Kern.)	248
Manager, Vijaya Bank Vs. RPFC – 2003 (III) LLJ 419 (Karn.DB)	247
Mangalore Ganesh Beedi Works Vs. A.P.F.C. - 2002 Lab.IC 1578 (Karn)	113
Mansa Nagrik Sahakari Bank Ltd. Vs. R.P.F. Commissioner-2003 III CLR 177 (Guj. H.C,)	21
Marathwada Gramin Bank Karmachari Sanghathan and another vs. Management of Marathwada Gramin Bank and others; Marathwas Regional Rural Bank Employees' Union vs. Management of Marathwada Gramin Bank	

and others – [2011 (9) SCC 620: 2011 (4) LLJ. 305: 2011 (4) LLN. 472: 2011 (4) Lab.I.C. 4449: 2011 (131) FLR. 754: 2011 LLR. 1130	119, 151
Mayur Biscuit Co. (P) Ltd. Vs. R.P.F.C.- (1999) 81 FLR 581 (Ori.DB)	199
Merta Oil Mills Co. Vs. R.P.F.C. – (1992) 65 FLR. 537 (Raj.).	35
Mettur Industries Vs. Velayutha Mudaliar- (1961) 1 LLJ 279	150
Midlands (P) Ltd. Vs. R.P.F.C. and another- 1994 (I) LLJ 1230 (All)	199, 200
Minerva Stores Vs. R.P.F.C. – 1978 Lab.I.C. 1160	192
Mohammed Ali Jinnah, Prop. M.A.J. Cins Part, Trichy Vs. APFC–2010-III-LLJ-765-(Mad.)	243
Mohd. & Sons Vs. J.M. Pandya- 1979 Lab.IC (NOC) 115 (Raj)	115
Mohd. Ali & Ors Vs. UOI & Another – 1963 (A) LLJ 536; AIR 1964 SC 980	6, 126
Mohmadali Vs. Union of India– AIR 1964 SC 980; (1963) 1 LLJ 536	5
Moideen Beary Bajpe, SK Vs. R.P.F.C. Karnataka- [UP No. 3075 / 1974]	35
Mukhtiar Sing Sodhi Vs. RPFC, -1972 ALL LJ 265	89
Murarka Paints and Varnish Work Ltd. Vs. U.O.I. – 1976 Lab.IC 1953.	212
Mysore State Coop. Printing Works Ltd. Vs. R.P.F. Commissioner- 1976 Lab.IC 1307 (Kant)	127

"N"

N. Sathisan Enforcement Officer (Recovery) Vs. P. Velappan Nair and Others- CRP NO. 504/1992 F. pronounced on 17.9.1992 – unreported judgement	249
N.K. Jain vs. C.K. Shah- (1991) 2 SCC 495; 1991 SCC (L&S) 656; 1991 Lab.I.C. 1013	108, 117, 175, 289
Narammal and another Vs. Kanthani and others- [1992 (2) MLJ 538 (Mad)	140
National Thermal Power Corp. Ltd. Vs. R.P.F.C.- 1998 (2) CLR 561 (Cal.-DB)	198, 201
Navedac Prosthetic Centre Vs. R.P.F.C.- (1996) 2 LLN. 738 (P&H)	47
Nazeena Traders (P) Ltd Vs. RPFC – AIR-1965 AP 200; 1966 (1) LLJ 334	9, 27, 42, 51, 126
Navnit Lal K Shah (Dr.) vs. Union of India-2003 (III) CLR 904 (Bom.)	214
Neyveli Lignite Corpn. Ltd. Vs. R.P.F.C. Madras and others – 1997 (i) CLR-699. (Mad.)	243

"O"

Om Roller Flour Mills Vs. U.O.I. – 2002 (3) LLJ 228; 2002 Lab.IC 1221; 2002 (94) FLR 908; 2002 LLR 683	223
Organo Chemical Industries Vs. Union of India- (1979) 4 SCC 573; 1980 SCC (L&S) 92; (1979) 2 LLJ 416	209, 214, 215
Orissa Cement Ltd. Vs. Union of India- AIR 1962 SC 1402; (1962) 1 LLJ 493	115

"P"

P.F. Inspector, Vijaywada Vs. Sivarama Krishna Industries and others-1992 (I) LLN 248 (AP)	295
P.M. Patel and Sons and other Vs. U.O.I. AIR 1987 SC 447; 1986 Lab.I.C. 1410; 1986 (I) LLJ.88 (SC)	38
P.V. Joseph Vs. Official Liquidator and Others- 2002 (100) FJR 197	242
Padiyur Sarvodaya Sangh Vs. Union Of India [(1999) 2 LLN 224 (Mad)	115
Parvati Construction Co. Vs. Rajasthan Housing Board-(1998) 2 LLJ 970 (Raj)	117
Patwardhan Tailors Poona Vs. Their Workmen- 1960 (I) LLJ.722	34

Table of Cases

Pathankot Janta Cooperative Labour & Construction society Ltd. and another vs. State of Punjab Through Secretary, Irrigation, Punjab, Chandigarh & other – [2011 LLr. 1162 (P & H H.C.)	218
Pearly Andrew Franz Vs. Official Assignee- AIR 1966 Bom 121; (1965) 2 LLJ 478	150
Petroleum Workers Union Hindustan Petroleum Corp. Ltd. Chennai and other Vs. HPCL Mumbai and others – 2004 (2) LLN 451	116
Pfizer Employees' Union and other Vs. R.P.F,C. and others – 2000 (103) FJR 120	174
Poona Shims Pvt. Ltd. Vs. V.P, Ramaiah, Regional P.F. Commissioner and another- 2007 LLR 488 (Bom)	215
Pragati Metal Works Vs. The RPFC-2001 (89) FLR 981	244
Prakash Cotton Mills (P) Ltd. Vs. State of Bombay 1957(2)LLJ.490	9, 51
Prantiya Vidyut Mandal Mazdoor Federation and others Vs. Rajasthan State Electricity Board and others- 1992 Lab.IC 1790; 1993 (1) LLJ 222 (SC)	112
Premier Stud and Chaplets Co. Vs. State – (1980) 56 FJR 611	289
Proto Pumps and Motors Pvt. Ltd. Vs. Asstt. P.F. Commissioner, EPFO, Surat and others – 2004 Lab.IC 2993; 2004 LLR 1145	116
Provident Fund Inspector Vs. Jhoomarlal Swarooplal Tiwari- (1994)69 FLR (Sum) 22	86
Provident Fund Inspector Vs. Ram Kumar- 1983 Lab.IC 717 (P&H)	126, 278, 295
Provident Fund Inspector Vs. Venkatachalam Chettiar- (1970) 1 LLJ 455	89
Provident Fund Inspector, Kota Vs. Smt Bhogi Bai and Others – 2008 (118) FLR 687 (Raj.)	288

"Q"

'Nil'

"R"

R. Ramanathan Chettiar Jewellers Vs. Regional Commissioner, EPF- (1998) 2LLJ 945; 1998 4 LLN 783; (1999) 1 FLR 559 (Mad)	113
R.K.L. Gupta Vs. Ram Babu Lal- 1970 (I) LLJ.390	175
R.N.T. Estates Ltd. Vs. U.O.I. 1989 Lab I.C. N.O.C. 177 (Cal.)	212, 243
R.P.F. Commissioner Vs. Puttamma, (1999) 1 LLJ 377; (1999) 1 CLR 820 (Kant)	150
R.P.F. Commissioner Vs. S. D. College -(1997) 1 SCC 241; 1997 SCC (L&S) 449; 1997 Lab.IC 910	214
R.P.F.C Vs. K.T. Rolling Mills Ltd. -1995 (1) LLJ 882 (SC)	213
R.P.F.C., EPF Vs. Southern Alloy Foundries (P) Ltd.- 1981 Lab.IC 472 (Mad-DB)	113
R.P.F.C. Mangalore Vs. Jamiyyatul Falsh, Mangalore and Another– 2010-LLJ-652: 2010 (2)Lab.I.C. 1365 (Karn.)	211
R.P.F.C. Mangalore Vs. Karnataka Forest Plantation Corps. Ltd. Bangalore. 2000 Lab I. C. 1268.	243
R.P.F.C. T.N. Vs. Snap Top Machines Accessories India (P) Ltd. – 2002 (1) CLR 437 (Mad-DB)	213
R.P.F.C. Vs. Dharamsi Morarji Chemicals Co. Ltd. – 1998 (II) CLR 151 (SC)	30
R.P.F.C. Vs. Glamour Prop. S.H. & Sons.- 1982 Lab.I.C. 1787	192
R.P.F.C. vs. Dr. O. P. Mittal and another-2011 LLR. 1254 (P. & H. HC)	12
R.P.F.C, Tirunellveli vs. Prabha Beverages Pvt. Ltd. And another-2009 LLR. 972 (Madras)	41
R.P.F.C. Vs. Shrikrishna Metal Mfg. Co.- AIR 1962 SC 1536	42
R.P.F.C. Vs. T.S. Hariharan – AIR 1971-SC 1519; 1971 (I) LLJ. 416	32, 35
R.P.F.C. W.B. Vs. The Gauripore Co. Ltd.- 1992 Lab.IC 1515 (Cal.)	292
R.P.F.C., Jaipur Vs. M/s Naraini Udyog and others-1996 (2) LLJ. 1063 (SC)	30

Case	Page
RPFC Vs. Shibu Metal Works – 1965 (1) LLJ 473	9, 27, 51
RPFC Vs. Shiv Kumar Joshi – 2000 Lab. I.C. 232 (SC)	8
R.P.F.Commissioner vs. Harihar Polyfibres – (1991) 2 LLN 948; 1992 LabIC 202; (1992) 1 CLR 517 (Kat-DB) reversing Harihar Polyfibres vs. RPFC- (1990) 1 CLR 342; 60 FLR 195; 1991) 2 LLJ 477	151
R.P.F.Commissioner Vs. K.R Subbaier Tape Factory- (1966) 2 LLJ 676; AIR 1967 Mad.129 (DB).	127
Regional P.F. Commissioner vs. M/s Nath Traders and others- 2007 (1) Lab.I.C. 826 : 2007 LLR. 378 (Delhi HC)	31
The Regional P.F. Commissioner, Mumbai vs. M/s syndicate Overseas Pvt. Ltd. – 2001 LLR 953 (Bom. H.C.)	113
Regioal P.F. Commissioner vs. Sanatan Dharma Girls Secondary School & others – AIR 2007 SC 276: 2007 I LLJ 458: 2007 (1) SCC 268: 2007 (112) FLR 314	25
Rabindra Chamaria and others Vs. Registrar of Companies, W.B., AIR 1992 SC 398; 1992 (I) LLJ 313 (SC)	292
Radha Krishan Vs. R.P.F.C.- AIR 1967 MP 157	195
Raghunandan Prasad & Co. Vs. Union of India- 1989 Lab.I.C. 1701; (1989) 1 LLN 788; (1989) 42; (1989) 1 CLR 641 (Raj. DB)	47
Railway Employees' Cooperative Banking Society Vs. U.O.I.- 1980 Lab.I.C. 1212 (Raj.)	35
Ram Kripal Prasad and others Vs. State of Bihar – AIR 1986 Patna 254 (F.B.)	290, 295
Ramesh Metal Works Vs. State, (1962) 1 LLJ 169: AIR 1962 All 227	10, 52
Rashtriya Mill Mazdoor Sangh and others Vs. R.P.F.C. Bombay and others – 1991 Lab.IC 1572 (Bom)	141
Ratanlal Vs. R.P.F.C. – 1977 Lab.I.C. 1765 (Del)	48
Raynold Pens India Pvt. Ltd. & Other vs. R.P.F.C. (II), Chennai – 2011-LLR 876 (Mad)	112
Recovery Officer and APFC Vs. Kerala Financial Corpn. –[2002 III CLR 191 (Ker.DB)	242
Rhone Poulenc Employees' Union Vs. R.P.F. Commissioner –(1996) 2 LLJ 1001; (1996) 3 LLN 709 (Bom.)	165, 172

"S"

Case	Page
S. Ganpathy Vs. Mahalaxmi Textile Mills Ltd. And others – 1989 Lab,IC (NOC) 200 (Mad.)	293
S.H. Salve Kadam & Co. Vs. R.P.F.C.- 1981 Lab.IC 568 (Kar.)	295
SK Nasiruddin vs. C.P.F. Commissioner - (1997) 75 FLR 471	116
S.K. Nasiruddin Beedi Marchant (P) Ltd. Vs. R.P.F.C. and other- 1991 (I) LLJ.19	37
S.P. Abdul Rahim and Sons Vs. R.P.F.C. and another- 1996 (I) LLJ. 1134 (Mad.)	38
M/s. Sachdeva Maternity & General Hospital vs. Presiding Officer, E.P.F Appellate Tribunal & another- 2015 LLR. 837 (P 7 H H.C.)	31
Sahara Zila Khadi Gramodyog Sangh Vs. Union of India- (1996) 2 CLR 678; (1996) 3 LLN 246 (Pat.DB)	48
Sampath Kumaran & Co. vs. R.P.F.C. –1974 Lab.I.C. 602; (1973 44 FJR 191	43
Sampat Mal Lodha vs. State of Rajasthan – 1988 (72) FJR 11 (Raj.)	292
Sangam Spinners Vs. R.P.F.C.-I- 2008(I)CLR424 (SC); 2008-I-LLJ. 661(SC)	28, 209
Sasidharan Vs. R.P.F. Commissioner- 1982 Lab.IC 597 (Ker)	127
Satish Plastic Vs. R.P.F.C.- (1982) 44 FLR 207	34
Sayaji Mills Ltd. Vs. R.P.F.C.-AIR 1985 S.C. 323; 1985 SCC (L&S) 310	9, 27, 42

Table of Cases

Case	Page
Security Guards Board of Greater Bombay and Thane District and others Vs. R.P.F.C. – 1991 Lab IC 1855 Bom.	24
Shanti Vihar Hotels Ltd. And other Vs. P.F. Inspector, Madras – 1992 MLJ (Cr.) 59 (Mad)	296
Shapoorji Nusserwanji & Co. Vs. Trustees of E.P.F.- (1970) 37 FJR 569 (Bom)	48
Shree Changdeo Sugar Mills and other Vs. U.O.I. and another- 2001 (2) SCC 519; 2001 SCC (L&S) 457; AIR 2001 S.C. 557; 2001 (88) FLR 939	113
Shree Kutchi Oshwal Mahila Mandal vs. U.O.I. and others, - 1992 Lab.I.C. 1449 (Bomb.)	34
Shree Mahila Griha Udyog Lijjat Papad vs. U.O.I. and another- 1994 Lab.I.C. 1308 (M.P.); (1994) 2 LLJ. 610	34
Shree Mahila Griha Udyog Lijjat Papad vs. U.O.I. and another-1999 (4) LLN. 64 (SC)	34
Shrikanta Datta Narasimharaja Wodiyar Vs. Enforcement Officer, Mysore- (1993) 3 SCC 217;1993 SCC (L&S) 751; (1993) 2 LLN 69	10, 27, 52, 88, 292
Silver Jublee tailoring Vs. Chief Inspector of Shops and Establishments and another-1974 (I)-SCR 747	33
Sindri Workers Union Vs. Commissioner of Labour" – AIR 1959 Pat. 36; 1959 (2) LLJ- 53.	21
SLM Manek Lal Industries Vs. R.P.F.C. [1997 (2) LLJ-283 (Guj.)	8, 248
Smt. Om Wati Vs. Delhi Transport Corpn. New Delhi and others-1988 Lab,IC 500 (Delhi)	140
Som Prakash Rekhi Vs. UOI- (1981) 1 SCC 449; 1981 SCC (L&S) 200; (1981) 1 LLJ 79	151
South India Research Institute Vs. R.P.F. Commissioner- (1981) 59 FJR 160 (AP)	127
Sree Gopikrishan Engineering (P) Ltd. Vs. R.P.F.C., W.B.- [1986 Lab.I.C. 2066 (Cal.)	192
Sri Angappa Spinning Mills and others Vs. R.P.F.C. TN- 1986 Lab.I.C. 458	243
Sri Varadaswami Transport (P) Ltd. Vs. RPFC, Madras- AIR 1965 Mad. 466; 1966 (I) LLJ.699	18
Standard Chartered Bank Vs. U.O.I – 2002 (II) LLJ 754 (Cal.)	224
State Bank of Mysore Vs., R.P.F. Commissioner, Bangalore–1999 (I) 316 (Karn.)	248
State of Bihar vs. Bhadani -AIR 1959 Pat. 9; (1959) 1 LLJ 157	293
State of Bihar Vs. Deokaran Menshi – AIR 1973 SC 908	289
State of Gujrat Vs. Indequip Engineering Ltd. –(1979) 2 GLR 784	296
State of Orissa Vs. Dr. (Miss) Bina Pani dei – AIR 1967 SC 1269	211
State of Madras vs. V.G. Row, AIR 1952 SC 196	85
Sukchain & Co. Vs. F.C.I. – 1985 (65) FJR 337	195
Sundaram Finance Corporation & another Vs. R.P.F.C. Madras & Others- 1989 (I) MLJ. 356	46
Sunderam Industries Ltd vs. R.P.F. Commissioner-(1996) 88 FJR 13; (1996)72 FLR 461 (Kant)	129
Surya Roshni Ltd. Vs. EPF- 2011- LLR 568 (M.P.)	112
Swasik Textile Engineers (P) Ltd. Vs. Virijibhai Mavjibhai Rathod- 2008 CLR 953 (Guj)	114
Syed Abdul Azeez Khan Vs. Flower- (1967) 1 LLJ 796; 1968 LabIC 441 (Mad).	150

"T"

Case	Page
T.K. Meenaxi & Another Vs. Steel Authority of India & Others – 2000 (6) SCC 493 : AIR 2000 SC 1596	5
T. Marimuthu Handloom Factory, Madurai vs. R.P.F.C. Madras- 1990 Lab.IC 2030 (Mad)	194
Tapan Kumar Battacharyya Vs. Asstt. P.F. Commissioner and Others– 2010-III-LLJ-700 (Cal.)	241

Case	Page
Tata Engineering and Locomotive Co. Ltd. Vs. U.O.I.- 1991 Lab.I.C. 49; 2 CLR 595; 62 FLR 191 (Bom.); (1990) 2 LLN 1194	35
Tata Iron & Steel Co. Ltd. Vs. Bir Singh- (1983) 63 FJR 32 (Pat)	150
The ACME Company Ltd. Vs. U.O.I. – 2005(I) LLJ.250; 2004 LLR 1054	47
Tin Plate Co. of India Ltd. Vs. Presiding Officer, E.P.F. Appellate Tribunal, New Delhi –2003(2) LLJ.997; 2003 (79) FLR 923	196
Titagarh Paper Mills Co. Ltd. Vs. Workmen- AIR 1959 SC 1095; 1959 Supp (2) SCR 1002; (1959) 2 LLJ 9	111
Transport Corporation of India Ltd. Vs. R.M. Gandhi and others- 1991 Lab.I.C. 2017 (Bom); (1992) 64 FLR 697	290
Travencore Rayons Ltd. Vs. Provident Fund Officer and others – 1989 (I) LLJ 414 (Ker.)	293

"U"

Case	Page
Uma Shankar Srivastava Vs. State of U.P.- S.C. N. Vol. No. VI P.19 dated 16.10.1964	30
Union of India Vs. Hira Devi- AIR 1952 SC 227	150
Union of India Vs. Murugan Talkies – (1996) 1 SCC 504; 1996 SCC (L&S) 326	118
Union of India Vs. Narayan Bannppa Pakkanavar, -1989 Lab. I.C. 854 (Kant).	12, 86
Union of India Vs. Shree Digamber Jain Secondary School and others– 2003 I CLR 233 (Raj. DB)	25
Universal Brakes (P) Ltd., Coimbatore vs. Pesiding Officer, EPF Appellae Tribunal and others – 2011 III CLR 662 (Mad. H.C.)	114
Universal Paper Mills Ltd. and others Vs. R.P.F.C. and others – 20001 (2) LLJ 1193; 2001 (91) FLR 591; 2002 LLR 41; 2001 (99) FJR 199	8, 248
Unni Mammu Haji Vs. State of Kerala – 1989 (2) LLJ 493 (Ker.)	24
Usha Sales Ltd. Vs. R.P.F. Commissioner- 1980 Lab.IC 546; (1980) 1 LLN 452 (Del-DB)	114

"V"

Case	Page
Vallabhaneni Ratnakumari Vs. Katta Subbarvamma- (1994) 2 LLJ 81	150
Varadakkal Vs. the RPFC and another- 2001 (1) CLR 770; 2002 (1) LLJ 1018	141
Victoria Jubilee Technical Institution Vs. R.P.F.C.- 1980(I) LLJ. 254	28
Vijay Kumar and others Vs. Whirlpool of India and others- 2008 LLR 227 (SC)	117
Vikram Poddar vs. RPFC and others – 2001 (2) LLJ 518; 2001 (2) LLN 78	249
Virendra Vs. State of Punjab- AIR 1957 SC 89685	
Vishwa Bharati Welfare Printing Press vs. R,P,F,C, Hyderabad – 1979 Lab.IC 269	212

"W"

'Nil'

"X"

'Nil'

"Y"

Case	Page
Younus Mohammed Vs. R.P.F.C. and others – 1987 Lab.IC 1089 (MP);	195

"Z"

'Nil'

www.ingramcontent.com/pod-product-compliance
Lightning Source LLC
Chambersburg PA
CBHW082319220526
45470CB00008B/2356